MASTERING TALLY.ERP 9

MASTERING TALLY.ERP 9

DINESH MAIDASANI
B.A., Dip. Comp. Sc.

(An Imprint of Laxmi Publications Pvt.Ltd.)

An ISO 9001:2008 Company

BENGALURU • CHENNAI • COCHIN • GUWAHATI • HYDERABAD
JALANDHAR • KOLKATA • LUCKNOW • MUMBAI • RANCHI • NEW DELHI
BOSTON (USA) • ACCRA (GHANA) • NAIROBI (KENYA)

MASTERING TALLY.ERP 9

Printed and bound in India
Typeset at Kalyani Computer Services, Delhi
First Edition: 2011; Reprint : 2014
ISBN 978-93-80298-57-3

Branches

✆	Bengaluru	080-26 75 69 30	
✆	Chennai	044-24 34 47 26,	24 35 95 07
✆	Cochin	0484-237 70 04,	405 13 03
✆	Guwahati	0361-254 36 69,	251 38 81
✆	Hyderabad	040-27 55 53 83,	27 55 53 93
✆	Jalandhar	0181-222 12 72	
✆	Kolkata	033-22 27 43 84	
✆	Lucknow	0522-220 99 16	
✆	Mumbai	022-24 91 54 15,	24 92 78 69
✆	Ranchi	0651-220 44 64	

Published in India by

An ISO 9001:2008 Company
113, GOLDEN HOUSE, DARYAGANJ,
NEW DELHI - 110002, INDIA
Telephone : 91-11-4353 2500, 4353 2501
Fax : 91-11-2325 2572, 4353 2528
www.laxmipublications.com info@laxmipublications.com

C—
Printed at:

Contents

1 Introduction to Tally.ERP 9

New Features in Tally.ERP 9 Series A Release 1.0

Some of the new features in Tally.ERP 9 include:

Remote Access

Tally.ERP 9 provides remote capabilities to its users to access data from anywhere. Using Tally.NET features, the user can create remote users (ids), authorize & authenticate them to access company remotely. Currently, the remote connectivity allows the user to view/display the required information on his system instantly.

The process for remote access is as follows:

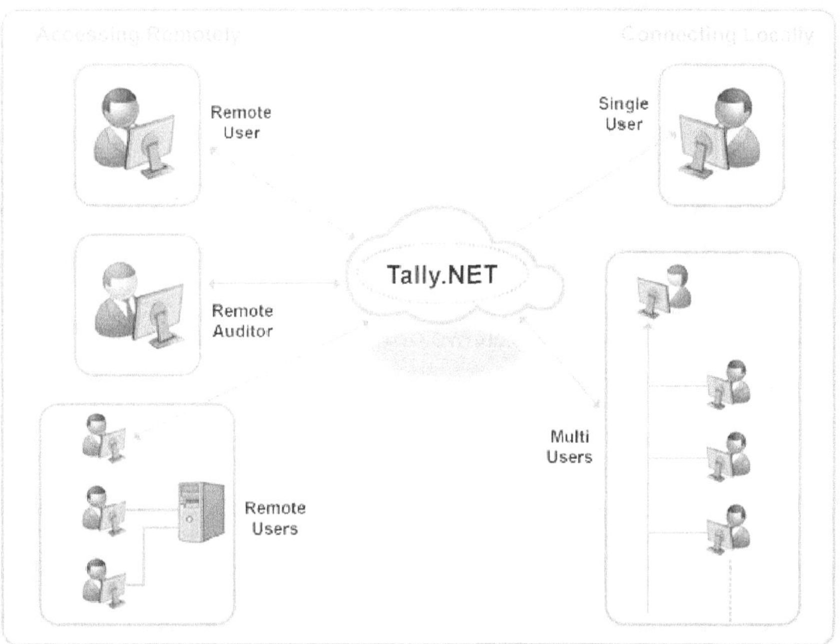

Fig. 1.1 Opening Screen

- Start Tally.ERP 9, load the required company and connect to Tally.NET
- Enter the remote user ID at the remote login location to access company data from Tally.ERP 9 Licensed / Educational.

Requirements for Remote Connectivity

At the Customer's Location:

- A valid Internet connection

- A valid Tally.ERP 9 License with a Tally.NET subscription
- Create and authorise remote users for a Company that has to be accessed remotely
- Load & Connect the Company to Tally.NET for remote access.

For the company to be accessed by the Remote User the computer has to be kept on and Tally.ERP 9 with company loaded.

At the Remote Location:

- A valid Internet connection
- Tally.ERP 9 (Licensed/Education)
- A valid remote User ID and Password.

Benefits of Remote Access:

- Provides anytime, anywhere access to required information
- Allows you to access Reports & Statements on the move to keep yourself updated with the latest Business happenings.
- Enhances response time to customers (For *e.g.*, Sales staff can access Customer's Outstanding Statement for immediate reference/discussion.)
- Easy access to financial information for faster & timely decision making.

Data Security:

- The Remote connectivity is initiated with a secured Handshake between two computers using Tally.NET environment.
- Customer can allow / disallow access to the Company Data for remote users at any point of time.
- Data resides on the Customer's Computer only.
- Encrypted Data is transferred between two computers on request.
- The customer can assign Security controls to remote users depending upon what access to be given.
- For the Remote user(s) Back up / Restore options will not be available in the remote location.

Remote TDL's

During Remote Access, the additional TDL's running at the customer's place will also be available to the Remote User at the remote Location.

The user experience remains the same either working locally on Customer's Computer or from a Remote Location. It is recommended to use Broadband connections to enjoy the best Remote experience.

Tally.NET

Tally.NET is an enabling environment which works behind the scenes to facilitate various Internet based services in Tally.ERP 9. Each Tally.ERP 9 is enabled for Tally.NET Services by default. Tally.NET provides the following services/capabilities in this release of Tally.ERP 9:

Tally.NET Features

- Create and maintain Remote Users
- Remote Access
- Control Centre

- Support Centre
- Synchronization of data (via Tally.NET)
- Product updates & upgrades.

The following services will be available in the forthcoming releases:

- Online help capability in the form of reference Manuals, Articles and FAQ's
- Access information from Tally.ERP 9 via SMS from mobile
- Employer Recruitment Test.

Simplified Installation Process

Tally.ERP 9 comes with a new enhanced installer, which allows the user to configure different settings from a single screen, as per requirements.

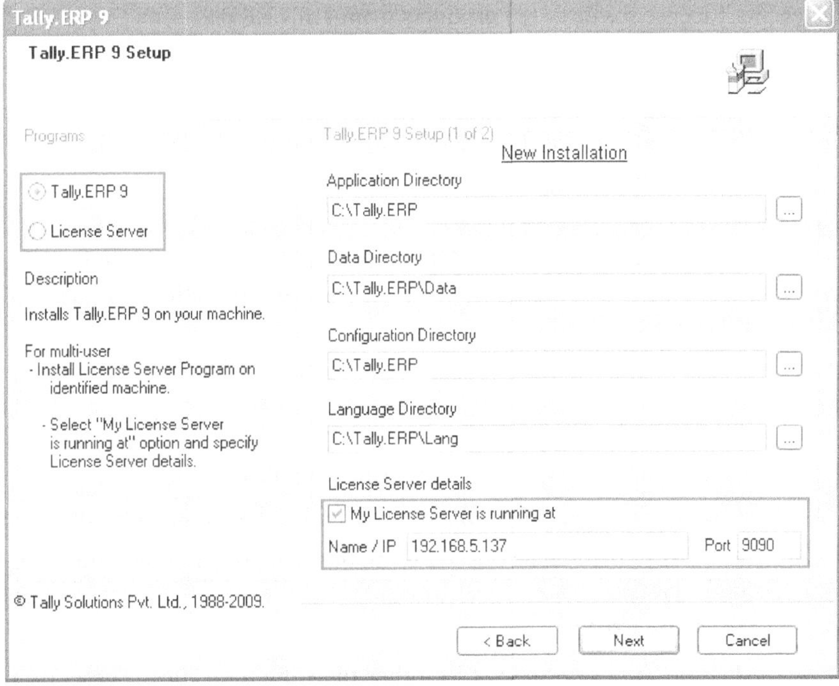

Fig. 1.2 Installing Tally.ERP 9

New Tally.ERP 9 Installer

The new installer allows the user to install Tally.ERP 9 application as well as License Server, however you may choose to install either of them one after the other.

Using the new Installer, the user can install Tally.ERP 9 and License Server separately on different Computers/folders or same folder.

- While installing Tally.ERP 9, the user can specify the path for Application, Data, Configuration and Language files to be stored.
- While Installing Tally.ERP 9 on the Client machine in a multiuser environment, the user is required

to provide the Computer Name / IP Address and Port Number of the computer, where the License Server is installed & running.

Uninstaller:

The Uninstaller wizard similar to the Installer, also provides flexibility to uninstall either Tally.ERP 9 application or License Server separately or both together. If only License Server is uninstalled, then Tally.ERP 9 will switch to Education mode on the Client Computer.

Tally Admin Tool

The TallyAdmin tool is a new component that has been introduced with Tally.ERP 9 which enables the user to perform the following activities without starting Tally.ERP 9:

- Initiate License Service operations.
- Display the active Tally.ERP 9 License Servers in a LAN.
- Administer Site License for different products from Tally.ERP 9.
- Check network connections between the computers designated as Client and Server.
- Convert TCP and TSF files of Tally 9 to the format compatible with Tally.ERP 9.

The Tally Admin Tool is available in the Tally.ERP 9 application folder, on installation.

Introduction to TDL Server DLL Component

Tally.ERP 9 onwards, a new component TDLServer.DLL has been introduced, which gets copied to the folder in which Tally.ERP 9 has been installed. All the default TDL files of Tally have been integrated in this component. On invoking Tally.ERP 9, these TDL's will be loaded. The user TDL's will be subsequently loaded as usual from Tally.ini.

The componentization will result in a more robust application. The benefits of this componentization are as follows:

- In case of any updates/ changes in TDL, only TDLServer.dll file needs to be downloaded and not the entire Tally application which enables faster downloads.
- This will help in dynamic loading and unloading of TDL Files while Tally application is running.
- Forthcoming Tally Developer will be directly using this component, thus eliminating the need for a separate DefTDL.dat file.

Unified File Format for Tally.ERP 9

The Tally.ERP 9 application folder contains files other than the data files. These are referred to as secondary files. From this release onwards the file format of all the secondary files have been standardized.

TCP Files

All the TDL files which were compiled for previous versions of Tally as .tcp have to be converted to a new format. Mentioned below are the ways in which this can be done.

The TDL files in txt format does not require this conversion.

Conversion of Tally 7.2 tcp Files to Tally.ERP 9 Format

Tally7.2 tcp files can be migrated to Tally.ERP 9 format using the Tally72Migration tool available in the Tally.ERP 9 folder. Migration process is the same as earlier.

Conversion of Tally 9 tcp Files to Tally.ERP 9 Format

- Automatic Conversion Process: When Tally.ERP 9 is installed in the existing Tally 9 folder then all the files with .tcp extension included in the "tally.ini" file are automatically converted to the Tally.ERP 9 compatible format. The original ".tcp" file is renamed as "<filename>.tcp.BAK". The name of the file which is converted to new format is same as the original filename. The original TCP file is retained as a backup file:

- Manual Conversion Process: To manually convert the files in the new format use the Conversion tab of Tally Admin Tool.

  It is mandatory to specify the File Type. The file Type can be TSF or TCP.

- TSF: Converts tally configuration file from old format to new format e.g. tallysav.tsf to tallycfg.tsf
- TCP: Converts TCP file from old format to new format.

In the Source File box specify the name of file to be converted.

In Destination File box provide the name for the converted file.

Start Tally.ERP 9 and check the status of your TDL file. [Go to Gateway of Tally, click F12:Configuration > Functions and Features] If the status is Active, then the tdl is compatible to Tally.ERP 9 format. If the status is Error, then scroll down to the line and press enter to know the details. Then make the TDL syntactically compatible as per the Tally.ERP 9 standards.

Configuration File

Manually the file "Tallysav.tsf" can be converted to the new standardized format by selecting "TSF" as the file type in the Conversion tab of Tally Admin Tool. Ensure that the destination file name is "Tallycfg.tsf"

Licensing in Tally.ERP 9

Tally.ERP 9 launches a new Licensing mechanism which is simple, user-friendly and addresses all the licensing activities from a single screen for users across segments of business. Besides, allowing activation of Single User (Silver) and Multi User (Gold) license, it also extends the feature to Multi-Site Licensing.

The salient features of Licensing are:

- License Activation is simple and easy two step process.
- Introducing the concept of an Account for better management & administration of Licenses through the Control Centre.
- Provide your Account ID and Password to reactivate license.
- The flexibility and compatibility to centrally manage multiple licenses across locations in a secured environment.
- Removes all licensing data from your computer for a particular instance of license.

Site Licensing

A new concept of Site Licensing is introduced from Tally.ERP 9. A site refers to activation of Tally.ERP 9 Single or Multi User license. The site licensing is broadly classified into two categories namely Single Site and Multi-Site.

- **Single Site**: A single instance of Tally.ERP 9 Silver or Gold license is active at a time under an Account.
- **Multi Site**: Is more than one active Tally.ERP 9 Silver or Gold licenses on different machines under a single account comprising of same or different Serial numbers.

Advantages:

- Centrally configure Sites / License across locations.
- An Account is created using your E-Mail ID provided in the activation form.
- All the serial numbers are assigned to the Account.
- User can split an Account or merge two or more Accounts.
- The Account information is accessible using the Account ID and Password.

Licensing Mechanism

- Provide the required details and your E-Mail ID in the activation form.
- On processing the request an encrypted (not in readable format) license file is generated and needs to be decrypted using a set of character and numbers called key.

Control Centre

Control Centre is a new feature being introduced with Tally.ERP 9. This utilises Tally.NET as an interface between the end user and Tally.ERP 9 installed at different locations. With the help of Control Centre, you will able to:

- Create users with predefined Security levels
- Centrally Configure & manage your Tally.ERP 9
- Surrender, Confirm or Reject activation of a Site
- Maintain Account related information.

Following are brief descriptions of the features of the Control Center:

Create Users with predefined Security Levels

Using the Control Centre feature, the Account Administrator can create users and map them to a predefined security level and authorise them to access a Site/Location linked to that Account. Further, the system administrator can also create Remote users (Tally.NET Users & Tally.NET Auditors) and allow / disallow them to remotely access the data.

The predefined security levels in Tally.ERP 9 are:

- Owner - This security level refers to the ownership for the complete Account. The Owner can create Standard Users or Owners with required permissions.
- Standard User - Created by the Owner with required permissions.

Centrally Configure and Manage your Tally.ERP 9

The Control Centre provides the flexibility to create (or change) the master configurations set for an Account and apply them to one or more sites (all sites) belonging to that Account.

The following master configurations set can be made from the Control Centre:

- Add/Modify the Tally.ini parameters
- Assign TDL's to a site or all the sites under an Account
- Permit or Deny changes to the local configurations.

The master configurations set created, is applied initially to the Account centrally, which is then inherited by the site(s) on updation of license, based on the site level permissions defined by the Account Administrator.

Surrender, Confirm or Reject Activation of a Site

The Account Administrator is authorised to surrender, confirm a site license or Reject the request received on activation from another site.

Maintain Account Related Information

Allows you to maintain information about the organisation. Based on the requirements, the Account Administrator can merge multiple accounts into one or split an account into multiple accounts for easy and better management.

Support Centre

Tally.ERP 9 provides a new capability known as Support Centre, wherein a user can directly post his support queries on the functional and technical aspects of the Product. Using Support Centre feature, the user can view all the support queries reported via Support Centre and also through other modes viz., Email, Calls, etc.

The Support Centre feature facilitates viewing queries for an activated license along with the Status, *i.e.*, Closed / Pending and Ticket Summary. The report is viewed based on Date, Status and Location.

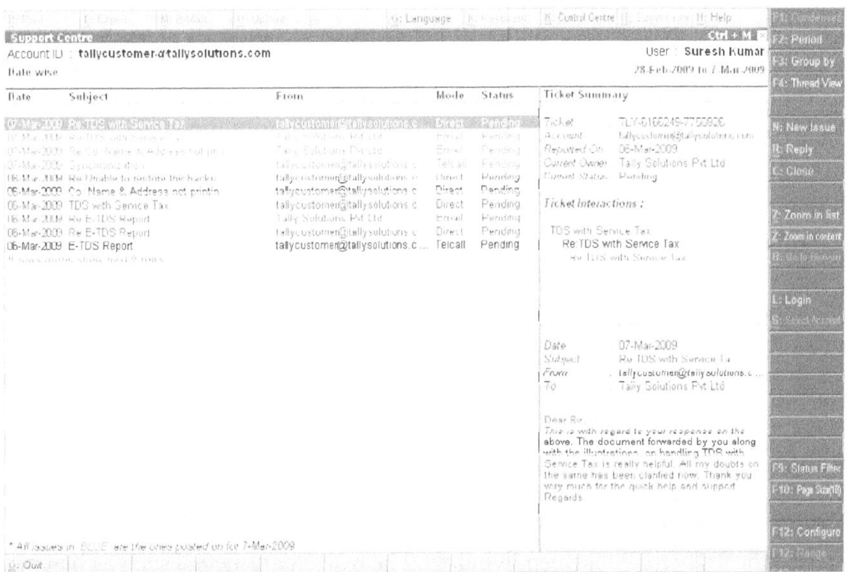

Fig. 1.3 Support Centre

Faster Reach for Help and Support

The Support Centre makes it easy and convenient to reach out Tally Support, including the Tally Service Partner, for any product help and support, by a click of a button from within the product.

Access Solutions to your Problems any time

This feature facilitates instant reference to the solutions provided for your queries at any point of time.

Avoid Repeated Explanations

Availability of information on the issues, interactions and resolutions, to the entire Tally Support Team, including the Tally Service Partners largely reduces the possibilities of repeated explanations on the issues/ support queries and thereby ensures quality help and support.

Track your Issues on Real-time basis

Support Centre enables you to track the status of your queries including the full chain of interactions irrespective of the mode of communication. If you have posted a query from the Support Centre within Tally. ERP 9 and then interacted over the phone, you will be able to see both the interactions.

Access Issues of any Location/Site

In case of Multi-site License, you can view the details of issues of any location /site from any of your Location(s).

Reach out to your nearest Partner instantly

You can search for a service partner and post your queries instantly.

Access your Support Centre remotely from any Tally.ERP 9

As an authorized Tally.NET user, Support Centre feature can be accessed remotely from any Tally.ERP 9 (active or in Educational mode) from anywhere. Support Centre also allows you to Select the required account from the list of User Accounts in case your ID (user name) is linked to multiple accounts.

Configure Tally.ERP 9 from Tally.ERP 9

The user can make all the necessary changes to the product configuration from Tally.ERP 9 itself by going to Data Configuration, TDL Configuration, Advanced Configuration and Licensing options available under F12:Configurations from Gateway of Tally. This provides a flexible option for the user to make changes in the Tally.ini file (Configuration file) and apply them from the application itself.

- **Data Configuration** - To specify the default Companies that should load during start up and path for the data files, language files, Confide files.
- **TDL Configuration** - Displays the additional TDL's (Local TDL's, Account TDL's, and Remote TDL's) and the user can specify the Local TDL's that need to be loaded. The TDL's specified will be loaded dynamically (without restarting Tally.ERP 9).
- **Advanced Configuration** - To configure Tally.ERP 9 as Server/Client/none, as ODBC Server and the port configured for ODBC or Data Sync.
- **Licensing** - To configure the License path in a Multiuser environment.

New Look & Feel

Resizing Screens

The user can resize the Tally.ERP 9 screen/window. The resize parameters such as height and width are defined in the Tally.ini file. The user can compare identical reports of different companies by changing the screen size for the two instances of Tally.ERP 9.

Multiple Selection Capabilities

The user can now select multiple lines in a Report at single instance. On selecting multiple lines, the user can delete or hide line(s) based on the requirement of the report.

Bottom Button Toolbar

Another new component that has been introduced in a set of buttons located at the bottom part of every report and Data Entry screen. Click on the button or press the relevant keys to perform the required task.

Information Panel

A new component titled Information Panel or Info Panel has been introduced which is located in the

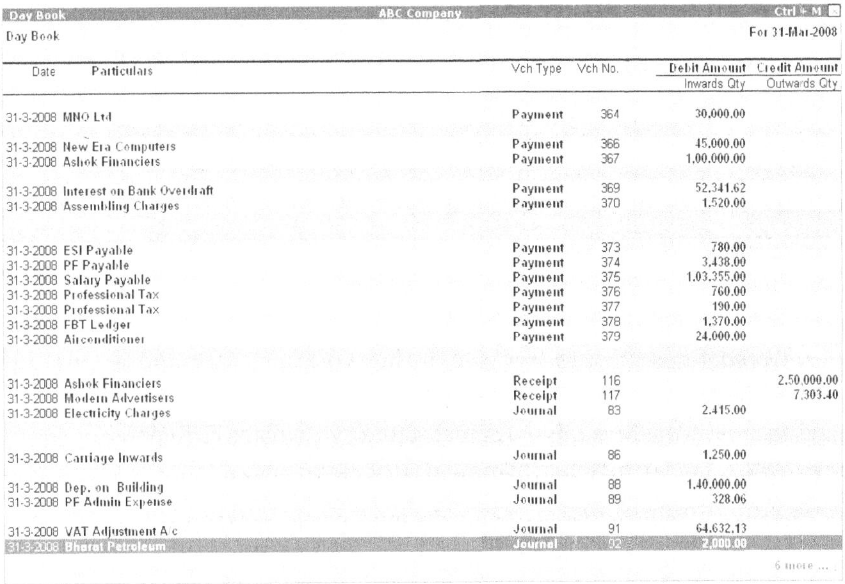

Day Book ABC Company Ctrl + M

Day Book For 31-Mar-2008

Date	Particulars	Vch Type	Vch No.	Debit Amount Inwards Qty	Credit Amount Outwards Qty
31-3-2008	MNO Ltd	Payment	364	30,000.00	
31-3-2008	New Era Computers	Payment	366	45,000.00	
31-3-2008	Ashok Financiers	Payment	367	1,00,000.00	
31-3-2008	Interest on Bank Overdraft	Payment	369	52,341.62	
31-3-2008	Assembling Charges	Payment	370	1,520.00	
31-3-2008	ESI Payable	Payment	373	780.00	
31-3-2008	PF Payable	Payment	374	3,438.00	
31-3-2008	Salary Payable	Payment	375	1,03,355.00	
31-3-2008	Professional Tax	Payment	376	760.00	
31-3-2008	Professional Tax	Payment	377	190.00	
31-3-2008	FBT Ledger	Payment	378	1,370.00	
31-3-2008	Airconditioner	Payment	379	24,000.00	
31-3-2008	Ashok Financiers	Receipt	116		2,50,000.00
31-3-2008	Modern Advertisers	Receipt	117		7,303.40
31-3-2008	Electricity Charges	Journal	83	2,415.00	
31-3-2008	Carriage Inwards	Journal	86	1,250.00	
31-3-2008	Dep. on Building	Journal	88	1,40,000.00	
31-3-2008	PF Admin Expense	Journal	89	328.06	
31-3-2008	VAT Adjustment A/c	Journal	91	64,632.13	
31-3-2008	Bharat Petroleum	Journal	92	2,000.00	

6 more ...

Fig. 1.4 New Look Day Book

bottom part of the Tally.ERP 9 screen. The Info Panel has five blocks namely Product, Version, Edition, Configuration and Calculator. The user can click on any one of these blocks to view the detailed information.

Product

Displays the logo and product name. The user can click on this section to go to Tally Solutions website to view the latest happenings.

Version

This part of the Info Panel displays the Release, Build, Date on which the recent License Update is done. In case Tally.ERP 9 is not updated with the recent Release/Build, the info panel will take you to the Download Center get the latest update. The user can also click on as on Date to update the License. It also displays the information on the Type of License (Silver/Gold/Auditors' Edition).

License

Displays the Serial Number, Site ID, Account ID and Tally.NET subscription details.

Configuration

Displays the Stat and Client Server Information. Stat Information will take the user to the Download center to download the Latest Stat file. The Client Server Information will allow the user to reconfigure the settings. The Additional TDL's loaded will also be shown in this section.

During Voucher Entry or while viewing reports the information panel is hidden to provide additional working space. However, you can click on the directional arrows to restore the information panel as and when required.

Calculator

Displays the Connection status while connecting to Tally.NET, during Data Sync, and Remote connectivity. This can also be used as Calculator.

Enhanced Payroll Compliance

Payroll in Tally.ERP 9 is now simplified & enhanced to handle all the functional, accounting and statutory requirements of your business. The following Statutory features and processes have been incorporated for faster, better and accurate payroll processing.

Payroll Statutory Features

The following statutory features have been incorporated in Tally.ERP 9:

Employees Provident Fund (EPF)

- Provides automated computation and deduction/contribution of Employees & Employer's Contribution towards Provident Fund.
- Provides a predefined PF process to expedite voucher entry and accurate processing of contributions.
- Generates the following Monthly / Annual statutory Challans & Reports:
- Form 12A: Statement of PF Contribution during a particular month
- Form 5: Details of the Employees joining during a particular month
- Form 10: Details of the Employees leaving during a particular month
- PF Combined Challan: Monthly Challan form to be submitted to the bank while paying the PF amount
- PF Monthly Statement
- Form 3A: Employee wise Annual Payment details
- Form 6A: Annual Statement of PF contribution
- Facilitates automated computation and payment of following administrative charges with the help of predefined processes.
- PF Administration Charges @ 1.10%
- Employees' Deposit-Linked Insurance Scheme (EDLI) @ 0.5%
- EDLI Administration Charges @ 0.01%
- Other Admin Charges (inspection charges, interest paid etc).

Employees State Insurance (ESI)

- Provides automated computation and deduction/contribution of Employees & Employer's Contribution towards Employees State Insurance.
- Provides predefined ESI process to expedite voucher entry and accurate processing of contributions.
- Generates the following Monthly / Half Yearly statutory Challans & Reports:
- ESI Monthly Statement
- ESI Monthly Payment Challan: Challan form to be submitted to the bank while paying the paying the ESI amount.
- Form 3: Monthly Declaration form
- Form 5: Half Yearly Return of ESI Contributions
- Form 6: Half Yearly Employee Register.

Professional Tax (PT)

- Provides automated computation and deduction of Professional Tax based on user-defined Slab rates.
- Provides predefined PT payment process to expedite voucher entry and accurate payment of Professional Tax.
- Generates following PT Reports:
- PT Computation Report: Print reports with Slab-wise details of Professional Tax by the Employer.
- PT Statement: Print monthly reports with Employee wise details of Professional Tax.

Payroll Processes

The following pre-defined payroll processes have been provided to automate different functions in Payroll:

- Salary Process – Automates the Computation of Salary
- PF Process – Automates the Computation of Employer PF Contribution
- ESI Process – Automates the Computation of Employer ESI Contribution
- Salary Payment – Automates the Payment of Salary
- PF Challan – Automates the Payment of PF
- ESI Challan – Automates the Payment of ESI
- Professional Tax Payment – Automates the Payment of PT.

Excise for Manufacturers

Tally.ERP 9 provides a complete solution for Excise related Business requirements for versatile industries. Salient features of Excise in Tally.ERP 9 are:

- The new Excise module allows you to maintain the required Central Excise records for multiple excise units of Traders /Manufactures in a single company.
- Excise module handles Ad valorem, Ad Quantum, MRP based Valuation Method for Excise Duty calculation, and also Expenses / Income can be apportioned for calculation of assessable value either by Value or by Quantity. Additional Expenses / Income can be apportioned for calculation of assessable value, both by Value or by Quantity.
- The user can maintain a Single Excise invoice book for all purposes of removals as per the requirement of Rule 11 and an option is provided to maintain the multiple Excise invoice book for a given Excise unit, the Serial number of Excise book will be generated as running series & with a check for duplicate numbers.
- The Excise Duty types & it's Calculation Method are Pre-defined for error free calculation.
- Items can be classified as per tariff (CETSH/HSN) number, and to support error free calculation duty types and calculation methods can be pre-defined with options provided to manage excise duty for Exempt and Special Rates.
- An option is provided to avail CEVAT Credit during purchase entry or avail partial/full credit in a separate entry. Input Service Tax can also be taken as input credit towards Excise duty payable.

Excise Manufacturing Reports in Tally.ERP 9

- Personal Ledger Account (P.L.A.): This is to be submitted on a monthly basis with the details of Excise duty payments and payable.

- ER1: Monthly return for production and removal of Goods and other relevant particulars.
- G.A.R.-7: Proforma for Central Excise duty payments.
- CENVAT Credit on / Capital Goods Availed / Utilized Account: Details of CENVAT Credit availed and utilized for capital goods.
- Record of CENVAT Credit Allowable on Capital Goods (RG23 C Part II).
- Quantitative Account of Capital Goods on which CENVAT Credit Availed (RG23 C).
- CENVAT Credit on Inputs availed / Utilised Account.
- Records of CENVAT Credit Allowable on Inputs (RG23 A PartII).
- Quantitative Account of Inputs on which CENVAT Credit Availed (RG23 A).
- Rule 11 Invoice: The Excise invoice can be generated as per Rule 11 requirements.
- Daily Stock Account (RG 1 Register): Provides RG1 Register as prescribed the excise dept. for daily entry of production and removals.
- Statutory Sales Register: provides complete details of Excise sales of finished goods.

Auditors' Edition of Tally.ERP 9

Tally.ERP 9 offers a special Gold Auditors' Edition, which provides Audit and Compliance capabilities exclusively for Chartered Accountants. The current release provides the following tools:

- Tax Audit
- Statutory Compliance

Using Tally.ERP 9, Chartered Accountants can provide Audit and Compliance services to their clients in the following scenarios:

Audit at CA's office by accessing local data

The Auditors' Edition includes the Audit/Compliance capabilities as a default feature without any dependency on Tally.NET for Authentication. When the Client's data is locally available at CA's office, the Auditor can perform the Audit or Verification as the Tax Audit and Statutory Compliance features are available by default.

Audit at Client's place by accessing local data

When the Auditor wants to use the Auditors' License from Clients Office to provide the Audit or Compliance Service, the Internet Connection and Tally.NET subscription is required. The Client should have authorized the Chartered Accountant as Tally.NET Auditor for the Company. In this scenario, Tally.NET is used to Authenticate the Auditor and fetch the Auditors' License on the Client's Tally.ERP 9. The Auditor can then open the Company and perform Audit or Verification in the same way as it is done in the Auditor's office with Local data using the Auditor's License.

In this scenario, the Auditor should have a valid Tally.NET subscription to perform Audit.

Audit Remotely by accessing Client's data from anywhere

When the Auditor wants to access the Client's Data Remotely and provide Audit and Compliance services from his office (or from any other remote location), the internet connection and valid Tally.NET subscription is a must for both Auditor and Client. The Client should have authorized the Chartered Accountant as Tally.NET Auditor and Connect the Company to Tally.NET at the time of Audit/ Verification process. The Auditor will Login as Remote User and provide the Auditor's Username and

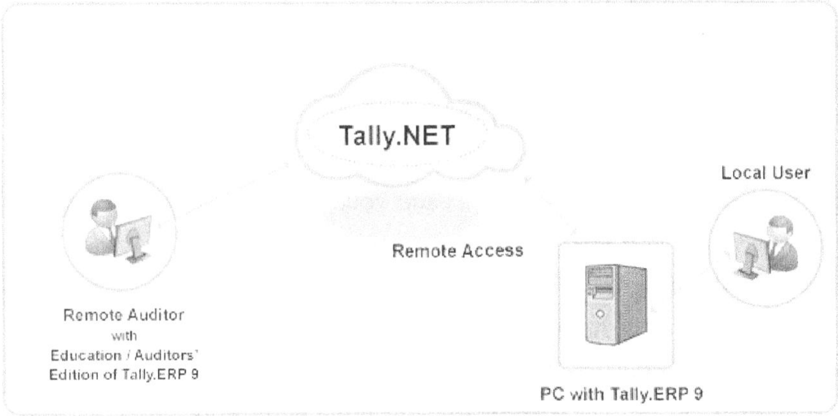

Fig. 1.5 Remote Auditor

Password to view the Companies that are available for Audit (Connected) belonging to various Client's based on the Access provided. The Auditor can open the required Company to perform the Audit/ Verification and save the Audit/Verification Notes.

The user experience essentially remains the same in all the three scenarios.

Tax Audit

The Tax Audit feature in Tally.ERP 9 enables the auditor to compile information in comparatively less time with required accuracy to form his opinion and print Annexures as required for Tax Audit under Section 44AB. The following Clauses are available with respect to Form 3CD:

- Bonus PF, ESI Recoveries (Clause 16)
- Amounts inadmissible u/s 40A(3)(Clause 17(h))
- Payments u/s 43B (Clause 21)
- Employer's Contribution
- Tax Collected at Source
- Service Tax
- Value Added Tax
- Loans / Deposits Accepted (Clause 24(a))
- Loans / Deposits Repaid (Clause 24(b))
- Fringe Benefits Tax (Annexure II).

Statutory Compliance

Statutory Compliance is a comprehensive tool available with Auditors' Edition to provide Compliance services for the following Direct and Indirect Tax modules available in Tally.ERP 9.

- Value Added Tax (VAT)
- Service Tax
- Fringe Benefit Tax (FBT)
- Tax Collected at Source (TCS).

The salient features for Statutory and Compliances are:

- Taxation based in-built rules to classify the Masters and Vouchers as Possibly Incorrect (not created as per the recommended setup for each Taxation)
- Reasons for Possibly Incorrect Masters and Vouchers
- Auditor can concentrate only on Possibly Incorrect and save time
- No need for 100% verification of Masters and Vouchers (for other than Possibly Incorrect)
- Taxation based Payable & Paid information
- Taxation based Due Dates
- Random verification of In Accordance Masters and Vouchers
- Provision to raise Clarification on Master and Vouchers from Clients
- Provides facility to record Verification Remarks using Verification Note.

Major Enhancements

Some of the major functionality changes in Tally.ERP 9 include,

- TDS Compliance
- Data Synchronization
- Size and Performance
- FBT.

Tax Deducted at Source (TDS)

The TDS feature in Tally.ERP 9 has been revamped to handle all the functional, accounting and statutory requirements of your business in an accurate and simplified manner. The new/enhanced TDS features are:

- Option provided to the user to deduct the TDS at the time booking the Expense itself.
- The user can deduct the TDS in a single Voucher at the end of the month for all TDS related Expenses/ Advance Payments booked during a particular month.
- Provides an option to have a single Expense Ledger for multiple Nature of Payments. This will reduce the need to create Nature of Payments wise separate Ledgers.
- The user can have a single TDS Duty Ledger for multiple Nature of Payments. This will reduce the need to create multiple Duty Ledgers.
- Both TDS related and non-TDS related Expenses can be booked in a single Voucher. You can also deduct the TDS at the time of Voucher entry or later.
- Handling TDS for Non-Residents (Sec.195) Payments.
- Tally.ERP 9 handles TDS deductions where payment to the contractor or the sub-contractor exceeds Rs.20, 000 in a single payment or Rs. 50,000 in aggregate during a financial year as prescribed under section 194C.
- Surcharge Retrospective Calculation – Once the Surcharge Exemption Limit exceeds for a particular Nature of Payment for a Particular Vendor, the Surcharge will be calculated for the previous payments also.

- Facility to Print (Hard Copy) and Export Form 26, 26Q & related Annexures, Form 27, 27Q & related Annexures and Form 16A.
- Provides the option to configure the Lower / Zero rate, Ignore IT / Surcharge Exemption Limit in the Party Creation screen. This will facilitate faster data entry as the user need not remember the party TDS details at the time of Voucher entry.

TDS related Reports in Tally.ERP 9:

- TDS Computation Report – This report will help the user to manage the TDS deductions.
- TDS Challan (ITNS 281) printing – Monthly challan based on the TDS sections.
- TDS Outstanding Reports – Displays the details of the TDS Outstanding for the selected period.

This can be filtered based on:

- TDS Payable
- Nature of Payment wise
- Party wise.
- TDS Exception Reports – This report will display the details of the vendor which are not having the required details for e-TDS filing (There are certain pre-defined fields to captured and validated before e-TDS filing). e.g. TDS parties not having PAN details.
- Form 16A – TDS Certificate to be provided to the vendors either at the time of Payment or at the end the year (Annually).
- Form 26 & Annexure – Annual returns of TDS deducted and paid.
- Form 26Q & Annexure – Quarterly returns of TDS deducted and paid.
- Form 27 & Annexure – Annual returns for Non-Residents for TDS deducted and paid.
- Form 27Q & Annexure – Quarterly returns for Non-Residents for TDS deducted and paid.
- e-TDS – Generates the required file for filing the TDS returns electronically.
- Form 27A – Covering Letter for e-TDS returns.

Data Synchronization Changes

Using Direct – Client and Server Capability

Direct- Client and Server capability for Synchronization through a private network will be incorporated as a default feature of Tally.ERP 9 Series A release 1.0 onwards.

Using Tally.NET Server

The process of Data Synchronization using TallyLink Server has been changed in Tally.ERP 9. Going forward Synchronization will be available as a service through the Tally.NET Framework. The user will be able to use Tally.ERP 9 Silver (SU) at both the ends to Synchronize data.

To use this service the Tally Server Company has to be Connected to Tally.NET server at the time of Synchronization.

Tally.NET Server (TNS) will be used for Synchronization instead of TRB Server.

In Sync Configuration, under TallyLink Configuration, the options "Use Tally Link" & "Connect to Tally Link Server" have been removed.

Size and Performance Changes

Automatic caching based on system memory

Report generation involving large amount of data was always impeded by the problem of high memory usage. In Tally.ERP 9, a new feature has been introduced to overcome this hurdle. The application now uses an automatic caching based on the memory of the system it is running on. This results in the usage of lesser memory even with higher data volumes. Reports which were running out of memory or consuming a large amount of virtual memory on a 2GB system, will now respond even on a 1GB system. This can be observed by generating a report, say a day book containing 50,000 to 100,000 vouchers on a 512MB machine using the last major release as well as this release.

Faster Data Entry

The data entry speed has been considerably increased in scenarios where there are a large number of 'Tracking numbers' and 'list of pending orders'. In other words, the time taken to make a single entry has been reduced due to the faster retrieval and display of tables for selection of tracking numbers and pending orders.

Application size reduction by three-fourth

A faster, powerful and a SMALLER Tally.ERP 9 application! The application has been redesigned to drastically reduce its size. The "exe" file of the application has been reduced to approximately three-fourth the size of earlier versions. To be more precise, it has been reduced from 10.7 MB to 1.96 MB. This will result in faster installation, loading, and opening of the application, thereby enhancing the overall user experience.

DATA SIZE Reduction

The data size for Tally.ERP 9 has been effectively reduced to 40%. This will help in enhancing the overall performance of the application.

Data rewrite is mandatory in this release.

Performance

- GST Analysis Report - Performance of GST Analysis Report (Singapore) for a specific period has improved compared to Tally 7.2 and Tally 9 (earlier releases).
- Bank Reconciliation Statement- Performance of Bank Reconciliation statement for a specific period has improved compared to earlier releases of Tally 9.
- Memory and performance is Optimized for long reports like daybook based on vouchers.

Fringe Benefits Tax

The following enhancements are made in the Fringe Benefits Tax feature of Tally.ERP 9:

- FBT Annual Returns in Form ITR 8 along with FB I schedule displaying the details of computation of Fringe Benefits & Fringe Benefits Tax is available.
- Exemption Amount field is provided for FBT transactions to capture exemption amount and to accurately calculate the FBT on the assessable value.
- F12: Configuration option in FBT Computation allows you to view FBT, Surcharge, Education Cess and Secondary Education Cess details in Separate columns, by enabling Show Tax Details.

TDL Enhancements for Tally.ERP 9

In Tally.ERP 9, major changes have been provided by the platform to enhance the TDL capabilities which helps the programmer to develop and deploy quick and efficient solutions with ease. Major improvements have taken place in terms of language usage standardisation and performance improvements.

Breakthrough enhancements at the Collection level to provide capabilities of Remoting and Advanced Reporting. Collection is now a complete Data Processing Artefact in TDL.

Let us now have an overview of the major enhancements that have taken place in the areas mentioned below. A detailed documentation for each of these enhancements is available in our document "TDL Enhancements for Tally.ERP 9". This document along with corresponding Sample TDL's can be downloaded from our website.

Attributes and Modifier Enhancements

Based on user requirements and analysis many new attributes have been introduced. These have impacted the programmer in a way that has reduced their deployment time to cater to functional requirements. Some of the new usage have improved the performance drastically.

The behaviour and syntax of many attributes and modifiers have been changed to maintain consistency and ease of code. The sequence of evaluation of attributes and modifiers have been standardised. Mentioned below is the complete set of new Attributes and Modifiers.

- Report Attribute – Full Screen
- Key attributes – Scope
- Part attribute – Retain Focus
- Field attributes – Tool Tip, Set By Condition
- Collection Attribute – Subtitle
- New Modifier – Switch.

Mentioned below is the list of existing attributes and modifiers for which the behaviour has been changed.

- Attribute Set As and Info – When both are specified, Info takes Precedence
- Enhanced syntax of Local – Now can be nested
- Format Attribute
- Attribute Sync
- The sequence of evaluation of Attributes and Modifiers
- Modifier-Use
- Standardization of Modifiers Add/Delete/Replace across definitions.

Enhanced Special Symbols

New special symbols have been introduced to take care of Multiline commenting(/* */), reinitializing definitions(*). The existing system formulas can now be modified for optimized performance using the extended behaviour of '#'

New Method Formula Syntax with Relative Object Specification

The $ operator has been enhanced with a new capabilities. This allows direct access to any object method including its sub-collections to any level with a dotted notation framework. Using the new capability, there is no need to repeat a line over a sub-collection to access it. The values from any object anywhere can be accessed without making the object as the current object in context.

Enhancements-Object Association & Object Access via Interface Object

In TDL, Interface Object exists in context of any data object. Every Interface object needs to be associated with some data object. In the absence of any explicit object association, Interface object will get associated with Anonymous object. TDL programmer can explicitly associate Interface objects like Report, Part, Line and Field with data object. There have been changes either in the form of syntax improvements or with the introduction of new attributes like "Object Ex" at the part level.

From this release onwards, data objects in associated with Interface objects can be accessed using the new Interface object access syntax. Now it is possible to identify an Interface object using Access Name and then use the enhanced method formula syntax to access the Data Object associated with it. Data object which is associated to Interface Object can be accessed with the following 2 step procedure.

- Identifying Part and Line Interface object with 'Access Name'
- Value/Collection Extraction.

Bracket Support in Language Syntax

Prior to this release, the usage of TDL language token bracket ('(' and ')') was restricted as mathematical operator only. From this release onwards brackets can be used in the following scenarios.

- During the function call to enclose the function parameter.
- In the language syntax for nesting formulas.
- As a Mathematical Operator.

Action Enhancements

Key action is enhanced to perform various operations on multiple lines. Multiline selection capability is possible with the help of two attributes Scope(Key definition) and Selectable (Part and Line definition). Some New and Changed Actions are mentioned below:

New Actions

- Modify Object
- Set Object Values
- Browse URL
- HTTP Post.

Enhanced Actions

- Print
- Mail
- Export
- Upload.

User Defined Functions in TDL

This is one of the breakthrough changes which has taken place at the platform level. We all know that TDL is a definition language which provides capability for rapid development. But now TDL is procedural as well. With the introduction of Functions/Procedures as a part of Tally.ERP 9 family the TDL capabilities have reached a new dimension.

This will help the application programmers to develop their own functions for achieving business functionality. Their will be a decrease in platform dependency for particular business function. The resultant would be faster development cycles for business modules.

Collection Enhancements

Collection, the data processing artefact of TDL provides extensive capabilities to gather data not only from Tally database but also from external sources using ODBC, DLLs, and HTTP and so on. A set of new capabilities have been added to Collection which provides far more flexibility and power in the hands of the TDL programmer. This will allow writing significantly complex reports with ease and still delivering enhanced performance with high volume of data.

The following are the capabilities which have been achieved using new collection enhancements.

Aggregation & Summarization

A major technological advancement in this release of Tally.ERP 9 is "Data Roll up in TDL Collection – GROUP BY". This will now facilitate the creation of large summary tables of aggregations in a single shot using the new attributes of the Collection description. This allows us to Walk down the object hierarchies and gathers values and summarizes them in one scan. Overall it reduces the TDL code complexity, resource requirement and increases performance drastically in case of reports generated using this new capability.

Collection re-use, extraction and chaining

A collection can extract information from other collections including its sub-objects with the choice of method(s), filter(s) and sort-order. Source Collection within a collection, collection(s) can be chained. In other words, Summary Collection can be used as Source Collection for some other Collection and so on.

Indexed or Searchable Collection on TDL defined keys

The capabilities discussed above extend the data gathering capabilities of TDL. However business reporting in general and in Tally uses hierarchical presentation or columnar presentation rather than simple table representation. If Report is having two or more dimensions like Ledger and Cost Centre and so on, a simple repeat on the summarized collection will not suffice. In order to improve performance indexing capability has been introduced which will work with a key combination.

Usage as Tables

TDL allows to display the values obtained from the collection as a pop-up table. Earlier the values of voucher and the ODBC data can't be displayed as a collection. Now all limitations pertaining to usage of Collections as Tables have been completely eliminated. Any collection which can be created in TDL can be displayed as a table now. Collection with aggregation and XML Collections can also be used as Tables.

Integration Capabilities using HTTP XML Collection

Collection capability has been enhanced to gather live data from HTTP/web-service delivering XML. The entire XML is automatically now converted to TDL objects and is available natively in TDL reports as $ based methods. Reports can be shown live from an HTTP server. The attributes in collection for gathering XML based data from a remote server over HTTP are RemoteURL, RemoteRequest, XMLObjectPath, and XMLObject.

Dynamic Object support for HTTP-XML Information Interchange

When a collection is used for editing (alter/create), objects are dynamically added to the collection when a new line is repeated over the same. The type of object which is added depends on the specification in the TYPE attribute. In case the TYPE attribute is not specified it defaults to adding a standard empty object.

However the following holds true for a COLLECTION keeping in mind the latest enhancements.

- It can be made up of multiple types of objects (say Ledgers and Groups).
- It can have TDL defined objects which are retrieved from XML file.They are specified using XML Object.
- It can have aggregated objects.

Depending solely on the TYPE attribute for deciding the object type is a constraint with respect to the above facts. This is now being removed with the introduction of a new attribute which will independently govern the type of object to be added to the collection on-the-fly. A new attribute NEW OBJECT is now supported for collection.

Collection Capabilities for Remoting

Enabling access to your organizational data in an 'any-time, any-where' and yet being truly usable is what Tally.ERP 9 delivers. With Tally.NET enabled remote access, it will be possible for any authorized user to access Tally.ERP 9 from anywhere.

Major Enhancements have taken place at the collection level to achieve remoting capabilities. The attributes Fetch, Compute and AggrCompute provided at the collection level and FetchObject and FetchCollection at the report level significantly help in above functionality.

For detailed documentation, refer to Writing Remote Compliant TDL for Tally.ERP 9 on Tally Website.

Minor Enhancements

Accounting Masters

- In the Group Creation /Alteration screen, the option No Appropriation has been removed as it had the same behaviour of Not Applicable.
- On disabling TDS / TCS, in the Ledger Alteration, Tally.ERP does allow the manual selection of State.
- The field Rounding Method is provided in Ledger masters grouped under Duties & Taxes, Direct Expenses, Indirect Expenses, Direct Income, Indirect Income, Current Asset, Current Liability, Sales Accounts, Purchase Accounts and Primary Group in Purchase/Sales Invoice mode only.

Accounting Reports

- F8: Other Report option is disabled in Statistics and Group Payment Performance under Group Summary.

Accounting Vouchers

- In sales invoice, the Company's/Buyer's Tax Registration numbers will be printed in the order given below:
- Company's VAT TIN No.
- Company's CST No.
- Company's Service Tax No.
- Buyer's VAT TIN/Sales Tax No.
- Buyer's Service Tax No.
- The Option 'Show Ledger Current Balances' in F12: Voucher Configuration is now applicable for Ledgers in Invoice Format. If this field is set to NO, the Current Balance of ledgers will not be displayed in the invoices.

- A Purchase order entered in a company with GST Registration number can be exported using Excel (Spreadsheet) or HTML format.
- Application supports the printing of Inventory Details for Debit Note, Credit Note, Payment, Receipt and Journal entered in voucher mode, by enabling the option Print Inventory Details in F12: Print Configuration.
- A Facility to print the serial number for each item in the Sales Invoice has been provided.
- An option has been provided to print the system date and time in all the reports including the Invoice.

Company Master

- Enhanced Company Creation Master with user friendly interface is provided.
- The F12 Configuration options are modified for all the masters. The F12: Configuration screen will now display only relevant configurations depending upon the selected Master/Voucher/ Feature.
- A new option Disallow Opening in Educational Mode is provided in the Company Creation/ Alteration mode as an additional scattier control measure to prevent the users from opening the particular Company in Educational Tally.ERP 9. This will appear only if the Security Control feature is enabled.

This feature will help to ensure that the unauthorised users does not open and view/alter/delete the Company data from Educational version of Tally.ERP 9. The users will be restricted to open the data without the Account TDL's being loaded (which may have certain restrictions) in Educational Mode.

Cost Categories/Cost Centres

- Cost Centres will appear along with Cost Centre Class in all Vouchers.

CST

- In CST Forms Issueable / Receivable report, F12: Configure option is provided to sort details of Party in an alphabetical order.

Email

- SSL Interfaces are provided to enable the user to E-mail the required information from Tally.ERP 9 to external Mail servers. e.g. now you can use Gmail service to send e-mail through Tally.ERP 9.

Excise for Dealers

- In Excise Sales Invoice, Supplier Details for Stock item displays Rate of Basic Excise Duty and Excise Duty Per Unit along with supplier details and quantity purchased in the List of Purchases table.
- A separate column has been provided to display the Special Additional Duty in the printed format of Excise Purchase Invoice.
- In Gujarat Excise Sales invoice, a separate column has been added to display the HSN Code.
- In an Excise Purchase Invoice, an option has been provided to create a ledger under Manufacturer/ Importer Details section in Supplementary Details screen.

- Configuration Use Excise Format in F12: Configuration is displayed only on enabling the option Allow Excise rules for Invoicing in F11: Features.

Fringe Benefits Tax

- Verification Details is provided in the FBT Print Configuration screen for FBT Returns to capture the Designation, Date and Place details.

Final Accounts

- If the option Income/Expense Statement instead of P & L is enabled in F11: Accounting Features, then in Income and Expenses A/c report, F12: Configure displays Show Vertical Income & Expense Stmt. instead of Show Vertical Profit & Loss.
- In Statistics report, a facility has been provided to sort the voucher types using the configuration Sort by Parent Voucher Type.

Installation

The language support for Bahasa Indonesia and Bahasa Melayu has been provided for Windows 98 & Windows NT operating system also.

Inventory Masters

- In the Stock Group and Stock Item creation and alteration screen, a minimum width of 30 characters is provided to ensure visibility of names entered.

Inventory Vouchers

- The option "Show using Alternate Units" is provided in F12: configure of Stock Vouchers screen to display the alternate unit details for stock items.

Job Costing

- In Material Consumption Stock Summary report, Alt+C – New column will now display the details of all the Godowns, related to a particular Job/Project instead of other Job/Project (Cost Centre) details.

Licensing

- A Confirmation message is displayed when the user opts to surrender the licensed version of Tally.ERP 9.
- In the process of activating license, an hour glass will be displayed as an indicator to show the progress of activation.

Multi-currency

- Bank Reconciliation displays the accurate Closing Balance of Transacted Currency as per Company Books and Actual Balance, when "Show Forex Transactions only" is activated in F12: Configure.

Payroll & Statutory

- The Payslip when emailed in HTML format contains the Company Name and Address.
- In the Pay Head Master, an option has been provided to round off the Gratuity amount.
- The Option 'Show Zero Value Payslips Also' is provided in Multi Payslip Printing to print the Blank Payslips.
- In Paysheet, the Grand Total of Attendance is displayed and the user can drill down to Attendance Voucher from Attendance details.

- Position Index for Reports of the Employee is set as Default Sorting Method for all the Payroll Reports, in addition Alphabetical (increasing) and Alphabetical (decreasing) options are added to the Sorting Methods list of Pay Sheet Configuration.
- Tally.ERP 9 now allows the user to group the (Income Tax) TDS Pay Head under Duties & Taxes and Salary Payable Pay Head under Provisions.
- The option Show new joinees only has been renamed as Show zero valued Employees also in F12: Configuration of Gratuity Report.
- In Pay sheet report the option "Display Attendance/Production Types in Tail Units?" is provided under F12: Configure.
- New Pay Head Type Bonus has been provided in the Pay Head masters creation.
- In International Version of Tally Gratuity Report Option has been provided in Payroll Reports Menu.
- The Payroll Info. menu order has been changed as shown below:
- Employee Groups
- Employees
- Units (Work)
- Attendance/Production Types
- Pay Heads
- Salary Details
- Voucher Types.
- The shortcut key for Payroll Reports (payroll statutory reports) under Statutory Reports has been changed from A to P.
- The option Payroll Configuration will be available by default in the F12: Configurations screen, whether the Company is selected or not.
- Professional Tax Pay Head can now be created with Calculation Period as both Month and Period. This will support the Professional Tax Computation either monthly or Periodically(Half Yearly) as required by some of the states (*e.g.*, Tamil Nadu).

POS

- Party Details can now be entered and Printed in the POS Invoice.

Printing

- The Option "Print Narration for Each Entry" is provided in F12: Invoice printing Configuration to print narration for each entry in Purchase or Sales voucher.
- The Option "Print Narration" is provided in F12: Configure (Physical Stock Printing Setup) to print Narration in Physical Stock Voucher. The same facility is provided to print Stock Journal Voucher.
- Print Configuration is provided for Rejections In and Rejections Out Voucher Types.

- The Title provided in Print configuration screen of Payment/Receipt/ Journal/Debit Note/Credit Note voucher is changed from Printing Setup to Printing Configuration.

Reports

- Alt + Enter key has been provided for Remote as well as Local users, to facilitate to drill down to voucher level in Display mode.
- Ctrl + Enter key has been provided for Remote as well as Local users, to facilitate to drill down to voucher level in Alteration mode.

Security Control

- A warning message "Forgetting your password will render your data unusable!!" will be displayed when the user is setting or changing the Admin User Name and/or Password in Company Creation/alteration screen.

Service Tax

- In Sales Register columnar report, a separate column has been provided for displaying the Service Tax Registration number.
- In Service Tax Payables report, F4: Category button has been added to filter the services provided, based on the service category.
- According to the new notification the "Focal Bank Details" has been withdrawn from Company F11: Statutory and Taxation under Company Service Tax Details.
- Options have been provided to Display/Alter the Exemption Notification Number in item invoice.
- In service tax payment voucher, cheques/Draft/Pay order No and Bank Name fields are provided under 'Payment Details' sub screen in 'Provide details' field.
- Option to enter Challan No. and Challan Date is provided under Payment Details in Service Tax GAR 7 Payment Voucher, which will get printed in ST3 Form.
- Cost centre allocation has been provided for Service Tax ledgers created under Duties and Taxes while recording Sales Vouchers.
- The Service Tax Invoice captures Company's PAN Number after Buyer's Service Tax Number.

VAT

- In the voucher class screen of sales voucher type, the Calculation Methods Additional Tax and Cess on VAT can be selected only if the VAT Classification is selected in the respective sales ledger.
- When a Company opts for Composition to Regular VAT and tries to pass a purchase entry during composition period, in Purchase Accounting Allocation Screen VAT/TAX Class displays Composition VAT Classifications for selection.
- When a MRP Stock Items Invoice is printed with VAT Analysis, total MRP Assessable Value is displayed as Net Value under VAT analysis.
- Payment Details are now supported for Haryana VAT Forms and CST Form.
- Payment Details are now supported for Himachal Pradesh VAT Forms and CST Form. Issues Resolved.

Accounting Masters

- Opening Balance Bill Details in the ledger master are neither being updated nor erased when the Opening Balance is altered in the ledger. This issue has been resolved.

Accounting Reports

- On selecting Budget Variance and then selecting any particular month in Stock Item Monthly Summary, the error message Memory Access violation is being displayed. This issue has been resolved.
- In Purchase/Sales Voucher Register report, where the sort option is selected as Amount-wise (Decreasing) and Amount-wise (Increasing), the amount as per the selected method is not being displayed. This issue has been resolved.
- In case of a journal entry consisting of a sundry creditor ledger, the Day Book Extract report of Journal voucher is not displaying Sundry Creditors under Current Liabilities. This issue has been resolved.
- The Post Dated vouchers report displays regular vouchers along with post dated vouchers when the report period was changed. This issue has been resolved.
- Date range is not refreshing while viewing Outstanding Report from the Ledger Report. This Issue has been resolved.
- A credit note entry made in voucher mode, is displaying the invoice format without Party name when printed from Multi Voucher Printing option. The same entry when made in invoice mode, displays the invoice format with party name when printed from Multi Voucher Printing. This issue has been resolved. The credit note entry made both in voucher and invoice mode, when printed from Multi Voucher Printing option is displaying the Party name.
- In case of multi year data, date range provided for previous year in ledger outstanding report from respective Ledger account is not being displayed as per the specified date range. This issue has been resolved.
- On pressing Enter on the exploded line of Group Vouchers; it would display Forex Gain / Loss Statement as the report heading. This issue is resolved and it does not allow to drill down.
- In the Outstanding Ledger Report, when Show Bills of following type is set to Debit Bills in F12: Configure, both credit and debit bills are displayed in the report. This issue has been resolved and only Debit Bill are displayed when Show Bills of following type is set to Debit Bills in F12: Configure.

Accounting Vouchers

- In sales invoice, if one VAT ledger is selected and then changed to another VAT ledger before saving the entry, the percentage and amount are not being refreshed. This issue has been resolved and the VAT Percentage and amount are now being calculated on the basis of the reselected VAT ledger.
- A voucher class consisting of multiple excise duty ledgers with Type of Calculation based On Item Rate calculates the amount of duty on the item for all excise ledgers included in the voucher class and displays it in the Excise Sales Invoice. This issue has been resolved. The calculation of excise duty on an item is now being displayed only for the relevant excise ledger.
- On activating Use Additional Description(s) for Ledger Name in Invoice Configuration, the Description of Ledger screen is not being displayed for Accounts only companies. This issue has

been resolved. The Description of Ledger screen is now being displayed even for Accounts only companies.

- When the same Bank Ledger is selected for both Cheque and Card Payment fields in POS Invoice entry, the amount displayed in both the fields was the same, when opened in alteration mode. This issue has been resolved.
- On changing the invoice date in a Sales Invoice entered with voucher class having discount ledger and method of calculation set to As User Defined Value, in the alteration mode, the percentage entered is not being displayed. This issue has been resolved.
- In a Sales / Purchase Invoice containing two different VAT sales/ purchase ledger, the sales/ purchase figure of an item is modified either by changing the rate, quantity or the sales/purchase amount directly. After this modification, the sales/purchase value is not being picked up automatically in the "Assessable Value" field. This issue has been resolved.
- When a single excise stock item is accounted in a sales voucher with the Voucher Class containing Multiple Excise Ledgers with different Rates (Grouped under Duties & Taxes) and Type of calculation as Tax based on Item Rate, the Excise amount is being calculated for all the Excise Ledgers. This issue has been resolved.
- When a voucher is recorded with the selection of Voucher class having Excise duty ledgers set to calculate the Excise on Current Sub Total and the option Calculate Tax on current Sub-Total is activated in F12: Configure, the Excise amount is calculated based on the Current Subtotal. But, if the same voucher is altered by deactivating the option Calculate Tax on current Sub-Total, the Excise amount is calculated based on the Item Rate and not on the current sub-total. This issue has been Resolved and now the excise amount is calculated correctly.
- On creating a POS invoice with different amounts entered in the Credit/Debit Card Payment and Cheque fields with the same bank ledger in the voucher creation mode and then on opening this invoice in the alteration mode, the same amount is being displayed in both fields. Apart from that, the entries are not being saved in the alteration mode. This issue has been resolved and the values entered in the above mentioned fields are being retained with the flexibility to save the changes made to the invoice.
- While altering a Sales Invoice, the VAT/TAX Class does not appear for the second and subsequent items. This issue has been resolved and the VAT/TAX class is now displayed for any number of items added to the sales invoice in the alteration mode.
- When the option Maintain Bill wise Details is not enabled under F11: Accounting Features, a Ledger created under Sundry Debtors or Sundry Creditors Group with Opening Balance allows the mentioning of Bill-wise Break-up for the amount. This issue has been fixed.

Audit Features

- A voucher accepted during Audit and then deleted displays particulars as DELETED – Audit Voucher in Audit Listing. On pressing Enter to view such a voucher, Ledger Forex Gain/Loss report is being displayed. This issue has been resolved.

Budgets and Credit Limits

- The function Sales Voucher Registers with Extract of all vouchers, crashes when Budget Variance is selected. This issue has been resolved and the Budget variance button has been removed from the Sales Register, Purchase Register, Journal Register under Accounts Books, Bill Outstanding

Reports of Sundry Debtors and Creditors, Stock Items, Stock Transfers, Physical Stock Register under Inventory Books and Memorandum Vouchers under Exception Reports, as it is not required.

Cost Categories

- The Cash Book is displaying cost centre details only when printed from Multi Column Cash/ Bank and not from Account Books of Multi Account Printing menu. This issue has been resolved.

Crash/MAV

- While Filtering the Stock Items with Stock Groups from Sales Register, the application crashes with the error message "Memory Access Violation". This issue has been resolved.
- While Printing any report if the Key combination Alt+U is pressed instead of Alt+I to select the print preview option in the Print Configuration screen, the application crashes with the error message "Memory Access Violation". This issue has been resolved.

Data/TCP Migration

- On migrating data from Tally 7.2 to Tally 9, the order reference number entered in supplementary details of some of the sales invoices are getting changed. This issue has been resolved and the order reference number entered in every sales invoice is now being retained even after migrating data from Tally 7.2 to Tally.ERP 9.

Excise for Dealers

- When multiple Purchases pertaining to a single Item are adjusted in a Excise Sales Invoice, the values of such entries are capturing only the first item in the Excise Stock Register/Excise Purchase Bill Register. This issue has been resolved.
- In the detailed format of Excise Stock Register and Purchase Bill Register report, the address of the party is not being displayed in the Name and Address of the Party column only for the first entry. This Issue has been resolved and the address of the party is now being displayed for all entries in the detailed format of Excise Stock Register and Purchase Bill Register.
- Excise Opening Stock Entry details do not appear in the Excise Stock Register and when the sales invoice raised against the opening stock is printed, Excise Pass on Duty Values and Excise Purchase Section Duty Values do not appear in the printed Sales invoice. This issues have been Resolved.

Export/Import

- When Stock Items with Part Numbers are exported using Excel (spreadsheet) format, the Part Numbers are displayed with a negative sign in the Excel sheet. This issue has been resolved and the part numbers of the stock items are now being displayed correctly in the Excel sheet.
- On exporting any of the Ledger vouchers from Tally to Excel Spread Sheet, the Debit/Credit Balances are interchanged (Debit balance is shown as credit and the credit balance is shown as debit) in Excel. This issue has been resolved.
- When Vouchers without Effective Date are imported in SDF format, the application displays the error message crashes with error message Memory Access Violation. This issue has been resolved and vouchers can now be imported even when the effective date is not mentioned in the voucher.
- When Ledgers are exported in ASCII format from Multi Account Printing as Group of Accounts by enabling the option Start fresh page for each Account in Print Configuration screen, the exported text file displays the group ledger which was debited even in the Credit field. This issue has been resolved.

- When the Bank Reconciliation Statement is exported using Excel Format, the details are not being displayed in the appropriate columns and the Balance as per Bank and Company Books is being displayed twice. This issue has been resolved.
- Compound Units are not getting exported to Excel. This issue has been resolved and compound units can now be exported to excel as text and not as a number.

Final Accounts

- The column heading separator lines do not appear when a new column is inserted in the Profit and Loss Account. This issue has been resolved and the column heading separator lines appear in the Profit and Loss Account.

Fringe Benefit Tax

- FBT Challan Reconciliation displays even the Reconciled Vouchers, when the option Show Reconciled vouchers is not activated in F12: Configure. This issue has been resolved.
- When a FBT Payment entry is passed without using the FBT helper, the application allows the entry in the To field, a date prior to the date mentioned in the From field in the FBT Payment Details screen. This issue has been resolved.
- On entering only the month in FBT Filters, the first day of the month was being displayed as date in both From Date and To Date fields.This issue has now been resolved.
- The Additional Education Cess @ 1% applicable only from April 2008, is being calculated and displayed in the FBT Computation report generated for the period 2006-07. This issue has been resolved and now the Additional Education Cess @ 1% is not considered in the FBT Computation report of the previous year.
- While generating the FBT Computation report for a financial year, the application hangs if the volume of data is high. This issue has been resolved and the FBT Computation report now displays the details like any other report regardless of data size.
- In the FBT Computation Report, Tax is being calculated even on the Credit Value of Expenditure and as a result the Grand Total of Net expenditure amount is being displayed with a negative sign.This issue has been resolved.
- FBT Ledger created in FBT Filters sub screen is not displayed in the List of FBT Ledgers for selection. This issue has been resolved.
- The FBT Payment entry marked as optional is affecting the FBT Computation report as it was being considered as a regular payment entry. This issue has now been resolved.
- The value calculated by using FBT Filters in Payment voucher was more than the amount displayed in FBT Computation report. On restoring the data backup of company enabled for FBT, the Company FBT Assessee Details were missing in both Statutory & Taxation Features and FBT Challan. On activating the FBT feature, the amount displayed in FBT Challan is more than the amount displayed in the FBT Computation report. This issue has been resolved. The value displayed in FBT Computation report is captured in FBT Payment voucher on using the auto fill option and the Company FBT Assessee Details are also retained even after restoring the data.
- FBT Computation amount is not matching with the FBT payment amount during FBT Payment

Entry. It shows a difference of Rs.1/-. This happens due to rounding off. This issue has been resolved.

- FBT Computation report captures and prints the period including the post dated voucher date, when the post dated entry is passed using the ledgers for which FBT option is not enabled. This issue has been resolved.

Inventory Masters

- After deleting the components/items used in Bill of Material (BOM), the application has to be reloaded or the item has to be renamed. This issue has been resolved, and the Components/items can now be deleted without reloading the application or renaming the item.
- When Use expiry dates option is changed from Yes to No and again to Yes, the tag name of Allow use of expired batches does not appear. This issues has been resolved and Allow use of expired batches is now displayed when Use expiry dates is changed.
- In the Stock Ageing Analysis report Company Name and Address is not getting printed from the second page onwards. This issue has been resolved.

Inventory Vouchers

- The voucher number of Sales Order is getting reflected in Delivery Note. Hence, the voucher number subsequent to that of sales order is being displayed as the reference number in delivery note. This issue has been resolved.
- On printing a sales invoice in simple format with tracking details for more than one Delivery Note, only one delivery note number was being captured and printed. This issue has been resolved. Multiple delivery note numbers are now being printed in a single sales invoice.
- In the stock item allocation screen of sales order, when Any was selected under godown for a particular stock item, a warning message Negative Stock! is displayed even though there is a closing balance of that item in other godowns. This issue has been resolved. On selecting Any as godown, the warning message Negative Stock! is not displayed if there is closing balance of stock items in other godowns.
- The reference number entered in sales invoice is not being captured in the Bill-wise details screen, if the method of voucher numbering is set to None in the sales voucher type alteration screen. This issue has been resolved.
- In a Manufacturing Journal, for a Stock Item with Component List details (BOM) if the amount is entered for the Component item without defining the rate, then Rate of the Component item is not being calculated automatically (Left blank) based on the quantity and amount. This issue has been resolved and Rate is calculated based on the Quantity and amount specified.
- When a Stock item, allocated with the amount of Expenses on purchase is transferred from one godown to another using Stock Journal, the Rate displayed for the item in Destination Column does not include the expenses on purchase. This issue has been resolved.
- When a Sales Invoice is printed in simple format, Delivery Note date is not being printed, even when the details are entered in the invoice dispatch details. This issue has been resolved and the Delivery Note date is printed in the sales invoice.
- In a sales invoice, if a reference is provided and if "Use defaults for bill allocation" is set to No then reference is captured in Bill wise window. If reference is not provided then the voucher number is captured. This issue has been resolved.

- The Tracking number used in 'Rejection In' is not being displayed in Item Allocation screen of Credit note (As Voucher mode). This issue has been resolved.
- For a Company in which VAT and Use different Actual & Billed Quantity features are enabled, "Calculate MRP on billed quantity" option is not being saved in F12: Invoice / Orders Entry configuration once you quit the application and reopen it. This issue has been resolved.
- On making a sales entry by selecting multiple godowns in the Inventory allocation screen, a warning message showing wrong negative stock is displayed. This issue has been resolved and the warning message displays the correct negative stock value.
- After enabling "Use Common Table for stock items" using CTRL+ALT+F12 from Gateway of Tally, quantity was being displayed in "List of items" in the following voucher types: • Stock journal • Rejection in • Rejection out • Physical Stock. This issue has been resolved and the List of Items is not displayed in the above Vouche types when the option Use Common table for stock items is enabled.
- On taking a printout of the Rejection In voucher, it prints the heading as Rejection In number instead of Order No. This issue has been resolved.

Inventory Reports

- On viewing the stock summary report through F9: Inventory Reports from the Ledger Report screen, the closing stock value is displayed as NIL. This issue has been fixed.

Job Costing

- In the Job Work Analysis report, the Consumption does not consider the Cost of Sales. This issue has been resolved.

Licensing

- Multi-Account Printing menu is not being refreshed when the license is activated or surrendered. It takes effect only when the application is restarted. This issue has been resolved.

Multi-currency

- In the Bank Ledger Voucher report, if a voucher is altered by drilling down from the report, the Opening and Closing Balances of Ledger Voucher report are displayed in the base currency instead of the Foreign currency, if 'Show Forex details' also' and 'Show Forex Transactions only' are enabled in F12: Configure. This issue has been resolved and on altering a voucher containing foreign currency, opening and closing balances appear in foreign currency only.
- On reconciling a bank account containing foreign currency transaction, the Balance is different as per Company Books. This issue is resolved and now it displays the correct reconciled values.
- On viewing any ledger account with the Show Forex Transactions option set to "Yes", it displays the transacted values in foreign currency but opening and closing balances are displayed in the base currency. This has been resolved and it now displays the opening and closing balance in foreign currency.

ODBC/Export/Import

- A Purchase Invoice consisting details of Company's Address and E-Mail ID, when exported in HTML format displays the error message 'Part:EXPINV Purchaser'. This issue has been resolved. The Purchase Invoice is now being exported in HTML format along with the Company's address & Email-ID.

- When Sales Register is exported in HTML or Excel (Spreadsheet) format or printed by enabling Show Columnar Register with Type of Column as All Items (in one col.) the report was being exported/printed in multiple columns. This issue has been resolved.
- On exporting Employee masters in XML format from List of Accounts, all the accounts and payroll masters were also being exported along with employee masters. This issue has been resolved.

Optional & Scenario management

- In the Post Dated Voucher Report, optional voucher is also being displayed. This issue has been resolved.

Payroll & Statutory

- Drill down in Expat Reports, displays the repeated information. This issue has been resolved and the option to drill down from Expat Reports has been removed.
- The option to drill down from Attendance Sheet to Attendance voucher is not functioning. This issue has been resolved.
- The Payment Advice is displaying the monthly instalment of loan amount recovered from employee's salary, even though it is not included in payment voucher. This issue has been resolved.
- In the Pay Head creation screen, if the pay head name is entered and then altered, the changed name is not being displayed in the field Name to appear in Payslip. This issue has now been resolved.
- When the positive attendance type is used in the Pay Head, Payroll was not being calculated for employees who resign before/prior to the date for which the attendance voucher was recorded. This issue has been resolved.
- When Payslips are printed through Multi Payslip Printing by enabling the option Remove Zero Entries, the application still prints blank payslips for deactivated/zero entry employees. This Issue has been resolved and now only the payslips with the entries are printed, when the option Remove Zero Entries is enabled in Multi Payslip Printing.
- When you drill down from the attendance value of the employee in Attendance sheet, Voucher Details are not being displayed in the Attendance Voucher. This issue has been resolved.
- When the Employee Voucher Report is printed, the title of the report is getting printed as Cost Centre instead of Employee. This issue has been resolved.
- Print Configuration Screen of Multi Payslip Printing is not aligned properly. The alignment has now been rectified.

POS

- After recording a POS transaction, the Sales Invoice Printing configuration screen title, is being displayed as 'POS Invoice Printing Configuration' instead of "Invoice Printing Configuration". This issue has been resolved.
- In the alteration mode, List of Ledgers Accounts is not being displayed, when the cursor is in the Credit/Debit Card payment field in a POS Voucher with a Class. This issue has been resolved.
- When the Rate of Expense is altered in a POS voucher with class in the alteration Mode, the Amount is not being calculated properly. This issue has been resolved.

- In the alteration mode, when the Sales Ledger is changed in a POS invoice, the VAT/Tax Class is not being refreshed as applicable to the changed sales ledger. In addition to this, on changing the VAT Ledger the VAT Percentage is Not being changed. This issue has been resolved.
- The application malfunctions when a POS Invoice with a Class (voucher Class is created with 'Type of Calculation' set to "As Total Amount Rounding" under Additional Accounting Entries) is altered. This issue has been resolved.
- On creating a POS Invoice in multi-payment mode with the same bank ledger selected for Credit /Debit Card Payment and Cheque fields with different values, and then opening it in the alteration mode, the amount is repeated in the Credit/Debit Card Payment and Cheque fields. This issue is resolved and amount name does not get repeated.

Printing

- Documents are not printed correctly on HP 1005, 3050 & 2600 N, Samsung ML-4600 Printer and Canon LBP 1120 printers. This issue has been resolved.
- The report title of a Credit Note is being displayed as Cash Voucher, when printed from Multi Voucher Printing option of Multi Account Printing menu. This issue has been resolved and the report titles now display the names of the respective vouchers selected in the Printing Vouchers screen.
- In Day Book – Sales Register, if the Sorting Method was set to Alphabetical (Decreasing/ Increasing), the vouchers were displayed in the order set, but the same was not being reflected in printed format. This issue has been resolved.
- When the invoice title is not defined either in the Sales Voucher Type or in the F12: Invoice Print Configuration, Sales Invoice is printed without title. This issue has been resolved and now "Invoice" is set as Default Title, when the title is not defined in the Voucher Type or in the F12: Invoice Printing Configuration.
- In Multi Account Printing, if the ledger is printed as Group of Account with Debit/Credit entries only, by setting the option Start fresh page for each Account to No, a blank report is being displayed. This issue has been resolved.
- Changes made to Print Configuration settings for Debit Note are not affecting the print. This issue has been resolved.
- While printing a cheque with a ledger grouped under secured/unsecured loans in the payment voucher, the Ledger name does not get printed on the cheque. This issue has been resolved.
- When a credit note is printed by enabling the option 'Print Quantity Column' in Print configuration, the Quantity Column was not getting printed in the credit note. This issue has been resolved.
- While printing the Confirmation of Accounts for Sundry Creditors, the purchase Voucher number is getting printed instead of purchase reference details. This issue has been resolved.
- While printing the Group of Accounts from Multi Account Printing with the option Start fresh page for each Account set to No, the references and inventory details are not printed, even if the options Show Bill wise Details also & Show Inventory Details also are set to Yes. This issue has been resolved.

- Heading in the Print Preview of Rejection In voucher type is displayed as Order No instead of Rejection In No. This issue has been resolved.
- While printing the Rejection In/Rejection Out vouchers, the Batch Number, Manufacturing Date and Expiry Date is not being printed. This issue has been resolved.
- While printing multiple vouchers using Multi Account Printing, from page three onwards, the vouchers are carried over to the next page. This issue has been resolved.
- When we are printing from Multi Account Printing > Account Books > Ledger > All Accounts or Group of Accounts and set Yes to Start fresh page for each Account in the Page Details section, Page: 1 of 1 is displayed even though number of Ledgers to print are more than one. This issue has been resolved.
- When the Page Range is set to Odd/Even or Front /Back, user should be able to navigate between the pages. Currently, only 'Home' and 'End' buttons work i.e. user can go only to first page or last page. Page-up, Page-down, and arrow keys are not working in the Print Preview mode. This issue has been resolved.

Rewrite/Backup/Restore/Split

- On successfully taking a backup on a removable device it is found that all the files in the removable files drive are deleted. This issue is now resolved and on successfully taking backup on the removable drive, the Tally backup file gets added to the device.

Service Tax

- In the process of Splitting the company data of two financial years (2006-2008), wherein Service Tax sale and receipt records are in One financial Year (2006-2007) and The Service Tax payment records are in another financial year (2007-2008), Service Tax paid is displayed as Input Credit in the new company split from 1-4-2007. This issue has been resolved.
- The Service Tax amount is not being captured in the Bill wise Details screen while passing a Journal Voucher. This issue has been resolved and the Service Tax Amount is captured in the bill-wise details screen.

Synchronization

- When the user tries to synchronize the data containing the '<' or '>' symbol specified either in narration or ledger or stock item name field or in any other field, the application displays the XML tag (< or >) in the calculator panel without terminating the Synchronization process. This issue has been resolved.

Tax Collected at Source

- When a TCS payment entry is recorded using TCS Helper with the option Show Bill wise details in F12: Configure enabled, Bill-wise details for TCS Tax Ledger displays TDS Details for instead of TCS Details for. This issue has been resolved.
- In the alteration screen of sales invoice, on changing the sale value, the TCS surcharge amount is not being changed as per the new gross value. This issue has been resolved.
- When TCS (Tax) Ledger is included in a Sales Invoice in alteration mode, the TCS amount is not being calculated. This issue has been resolved.

TDL issues

- Rate type is not working in Batch wise details during Stock item creation, but is working in the alteration mode. This issue has been resolved and Support for using Rate type in batch-wise details in Creation mode has now been provided.

VAT

- In a sales invoice of a company with Accounts Only feature, the Output VAT amount of transaction involving two different VAT rates is calculated on the current sub-totals and not the assessable value. This issue has been resolved and now the output VAT amount is being calculated on the assessable value of respective sales ledgers.
- On switching from a company with Accounts with Inventory feature to a company with Accounts only feature, when a Sales transaction using an Accounting Invoice with multiple VAT rates is entered, the Output VAT for the second VAT classification appears incorrectly and an incorrect value is displayed in the Computation statement. This issue has been resolved and the Output VAT values are being displayed correctly.

2 Installation and Licensing of Tally.ERP 9

Pre-Installation

To install Tally.ERP 9 the user needs to have administrator rights (Create, Write, Update, Modify and Delete permissions). Multilingual users must ensure that the operating system supports multiple languages. The Hardware requirements and Operating system required for a Client-Server and a standalone computer are as described below:

Hardware Requirements for Tally.ERP 9

Processor	Intel Pentium IV or above and equivalent
Memory	256 MB Recommended is 512 MB RAM or more
Free Hard Disk Space	40 MB Minimum (Excluding data)
Monitor Resolution	800 x 600Recommended 1024 x 768 or Higher

Operating System required for

Single User	Microsoft Windows 98/ME/NT/2000/2003/2008/XP/Vista
Multi-User	The Tally License Server can be installed only on Windows NT/2000/2003/ XP/Vista

Installing Tally.ERP 9 - Single User

You can install Tally.ERP 9 using one of the following methods:

Method 1:

· Double click the install.exe icon on the CD.

Method 2:

- Click START from Windows.
- Select RUN.
- TYPE <CD drive>:\INSTALL.
- Press ENTER.

Follow the instructions displayed on your screen to proceed with the installation of Tally.ERP 9.

1. The Tally.ERP 9 Setup Wizard screen is displayed as shown.
2. Click Next to continue with the installation
3. The Tally.ERP 9 Setup screen appears

    3.1 In the Programs section check select Tally.ERP 9.

    3.2 In the Tally.ERP 9 Setup section, you can accept the default directories as shown or click on

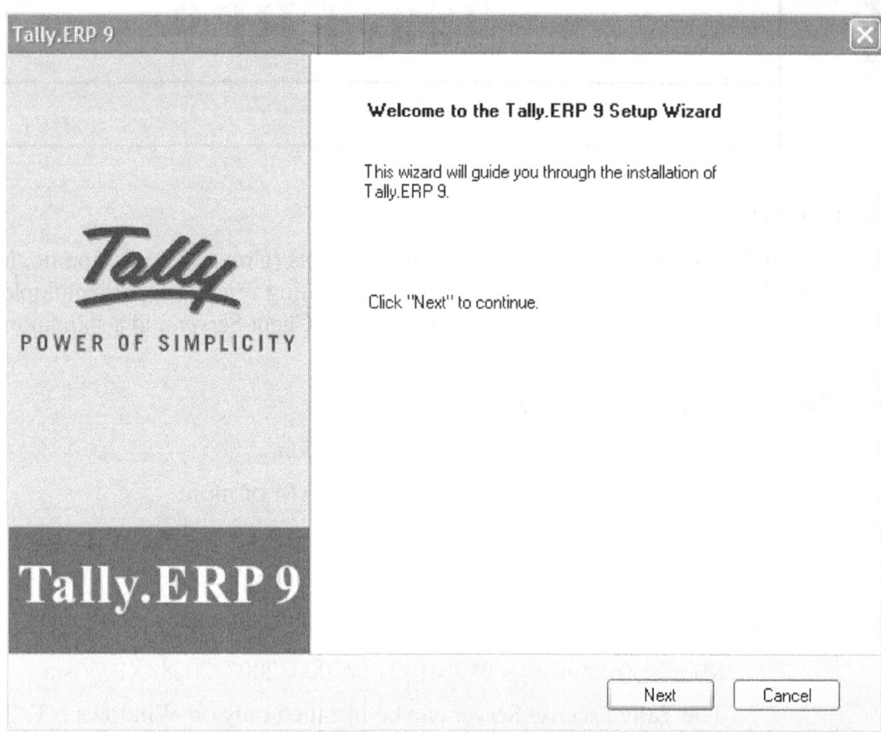

Fig. 2.1 Starting Installation

Tally.ERP 9

Tally.ERP 9 Setup

Programs

Tally.ERP 9

License Server

Description

Installs Tally.ERP 9 on your machine.

For multi-user
- Install License Server Program on identified machine.
- Select "My License Server is running at" option and specify License Server details.

Tally.ERP 9 Setup (1 of 2)

New Installation

Application Directory

C:\Tally.ERP9

Data Directory

C:\Tally.ERP9\Data

Configuration Directory

C:\Tally.ERP9

Language Directory

C:\Tally.ERP9\Lang

License Server details

My License Server is running at

Name / IP Port

© Tally Solutions Pvt. Ltd., 1988-2009.

< Back Next Cancel

Fig. 2.2 Installation 1st Step

the buttons provided next to the respective text boxes to change the path of Application Directory, Data Directory, Configuration Directory and Language Directory.

3.2.1 **Application Directory** – The program files reside in this directory.

3.2.2 **Data Directory** – by default Tally.ERP 9 data is stored in C:\Tally.ERP 9\Data. During the installation process, the wizard detects and retains the data path of previously installed version of Tally.ERP 9.

3.2.3 **Configuration Directory** – by default the configuration files reside in the application directory.

3.2.4 **Language Directory** – by default the Language files with the extension .dct are stored in the application directory.

4. Click Next.
5. In the Country/Language Selection screen, check Install Operating System Language Support to install Tally.ERP 9 with multi-lingual support.

   To use Tally.ERP 9 in English only, uncheck Install Operating Systems Language Support
6. By default, India/SAARC appears in the Country Selection. Select Others if you are not residing in India or any of the SAARC countries.

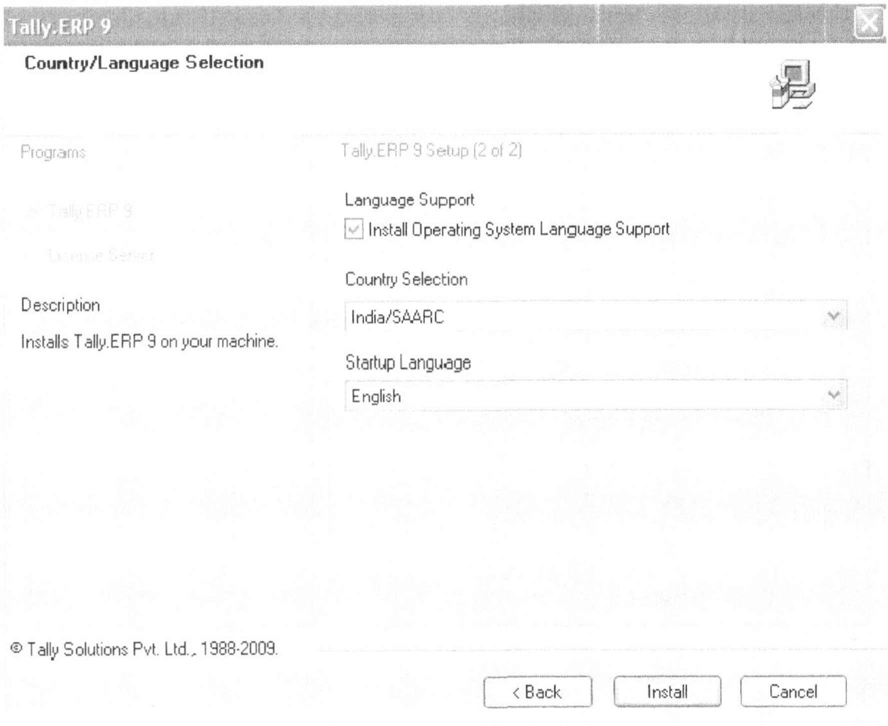

Fig. 2.3 Installation 2nd Step

7. Click Install.
8. The Setup Status screen is displayed as shown next.
9. You will be prompted for the language support files in the Files needed screen, insert operating

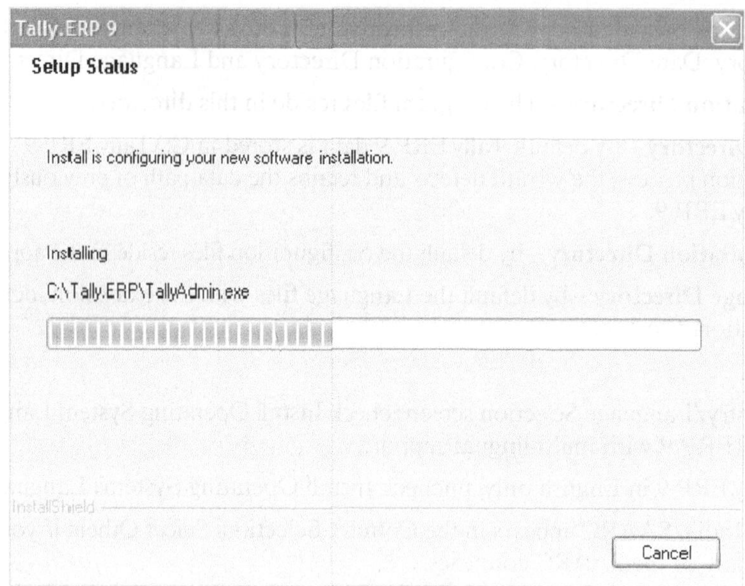

Fig. 2.4 Setup Status

systems CD in the drive or click Browse and select the i386 folder where the required language support files reside on your computer.

10. Click OK to install Language Support.

    Incase you click Cancel or do not have the operating system CD, The language support will not be available.

11. In the installer screen click Finish to complete Tally.ERP 9 Setup.
12. Click Finish to complete Tally.ERP 9 Silver Installation.

To start the Tally.ERP 9 application, double click the Tally.ERP 9 icon on the desktop.

Installing Tally.ERP 9 – Multi User (Server)

You can install Tally.ERP 9 using one of the following methods.

Method 1:

- Double click install.exe icon on the CD.

Method 2:

- Click START from Windows.
- Select RUN.
- TYPE <CD drive>:\INSTALL.
- Press ENTER .

Follow the instructions displayed on your screen to proceed with the installation of Tally.ERP 9.

1. The Tally.ERP 9 Setup Wizard screen is displayed as shown.
2. Click Next to continue.

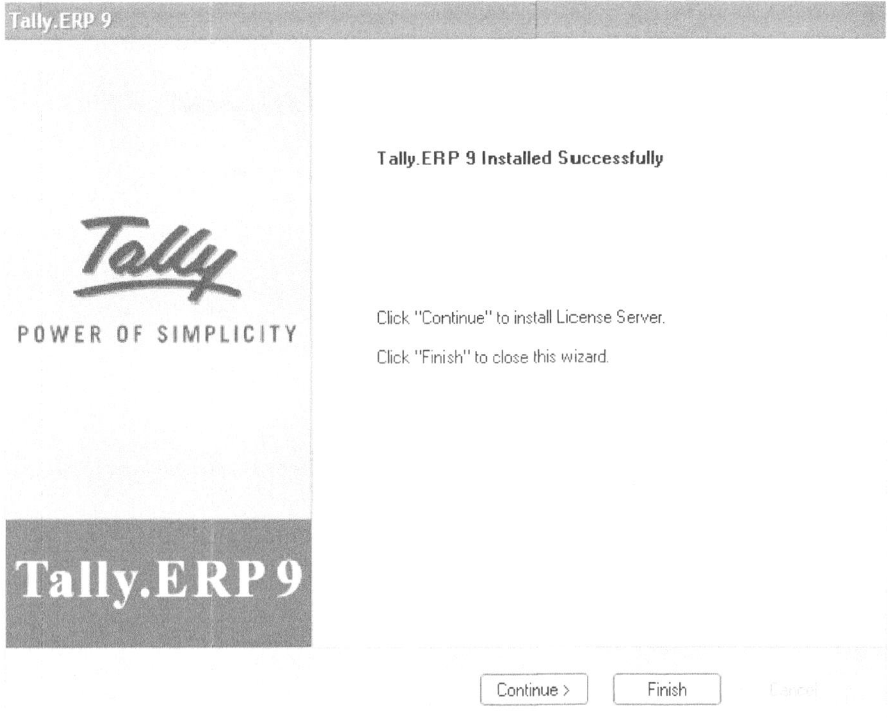

Fig. 2.5 Installation Complete

3. The Tally.ERP 9 Setup screen appears.
4. To install the Tally.ERP 9 Licence Server select the option License Server in the Programs section of the Tally.ERP 9 Setup screen.
5. Accept the default License Server Directory and Port Number or specify the License Server Directory name and Port Number in the Tally.ERP 9 setup screen.

   The Port number provided during installation is captured and displayed as a parameter to LicServerPort in the Tally.ini file.
6. Click Install.
7. The Setup Status is displayed as shown.
8. Once the installation process is completed, the Installation Successful screen is displayed as shown.
9. Click Finish to complete the installation process.

Installing Tally.ERP 9 - Multi User (Client)

You can install Tally.ERP 9 using one of the following methods.

Method 1:

- Double click install.exe icon on the CD.

Method 2:

- Click START from Windows.

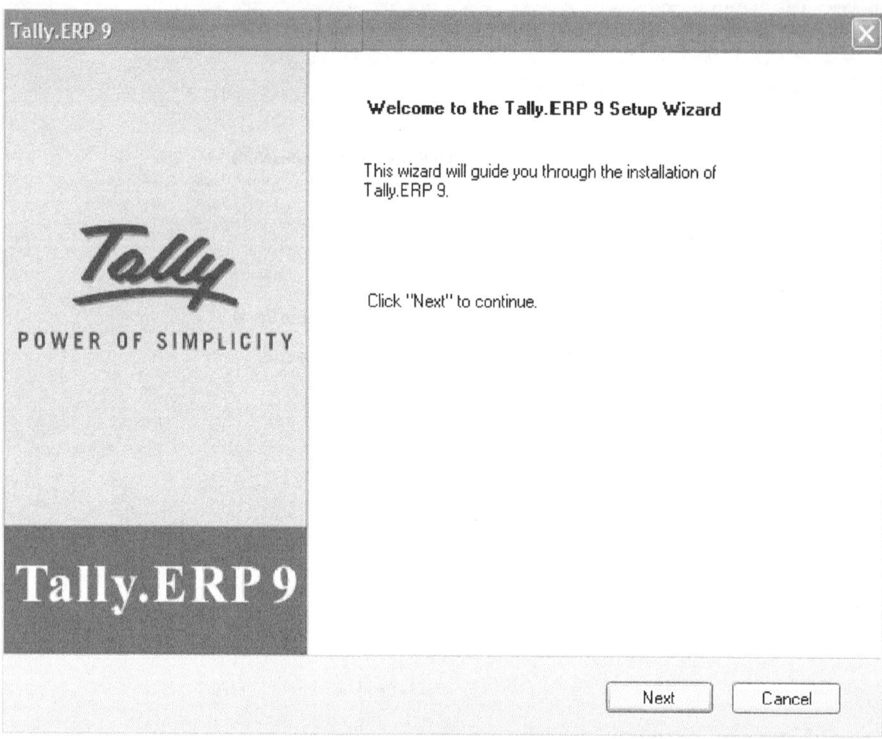

Fig. 2.6 Starting Installation of Multi-user

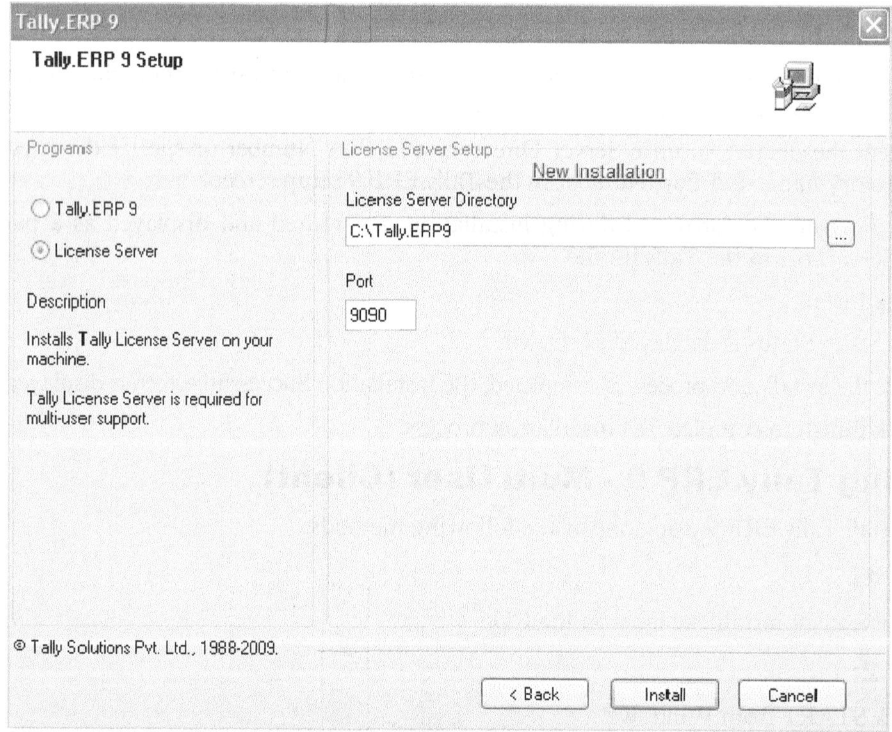

Fig. 2.7 License Server Setup

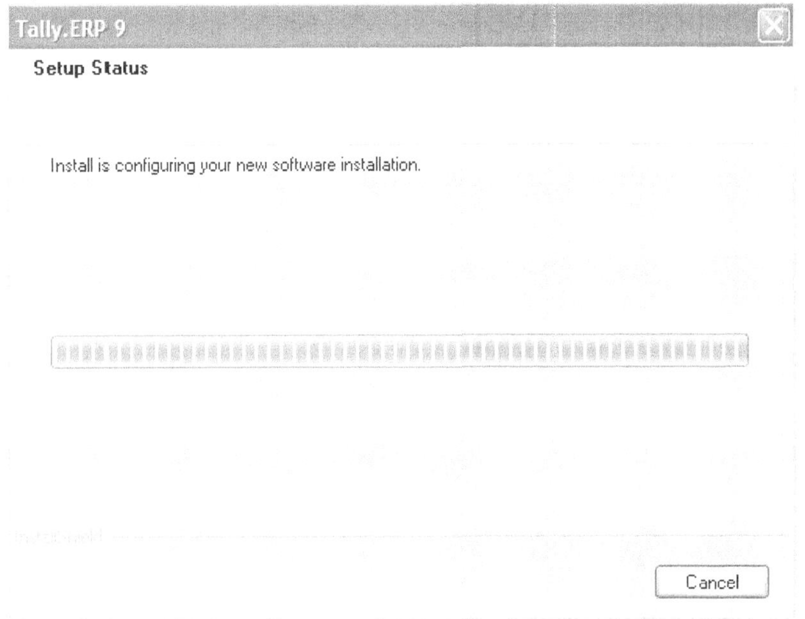

Fig. 2.8 Server Setup Progress

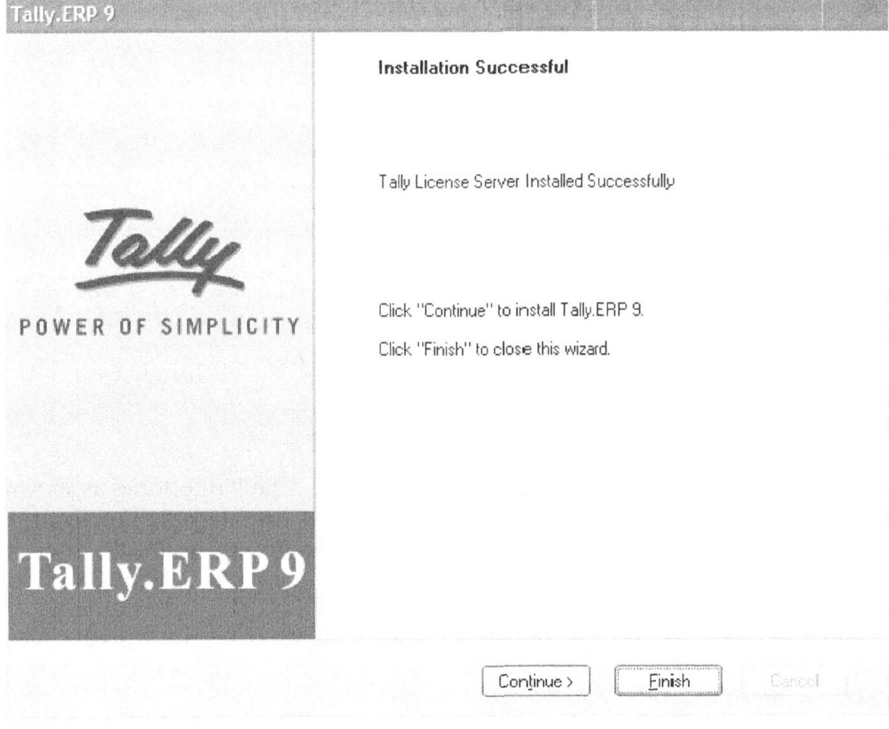

Fig. 2.9 Server Setup Complete

- Select RUN.
- TYPE <CD drive>:\INSTALL.
- Press the ENTER key.

Follow the instructions displayed on your screen to proceed with the installation of Tally.ERP 9.

1. The Tally.ERP Setup Wizard screen is displayed as shown.
2. Click Next to continue with Installation.
3. The Tally.ERP 9 Setup screen appears.

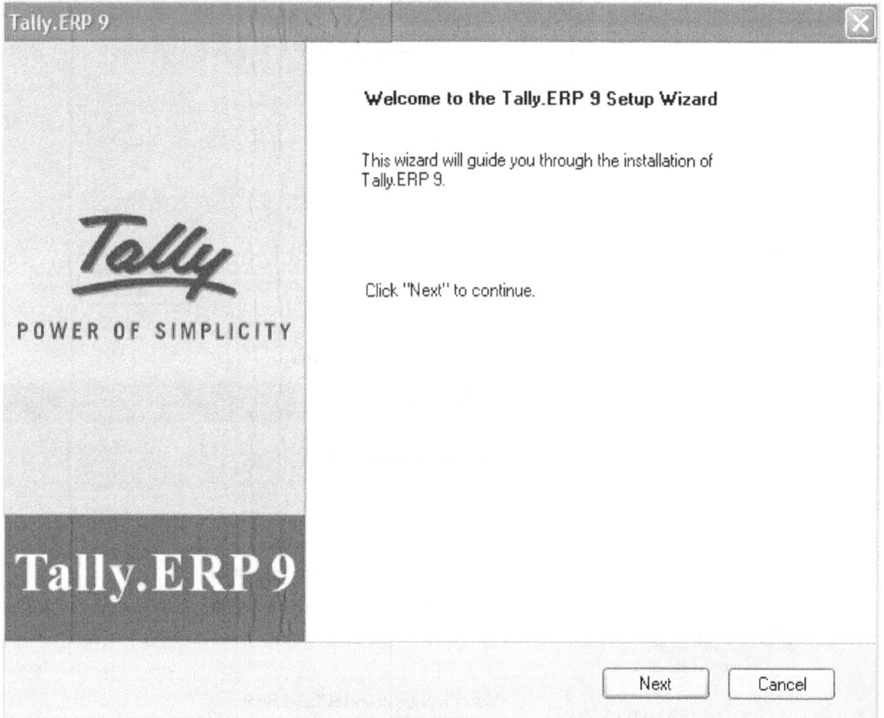

Fig. 2.10 Installation of Multi User

3.1. In the Programs section, select the option Tally.ERP 9

3.2. In the Tally.ERP 9 Setup section, you may accept the default directories as shown or click on the buttons provided next to the respective text boxes to change the Application Directory, Data Directory, Configuration Directory and the Language Directory.

3.2.1. **Application Directory** - The program files reside in this directory.

3.2.2. **Data Directory** – By default Tally.ERP 9 data is stored in C:\Tally.ERP 9\Data. The user can change the data directory by clicking on the button provided next to the text box and type in the new path.

3.2.3. **Configuration Directory** – by default the configuration files reside in the application directory. Specify the path in case you want the files to be saved elsewhere on your system.

3.2.4. **Language Directory** – by default the Language files (.dct) are stored in the application directory.

4. Enter the Name/IP Address of the Tally.ERP 9 License Server and port number in the Port field. This will enable the Tally.ERP 9 Client to establish a connection with the license server using the dedicated port.
5. Click Next.
6. In the Country/Language Selection screen, check Install Operating System Language Support to install Tally.ERP 9 with multi-lingual support.

   To use Tally.ERP 9 in English only, uncheck Install Operating Systems Language Support.

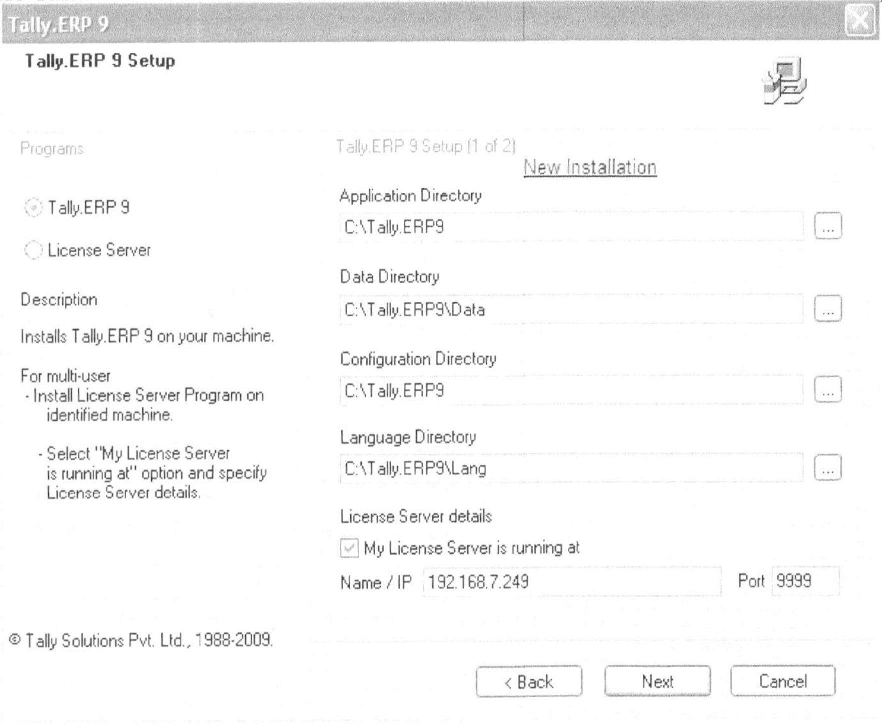

Tally.ERP 9
Tally.ERP 9 Setup
Programs
Tally.ERP 9
License Server
Description
Installs Tally.ERP 9 on your machine.
For multi-user
- Install License Server Program on identified machine.
- Select "My License Server is running at" option and specify License Server details.
© Tally Solutions Pvt. Ltd., 1988-2009.
Tally.ERP 9 Setup (1 of 2)
New Installation
Application Directory
C:\Tally.ERP9
Data Directory
C:\Tally.ERP9\Data
Configuration Directory
C:\Tally.ERP9
Language Directory
C:\Tally.ERP9\Lang
License Server details
My License Server is running at
Name / IP 192.168.7.249 Port 9999
< Back Next Cancel

Fig. 2.11 Setup Part 1/2

7. By default, India/SAARC appears in the Country Selection. Select Others if you are not residing in India or any of the SAARC countries.
8. Click Next.
9. Click Install.
10. The Setup Status is displayed as shown below.
11. You will be prompted for the language support files in the Files Needed screen, insert operating systems CD in the drive or click Browse and select the i386 folder where the required language support files reside on your computer.
12. Click OK to install Language Support.

    Incase you click Cancel or do not have the operating system CD, The language support will not be available.

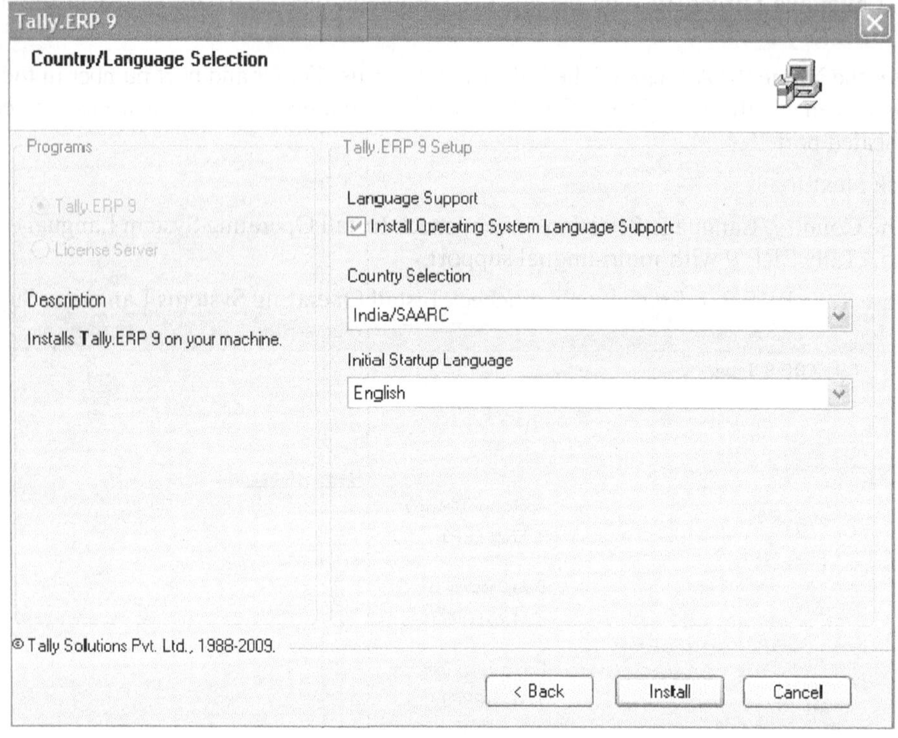

Fig. 2.12 Setup Part 2/2

13. In the installer screen click Finish to complete Tally.ERP 9 Setup.

On successful installation of Tally.ERP 9, double click on the Tally.ERP 9 icon on the desktop to start Tally.ERP 9

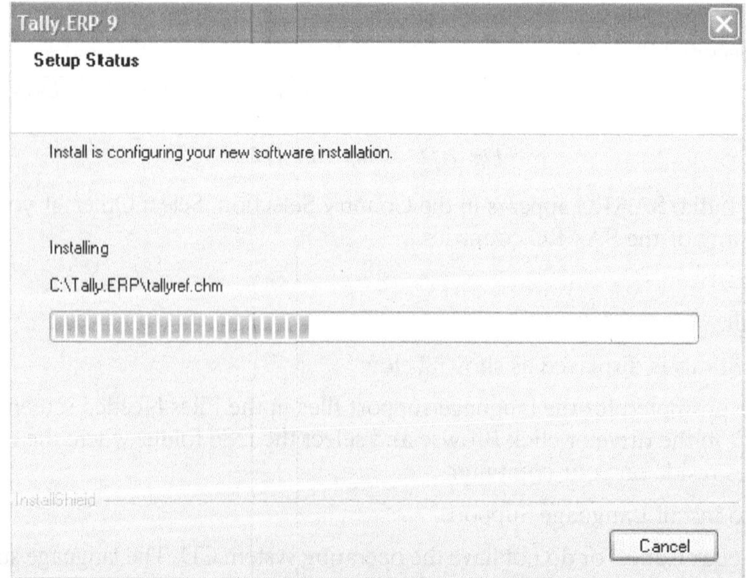

Fig. 2.13 Setup Progress

Licensing

Tally.ERP 9 brings a simple and user-friendly Licensing mechanism, which addresses many of the licensing activities across segment of users. You can activate a Single User (Silver) or Multi User (Gold) license or Multi-Site License.

Features of Licensing:

- Simple and easy to use
- Flexibility to configure settings based on Single User / Multi-user / Multi-Site.
- Brings in the concept of Account for better management & administration of Licenses.
- Activation / Reactivation is possible with Account ID and Password.
- Central Management of multiple License running at different sites in a secured environment.

Site Licensing

A new concept known as Site Licensing is introduced from Tally.ERP 9. A site refers to a single instance of Tally.ERP 9 installed and activated. The site licensing is broadly classified into two categories namely Single Site and Multi-Site

Single Site: A single instance of Tally.ERP 9 Silver or Tally.ERP 9 Gold license running.

Multi Site: More than one instance of Tally.ERP 9 Silver or Tally.ERP 9 Gold license is running at different locations under the single Account comprising of same or different serial numbers.

Activate License

The Licensing Operations Startup screen will appear only when Tally.ERP 9 is unable to detect the a valid license on your computer for any one of the reasons mentioned below.

- You have installed Tally.ERP 9 for the first time on your computer.
- Reinstalled Tally.ERP 9 after changing the hardware or formatting the Hard Disk.

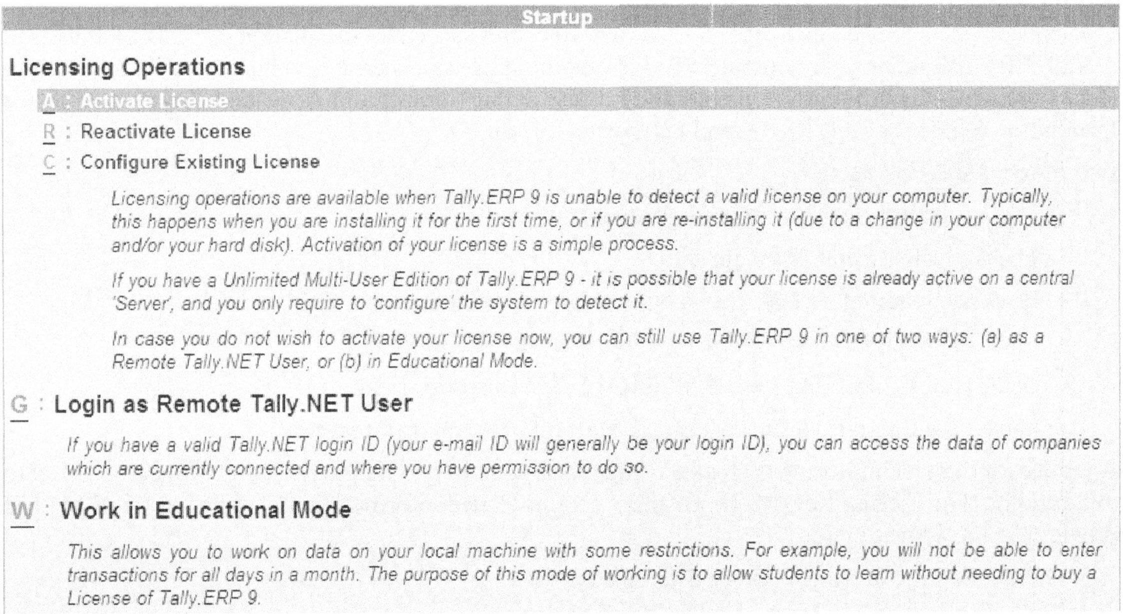

Fig. 2.14 Licensing Operations

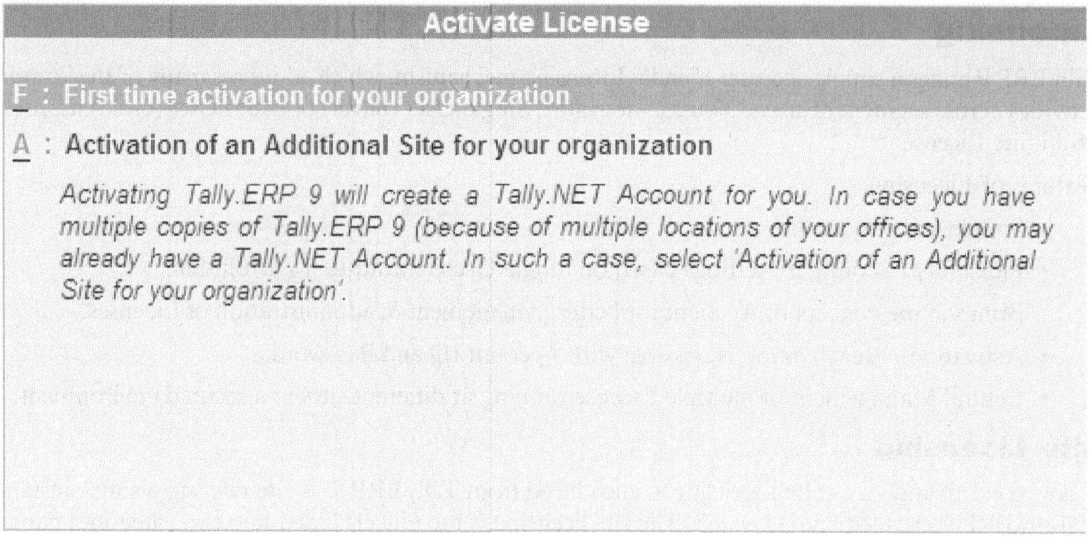

Activate License

F : First time activation for your organization

A : Activation of an Additional Site for your organization

Activating Tally.ERP 9 will create a Tally.NET Account for you. In case you have multiple copies of Tally.ERP 9 (because of multiple locations of your offices), you may already have a Tally.NET Account. In such a case, select 'Activation of an Additional Site for your organization'.

Fig. 2.15 Activate Licensing

To activate a license follow the steps shown :

- Select Activate License.
- The Activate License screen appears as shown.

The Activate License has two option which allow you to activate the license based on your requirement.

- First time activation for your organization: allows you to activate a single site license.
- Activation of an additional Site for your organization: allows you to activate the next or consecutive site licenses for your organization.

First Time Activation for your Organization

You can activate a Single Site license for the first time after successful installation of Tally.ERP 9 Silver or Tally.ERP 9 Gold on your computer. To activate the single site license, you must have Administrative Rights or login as an administrator, enter the License Serial Number and Activation Key printed on the Installation Guide for Tally.ERP 9 and enter your E-Mail ID.

In the Activate License screen:

- Select First time activation for your organization
- The Activate License form appears
- Enter the required License Serial Number in the Serial Number field
- Enter the required Activation Key in the Activation Key field
- Enter your E-Mail ID in the E-Mail ID of Administrator field
- Repeat the Email-ID in the Repeat (E-Mail ID of Administrator) field.

A unique account identification is created using this E-Mail Id and the license serial number is linked to this account. The License Key, Password and Account related information are mailed to the E-Mail Id provided in the activation form.

- Press Enter to activate a Single Site License.

Activate License

Serial Number : 702046089
Activation Key : PGT5H254T

E-Mail ID of Administrator : sysadmin@abccompany.com
Repeat (E-Mail ID of Administrator) : sysadmin@abccompany.com

Activating your License is a simple two-step process. Once your Serial Number and Activation Key are confirmed, you will receive an E-Mail giving you some important details:

1. Your Tally.NET Account ID (which you may later modify)
2. A License Key (which you will require to complete the Activation process)
3. Details on how to access your Tally.NET Account and use it effectively for your organization.

Please remember that the Activation process can be completed only with the 'License Key' which is sent in the E-Mail to the Administrator. It is important, therefore, that a valid E-Mail is given.

Fig. 2.16 Activate Licensing with Serial Number

- Tally.ERP 9 searches for the availability of Internet Connectivity on your computer

Internet Connection is Available:

- Tally.ERP 9 displays a message Congratulation! Your activation Request has been processed.
- The Tally_lck.lic file is created which resides in the default Tally.ERP 9 directory.
- Proceed to section titled Procedure to Unlock License File.

Internet Connection is not Available:

- Tally.ERP 9 displays a message Could not Connect to Internet, Do you want to Generate the License File Offline.
- Press Y or click Yes to proceed with the Offline Licensing.
- Tally.ERP 9 displays a message Your Offline Activation Request has been Created Successfully. A license request file titled Tally_req.lic is generated and stored in the default Tally.ERP 9 folder.
- Copy the Tally_Req.lic file onto a pen drive/CD and transfer it to another computer with Internet Connectivity and Tally.ERP 9. On this computer, Tally.ERP 9 could be in Educational mode.
- Start Tally.ERP 9 on this computer
- Go to Gateway of Tally > F12: Configure > Licensing > Send External Request
- Tally.ERP 9 displays a message Offline Response File Tally_lck.lic Generated Successfully. The Tally_lck.lic is created and stored in the default Tally.ERP 9 directory.

Startup

Licensing Operations

A : Activate License

R : Reactivate License

Q : Send External Request

C : Configure Existing License

Licensing operations are available when Tally.ERP 9 is unable to detect a valid license on your computer. Typically, this happens when you are installing it for the first time, or if you are re-installing it (due to a change in your computer and/or your hard disk). Activation of your license is a simple process.

If you are a user of Tally.ERP 9 Multi-User - it is possible that your license is already active on a central 'Server', and you only require to 'configure' the system to detect it.

In case you do not wish to activate your license now, you can still use Tally.ERP in one of two ways: (a) as a Remote Tally.NET User, or (b) in Educational Mode.

G : **Login as Remote Tally.NET User**

If you have a valid Tally.NET login ID (your e-mail ID will generally be your login ID), you can access the data of which are currently connected and where you have permission to do so.

W : **Work in Educational Mode**

This allows you to work on data on your local machine with some restrictions. The purpose of this mode of working is to allow students to learn without needing to buy a License of Tally.ERP. For example, you will not be able to enter transactions for all days in a month.

1 more ...

Fig. 2.17 Send External Request

- The License Key to activate the Tally.ERP 9 license and the Password are emailed separately to the email id provided in the activation form.
- Copy Tally_lck.lic and transfer it to the default Tally.ERP 9 application folder of the computer where Tally.ERP 9 has to be activated.
- Start Tally.ERP 9
- Proceed to section titled Procedure to Unlock License File.

Procedure to Unlock License File:

- Access your mail and retrieve the unlock key before proceeding to unlock the license file.
- In the Startup screen select Unlock License.
- Type the Unlock Key retrieved in unlock field and press Enter.

Unlock License

Unlock Key : 8ZR46NX3N

Unlock Key has been sent to the E-Mail ID you had provided in the Activation / Reactivation form.

On successfully unlocking the license file, Tally.ERP 9 displays the following message.

On starting Tally.ERP 9, the License Serial Number and Account ID are displayed under the Version and Licesing tab of the information panel respectively.

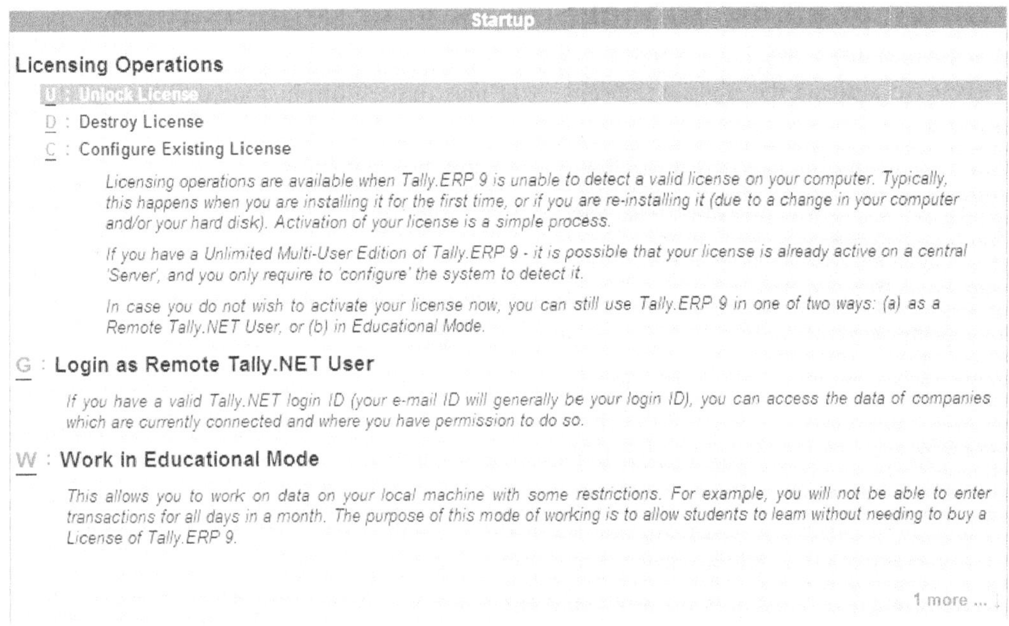

Fig. 2.18 Unlocking License

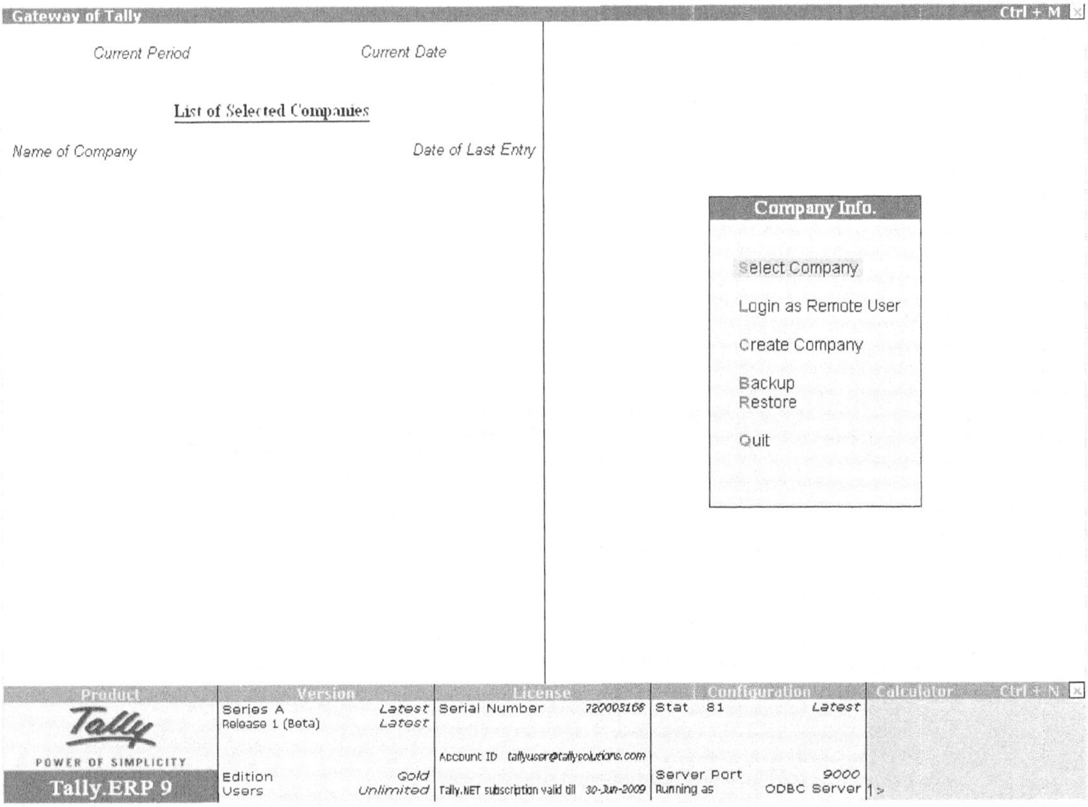

Gateway of Tally — Ctrl + M

Current Period *Current Date*

List of Selected Companies

Name of Company *Date of Last Entry*

Company Info.

Select Company
Login as Remote User
Create Company
Backup
Restore
Quit

Product	Version		License		Configuration		Calculator
Tally POWER OF SIMPLICITY	Series A	*Latest*	Serial Number	*720003168*	Stat 81	*Latest*	
	Release 1 (Beta)	*Latest*	Account ID	*tallyuser@tallysolutions.com*			
Tally.ERP 9	Edition	*Gold*			Server Port	*9000*	
	Users	*Unlimited*	Tally.NET subscription valid till	*30-Jun-2009*	Running as	ODBC Server	1 >

Fig. 2.19 Displaying Serial Number

Activation of an Additional Site for your Organisation

You can use this option to activate a Multi Site License for the first time after successful installation of Tally.ERP 9. To activate the multi site license you must have Administrative Rights or login as an administrator.

To activate the Multi Site license for the first time follow the steps shown:

- Select Activation of an Additional Site for your Organisation.
- The Activate Site License form.
- Enter the License Serial Number in the Serial Number field.
- Enter the Activation Key in the Activation Key field.

The License Serial Number and Activation Key is printed on Installation Guide for Tally.ERP 9.

- Enter the required Account ID in the Account ID field. The Account ID is created by dealing Tally partner and provided to you. In case you had activated a single site license earlier, you can use the same Account ID.
- Enter the required Site Name in Site ID field. This will enable you to distinguish between sites that are activated using the same serial number in case of multi site.
- Enter your E-mail address in the E-Mail ID of the Site Administrator field. The License Key, Password and account related information will be emailed to the E-Mail ID provided.
- Ensure that you re-enter the same Email ID in Repeat (E-Mail ID of the Site Administrator) for the purpose of confirmation.
- Tally.ERP 9 searches for the availability of Internet Connectivity on the users computer.

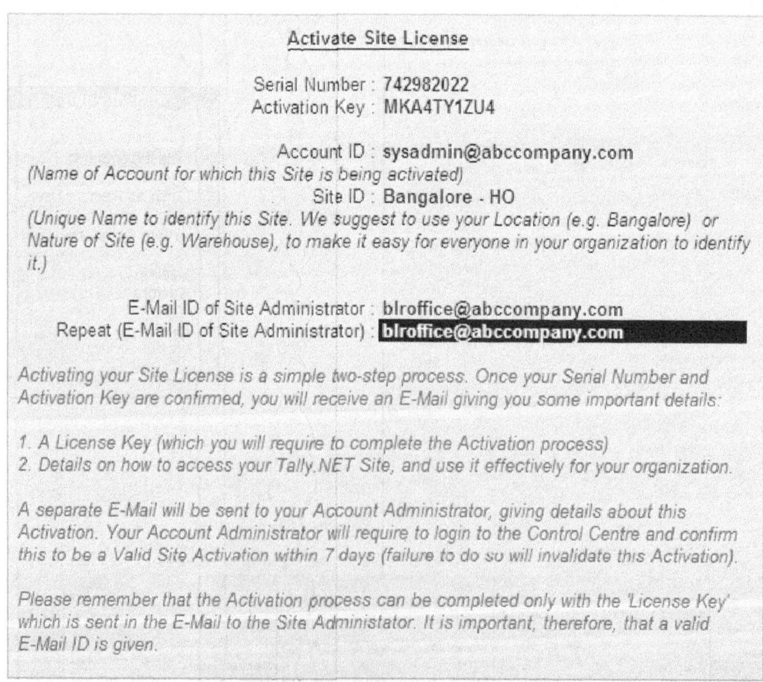

Activate Site License

Serial Number : 742982022
Activation Key : MKA4TY1ZU4

Account ID : sysadmin@abccompany.com
(Name of Account for which this Site is being activated)
Site ID : Bangalore - HO
(Unique Name to identify this Site. We suggest to use your Location (e.g. Bangalore) or Nature of Site (e.g. Warehouse), to make it easy for everyone in your organization to identify it.)

E-Mail ID of Site Administrator : blroffice@abccompany.com
Repeat (E-Mail ID of Site Administrator) : blroffice@abccompany.com

Activating your Site License is a simple two-step process. Once your Serial Number and Activation Key are confirmed, you will receive an E-Mail giving you some important details:

1. A License Key (which you will require to complete the Activation process)
2. Details on how to access your Tally.NET Site, and use it effectively for your organization.

A separate E-Mail will be sent to your Account Administrator, giving details about this Activation. Your Account Administrator will require to login to the Control Centre and confirm this to be a Valid Site Activation within 7 days (failure to do so will invalidate this Activation).

Please remember that the Activation process can be completed only with the 'License Key' which is sent in the E-Mail to the Site Administator. It is important, therefore, that a valid E-Mail ID is given.

Fig. 2.20 Additional Site Information

Internet Connectivity is Available:

- The Tally_lck.lic file is created which resides in the default Tally.ERP 9 folder,
- The Unlock Key is emailed to the Site Email ID provided in the activation form.
- Tally.ERP 9 displays a message License Updated Successfully.
- Proceed to section Procedure to Unlock License File.

Internet Connectivity is Not Available:

- Tally.ERP 9 displays a message Could not Connect to Internet, Do you want to Generate the License File Offline.
- Accept to generate the Tally_req.lic offline, which resides in the default Tally.ERP 9 folder. Copy the Tally_Req.lic file onto a pen drive/CD and transfer it to another computer with Internet Connectivity and Tally.ERP 9.

Could not connect to the internet!
Do you want to continue activation in offline mode?
Yes or No

- Start Tally.ERP 9
- Go to Gateway of Tally > F12: Configure > Licensing > Send External Request
- The License Key and Password to access the Support Centre is mailed separately to the email id provided in the activation form.
- The Tally_resp.lic is created and stored in the default Tally.ERP 9 directory, transfer this file to the default Tally.ERP 9 folder of the computer where Tally.ERP 9 has to be activated.
- Start Tally.ERP 9

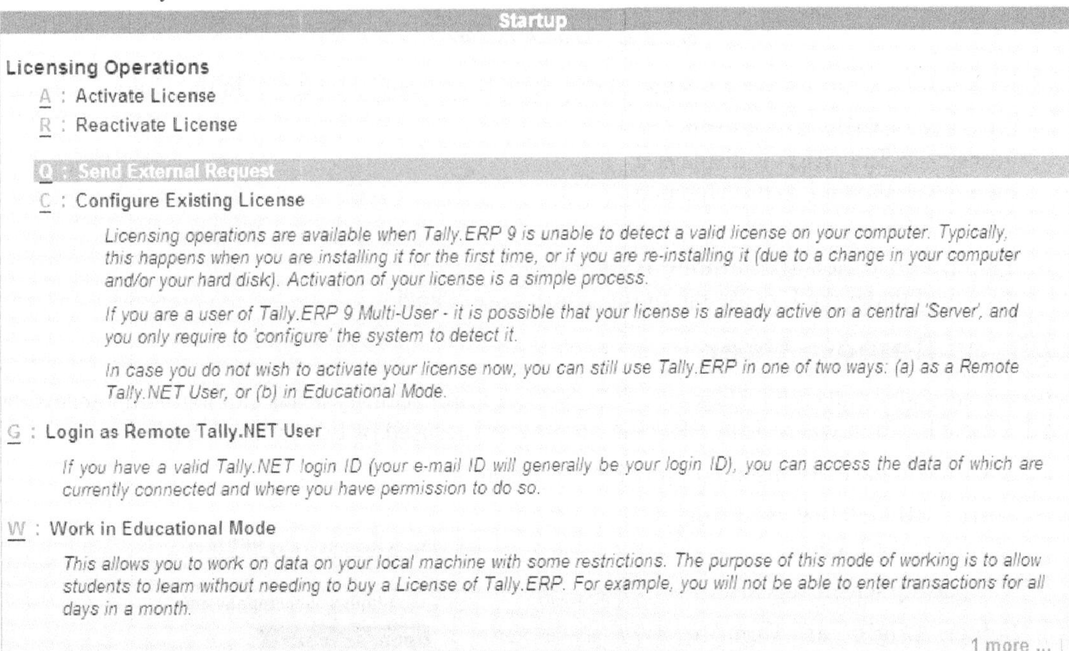

Fig. 2.21 Send External Request Screen

Common Procedure to Unlock License:

- Access your email and retrieve the unlock key before proceeding to unlock the license file.
- In the Startup screen, select Unlock License

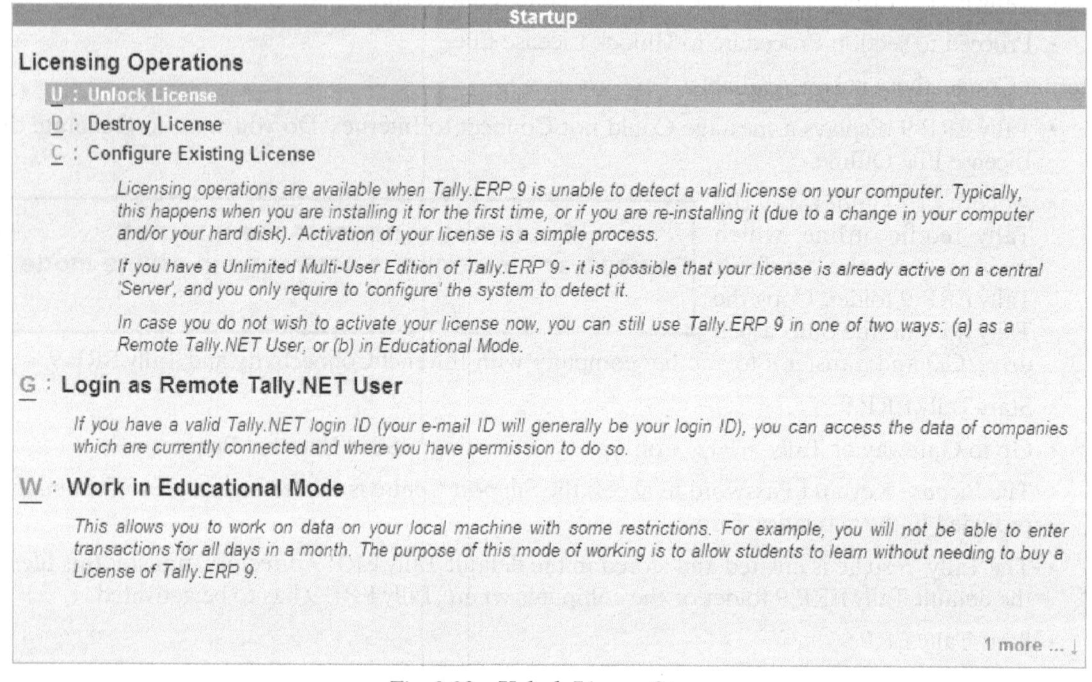

Fig. 2.22 Unlock License Screen

- In the Unlock License screen, enter the Unlock Key received by email in the Unlock Key field.
- On successfully unlocking the license file Tally.ERP 9 displays a message as shown License Updated Successfully.
- The License Serial Number is displayed under the License tab of the Information Panel.

Login as Remote User

Users created under Tally.NET User or a Tally.NET Auditor security levels can login and access data from a remote location where Tally.ERP 9 is running in Licensed or Educational mode.

- In case you have not installed Tally.ERP 9, Install it.
- Start Tally.ERP 9 without activating the License.
- The Startup screen appears.
- Select Login as Remote Tally.NET User.

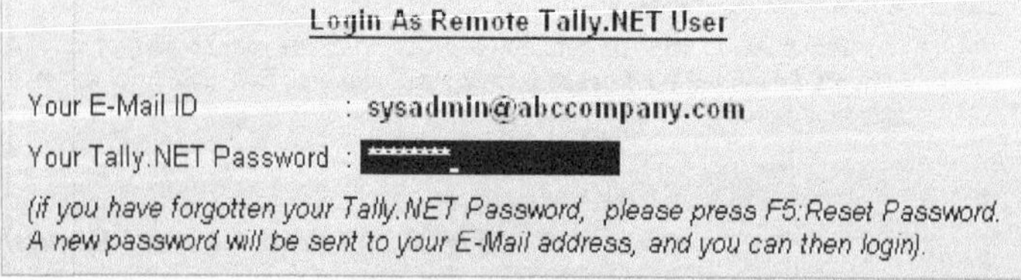

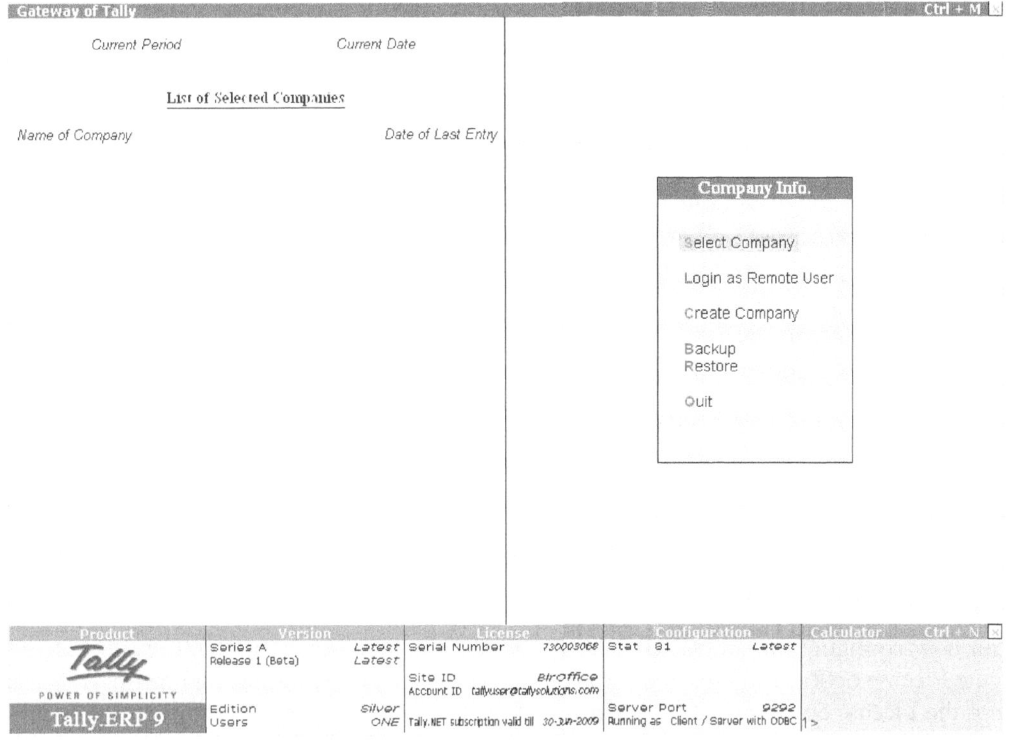

Fig. 2.23 Opening Screen with Serial Number displayed

- The Login As Remote Tally.NET User screen appears
- Enter your Tally.NET ID in Your E-Mail ID field
- Enter your Tally.NET password in the Password field.

Work in Educational Mode

Work in Educational Mode is an option available in the Startup screen to the future users of Tally.ERP 9. The future users can install and have live experience on the features and reports available in Tally.ERP 9, whereas Tally.NET User and Tally.NET Auditor can login from a remote location, view reports or scrutinise data while Tally.ERP 9 works in Educational mode.

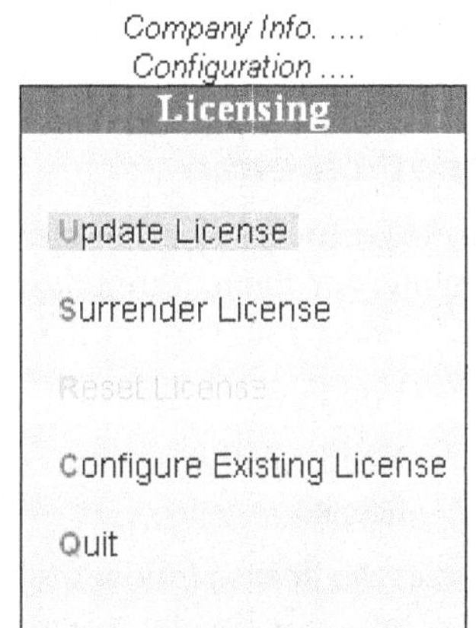

Update License

The procedure to update Tally.ERP 9 license for Single Site and Multi Site is similar. You require updating the license information when the TDL/ General configuration assigned to the Account have to be applied to the respective site or when you renew/subscribe for Tally.NET. To update the license ensure that your computer is connected to Internet.

Go to Gateway of Tally or from the Company Info menu

- Press F12: Configure > Licensing

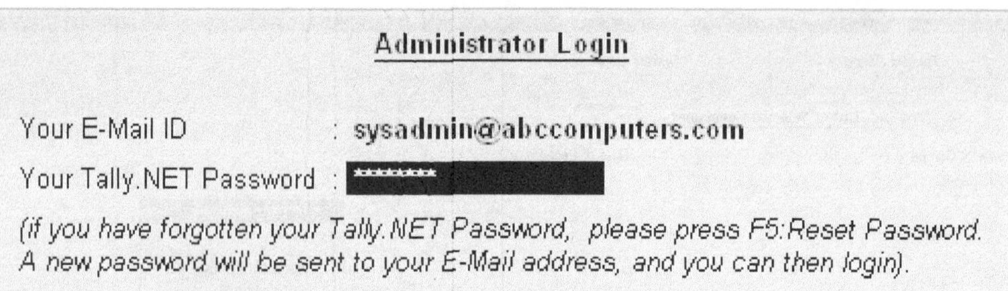
Administrator Login

Your E-Mail ID : sysadmin@abccomputers.com

Your Tally.NET Password : **********

(if you have forgotten your Tally.NET Password, please press F5:Reset Password. A new password will be sent to your E-Mail address, and you can then login).

Fig. 2.24 Login Screen

- In the Licensing screen
- Select Update License
- The Administrator Login screen appears
- Provide the your Account ID in Your E-Mail ID field
- Provide your account password in Your Tally.NET Password field
- Tally.ERP 9 displays the message License Updated Successfully.

Configure License

You can now configure the Tally.ERP 9 license without actually opening the Tally.ini file using the Configure License option available in the Startup screen. The Configure Existing License will accept the Name of the License Server or the IP Address and the Port number. These parameters are updated into the Tally.ini file.

To configure the Tally.ERP 9 license follow the steps shown:

- In the Startup screen
- Select Configure Existing License.

The Configure Existing License screen appears

- Provide the required License Server Name / IP Address in Tally License Server field.
- By default, Tally.ERP 9 uses port 9090. In case you want to use another port then provide the required Port Number in Port field.
- Accept to save the license server details and the port number in Tally.ini file.

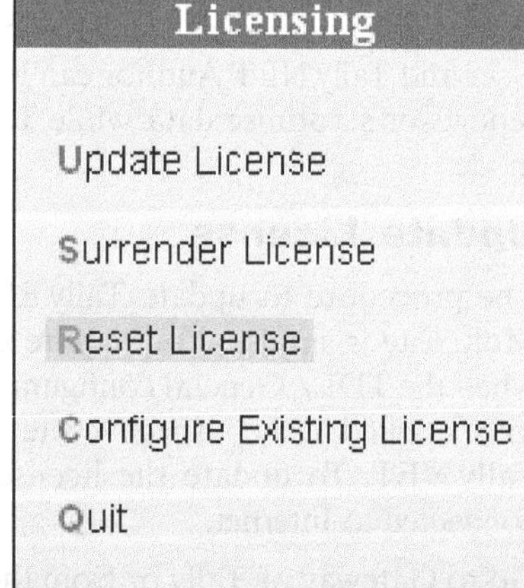

Reset License

The Reset License option clears licensing information from your computer for the required license serial number. You can reset the license under following circumstances:

- You have not received an email containing the Unlock Key.
- Need to clear license information for a subscription based license.

To reset the license follow the steps shown:

- Go to Gateway of Tally > F12: Configure > Licensing

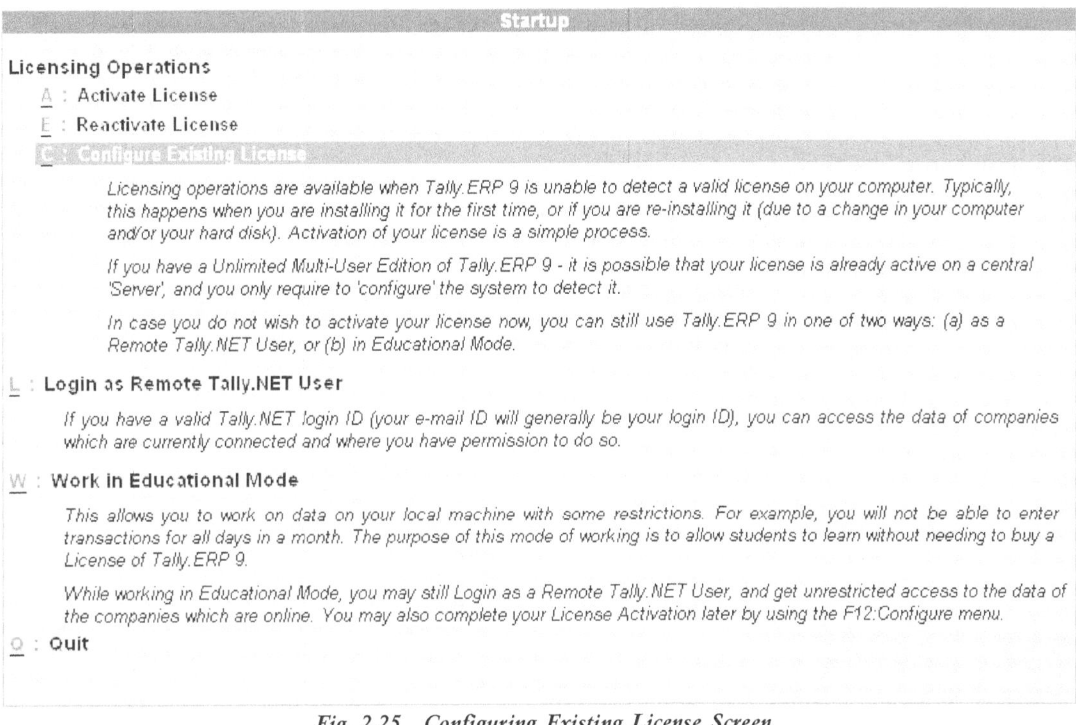

Fig. 2.25 Configuring Existing License Screen

- Select Reset License
- Tally.ERP 9 prompts a message as shown:
- Press Y or click on Yes to reset license.
- Tally.ERP 9 displays a message License Reset Successfully!

You are about to Reset your License. Continue ?

Yes or No

Admin Tool

In a multi user environment set-up one computer is designated as the License Server and all other computers are designated as License Clients. You can install the Tally License Service (License Server) only the computer designated as License Server and install Tally.ERP 9 only on the computers designated as the License Clients.

Tally Admin Tool

The Tally Admin tool is a license administration utility that resides in the default Tally.ERP 9 folder and helps you to administer the licenses of Tally products.

- To start the Admin Tool double click on TallyAdmin.exe.
- The Tally Admin tool is displayed as shown:
- The TallyAdmin tools screen has two tabs namely.
- Licensing is further classified into.
- Service Operations.
- License Servers.

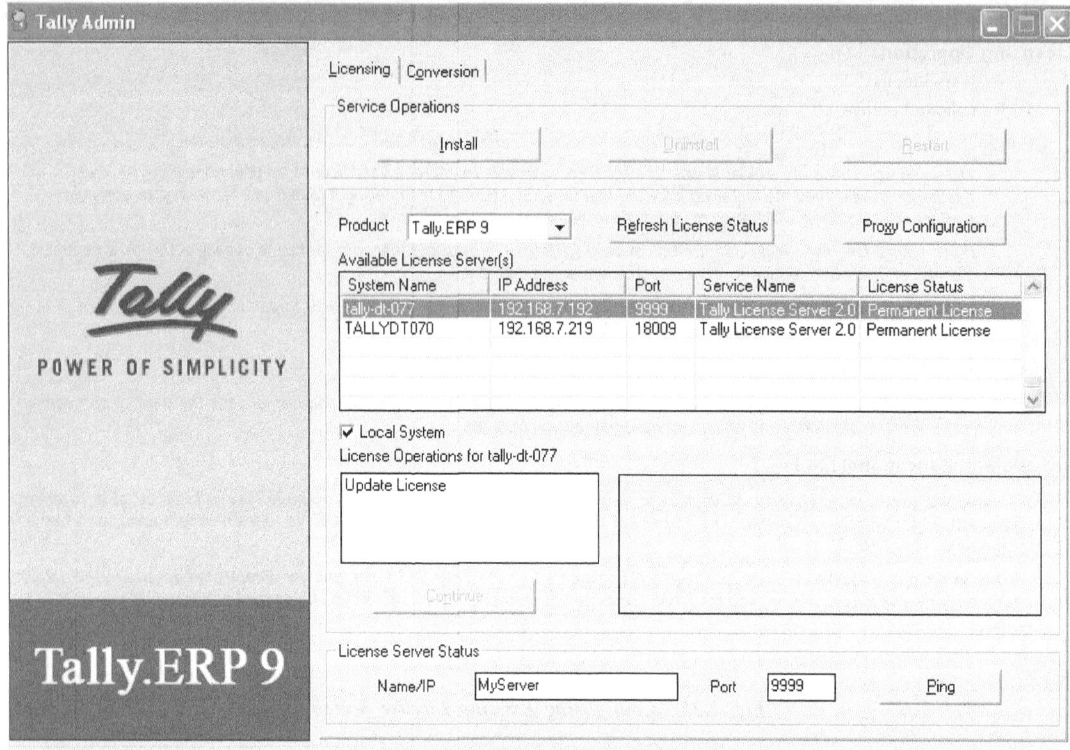

Fig. 2.26 Tally Admin Tool Screen

- License Operations.
- License Server Status.
- Conversion: Converts TCP and TSF files from earlier version of Tally 9 to a format compatible with Tally.ERP 9.

Service Operations

- **Install** : Set up/run the license service in the background on the computer designated as Server. On starting the License Service, a message Tally License Server Installed and Started Successfully is displayed.
- **Uninstall** : Removes the license service from the Server. On removing the License Service displays a message Tally License Server uninstalled successfully.
- **Restart** : Restart the License Server once again. On restarting the license server a message Tally License Server restarted successfully is displayed.

Product: Select the required Product and click Refresh License to get the most recent information on licenses running for that product.

Proxy Configuration: Will allow the user to configure the proxy server, if required. Click Proxy and enter the Proxy Server URL using which you can access the internet, in case the proxy server requires authentication enter the required Username and Password.

Available License Servers : will display the list of license servers available within the LAN along with the System Name, IP Address, Port and License Status for different products of Tally.

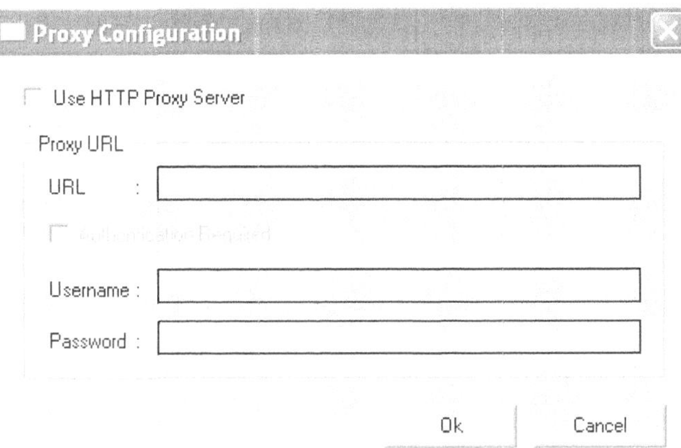

Note: Check Local System to activate a license from the client machine.

License Operation for: Depending on the License Status displayed for the system, the licensing operations are available. When the License Status is displayed as Permanent License, the licensing operation available is Update or when the license status is displayed as No License you can Activate License or Reactivate License based on your requirement.

Activate License: This option is available, only when the user starts the TallyAdmin tool for the first time after installation of Tally.ERP 9 or when the License Status is displayed as No License. You can activate a Single Site or Multi Site license, using this option. The detailed steps for activating a single site and multi site license is discussed in the chapter Activating Tally.ERP 9 Single Site and Multi Site respectively.

Reactivate License: This option is available only when the user starts the TallyAdmin tool after installation or after surrendering the license of Tally.ERP 9. You can Reactivate a Single Site or Multi Site license using this option. The detailed steps for activating a single site and multi site license is discussed in Reactivating Tally.ERP 9.

Update: will update the most recent license information on your system. You can select this option to download the TDL/General configuration assigned to the account which are intern applied to the respective site or when you renew/subscribe for Tally.NET.

License Server Status (for License Clients)

Name/IP: Enter the Name/IP Address of the computer designated as the License Server.

Port: is the dedicated port number to which the License Server is listening.

Ping: Click Ping to check the status of the License Server.

License Server Status
Name/IP MyServer Port 9999 Ping

Surrender License

In case the user desires to use Tally.ERP 9 on another computer, surrender the activated license. You have to surrender the Tally.ERP 9 license in one of the following scenarios:

1. Format the hard disk
2. Reinstall the operating system
3. Add new hardware or drivers
4. Reactivate the same license on another computer.

To surrender the single site license, you have to execute the following steps:

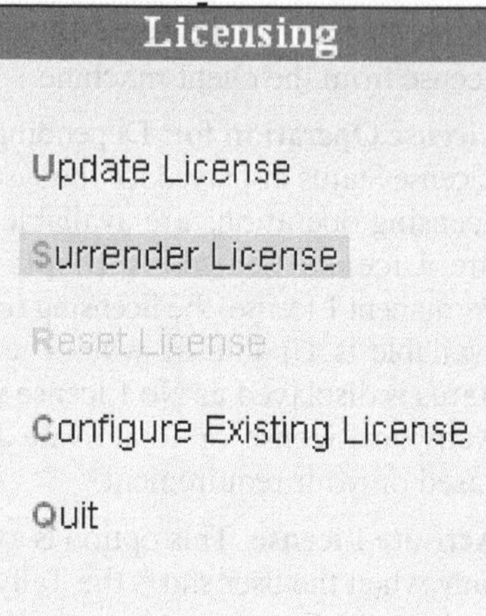

From the Company Info menu or Gateway of Tally

- Press F12: Configure > Licensing
- Select Surrender License
- Tally.ERP 9 prompts you with a message as shown below

You are about to Surrender your License. Continue ?

Yes or No

- Press Y or click on Yes to surrender license
- Tally.ERP 9 displays a message License Surrendered Successfully.

3 Data Migration

Introduction

Data created in Tally 7.2 or TCP (Tally Compliant Product) files created for use with Tally 7.2 cannot be used with Tally.ERP 9. Hence, Data and TCP files need to be upgraded for use with Tally.ERP 9. The Tally Data Migration Tool helps users to upgrade Data and TCP files in order to be compliant with Tally.ERP 9. A valid Tally.ERP 9 license is required to upgrade Data or TCP files from Tally 7.2 to Tally.ERP 9.

Tally 6.3 users can use the migration tool to rewrite data to Tally 7.2 and then migrate to Tally.ERP 9. A logical migration of data from the earlier version of Tally 9 will occur when you load the company for the first time in Tally.ERP 9.

To Start the Migration Tool

By default the Tally Data Migration Tool is available in the Tally.ERP 9 folder.

To start the migration tool double click on the tally72migration.exe.

The Tally Data Migration Tool and Tally.ERP 9 screens open simultaneously.

The Migrate Company menu has the following options:

tally72migration.exe

- **Migrate Data** – allows the user to upgrade Tally 7.2 data to Tally.ERP 9.
- **Migrate TCP** – allows the user to upgrade TCP files created in Tally 7.2 to Tally.ERP 9.
- **Restore 7.2 Backup** – allows the user to restore data backup taken in Tally 7.2.

Migration Messages Pane

The migration status is displayed in the Migration Messages pane.

Calculator Pane

The Calculator pane in the Tally.ERP 9 screen displays any error messages that appear during the migration process.

Migrating Tally7.2 Data to Tally.ERP 9

Customers using Tally 7.2 have to execute the steps shown in order to upgrade their existing data from Tally 7.2 to Tally.ERP 9.

1. Double click on the Tally7.2migration.exe.
2. Tally Data Migration and Tally.ERP 9 start simultaneously in separate screens.
3. As soon as Tally.ERP 9 is loaded, a message Ready for Migration appears in the Migration Messages Pane.
4. Select Migrate Data.

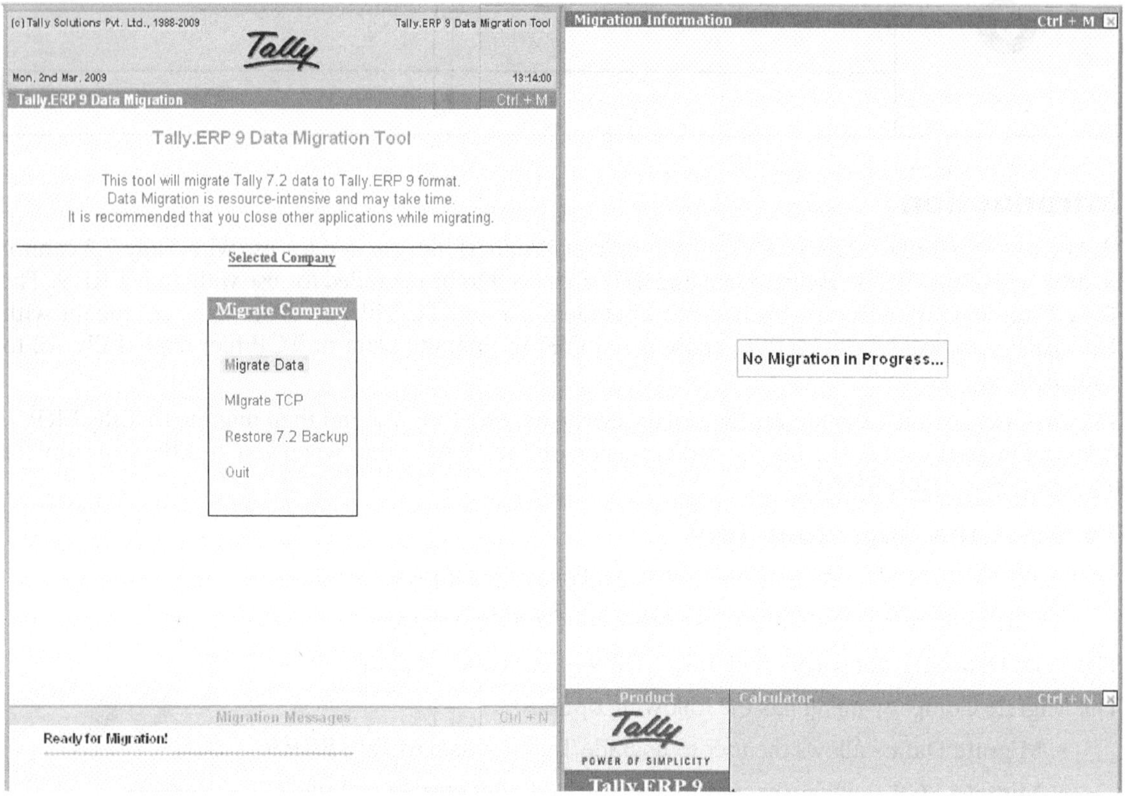

(c) Tally Solutions Pvt. Ltd., 1988-2009 Tally.ERP 9 Data Migration Tool

Mon, 2nd Mar, 2009 13:14:00

Tally.ERP 9 Data Migration Ctrl + M

Tally.ERP 9 Data Migration Tool

This tool will migrate Tally 7.2 data to Tally.ERP 9 format.
Data Migration is resource-intensive and may take time.
It is recommended that you close other applications while migrating.

Selected Company

Migrate Company

Migrate Data
Migrate TCP
Restore 7.2 Backup
Quit

Migration Messages Ctrl + N

Ready for Migration!

Migration Information Ctrl + M

No Migration in Progress...

Product Calculator Ctrl + N

Tally POWER OF SIMPLICITY Tally.ERP 9

Fig. 3.1 Data Migration Screen

5. The Select Company for Migration appears.
6. Specify the data path, if required.

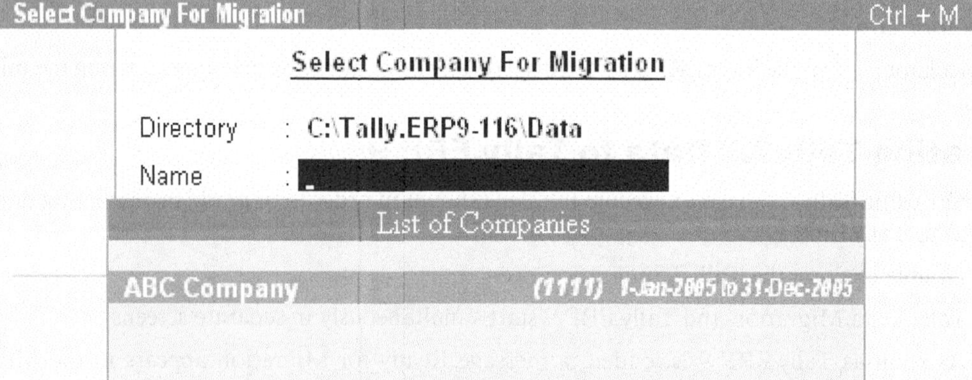

Fig. 3.2 Select Company for Data Migration

7. Select the required company from the List of Companies.
8. Incase the company selected contains Payroll data; Tally.ERP 9 prompts a message as shown:

Information!

This company has Payroll feature enabled!

You need to follow few post migration steps to configure Payroll

Please refer to help document for details

(Press 'Enter' to Continue)

Fig. 3.3 Payroll Prompt Screen

9. Press Enter to continue with Migration.
10. Tally.ERP 9 displays a message Continue Migration Yes or No.

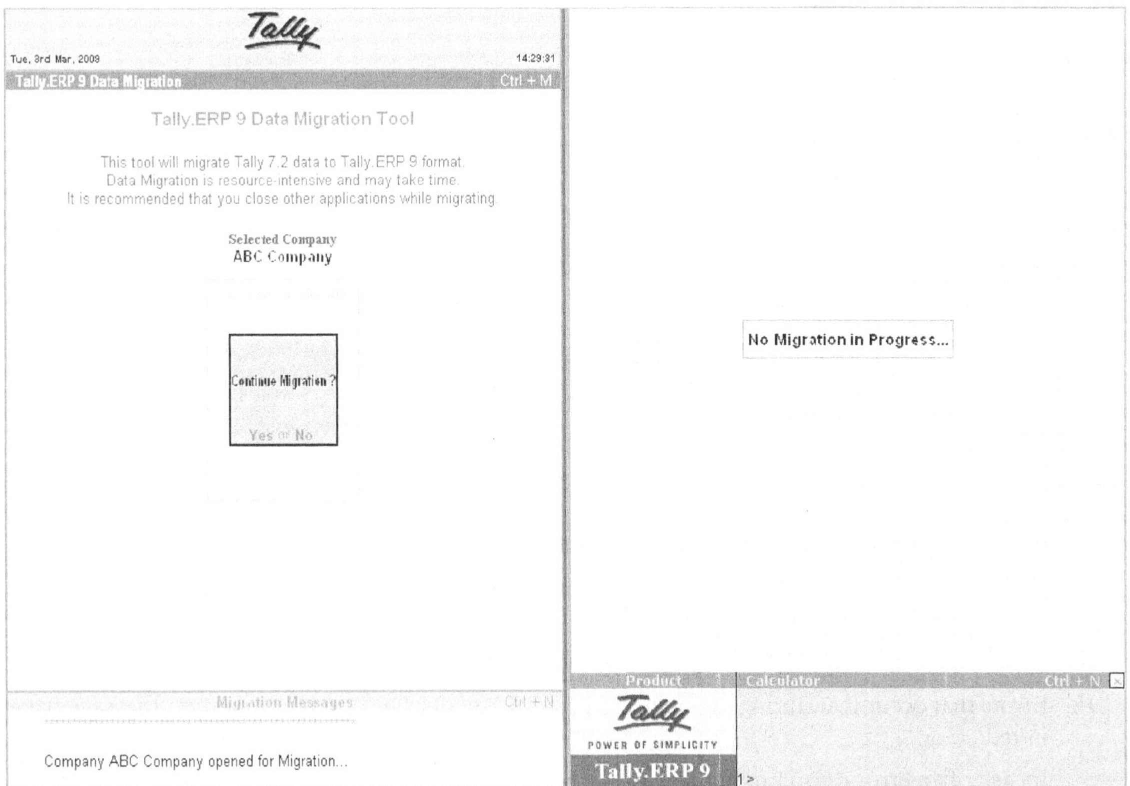

Fig. 3.4 Continue Migration Screen

11. Press Yes to start data migration from Tally 7.2 to Tally.ERP 9.
12. The Migration Information screen displays the Types of Masters and Types of Vouchers that need to be migrated from Tally 7.2.

13. Tally.ERP 9 displays a message Migrate Yes or No
14. Press Y or click on Yes to proceed with migration.
15. During the migration process, the calculator pane of Tally.ERP 9 displays the number of Masters and Vouchers migrated to Tally.ERP 9.

    Certain un-used Voucher Types are removed from Tally.ERP 9, hence there will be a mismatch in Voucher Type Master Statistics.

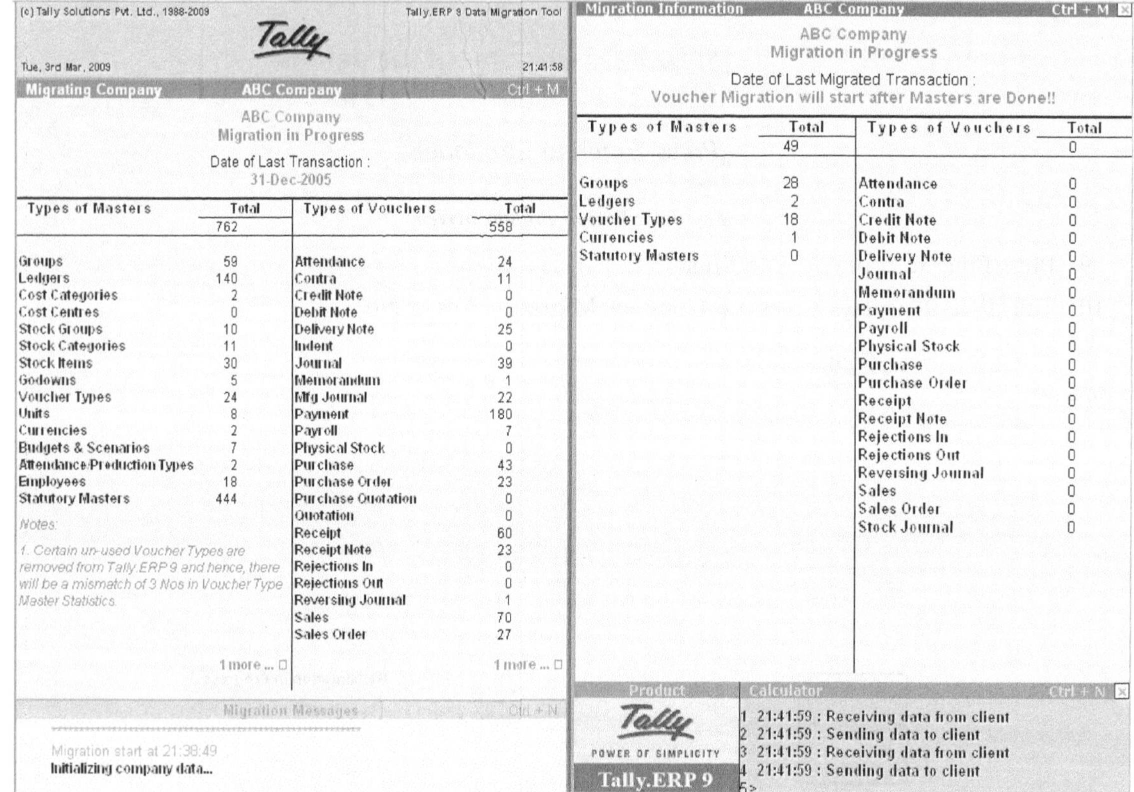

Fig. 3.5 Data Migration Progress

16. Employee Masters have been split into Employees and Employee Groups.

    On successfully completing the migration process, Tally.ERP 9 will display a message Migration Completed Check Statistics.

17. On pressing any key a Congratulatory message appears as shown:
18. Errors that occur that during the migration process are displayed in the Migration Message pane in red color.

    Incase of an error during migration, it is advised to rewrite the data by pressing Ctrl + Alt + R from the migration tool and then start migration of data to Tally.ERP 9.

19. The migrated company data is stored in the default Tally.ERP 9 folder and prefixed with a zero. The company folder will appear as shown.

Caution

Tally.ERP 9 will warn the user with a message as shown, when the user want to migrate the same company from Tally 7.2 to Tally.ERP 9 once again.

00002

Changes that occur after Successful Migration to Tally.ERP 9.

- The Payroll Deduction ledgers created under the group Duties and Taxes in Tally 7.2 are migrated as Pay Heads grouped under Current Liabilities.
- The Payroll Deduction ledgers created under the group Direct or Indirect Expenses in Tally 7.2 are migrated as Pay Heads grouped under Current Liabilities.
- The Payroll Deduction ledgers created under the group Loans & Advances (Assets) in Tally 7.2 are migrated as Pay Heads grouped under the pay head type Loans and Advances.
- Any Attendance type created with unit Month will appear prefixed with ATTD- followed by the name of the Attendance Type.

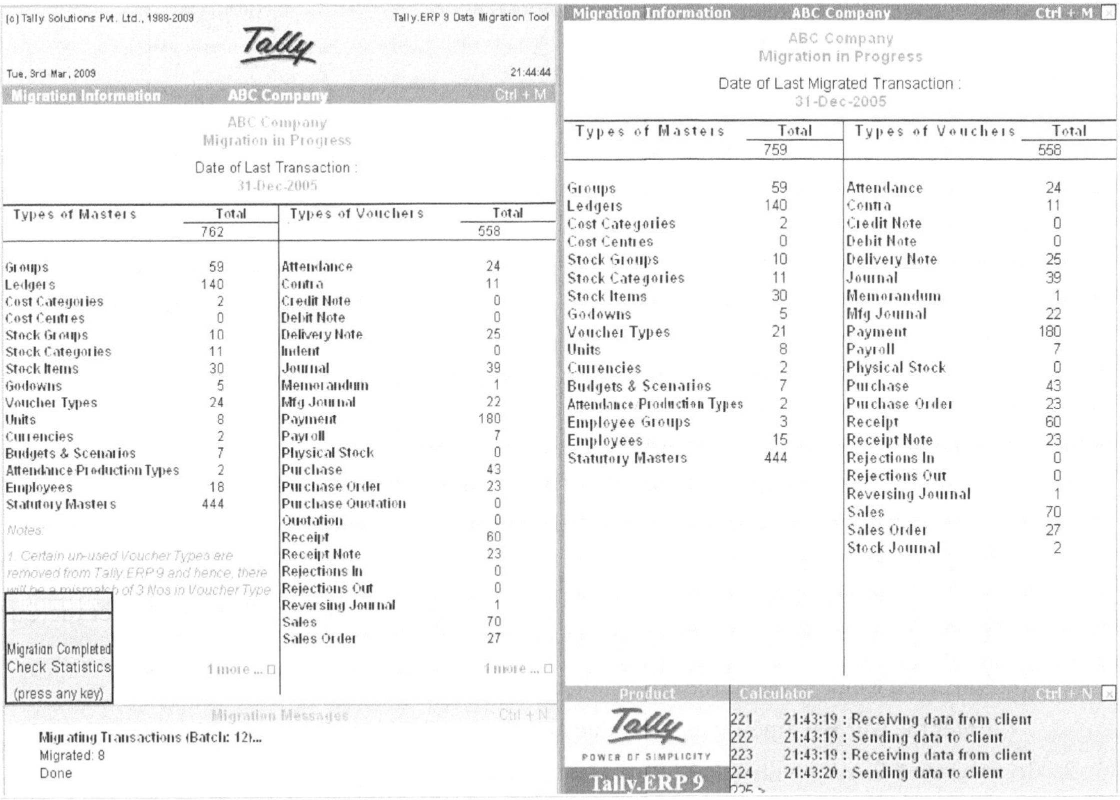

(c) Tally Solutions Pvt. Ltd., 1988-2009 Tally.ERP 9 Data Migration Tool

Tally

Tue, 3rd Mar, 2009 21:44:44

Migration Information ABC Company Ctrl + M

ABC Company
Migration in Progress

Date of Last Transaction :
31-Dec-2005

Types of Masters	Total	Types of Vouchers	Total
	762		558
Groups	59	Attendance	24
Ledgers	140	Contra	11
Cost Categories	2	Credit Note	0
Cost Centres	0	Debit Note	0
Stock Groups	10	Delivery Note	25
Stock Categories	11	Indent	0
Stock Items	30	Journal	39
Godowns	5	Memorandum	1
Voucher Types	24	Mfg Journal	22
Units	8	Payment	180
Currencies	2	Payroll	7
Budgets & Scenarios	7	Physical Stock	0
Attendance Production Types	2	Purchase	43
Employees	18	Purchase Order	23
Statutory Masters	444	Purchase Quotation	0
		Quotation	0
		Receipt	60
		Receipt Note	23
		Rejections In	0
		Rejections Out	0
		Reversing Journal	1
		Sales	70
		Sales Order	27
1 more ...		1 more ...	

Notes:
1. Certain un-used Voucher Types are removed from Tally.ERP 9 and hence, there will be a mismatch of 3 Nos in Voucher Type

Migration Completed
Check Statistics
(press any key)

Migration Messages Ctrl + N

Migrating Transactions (Batch: 12)...
Migrated: 8
Done

Migration Information ABC Company Ctrl + M

ABC Company
Migration in Progress

Date of Last Migrated Transaction :
31-Dec-2005

Types of Masters	Total	Types of Vouchers	Total
	759		558
Groups	59	Attendance	24
Ledgers	140	Contra	11
Cost Categories	2	Credit Note	0
Cost Centres	0	Debit Note	0
Stock Groups	10	Delivery Note	25
Stock Categories	11	Journal	39
Stock Items	30	Memorandum	1
Godowns	5	Mfg Journal	22
Voucher Types	21	Payment	180
Units	8	Payroll	7
Currencies	2	Physical Stock	0
Budgets & Scenarios	7	Purchase	43
Attendance Production Types	2	Purchase Order	23
Employee Groups	3	Receipt	60
Employees	15	Receipt Note	23
Statutory Masters	444	Rejections In	0
		Rejections Out	0
		Reversing Journal	1
		Sales	70
		Sales Order	27
		Stock Journal	2

Product Calculator Ctrl + N

Tally POWER OF SIMPLICITY Tally.ERP 9

221 21:43:19 : Receiving data from client
222 21:43:19 : Sending data to client
223 21:43:19 : Receiving data from client
224 21:43:20 : Sending data to client

Fig. 3.6 Data Migration Information

- Incase the user had migrated data containing attendance entries for the current month, whose Payroll is yet to be processed, such entries will become Production Type Entries. It is suggested that the user re-enter attendance entries for the current month after migration and then process the Payroll.
- On successful migration the Attendance Types will change to Production Types, therefore the YTD details are not retained and the migrated Attendance types are pre-fixed with ATTD-

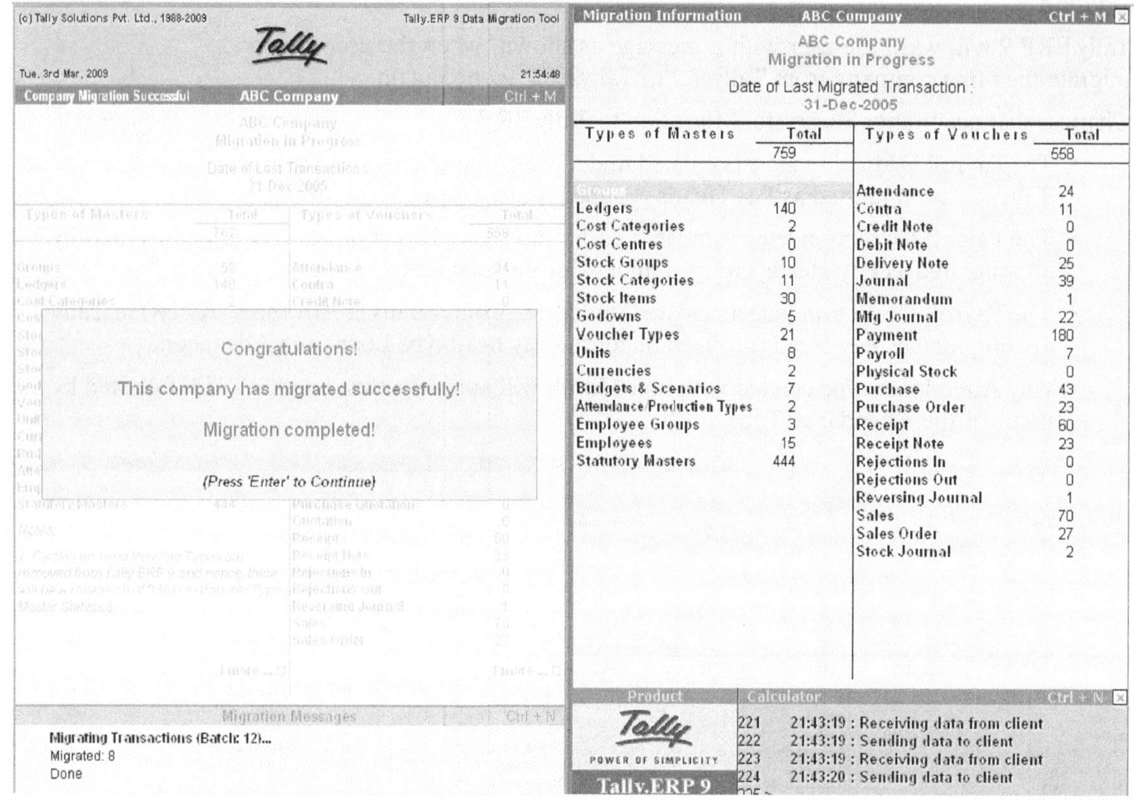

Fig. 3.7 Data Migration Completed Screen

Follow the procedure to display the accurate YTD details in the Payslip:

1. To generate a Payslip with YTD Details for any of the earlier months:
   - Create/Alter the Attendance Voucher for the respective month
   - Select the Employee
   - To Nullify the YTD details, select the ATTD- prefixed Attendance Type and enter the Cur Bal value with a Negative sign in the Value field
   - Select the Employee and the Attendance type
   - Enter the Cur Bal amount as the Value and Accept the Voucher.
2. To generate a Payslip with YTD Details from the Current month onwards:
   - Create/Alter the Attendance Voucher for the previous month
   - Select the Employee
   - To Nullify YTD details, select ATTD- prefixed Attendance Type and enter the Cur Bal value with a Negative sign in the Value field
   - Select the Employee and the Attendance type
   - Enter the Cur Bal amount as the Value and Accept the Voucher.

Selected Company
ABC Company

Information!

This company has Payroll feature enabled!

You need to follow few post migration steps to configure Payroll

Please refer to help document for details

(Press 'Enter' to Continue)

Fig. 3.8 Caution Screen

Additional Information

Once the migration of Data from Tally 7.2 to Tally.ERP 9 is completed, two important log files are created in the folder containing the tally72migration.exe.

`migration.err`

The migration.err file contains the errors, if any, which occur during migration.

`migration.log`

The migration.log file provides the user with the following migration details :

1. Date of Migration
2. The Name of the company opened for migration
3. Migration Start time
4. Time taken and the Migrate data information, *i.e.*, Masters, Vouchers and Reports from Tally 7.2 to Tally.ERP 9
5. Lists the number of errors, if any
6. Migration End time
7. The Migration tool closing 7.2 company ABC Company and Closed information of the migrated company.

Migrating Group Companies

To migrate Group companies:

1. Migrate each member company individually from Tally 7.2 to Tally.ERP 9
2. On successful migration of the companies, re-create the Group company in Tally.ERP 9.

Post Migration Steps for Payroll Data in Tally.ERP 9

On successful migration of the Payroll data from Tally 7.2 to Tally.ERP 9, the user has to configure the following settings for the Pay Heads:

1. Enable the Payroll Statutory Features:
    - From Gateway of Tally > Press F11: Features > F3: Statutory Feature
    - Set Yes to Enable Payroll Statutory
    - Set Yes to Set/Alter Payroll Statutory Details
    - In the Payroll Statutory screen

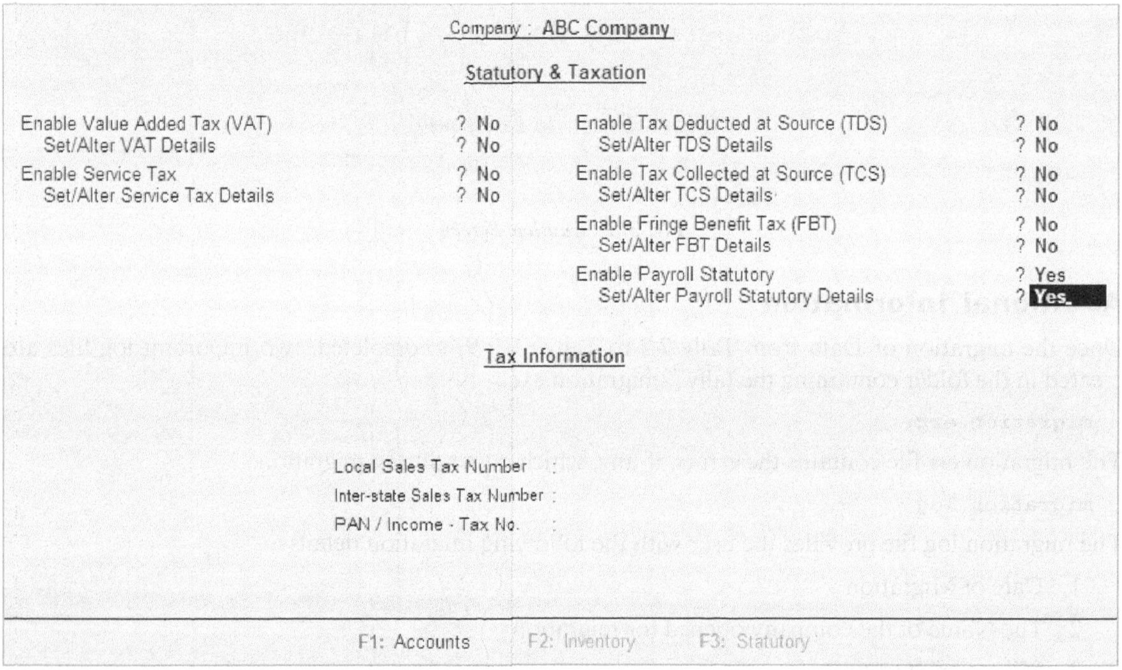

Company : ABC Company

Statutory & Taxation

Enable Value Added Tax (VAT)	? No	Enable Tax Deducted at Source (TDS)	? No
Set/Alter VAT Details	? No	Set/Alter TDS Details	? No
Enable Service Tax	? No	Enable Tax Collected at Source (TCS)	? No
Set/Alter Service Tax Details	? No	Set/Alter TCS Details	? No
		Enable Fringe Benefit Tax (FBT)	? No
		Set/Alter FBT Details	? No
		Enable Payroll Statutory	? Yes
		Set/Alter Payroll Statutory Details	? Yes

Tax Information

Local Sales Tax Number :
Inter-state Sales Tax Number :
PAN / Income - Tax No. :

F1: Accounts F2: Inventory F3: Statutory

Fig. 3.9 Statutory and Taxation Screen

- The user has to enter the Provident Fund Company Code, Company Account Group Code and Company Security Code
- The user has to enter the Employees State Insurance Company Code, ESI Branch Office and Standard Working Days. By default, 10, 000 is displayed as the eligibility amount for ESI in Eligibility Amount field
- Press Enter to accept and return to the Statutory & Taxation screen
- Press Escape to return to Gateway of Tally.

2. Select the Pay Heads, Pay Type, Group, Calculation Type and provide Computation Info.

Non Statutory Pay Heads:

- Select the respective Pay Head Type from the list of Pay Head Types
- Select the respective Group from the List of Groups for the Pay Head

Payroll Statutory Details

Provident Fund

Company Code :
Company Account Group Code :
Company Security Code :

Employee State Insurance

Company Code :
ESI Branch Office :
Eligibility Amount :
Standard Working Days (per month) :

- Select the respective Calculation Type from the List of Calculations
- Select the respective Computation Type from the List of Computation On
- In the Computation On Specified Formula select the Pay Head from the List of Pay Heads
- Enter the Effective From date
- In Slab Type column select Percentage from the List of Slabs.

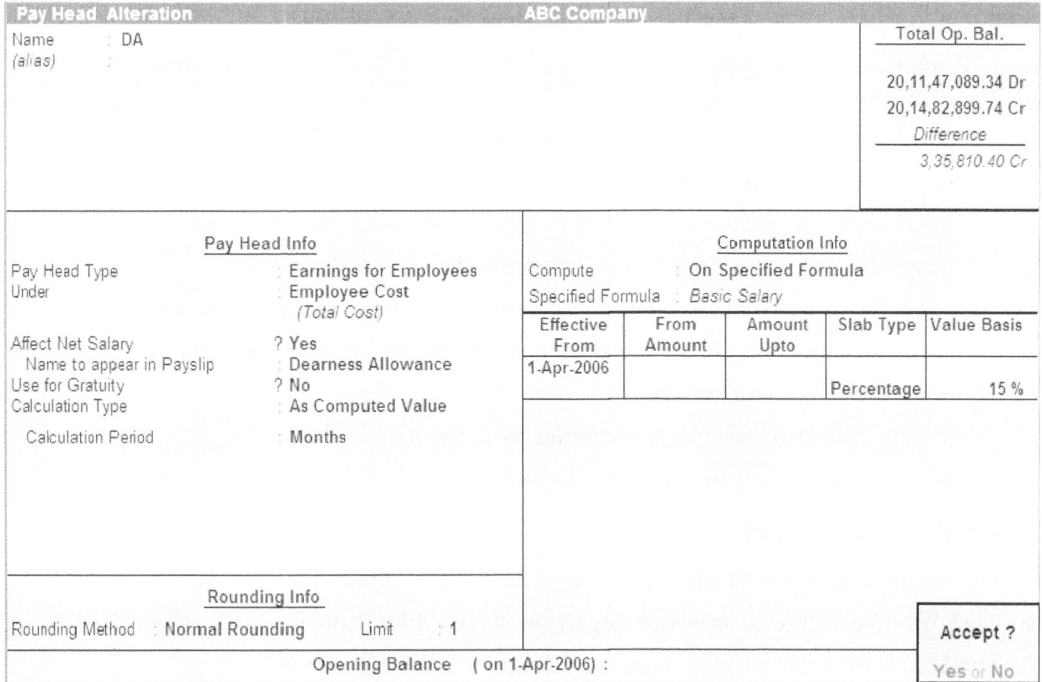

Pay Head Alteration ABC Company

Name : DA
(alias) :

Total Op. Bal.
20,11,47,089.34 Dr
20,14,82,899.74 Cr
Difference
3,35,810.40 Cr

Pay Head Info

Pay Head Type : Earnings for Employees
Under : Employee Cost
(Total Cost)
Affect Net Salary ? Yes
Name to appear in Payslip : Dearness Allowance
Use for Gratuity ? No
Calculation Type : As Computed Value
Calculation Period : Months

Computation Info

Compute : On Specified Formula
Specified Formula : Basic Salary

Effective From	From Amount	Amount Upto	Slab Type	Value Basis
1-Apr-2006			Percentage	15 %

Rounding Info

Rounding Method : Normal Rounding Limit : 1

Opening Balance (on 1-Apr-2006) :

Accept ?
Yes or No

Fig. 3.10 Pay Head Alteration Screen

- Enter the required value in the Value Basis column.

Pay Head Alteration ABC Company

Name : Employee Provident Fund
(alias) :

Total Op. Bal.
20,11,47,089.34 Dr
20,14,82,899.74 Cr
Difference
3,35,810.40 Cr

Pay Head Info

Pay Head Type : Employees' Statutory Deductions
Statutory Pay Type : PF Account (A/c No. 1)
Under : Current Liabilities

Affect Net Salary ? Yes
Name to appear in Payslip :

Calculation Type : As Computed Value
Calculation Period : Months

Computation Info

Compute : On Specified Formula
Specified Formula : Basic Salary

Effective From	From Amount	Amount Upto	Slab Type	Value Basis
1-Apr-2006			Percentage	12 %

Rounding Info

Rounding Method : Normal Rounding Limit : 1

Accept ?
Yes or No

Opening Balance (on 1-Apr-2006) : 5,08,679.80 Cr

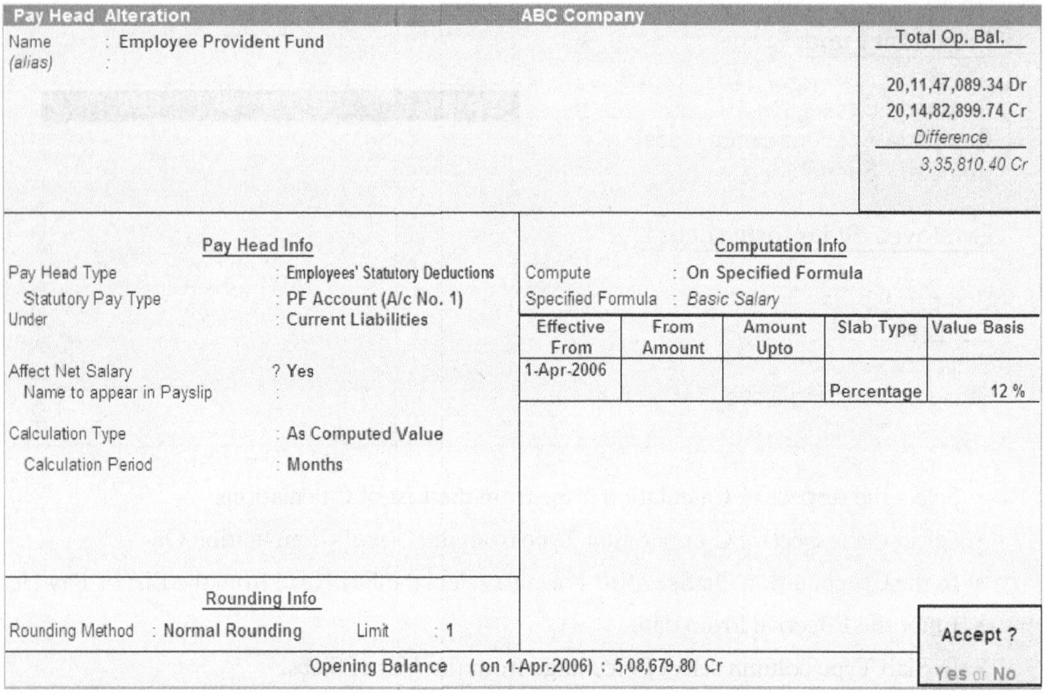

Fig. 3.11 Enter the Value Basis Information

Statutory Pay Heads:

- Select the respective Pay Head Type from the List of Pay Head Types
- Select the respective Statutory Pay Type from the Employees Statutory Deductions
- Select the respective Group from the List of Groups for the Pay Head
- Select the respective Calculation Type from the List of Calculations
- Select the respective Computation Type from the List of Computation On
- In the Computation On Specified Formula select the Pay Head from the List of Pay Heads
- Enter the Effective From date
- In Slab Type column select Percentage from the List of Slabs
- Enter the required value in the Value Basis column.

Migrating TCP Files

To migrate the TCP files from Tally 7.2 to Tally.ERP 9 follow the steps mentioned below:

1. Click Migrate TCP to commence migration of TCP files from Tally 7.2 to Tally.ERP 9
2. The Migration utility displays a message Migrate TCP(s) Yes or No
3. Accept to continue with the migration of TCP Files

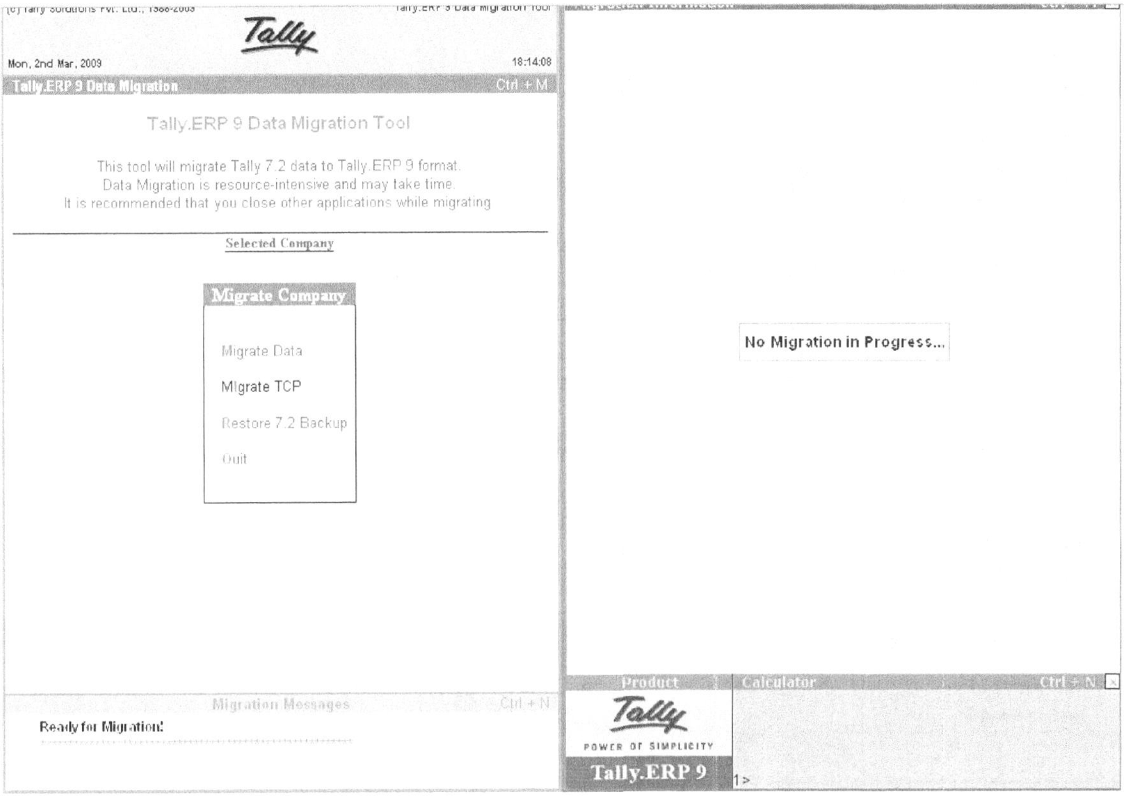

Mon, 2nd Mar, 2009 18:14:08

Tally.ERP 9 Data Migration Ctrl + M

Tally.ERP 9 Data Migration Tool

This tool will migrate Tally 7.2 data to Tally.ERP 9 format.
Data Migration is resource-intensive and may take time.
It is recommended that you close other applications while migrating

Selected Company

Migrate Company

Migrate Data
Migrate TCP
Restore 7.2 Backup
Quit

No Migration in Progress...

Migration Messages Ctrl + N

Ready for Migration!

Product Calculator Ctrl + N

Tally POWER OF SIMPLICITY Tally.ERP 9

Fig. 3.12 Migrating TCP Screen

4. On successfully migrating the TCP file from Tally 7.2 to Tally.ERP 9, a message is displayed shown below:

5. Press Enter to continues.

Post Migration Observations for the TCP files

1. The migrated TCP file is saved in the same folder where Tally 7.2 TCP file resides.

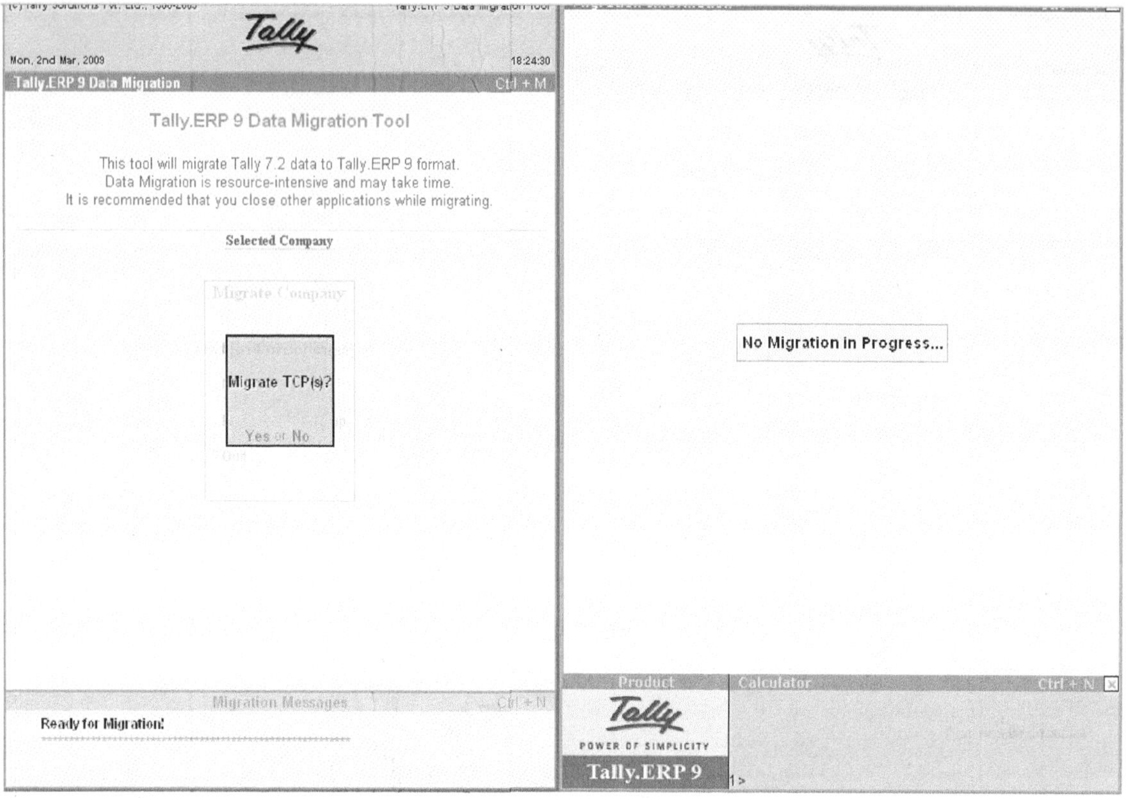

Fig. 3.13 Confirmation of Migration

2. The migrated TCP filename is suffixed with the digit 9 as shown and appears similarly in the Tally.ini.

```
User TDL = Yes

tdl = c:\tally\allmenuactive729.tcp
```

Restoring 7.2 Backup

To restore the backup of data created in Tally 7.2 the user has to follow the steps shown:

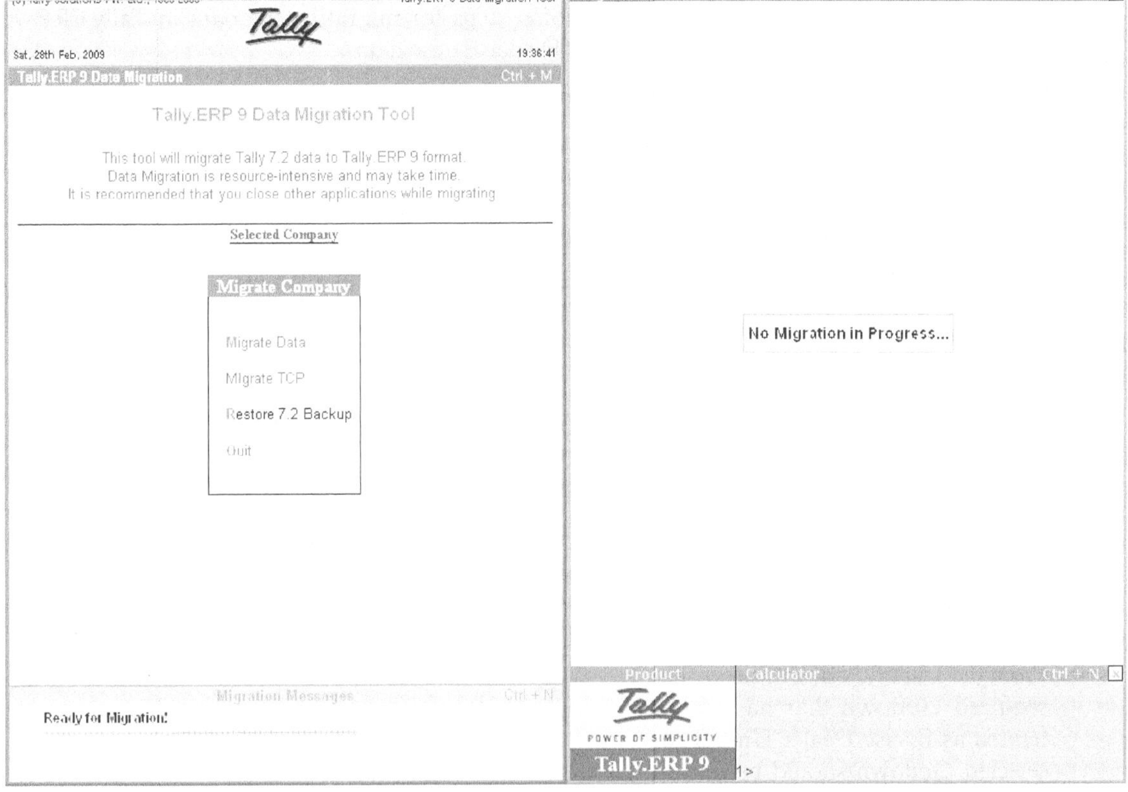

Fig. 3.14 Restoring Data Screen

1. Select Restore 7.2 Backup to restore the Tally 7.2 data backup
2. In the Restore Companies on Disk screen enter the path for
   - Destination – is the folder where the data backup has to be restored
   - Source – is the folder which contains the data backup
3. Select the company which has to restored from the List of Companies
4. Accept to restore the data backup
5. The restored data of Tally 7.2 is available in the destination folder
6. The user can proceed with Migrating Data to Tally.ERP 9.

Migrating Dealer Excise Data

Migration of Dealer Excise data from Tally 9 to Tally.ERP 9.

There are two ways of Migrating Dealer Excise data depending upon feature enabled in the data.

- Maintain Multiple Godown is set to No
- Maintain Multiple Godown is set to Yes.

Maintain Multiple Godown is not Enabled

In Dealer Excise data of Tally 9, where Maintain Multiple Godown option in F11 – Features is not enabled . Then, you need not perform any additional steps for migrating the data in Tally.ERP 9. Tally.ERP 9 will Rewrite and after and migrate the Dealer Excise data.

Maintain Multiple Godown is Enabled

In Dealer Excise data of Tally 9 where Maintain Multiple Godown option in F11 – Features is enabled. Then you need to perform the steps shown below before Rewrite. On successfully rewriting the data in Tally.ERP 9 go to Gateway of Tally > Display > Exception Reports > Excise Dealer

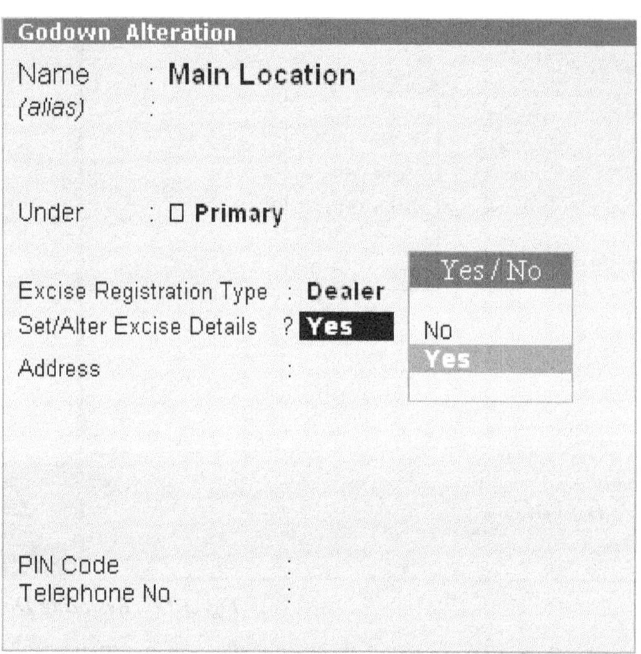

Tally.ERP 9 will display Godown names and List of Voucher types used by these Godowns

From the list of Godown select the required godown that has to be created as Excise Dealer Unit.

Steps for setting Godown as Excise Dealer Unit:

1. Go to Gateway of Tally > Inventory Info > Godowns > Alter.
2. From the List of Godown, select the required Godown that has to be treated as Excise Dealer Unit. The selected Godown should be under Primary.
3. In Excise Registration Type, select as Dealer from List of Registration Types.
4. Set Yes to Set/Alter Excise Details.
5. Specify the required Excise Details in Excise Details screen.
6. Similarly, you are required to alter the details for the remaining Godowns which are under Primary and group them under the Godown which has been treated as Excise Dealer Unit and select Not Applicable in Excise Registration Type.
7. The completed Godown Alteration screen appears as shown.

Godown Alteration
Name : Main Location
(alias) :
Under : Primary
Excise Registration Type : Dealer
Set/Alter Excise Details ? Yes
Address : No 33, Chickpet
Bangalore
PIN Code : 560012
Telephone No. : 40014001
Accept ?
Yes or No

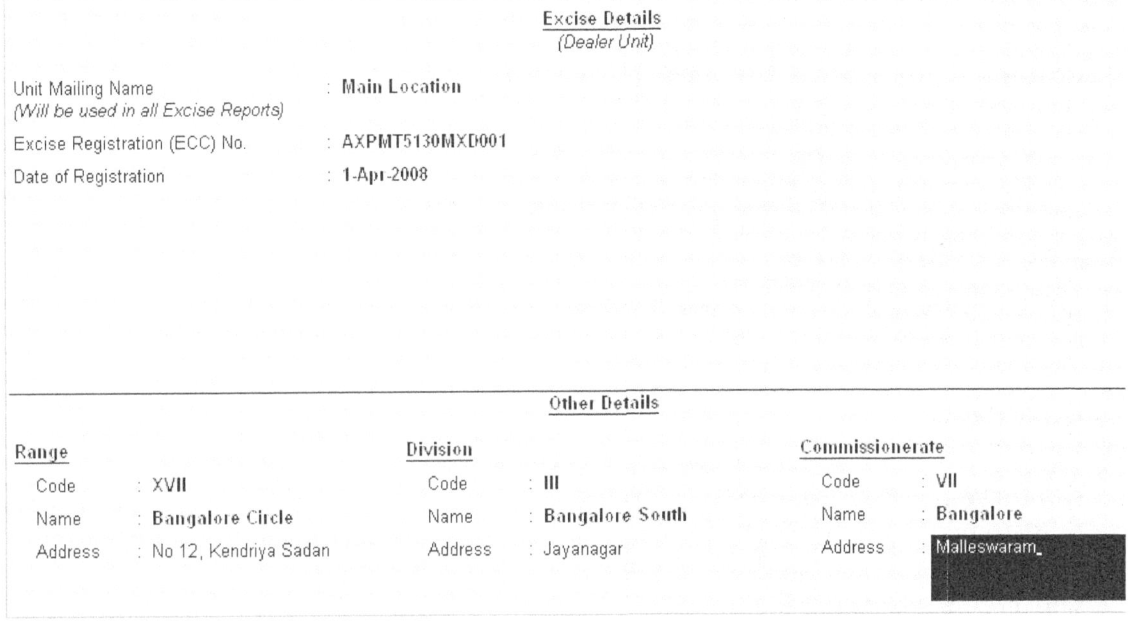

Fig. 3.15 Excise Details Screen

Alter Voucher Types

Voucher Types which were enabled for Excise in Tally 9 need to be altered in Tally.ERP 9.

Steps for altering Voucher Types:

1. Gateway of Tally > Accounts Info. > Voucher Types > Alter
2. Select the required Voucher Type that has to be altered for Dealer Excise
3. In Voucher Type Alteration screen, set Yes to Use for Excise
4. Select the Default Excise Unit
5. Save the alteration in the Voucher type.

Note: In the Voucher Type Alteration screen set Yes to Use for Excise for each Voucher Type used for Excise in Tally 9 as it allows you to alter only once.

After doing the above changes, you have to re-migrate the data for Dealer Excise.

Steps for Re-migration

1. Go to Gateway of Tally > press Alt + Ctrl + M to migrate the data.
2. In the Migrate Data screen, select All Items from the List of Modules to migrate.
3. On successfully migration, re-check and compare the statistics of the migrated data with the old data.

Migrating TDS Data

Pre Migration

Before migrating the data to Tally.ERP 9 TDS, deduct TDS for all pending Bills of all Parties even though they have not crossed the exemption limit. You can ignore the exemption limit by configuration at the master level.

Vouchers Considered for TDS Migration

The TDS migration will happen only for

- TDS Deduction Voucher
- Advance payment voucher where TDS is deducted in the same voucher.

Migration Flow

Migration will happen based on the supplier Ledger. Before the actual migration Tally checks for the validity of all transactions for a supplier and if any error is found it skips that supplier or skips the transaction depending upon the type of data error.

Data Errors

Data Errors in TDS Migration can be categorized as follows:

1. **TDS Process Flow Error**: This type of error not only affects the particular transaction in which it is identified but also the subsequent transactions. When this type of an error is identified in a transaction, all the transactions for that supplier will not be migrated.

Reasons for Non-migration

- Gross amount is empty.
- Gross amount is equal or less than the previous deduction's gross amount.

  How to find non-migrated vouchers?

  - In Tally.ERP 9 the non-migrated vouchers can be tracked from.
  - Go to Gateway of Tally > Statutory reports > TDS Reports > Exception Report >Track Migrated Vouchers.
  - To find the non-migrated vouchers based on bill details.
  - Go to Gateway of Tally > Statutory Reports > TDS Reports > Exception Report > Track Migrated Bills.

2. **Transaction Error**: This type of error affects only the particular transaction in which it is identified. When this type of an error is identified in a transaction, the particular transaction will not be migrated.

Reasons for Non-migration:

- Multiple duty ledger or supplier selected in a deduction voucher
- Multiple party bill adjustment done in a single deduction transaction
- In party bill adjustment, normal bill is adjusted instead of corresponding TDS liability bill.

However in both the above cases, you can correct the data and re-migrate by pressing Ctrl+Alt+M from Gateway of Tally.

Assessable Value & TDS Calculation

In old TDS there was no concept of Assessable value (Gross Value concept was used) which is required for TDS statutory reports at each Nature of Payment level of a transaction. Tally.ERP 9 supports assessable value concept in new TDS. To calculate Assessable Value for old TDS data while migrating, Tally sorts the supplier vouchers based on the sequence of entry and identifies the Assessable value from the deduction voucher by applying the following formula:

Assessable Value for the Deduction = (Current Deduction's Gross Amount –Previous Deduction's Gross Amount).

Tally re-calculates the tax amount by applying the stored percentages. If there is a difference between Calculated Tax and Actual Tax stored in the deduction voucher, the difference will be treated as below:

1. In case the difference amount less than or equal to Rs. 3/- (plus or minus), it is considered as rounding-off issue and adjusted in Income Tax.
2. In case the amount is more than Rs.3 (plus or minus):
   - if it is negative, it will be treated as Surcharge Reversal and adjusted in Surcharge.
   - if it is positive difference, it will be treated as extra Surcharge Deduction and adjusted in Surcharge.

TDS Migration in different scenarios

1. Single liability booked with multiple deductions - this case will be true only in case if the Surcharge got activated in between either by crossing the limit or ignoring at the master level. In any case, it will create only one tax reference in the liability voucher provided the same bill is adjusted in both the deduction voucher in old TDS.
2. Multiple liability but single deduction – Tally.ERP 9 will update only one liability voucher which is got adjusted in deduction voucher.

   For Example:

   There are 3 liabilities booking vouchers b001, b002 and b003 booked for rent amounting Rs 100000 each respectively. Single deduction voucher is passed for all the 3 vouchers and adjusted against only with 3rd bill (b003).

   How Tally.ERP 9 will handle the migration for the above example:

   - First two vouchers will never get migrated.
   - It will migrate only the third voucher since it is adjusted in the deduction voucher for the entire assessable value of Rs.3,00,000/–.
3. Liability booked but deduction is not done- In this scenario, we will not be able migrate only liability vouchers since it does not have any deduction information. Need to follow the first step mentioned in Prerequisite before migration.
4. If the same TDS tax reference is used for two different deduction vouchers of the same or different party for same nature of payment. And a single TDS payment is made for that TDS tax reference.

   Tally.ERP 9 will not migrate the second deduction voucher. However you can correct reference of second deduction voucher and re-migrate by pressing Ctrl+Alt+M from Gateway of Tally.

   And for TDS payment you have to manual correct the reference by going in alteration screen.

Post Migration

1. If zero rates are applicable for a transaction, that transaction will not get migrated since it does not have any deduction for it. The same effect has to be manually given in new TDS by altering

the voucher for the assessable value. Other wise, the same will not be considered for exemption limit calculation.

2. Lower deduction details will not be migrated since earlier it was configured at the supplier level and applicable for all nature of payments.

   In Tally.ERP 9, the same can be configured for each nature of payment. Because of which the same has to be configured once after the migration.

3. The configuration of ignoring IT exemption limit was set in duty ledger and applied across all the suppliers in previous TDS.

   However in Tally.ERP 9 the same can be configured for each supplier and for each nature of payment. Because of which it requires one time manual configuration after the migration.

   If this is not set and any TDS deduction is found without crossing the exemption limit (due to previous configuration in the old TDS), will be shown in negative in computation report.

4 Creating Masters in Tally.ERP 9

Accounting Information

Accounts Info menu lists the masters through which you can provide the details of your company's accounts.

Go to Gateway of Tally > Accounts Info.

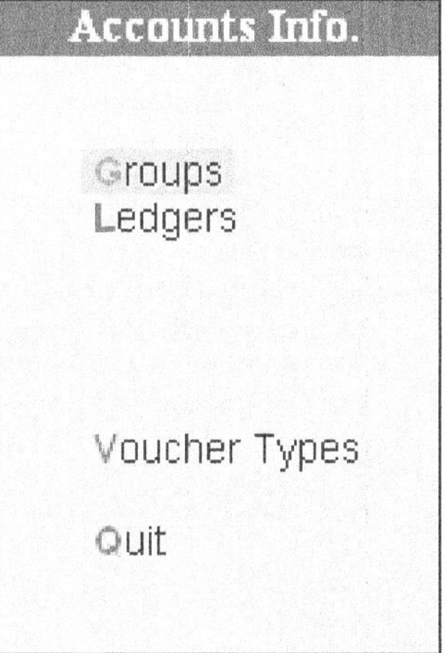

Configuring F12 Configure and Setting F11: Features

F12: Configure and F11: Features help you to organize the information and the level of details as per requirement. You can modify/alter the settings in F12: Configure and F11: Features at any point of time.

Go to Gateway of Tally > F11: Features > F1: Accounting Features

There are various settings available under Accounting/Inventory/ Statutory & Taxation Features, which determine the information to be entered in transaction entries.

F12: Configurations

To set F12: Configure for Accounts and Inventory Masters

Go to Gateway of Tally > F12: Configure > Accts/Inv Info.

By default, Accounts/Inventory Masters settings are set to No. Features that you require can be set to Yes. Typically, they are additional fields that appear during Masters Creation which enable you to obtain more information and detailed analysis.

Functions in Accounts Info. Menu

Accounts Information contains the masters. Each master has Create, Alter and Display functions.

Single Group option is useful when you wish to work on one Group at a time. Multiple Group option is very useful when you are working on many sub-groups at a time and saves a lot of time. Once a sub-group is created, it behaves exactly like a Group.

Create

The Create option is used to create new masters.

Display

The Display option is used to view the Master information. Master information cannot be modified in Display mode.

Alter

The Alter option allows you to view and make the necessary changes to the master information. This does not allow the creation of masters.

Company: ABC Company

Accounting Features

General		Invoicing	
Integrate Accounts and Inventory	? Yes	Allow Invoicing	? Yes
Income/Expense Statement instead of P & L	? No	Enter Purchases in Invoice Format	? Yes
Allow Multi-Currency	? No	Use Debit/Credit Notes	? No
		Use Invoice mode for Credit Notes	? No
		Use Invoice mode for Debit Notes	? No
Outstandings Management		**Budgets & Scenario Management**	
Maintain Bill-wise Details	? Yes	Maintain Budgets and Controls	? No
(for Non-Trading A/cs also)	? No	Use Reversing Journals & Optional Vouchers	? No
Activate Interest Calculation	? No	**Other Features**	
(use advanced parameters)	? No	Enable Cheque Printing	? No
Cost/Profit Centres Management		Set/Alter Cheque Printing Configuration	? No
Maintain Payroll	? No	Allow Zero valued entries	? No
Maintain Cost Centres	? No		
Use Cost Centre for Job Costing	? No		
More than ONE Payroll / Cost Category	? No		
Use Pre-defined Cost Centre Allocations during Entry	? No		

F1: Accounts F2: Inventory F3: Statutory F5: Audit

Fig. 4.1 Accounting Features Screen

Master Configuration

Allow ALIASES along with Names ? Yes
Allow Language ALIASES along with Names ? No

Accounts		Inventory	
Allow ADVANCED entries in Masters	? Yes	Allow ADVANCED entries in Masters	? No
Use ADDRESSES for Ledger Accounts	? Yes	Use PART NUMBERS for Stock Items	? No
Use CONTACT DETAILS for Ledger Accounts	? No	Use Description for Stock Items	? No
Add NOTES for Ledger Accounts	? No	Use REMARKS for Stock Items	? No
		Use ALTERNATE UNITS for Stock Items	? No
		Allow Std. Rates for Stock Items	? No
		Specify Default Ledger Allocation for Invoicing	? No
		Allow Component list details (Bill of Materials)	? No
		Use ADDRESSES for Godowns	? No

Fig. 4.2 Master Configuration Screen

Groups

Groups are collection of Ledgers of the same nature. Account Groups are maintained to determine the hierarchy of Ledger Accounts which is helpful in determining and presenting meaningful and compliant reports.

has the flexibility of setting user required chart of accounts. You can group the Ledger accounts under the required Groups at the time of creating the chart of accounts or you can alter them at any time.

The Group behavior is classified into Capital or Revenue and more specifically into Assets, Liabilities, Income and Expenditure. The Groups ascertain whether the same will affect Profit and Loss Account which is revenue in nature or Balance Sheet which is capital in nature.

A Discussion on Each of the Reserved Groups

Capital Account

This records the Capital and Reserves of the company. The ledgers that belong to Capital Accounts are Share Capital, Partners' Capital A/c, Proprietor's Capital Account and so on.

Reserves and Surplus [Retained Earnings]

This contains ledgers like Capital Reserve, General Reserve, Reserve for Depreciation and so on.

Current Assets

Current Assets record the assets that do not belong either to Bank Accounts or to Cash-in-Hand sub-groups.

Bank Accounts

Current account, savings account, short term deposit accounts and so on.

Cash-in hand

Tally.ERP 9 automatically creates Cash A/c in this group. You can open more than one cash account, if necessary.

Note: An account under Cash-in-hand group or Bank Accounts/Bank OCC A/c group is printed as a separate Cash Book in the traditional Cash Book format and does not form part of the Ledger.

Deposits (Asset)

Deposits contain Fixed Deposits, Security Deposits or any deposit made by the company (not received by the company, which is a liability).

Loans & Advances (Asset)

This records all loans given by the company and advances of a non-trading nature (example: advance against salaries) or even for purchase of Fixed Assets. We do not recommend you to open Advances to Suppliers' account under this Group. For further details, please refer to the section on Common Errors.

Stock-in-hand

This group contains accounts like Raw Materials, Work-in-Progress and Finished Goods. The balance control depends on whether you have selected Integrated Account-cum-Inventory option while creating the company. (refer to Company creation section for more details) Let us consider these options:

Integrated Accounts-cum-Inventory

This option has a significant effect on the Balance Sheet and Profit & Loss Account. If set to Yes, it brings the stock/inventory balance figures from the inventory records and provides a drill down to the Stock registers from the Balance Sheet.

You are not allowed to directly change the closing balance of an account under this group. You are allowed to pass transactions in Inventory records and the account balances are automatically reflected in the Balance Sheet as Closing Stock.

Non-integrated Accounts-cum-Inventory

If Integrated Account-cum-Inventory option is set to No, it ignores the inventory books figures and picks up manually entered closing stock balances from the ledger account created. This provides the facility to maintain accounts separately and inventory separately.

You are not allowed to pass transactions if your accounts that come under this Group. It allows you to hold opening and closing balances only. Since no vouchers can be passed for these accounts, they are the only accounts for which the closing balances can be directly altered (by an authorised user only).

Sundry Debtors

For customer accounts refer to common and possible errors in grouping of accounts section.

Current Liabilities

Accounts like Outstanding Liabilities, Statutory Liabilities and other minor liabilities can be created directly under this group. Sub-groups under Current Liabilities are Duties and Taxes, Provisions and Sundry Creditors.

Duties and Taxes

Duties and Taxes contain all tax accounts like VAT, CENVAT, Excise, Sales and other trade taxes and the total liability (or asset in case of advances paid) and the break-up of individual items.

Provisions

Accounts like Provision for Taxation, Provision for Depreciation and so on are recorded under Provisions.

Sundry Creditors

For trade creditors, refer to common and possible errors in grouping of accounts section.

Investments

Group your investment accounts like Investment in Shares, Bonds, Govt. securities, long term Bank deposit accounts and so on. This allows you to view the total investments made by the company.

Loans (Liability)

Loans that a company has borrowed, typically long-terms loans.

Bank OD Accounts [Bank OCC Accounts]

provides you with distinct types of Bank Accounts,

Bank OCC A/c

To record the company's overdraft accounts with banks. For example, Bill Discounted A/c's and Hypothecation A/c's etc.

Note: An account under Bank OCC A/c group is printed as a separate Cash Book in the traditional Cash Book format and does not form part of the Ledger.

Secured Loans

Term loans or other long/medium term loans, which are obtained against security of some asset. does not verify the existence of the security. Typical accounts are Debentures, Term Loans, and so on.

Unsecured Loans

Loans obtained without any security. Example: Loans from Directors/partners or outside parties.

Suspense Account

In modern accounting, many large corporations use a Suspense Ledger to track the money paid or recovered, the nature of which is not yet known. The most common example is money paid for Travelling Advance whose details will be known only upon submission of the TA bill. Some companies may prefer to open such accounts under Suspense Account.

Loans and Advances (Asset) group.

The Suspense Account is a Balance Sheet item. Any expense account even if it has 'suspense' in its name, it should be opened under Revenue group like Indirect Expenses and not under Suspense Account group.

Miscellaneous Expenses (Asset)

This group is typically used for legal disclosure requirements such as Schedule VI of the Indian Companies Act. It should hold incorporation and pre-operative expenses. Companies would write off a permissible portion of the account every year. A balance remains to an extent that cannot be written off in Profit & Loss Account. Tally.ERP 9 does not show loss, carried forward in the Profit & Loss Account, under this group. The Profit & Loss Account balance is displayed separately in the Balance Sheet.

Branch/Divisions

This maintains ledger accounts of all your company's branches, divisions, affiliates, sister concerns, subsidiaries and so on. Tally.ERP 9 permits Sales and Purchase transactions to take place with accounts opened here. Remember, these are their accounts in your books and not their books of accounts. Just treat them as any other party account. If you wish to maintain the books of a branch/division on your computer, you must open a separate company. (Tally.ERP 9 allows maintenance of multiple company accounts).

Revenue — Primary Groups

Sales Account

You can classify your sales accounts based on Tax slabs or type of sales. This also becomes a simple mechanism for preparation of Tax returns.

Examples:

- Domestic Sales
- Export Sales.

Now under Domestic Sales open the following ledgers:

- Sales (10%)
- Sales (5%)
- Sales (exempt).

You can even open an account as Sales Returns under the group Domestic Sales to view your net sales after returns (or the returns may be directly passed through Journal against the specific Sales account).

Note: Do not create customer accounts under this group. For more details, refer to common and possible errors in grouping of accounts section.

Purchase Account

This is similar to sales accounts, except for the type of transactions.

Direct Income [Income Direct]

These are Non-trade income accounts that affect Gross Profit. All trade income accounts fall under Sales Accounts. You may also use this group for accounts like Servicing, Contract Charges that follow sales of equipment.

For a professional services company, you may not use Sales Account group at all. Instead, open accounts like Professional Fees under this group.

Indirect Income [Income Indirect]

These are miscellaneous non-sale income accounts. Example: Rent Received and Interest Received.

Direct Expenses [Expenses Direct]

These are Manufacturing or direct trading expenses. These accounts determine the Gross Profit of the company.

Indirect Expenses [Expenses Indirect]

All administrative, selling or non-direct expenses.

Profit & Loss Account is a reserved primary account in Tally.ERP 9. You can use this account to pass adjustment entries through journal vouchers. For example, transfer of profit or loss account to Capital or Reserve account.

Common and Possible Errors in Grouping and Account Classification

Debtor/Creditor classification

Accounts of parties with whom your company is trading should be opened under any of the following groups (or sub-groups under them):

- Sundry Debtors
- Sundry Creditors
- Branch/Divisions.

Sales and Purchase account groups are meant for revenue accounts and are reflected in the Profit & Loss Account. If you open party accounts under these groups, it becomes difficult to pass sales or purchase voucher transactions.

For example, in a sales voucher transaction entry, you must debit an account, which can be sundry debtor, branch/division or even a sundry creditor. Moreover, other facilities like bill-wise allocation and tracking will not be available unless the accounts belong to one of these groups.

Opening two accounts of the same party

Tally.ERP 9 classifies debtors, creditors and branch/divisions for convenience. This helps you in the process of keeping the accounts of a particular group together during display and analysis. Thus you can pass both sales and purchase entries for a party account placed under Sundry Debtors. Use the classification depending on the most natural group for the party.

For example, parties from whom you buy frequently can be placed under Sundry Creditors, as that is the natural place to look for their account. Tally.ERP 9 does not restrict the accounts from having obverse balances. Thus, a Sundry Debtor can have a credit balance depending on the state of his account.

Therefore, you need not open two accounts for the same party - one under Sundry Debtors and another under Sundry Creditors. Tally.ERP 9 restricts opening of two identical ledger accounts. In such cases, you may decide to circumvent by marking one account as "A & Co - S/Dr" and another "A & Co - S/Cr". This will allow you to have two accounts of the same party under two groups, but you will lose the advantage of analyzing net position at a single instance. It is always better to maintain a single account to obtain best benefits.

Expenditure items are entered under Liabilities group. For example, the expenditure item Rates & Taxes under the group Duties and Taxes.

The group Duties and Taxes is specifically meant to handle taxation liabilities of your company. Rates & Taxes and other statutory expenses should be placed under Indirect Expenses.

Simply adhering to the reserved groups may be sufficient for many organizations. For greater diversity, Tally.ERP 9 allows you to create your own groups, either as sub-groups or primary groups. Groups can be sub-classified to practically an unlimited level, giving you a virtual accounting tree. At the lowest level, of course, would be the ledger account.

Pre-defined Groups in Tally.ERP 9

By default, Tally.ERP 9 provides a list of Groups called pre-defined groups. The Primary Group cannot be deleted, however, it can be renamed which is not suggested. The user can create any number of Primary Groups and Sub Groups which are again grouped under a Primary Group/Sub Group.

There are 28 pre-defined Groups in Tally.ERP 9, out of which 15 are Primary Groups and 13 are Sub-Groups.

15 Primary Groups	**13 Sub Groups**
Branch / Divisions	Bank Accounts
Capital Account	Bank OD A/c
Current Assets	Cash-in-hand
Current Liabilities	Deposits (Asset)
Direct Expenses	Duties & Taxes
Direct Incomes	Loans & Advances (Asset)
Fixed Assets	Provisions
Indirect Expenses	Reserves & Surplus
Indirect Incomes	Secured Loans
Investments	Stock-in-hand
Loans (Liability)	Sundry Creditors
Misc. Expenses (ASSET)	Sundry Debtors
Purchase Accounts	Unsecured Loans
Sales Accounts	
Suspense A/c	

Out of the 15 Primary Groups, 9 Primary Groups appear in the Balance Sheet which are Capital in nature and 6 Primary Groups appear under Profit & Loss Account which are Revenue in nature.

13 Sub Groups are classified under the 15 Primary Groups and they appear in the Balance Sheet.

Pre defined Sub Groups	Under
Bank Accounts	Current Assets
Bank OD A/c	Loans (Liability)
Cash-in-hand	Current Assets
Deposits (Asset)	Current Assets
Duties & Taxes	Current Liabilities
Loans & Advances (Asset)	Current Assets
Provisions	Current Liabilities
Reserves & Surplus	Capital Account
Secured Loans	Loans (Liability)
Stock-in-hand	Current Assets
Sundry Creditors	Current Liabilities
Sundry Debtors	Current Assets
Unsecured Loans	Loans (Liability)

Creating a Group

There are two options for creating Groups in Tally.ERP 9:

Single Group – We can create only one Group by using Single Group creation screen.

Multiple Groups – We can create multiple Groups by using Multiple Group Creation screen.

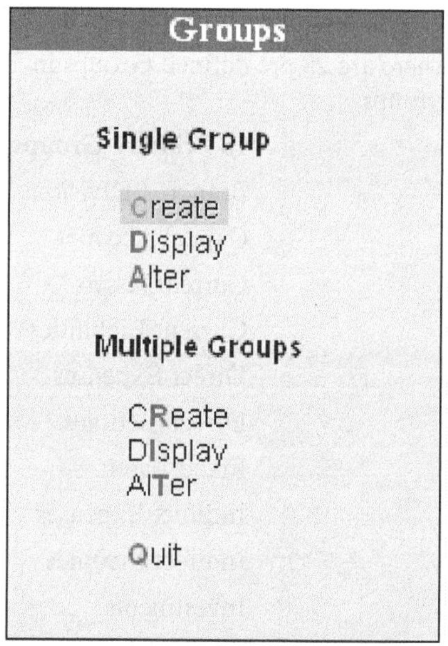

Creating a Single Group

Go to Gateway of Tally > Accounts Info. > Groups > Create under Single Group

The Group Creation screen is displayed as shown:

Name of Group

Enter the name of the Group to be created. For example "Administrative Expenses" in the name field.

Alias

Enter an alias name to allow access to the group using the Alias in addition to its name or leave it blank. For example, for Administrative expenses, you can enter Office Expense or even an alphanumeric code, say E001, as an alias

Under

Specify under which existing (Parent) group the sub-classification is required.

Group Creation
Name : **Administrative Expenses**
(alias) : Office Expenses
Under : **Indirect Expenses**
Accept ?
Yes or No

Note: If it is a new primary group, select Primary (requirement of a new primary group is very rare, but the option exists). Creation of new Primary Group is not allowed if Allow Advanced entries in Masters is set to No in F12: Configure. You can also create a new Parent Group by using Alt+C.

Tally has the flexibility of creating the related Masters from specified screens:

Button	*Shortcut Keys*	*Behaviour*
L: Ledgers	Ctrl+L	Navigate to Ledger Creation screen
V: Vch Types	Ctrl+V	Navigate to Voucher Creation Screen

Creating a Group with advanced usage

Go to Gateway of Tally > Accounts Info > Groups > Create under Single Group > select F12 configure (Group Configuration) and enable Allow Advanced entries in Masters under Accounts Masters.

Group Configuration	
Allow ALIASES along with Names	? Yes
Allow Language ALIASES along with Names	? No
Allow ADVANCED entries in Masters	? Yes

Creation of 'Printing' Group under Primary Group:

- Advanced options.
- Nature of Group.

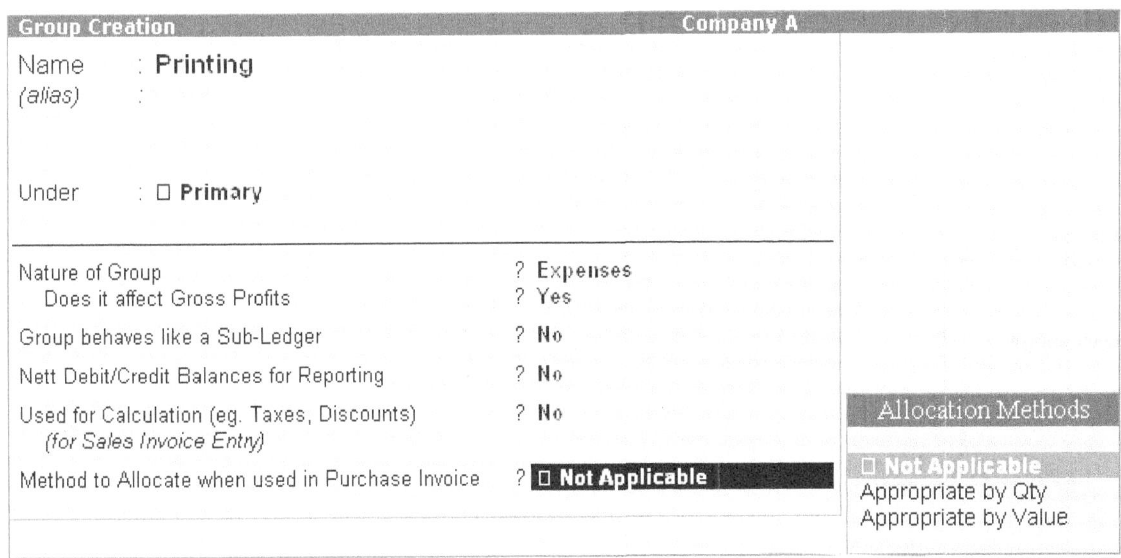

Fig. 4.3 Group Creation Screen

If a group (*e.g.*, Printing) is created under Primary, you must select the appropriate option from the list whether it is an asset, liability, income or expenses. If you select an income or expenses you should specify whether it will affect the gross profits or not by suitably setting the option Does it affect Gross Profits? to Yes/No.

If the option is selected as Yes, the Group will appear under Trading Account and if the option is selected as No, the Group will appear under Profit & Loss Account.

You can use this concept when you wish to segregate your profits into Operative Profit and Net Profit. This helps you when you want to consider other revenue accounts in addition to Direct instead of Gross and Net Profit.

Normally, Tally.ERP 9 calculates Gross Profit using Opening Stock, Purchase Accounts, Direct Expenses, Sales Accounts, Direct Incomes and Closing Stock only. To make other accounts contribute to this, without classifying under these reserved heads, set this option to Yes.

Group behaves like sub-ledger

This option will allow such Groups to behave as defined in the Master to act as equal to the behavior of Ledger.

When Group behaves like sub-ledger is set to No, the same will display all the Ledgers grouped under the same in detailed mode.

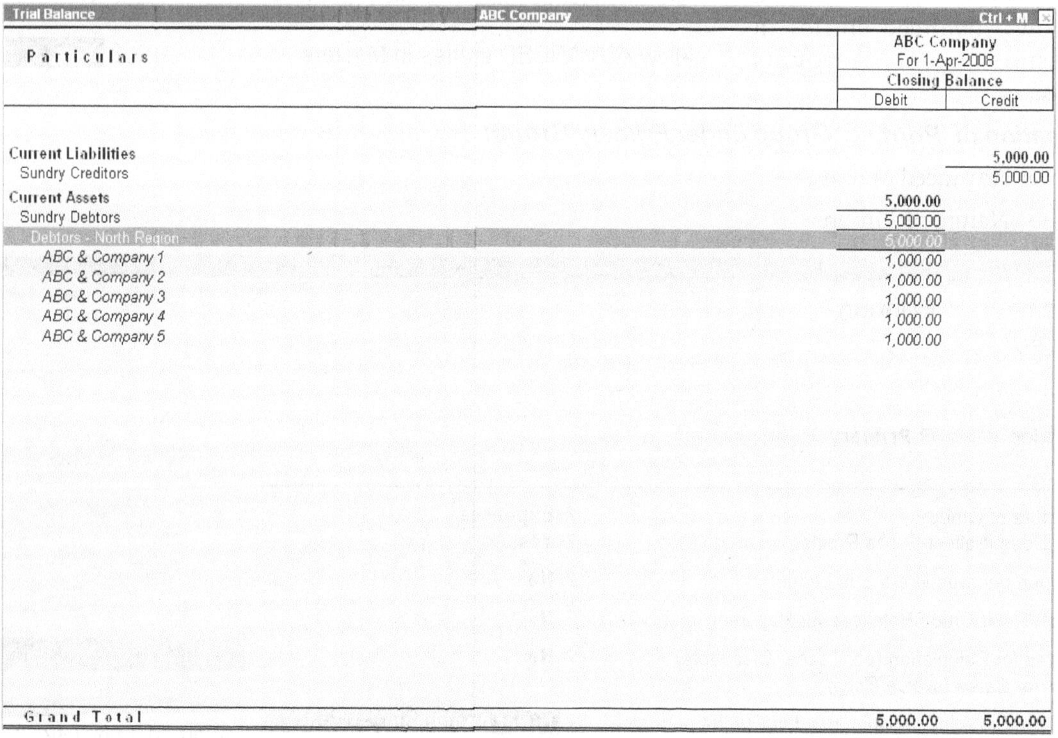

Trial Balance — ABC Company — Ctrl + M

Particulars	ABC Company For 1-Apr-2008 Closing Balance Debit	Credit
Current Liabilities		**5,000.00**
Sundry Creditors		5,000.00
Current Assets	**5,000.00**	
Sundry Debtors	5,000.00	
Debtors - North Region	*5,000.00*	
ABC & Company 1	*1,000.00*	
ABC & Company 2	*1,000.00*	
ABC & Company 3	*1,000.00*	
ABC & Company 4	*1,000.00*	
ABC & Company 5	*1,000.00*	
Grand Total	5,000.00	5,000.00

Fig. 4.4 Trial Balance Screen

When the Group behaves like sub-ledger is set to Yes, the same will not display the Ledgers grouped under the same in detailed mode.

The same is helpful in reports when there is a large number of Ledgers under any Group.

Nett Debit/Credit Balances for Reporting

Setting this option to Yes will display either the net debit or credit balance in the report (whichever is higher). If this is set to No, both debit and credit balances will be displayed in the report.

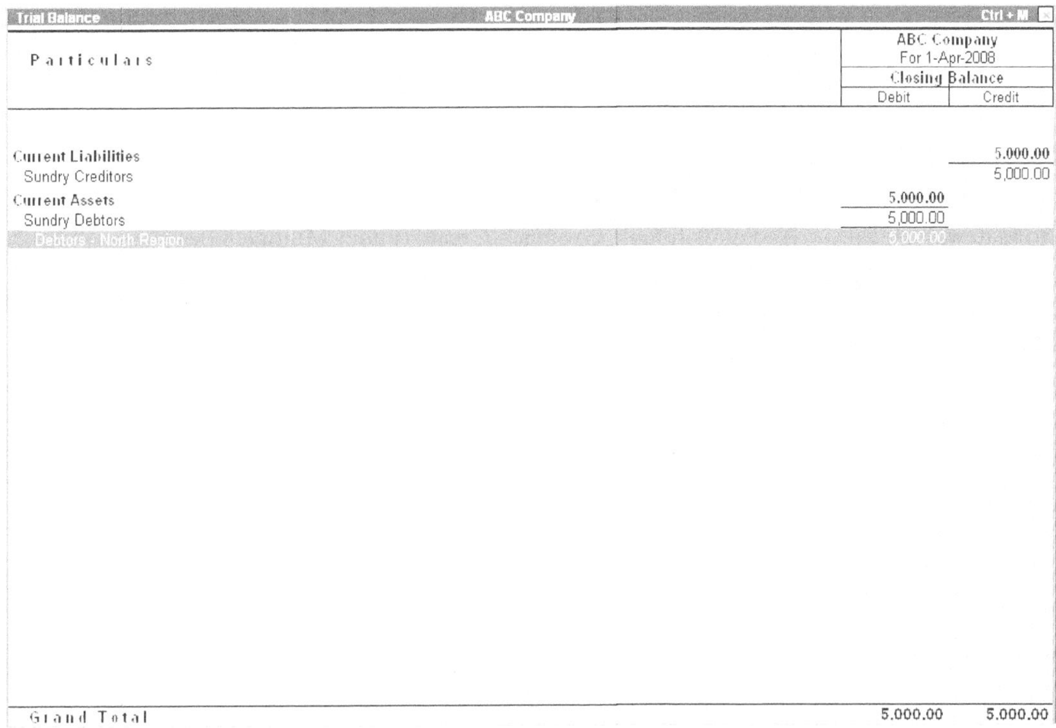

Fig. 4.4a Trial Balance Grouped Screen

Used for Calculation (e.g. taxes, discounts)

Set this option to Yes if ledgers under this group would have percentages for discounts/taxes to be used in invoice entry. This gets reflected while passing voucher entry in Invoice mode and for automatic calculations.

Method to allocate when used in purchase invoice

Select the appropriate allocation method from the list. This is used to allocate the expense of the Item in the ratio of the quantity or value.

Buttons in Group Creation Screen with advanced usage:

Button	*Shortcut Keys*	*Behaviour*
L: Ledgers	Ctrl+L	Navigate to Ledger Creation screen
S: Cst Cat	Ctrl+S	Navigate to Cost Category Creation screen
C: Cst Ctr	Ctrl+C	Navigate to Cost Centre Creation screen
O: Employee Groups	Ctrl+O	Navigate to Employee Groups Creation screen
E: Pay Heads	Ctrl+E	Navigate to Pay Head Creation screen
P: Employee	Ctrl+P	Navigate to Employee Creation screen
T: Attd Type	Ctrl+T	Navigate to Attendance/Production Type Creation screen
U: Units	Ctrl+U	Navigate Unit Creation screen
B: Budget	Ctrl+B	Navigate to Budget Creation screen

V: Vch Types Ctrl+V Navigate to Voucher Type Creation screen

The default buttons available are Ledgers and Voucher Types and the rest of the options displayed based on the features enabled in F11:F1: Accounting features.

Creating Multiple Groups

You can create Multiple Groups, by selecting this option.

Go to Gateway of Tally > Accounts Info. > Groups > Create (under Multiple Groups)

You can create any number of Groups under an already created/ selected Group. In this mode of group creation, the sub-groups will automatically inherit the characteristics of their parent groups.

You can also create any number of Groups under different Groups by selecting All Items in "Under Group" field.

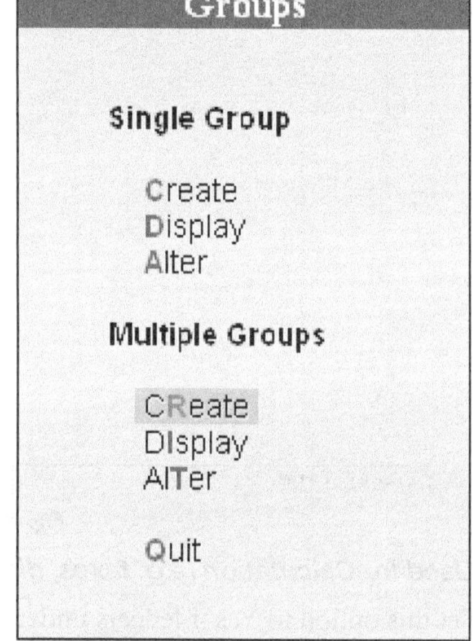

Under Group

Select the parent group under which you want the new groups to be created from the List of Groups. The group selected is displayed in the Under Group field.

Name of Group

Enter the name of the Group.

Under

If you select any group other than All Items in the Under Group field, then this column is filled in automatically with the selected Group name and the cursor skips this column. This speeds up data entry.

If you select All Items in the Under Group field, the cursor does not skip this field and allows you to enter the parent group of each of them.

Multi Group Creation Company A Ctrl + M

Under Group : **Sundry Creditors**

S.No.	Name of Group	Under
1.	Creditors - Raw Materials	Sundry Creditors
2.	Creditors - Consumables	Sundry Creditors

Multi Group Creation Company A Ctrl + M

Under Group : □ **All Items**

S.No.	Name of Group	Under
1.	Factory Expenses	Direct Expenses
2.	Staff Welfare Expenses	Indirect Expenses

Note: To change individual group behavior created using multiple groups, use single group alter option.

Buttons in Multiple mode Group creation

Button	*Shortcut Keys*	*Behaviour*
F4: Parent	F4	The Parent Group can be changed
L: Ledgers	Ctrl+L	Navigate to Ledger Creation screen
S: Cst Cat	Ctrl+S	Navigate to Cost Category Creation Screen
C: Cst Ctr	Ctrl+C	Navigate to Cost Centre Creation Screen
O: Employee Groups	Ctrl+O	Navigate to Cost Centre Creation Screen
P: Employee	Ctrl+P	Navigate to Employee Creation Screen

Note: The default buttons available are Parent and Ledger and the rest of the options displayed are based on the features enabled in F11:F1 Accounting feature.

Displaying a Group

You can display the Groups in Single mode or Multiple mode.

Single Mode:

Go to Gateway of Tally > Accounts Info. > Group > Display (under Single Group).

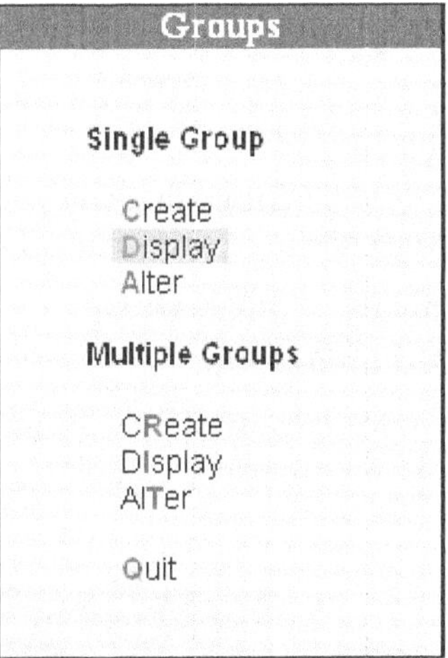

Select the name of the Group from the List of Groups. You cannot make any changes in the Display mode.

Displaying a Single Group

Group Display — Company A

Name : **Administrative Expenses**
(alias) : Office Expenses

Under : **Indirect Expenses**

Group behaves like a Sub-Ledger	? **No**
Nett Debit/Credit Balances for Reporting	? **No**
Used for Calculation (eg. Taxes, Discounts) *(for Sales Invoice Entry)*	?
Method to Allocate when used in Purchase Invoice	? □ **Not Applicable**

Multiple Mode:

Go to Gateway of Tally > Accounts Info > Group > Display (under Multiple Group).

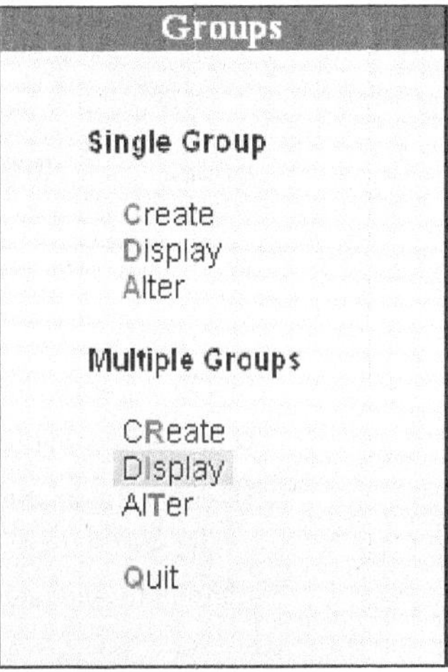

Displaying Multiple Groups

Select the Group from the List of Groups to display all the Groups under the selected Group or select All Items to display all Groups. The Multi Group Display screen lists Groups and the corresponding details of the Groups.

Multi Group Display	Company A	Ctrl + M
Under Group : **Sundry Creditors**		

S.No.	Name of Group	Under
1.	Creditors - Consumables	Sundry Creditors
2.	Creditors - Raw Materials	Sundry Creditors

Button:

F4: New Parent (Ctrl+F4) - You can navigate to select any other Group in the display mode by selecting this button from the Button Bar.

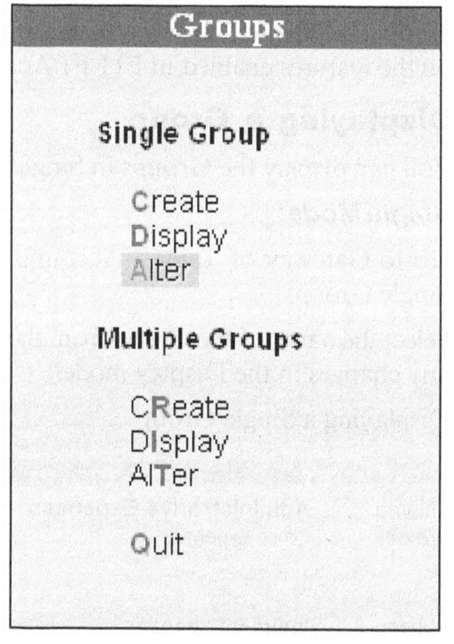

Altering a Group

You can alter the Groups in Single mode or Multiple mode.

Single mode

Go to Gateway of Tally > Accounts Info. > Group > Alter (under Single Group)

Select the Group that you wish to alter from the List of Groups. Make the necessary changes and click Yes to save the changes.

Altering a Single Group

Multiple Mode

Go to Gateway of Tally > Accounts Info. > Group > Alter (under Multi Groups).

Group Alteration Company A

Name : **Administrative Expenses**
(alias) : Office Expenses

Under : **Indirect Expenses**

Group behaves like a Sub-Ledger ? **No**
Nett Debit/Credit Balances for Reporting ? **No**
Used for Calculation (eg. Taxes, Discounts) ? **No**
(for Sales Invoice Entry)
Method to Allocate when used in Purchase Invoice ? **Not Applicable**

Fig. 4.5 Group Alteration Screen

Altering Multiple Group

Select the Group for which you want to alter from the List of Groups. In Multi Group Alteration screen, make the necessary changes and click Yes to save changes.

Deleting a Group

Go to Gateway of Tally > Accounts Info > Groups > Single/ Alter

The Delete function is performed through the single alteration mode. You cannot delete groups from the Multiple Alteration mode.

Select the Group to be deleted.

Press Alt+D to delete.

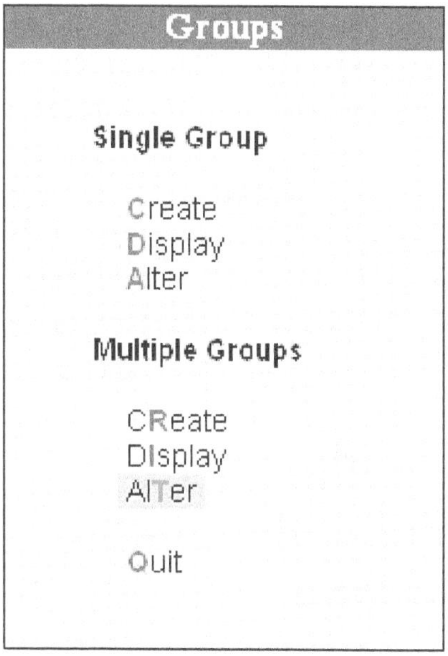

Groups

Single Group

Create
Display
Alter

Multiple Groups

CReate
DIsplay
AlTer

Quit

Managing Groups in Multiple Companies

Copying masters from one company to another

Master information is the same for most group companies and it is certainly beneficial to maintain same group structure and ledgers. This becomes necessary if you have a parent company with subsidiaries or branches. This ensures uniformity of reports in all companies and proper consolidation of accounts. To avoid the tedious process of re-creating masters in other companies, Tally.ERP 9 enables you to copy the groups created in one company to another in alteration mode.

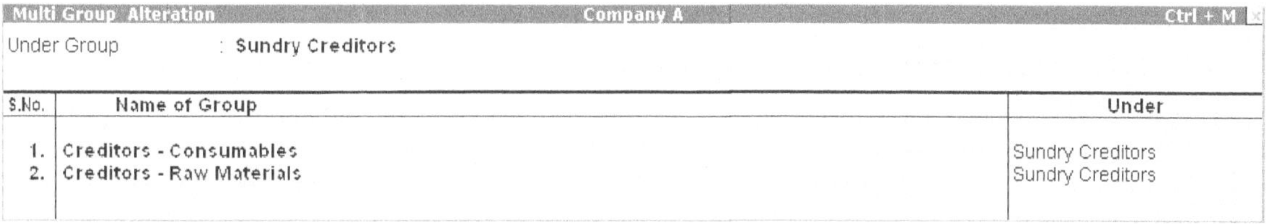

Multi Group Alteration — Company A — Ctrl + M

Under Group : Sundry Creditors

S.No.	Name of Group	Under
1.	Creditors - Consumables	Sundry Creditors
2.	Creditors - Raw Materials	Sundry Creditors

Copying a single group from one company to another

To copy the masters from one company to another, you need to select both the companies i.e., Source Company (from where the Master has to be copied) and Destination Company (To the company in which we have to copy the Master) in Gateway of Tally to switch between companies.

Go to Gateway of Tally > Select Company ABC Company

Go to Gateway of Tally > Select Company XYZ Company

The source company should be listed first in the Gateway of Tally (ABC Company)

Go to Gateway of Tally > Accounts Info. > Groups > Single Group > Alter

1. Select a particular group, for example select Southern Debtors created under Sundry Debtors.
2. Select F3: Company Button: to switch over to the destination company (XYZ Company).
3. Accept the screen, after making alterations, if any.

If the parent of the group does not exist, you will not be able to accept the screen without selecting a parent in the destination company.

Once you accept the screen, you are taken back to the source company list of groups. The same group now exists in the destination company.

Copying multiple groups from one company to another

1. Select ABC Company and XYZ Company from the Gateway of Tally. The source company should be listed first in Gateway of Tally (ABC Company).
2. Go to Gateway of Tally > Accounts Info > Groups > Multiple Groups > Alter > Select a particular Group or All Items from the list.
3. Click on F3: Company button or press F3 key to switch over to the destination company.
4. Accept the screen, after making additions/alterations, if any.
5. Once you accept the screen, you are taken back to the source company List of Groups. The same group now exists in the destination company. The above method of copying masters is possible only if the books of accounts are maintained on the same computer.

The above methods can be also used for copying other masters like ledgers, cost categories and cost centres.

Ledgers

A Ledger is the actual account head to which you identify a transaction and . must be used in all Accounting Vouchers. Without a ledger we cannot record any transactions.

Ex: Purchase, payments, sales, Receipts, etc, all these accounts heads are ledger Accounts.

All Ledgers have to be classified into Groups. Classification of Ledgers to the appropriate groups is very important. These Groups and Ledgers are classified to Profit & Loss or Balance Sheet. The creation and usage of Groups in Tally.ERP 9 has been explained earlier. Now you will learn how Tally.ERP 9 works with Ledgers.

Pre-defined Ledgers in Tally.ERP 9

There are two pre-defined ledgers available in Tally.ERP 9, they are:

Cash

This Ledger is created under the Group Cash-in-hand. You can enter the opening balance as on the date of books beginning from. You can also alter the name and even delete the Ledger.

Profit and Loss Account

This Ledger is created under the Group Primary. Previous year's Profit or Loss is entered as the opening balance for this ledger. The balance entered here is treated as the opening profit/loss and shown in the Balance Sheet as opening balance of Profit and Loss account in the Liabilities side.

You cannot delete this ledger, but you can modify the same.

Creating a Ledger

Go to Gateway of Tally > Accounts Info. > Ledgers

You can create either Single or Multiple Ledgers.

Importance of Grouping and Accounting Classifications

Debtor/Creditor Classification

1. Placing individual party accounts under Sales or Purchase Accounts groups:

Accounts of parties with whom your company has trade relationship must be opened under one of the following groups (or sub-groups under them) only:

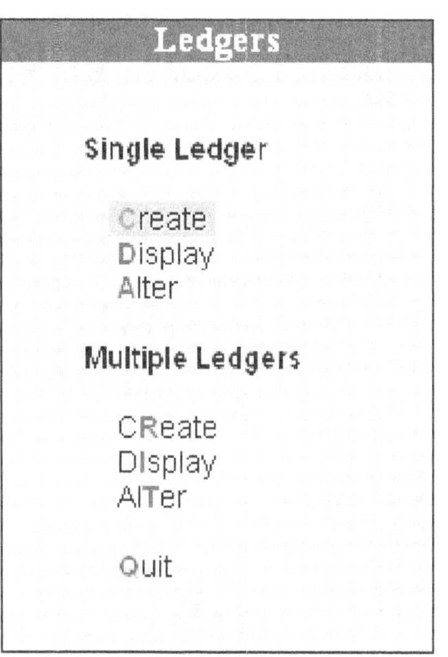

- Sundry Debtors
- Sundry Creditors
- Branch/Divisions

Sales and Purchase account groups are meant for revenue accounts and would be reflected in the Profit & Loss Account. If you open party accounts under these groups, you will find it difficult to pass sales or purchase voucher transactions. For example, in a sales voucher transaction entry, you must debit an account which is a sundry debtor, branch/division or even a sundry creditor (why a creditor? - it will be explained soon). Moreover, other facilities like bill-wise allocation and tracking will not be available unless the accounts belong to one of these groups.

2. Opening two accounts of the same party

For convenience Tally.ERP 9 has separately classified debtors, creditors and branch/divisions. There is no operational distinction except for the purpose of keeping the accounts of a particular group together during displays and analysis. You can pass both sales and purchase entries for a party account placed under Sundry Debtors.

We recommend that you use the classification depending on the most natural group for the party. For example, parties from whom you buy more frequently then you sell to can be placed under Sundry Creditors, as that would be the natural place for you to look for his account.

Tally.ERP 9 does not restrict the accounts from having obverse balances. Thus, a Sundry Debtor can have a credit balance depending on the state of his account.

Note: You need not open two accounts of the same party - one under Sundry Debtors and another under Sundry Creditors.

Remember, Tally.ERP 9 restricts you from opening two identical ledger accounts. Of course, you may decide to circumvent by marking one account as A & Co - S/Dr and another A & Co - S/Cr. Doing this would allow you to have two accounts of the same party under two groups, but you would lose the advantage of analyzing his net position at one instance. We recommend that you maintain a single account to obtain best results.

3. Placing expenditure items under a Liabilities group, e.g., the expenditure item 'Rates & Taxes' under the group 'Duties and Taxes'.

The group Duties and Taxes is specifically meant to handle taxation liabilities of your company. Rates & Taxes and other statutory expenses should be placed under Indirect Expenses.

Creating a Single Ledger

The creation of a Ledger depends on the features you have selected under F11: Features of your company and F12: Configure. By default, Tally.ERP 9 contains two Ledger accounts namely, Cash (Under Cash-in- Hand) and Profit and Loss Account (direct Primary Account). You need to create all other accounts heads. There are no restrictions in Ledger creation except that you cannot create another Profit & Loss A/c. Any number of Cash Accounts may be created in any other name for ex: Petty Cash.

Go to Gateway of Tally > Accounts Info > Ledgers > Create

Ledgers can be created in Normal mode or in Advance mode.

Creating Ledger in Normal Mode

Go to Gateway of Tally > Accounts Info > Ledgers > Single Ledger > Create

Name

Enter the Name of the account. You can provide the full name of the account. Tally.ERP 9 fits it all in. Press Enter to move to the next field. Tally.ERP 9 does not allow the entry of duplicate names. The uniqueness check is made here itself.

Note that the punctuation and other non-relevant information are ignored by Tally.ERP 9 in its recognition of a name. Thus, CST, C.S.T. and C. S. T. are all considered as same.

Ledger Creation		ABC Company
Name	: A's Capital Account	Total Op. Bal.
(alias)	:	
		5,00,000.00 Cr
		Difference
		5,00,000.00 Cr
Under	: Capital Account	
	Opening Balance (on 1-Apr-2008) : 5,00,000.00 Cr	

Tally.ERP 9 converts the first letter of all relevant words to upper case, which helps you; speed up data entry.

Alias

Enter an alias name if required. You can access the Ledgers using the original name or the alias name.

Under

All accounts must be classified under their appropriate Groups. Select the Group under which the Ledger is created from the List of Groups. (To create a new Group from this field press [ALT + C]). A wrong classification would affect the treatment of the Ledger account in final statements and during voucher entry.

You can, alter a Ledger account to change its group classification at any time. Refer Importance of Grouping and Accounting Classifications: for more details in Grouping

Opening Balance

If yours is an existing company whose books you are entering into Tally.ERP 9, Opening Balance would be applicable in circumstances where the Ledger is an asset or a liability and if it has a balance in the account as on the date of beginning of books in Tally.ERP 9.

Tally.ERP 9 recognizes normal accounting principles of debit balances for Assets and credit balances for

Liabilities. It accepts the reverse for obverse balances. Revenue accounts normally do not have balances. Tally.ERP 9, however, permits you to give balances even for such accounts - You may be transferring your books on to Tally.ERP 9 in the middle of the year and may not have closed them in your earlier system. Hence, you may specify whether the balance is Debit or Credit. Simply D or C would suffice.

Creating a Purchase / Sales Ledger

Go to Gateway of Tally > Accounts Info > Ledgers > Create

Inventory values affected: This is applicable for Companies maintaining Accounts with Inventory. Inventory allocation is required for Accounts like Sales, Purchase, Receipt note, Delivery note, etc. However, Tally.ERP 9 does not restrict to particular accounts as you may have the need to affect inventory with accounts like Customs Duty, and perhaps, direct expenses related to purchases such as Freight Inwards.

Cost Centres are applicable: Tally's concept of Cost Centres allows an additional dimension to a transaction. .

You have set Maintain Cost Centres to Yes in F11: Features:F1:Accounting Features, to get this option in the Ledger creation screen. If any of the transactions need to be allocated to any particular Cost Center (Which involves this ledger) set this option to Yes.

Activate Interest calculation: Set this option to Yes to enable Tally.ERP 9 to calculate interest automatically based on the interest rate and style of calculation specified for this ledger account.

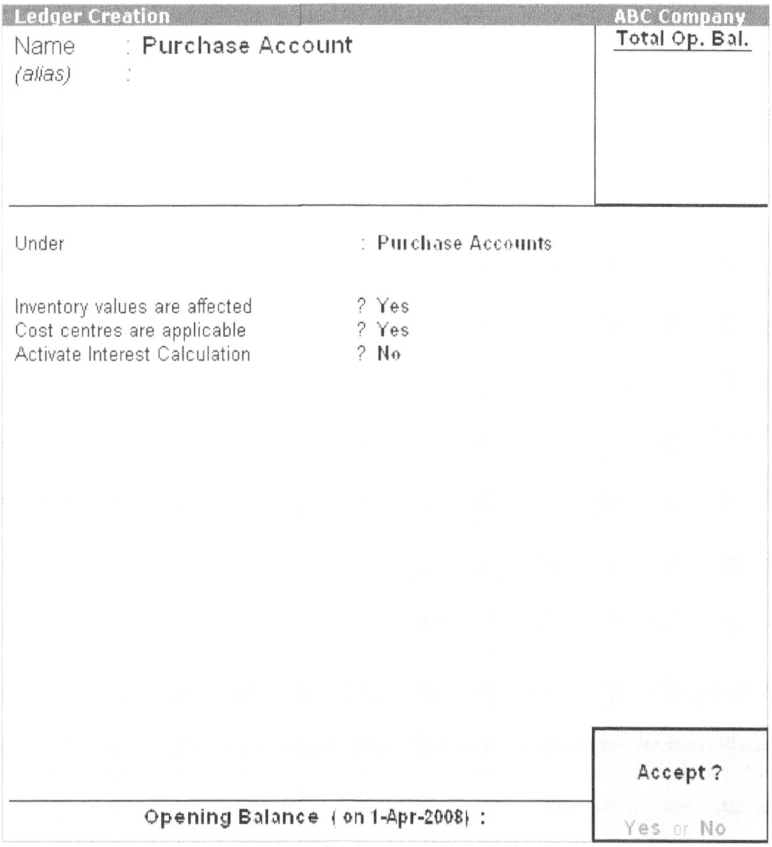

Ledger Creation ABC Company

Name : Purchase Account

(alias) :

Total Op. Bal.

Under : Purchase Accounts

Inventory values are affected ? Yes

Cost centres are applicable ? Yes

Activate Interest Calculation ? No

Opening Balance (on 1-Apr-2008) :

Accept ?

Yes or No

Use advanced parameters: The advanced parameters are particularly useful where interest rates change from time to time. Set this option to Yes to enable this.

Creating a Expenses / Income Ledger

Go to Gateway of Tally > Accounts Info > Ledgers > Create

Inventory values affected: This is applicable for Companies maintaining Accounts with Inventory. Inventory allocation is required for Accounts like Sales, Purchase, Receipt note, Delivery note, etc. However, Tally.ERP 9 does not restrict you to particular accounts as you may have the need to affect inventory with accounts like Customs Duty, and perhaps, direct expenses related to purchases such as Freight Inwards.

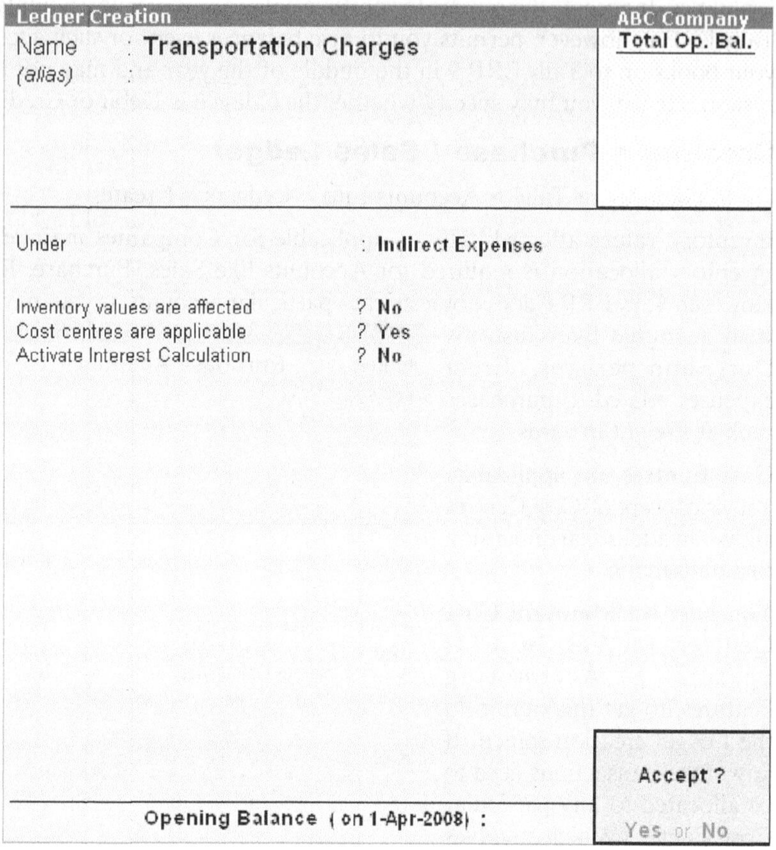

Cost Centres are applicable: Tally's concept of Cost Centres allows an additional dimension to a transaction. .

You have set Maintain Cost Centres to Yes in F11: Features:F1:Accounting Features, to get this option in the Ledger creation screen. If any of the transactions need to be allocated to any particular Cost Center (Which involves this ledger) set this option to Yes.

Activate Interest calculation: Set this option to Yes to enable Tally.ERP 9 to calculate interest automatically based on the interest rate and style of calculation specified for this ledger account.

Use advanced parameters: The advanced parameters are particularly useful where interest rates change from time to time. Set this option to Yes to enable this.

Ledger Creation ABC Company

Name : Transportation Charges

(alias) :

Total Op. Bal.

Under : Indirect Expenses

Inventory values are affected ? No

Cost centres are applicable ? Yes

Activate Interest Calculation ? No

Accept ?

Yes or No

Opening Balance (on 1-Apr-2008) :

Creating a Party Ledger

Go to Gateway of Tally > Accounts Info > Ledgers > Create

The Party Ledger account screen is displayed as shown:

Currency of Ledger: Tally.ERP 9 allows you to maintain Ledgers in any currency and the amount is reflected in the selected currency. But it is strongly advised that you maintain the currency of the Ledger as the Base currency.

Only foreign currency bank accounts are maintained in foreign currency and other ledgers are maintained in Base Currency. Nevertheless you can enter transactions in any other currency.

To create/maintain ledgers in multiple currency, set Allow Multi Currencies to Yes under F11: Features.

You can always create a new currency from this field by pressing Alt+C.

Maintain Balances Bill-by-Bill: This option is applicable when you want the balances to be maintained Bill by Bill or Bill wise. Normally, this option is useful for Ledgers falling under Sundry Debtors & Sundry Creditors. If you set this option to Yes, while entering the opening balance in the Opening Balance field at the end of Ledger Creation screen and press Enter, the Bill-wise Breakup screen of the Ledger created is displayed as shown.

Date: Since you are giving the break-up of the Opening Balance, the date of the bill would naturally be

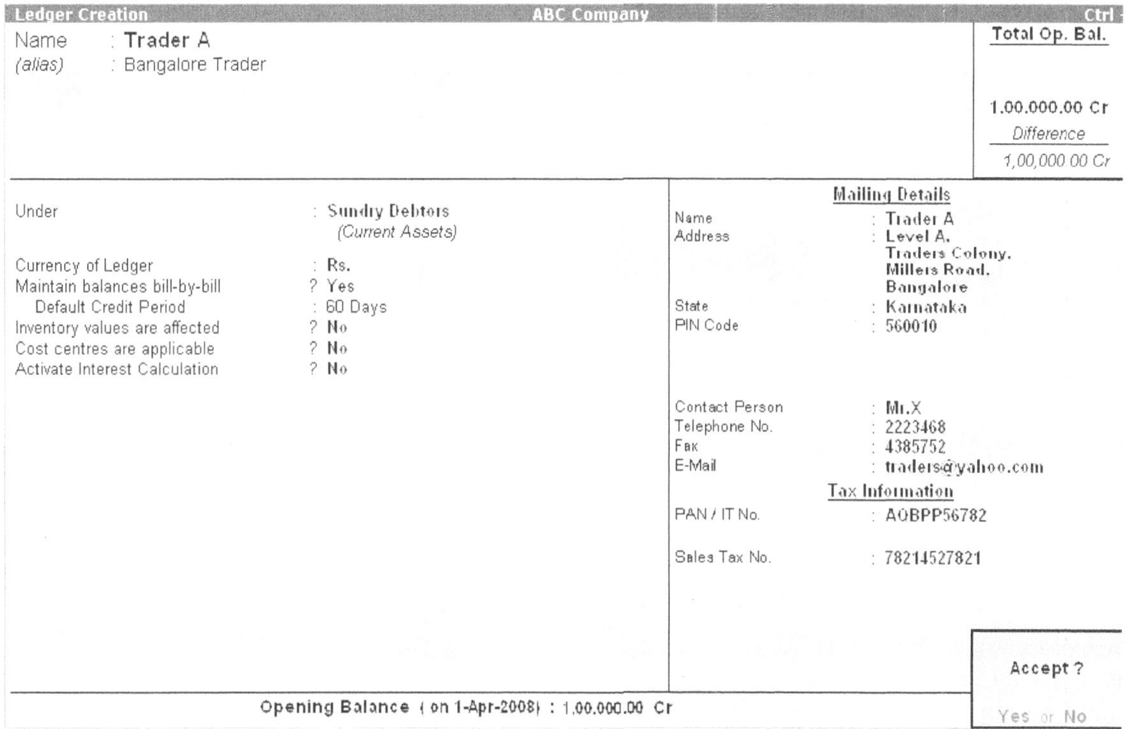

Fig. 4.6 Ledger Creation Screen

prior to the accounting period. By default Tally.ERP 9 takes last date of your previous accounting period, e.g., 31 March 2008. Change it, if necessary.

Name: Enter a Name to which you can later refer when adjusting the bill. You can enter the Bill number or Document number.

Due date (or credit days): For the Ledgers under Sundry Debtors and Creditors, give the credit period or the date when the bill is due.

Note: During transaction entry, there would be another concept-that of effective date. If you opt for using effective dates instead of bill dates the due date would be calculated accordingly.

Amount: For the amount of the bill due, you can give particulars of all the pending bills one by one.

If the total amount of all your bills covers the Opening Balance, the On Account becomes NIL. You could have Bills totaling beyond the Opening Balance. In the screen shown below, there are two bills 50,000, 25,000. Now, if the balance brought forward is 1,00,000/- , the On Account amount will reflect 25,000/-. If you obtain the bill particulars at a later date, you can alter the ledger to enter these details, which will nullify On Account.

Default Credit Period:

The Credit period may be given for Sundry Debtors and Sundry Creditors. The number of Credit days or period can be defined in various ways:

- **Days**: If there is no suffix given to the number of credit days, then it is taken as Days. For Ex: If you enter just the number 5, then it is considered as 5 Days.

- **Weeks**: If W is given as suffix to the number of credit period, then it is taken as Weeks. For Ex: If you enter 5 W, then it is taken as 5 Weeks.
- **Months**: If M is given as suffix to the number of credit period, then it is taken as Months. For Ex: If you enter 5 M, then it is taken as 5 Months.
- **Year**: If Y is given as suffix to the number of credit period, then it is taken as Year. For Ex: If you enter 5 Y, then it is taken as 5 Years.

Bill-wise Breakup of : **Trader A**
Upto: **Rs. 1,00,000.00 Dr**

Date	Name	Due Date, or Credit Days	Amount	Dr/ Cr
31/3/2008	**001**	**1-Aug-2008**	**50,000.00**	**Dr**
31/3/2008	**002**	**30-Sep-2008**	**50,000.00**	**Dr**
			1,00,000.00	**Dr**
		On Account:		
			1,00,000.00	**Dr**

Bill-wise Breakup of : **Trader A**
Upto: **Rs. 1,00,000.00 Dr**

Date	Name	Due Date, or Credit Days	Amount	Dr/ Cr
31/3/2008	**001**	**1-Aug-2008**	**50,000.00**	**Dr**
31/3/2008	**002**	**30-Sep-2008**	**25,000.00**	**Dr**
			75,000.00	**Dr**
		On Account:	**25,000.00**	**Dr**
			1,00,000.00	**Dr**

Inventory values affected: This is applicable for Companies maintaining Accounts with Inventory. Inventory allocation is required for Accounts like Sales, Purchase, Receipt note, Delivery note, etc.. However, Tally.ERP 9 does not restrict you to particular accounts as you may have the need to affect inventory with accounts like Customs Duty, and perhaps, direct expenses related to purchases such as Freight Inwards.

Cost Centres are applicable: Tally's concept of Cost Centres allows an additional dimension to a transaction. .

You have set Maintain Cost Centres to Yes in F11: Features:F1:Accounting Features, to get this option in the Ledger creation screen. If any of the transactions need to be allocated to any particular Cost Center (Which involves this ledger) set this option to Yes.

Activate Interest calculation: Set this option to Yes to enable Tally.ERP 9 to calculate interest automatically based on the interest rate and style of calculation specified for this ledger account.

Use advanced parameters: The advanced parameters are particularly useful where interest rates change from time to time. Set this option to Yes to enable this.

Statutory Information: This functionality is available only, if you have enabled at least one of the options under F11: Features> F3: Statutory & Taxation. Based on the options enabled under F3: Statutory & Taxation, the respective fields will be displayed in the Statutory Information section.

Mailing Details: is applicable only for party accounts like Sundry Debtors, Creditors and Branch Divisions, Branch/Divisions, Bank & Bank OCC A/c, Loans & Advances Assets, Loans & Advances Liabilities, Secured & Unsecured Loans, etc. These are used in mailing outputs like statement of accounts.

Tax Information: The Tax Information consists of the default fields PAN/IT No. and the TIN/SALES Tax No. Based on the features you enable in F11: Features> F3: Statutory & Taxation, additional fields will appear under Taxation.

Percentage of Calculation: This field is applicable only for Ledgers created under the Group Duties and Taxes, or for Ledgers created under any Group for which Used for Calculation is enabled in the Group Creation screen.

Option Bank Reconciliation in Ledger master creation screen: Effective date for Reconciliation option will appear when a ledger is created under Bank Account group. Give the date of reconciliation on which you would like to reconcile the voucher.

Ledger Creation ABC Company
Name : National Bank Total Op. Bal.
(alias) :

Under : Bank Accounts
(Current Assets)

Currency of Ledger : Rs.
Cost centres are applicable ? No
Activate Interest Calculation ? No
Effective Date for Reconciliation ? 1-Apr-2008

Opening Balance (on 1-Apr-2008) : 2,50,000.00 Dr

Creating a Duty and Taxes Ledger

Go to Gateway of Tally > Accounts Info > Ledgers > Create

The Group Duties and Taxes is used for automatic tax calculation. You need to specify the rate of tax *e.g.*, 5%, 10%, 12.5% etc. You can use an automatic Discount calculation facility by specifying a negative percentage in this field. On entering a percentage, a new field Method of Calculation is displayed.

Creating a Current Liabilities / Assets Ledger

Go to Gateway of Tally > Accounts Info > Ledgers > Create

Inventory values affected: This is applicable for Companies maintaining Accounts with Inventory. Inventory allocation is required for Accounts like Sales, Purchase, Receipt note, Delivery note, etc. However, Tally.ERP 9 does not restrict to particular accounts as you may have the need to affect inventory with accounts like Customs Duty, and perhaps, direct expenses related to purchases such as Freight Inwards.

Cost Centres are applicable: Tally's concept of Cost Centres allows an additional dimension to a transaction.

You have set Maintain Cost Centres to Yes in F11: Features: F1:Accounting Features, to get this option in the Ledger creation screen. If any of the transactions need to be allocated to any particular Cost Center (Which involves this ledger) set this option to Yes.

Activate Interest calculation: Set this option to Yes to enable Tally.ERP 9 to calculate interest automatically based on the interest rate and style of calculation specified for this ledger account.

Use advanced parameters: The advanced parameters are particularly useful where interest rates change from time to time. Set this option to Yes to enable this.

Creating a Ledger with Advanced Usage

The information required for creating Ledgers depends on the features selected by you under F11: Features and F12: Configure. The Ledger Creation screen will have additional fields depending on your feature settings for your company. If you set the field Allow ADVANCED entries in Masters in F12: Configure (Ledger Configuration) as Yes, you can work in Advanced.

Enable the following features in F11:Features (F2:Accounting Features):

- Allow Multi-Currency
- Maintain Billwise Details
- Maintain Cost Centres
- Activate Interest Calculation

Enable all the options under Accounts Masters in F12: Configure (Ledger Configuration):

Creating Multiple Ledgers

You can create multiple Ledgers at a time in this mode. This will save the time of the user.

Go to Gateway of Tally > Accounts Info > ledgers > Multiple ledgers > Create

Under Group

Select the name of the group under which you want to create the Ledgers from the List of Groups.

Below this field, the other fields are

Ledger Creation — ABC Company

Name : Local Taxes — Total Op. Bal.
(alias) :

Under : Duties & Taxes (Current Liabilities)
Currency of Ledger : Rs.
Type of Duty/Tax : Others
Inventory values are affected ? No
Cost centres are applicable ? No
Activate Interest Calculation ? No
Percentage of Calculation (eg 5) ? 4 %
Method of Calculation :
Rounding Method :

Opening Balance (on 1-Apr-2008) :

Ledger Creation — ABC Company

Name : Furniture and Fixtures — Total Op. Bal.
(alias) :

Under : Fixed Assets

Opening Balance (on 1-Apr-2008) :

Accept ?
Yes or No

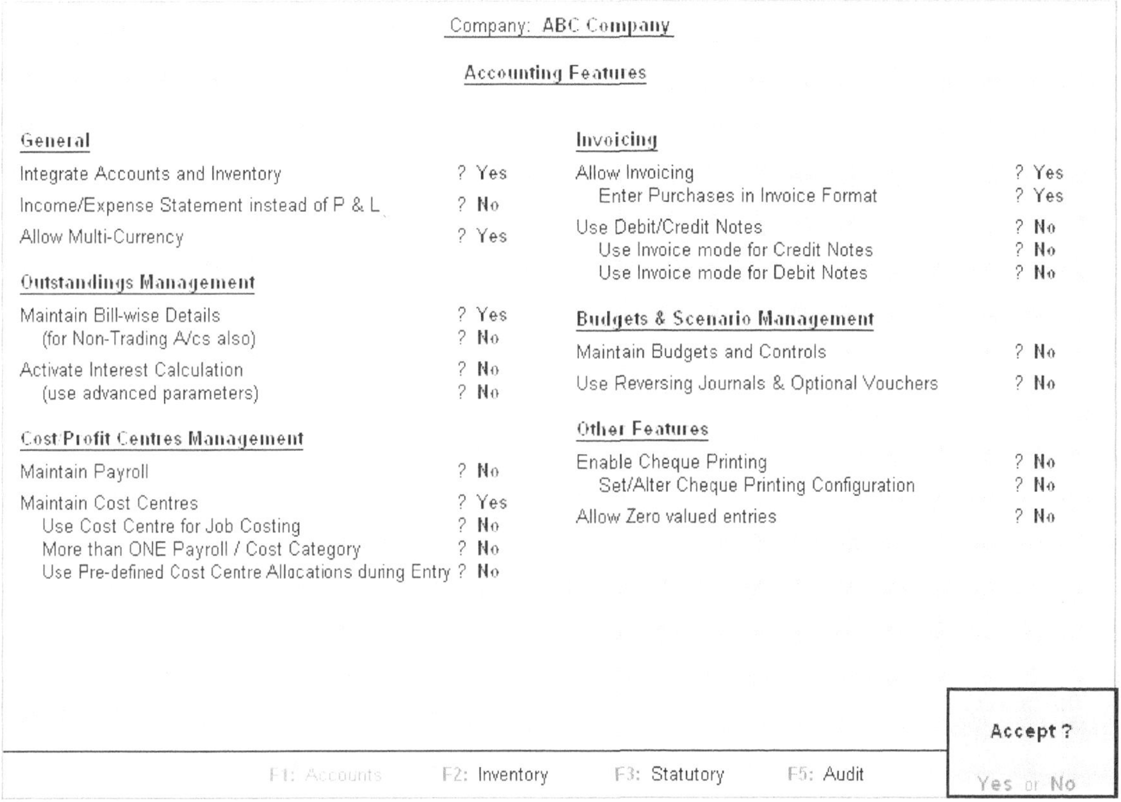

Company: ABC Company

Accounting Features

General

Integrate Accounts and Inventory	? Yes
Income/Expense Statement instead of P & L	? No
Allow Multi-Currency	? Yes

Outstandings Management

Maintain Bill-wise Details	? Yes
(for Non-Trading A/cs also)	? No
Activate Interest Calculation	? No
(use advanced parameters)	? No

Cost/Profit Centres Management

Maintain Payroll	? No
Maintain Cost Centres	? Yes
Use Cost Centre for Job Costing	? No
More than ONE Payroll / Cost Category	? No
Use Pre-defined Cost Centre Allocations during Entry	? No

Invoicing

Allow Invoicing	? Yes
Enter Purchases in Invoice Format	? Yes
Use Debit/Credit Notes	? No
Use Invoice mode for Credit Notes	? No
Use Invoice mode for Debit Notes	? No

Budgets & Scenario Management

Maintain Budgets and Controls	? No
Use Reversing Journals & Optional Vouchers	? No

Other Features

Enable Cheque Printing	? No
Set/Alter Cheque Printing Configuration	? No
Allow Zero valued entries	? No

F1: Accounts F2: Inventory F3: Statutory F5: Audit

Accept ?

Yes or No

Fig. 4.7 Accounting Features Screen

arranged in a table. The cursor rests at the field Name of Ledger.

The other fields in the column are:

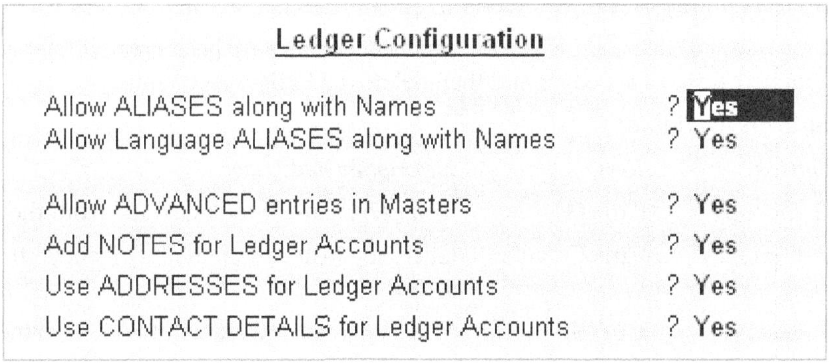

Sl.No

This is auto generated.

Name of Ledger

Enter the name of the Ledger.

Ledger Configuration

Allow ALIASES along with Names	? Yes
Allow Language ALIASES along with Names	? Yes
Allow ADVANCED entries in Masters	? Yes
Add NOTES for Ledger Accounts	? Yes
Use ADDRESSES for Ledger Accounts	? Yes
Use CONTACT DETAILS for Ledger Accounts	? Yes

Under

If you select All Items in Under Group field, you have the option to select the group in this column. You can even create a new group from this field by pressing Alt+C. If you have selected any other Group in Under Group, the selected group in Under Group gets displayed here automatically and the cursor skips this column.

Opening Balance

This is the balance remaining when you first enter your books on Tally.ERP 9, *i.e.*, the date of beginning

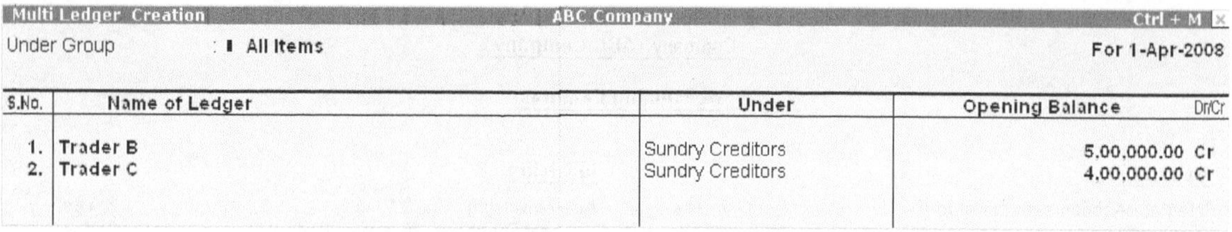

Multi Ledger Creation	ABC Company		Ctrl + M
Under Group : All Items			For 1-Apr-2008
S.No. Name of Ledger	Under	Opening Balance	Dr/Cr
1. Trader B	Sundry Creditors	5,00,000.00	Cr
2. Trader C	Sundry Creditors	4,00,000.00	Cr

Fig. 4.7a Multiple Ledger Creation

of books. If you have opted to maintain balances bill-by-bill, you must give the bill details. (Refer Creating a Ledger- Advanced Usage for more details on this)

Dr/Cr

Specify whether the Opening Balance is Debit or Credit. Tally.ERP 9 follows the normal accounting principals of accounting. (Refer Creating a Ledger - Advanced Usage for more details on this).

Displaying / Altering a Ledger Account

Information under Display and Alter is the same. Display option does not permit any modification. Alter option permits you to alter the information.

You are allowed to alter any information of the ledger master with the exception of the Closing Balance of a ledger account, if any, other than closing balance of accounts under the group Stock-in-hand.

Go to Gateway of Tally > Accounts Info. > Ledgers > Display or Alter

Modification of Account Ledgers is possible under Single Ledgers as well as Multiple Ledgers option. However under Multiple Ledgers, all the fields are not available for alteration

Deletion:

You can delete the ledger if no vouchers have been created under this ledger.

Go to Gateway of Tally > Accounts Info > Ledgers > Alter > Press Alt+D

If you want to delete a Ledger for which Vouchers have been created, then you have to first delete all the Vouchers from that Ledger and then delete the Ledger Account.

Buttons available:

Buttons	*Keys*	*Description and Usage*
G: Groups	Ctrl+G	You can create "Stock Group" from the Stock Item Creation screen
E: Currency	Ctrl+C	Currency You can create "Currency" from the Stock Item Creation screen
S: Cst Cat	Ctrl+S	You can create " Cost Category" from the Stock Item Creation Screen
C: Cst Ctr	Ctrl+C	You can create "Cost Center" from the Stock Item Creation screen
B: Budget	Ctrl+B	You can create "Budget" from the Stock Item Creation Screen
V: Vch Types	Ctrl+V	You can create "Voucher Type" from the Stock Item Creation screen

Voucher Types

There are 18 different pre-defined Voucher types in Tally.ERP 9. Voucher type pertains to both Accounting and Inventory. These are used for recording various transactions according to the user needs.

Examples include Cash Payment Vouchers and Bank Payment vouchers where the relevant predefined voucher is Payment Voucher. You may have two or more sets of Sales Vouchers for different kinds of sales transactions, *e.g.*, Credit Sales, Cash Sales, etc.

If a voucher type is created, you can:

- Have the different Voucher numbering methods.
- Give own prefix and suffix details for the voucher numbering.
- Use the Effective Dates for the vouchers.
- By default, make some vouchers optional if required.
- Decide to have the Common Narration or Narration for each entry.
- Automate the printing immediately after saving the vouchers.
- Get separate reports for each type of voucher.

Pre-defined Voucher Types in Tally.ERP 9

Go to Gateway of Tally > Display > List of Accounts > Ctrl+V [Voucher Types]

Or

Go to Gateway of Tally > Accounts info / Inventory Info > Voucher types > Alter

Alter a predefined voucher type

Even if you do not need extra voucher types, you would normally alter the predefined voucher types to customize them according to your needs, e.g., to control their numbers.

Go to Gateway of Tally > Accounts info / Inventory Info > Voucher types > Alter.

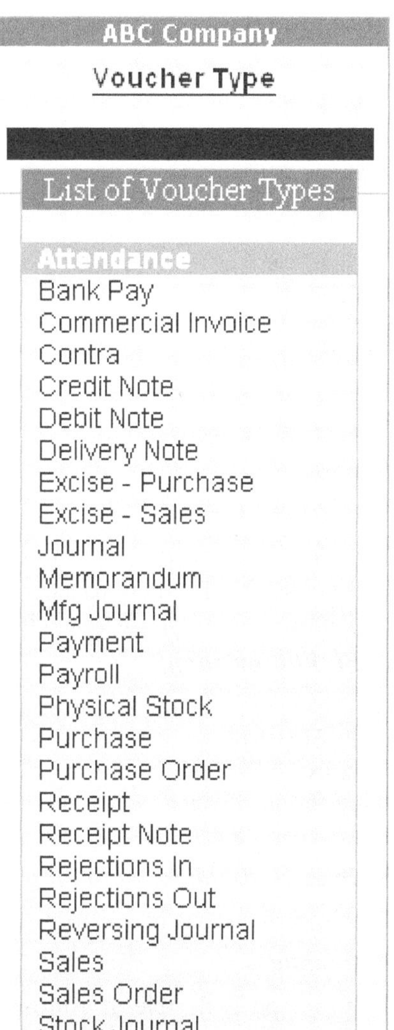

Creating a Voucher Type

Go to Gateway of Tally > Accounts Info/ Inventory Info > Voucher Type > Create.

The Voucher Type creation screen is divided into three sections depending on various settings.

- General
- Printing
- Voucher Class.

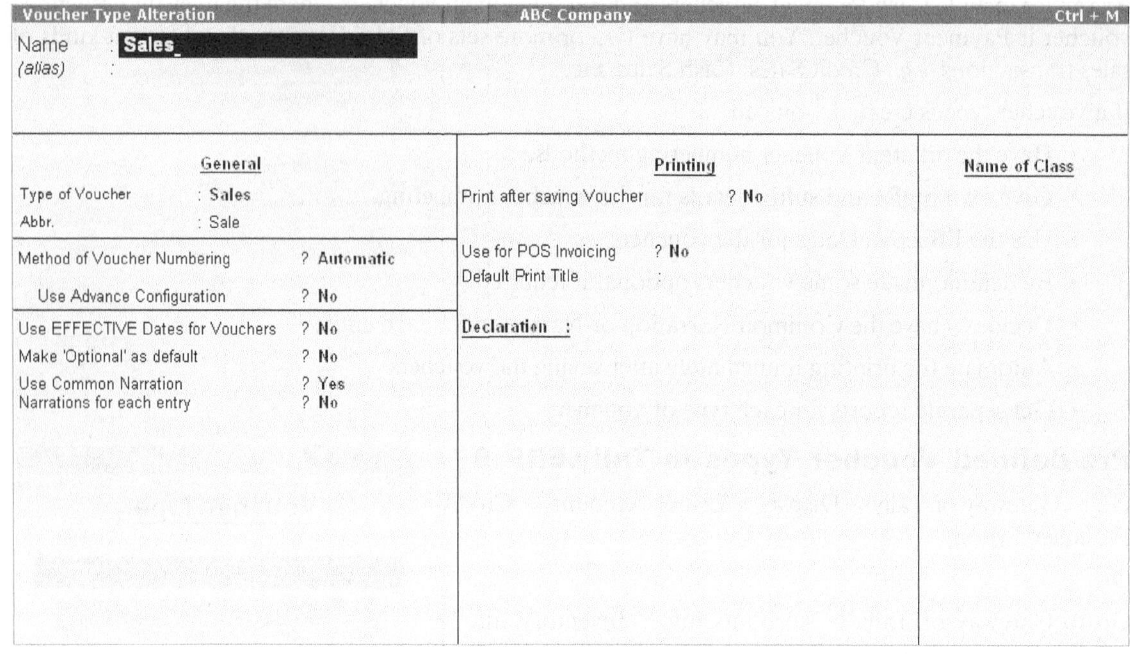

Fig. 4.8 Voucher Creation

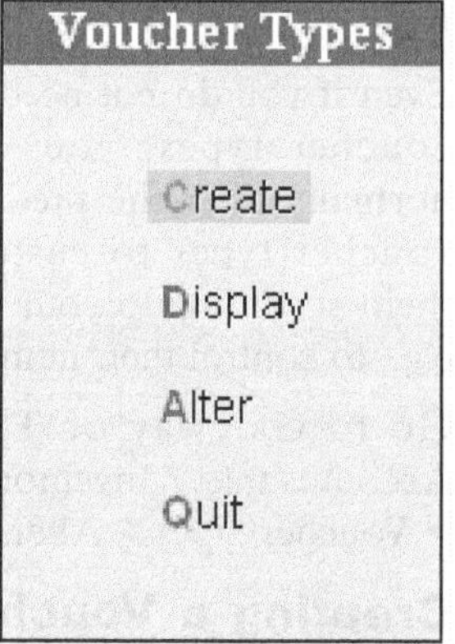

Name

Give the name of the new voucher type, *e.g.*, Sales Invoice.

Alias

Give the alias, if required.

General

Type of Voucher

The type of voucher should be any one of the predefined voucher types (already listed). The new voucher type would inherit the properties of this predefined voucher type. It would function exactly like the predefined voucher.

Abbr (Abbreviation)

An abbreviation is required particularly for unformatted reports, which do not use compressing techniques. (Tally.ERP 9 allows printing of both formatted and unformatted reports). Even if the Abbreviation is not specified, Tally.ERP 9 automatically sets a default name for the Voucher. In this example, Sale is the abbreviation. Though there is no restriction on the length of the abbreviation, it should preferably consist of five characters or less.

Method of Voucher Numbering

This is, perhaps, one reason for your opting for a new voucher type. There are three methods available:

Automatic

This method is flexible. If Automatic method is selected, then Tally.ERP 9 numbers the vouchers automatically.

Voucher Type Creation ABC Company Ctrl + M

Name : Sales Invoice
(alias) :

General		Printing		Name of Class
Type of Voucher	: Sales	Print after saving Voucher	? No	
Abbr.	: Sale			
Method of Voucher Numbering	? Automatic	Use for POS Invoicing	? No	
Use Advance Configuration	? No	Default Print Title	:	
Use EFFECTIVE Dates for Vouchers	? No	Declaration :		
Make 'Optional' as default	? No	"I/We declare that goods sold under this invoice/bill/cash is given under our registration certificate and the transactions has been effected by me us and accounted for the turnover".		
Use Common Narration	? Yes			
Narrations for each entry	? No			

Accept ?
Yes or No

Fig. 4.9 Sales Voucher Creation

Manual

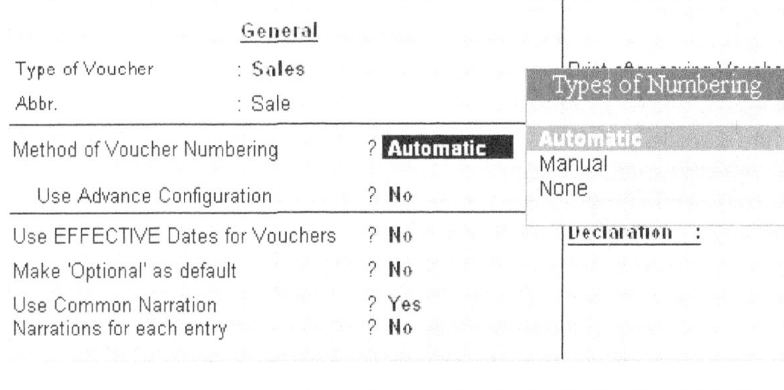

This method allows you to number the vouchers manually. It does not check for the sequence of the numbers and permits you to specify anything that you wish in the voucher number field. However, you may choose to prevent entry of duplicate numbers. If you would like to do so, then set Prevent Duplicates to Yes.

Method of Voucher Numbering ? Manual
Prevent Duplicates ? Yes

1. Prevention of Duplicates is possible if you enable the option at the time of creation. You may enable it later (by alteration) only if there are no transactions of this voucher type.
2. If you face difficulty due to existing transactions, just create another voucher type for preventing duplicates of subsequent voucher numbers.

None

This will disable numbering of such vouchers. If you select this method, no further information is required.

Use Advance Configuration

If the Method of Voucher Numbering is set to Automatic, then an additional field to set the advanced configuration for the Voucher type is displayed. Setting this field to Yes, Voucher Type Creation (Secondary) screen is displayed.

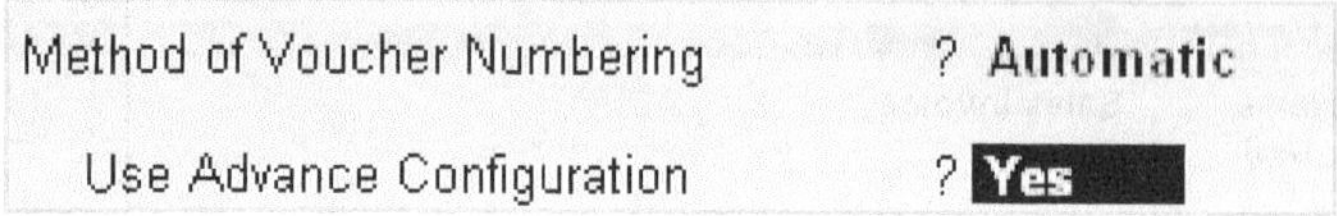

Method of Voucher Numbering ? **Automatic**
Use Advance Configuration ? **Yes**

A further discussion on these options is necessary.

Use EFFECTIVE dates for vouchers?

Select Yes if you want to enter effective dates for vouchers. You would opt for this if you have instances where a transaction under consideration for overdue/ageing analysis is recorded currently but will come into effect from another date. If the effective date is entered, the overdue/ageing will be considered from the effective date and not from voucher date.

Make Optional as Default

Setting this option to Yes, will set your Voucher to Optional Voucher by default. Refer to Optional Vouchers for further details.

Note: For Memorandum and Reversing Journal voucher the option Make Optional as Default will not be shown.

Use common narration?

Select Yes to give a common narration for the entire voucher. Tally.ERP 9 vouchers can have multiple entries. Hence, you may wish to give a common narration for all the entries of the voucher. Select No, if you do not want a common narration.

Example of common narration in a voucher:

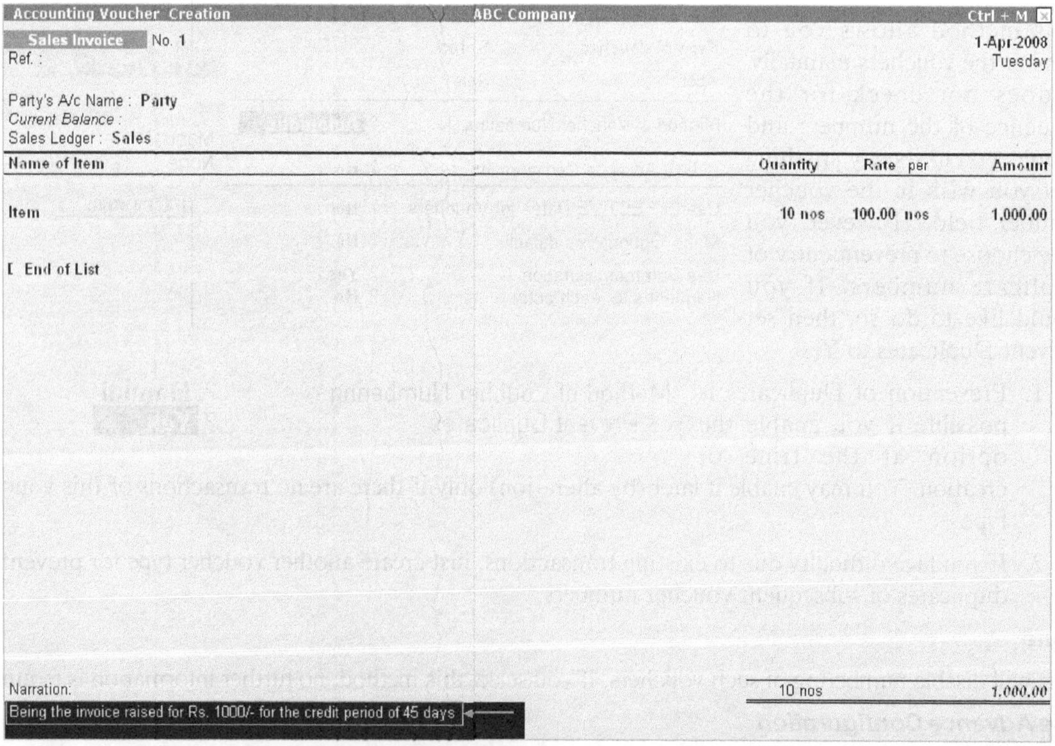

Accounting Voucher Creation ABC Company Ctrl + M
Sales Invoice No. 1 1-Apr-2008
Ref. : Tuesday
Party's A/c Name : Party
Current Balance :
Sales Ledger : Sales

Name of Item	Quantity	Rate per	Amount
Item	10 nos	100.00 nos	1,000.00
[End of List			

Narration: 10 nos 1,000.00
Being the invoice raised for Rs. 1000/- for the credit period of 45 days

Fig. 4.10 A Voucher

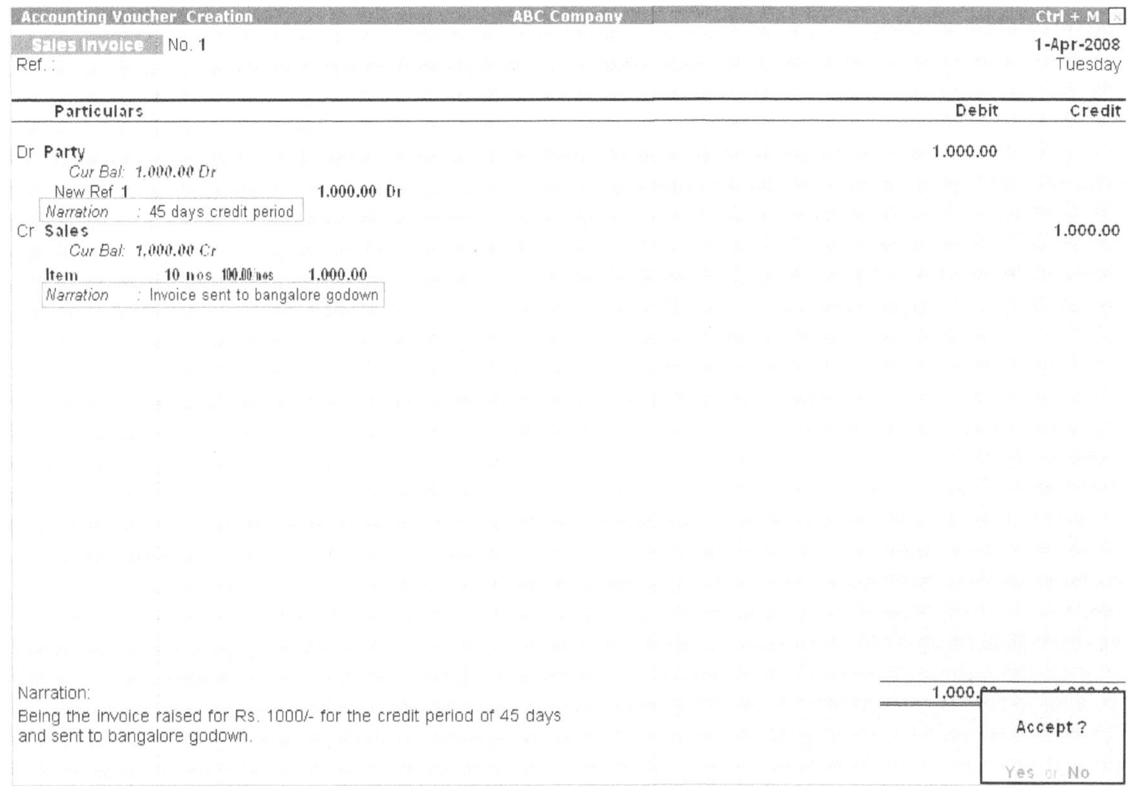

Fig. 4.11 Giving Narration to the Voucher

Narrations for each entry

Select Yes, if you want to give a separate narration for each entry of a voucher. This would be applicable for a multiple entry voucher where you want separate details for each entry. Select No if you do not want a separate narration for each entry.

Note: To get the Narration for each entry raise the sales in As Voucher and for Payment or Receipt vouchers, set Use Single Entry mode for Pymt/Rcpt/Contra to No in F12:Configurations.

For Delivery Note, Receipt Note, Sales order, Purchase order, Physical Stock, Stock Journal, Rejection In and Rejection Out, the option Narration for each entry is deactivated.

Printing

Print after saving voucher

Select Yes to print every voucher after entering it, else select No. This is suitable for an online environment where you use Tally.ERP 9 printed vouchers as the formal voucher. Remember, that the transaction is already recorded and posted and should you wish to make corrections to the printed voucher, you must alter the Tally.ERP 9 voucher online and print it again.

Note: If we select Receipt as Type of Voucher the option Print Formal Receipt after saving will be displayed. Depending on the Type of Voucher you have selected to create or alter, different printing features appear in this field.

Use for POS Invoicing

If you would like to use the sales invoice as POS invoice then set this option to Yes.

Default Print Title

If you would like to give the default print title for POS Invoice then specify the same. So when ever you print the POS Invoice this title will be printed.

Name of Class

You can create classes by entering the class name in this section.

Stock Journal Voucher Type

The option Use Manufacturing Journal will be enabled for Stock Journal Voucher type

Voucher Type Creation | ABC Company | Ctrl + M

Name : **Stock Journal Voucher**
(alias) :

General		Printing		Name of Class
Type of Voucher	: Stock Journal	Print after saving Voucher	? No	
Abbr.	: Stk Jrnl			
Method of Voucher Numbering	? Automatic			
Use Advance Configuration	? No			
Use EFFECTIVE Dates for Vouchers	? No			
Make 'Optional' as default	? No			
Use Common Narration	? Yes			
Use as a Manufacturing Journal	? Yes			

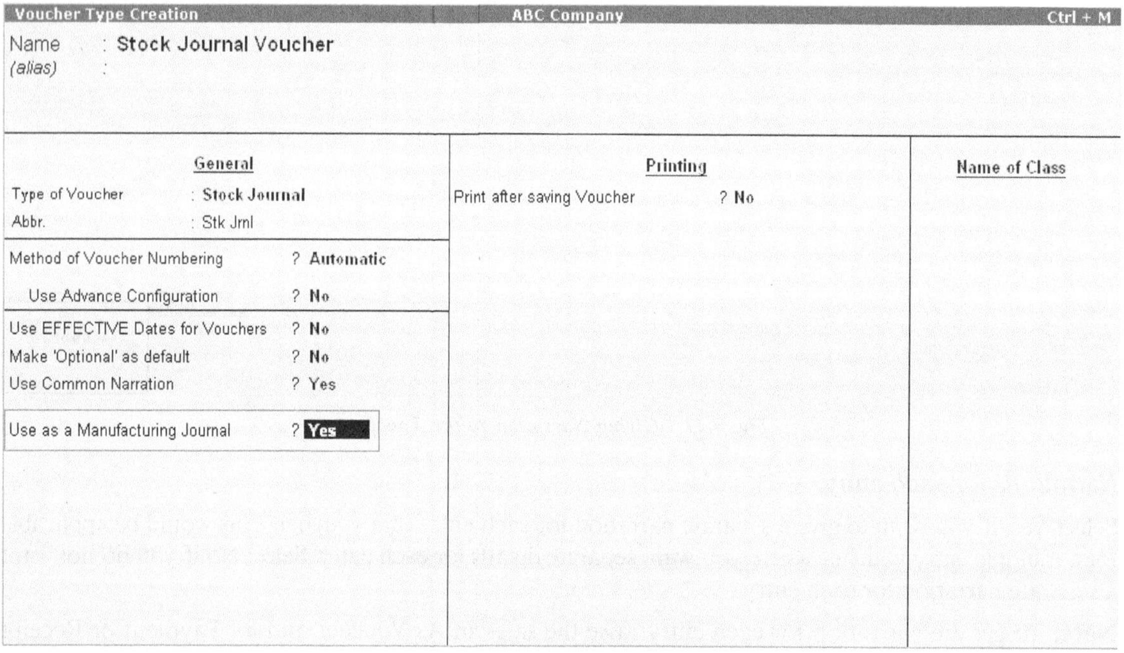

Fig. 4.12 Stock Journal Voucher

Creating a Voucher Type with Advanced Configuration

If the Method of Voucher Numbering is set to Automatic, then an additional field to set the advanced configuration for the Voucher type is displayed. On setting this field to Yes, the Voucher Type Creation (Secondary) screen is displayed.

The Voucher Type Alteration will appear as shown :

Method of Voucher Numbering	? Automatic
Use Advance Configuration	? Yes

Starting number

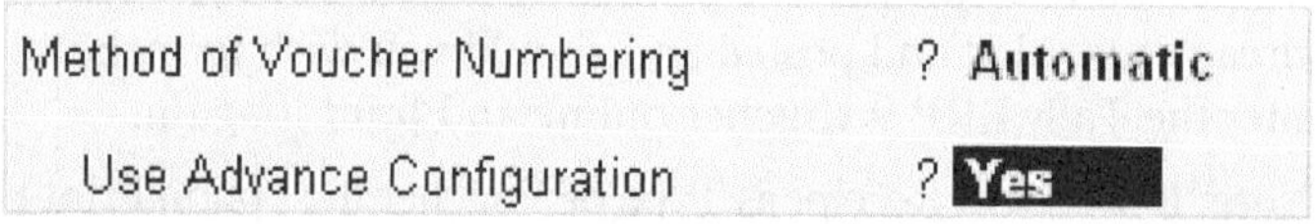

Give the number for the first voucher. Usually it is 1. You can set it to any number you want. Tally.ERP 9 will auto-increment from this number for subsequent vouchers. However, the numbering of vouchers also depends on other variables selected by you, explanations of which will follow hereafter.

Voucher Type Alteration (Secondary) ABC Company Ctrl + M

Starting Number ? 1
Width of Numerical Part : 3
Prefill with ZERO ? Yes

Restart Numbering			Prefix Details		Suffix Details	
Applicable From	Starting Number	Particulars	Applicable From	Particulars	Applicable From	Particulars
1-Apr-2008	1	Yearly	1-Apr-2008	ABC	1-Apr-2008	2008

Fig. 4.13 Creating a Voucher with Advanced Configuration

Width of Numerical Part

You may leave it blank to let Tally.ERP 9 automatically adjust the width according to the number. However, if you would like to have a specific width to be fixed then set the same. e.g., 3.

Prefill with ZERO

When the width is specified, the digits before the voucher number are left blank if this option is set to 'No'.

For example, Sales Invoice No: 1

If this option is set Yes, it pre-fills the space with zeroes based on the width of numerical part specified.

For example, if the Width of Numerical Part is specified as 3, and if Pre-fill with Zero is set to Yes, then it display the voucher number as below:

Sales Invoice No: 001.

If Width of Numerical Part is specified as 4, then it displays the voucher number as below:

Sales Invoice No: 0001 and so on.

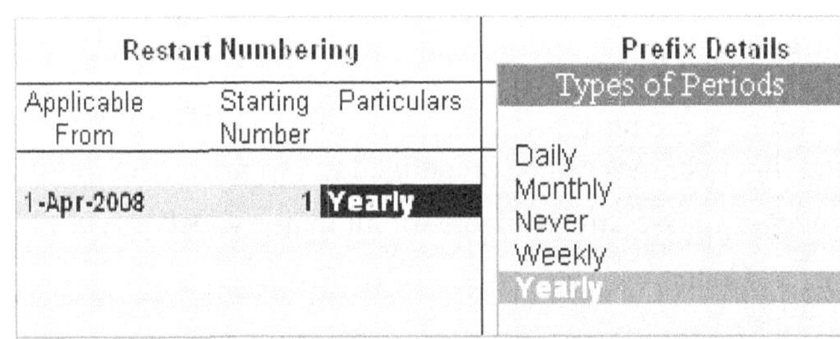

Restart Numbering			Prefix Details
Applicable From	Starting Number	Particulars	Types of Periods
1-Apr-2008	1	Yearly	Daily Monthly Never Weekly Yearly

Restart Numbering

Voucher Numbering may be restarted with the starting number (as specified) at intervals selected by you - Daily, Monthly, Never, Weekly or Yearly. You must give the date when the numbering should restart in the field Applicable from. The date must be the first day of the month. You can specify more than one Restart dates. For example, should you wish to renumber your vouchers from 01 June 08 on a yearly basis, you must specify it in the next field. This would retain the numbering system in the prior period. If, however, you want to change the numbers from the beginning from monthly to yearly basis, simply alter the first field itself.

Prefix Details

If you want the voucher numbers to be prefixed with some fixed information, enter the information here. Examples of prefix details are:

month of the voucher - April/

company info like ABC/

even fixed number series like 1000

Note: The numeric portion begins immediately after the prefix information. Therefore, be sure to give a space or a slash '/' or some special character to highlight a separation, e.g. we have specified April/. The slash would cause the voucher number to appear as April/001, otherwise it would appear as April001. This facilitates simple usage for fixed number series appearing as 200100001 where 2001 is the prefix, and 00001 is the starting number with a width of 5, and with leading zeros.

You can choose different prefix information for different periods or continue with one. The prefix continues from the date you mention under Applicable from till the next date that you may give under Applicable from. Hence, we have chosen to change the prefix from April to May when the month changes. Please note, however, that if we omit to change the prefix for the subsequent months (*i.e.*, do not give Applicable from date for the month), your voucher numbers for even June, July, *etc.*, would contain the prefix 'May'.

Suffix Details

You can also give fixed suffix information for the voucher number. The same rules and effects as for Prefix Details are applied.

The Sales Invoice voucher number looks like this:

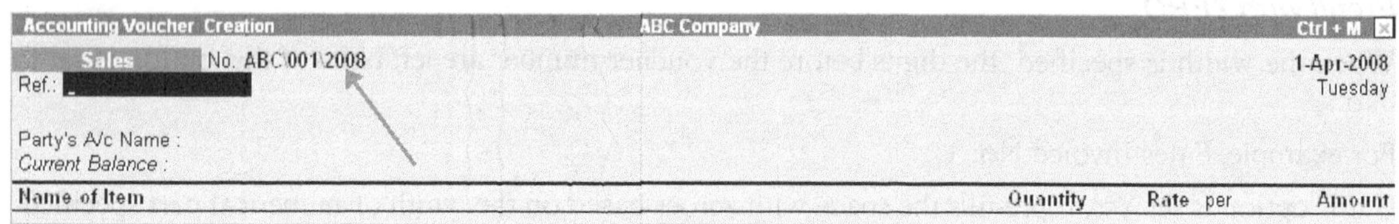

Fig. 4.14 Accounting Voucher with voucher number

Voucher Class

Voucher Classes are used to automate Accounting Allocations in transactions. It is a table for predefining the entries to make Invoice entry a simple task. This is particularly useful in sales invoicing where the nominal ledger accounts, to be credited for each item of sale is defined once. During voucher entry, the accounting credits for items sold are done automatically. Additional accounting entries like, tax, freight, and other charges can be predefined to be carried out untouched during actual invoicing.

Voucher Classes are available for all major voucher types like:

- Contra

- Payment
- Receipt
- Journal
- Sales
- Credit Note
- Purchases
- Debit Note
- Sales Order
- Purchase Order
- Delivery Note
- Stock Journal.

Creating a Purchase Voucher Class

Purchase Voucher Classes are templates where you can restrict accounts to be used in entries as well as automate accounting entries for items and expenses.

You can either alter the existing Purchase Voucher Type or create a new voucher type based on the requirements.

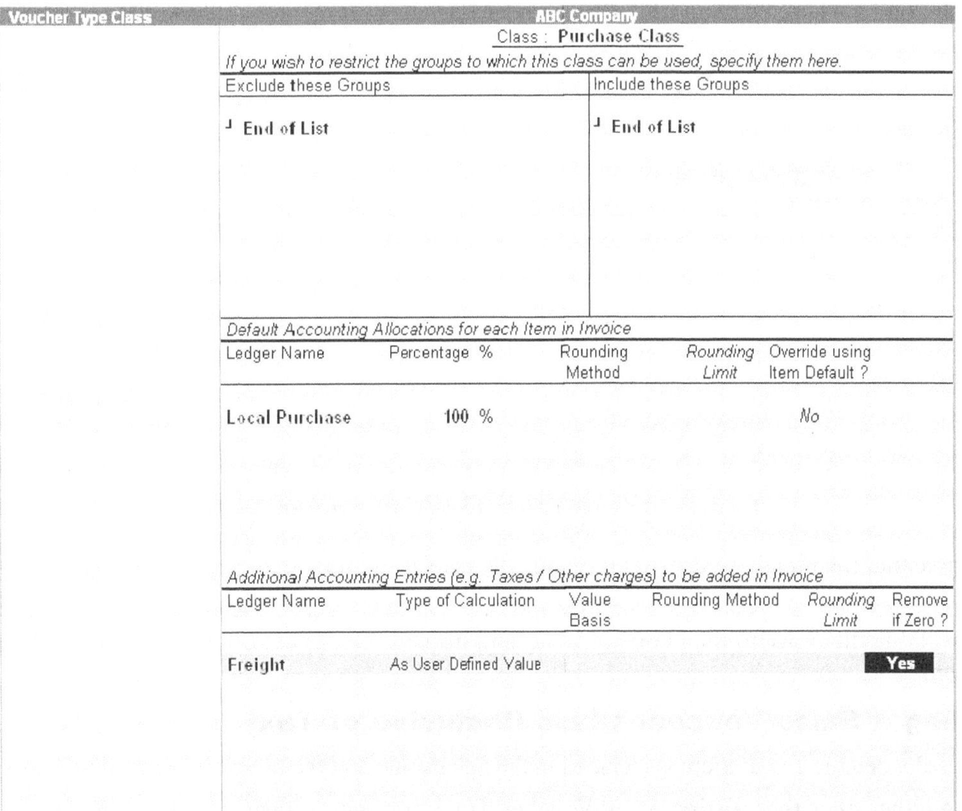

Fig. 4.15 Voucher Type Class

Go to Gateway of Tally > Accounts Info > Voucher Type >Alter > Purchase

Give a name to the class under Name of Class say Purchase Class. You can create more than one class. (Make sure that Enter Purchases in Invoice Format in F11 feature is enabled to create class). Create the class as follows:

Default Accounting Allocations

All the stock items that will be entered in the voucher using this class will be automatically allocated to this Ledger account Local Purchases. Of course, the stock item record remains as it is and can be viewed separately.

Pass a Purchase entry using the created Purchase Class:

Go to Gateway of Tally > Accounting Vouchers > F9 Purchase > and select the Class.

1. Select the Supplier Account.

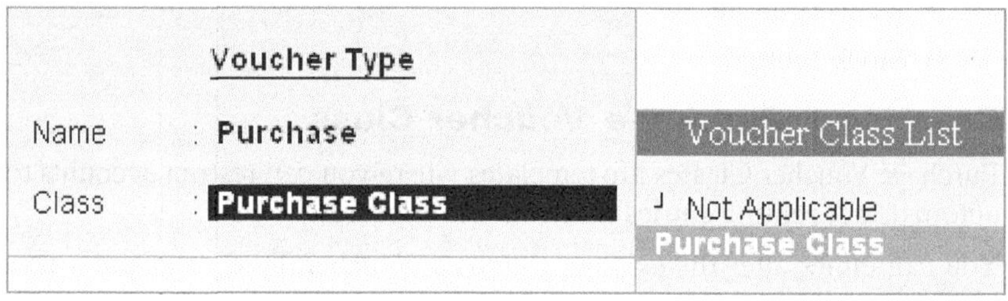

You will observe that the Ledger Accounts grouped under Sundry Debtors are also listed as you have not specified any condition to exclude Sundry Debtors Group. If you have specified Sundry Debtors under Exclude option, then Tally would have displayed the Ledgers excluding those Ledgers grouped under Sundry Debtors.

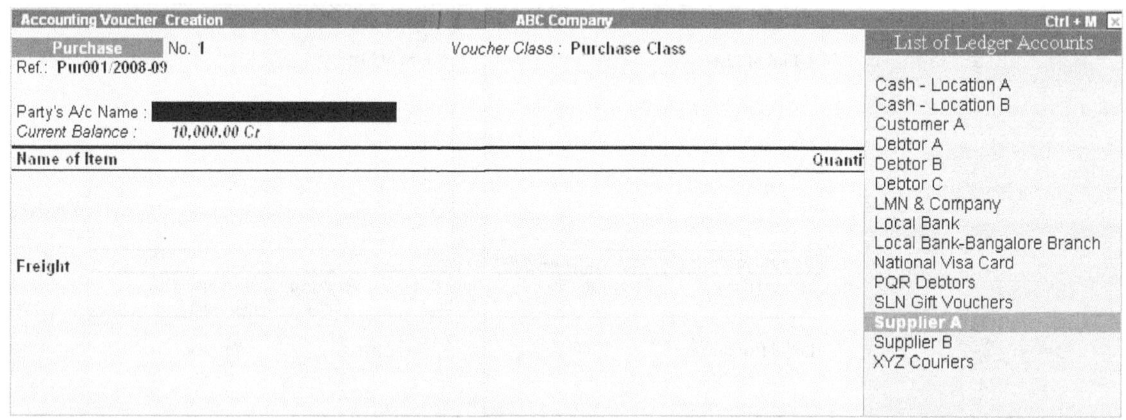

Fig. 4.16 Selecting Ledger Accounts for Purchase Voucher

Please note that the Freight Ledger is automatically displayed and the user has to only specify the value.

Once you select Item B, specify the Quantity and rate, the value will be automatically calculated and the cursor will directly move to the Name of Item field instead of popping up the Accounting Allocations for screen.

Creating a Sales Voucher Class (Inclusive of Tax)

This is used when the Tax amount is included in the Sales value and the same is illustrated with an example.

You can either alter the existing Sales Voucher Type or create a new voucher type based on their requirements.

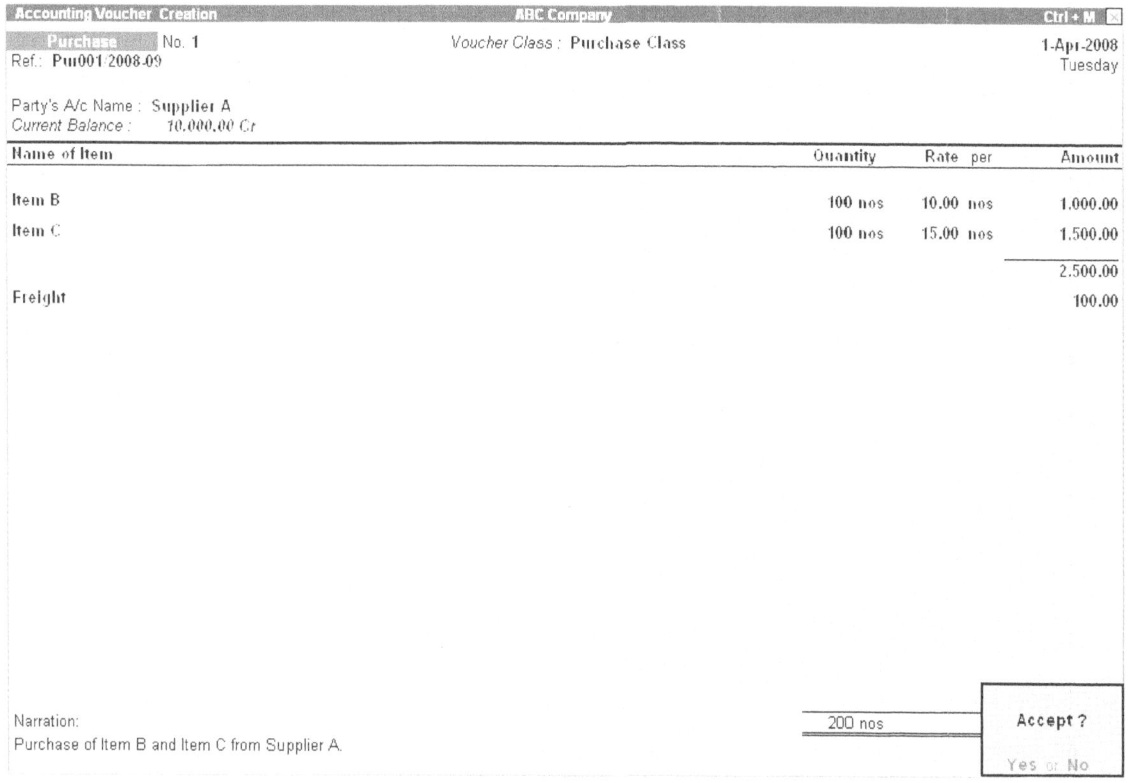
Accounting Voucher Creation | ABC Company | Ctrl + M

Purchase No. 1 | Voucher Class : Purchase Class | 1-Apr-2008 Tuesday

Ref.: Pur001/2008-09

Party's A/c Name : Supplier A

Current Balance : 10,000.00 Cr

Name of Item	Quantity	Rate per	Amount
Item B	100 nos	10.00 nos	1,000.00
Item C	100 nos	15.00 nos	1,500.00
			2,500.00
Freight			100.00
	200 nos		

Narration:
Purchase of Item B and Item C from Supplier A.

Fig. 4.17 Purchase Voucher

Go to Gateway > Accounts Info > Voucher Types > Alter > Sales

Give a name to the class under Name of Class say Sales Class B. You can create more than one class. Specify the table of class as below:

Now pass Sales Invoice and check,

Go to Gateway of Tally >Accounting Vouchers > F8 Sales. select Sales Class B

The total value of the sale is Rs. 1500/=. Select the entry in alteration mode, move the cursor till the amount field and check.

The total value is allocated to Sales and Tax Ledgers, as defined in the voucher class.

Creating a Sales Voucher Class with Override using Item default

You can either alter the existing Sales Voucher Type or create a new voucher type based on their requirements.

Go to Gateway > Accounts Info > Voucher Types > Alter > Sales

Give a name to the class under Name of Class say Sales Class A. You can create more than one class. Specify the table of class as shown:

Override using Item Default:

Item default refers to the Default Ledger account that you had set for a Stock Item. It is possible to enter

Voucher Type Class	ABC Company

Class : Sales Class B

If you wish to restrict the groups to which this class can be used, specify them here.

Exclude these Groups	Include these Groups
┘ End of List	┘ End of List

Default Accounting Allocations for each Item in Invoice

Ledger Name	VAT/Tax Class	Percentage %	Rounding Method	*Rounding Limit*	Override using Item Default ?
Sales 4 %	Sales @ 4%	96.15 %	┘ Not Applicable		*No*
Output Vat 4%	Output VAT @ 4%	3.85 %			

Additional Accounting Entries (e.g. Taxes / Other charges) to be added in Invoice

Ledger Name	Type of Calculation	Value Basis	Rounding Method	*Rounding Limit*	Remove if Zero ?

Fig. 4.18 Selecting Sales Options

Accounting Voucher Creation | ABC Company | Ctrl + M

Sales No. 2 | *Voucher Class :* Sales Class B | 1-Apr-2008 Tuesday

Ref.: Sale02/2008-09

Party's A/c Name : Customer A

Current Balance : *4,091.25 Dr*

Name of Item	Quantity	Rate	per	Amount
Item E	100 nos	15.00	nos	1,500.00

100 nos

Narration:
Sale of Item E to Customer A.

Accept ?
Yes or No

Fig. 4.19 Sales Voucher

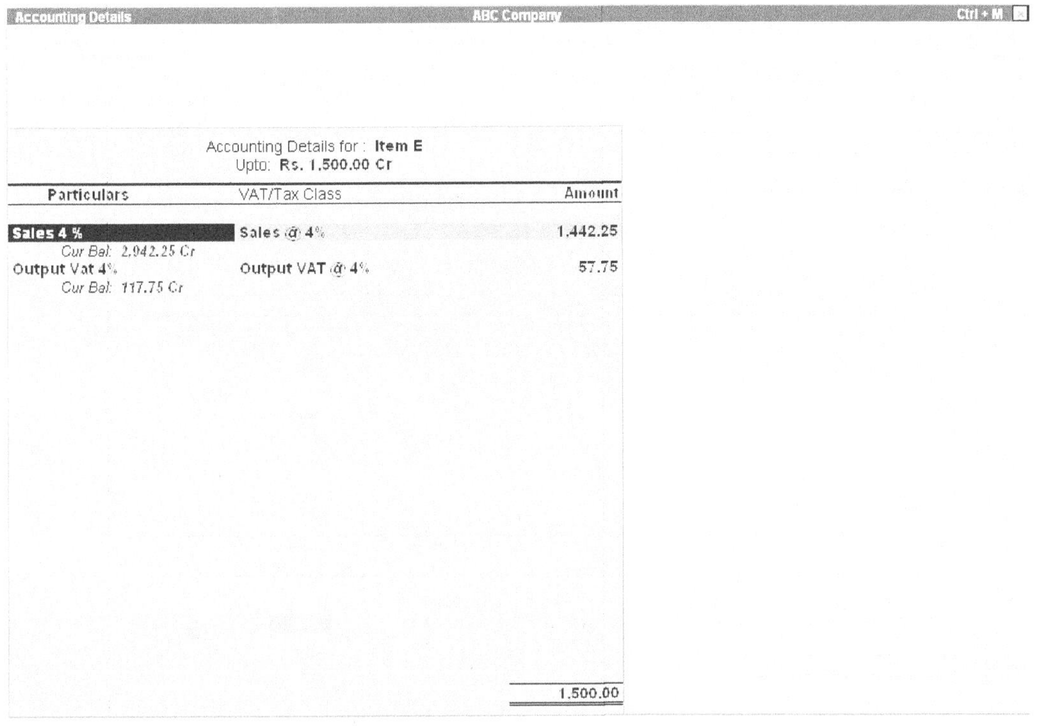

Fig. 4.20 Accounting Details for Sales Voucher

a Tax Invoice having multiple items with different VAT/Tax Rates. Item default refers to the Sales Ledger account that you may have set for a stock item.

If you set Override using Item default to Yes and specify a Sales Ledger in the Class Table, the sales Ledgers set in the item masters will still be considered.

Create Stock Item say Item D and Item E and set Yes to option Set/Modify Default Ledgers for Invoicing and specify as below: (To display this option, enable Specify Default Ledger Allocation for Invoicing in F12 configure).

Item D:

Item E:

Now pass the Sales entry and check:

Go to Gateway of Tally >Accounting Vouchers > F8 Sales > select Sales Class A

The VAT Ledgers are selected automatically.

Select Party's name and select Item D and Item E and check.

The Items will be automatically allocated to the Ledgers defined in Item Master and VAT calculation automates and facilitates the user to pass the entries faster and with ease.

Voucher Classes for Payment, Receipt and Contra Vouchers

Voucher Classes for Payment, Receipt and Contra Vouchers.

Voucher Type Class — ABC Company — Ctrl + M

Class : Sales Class A

If you wish to restrict the groups to which this class can be used, specify them here.

Exclude these Groups	Include these Groups
┘ **End of List**	┘ **End of List**

Default Accounting Allocations for each Item in Invoice

Ledger Name	VAT/Tax Class	Percentage %	Rounding Method	*Rounding Limit*	Override using Item Default ?
Sales 4 %	**Sales @ 4%**	**100 %**			*Yes*

Additional Accounting Entries (e.g. Taxes / Other charges) to be added in Invoice

Ledger Name	Type of Calculation	Value Basis	Rounding Method	*Rounding Limit*	Remove if Zero ?
Output Vat 4%	On VAT Rate	4% ┘	Not Applicable		Yes
Output Vat 12.5%	On VAT Rate	12.50% ┘	Not Applicable		**Yes**

Fig. 4.21 Giving name to Name of Class

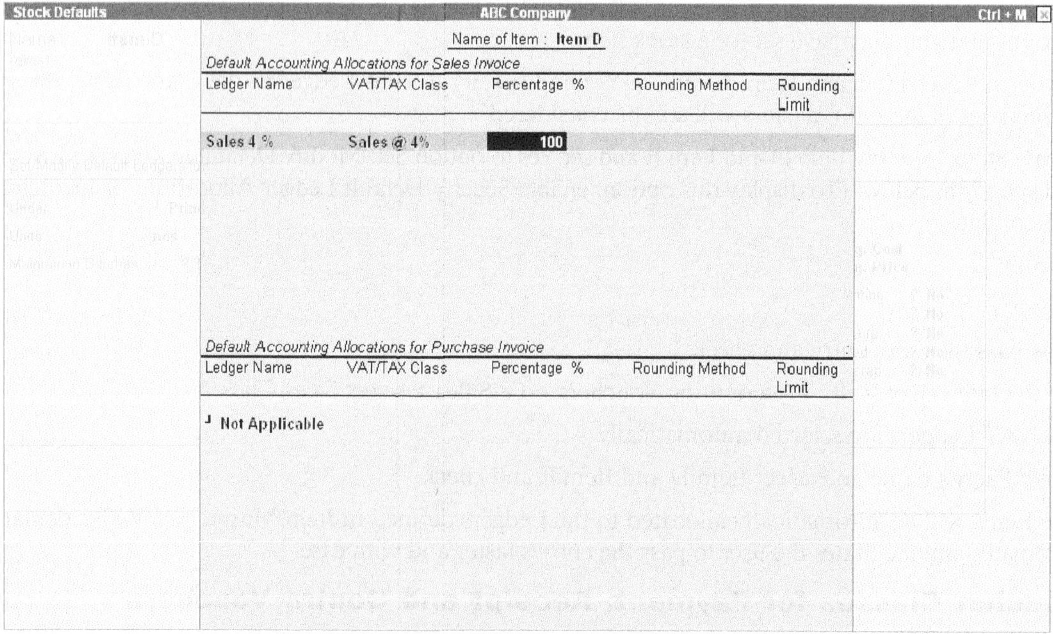

Fig. 4.22 Item D Sales Class

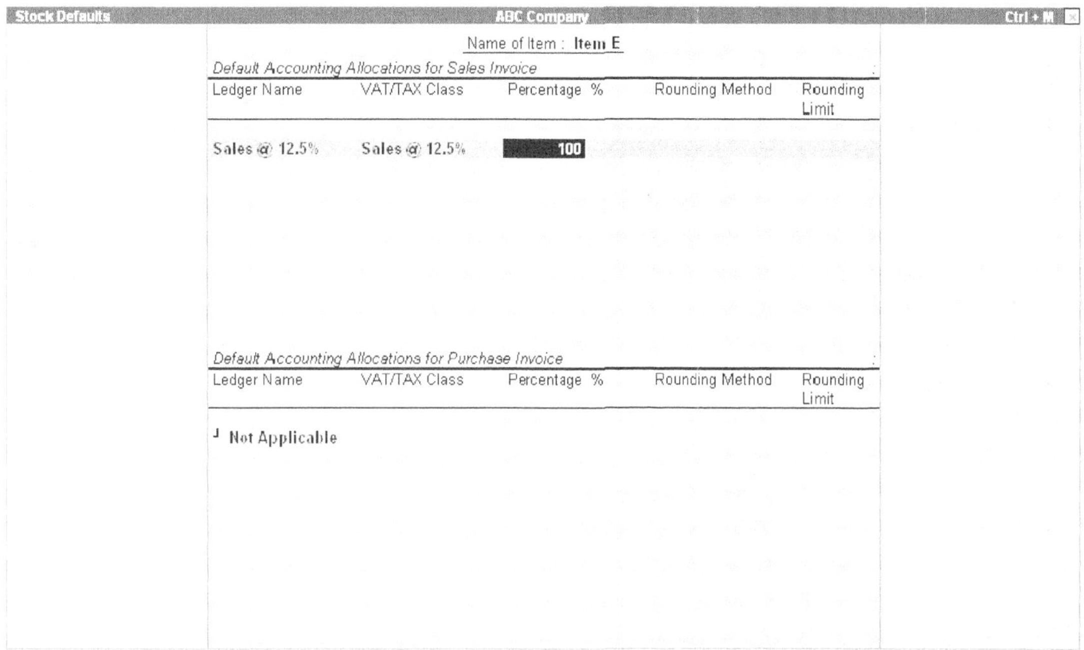

Fig. 4.23 Item E Sales Class

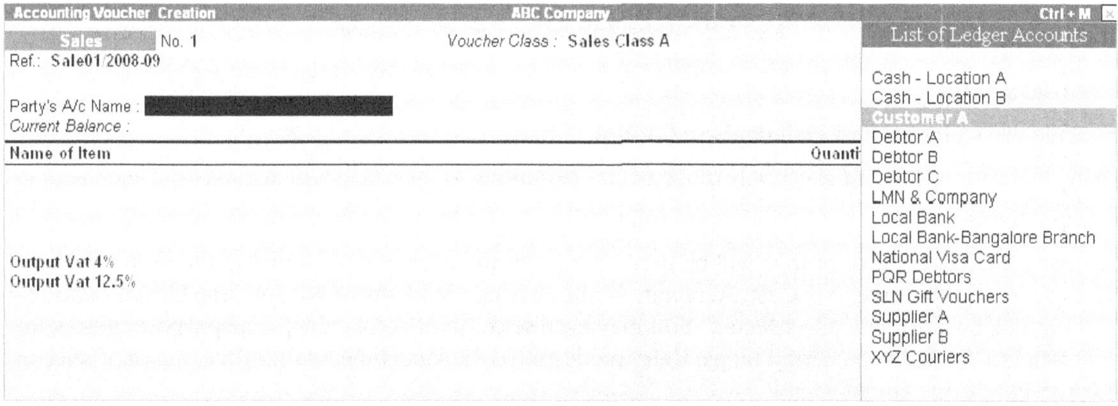

Fig. 4.24 Selecting Ledger

The primary intention of using classes for payment, receipt and contra vouchers is to enable data input in single entry or list mode rather than in Tally's traditional double entry mode.

Let us take an example of a Payment Voucher.

You can either alter the existing Payment Voucher Type or create a new voucher type based on your requirements.

Go to Gateway of Tally > Accounts Info > Voucher Types > alter Payment

Take the cursor to the Name of Class field. Give a name to the class say Cash Payment. You can create more than one class.

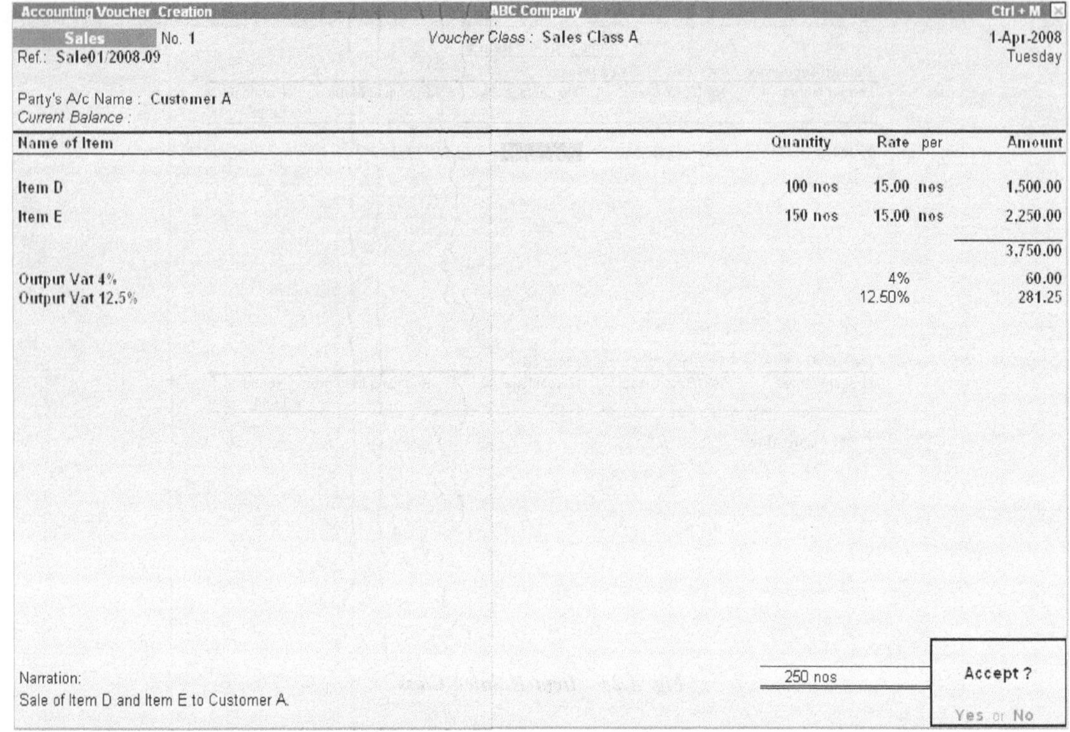

Fig. 4.25 Sales Accounting Voucher Creation

The Class Table

Exclude these Groups and Include these Groups.

Using this option, you can select only those groups pertaining to the Class, which makes the entry simpler.

Ledger Name

Selecting the ledger account that will be used to pay out the money will eliminate the need to select it during entry. In this case, it is Cash Account. While passing the payment voucher, the Cash-Location B account will be automatically selected. You may even select 'Not Applicable'. The purpose of selecting 'Not Applicable' will be, to permit Single Entry mode and at the same time retaining the option of selecting the account during entry.

Voucher Class for Journals

Voucher Classes in Journals is used to handle Forex Gain Loss Adjustments for companies having Multi-Currency Accounts. You would create a 'class' in the normal way (Accounts Info > Voucher Types > Alter > Journal). Having selected the class during Voucher Entry, you will find only those Ledger Accounts appearing which have a Gain/Loss to be adjusted as of the date of voucher and auto-calculation of these amounts.

Voucher Class for Debit Notes and Credit Notes

Voucher classes for Credit Notes are similar to sales invoices except for one important inclusion. You can set the class for interest entries to enable adjustment of interest payable. If the Interest option is selected, the other sales invoice-like options will not be available. A separate class may to be created for

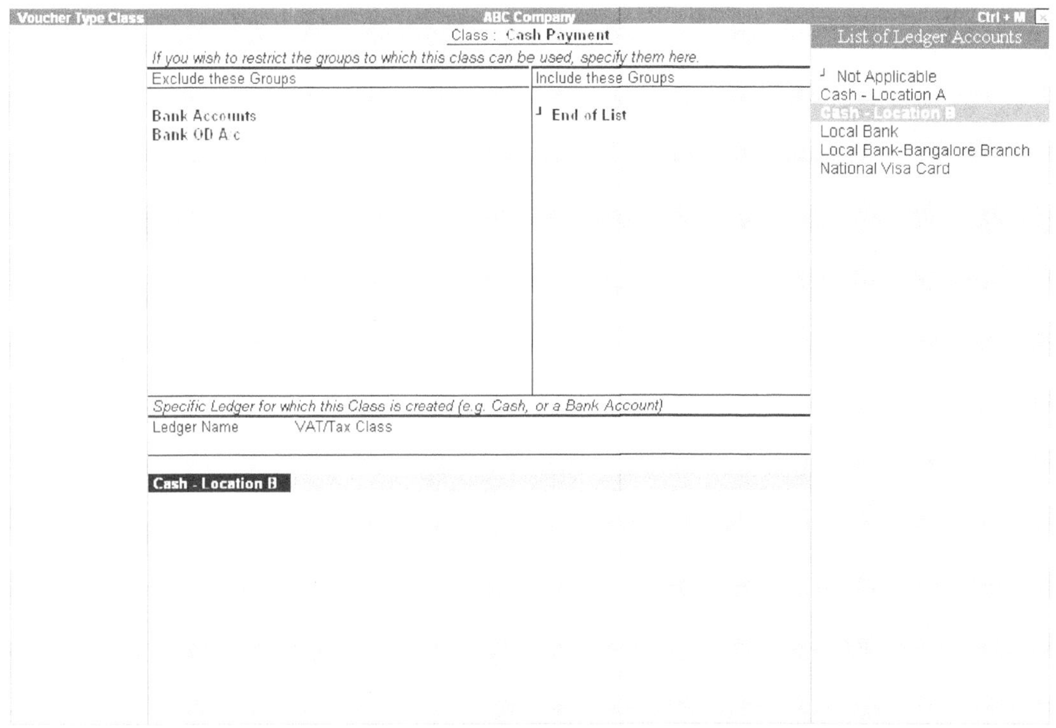

Fig. 4.26 Voucher Class for Payments

entries like Sales Returns. Since Sales and Purchase Invoice classes have already been dealt with, we shall not elaborate on this behavior anymore.

Debit Note classes can be set for interest entries only. Classes for other entries are not available as the invoice mode of entry is not possible for Debit Notes.

Creating a Payment Voucher Entry with Class

Select Accounting voucher from Gateway of Tally. Press F5: Payment. You have to select a class or Not Applicable, if no class is desired for this entry. If Cost Centre Class has been set, it can also be selected.

The entry will be made as follows:

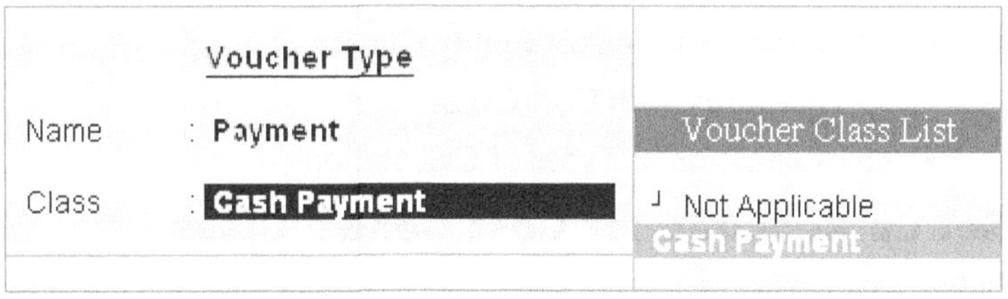

The Voucher Class is Cash Payment. Once the voucher class is selected, the Cash Ledger is automatically selected and you need to select only the Ledgers which are to be debited. Please note that the entry is not done in the regular Dr/Cr format. Data entry in Tally.ERP 9 is very rapid. This feature makes it much more faster!

Cost Centre Class

The purpose of Cost Centre Classes is to facilitate predetermined allocation of cost centres to Ledger accounts (like expenses and incomes) during voucher entry.

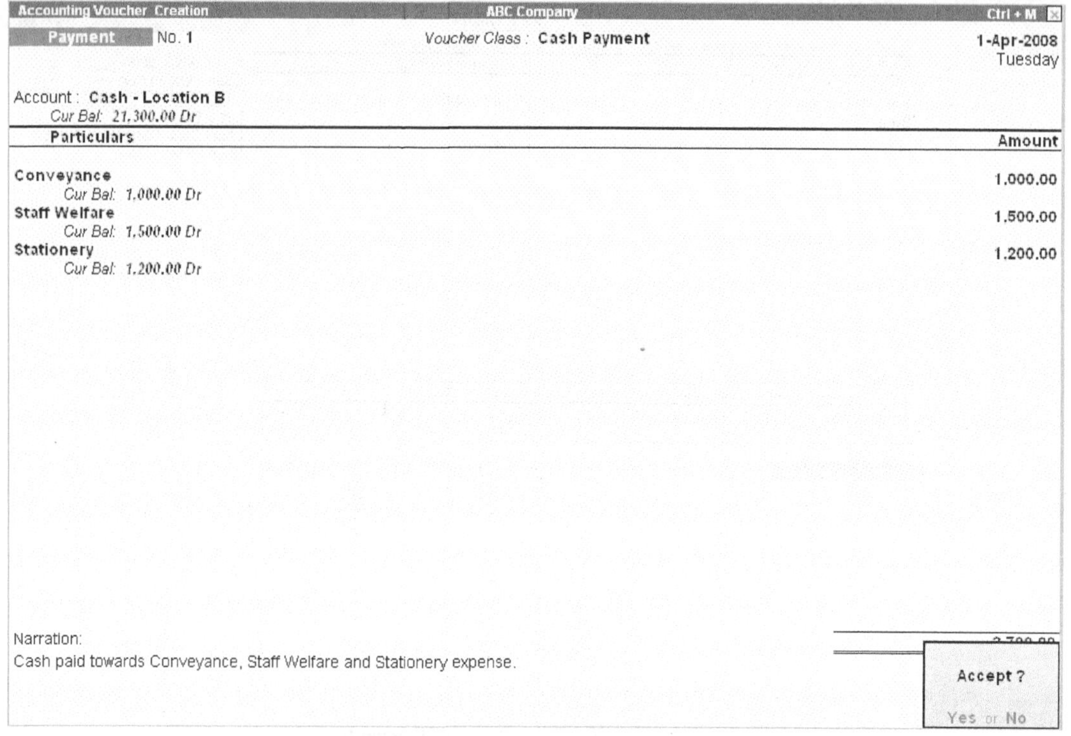

Fig. 4.27 Payment Voucher Entry with Class

How does it work?

The Automation of cost centre allocation involves creation of classes and predefining percentages for cost centres.

Cost centre classes affect all voucher types. In voucher entry, depending upon the cost centre class, the allocation will be carried out in the background without the allocation screen being displayed at all.

More:

- Set up required for Cost Centre Classes
- Voucher Entry with Cost Classes
- An explanation of Types of Calculation.

Set up Required for Cost Centre Class

Before you select classes, it is advisable to create the cost centre structure.

Define the Classes required and indicate which cost centres will be affected for each class. For example, you might have the following structure:

Divisions

1. Export
2. Wholesale
3. Retail.

Departments

1. Finance
2. Marketing.

Where Divisions and Departments are Cost Categories and the others are cost centres.

Now, you would like to allocate sales to the following Cost Centre Classes:

1. Export Class - to allocate 100% of Export sales to the cost centre Export
2. Wholesale Class - to allocate 100% of wholesale sales to the cost centre Wholesale
3. Retail Class - to allocate 100% of retail sales to the cost centre Retail.

You would also like to allocate all the sales (Export, Wholesale and Retail) to the Marketing Department.

Along with the above mentioned, you would also like to allocate Marketing Expenses on a pro-rata in the following manner:

1. Finance – 50%
2. Marketing – 50%

With this structure, let us now set up the classes.

Cost/Profit Centres Management

Maintain Payroll	? No
Maintain Cost Centres	? Yes
Use Cost Centre for Job Costing	? Yes
More than ONE Payroll / Cost Category	? Yes
Use Pre-defined Cost Centre Allocations during Entry	? Yes

Set up Cost Centre Classes

Go to Gateway of Tally > select F11: F1: Accounting Features

Set Use Pre-defined Cost Centre Allocations during Entry to Yes

(The other options can remain as previously set and are not discussed here.)

Click on Enter, which will pop up Auto Cost Allocations-Cost Centre Classes creation screen. Type the Class name and select the Categories and the respective cost centres. Specify the percentage of allocation. After entry, your auto-cost allocation screen will be displayed as shown:

Auto Cost Allocations

Cost Centre Classes

Name: ABC Company

Class Name	
Export Class	
Divisions	
Export	100 %
Department	
Marketing	100 %
Wholesale Class	
Divisions	
Wholesale	100 %
Department	
Marketing	100 %
Retail Class	
Divisions	
Retail	100 %
Department	
Marketing	100 %
Marketing Expenses	
Department	
Finance	50 %
Marketing	50 %

You have created the Cost Centre Classes as Export, Wholesale, Retail and Marketing Expenses. Divisions and Departments are cost categories. Export, Wholesale and Retail are cost centres under Divisions. Marketing and Finance are cost centres under Departments.

It is not necessary to have the same names for the classes and the cost centres, as shown in the above example.

Inventory Information

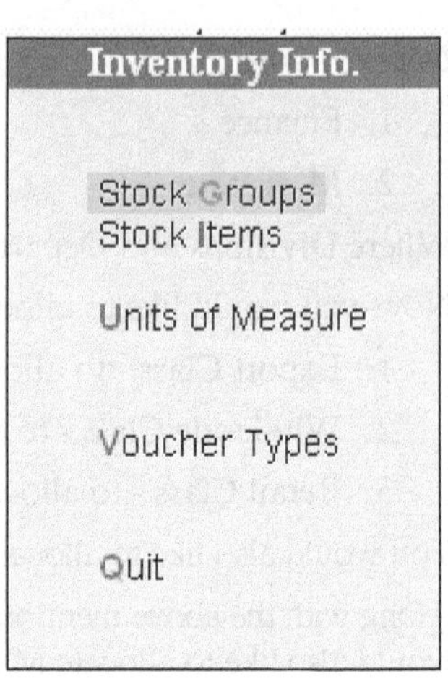

The Inventory Info menu, lists the inventory masters of the company, using which you can create, alter and display the inventory master details.

Go to Gateway of Tally > Inventory Info

Inventory Configurations & Features (F11 & F12)

Configuration of Inventory

By using F12:Configure, you can enable the required settings of Inventory Masters.

By default, the settings pertaining to Inventory Masters are set to No. If you set them to Yes, the features will be enabled. Typically, they are additional fields that appear during Masters creation which enable you to obtain more information and detailed analyses.

Note: If you press F12 anywhere in the Menu, it will take you to the configuration menu.

Features of Inventory

By using F11:Features, you can enable the various settings under inventory features which determine the information to be entered during transaction entries.

Functions in Inventory Info. Menu

Inventory information contains the inventory masters. Each master has Create, Display and Alter functions.

These three functions are grouped under:

1. Single
2. Multiple

In Single, you can execute the function on one master. In Multiple, you can execute the function on multiple masters.

Functions

Create

The Create option is used to create new masters. Any modification to the masters can be done only through the Alter mode.

Display

The Display option is used to view the Master information. Master information cannot be modified in Display mode.

Alter

The Alter option allows you to view and make the necessary changes to the master information. This does not allow creation of masters. In Alteration mode, you can delete the master. [Press ALT+D for deletion]

Stock Group

Stock Groups in Inventory are similar to Groups in Accounting Masters. They are helpful in the classification of Stock Items.

You can group Stock Items under different Stock Groups to reflect their classification based on some common features such as brand name, product type, quality, etc.

Grouping enables you to locate Stock Items easily and report their details in statements.

Example:

Stock Item	*Sub Group*	*Main Group*
Brand A - 19" TFT	Brand A	Grade One
Brand A - 17" CRT	Brand A	Grade One
Brand B - 19" TFT	Brand B	Grade Two
Brand B - 17" CRT	Brand B	Grade Two

You now have ready details of Grade One and Grade Two products, duly classified. You can also view the sub group classification.

Go to Gateway of Tally > Inventory Info. > Stock Groups

Stock Groups

Single Stock Group

Create
Display
Alter

Multiple Stock Groups

CReate
DIsplay
AlTer

Quit

Creating a Stock Group

Go to Gateway of Tally > Inventory Info. > Stock Groups > Create (under Single Stock Group)

A brief description on each of the fields in the Stock Group Creation screen follows:

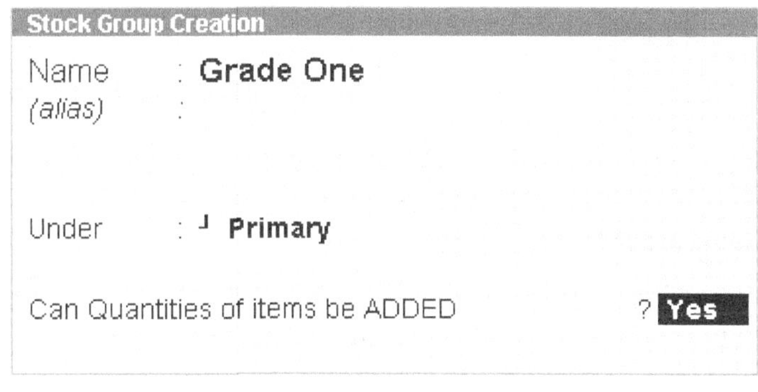

Name

Enter the name of the Stock Group to be created. For example, Grade One.

Alias

Enter additional name apart from primary name [if required]. You can create any number of additional names.

Under

Specify whether it is a primary group or a sub-group of another group, by selecting from the list.

Press Alt+C to create a parent group, if you do not have it in the list.

Can quantities of items be ADDED?

This field pertains to information on measuring the units of the Stock Items that you would categorise under the Stock Group.

The Stock Items categorised under the group should have similar units for them to be added up. You cannot add quantities in Kgs to quantities in Pcs.

Creating Multiple Stock Groups

Go to Gateway of Tally > Inventory Info. > Stock Groups > Create (under Multiple Stock Groups)

Select the parent group under which you want the new groups to be created from the "List of Groups".

A brief description on each field in the Multi Stock Group Creation screen is given below:

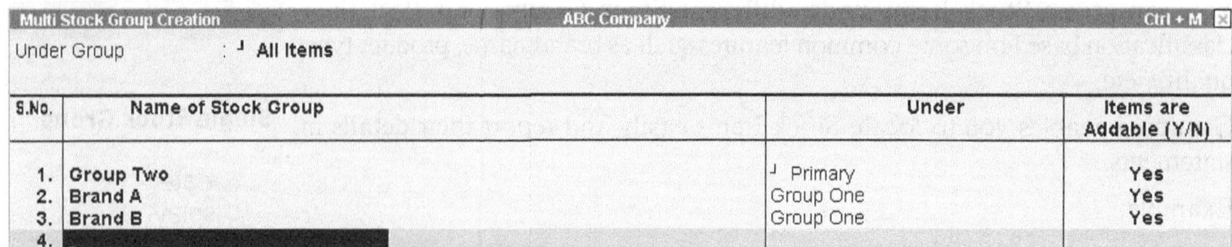

Multi Stock Group Creation ABC Company Ctrl + M

Under Group : ┘ All Items

S.No.	Name of Stock Group	Under	Items are Addable (Y/N)
1.	Group Two	┘ Primary	Yes
2.	Brand A	Group One	Yes
3.	Brand B	Group One	Yes
4.			

Fig. 4.28 Multi Stock Group Creation 1/2

Name of Stock Group

Enter the name of the Stock Group.

Under

If you select any group other than All Items in the Under Group field, then this column is filled in automatically with the selected Group name and the cursor skips this column. This speeds up data entry.

Multi Stock Group Creation ABC Company Ctrl + M

Under Group : Group Two

S.No.	Name of Stock Group	Under	Items are Addable (Y/N)
1.	Brand C	Group Two	Yes
2.	Brand D	Group Two	Yes
3.			

Fig. 4.29 Multi Stock Group Creation 2/2

If you select All Items in the Under Group field, the cursor does not skip this field and allows you to enter the parent group for each one of them.

Items are Addable? (Y/N)

You can select whether units of the Stock Items under Stock Group are to be added or not.

Buttons specific to Multi Stock Group Creation screen

Buttons	*Short cut keys*	*Description & Use*
F4: Parent	CTRL+F4	Allows you to change the parent for all sub groups.
F8: Skip Details	F8	Cursor will not go to Column Items are Addable (Y/N). If Items are addable is to remain the same as specified for further subgroup creation, use this button. The cursor skips the column which speeds up data entry.
C: Category	CTRL+C	Allows you to Create a Multi Stock Category.
I: Items	CTRL+I	Allows you to Create a Multi Stock Item.
O: Godown	CTRL+O	Allows you to Create a Multi Godown.

Displaying a Stock Group

You can display a Stock Group in Single mode and multiple mode.

Displaying Single Stock Group

Go to Gateway of Tally > Inventory Info. > Stock Groups > Display (under Single Stock Group)

Select the Stock Group whose particulars you want to display from the List of Groups.

The Stock Group Display screen is displayed as shown.

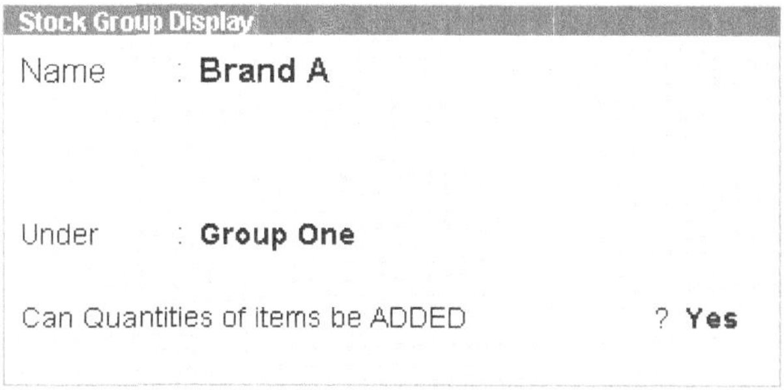

Stock Group Display
Name : Brand A
Under : Group One
Can Quantities of items be ADDED ? Yes

Buttons specific to stock group Display mode:

Buttons	*Short cut Keys*	*Description & Use*
C: Category	CTRL+C	Allows you to Display a Stock Category.
I: Items	CTRL+I	Allows you to Display a Stock Item.
U: Units	CTRL+U	Allows you to Display a Unit of Measure.
O: Godown	CTRL+O	Allows you to Display a Godown.
V: Vch Types	CTRL+V	Allows you to Display a Voucher Types

Altering a Stock Group

Go to Gateway of Tally > Inventory Info. > Stock Groups > Alter (under Single Stock Group)

Select the Stock Group from the List of Groups. The Stock Group Alteration screen is displayed as shown.

Stock Group Alteration
Name : Brand D
(alias) :
Under : Group Two
Can Quantities of items be ADDED ? Yes

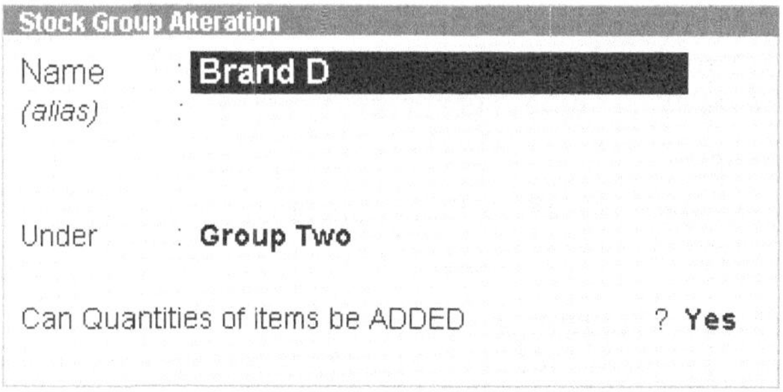

Make the necessary changes and click Yes to accept or press Ctrl+A to Save.

Deletion is possible only in the mode,. For deleting the Stock Group, Press ALT+D.

Note: You cannot delete a stock group, if it is used by any sub groups or stock items. In order to delete the Stock Group, first delete the relevant sub groups and Stock items.

Buttons specific to stock group Alter mode:

Buttons	*Short cut Keys*	*Description and Keys*
C: Category	CTRL+C	Allows you to Alter a Stock Category.
I: Items	CTRL+I	Allows you to Alter a Stock Item.
U: Units	CTRL+U	Allows you to Alter a Unit of Measure.
O: Godown	CTRL+O	Allows you to Alter a Godown.
V: Vch Types	CTRL+V	Allows you to Alter a Voucher Types

Stock Categories

Stock Category offers a parallel classification of stock items. Like stock Groups, classification is done based on similarity in behaviour.

For example,

Stock Item	*Sub Group*	*Main Group*	*Sub-Category*	*Main Category*
Brand A	19" TFT	Brand A	Grade One	TFT Monitor
Brand A	17" CRT	Brand A	Grade One	CRT Monitor
Brand B	19" TFT	Brand B	Grade Two	TFT Monitor
Brand B	17" CRT	Brand B	Grade Two	CRT Monitor

The advantage of Categorizing items is that you can classify the stock items (based on functionality) together – across different stock groups which enables you to obtain reports on alternatives or substitutes for a stock item.

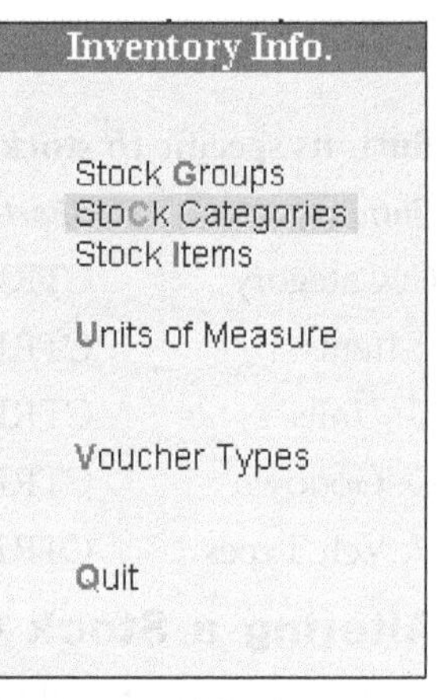

You now have the details of TFT and CRT products, duly classified. You can also view the Monitor classification.

For enabling Stock Category option in the Inventory Info menu, press F11 > Inventory Features > Set Yes for Maintain Stock Categories.

Go to Gateway of Tally > Inventory Info. > Stock Category

Creating a Stock Category

Go to Gateway of Tally > Inventory Info. > Stock Categories > Create (under Single Stock Category)

The Stock Category Creation screen is displayed as shown.

Stock Category Creation
Name : **Monitor**
(alias) :
Under : **Primary**
Accept ?
Yes or No

A brief description of each field in the Stock Category Creation screen is given below:

Name

Enter the name of the Stock Category.

Under

Specify whether it is a primary category or a sub-category of another category. Select Primary from the list, if you do not have a parent group. Use ALT + C to create a parent if you do not have the required category in the list.

Buttons specific to stock category creation:

Buttons	*Short Cut Keys*	*Description and Use*
G: Groups	CTRL+G	Allows you to Create a Stock Group.
I: Items	CTRL+I	Allows you to Create a Stock Item.
U: Units	CTRL+U	Allows you to Create a Unit of Measure.
O: Godown	CTRL+O	Allows you to Create a Godown.
V: Vch Types	CTRL+V	Allows you to Create a Voucher Types.

Creating Multiple Stock Categories

Go to Gateway of Tally > Inventory Info. > Stock Categories > Create (under Multiple Stock Category)

The Multiple Stock Category Creation screen is displayed as shown:

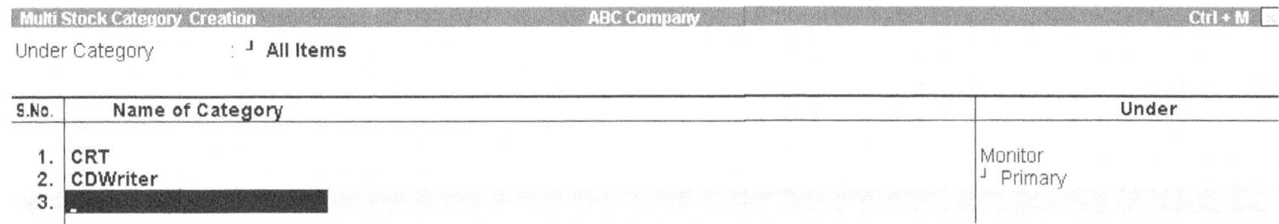

Fig. 4.30 Creating Multi Stock Category

A brief description of each field in the Multi Stock Category Creation screen is given below:

Under Category

This field will display the List of Categories. You can select a category for which a multiple sub-category can be created.

If you select All Items in List of categories, selection of parent category Under column is possible during creation of sub-category.

If you select specific category in List of Categories, that category will get populated automatically whenever creation of sub-category and cursor skips Under column.

Name of the category

Specify the name of the Stock Category.

Under

If you have select All Items in Under Category, you must specify a parent category in this column.

Buttons specific to Multi Stock Category screen:

Buttons	*Short Cut Keys*	*Description and Use*
F4: Parent	F4	Allows you to change the parent for all Categories.
G: Groups	CTRL+G	Allows you to Create a Multi Stock Group.
I: Items	CTRL+I	Allows you to Create a Multi Stock Item.
O: Godown	CTRL+O	Allows you to Create a Multi Godown.

Displaying a Stock Category

You can display a Stock category in Single and Multiple mode.

Displaying a Single Stock Category

Go to Gateway of Tally > Inventory Info. > Stock Categories > Display (under Single Stock Category)

Stock Category Display
Name : CRT
Under : Monitor

Select the Category for which you want to view the display details from the List of Categories.

The Stock Category Display screen shows the details entered in Stock Category Master.

Buttons specific to stock Category Display mode:

Buttons	*Short Cut Keys*	*Description and Use*
G: Group	CTRL+G	Allows you to Display a Stock Group.

I: Item	CTRL+I	Allows you to Display a Stock Item.
U: Units	CTRL+U	Allows you to Display a Unit of Measure.
O: Godown	CTRL+O	Allows you to Display a Godown.
V: Vch Types	CTRL+V	Allows you to Display a Voucher Types

Altering a Stock Category

Go to Gateway of Tally > Inventory Info. > Stock Categories > Alter (under Single Stock Category)

Select the Stock Category from the List of Categories.

The Stock Category Alteration screen is displayed as shown.

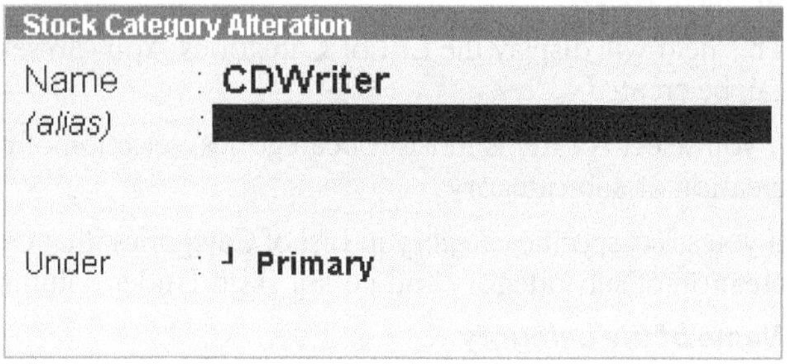

Stock Category Alteration

Name : CDWriter
(alias) :

Under : Primary

Make the necessary changes and click Yes to accept or press CTRL+A to Save.

Deletion is possible only in the alteration mode,. For deleting the Stock Category, Press ALT+D.

Note: You cannot delete a stock Category, if it is used by any sub Category or stock items. In order to delete the Stock Category, first delete the relevant sub Category and Stock items.

Buttons specific to stock group Alter mode:

Buttons	*Short Cut Keys*	*Description and Use*
G: Groups	CTRL+G	Allows you to Alter a Stock Group.
I: Items	CTRL+I	Allows you to Alter a Stock Item.
U: Units	CTRL+U	Allows you to Alter a Unit of Measure.
O: Godown	CTRL+O	Allows you to Alter a Godown.
V: Vch Types	CTRL+V	Allows you to Alter a Voucher Types.

Note: Godown buttons are visible only if you have opted for the same in F11: Features.

Altering Multiple Stock Categories

Go to Gateway of Tally > Inventory Info. > Stock Categories > Alter (under Multiple Stock Categories)

Select the Stock Category from the List of Stock Categories. The Multi Stock Group Alteration screen is displayed as shown:

Multi Stock Category Alteration ABC Company Ctrl + M

Under Category : All Items

S.No.	Name of Category	Under
1.	CDWriter	Primary
2.	Monitor	Primary
3.	CRT	Monitor

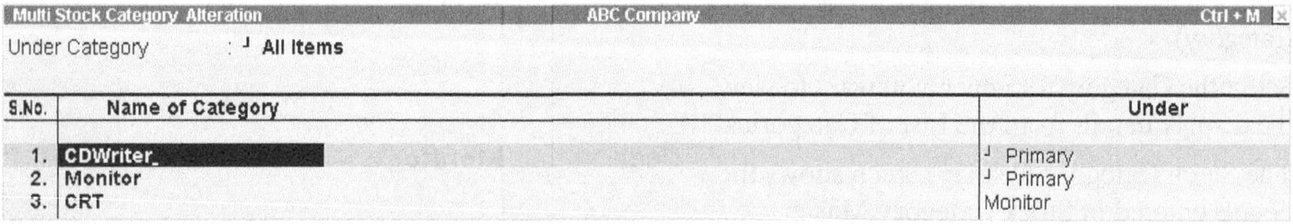

Fig. 4.31 Altering Multiple Stock Category

Make the necessary changes and click Yes to accept or Press CTRL+A to save.

Note: You cannot delete a Stock Category in multiple mode.

Buttons specific to Multi stock Category Alter mode:

Buttons	*Short Cut Keys*	*Description and Use*
F4:Parent	F4	Allows you select Stock Category from Under Category Field for changing the parent of sub Category.
F4: Parent	CTRL+F4	Allows you to select parent [Stock Category] from List of Category. You can able to alter the sub Category of selected Stock Category.
F6: Skip Names	F6	Cursor will not go to Column Name of Stock Category. If you want to alter only the details of Under Column then you can skip names.
F7: Skip Parent	F7	Cursor will not go to column Under. If you do not want to alter parent then you can skip parent.
G: Groups	CTRL+G	Allows you to Alter a selected stock Group in Multi-stock Group screen.
I: Items	CTRL+I	Allows you to Alter a selected Item in Multi Stock Item screen.
O: Godown	CTRL+O	Allows you to Alter a selected Godown in Multi Godown screen.

Stock Items

Stock Item refers to goods that you manufacture or trade. It is the primary inventory entity and is the lowest level of information on your inventory. You have to create a Stock Item in Tally.ERP 9 for each inventory item that you want to account for.

Go to Gateway of Tally > Inventory Info. > Stock Items

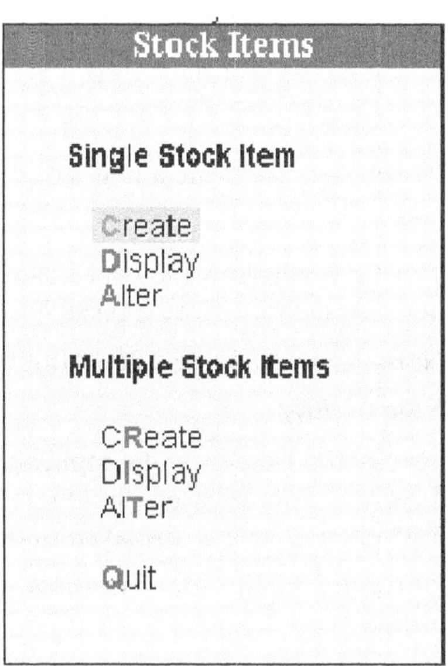

Creating a Stock Item

Two Modes of Creation:

1. Normal Mode
2. Advance Configuration Mode.

Creation of Stock item in Normal Mode:

Go to Gateway of Tally > Inventory Info > Stock Item > Single Create (under Single Stock Item)

Stock Item creation is displayed as shown:

A brief description of each field in the Stock Item Creation screen follows:

Name

Specify the name of the Stock Item.

Alias

Specify the Alias name of Stock Item (if required).

Under

This field will show the List of Groups. Here you can select the Stock Group to which the Stock Item belongs. By default, Primary Stock Group appears in this field.

Stock Item Creation			ABC Company
Name : **Brand A - 19" TFT**			
(alias) :			
Under : **Brand A**		**Tax Information**	
Units : **Nos.**		Rate of Duty (eg 5) : **16.50**	
		Tariff Classification :	
	Quantity	**Rate per**	**Value**
Opening Balance :	**5 Nos.**	**8,000.00 Nos.**	**40,000.00**

Fig. 4.32 Stock Item Creation Screen

Note: You can create a new stock Group by pressing ALT+C at this field.

Units

This field will show the Unit List. Here you can select the Unit of measurement applicable for the stock item. By default, Not Applicable appears in this field.

Note: You can create a new Unit by pressing ALT+C at this field.

Rate of duty

Specify the Rate of Duty applicable for the stock item. This field is used for the calculation of excise duty or if duty is based on item rate. During Invoicing, whenever you select a Stock Item, the Rate of duty entered here is displayed in the Invoice creation screen.

Note: In F11 Inventory features, if Allow Invoicing is set to No then Rate of Duty field will not be visible.

Tariff Classification

Specify the Tariff Classification for the item, if applicable.

This field will appear only when you specify a value in the Rate of Duty field.

Opening Balance

Specify the details of Opening Stock, if any, for the Stock Item as on the date of Beginning of Books.

In the Quantity Field, specify the stock item Quantity, say 5 Nos.

In the Rate Field, specify the stock item Rate, say Rs. 8000 per piece.

In the Value Field, Tally.ERP 9 automatically calculates the value by multiplying the Quantity and Rate. You can also edit the value, Tally.ERP 9 automatically refreshes the Rate field accordingly.

Note: If Unit field is Not Applicable then the cursor will move from Quantity and Rate Field.

Buttons specific to Single Stock item creation:

Buttons	*Short Cut Keys*	*Description and Use*
G: Groups	CTRL+G	Allows you to Create a Stock Group.
I: Items	CTRL+I	Allows you to Create a Stock Item.
U: Units	CTRL+U	Allows you to Create a Unit of Measure.
O: Godown	CTRL+O	Allows you to Create a Godown.
V: Vch Types	CTRL+V	Allows you to Create a Voucher Types.

Creating a Stock item in Advance Mode

Advance mode means enabling advance configuration and Features for stock item master in F12:Configure and F11:Features.

Shown below are the advance configuration parameters for stock item master under F12:Configure (Master Configuration) :

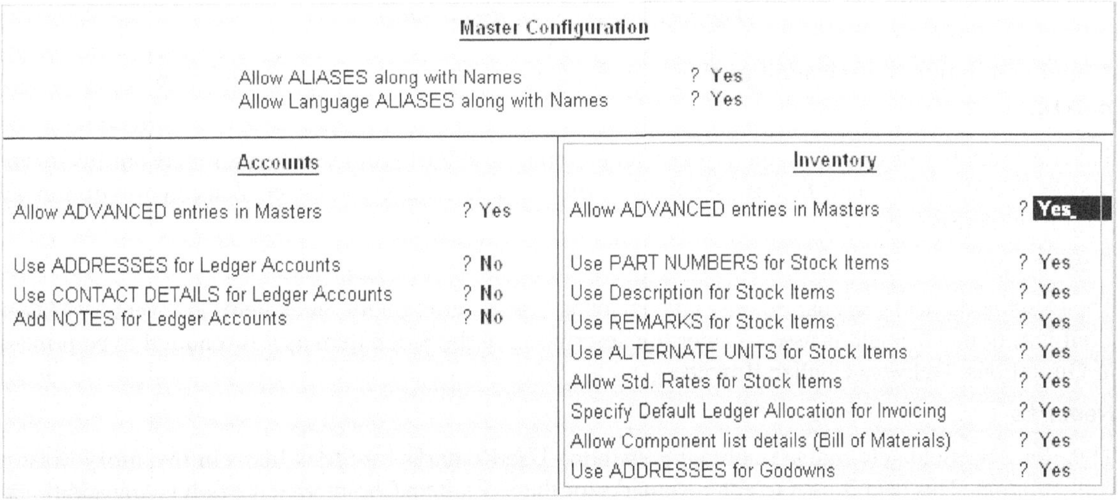

Master Configuration

Allow ALIASES along with Names	? Yes
Allow Language ALIASES along with Names	? Yes

Accounts

Allow ADVANCED entries in Masters	? Yes
Use ADDRESSES for Ledger Accounts	? No
Use CONTACT DETAILS for Ledger Accounts	? No
Add NOTES for Ledger Accounts	? No

Inventory

Allow ADVANCED entries in Masters	? Yes_
Use PART NUMBERS for Stock Items	? Yes
Use Description for Stock Items	? Yes
Use REMARKS for Stock Items	? Yes
Use ALTERNATE UNITS for Stock Items	? Yes
Allow Std. Rates for Stock Items	? Yes
Specify Default Ledger Allocation for Invoicing	? Yes
Allow Component list details (Bill of Materials)	? Yes
Use ADDRESSES for Godowns	? Yes

Fig. 4.33 Configuring Parameters of Stock Item Master

Shown below are the advance Features for stock items in F11:Features:

Note: You can configure the entire setup according to your requirements. According to the configuration in F12 and F11, stock item master fields will get added and removed.

Storage & Classification

Maintain Multiple Godowns	? Yes
Maintain Stock Categories	? Yes
Maintain Batch-wise Details	? Yes
(set Expiry Dates for Batches)	? Yes
Use different Actual & Billed Qty	? No

Go to Gateway of Tally > Inventory Info > Stock Items > Create (under Single Stock Item)

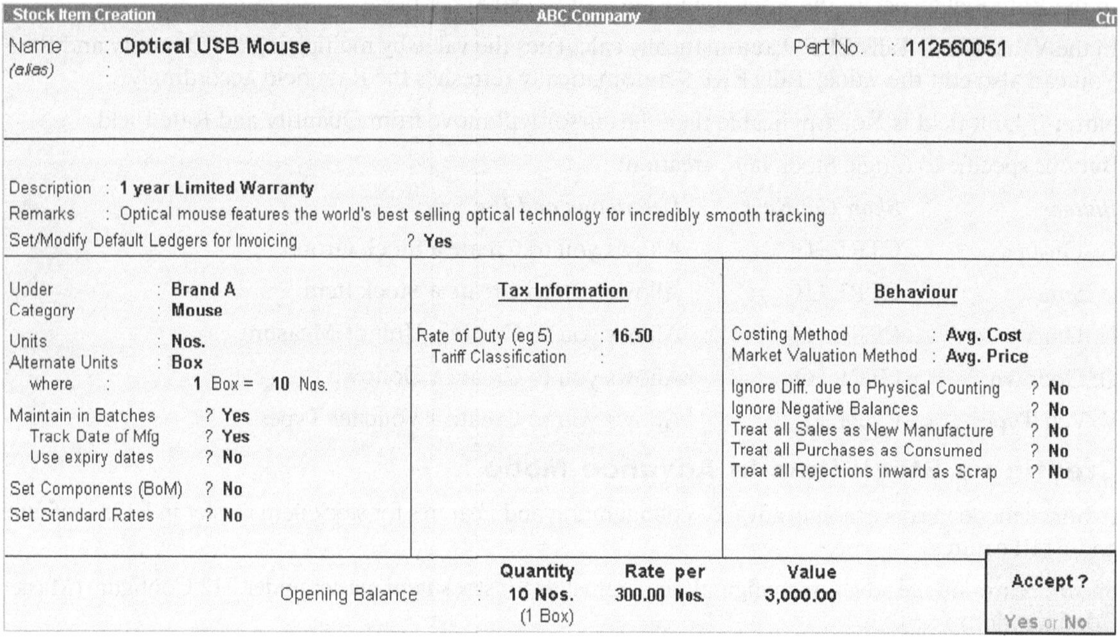

Stock Item Creation ABC Company Ctrl

Name : **Optical USB Mouse** Part No. : **112560051**
(alias) :

Description : **1 year Limited Warranty**
Remarks : Optical mouse features the world's best selling optical technology for incredibly smooth tracking
Set/Modify Default Ledgers for Invoicing ? **Yes**

Under : **Brand A**
Category : **Mouse**
Units : **Nos.**
Alternate Units : **Box**
where : **1** Box = **10** Nos.
Maintain in Batches ? **Yes**
Track Date of Mfg ? **Yes**
Use expiry dates ? **No**
Set Components (BoM) ? **No**
Set Standard Rates ? **No**

Tax Information

Rate of Duty (eg 5) : **16.50**
Tariff Classification :

Behaviour

Costing Method : **Avg. Cost**
Market Valuation Method : **Avg. Price**
Ignore Diff. due to Physical Counting ? **No**
Ignore Negative Balances ? **No**
Treat all Sales as New Manufacture ? **No**
Treat all Purchases as Consumed ? **No**
Treat all Rejections inward as Scrap ? **No**

	Quantity	Rate per	Value
Opening Balance :	**10 Nos.** (1 Box)	**300.00 Nos.**	**3,000.00**

Accept ?
Yes or No

Fig. 4.34 Single Stock Item Creation

A brief description of each additional field in Stock Item Creation screen is given below.

Part No.

This Part number field gets enabled only after enabling Use Part Number for stock items in Inventory Master Configuration. This field is used to enter the Vendors catalogue number. You can also optionally print it in reports/invoices.

Description

The Description field gets enabled only after enabling Use Description for Stock Items in Inventory Master Configuration. This field is used to enter the description of the Stock Item as it is required to be printed in Quotations, Delivery Challan/Invoice.

Remarks

This Remarks field gets enabled only after enabling Use Remarks for Stock Items in Inventory Master configuration. This field is used to enter Remarks for the Stock Item (for internal use only). Any additional details about the Item can be entered here.

Set/Modify Default Ledgers for Invoicing?

This option gets enabled only after enabling Specify Default Ledger Allocation for Invoicing in Inventory Master Configuration. Once you enable this option, a screen will be displayed for selecting the default ledger allocation for sales and purchase for the stock item.

Note: This option is useful only in case of Invoice entry through Voucher Class.

Category

This Category field gets enabled only after enabling Maintain Stock Categories in Inventory Master

Features. This field will show the List of Categories. Here you can select the Stock Category under which the stock Item belongs. By default, Not Applicable is displayed in this field.

Note: You can create a new stock category by pressing ALT+C at this field.

Alternate Units

This Alternate Units field gets enabled only after enabling. Use Alternate Units for Stock Item in Inventory Master Configuration. Alternate Units is another unit, apart from the main unit, which you can use for the Stock Item. This is particularly useful when you need to handle different units at different times.

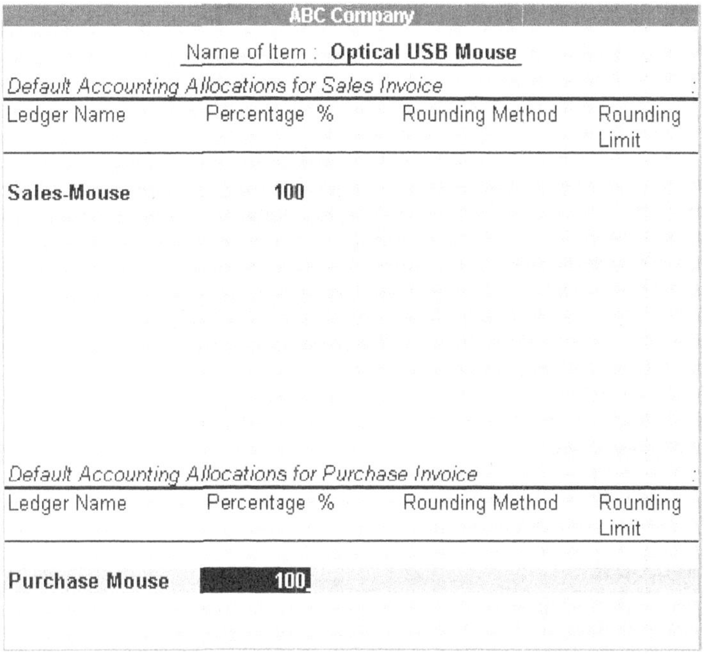

ABC Company

Name of Item : **Optical USB Mouse**

Default Accounting Allocations for Sales Invoice

Ledger Name	Percentage %	Rounding Method	Rounding Limit
Sales-Mouse	**100**		

Default Accounting Allocations for Purchase Invoice

Ledger Name	Percentage %	Rounding Method	Rounding Limit
Purchase Mouse	**100**		

Example:

1 Box contains 10 numbers of mouse. In some case, 1 Box contains 12 number of mouse. In this case, Alternate units is very useful. During entry, you can change the conversion factor between Box and number.

Maintain in Batches

This option gets enabled only after enabling Maintain Batch wise Details in Inventory Master Features. If you want to maintain the batch information of Stock Items, set the option Maintain in Batches to Yes.

Track Date of Mfg

This option is enabled only when Maintain in Batches? is set to Yes. If you want to specify the manufacturing date for the item, set Track Date of Mfg. to Yes.

Use Expiry Dates

This option gets enabled only after enabling Set Expiry Dates for Batches under Maintain Batch Wise Details option in Inventory Features. If you want to specify the expiry date of the item, set Use expiry dates to Yes. This option is useful for stock items like medicines, Food items, etc.

Set Component BOM

This option gets enabled only after enabling Allow Component List Details (Bills of Material) in Inventory Master Configuration.

Set Standard Rates

This option gets enabled only after enabling Allow Std. Rates for Stock Items in Inventory Master Configuration. This option helps you specify standard purchase rate and standard sales rates for the item.

The standards are effective from the specified dates and they continue to be used at these rates until the next date, where the standard rate changes.

Note: Standard Rates can also be used for valuation of closing stock.

Behaviour Group

Once you enable Allow Advanced Entries in Masters Behaviour Group option will be enabled.

Options available under Behaviour Group are:

Stock Item: **Optical USB Mouse**

Standard Cost			Standard Selling Price		
Applicable From	Rate	per	Applicable From	Rate	per
1-Apr-2008	100.00	Nos.	1-Apr-2008	120.00	Nos.
1-May-2008	105.00	Nos.	1-May-2008	135.00	Nos.
1-Jun-2008	110.00	Nos.	1-Jun-2008	150.00	Nos.

Costing Method

This field will display the List of Costing Method for valuating the Stock Item. Depending upon the stock item, you can select the costing method for valuating the Stock item.

Costing Methods

- At Zero Cost
- Avg. Cost
- FIFO
- FIFO Perpetual
- Last Purchase Cost
- LIFO Annual
- LIFO Perpetual
- Monthly Avg. Cost
- Std. Cost

A Brief description about each Costing Method:

At Zero Cost:

Cost of an item is considered as zero. For example, for defective items that have no commercial value.

Avg.Cost:

Periodic system:

This is also known as Weighted Average Cost. The weighted average cost for the whole year is computed as below:

$$\text{Average Cost} = \frac{\text{Total Inward Value for the Year}}{\text{Total Inward Quantity for the Year}}$$

Monthly system:

In monthly average cost, weighted average cost is determined on a monthly basis instead of annual.

FIFO (First-in, First-Out):

Periodic System

Under FIFO Periodic System, it is assumed that items purchased first are sold first under the current financial year (i.e., first lot from the opening stock of current year).

Perpetual System

Under FIFO Perpetual system, it is assumed that items purchased first are sold first across the financial year (i.e., first lot may be from previous year entry).

So cost of goods sold is based upon the cost of material received first in the period, while the cost of inventory is based upon the cost of material received last in the period.

Last Purchase cost

Last purchase cost is Last purchase rate. Cost of goods sold and Cost of inventory is based upon the Last purchase rate.

LIFO (Last-in, First-Out)

Periodic system

Under LIFO, it is assumed that items purchased last are sold first under the current financial year (i.e., first lot from the opening stock of current year).

Perpetual System

Under LIFO Perpetual system, it is assumed that items purchased last are sold first across the financial year (i.e., first lot may be from previous year entry).

So cost of goods sold is based upon the cost of materials received last in the period, while the cost of inventory is based upon the cost of material received first in the period.

Standard Cost

Standard Cost is Standard Rates specified in the Inventory master.

Cost of goods sold and Cost of inventory is based upon the Standard Rates.

Market Valuation Method

By using Market Valuation Method, you can determine the realisable worth of an Item.

Unrealised Profit of an Item = Closing value as per Costing Method – Closing value as per Market valuation method.

Select the appropriate method applicable for the Item from the Valuation Methods List.

Valuation Methods
At Zero Price
Avg. Price
Last Sale Price
Std. Price

At Zero Price

Realisable price of an item is considered as zero.

Example: For defective items that have no realisable value in the market.

Average Price

Weighted Average is computed as the sum of all invoice value / sum of all invoice quantity for the financial year.

Last Sale Price

Item is valued at Last Sale Price.

Standard Price

User specified rate applicable for the current date specified in Item master under Standard Rate is taken as the realizable rate.

Ignore Diff. due to Physical Counting

In Tally.ERP 9, you can record the physical stock as counted, using a physical stock voucher. If you wish to ignore the difference and continue with the stock as per books, set this option to Yes.

Ignore Negative Balances

If you set this to Yes, Tally.ERP 9 ignores the item in the stock reports, in case it has a negative balance.

Treat all Sales as New Manufacture

If you set this to Yes, whenever a sales entry is made, Tally.ERP 9 automatically updates the quantity and value in inward by treating the same entry as a New manufacture or purchase.

Treat all Purchases as Consumed

If you set this to Yes, then, whenever a purchase entry is made, Tally.ERP 9 automatically updates the quantity and value in outward by treating the same entry as consumed.

Treat all Rejections inward as Scrap

If you set this to Yes, then, whenever a rejection inward entry has been made [without tracking number],

Tally.ERP 9 automatically reduces the amount from the closing stock balance. In this case, you need not pass the credit note for reducing the value against rejection inward.

This is used for defective items returned by the customer.

Allow use of expired Batches

This option will get enabled once you enable the Use expiry dates under Maintain in Batches option.

If you set this to Yes, during selection of batches in voucher entry, expiry batches also get included in the List of Active Batch.

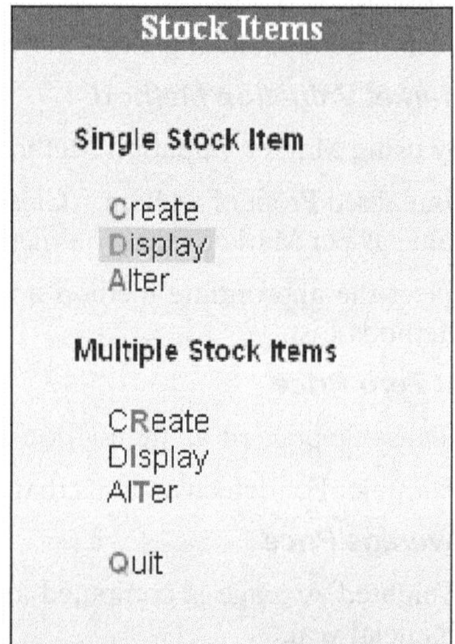

Displaying a Stock Item

You can display a single stock item master and multiple stock item masters.

Displaying a Single Stock Item

Go to Gateway of Tally > Inventory Info > Stock Items > Display (under Single Stock Item)

Select the Stock Item you want to display from the List of Items. The Stock Item Display screen is displayed as shown.

Displaying a Multiple Stock Item

Go to Gateway of Tally > Inventory Info > Stock Items > Display (under Multiple Stock Item)

Select a Stock Group or All Items from List of Groups to display the Stock Item under the selected group or All Items.

The Multi Stock Item display screen is displayed as shown.

Stock Item Display | ABC Company | Ct

Name : **Optical USB Mouse** Part No. : **112560051**

Description : **1 year Limited Warranty**
Remarks : Optical mouse features the world's best selling optical technology for incredibly smooth tracking
Set/Modify Default Ledgers for Invoicing ? **No**

Under : **Brand A**
Category : **Mouse**
Units : **Nos.**
Alternate Units : **Box**
where : 1 Box = **10** Nos.
Maintain in Batches ? **Yes**
Track Date of Mfg ? **Yes**
Use expiry dates ? **No**
Alter Components (BoM) ? **No**

Tax Information

Rate of Duty (eg 5) : **0**
Tariff Classification :

Behaviour

Costing Method : **Avg. Cost**
Market Valuation Method : **Avg. Price**
Ignore Diff. due to Physical Counting ? **No**
Ignore Negative Balances ? **No**
Treat all Sales as New Manufacture ? **No**
Treat all Purchases as Consumed ? **No**
Treat all Rejections inward as Scrap ? **No**

	Quantity	Rate per	Value
Opening Balance :	**10 Nos.** (1 Box)	300.00	**3,000.00**

Fig. 4.35 Displaying Multiple Stock Item 1/2

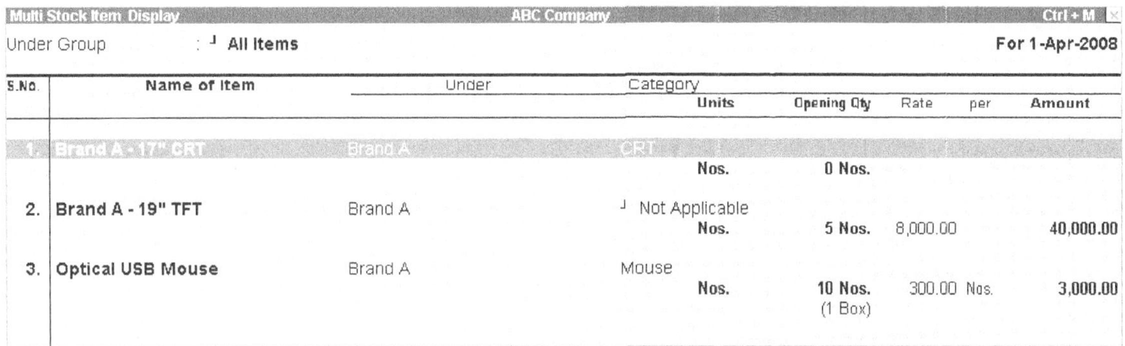

Multi Stock Item Display — ABC Company — Ctrl + M

Under Group : All Items — For 1-Apr-2008

S.No.	Name of Item	Under	Category	Units	Opening Qty	Rate	per	Amount
1.	Brand A - 17" CRT	Brand A	CRT	Nos.	0 Nos.			
2.	Brand A - 19" TFT	Brand A	Not Applicable	Nos.	5 Nos.	8,000.00		40,000.00
3.	Optical USB Mouse	Brand A	Mouse	Nos.	10 Nos. (1 Box)	300.00	Nos.	3,000.00

Fig. 4.36 Multiple Stock Item Display 2/2

Altering a Stock Item

You can alter a single stock item master and multiple stock item masters.

Altering a Single Stock Item

Go to Gateway of Tally > Inventory Info > Stock Items > Alter (under Single Stock Item)

Select the Stock Item you want to alter from the List of Items. The Stock Item Alteration screen is displayed as shown.

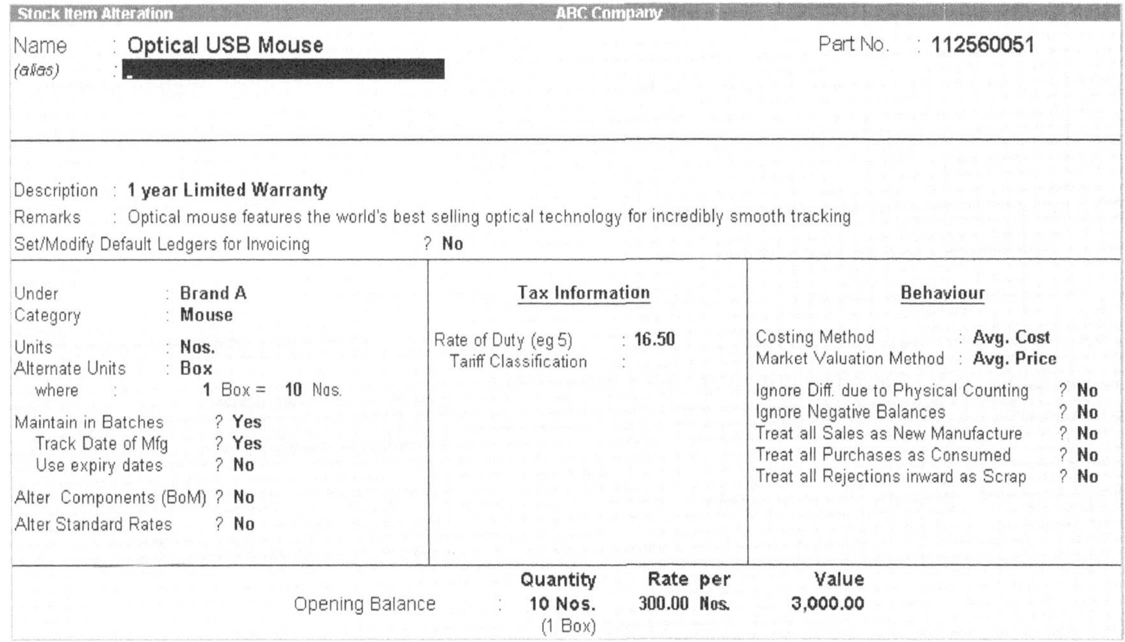

Stock Item Alteration — ABC Company

Name : Optical USB Mouse — Part No. : 112560051
(alias) :

Description : 1 year Limited Warranty
Remarks : Optical mouse features the world's best selling optical technology for incredibly smooth tracking
Set/Modify Default Ledgers for Invoicing ? No

Under : Brand A
Category : Mouse
Units : Nos.
Alternate Units : Box
where : 1 Box = 10 Nos.
Maintain in Batches ? Yes
Track Date of Mfg ? Yes
Use expiry dates ? No
Alter Components (BoM) ? No
Alter Standard Rates ? No

Tax Information
Rate of Duty (eg 5) : 16.50
Tariff Classification :

Behaviour
Costing Method : Avg. Cost
Market Valuation Method : Avg. Price
Ignore Diff. due to Physical Counting ? No
Ignore Negative Balances ? No
Treat all Sales as New Manufacture ? No
Treat all Purchases as Consumed ? No
Treat all Rejections inward as Scrap ? No

	Quantity	Rate per	Value
Opening Balance :	10 Nos. (1 Box)	300.00 Nos.	3,000.00

Fig. 4.37 Single Stock Item Alteration Screen

In the Alteration mode, you can change the item master settings.

If a transaction is entered for that item, it is not possible to alter the units and delete the stock item.

Altering a Multiple Stock Item

Go to Gateway of Tally > Inventory Info > Stock Items > Alter (under Multiple Stock Item)

Select a Stock Group or All Items from List of Groups to alter the Stock Item under the selected group or All Items.

The Multi Stock Item Alteration screen is displayed as shown.

Multi Stock Item Alteration — ABC Company — Ctrl + M

Under Group : All Items — For 1-Apr-2008

S.No.	Name of Item	Under	Category / Units	Opening Qty	Rate	per	Amount
1.	Brand A - 17" CRT	Brand A	CRT Nos.				
2.	Brand A - 19" TFT	Brand A	Not Applicable Nos.	5 Nos.	8,000.00	Nos.	40,000.00
3.	Optical USB Mouse	Brand A	Mouse Nos.	10 Nos. (1 Box)	300.00	Nos.	3,000.00

Fig. 4.38 Multiple Stock Item Alteration Screen

Note: In the Multi Stock Item Alteration screen, you can create an Item by specifying item name after the last item, but you cannot delete an item.

Units of Measurement

Stock Items are purchased or sold on the basis of quantity. The quantity is measured by Units. Hence, it is necessary to create Units of Measure. You can have simple units such as numbers, meters, kilograms, and pieces or compound units like box of 10 pieces [1box =10 pieces].

Go to Gateway of Tally > Inventory Info. > Units of Measure

Creating Simple Units of Measure

You can create Simple and Compound units.

Go to Gateway of Tally > Inventory Info > Units of Measure > Create

The Unit Creation screen is displayed as shown.

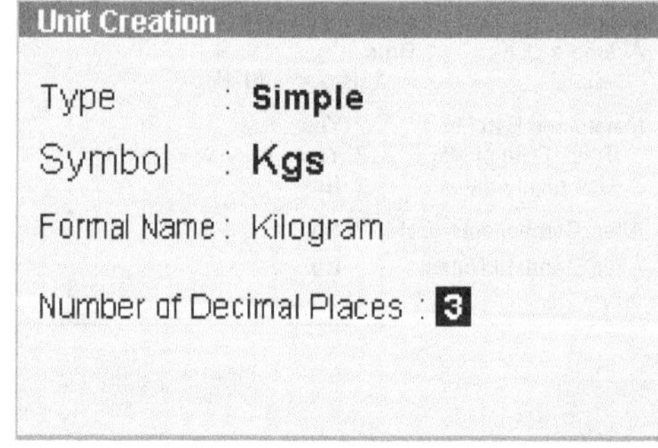

A brief explanation of each field in the Unit Creation screen is given below:

Type

This field will show the Type of Units.

1. Simple
2. Compound.

Simple units are nos, pcs, etc. Compound unit is a combination of two simple units.

By default Tally.ERP 9 will show the Simple unit for creating the unit of measure.

You can select the Compound Units by clicking on that field or by using SHIFT+TAB [cursor will go to the previous field].

Symbol

Define the symbol of the unit, *e.g.*, Nos. This symbol is used in all displays and printouts.

Formal Name

Specify the formal name of the symbol, *e.g.*, Numbers. This formal name is useful during the consolidation of data of different companies, where the symbols might be the same but are assigned to different units. The formal name will be used to match them.

Number of decimal places

In this field you can specify the decimal places for the Units from 0 to 4. This field is useful for Units measured in fractions.

Example:

Kilogram unit. 1.255 Kgs, here 1 is for Kg and fraction 255 is for gram. For this unit, number of decimal places required is 3.

Displaying a Units of Measure

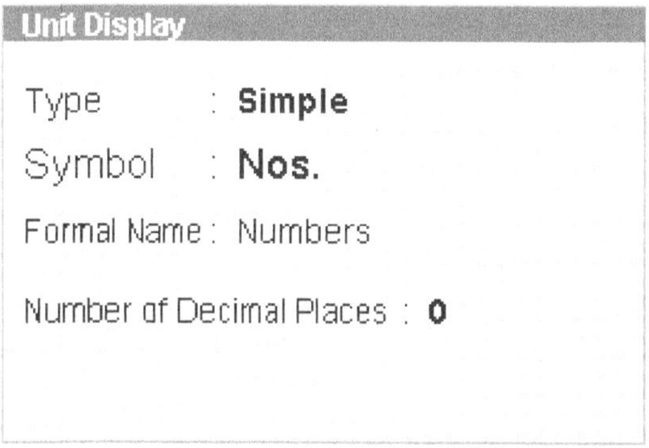

To display Units of Measure,

Go to Gateway of Tally > Inventory Info. > Units of Measure > Display

Select the Unit of Measure you would like to view from the Units list. You can select a compound unit or a simple unit from the list.

The Unit Display screen is displayed as shown.

In display mode it is not possible to make any changes.

Unit Display

Type : **Simple**

Symbol : **Nos.**

Formal Name : Numbers

Number of Decimal Places : **0**

Altering a Units of Measure

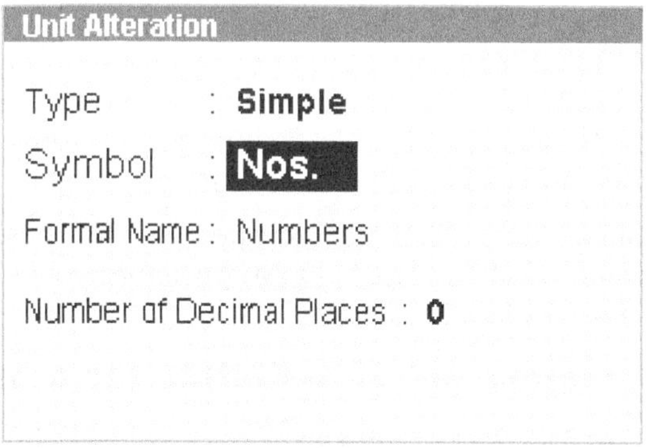

To alter Units of Measure

Go to Gateway of Tally > Inventory Info. > Units of Measure > Alter

Select the Unit of Measure you want to alter from the Units list. The Unit Alteration screen is displayed as shown.

Make the necessary changes and accept Yes to save or Press CTRL+A.

Note: In Alteration mode, you cannot alter the Number of Decimal places field.

Unit Alteration

Type : **Simple**

Symbol : **Nos.**

Formal Name : Numbers

Number of Decimal Places : **0**

You can delete a Unit of Measure from this screen by pressing Alt + D. However, you cannot delete a Unit of Measure that is part of a compound measure. You must delete the compound measure first.

Creating Compound Units of Measure

A Compound Unit is a relation between two Simple Units. Hence, before you create a Compound Unit, ensure that you have already created two Simple Units.

Example:

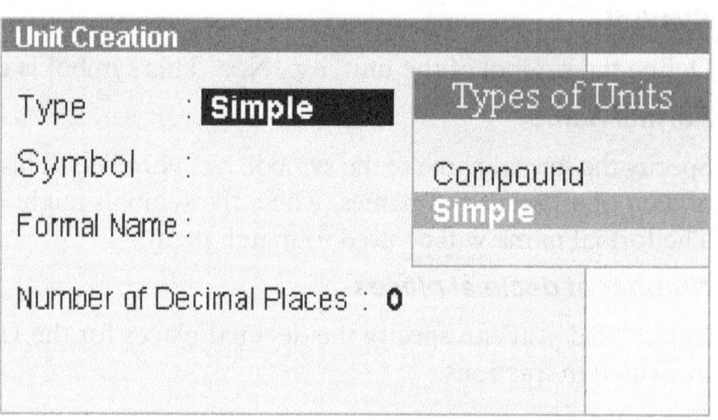

To Create Compound unit – Doz (Dozen) of 12 Nos (Numbers), you have to create two simple units, Doz (Dozen) and Nos (Numbers) and set the conversion factor as 12.

Go to Gateway of Tally > Inventory Info > Units of Measure > Create.

The Unit Creation screen is displayed as shown. Now Click on Type field or Press SHIFT + TAB or Press Backspace Key.

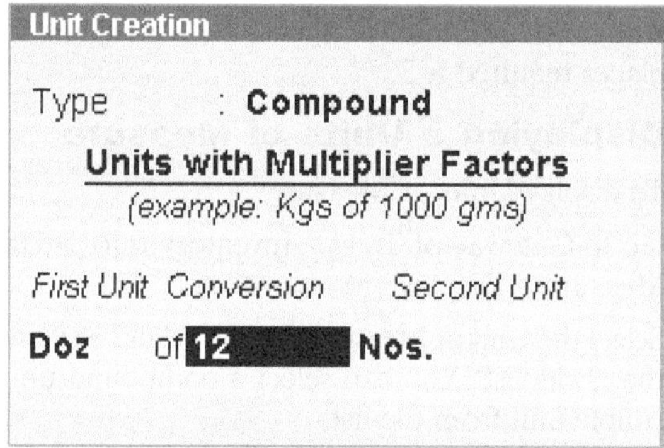

Select Compound from the Types of Units and press Enter. The Conversion field will be displayed for creating Compound unit.

Field Information:

First unit: Select the First unit from the Units List. In the above example, Dozen will be the First Unit.

Conversion: Specify the conversion Factor. In the above example, Conversion factor will be 12.

Second Unit: Specify the Second Unit from the Units List. In the above example, Number will be the Second Unit. This unit is also called Tail Unit.

Use CTRL + A or Accept the Screen for Saving of Compound Unit Creation.

Bill of Materials

A Bill of Materials is a list of constituent items along with quantity details that can be allotted for the manufacture of a certain product, by-product or likewise. This facilitates immediate reduction in stock of the item automatically. This process of listing the items that make up another item is made possible in Tally by enabling the Bill of Materials Facility.

Bill of Material (BoM) is created only for those items that are being assembled in-house. For trading items, you do not need a BoM. Therefore, you need to specify a BoM at the time of creating a Stock Item or when altering its master.

Creating Bill of Materials for a Stock Item

This is useful for manufacturing organisations and can be set up through F12: Configure. The Bill of Materials option is displayed in the Stock Item Creation screen only after entering a unit of measure in the Units field.

1. Go to Gateway of Tally > F12: Configure > Select Accts/Inventory Info > Set Allow Component List Details (Bill of Materials) to Yes

   OR

2. Go to Gateway of Tally > Inventory Info > Stock Items > Create > Press F12:Configure (Stock Item Configuration) and set Allow Component List Details (Bill of Materials) to Yes.

Master Configuration

Allow ALIASES along with Names	? Yes
Allow Language ALIASES along with Names	? Yes

Accounts		Inventory	
Allow ADVANCED entries in Masters	? Yes	Allow ADVANCED entries in Masters	? No
Use ADDRESSES for Ledger Accounts	? Yes	Use PART NUMBERS for Stock Items	? No
Use CONTACT DETAILS for Ledger Accounts	? Yes	Use Description for Stock Items	? No
Add NOTES for Ledger Accounts	? Yes	Use REMARKS for Stock Items	? No
		Use ALTERNATE UNITS for Stock Items	? No
		Allow Std. Rates for Stock Items	? No
		Specify Default Ledger Allocation for Invoicing	? No
		Allow Component list details (Bill of Materials)	? Yes
		Use ADDRESSES for Godowns	? No

Fig. 4.39 Allowing Bill of Materials in Master Configuration

A Bill of Material should be available while manufacturing an item. This is done through a stock journal. It is advisable to create a new voucher type, say, Mfg Journal which is based on Stock Journal.

Let us create a new Stock Item Television and specify its BoM.

Go to Gateway of Tally > Inventory Info. > Stock Items > Create.

The Stock Item Creation screen is displayed as shown.

Some information like Batches, Alt. Units etc. depend upon the company features, configuration and invoicing set-up.

Stock Item Configuration

Allow ALIASES along with Names	? Yes
Allow Language ALIASES along with Names	? Yes
Allow ADVANCED entries in Masters	? No
Use PART NUMBERS for Stock Items	? No
Use Description for Stock Items	? No
Use REMARKS for Stock Items	? No
Specify Default Ledger Allocation for Invoicing	? No
Use ALTERNATE UNITS for Stock Items	? No
Allow Std. Rates for Stock Items	? No
Allow Component list details (Bill of Materials)	? Yes

A pop-up list for the components is displayed which has to populated as shown next.

Unit of Manufacture

Specify the appropriate number of finished products that will be manufactured. While manufacturing and recording through a stock/manufacturing journal, record the item in multiples of this unit of manufacture. The components are multiplied by the same factor automatically. You are allowed to alter the components to reflect actual consumption, if there is a change from the BoM.

Item, Godown (Location) and Quantity

- Enter the name and quantity of the component. If there are multiple Godowns or Locations, specify the storage location for the item.
- Enter the options for all appropriate fields for the stock item and accept the screen.

Manufacturing Journal Entry

Go to Gateway of Tally > Inventory Vouchers.

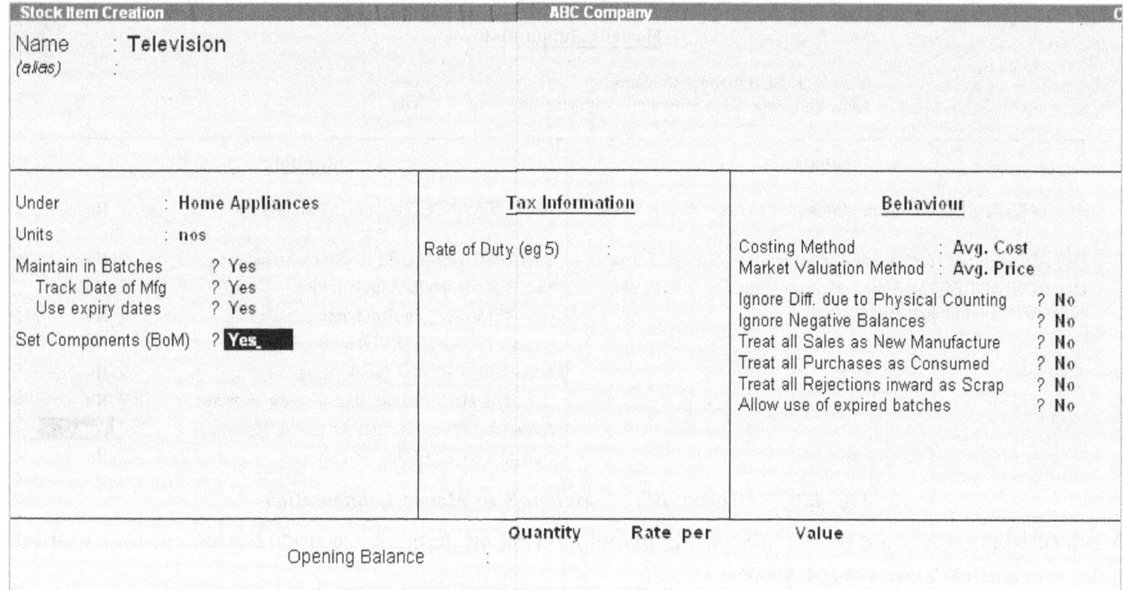

Fig. 4.40 Stock Item Screen

Select the button F7: Stk. Jrnl or press Alt + F7.

If you are creating a new voucher type Manufacturing Journal, a pop-up menu is displayed with the options default Stock Journal and Manufacturing Journal.

Select Manufacturing Journal and the following screen will be displayed.

Components of : Television
Unit of manufacture : 1.00 nos

Item	Godown	Quantity
Picture Tube	Raw Material Godown	1.00 nos
PCB Main Board	Raw Material Godown	1.00 nos
TV Tuner Card	Raw Material Godown	1.00 nos
Auto Amplifier	Raw Material Godown	1.00 nos
Stereo Speakers	Raw Material Godown	1.00 nos

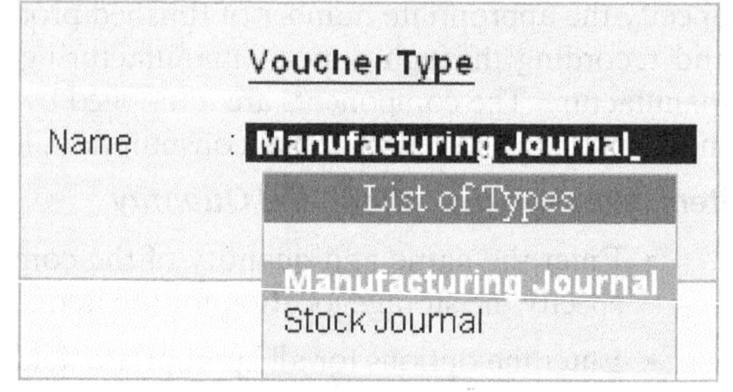

Locations / Godowns

Locations/Godowns are places where Stock Items are stored. You can monitor the location-wise movement of stock by creating multiple Godowns.

Example:

Suppose you have three Godowns, where you store the Goods. In Chennai, you have two Godowns and in Bangalore, one Godown.

You can create Godowns as shown below:

Godown	*Under*
Godown A	Chennai
Godown B	Chennai
Godown C	Bangalore.

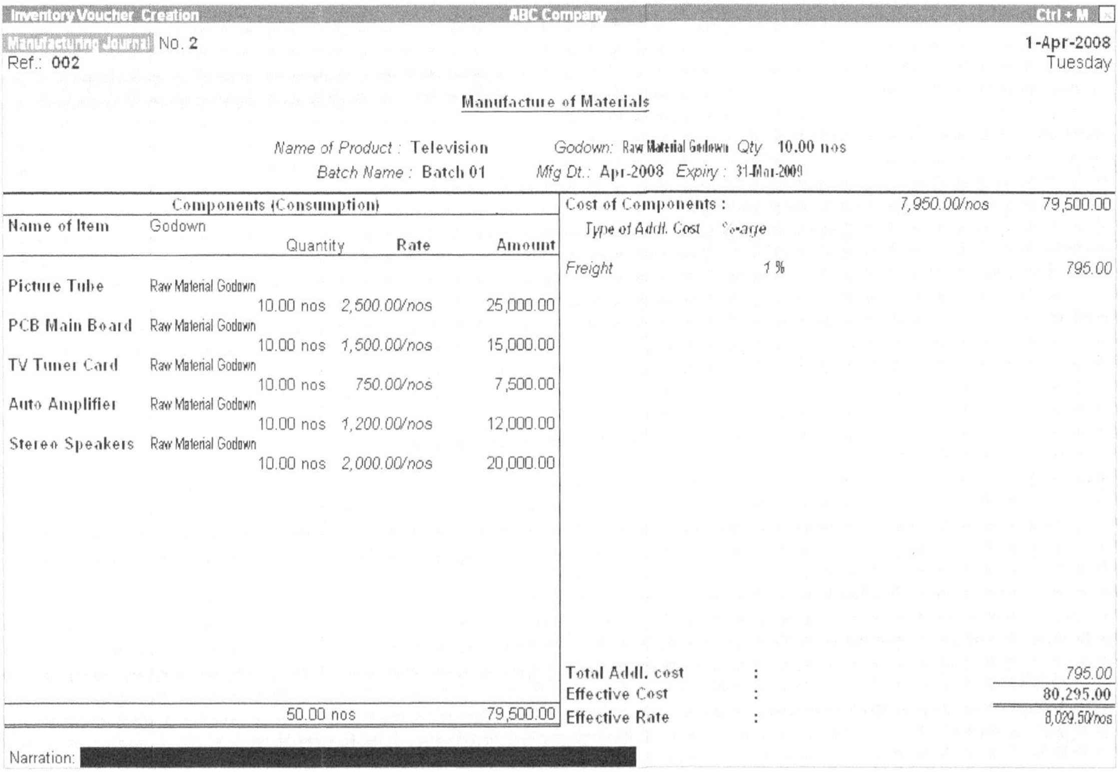

Inventory Voucher Creation | ABC Company | Ctrl + M

Manufacturing Journal No. 2 — 1-Apr-2008, Tuesday

Ref.: 002

Manufacture of Materials

Name of Product : Television *Godown:* Raw Material Godown *Qty* 10.00 nos

Batch Name : Batch 01 *Mfg Dt.:* Apr-2008 *Expiry :* 31-Mar-2009

Components (Consumption)				
Name of Item	Godown	Quantity	Rate	Amount
Picture Tube	Raw Material Godown	10.00 nos	2,500.00/nos	25,000.00
PCB Main Board	Raw Material Godown	10.00 nos	1,500.00/nos	15,000.00
TV Tuner Card	Raw Material Godown	10.00 nos	750.00/nos	7,500.00
Auto Amplifier	Raw Material Godown	10.00 nos	1,200.00/nos	12,000.00
Stereo Speakers	Raw Material Godown	10.00 nos	2,000.00/nos	20,000.00
		50.00 nos		79,500.00

Cost of Components :		7,950.00/nos	79,500.00
Type of Addl. Cost	*%-age*		
Freight	*1 %*		*795.00*
Total Addl. cost	:		795.00
Effective Cost	:		80,295.00
Effective Rate	:		8,029.50/nos

Narration:

Fig. 4.41 Manufacturing Journal Voucher

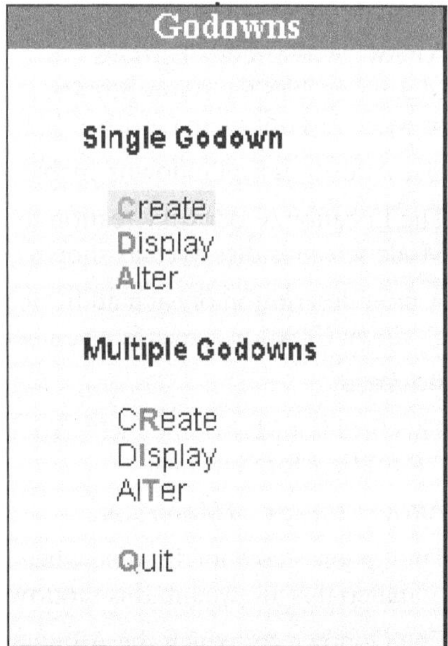

First you have to Create Chennai and Bangalore location and then you have to create Godowns under the respective location.

Tally.ERP 9 has a default Godown named Main Location. You can alter Tally's default godown and create a new one. Tally.ERP 9 permits the creation of any number of godowns, under groups and subgroups to match the structure you need.

Go to Gateway of Tally > Inventory Info. > Locations/Godowns.

Note

1: The term Locations is displayed in the Inventory Info. menu, if International is selected under Use Accounting Terminology of in the Gateway of Tally > F12:Configure screen. If India/SAARC is selected, the term Godowns is displayed.

2: You can create Locations/Godowns only if Maintain Multiple Godowns is enabled in F11: Features.

Creating a Location/Godown

You can create Locations/Godowns in Single mode and Multiple mode.

Creating a Single Location/Godown.

Go to Gateway of Tally > Inventory Info. > Locations/Godowns > Create (under Single Godown).

The Location/Godown Creation screen is displayed as shown:

Godown Creation

Name : Chennai Location_
(alias) :

Under : ┘ Primary

A brief explanation of each field in the Location/Godown Creation screen is given below:

Name

Specify the name of the Location/Godown.

Alias

Enter an alias name for the Location/Godown name, if required.

Under

Specify the Location/Godown under which the Location/Godown is to be categorised. Use Alt + C to create the parent Location/Godown if it is not in the list. Select Primary, if it is not a sub Location/Godown of any Location/Godown.

Creating a Single Location/Godown – Advance Mode:

Advance Mode indicates enabling certain options in Inventory master configuration screen in order to add or remove field which require in Godown Master.

In the Godown Master Screen, press F12, Master configuration screen is displayed as shown.

Godown Configuration

Allow ALIASES along with Names	? Yes
Allow Language ALIASES along with Names	? No
Use ADDRESSES for Godowns	? Yes

Allow Advanced Entries in Masters enables the Allow Storage of Materials option in Godown Master.

Use Addresses for Godowns enables the Address field in Godown Master.

The Location/Godown Creation in Advance Mode screen is displayed as shown.

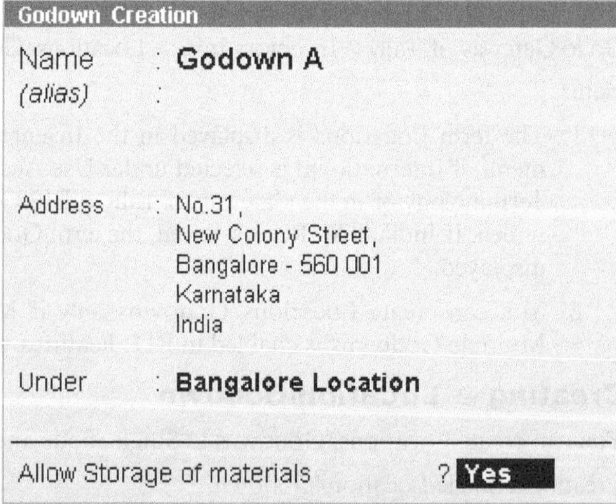

A brief description of each additional field in Godown Creation screen is given below.

Address

This field is a Multi-Line Field. You can enter the Address for Godown.

Allow Storage of Materials

This option is used for deciding whether storage of material is allowed in this Godown or not.

The Godown for which the Allow Storage of Materials is selected as No, will not appear in the Godowns list, during Voucher entry.

Example:

Godown A is under Chennai Location. Here, Chennai is a Location and Godown A is a place where material is stored.

For Chennai, Allow Storage of Materials is set to No, since this will not store the material. During Entry, Chennai will not get listed in the List of Godown.

For Godown A, Allow Storage of Material is set to Yes, since this will store the material. During Entry, Godown A will get listed in the List of Godown.

Creating Multiple Locations/Godowns

Go to Gateway of Tally > Inventory Info. > Locations/Godowns > Create (under Multiple Godowns)

The Multi Godown Creation screen is displayed as shown.

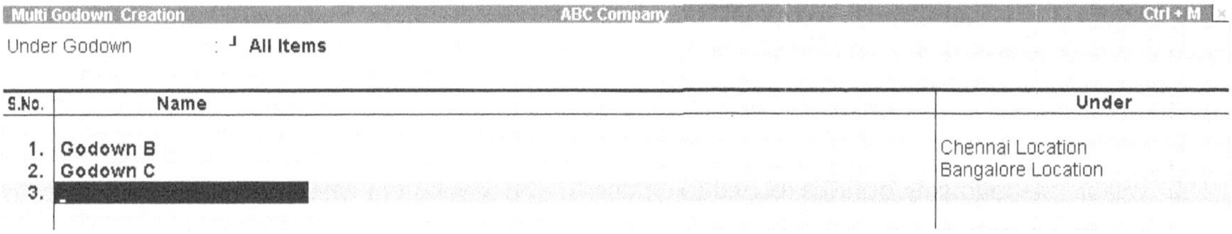

Multi Godown Creation ABC Company Ctrl + M

Under Godown : All Items

S.No.	Name	Under
1.	Godown B	Chennai Location
2.	Godown C	Bangalore Location
3.		

Fig. 4.42 Multi Godown Creation

Under Godown

Select the parent group under which you want the new Godowns to be created. If you select any Godown other than All Items, then all the new Godowns will be created under this Godown. Selecting All Items gives you the flexibility of specifying the parent of each new Godown created.

Name

Specify the name of the Godown.

Under

If you select All Items in the field Under Godown, you must specify a parent Godown here. If you select a Godown in the field Under Godown, that Godown will be displayed automatically in this column.

Displaying & Altering a Stock Location/Godown

You can display/alter the Godowns in single and multiple modes. It is similar to Displaying/Altering Stock Groups in single and multiple modes.

To display a single stock Location/Godown

Go to Gateway of Tally > Inventory Info. > Locations/Godowns > Display (under Single Location/Godown)

To display multiple stock Locations/Godowns at a time

Go to Gateway of Tally > Inventory Info. > Locations/Godowns > Display (under Multiple Locations/Godowns)

To alter a single stock Location/Godown

Go to Gateway of Tally > Inventory Info. > Locations/Godowns > Alter (under Single Location/Godown)

To alter multiple stock Locations/Godowns at a time

Go to Gateway of Tally > Inventory Info. > Locations/Godowns > Alter (under Multiple Locations/ Godowns)

You can delete a Godown/ location via Single Godown/Location Alter by pressing [Alt]+[D]. However, you cannot delete a Godown/location with sub-locations. The lower levels must be deleted first.

Batches & Expiry Dates

Batch details are used to identify the movement of the inventory in batches or lots. Although this is a requirement primarily of the pharmaceutical industry, the same can be used by other industries who maintain or manufacture perishable goods. Many organizations also purchase in lots in order to monitor the lots purchased individually. Hence, Tally.ERP 9 has used the term Batch/Lot.

Batches/Lots are also often used to monitor the date of manufacture, date of receipt or the expiry date.

Activating Batch-Wise Details

To Activate Batch-Wise Details in Tally.ERP 9,

1. Enabling Maintain Batch-wise details and Set Expiry Date for Batches in F11: Inventory Features.
2. Enable the following options related to batches in the Stock Item Master to Yes.
    a. Maintain in Batches
    b. Track date of manufacture
    c. Use Expiry Dates.

Manufacturing date & Expiry date for Batches

This feature is useful for businesses that deal in goods that have expiry dates like medicines, food and other perishables. During voucher entry, the date of the voucher is taken by default as the date of manufacture of the product. This can be changed but not to a date later than the voucher date. Expiry date cannot be a date prior to the voucher date.

Note: The manufacturing date cannot be later than the voucher date. The expiry date cannot be earlier than the manufacturing date.

Entering Batch-wise details for purchase voucher

Example:

Voucher Date: 1-10-2008. Purchase 250 nos. @ Rs.10 each. Batch no. SP-1062 having the manufacturing date 01-09-2005 and Expiry date 01-10-2008.

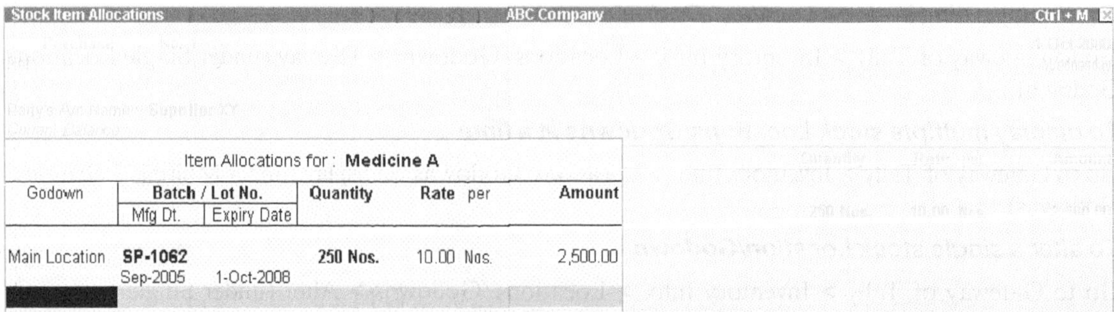

Stock Item Allocations — ABC Company — Ctrl + M

Item Allocations for : **Medicine A**

Godown	Batch / Lot No. (Mfg Dt. / Expiry Date)	Quantity	Rate	per	Amount
Main Location	**SP-1062** Sep-2005 1-Oct-2008	**250 Nos.**	10.00	Nos.	2,500.00

Fig. 4.43 Manufacturing and Expiry Date

In the manufacturing date field, by default it takes the voucher date in the format of month and year. In Expiry date filed, by default it set as Blank. You can specify the expiry date.

Selecting Batch-wise details for sales voucher:

Example:

Voucher Date:1-10-2008. Sales 100 nos. @ Rs.15 each against Batch no. SP-1062.

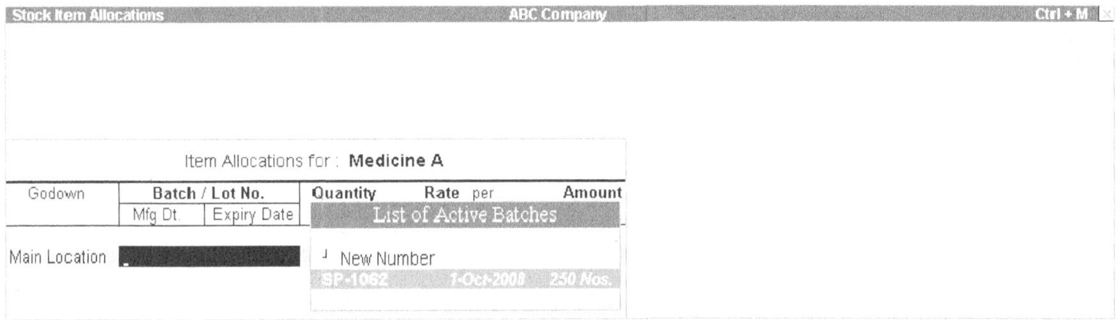

Fig. 4.44 Setting Expiry Date

In List of Active Batches, SP-1062 batch is displayed for selection,since the Expiry Date is not earlier to the Sale Voucher Date. If Sales voucher date is on 02-10-2008, Expiry Date is earlier than the Sale voucher date and it will not be displayed in the List of Active Batches.

This is because the option Honor Expiry Dates usage for Batches is set to YES in F12 Configure (Voucher Entry Configuration).

If you want to list the expiry batches during sales entry, set NO to Honor expiry Dates usage for batches in F12 Configure.

Inventory Voucher Types

There are 18 different pre-defined Voucher types in Tally.ERP 9. Voucher type pertains to both Accounting and Inventory. These are used for recording various transactions according to the user needs.

Examples include Cash Payment Vouchers and Bank Payment vouchers where the relevant predefined voucher is Payment Voucher. You may have two or more sets of Sales Vouchers for different kinds of sales transactions e.g. Credit Sales, Cash Sales, etc.

If a voucher type is created, you can:

- Have the different Voucher numbering methods.
- Give own prefix and suffix details for the voucher numbering.
- Use the Effective Dates for the vouchers.
- By default make some vouchers optional if required.
- Decide to have the Common Narration or Narration for each entry.
- Automate the printing immediately after saving the vouchers.
- Get separate reports for each type of voucher.

Creating an Inventory Voucher Type

Go to Gateway of Tally > Inventory info > Voucher types > Create

Pre- defined voucher types:

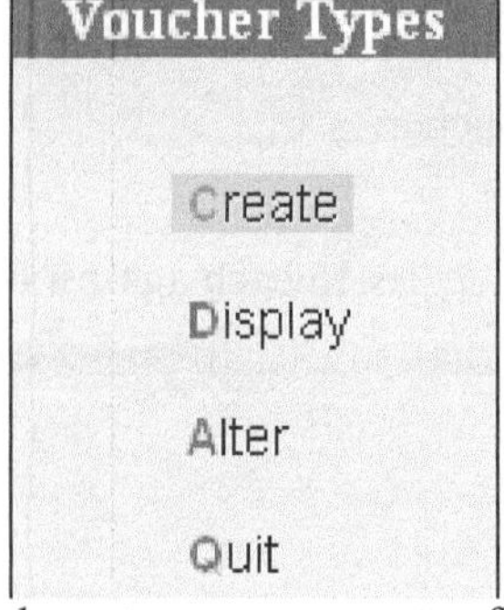

There are 18 pre-defined Voucher types in Tally.ERP 9. Voucher type pertains to both Accounting and Inventory. These are used for recording various transactions according to the user needs.

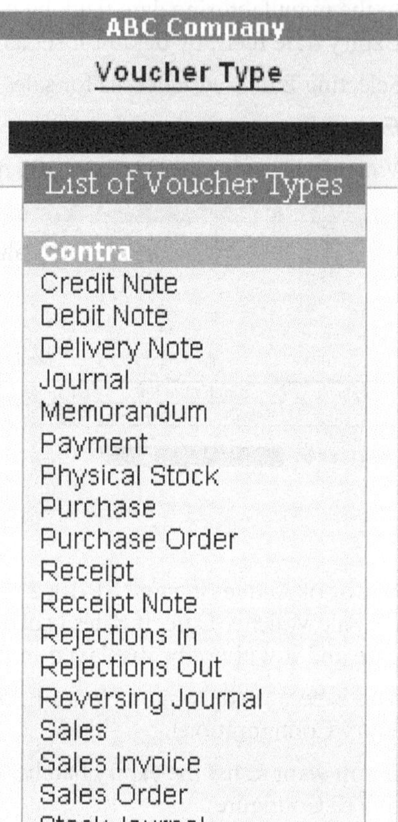

Examples include Cash Payment Vouchers and Bank Payment vouchers where the relevant predefined voucher is Payment Voucher. You may have two or more sets of Sales Vouchers for different kinds of sales transactions e.g. Credit Sales, Cash Sales, etc.

Alter a predefined voucher type

From Gateway of Tally > Inventory info > Voucher types > Alter

Even if you do not need extra voucher types, you would normally alter the predefined voucher types to customize them according to your needs, e.g., to control their numbers.

Creating a Manufacturing Journal Voucher Type

Go to Gateway of Tally > Inventory Info > Voucher Types > Create

Name

Enter the name of the Voucher for ex: Manufacturing Journal.

Type of Voucher

Select Stock Journal from the List of Voucher Types.

Method of Voucher Numbering

You can select the method of voucher numbering as required.

Use Advance Configuration

Enable the options as required.

Use a Manufacturing Journal

Set this option to Yes. Once this option is set to Yes, you will be able to pass the manufacturing Journal.

You can also alter the existing Stock Journal Voucher type and set Use as a Manufacturing Journal to Yes.

Go to Gateway of Tally > Inventory Info > Voucher type > Alter > Stock Journal

Note : Once the Stock Journal is set for Use as a Stock Journal. all stock journal vouchers will be treated as Manufacturing journals.

Inventory Voucher Class

Inventory Voucher Classes are used to automate Inventory Allocations in transactions. It is a table for

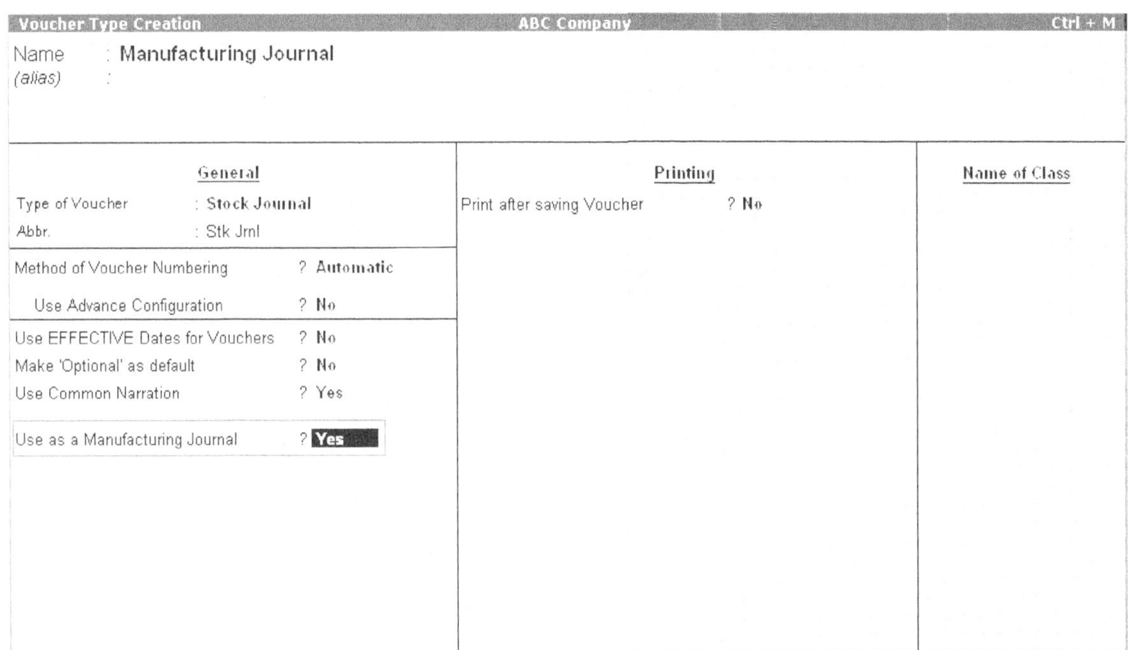

Fig. 4.45 Manufacturing Journal Voucher Type

predefining the entries to make Invoice entry a simple task. This is particularly useful in Stock Journals where the transfer of materials from one godown to another and vice versa has to be updated without updating the books of Accounts.

Creating Stock Journal Voucher Class

Stock Journal classes allow you to handle transfers from one location (Godown) to another, for companies having Multi-Location Inventory and at least two location/Godowns. Once the class is selected, you will need to specify the Destination and provide the list of items to be transferred. Through this class all items/batches thus selected will be exactly mirrored to the destination, including Batch Number, Rate and Value.

The user can either alter the existing Stock Journal or create a new voucher type based on the requirements.

Go to Accounts Info > Voucher Types > alter > Stock Journal.

Enter a name in the field Name of Class. (*e.g.*, Transfer).

Class: The Transfer screen is displayed. To create a class for inter-godown transfer, set the option Use Class for Inter-Godown Transfer to Yes.

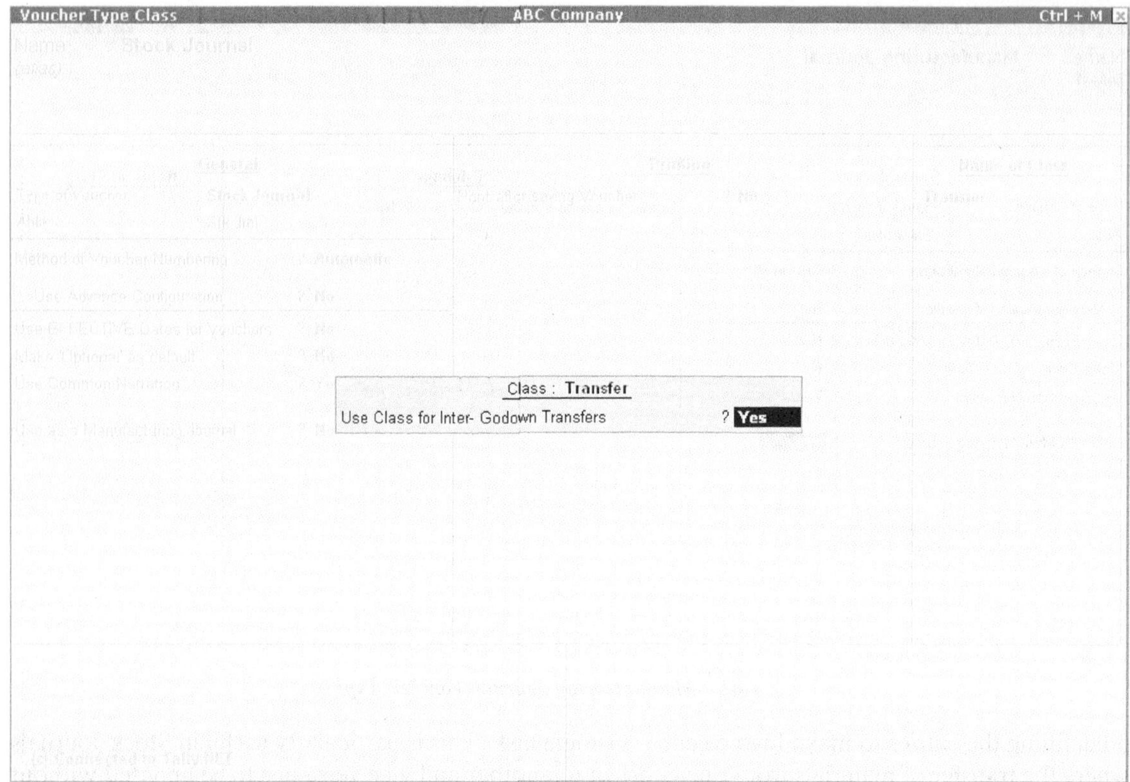

Fig. 4.46 Creating Stock Journal Voucher Class

5 Maintaining Company in Tally.ERP 9

Creating a Company

Creating a Company involves providing basic information about the company whose books of accounts are to be maintained in Tally.ERP 9.

```
Go to Gateway of Tally > (Alt+F3) Company Info. > Create Company
```

The Company Creation screen appears as shown :

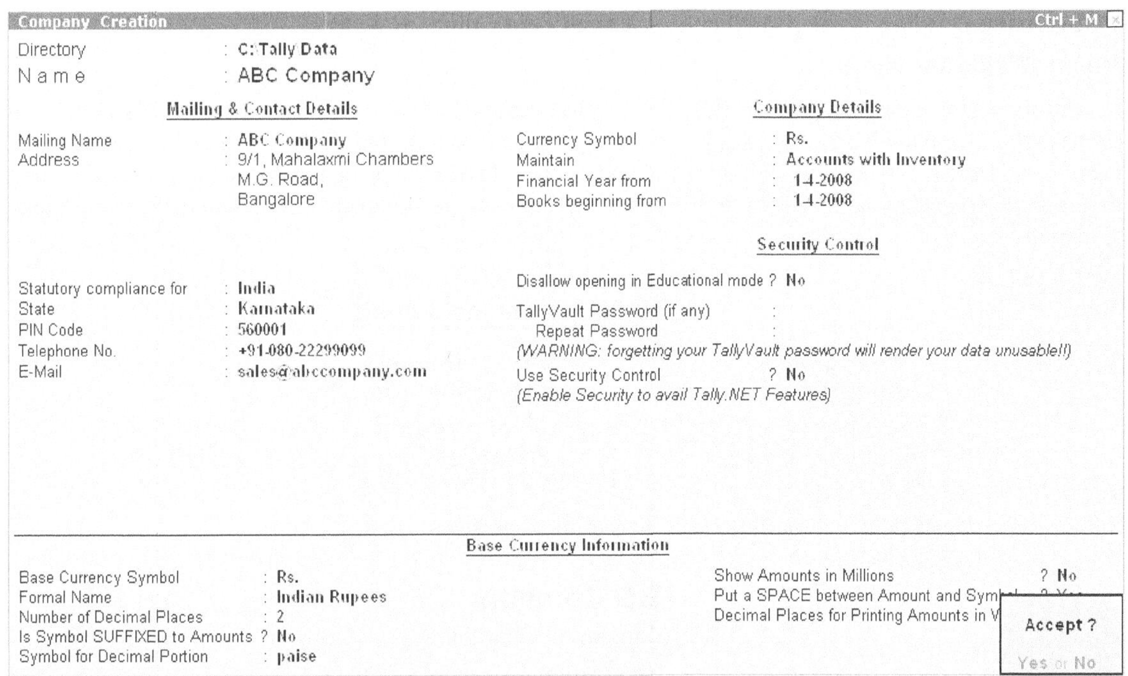

Fig. 5.1 Company Creation

A detailed explanation on each field is given:

Directory

The data path where you want the company to be created is specified in the Directory field.

This field is skipped by default when you create the company in the data path given in the Tally.INI file. If you want to change it, use the backspace key and modify it to the path required.

This is referred to as the Tally Anywhere concept – which is the ability to create/load companies in separate directories. The Directory field is displayed while selecting Select, Create, Backup, Restore and

Rewrite options for a company. By default, the cursor will skip the field, presuming that you wish to use the default data directory for your work. You may press Backspace to give a new path and work from there.

For example, the default Tally.ERP 9 data directory could be C:\TALLY.ERP\DATA. You may now wish to create a new company on C:\TALLY.ERP\PERSONAL, and some other companies on C:\TALLY.ERP\BRANCHES. The next time, the default directory displays C:\TALLY.ERP\DATA, and if you wish to work on the data of your branches, press Backspace and enter C:\TALLY.ERP\BRANCHES for the directory name. This displays the companies whose data is stored in that location in the List of Companies. You can even give the path of a network server or any other storage device.

Name

Enter the name of the company whose books are being opened. If you are a professional accountant and are maintaining the books of your clients, give the Client Company's name.

Mailing Name and Address

In addition to the Company Name, Tally.ERP 9 provides the facility to enter the Mailing Name field. It displays the Company Name by default. You may change it as required, if the mailing name is different from the Company Name. The mailing name and address details are picked up for inclusion in any report that needs the company name and address as heading. For example: Balance Sheets, Statement of Accounts, and so on.

Mailing & Contact Details

Mailing Name : **ABC Company**
Address : 9/1, Mahalaxmi Chambers
M.G. Road,
Bangalore

Tally.ERP's reports print the mailing name and address as given:

ABC Company
9/1, Mahalaxmi Chambers
M.G Road,
Bangalore

Tally.ERP 9 does NOT restrict the number of lines for the address details. Tally.ERP 9 accommodates all the entered information and vertically compresses the same.

Note: In the space provided for the Address details, observe the vertical compression as compared to the Mailing Name field where there is horizontal compression.

You can specify any length for the mailing name and you are permitted to give any number of lines for the address. The information is completely visible.

Tally.ERP 9 handles compressed information correctly while printing. It adjusts the reports accordingly.

Statutory compliance for

Select the Country from the List of Countries. The Statutory Features and Base Currency Symbol are enabled in accordance with the country selected. For example, if the accounts belong to a company in India, the base currency would be Indian Rupees. The Base Currency will appear with respect to the Country selected.

Selecting India from the List of Countries brings up a State, Pin Code and Telephone No. field.

State

You can select the appropriate state from the predefined list.

PIN Code

Specify the PIN Code (Postal Index Number) of the specified address.

Telephone

Enter the Telephone number.

E-mail Address

Enter the E-mail address that will be used to e-mail documents, reports and data from Tally.ERP 9.

Currency

Currency symbol is the symbol of the base currency, that is, the currency that will be used to maintain the books of account.

The symbol Rs. appears by default for India/SAARC Companies and the field is left blank for International Companies.

Maintain

Tally.ERP 9 displays a drop down for the Type of Company with two options Accounts only and Accounts with Inventory

Select Accounts only if you do not have any inventory transactions (suitable for professionals and corporate offices).

However, at a later date (if required) you can choose to alter the information as Accounts-with-Inventory. Select Accounts-with-Inventory, to maintain both financial accounts and inventory.

Financial Year From

In most countries, the books of accounts of a company are maintained for a stipulated period like, 12 months, 15 months, and so on. This stipulated period is referred to as the Financial Year.

The stipulated period of the financial year is 12 months in most countries. Tally.ERP 9 automatically considers 12 months from the date you give here as the Financial Year. For example, if you enter April 1, 2008 as the date, the Financial Year will be from April to March ending with March 31, 2009. If you enter October 1, 2008 as the Financial Year From then the financial year will be from October 2008 to September 2008 ending with 30th of September every year.

Tally.ERP 9 allows you to maintain data for multiple years by changing the period (Alt+F2) at the Gateway of Tally. In addition, you can also specify the date of actual establishment of the company (date of incorporation)

Books Beginning From

Tally.ERP 9 presumes that you wish to maintain books from the beginning of the financial year. Hence, Tally.ERP 9 displays the date given in Financial Year From field automatically.

The date for Books beginning from can be changed, in case of companies, which are incorporated in the middle of the year. If your company is new, you can opt to start the books of accounts from the date of actual establishment of the company (date of incorporation) but close books according to the Financial Year as specified by you. Tally.ERP 9 provides the required flexibility in such a case by allowing you to give the date when the books of accounts actually began. Tally.ERP 9 will open books from this date and close as on the last day of the Financial Year.

For example, if your company is established on August 19, 2008, the opening balances for all the accounts can be given as on August 19, 2008 even though the Financial Year given is April 1, 2008 (April to March financial year). The company's books will begin on August 19, 2008 and close on March 31, 2009, which ensures smooth transition to the next year.

This concept can be applied even when you are migrating to Tally.ERP 9 from any other system or from a manual accounting system on any day during the Financial Year. Close books in that other system on the previous day and start books on Tally.ERP 9 from this day. You are allowed to give opening balances of all Ledger accounts including Revenue accounts.

Disallow opening in Educational mode?

Set this option to Yes, if you don't want the company to be opened in Educational mode of Tally.ERP 9. Else, set this to No.

TallyVault Password

TallyVault is an enhanced security system, which allows for encryption of the company data. Encryption involves converting normally accessible Tally information into unrecognisable information, which can only be reconverted by authorised persons.

Give a password here and repeat the same in the Repeat field. This basically results in the creation of an encrypted company whose information is not accessible to users other than the password holder.

Use Security Control?

Set this to Yes, if you want to initiate a password-protected system to control access to Tally.ERP 9 data. Else, set this to No.

Security Control

Disallow opening in Educational mode ? Yes
TallyVault Password (if any) :
Repeat Password :
(WARNING: forgetting your TallyVault password will render your data unusable!!)
Use Security Control ? Yes
(Enable Security to avail Tally.NET Features)
Name of Administrator : Admin
Password : *****
Repeat Password : *****
Use Tally Audit Features ? Yes

Fig. 5.2 Security Control Screen

If you opt for security control, Tally.ERP 9 offers a comprehensive password based access control to different features of Tally.ERP 9 based on authority lists created by the Administrator. For more information refer Data Management in Tally.ERP 9.

Name of Administrator, Password, Repeat

Assuming the Tally Vault Password and Use Security Control is set to Yes enter the Name of Administrator, Password and Repeat in the respective fields.

Use TallyAudit Features

Tally Audit allows the administrator or an auditor profile user to track changes in accounting information. If you wish to use this facility, select Yes. Tally Audit will be available only to the administrator/auditor, through Display of Statements of Accounts. For more information refer Data Management in Tally.ERP 9.

On accepting the company creation screen, if you have specified Tally Vault password, Tally.ERP 9 prompts you to enter the TallyVault password as appears:

Then Tally.ERP 9 prompts you to enter the Name of User and Password (if any).

After verification Tally.ERP 9 imports the latest statutory masters. Wait till the screen shows that 100% of import is complete.

This completes the Company Creation process in Tally.ERP 9.

An explanation on the fields on the bottom of the Company creation screen follows:

Base Currency Information

The Base Currency Information is found in the bottom frame of the Company creation Screen. Base

Fig. 5.3 Using Password

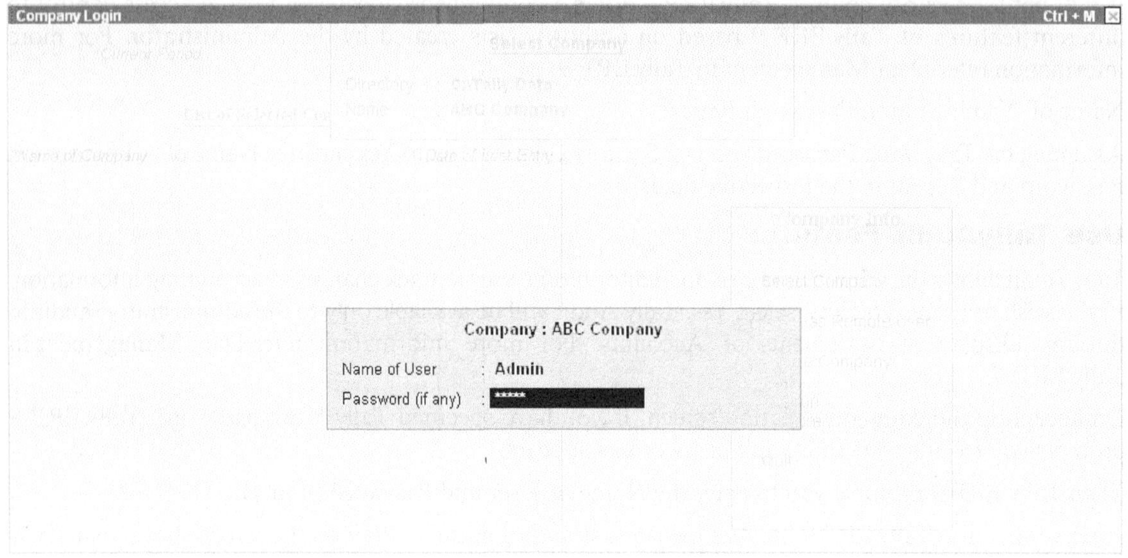

Fig. 5.4 Filling in the Password

Currency is the currency in which your accounts would be maintained. Financial statements are prepared in the base currency by default and these are normally required to be submitted to local statutory authorities. The Base Currency information in Tally.ERP 9 varies with the country selected for Statutory Compliance.

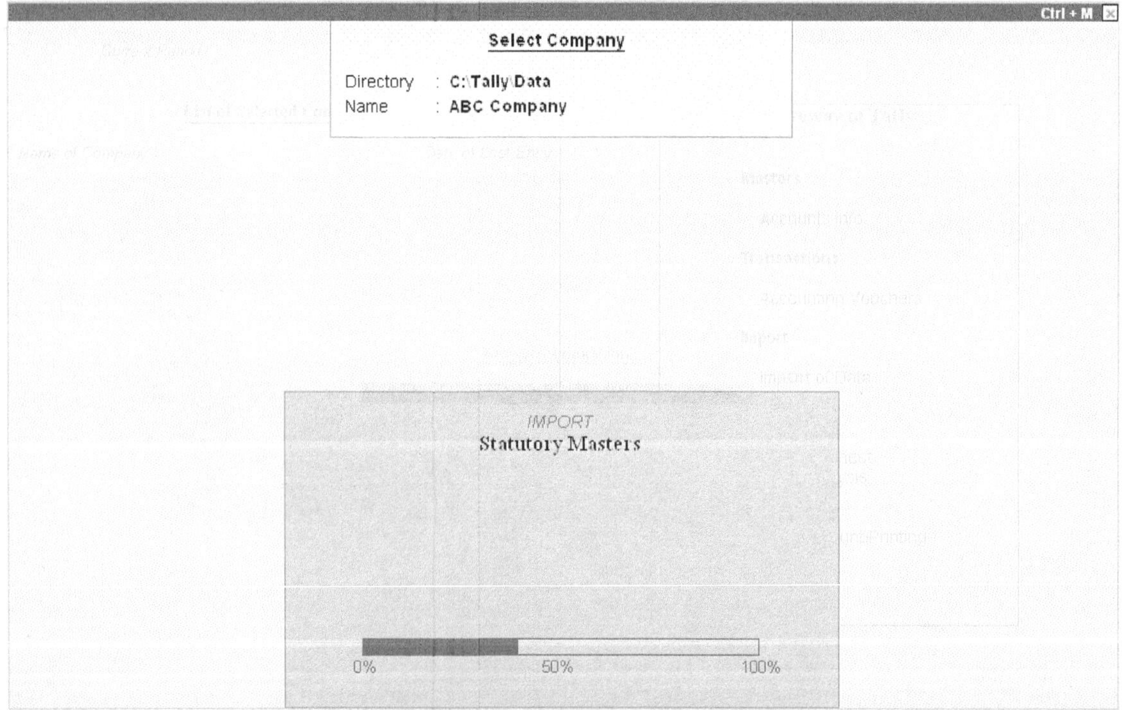

Fig. 5.5 Master being created

You can record transactions and raise invoices in foreign currency; and also maintain bank accounts or ledgers in foreign exchange, when required.

Base Currency Information

Base Currency Symbol	: Rs.		
Formal Name	: Indian Rupees		
Number of Decimal Places	: 2	Show Amounts in Millions	? No
Is Symbol SUFFIXED to Amounts	? No	Put a SPACE between Amount and Symbol	? Yes
Symbol for Decimal Portion	: paise	Decimal Places for Printing Amounts in Words	: 2

Base Currency Symbol

The currency symbol given earlier in the Company Creation screen is displayed here automatically.

Tally.ERP 9 uses this currency symbol in reports, wherever necessary.

Formal Name

Formal Name is the full name of the currency specified.

The Formal Name for the base currency is set to Indian Rupees for Indian Companies.

Number of decimal places

The number of decimal places for the base currency is set to 2, by default. However, you have the option of specifying up to 4 decimal places. Indian currency has 2 decimal places whereas certain other countries require 3 decimal places and so on.

Is Symbol Suffixed to Amounts

For countries, which specify the symbol after the amount (value) – this facility is provided. For example, Yen is specified after the amount (5000 Yen) unlike in India where the symbol is specified before the amount (Rs.5000).

Symbol for Decimal Portion

Enter the symbol for decimal portion.

Show Amounts in Millions

This is useful for companies, which require reporting the financial statements in millions. This is possible only if Allow Multi-Currency is enabled in F11: Accounting Features.

Put a space between Amounts and Symbol

This facility is provided to users who require a space between the amount and the symbol. However, putting a space between the amount and symbol could give an opportunity for misuse incase of cheque printing. Hence, the flexibility to turn this option on and off as required is provided.

Decimal Places for Printing Amounts in Words

You can specify the number of decimal places for printing the amount in words. This number should be equal to or lesser than the number specified in Number of Decimal places field in company creation or currency master screen which will appear in Invoice and Cheque printing screen. For example, if the currency is expressed upto 3 decimal places, the numeric to be printed in words can be restricted to 2 decimal places.

Company Information

The first step to get started in Tally.ERP 9, is to Create a Company. The initial screen appears as shown next: The Gateway of Tally screen is separated into six sections, namely Horizontal Button Bar, Main Area (Ctrl+M), Bottom Pane, Calculator Area (Ctrl+N), Task Bar and Button Bar.

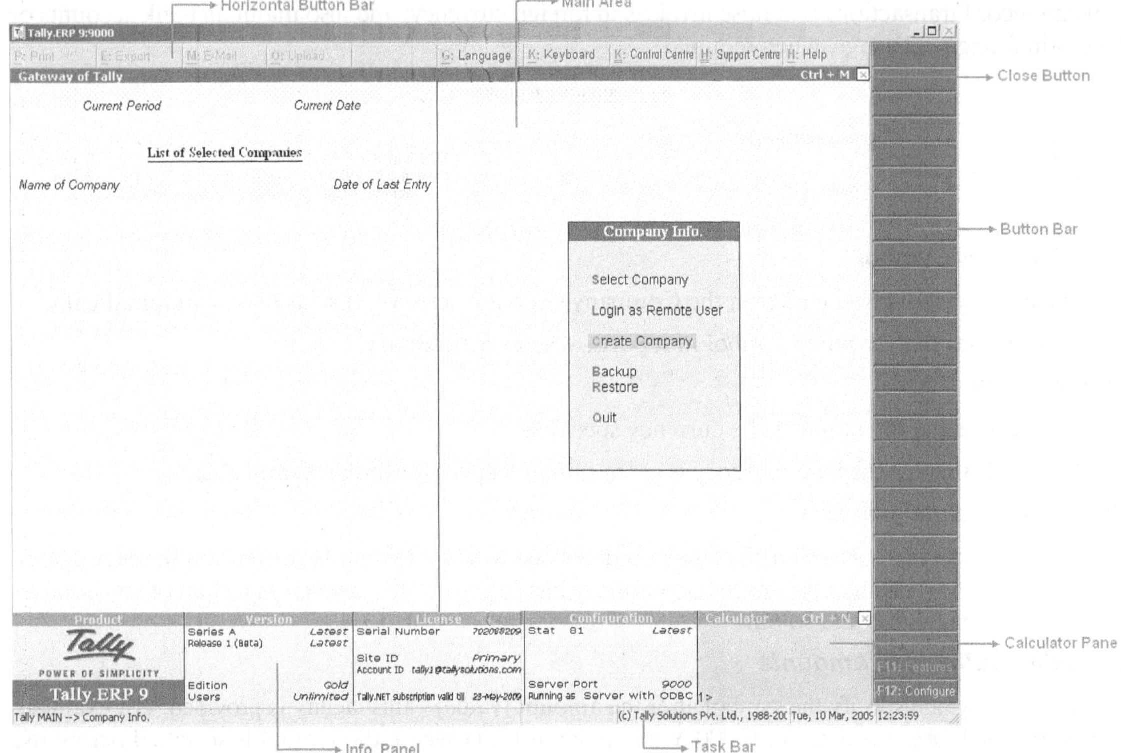

Fig. 5.6 Master Screen with Explanations

The elements of the Gateway of Tally screen are explained below:

Horizontal Button Bar

The Buttons, Print (Alt+P), Export (Alt+E), E-mail (Alt+M), Upload (Alt+O), Language (Ctrl+L), Keyboard (Ctrl+K), Control Centre (Ctrl+K), Support Centre (Ctrl+H) and Help (Alt+H) can be seen in the Horizontal Button Bar.

Control Centre (Ctrl+K) – To login control centre for account management.

Support Centre (Ctrl+H) – To access support incidents and queries and track the resolution status.

Help (Alt+H) – To access Tally.ERP's online context-sensitive help.

Main Area (Gateway of Tally)

The Main Area is separated into two:

1. Left-hand side area
2. Right-hand side area.

The left-hand side provides information on Current Period, Current Date and List of Selected Companies (Name of the company and the date when last entry has been made).

The right-hand side displays the Company Information menu such as Select a Company, Create a Company, Backup a Company or Restore a Company and so on.

Hot Keys

Hot keys are capitalized and are red in colour on all the menu screens. Using the Hot Keys in the Company Info Screen will take you to that particular screen or display the sub - menus within that Option.

Info. Panel

Tally.ERP 9 logo is displayed at the left of the Bottom Pane.

The Info. Panel contains the Version (every time a new release of Tally.ERP 9 is made, it is identified with a different release name like Release 3), License, Configuration blocks.

Version

This section displays the Release, Build, Edition details (Gold, Silver or Educational) and No of Users details.

Click on Version block of the Info. Panel to go to Product Details screen displaying Version and Edition Information of your Tally.ERP 9.

License

This section displays the Serial Number, Site ID, Account ID and Tally.NET Subscription details.

Click on License block of the Info. Panel to go to Tally.ERP 9 and Tally.NET Details screen displaying License, Remote License and Tally.NET Account Details of your Tally.ERP 9.

Product Details

Product Details

Tally.ERP 9 (press <Enter> to visit the TallyWeb and see full details about Tally.ERP 9)

This is 'Series A' of Tally.ERP 9, and you are running Release 1 (Beta), Build 130.

As of 9-Mar-2009, this is the latest Series, Release and Build.

(This information is automatically updated regularly)

Upgrade your installation (press <Enter> to visit the Download Center of the TallyWeb and get the latest programs and other information)

Edition Information

Auditors' Edition (press <Enter> to visit the TallyWeb and learn more about the various Editions of Tally.ERP 9)

This Edition of Tally.ERP 9 gives you Multi-User capability for Unlimited number of users on a LAN. The technical architecture of Tally.ERP 9 will give acceptable performance for upto 10 Users operating simultaneously. Going higher may slow the system down to some extent, and therefore, occasional spurts of larger number of users may continue to give acceptable usage.

This also gives you a range of functionality designed for Statutory Compliance Audit, Tax Audit, Statutory Audit and other related capabilities.

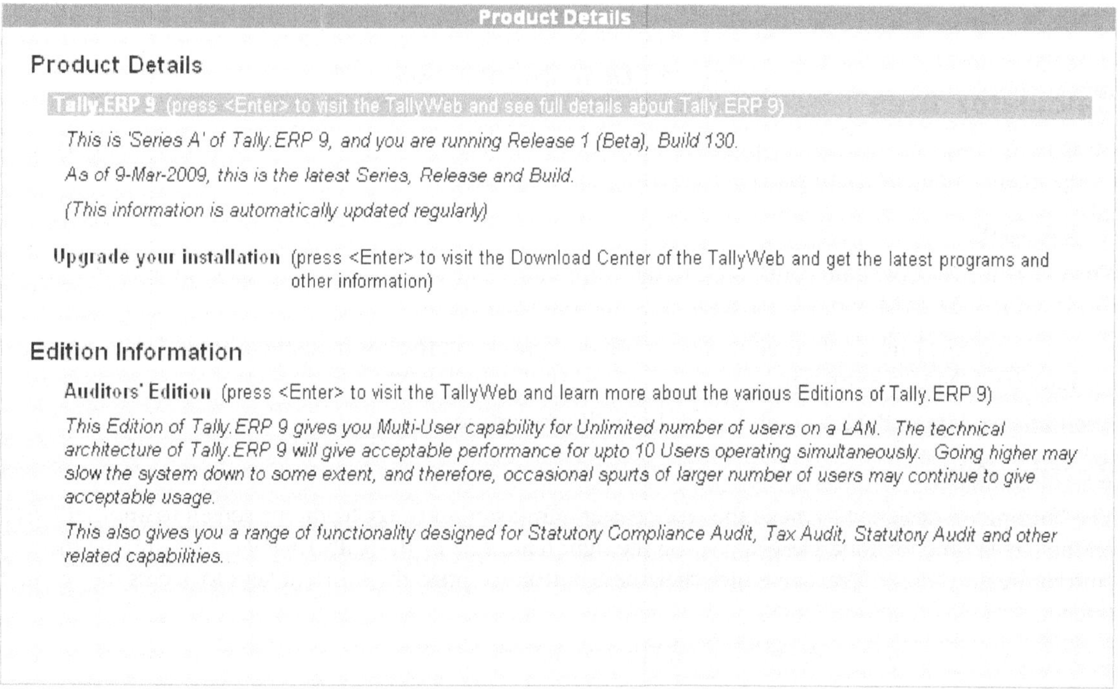

Fig. 5.7 Product Details License

Configuration

This section displays the Stat. file, Server Port and Running As details.

Click on Configuration block of the Info. Panel to go to Configuration Details screen displaying License, Remote License and Tally.NET Account Details of your Tally.ERP 9.

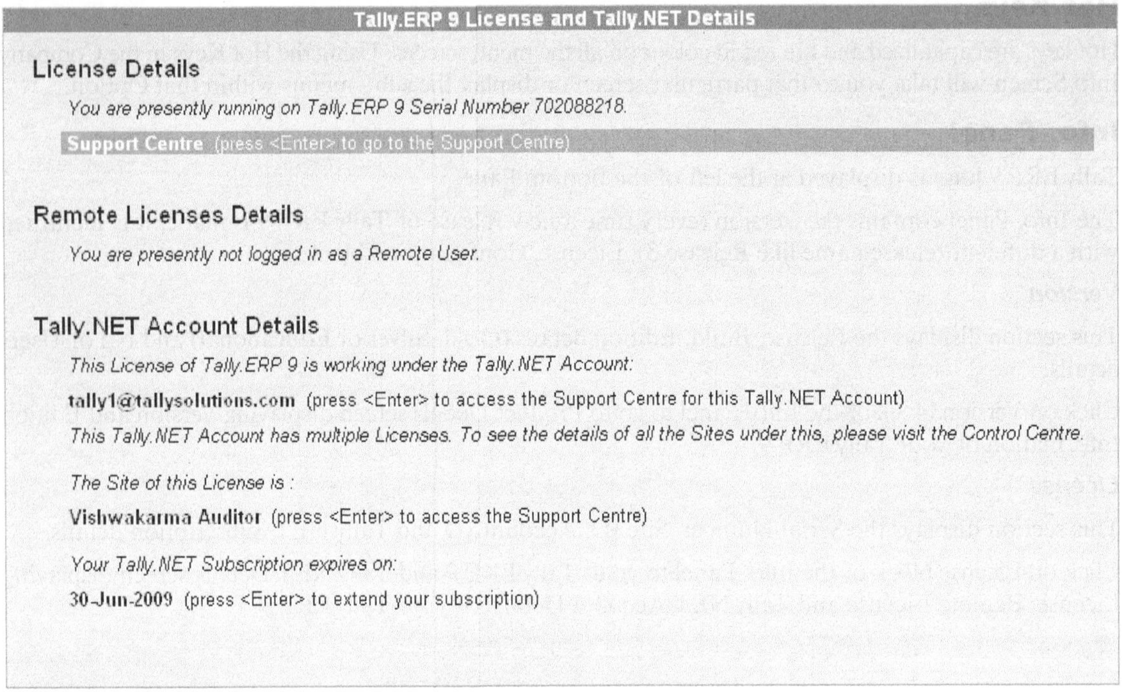

Tally.ERP 9 License and Tally.NET Details

License Details

You are presently running on Tally.ERP 9 Serial Number 702088218.

Support Centre (press <Enter> to go to the Support Centre)

Remote Licenses Details

You are presently not logged in as a Remote User.

Tally.NET Account Details

This License of Tally.ERP 9 is working under the Tally.NET Account:

tally1@tallysolutions.com (press <Enter> to access the Support Centre for this Tally.NET Account)

This Tally.NET Account has multiple Licenses. To see the details of all the Sites under this, please visit the Control Centre.

The Site of this License is :

Vishwakarma Auditor (press <Enter> to access the Support Centre)

Your Tally.NET Subscription expires on:

30-Jun-2009 (press <Enter> to extend your subscription)

Fig. 5.8 License and .NET details

Calculator Area

Press [Ctrl + N] to activate the calculator. Calculator Area is used for calculator functions. Any type of independent calculation can also be done using the calculator.

Task Bar

The Current Date (the date configured in the computer). The name of the day, date, month and year is displayed in DD, MM and YYYY format on the right-hand side.

System Time (the time configured in the computer) appears on the lower-right corner in Hour: Seconds: Minutes (HH/MM/SS) format.

The Path appears in the lower left corner in the Bottom pane.

Button Bar

The buttons are designed to make the work easier and faster and vary from one screen to another based on the screen functionality. They appear on the right hand side of the Tally.ERP 9 screen and the inactive buttons are greyed out. You can either click these buttons or press the shortcut keys to access the relevant screen.

The following are some of the buttons and their functions:

F1: Select Cmp – To select the company from the List of Companies and access data from other data directories on the local system or through the network. You can also access the Directory field by pressing [Backspace].

F12: Configure – To access the configuration settings to manage the information entered in Tally.ERP 9. For example, you can access the General Configuration to set country specific defaults, before creating a company.

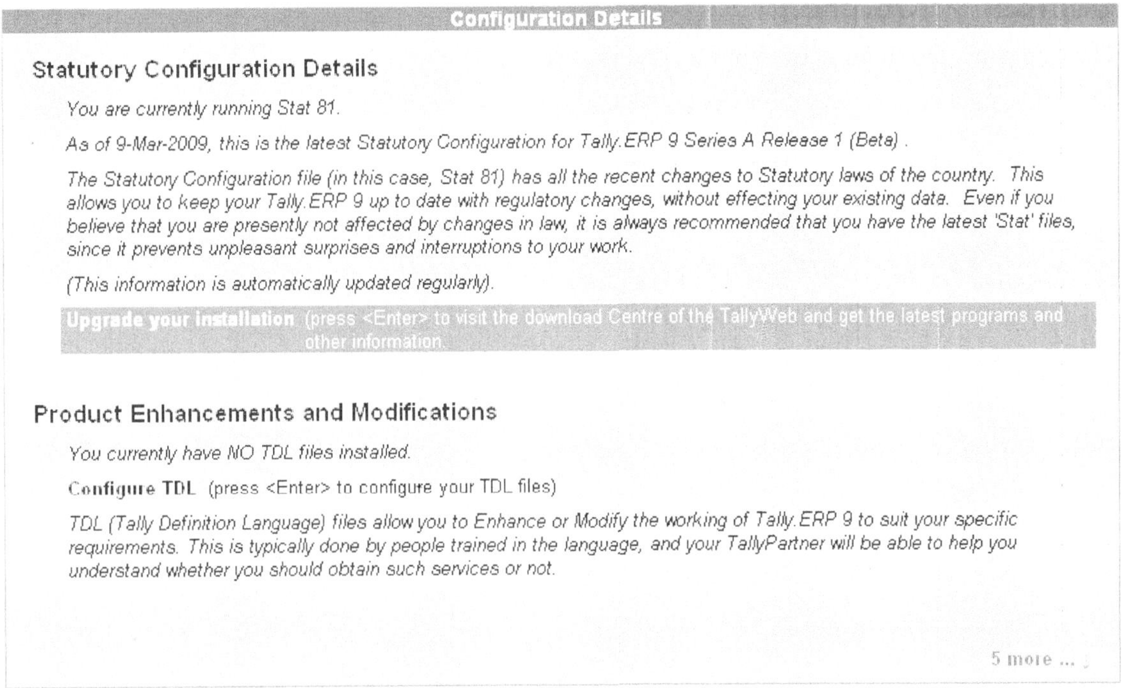

Configuration Details

Statutory Configuration Details

You are currently running Stat 81.

As of 9-Mar-2009, this is the latest Statutory Configuration for Tally.ERP 9 Series A Release 1 (Beta).

The Statutory Configuration file (in this case, Stat 81) has all the recent changes to Statutory laws of the country. This allows you to keep your Tally.ERP 9 up to date with regulatory changes, without effecting your existing data. Even if you believe that you are presently not affected by changes in law, it is always recommended that you have the latest 'Stat' files, since it prevents unpleasant surprises and interruptions to your work.

(This information is automatically updated regularly).

Upgrade your installation (press <Enter> to visit the download Centre of the TallyWeb and get the latest programs and other information.

Product Enhancements and Modifications

You currently have NO TDL files installed.

Configure TDL (press <Enter> to configure your TDL files)

TDL (Tally Definition Language) files allow you to Enhance or Modify the working of Tally.ERP 9 to suit your specific requirements. This is typically done by people trained in the language, and your TallyPartner will be able to help you understand whether you should obtain such services or not.

5 more ...

Fig. 5.9 Configuration details

Buttons where a character or function key is underlined indicates that you have to press underlined character or the function key along with [ALT] key.

Buttons where a character or function key is double underlined indicates, you have to press the character or the function key along with [CTRL] key.

- F1: Press the shortcut function key [F1] to select a company
- F1: Press [ALT+F1] to shut a company
- F8: Press [CTRL+F8] to select the Credit Note voucher
- Ctrl+M: Press Ctrl+M to access the Gateway of Tally
- Ctrl+N: Press Ctrl+N to access the Calculator frame.

Close Button

The Close Button in the upper right corner functions similar to the use of Esc in Tally.ERP 9. It brings you to back to the Gateway of Tally.ERP 9 from any screen.

Minimise Button

The Minimise button performs the standard Windows Operating System's function, allowing you to minimize Tally.ERP 9 and work on other applications. To restore Tally.ERP 9, click on the Tally.ERP 9 icon on the taskbar.

Information Panel

Information panel gives the information about the Product Version, Product License and Product Configuration

Company Info. Menu

The Company Info.(Information) menu appears as shown.

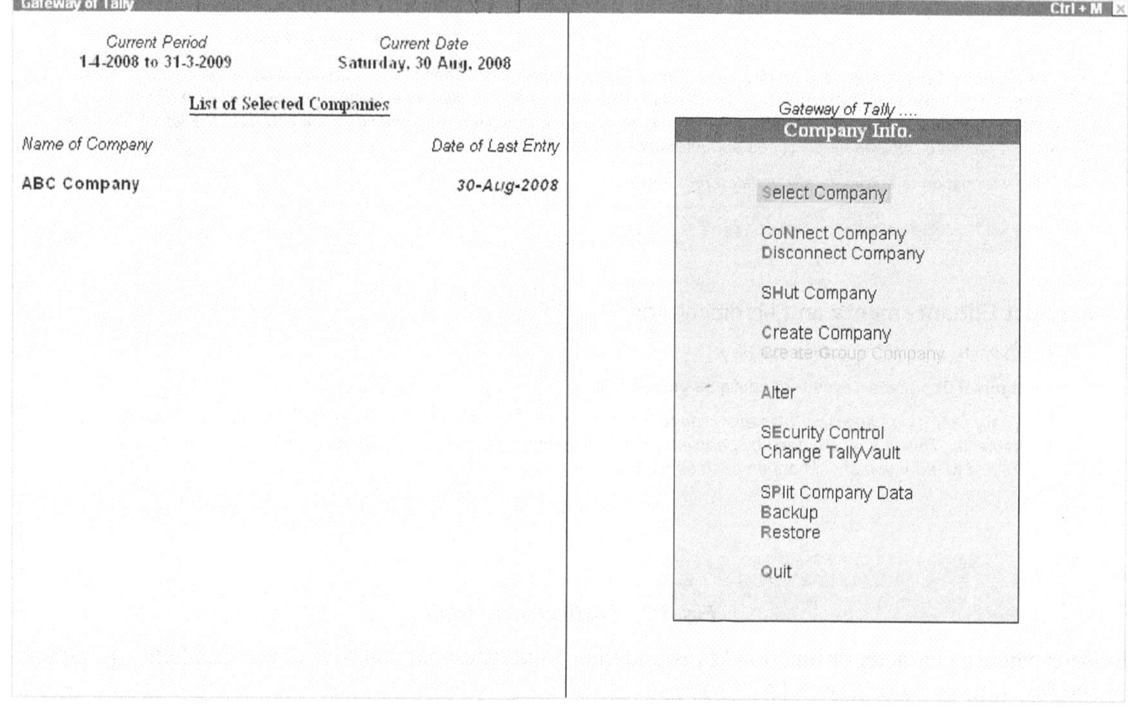

Fig. 5.10 Company Information Menu

The menu options in the Company Info. are as follows:

Select Company

Allows you to Select or load a company.

Connect Company

Allows you to Connect Company on Tally.NET.

Disconnect Company

Allows you to Disconnect Company from Tally.NET.

Shut Company

Allows you to shut a company.

Create Company

Allows you to create a Company.

Alter

Allows you to alter a company.

Security Control

Allows you to create Security Levels and users & passwords.

Change TallyVault

Allows you to secure the data by providing a TallyVault password.

Split Company Data

Allows you to split company data across multiple period.

Backup

Allows you to take a backup of the company data.

Restore

Allows you to restore a data backup.

Country Specific Configuration

The options available are Country Details, Style of Names, Style of Dates, Configuration of Numbers and Other Options.

```
Go to Gateway of Tally > F12:Configure > General
```

The Configuration settings of Country Details, Style of Names, Style of Dates and Configuration of

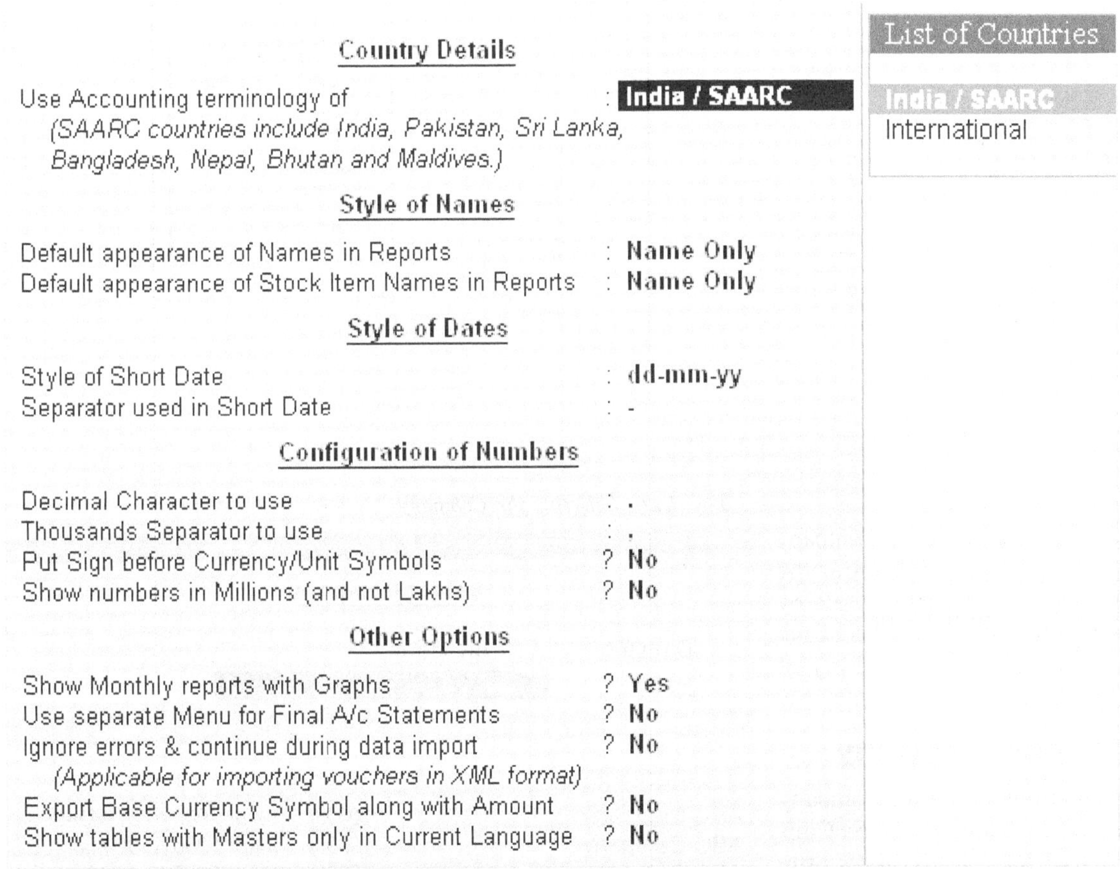

Country Details

Use Accounting terminology of : India / SAARC
(SAARC countries include India, Pakistan, Sri Lanka, Bangladesh, Nepal, Bhutan and Maldives.)

Style of Names

Default appearance of Names in Reports : Name Only
Default appearance of Stock Item Names in Reports : Name Only

Style of Dates

Style of Short Date : dd-mm-yy
Separator used in Short Date : -

Configuration of Numbers

Decimal Character to use : .
Thousands Separator to use : ,
Put Sign before Currency/Unit Symbols ? No
Show numbers in Millions (and not Lakhs) ? No

Other Options

Show Monthly reports with Graphs ? Yes
Use separate Menu for Final A/c Statements ? No
Ignore errors & continue during data import ? No
(Applicable for importing vouchers in XML format)
Export Base Currency Symbol along with Amount ? No
Show tables with Masters only in Current Language ? No

List of Countries
India / SAARC
International

Fig. 5.11 Selecting Country

Numbers are self-explanatory. The prime differences are in the use of terms like VAT in Europe and Sales Tax in Asia and America that have to be configured before creating a company. Refer the section Operations Configuration for details on the other fields.

Loading a Company

In order to load a company using the Select Company option, disable the default loading of a company in Tally.ini file. Set Default Companies to No OR place a semi-colon before Load = 00001 (company number - placing a semicolon means that the words following it in that line would not be executed. Each line is a separate command).

On double-clicking the Tally icon, the screen is displayed as shown:

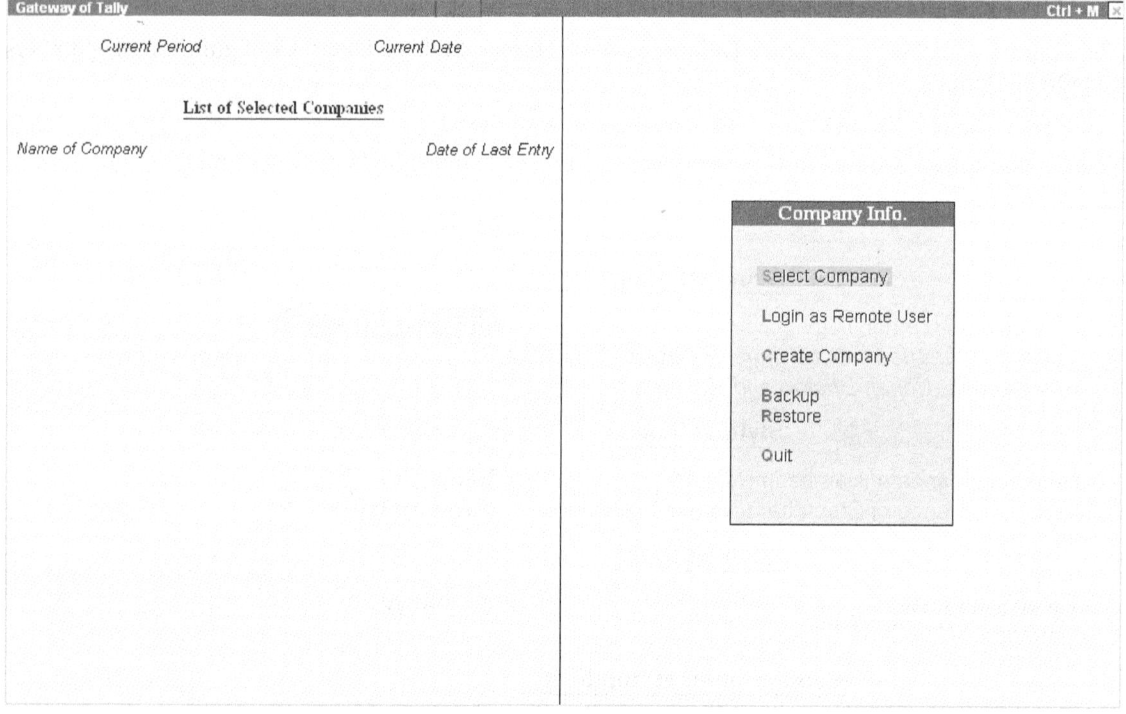

Fig. 5.12 Selecting the Company

You can use the Select Company option in two ways, from the Company Info. Menu OR by using the button F1: Select Cmp (available on the Gateway of Tally screen).

Select Company

Press Enter on Select Company or use the button F1: Select Cmp. Tally.ERP 9 displays the following screen:

Select Company

Directory : C:\Tally\Data

Name :

List of Companies

ABC Company	(10002)	1-Apr-2007 to 31-Mar-2009
ABC Company	(10003)	1-Apr-2008 to 31-Mar-2009
ABC Company	(10005)	1-Apr-2006 to 31-Mar-2007
ABC Company	(10006)	1-Apr-2005 to 31-Mar-2006

Tally.ERP 9 displays

1. Company Name (All the companies created are displayed)
2. **System-generated** code for each company displayed.

The Financial Year information relating to the number of years data present in the company.

Note: The system-generated code for each company is displayed to assist you in identifying which company you wish to work on in case you have multiple companies with the same name (as displayed in the above screen).

Select the required company to go to the Gateway of Tally for that company.

Loading a Company Automatically

When creating a company, Tally.ERP 9 creates a sub-directory under its \DATA directory for the company. The directory is allotted a number in serial order starting with 0001 (example – 10001, 10002...10009...10020, etc these are system generated codes for the company).

In order to automatically load a company, Tally.ERP 9 has to be configured appropriately From Data Configuration available in F12: Configuration from Gateway of Tally.

Note: You can also configure the above settings in Tally.ini file (available in the Tally.ERP 9 Directory).

Ensure that Default Companies is set to Yes and specify the company number which has to be loaded automatically, for example, Load = 10000

Note: You can specify any number here as per the information available in the data directory (10000 or 10002 or 10003, etc).

Example of sub-directories created by Tally.ERP 9 for different companies:

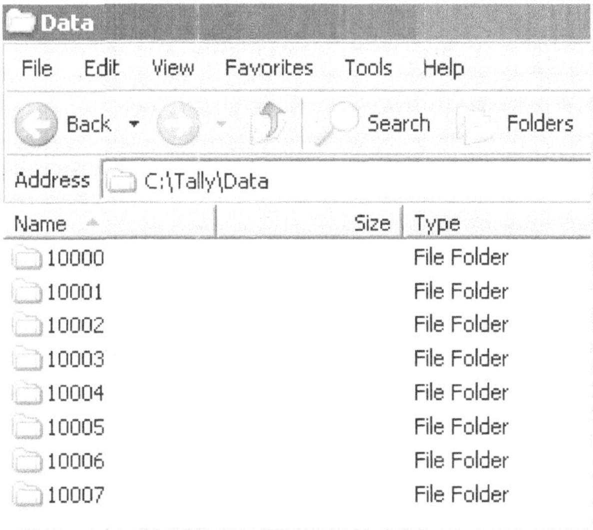

Gateway of Tally

Gateway of Tally is the screen that appears on selecting a company. The Gateway of Tally menu differs based on the type of company selected. An Accounts Only Company has a different Gateway of Tally menu from that of an Accounts-with-Inventory Company.

Gateway of Tally (Accounts-Only)

The Gateway of Tally menu of an Accounts Only company appears as shown below:

The Gateway of Tally screen is separated into 2 sections – Main Area (Ctrl+M) and the Button Bar.

Main Area

The left side of the Main Area gives information on:

1. Current Period – which is the currently loaded company's accounting period.

2. Current Date – This is the date of the last Voucher Entry for the selected company.
3. List of Selected Companies – This displays the name of the loaded company.

The Main Area gives information on:

1. Creation of Accounting Masters and Importing Master information.
2. Creation of Accounting Vouchers and Importing transaction information.
3. Viewing and printing financial reports using the information given in Masters and Transactions.

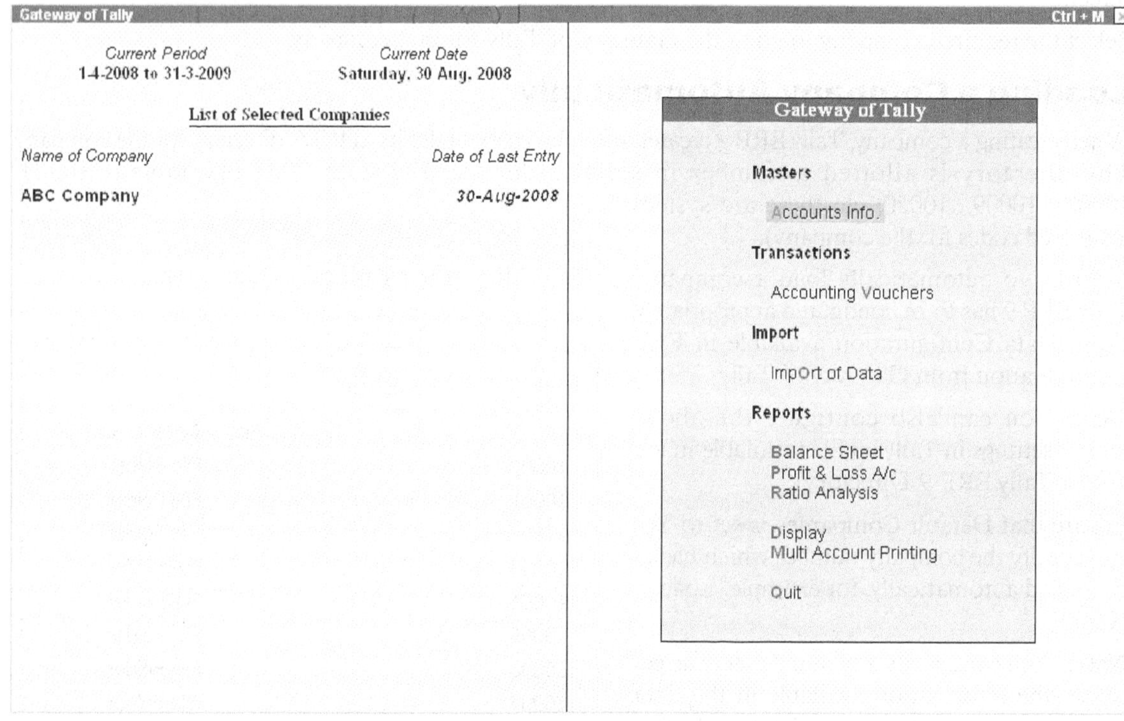

Fig. 5.13 Viewing the Company Information

Button Bar

The Button Bar displays the following buttons (keys):

1. F1: Select Cmp – To select a company.
2. F1: Shut Cmp – To shut or close the company.
3. F2: Date – To change the current date.
4. F2: Period – To change the period.
5. F3: Company – To select a different company.
6. F3: Cmp Info – To access the Company Info. Menu.
7. F4: Connect Company – To connect companies on Tally.NET.
8. F4: Disconnect Company – To disconnect companies from Tally.NET.
9. F11: Features – To access the Company features for a company.

10. F12: Configure – To access the configuration settings.

Note: You cannot load companies with the same name at the same time. The loaded or selected company will have to be shut first in order to load the other company.

Gateway of Tally (Accounts with Inventory)

The Gateway of Tally menu of an Accounts-with-Inventory company appears as shown next:

F12: Configurations in Tally.ERP 9

You can configure Tally.ERP 9 for masters, voucher entry, printing, connectivity, licensing, shop and other general settings by clicking on F12:Configure button or by clicking the F12 button on the keyboard.

Depending upon the screen, the configuration settings are displayed accordingly. For example, by using F12 in the voucher entry screen, the voucher entry configuration settings are displayed.

Configuration Menu

From any menu screen, when you click on F12:Configure button or click F12 on the keyboard, Tally.ERP 9 will display the configuration menu.

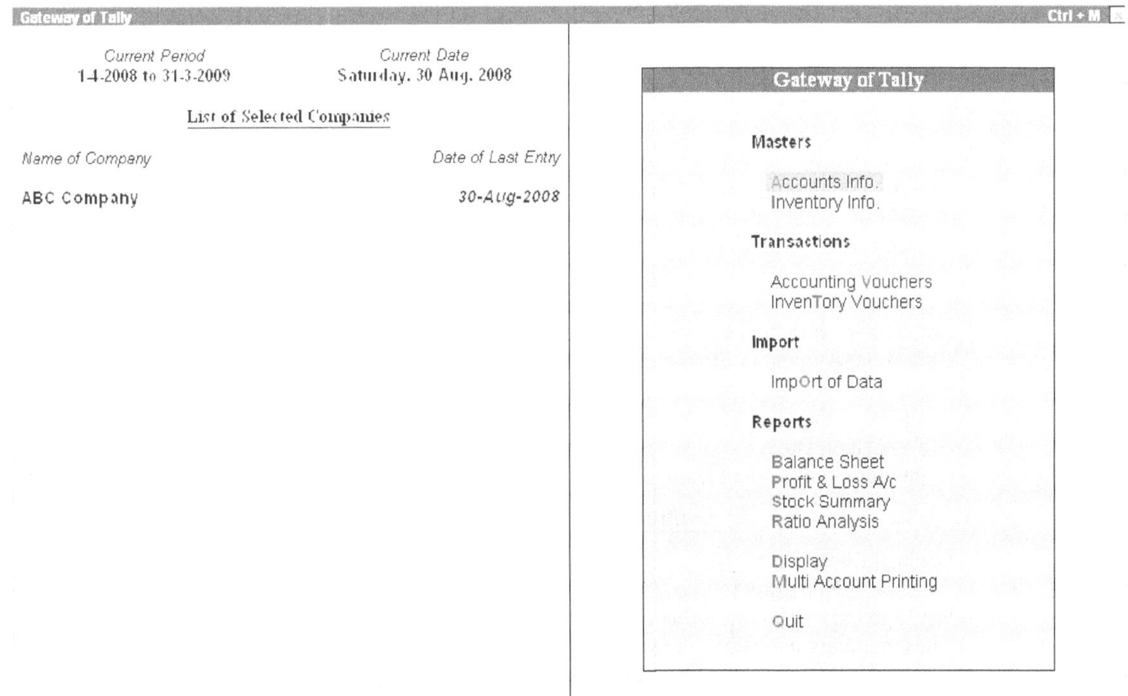

Fig. 5.14 Configuration Menu

Note:

1. Configuration settings apply to all the companies. You cannot set separate configuration for each company.
2. Configuration settings are saved in the file Tallycfg.tsf. By default, this file is available in the Tally.ERP 9 folder.

General

```
Go to Gateway of Tally > F12: Configuration
Menu > General
```

General Configuration Setting options:

Use Accounting Terminology of:

This option displays the List of Countries.

For setting the accounting terminology, select India/SAARC or International from the List of countries.

Default Appearance of Names in Reports:

This option displays the List of Name Styles for Ledgers.

By default, the name style of a Ledger is Name Only. You can change the name style by selecting from the List.

Default Appearance of Stock item Names in Reports:

This option displays Name style for stock items.

By default, the stock item name style is Name Only. You can change name style by selecting from the List.

Configuration

General
Numeric Symbols

Accts / Inventory Info.

Voucher Entry
Invoice / Orders Entry
PaYroll Configuration

Printing

Data Configuration
TDL Configuration
AdvanCed Configuration

Licensing

Quit

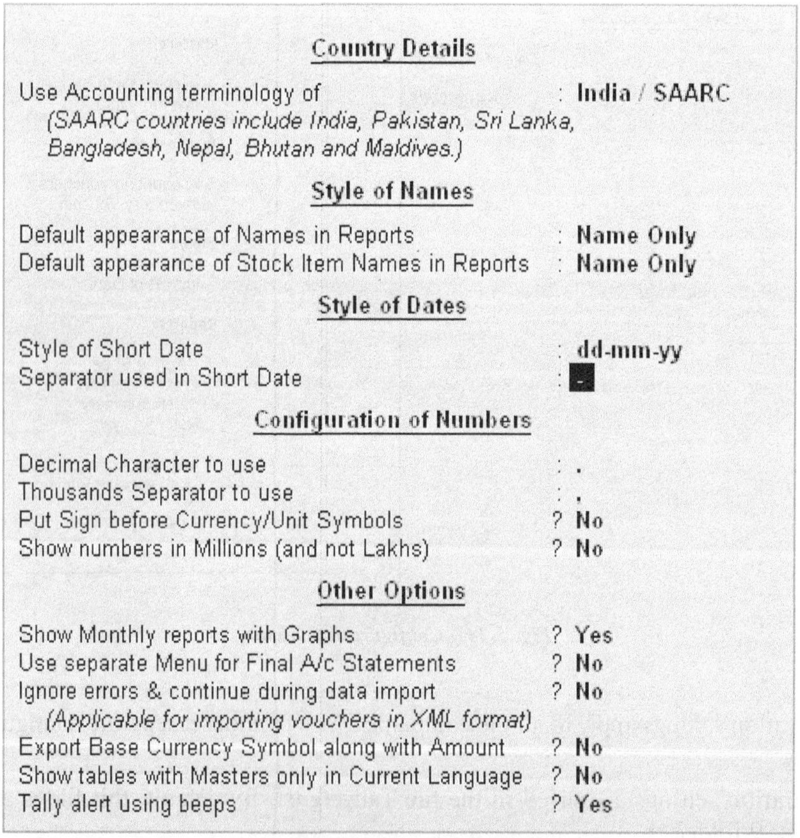

Country Details

Use Accounting terminology of : **India / SAARC**
(SAARC countries include India, Pakistan, Sri Lanka, Bangladesh, Nepal, Bhutan and Maldives.)

Style of Names

Default appearance of Names in Reports : **Name Only**
Default appearance of Stock Item Names in Reports : **Name Only**

Style of Dates

Style of Short Date : **dd-mm-yy**
Separator used in Short Date : **-**

Configuration of Numbers

Decimal Character to use : **.**
Thousands Separator to use : **,**
Put Sign before Currency/Unit Symbols ? **No**
Show numbers in Millions (and not Lakhs) ? **No**

Other Options

Show Monthly reports with Graphs ? **Yes**
Use separate Menu for Final A/c Statements ? **No**
Ignore errors & continue during data import ? **No**
(Applicable for importing vouchers in XML format)
Export Base Currency Symbol along with Amount ? **No**
Show tables with Masters only in Current Language ? **No**
Tally alert using beeps ? **Yes**

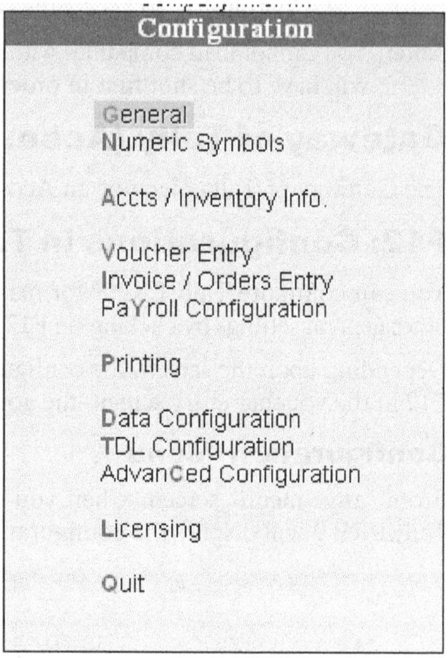

Fig. 5.15 Setting Configuration

Style of Short Date:

This option displays Style of Dates.

By default, date format is dd-mm-yy. You can change the date format by selecting a format from the List.

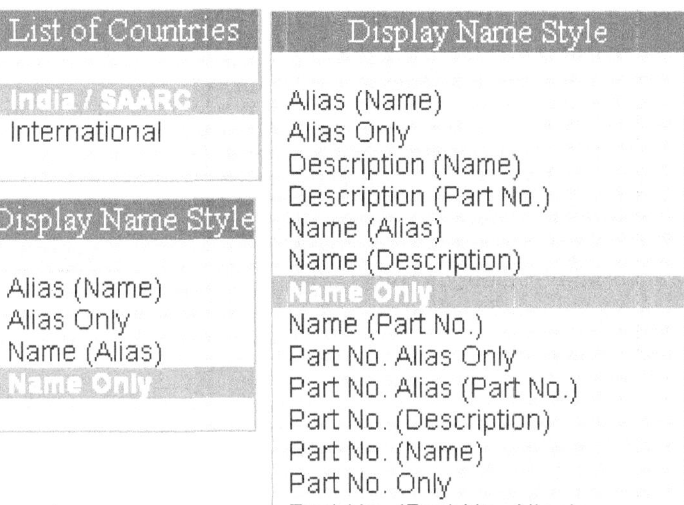

Separate Used in Short Date:

You can specify the separator for Date. By Default, hyphen ('-') is the separator.

Decimal character to Use:

You can specify a character for the decimal point.

Thousands Separator to use:

You can specify a character for the thousand separator.

Put Sign Before Currency or Unit Symbol:

If the option is set it to Yes, a Negative sign will be placed before the currency symbol, e.g. (-)$20. If the option is set it to No, a Negative sign will be placed after the currency symbol, *e.g.*, $(-)20.

Show numbers in Millions (and not Lakhs):

This option is used for showing numbers in Millions. If you set this option to Yes, the number will be displayed in Millions. If you set this option to No, the number will be displayed in Lakhs.

Show Monthly Reports with Graphs

By default this option is set to Yes. The reports are configured to display the Graphs in accordance with the numeric information. The graphs will not be displayed in the reports if this option is set to No.

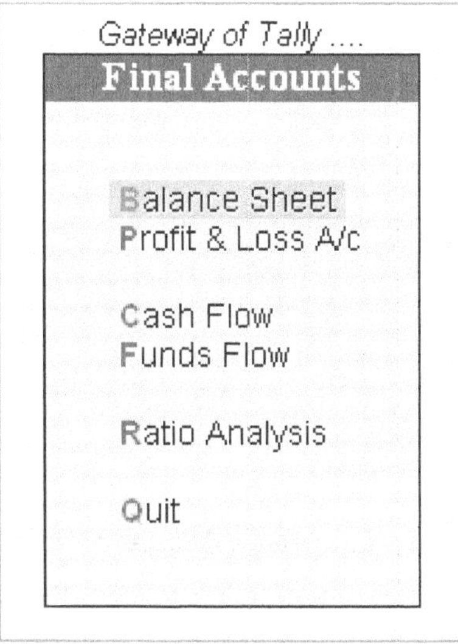

Use separate Menu for Final A/c Statements

By default, this option is set to No. If you set this option to Yes, a separate Menu Final Accounts will be displayed in Gateway of Tally. Under this menu, Balance Sheet, Profit & Loss A/c, Cash Flow, Funds Flow and Ratio analysis options are available.

Ignore errors & continue during data import

By default, this option is set to No. If you set this option to Yes , data will get imported even if errors are reported.

Numeric Symbols

This enables you to set the number styles. The default styles and symbols are specified. However, you have the option of changing them in the respective fields according to your preference.

For example, change negative sign from (-) to (+).

Accts / Inventory info.

```
Go to Gateway of Tally >
F12: Configure > Accts/
Inventory Info.
```

Here you can configure the details you want in the masters over and above those provided. You can access the F12: Configure screen from Accounts Masters and Inventory Masters when required.

Note: Depending upon the Company Features, option gets added in the Master configuration. For instance, if you enable VAT in F11 Statutory Feature, then the option Calculate VAT on MRP/Marginal gets added.

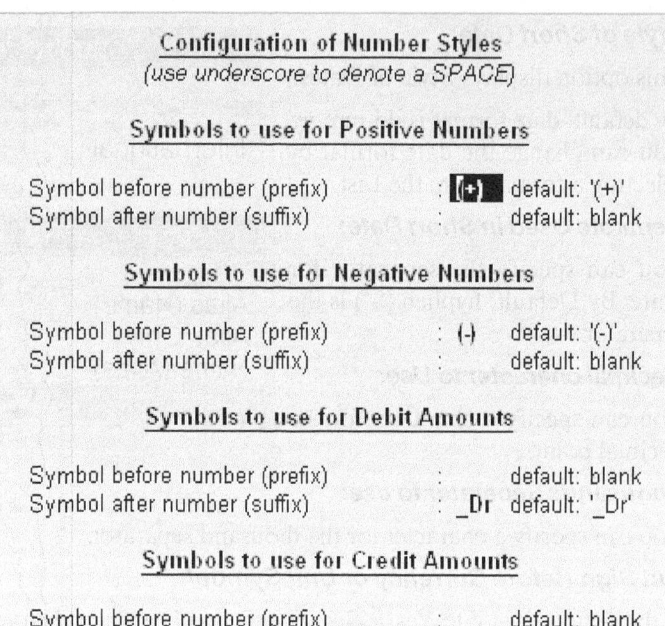

Configuration of Number Styles
(use underscore to denote a SPACE)

Symbols to use for Positive Numbers

Symbol before number (prefix)	: (+)	default: '(+)'
Symbol after number (suffix)	:	default: blank

Symbols to use for Negative Numbers

Symbol before number (prefix)	: (-)	default: '(-)'
Symbol after number (suffix)	:	default: blank

Symbols to use for Debit Amounts

Symbol before number (prefix)	:	default: blank
Symbol after number (suffix)	: _Dr	default: '_Dr'

Symbols to use for Credit Amounts

Symbol before number (prefix)	:	default: blank
Symbol after number (suffix)	: _Cr	default: '_Cr'

Master Configuration

Allow Aliases along with Names

Set this option to Yes to enter the Alias names in the Master.

Master Configuration

Allow ALIASES along with Names	? Yes
Allow Language ALIASES along with Names	? No

Accounts		Inventory	
Allow ADVANCED entries in Masters	? Yes	Allow ADVANCED entries in Masters	? No
Use ADDRESSES for Ledger Accounts	? Yes	Use PART NUMBERS for Stock Items	? No
Use CONTACT DETAILS for Ledger Accounts	? No	Use Description for Stock Items	? No
Add NOTES for Ledger Accounts	? No	Use REMARKS for Stock Items	? No
		Use ALTERNATE UNITS for Stock Items	? No
		Allow Std. Rates for Stock Items	? No
		Specify Default Ledger Allocation for Invoicing	? No
		Allow Component list details (Bill of Materials)	? No
		Use ADDRESSES for Godowns	? No

Fig. 5.16 Master Configuration

Allow Language Aliases along with Names

Set this option to Yes to enter the Alias names in any of the Indic Languages in the Master.

Accounts Masters

Allow Advanced Entries in Masters

Set this option to Yes, to enter some of the advanced information in the Ledger and Group Master. This information will be reflected in the reports.

Use Addresses for Ledger Accounts

Set this option to Yes to enter the Mailing Details in the ledger master. It is useful for a Customer ledger, a Party ledgers or Bank Accounts. Mailing Details like Name, Address, State, PIN Code and PAN / IT No. is entered in this section.

These details will appear in the printed reports.

Use Contact Details for Ledger Accounts

Set this option to Yes to specify the details of Contact person (if any) in the ledger creation screen.

You can specify the details like the Name of the Contact Person, Telephone Number, Fax Number and the E-Mail Id.

Add Notes to Ledger Accounts

Set this option to Yes and a new field to enter Notes appears in the Ledger master. This field allows you to enter any additional information about the ledger.

Note: The Contact Details for the ledgers appear only if Use Addresses for Ledger Accounts is set to Yes.

Inventory Masters

Allow Advanced entries in Masters.

Set this option to Yes to specify the behaviour of the Stock Item, in the Stock Item Master. For further details, please refer the section Stock Items.

Use Part Numbers for Stock Items

Set this option to Yes, to enter the Part Numbers of the Stock Item.

Use Description for Stock Items

Set this option to Yes to enter any Description of the Stock Item in the Stock Item Master.

Use Remarks for Stock Items

Set this option to Yes to enter your remarks or comments about the stock Item.

Use Alternate Units for Stock Items

Set this option to Yes to define an Alternate Unit for the Stock Item.

Allow Std. Rates for Stock Items

Set this option to Yes, to specify the Standard Purchase Cost and Standard Sales Price of the Stock Item.

Specify Default Ledger Allocation for Invoicing

Set this option to Yes, to Set or Modify Default Ledgers for Invoicing for the Stock Item.

This allows you to allocate default Sales/Purchase Ledgers which will be credited when a Stock Item is invoiced.

Allow Component list details (Bill of Materials)

Set this option to Yes, to define the Components (BOM) for the Stock Item. For further details, refer to the section Bill of Material.

Use Addresses for Godowns

Set this option to Yes, to enter the godown address in the Godown Master.

Voucher Entry

Go to Gateway of Tally > F12: Configure > Voucher Entry

By default, the above configuration options are displayed in the Voucher Entry configuration screen, which can be changed as per requirements.

Note: Depending upon the Company Features, options get added in Voucher Entry configuration. For instance, if you enable Allow Multi Currency option in F11 : Accounting Features, Show Forex Gain/Loss as on Voucher Date option gets added in voucher entry configuration.

Voucher Entry Configuration

Accounts		Inventory	
Skip Date field in Create Mode (faster entry!)	? Yes	Use Ref. Number in Stock Journal	? No
Use Single Entry mode for Pymt/Rcpt/Contra	? Yes	Warn on Negative Stock Balance	? Yes
Use Payment/Receipt as Contra	? No	Honor Expiry Dates usage for Batches	? Yes
Use Cr/Dr instead of To/By during entry	? Yes	Show Balances as on Voucher Date	? No
Warn on Negative Cash Balance	? Yes	Show Godown-wise Details	? Yes
Pre-Allocate Bills for Payment/Receipt	? No	Show Batch-wise Details	? Yes
Allow Cash Accounts in Journals	? No		
Allow Expenses/Fixed Assets in Purchase Vouchers	? No		
Allow Income Accounts in Sales Vouchers	? No		
Show Inventory Details	? Yes		
Show Table of Bill Details for Selection	? Yes		
Show Bill-wise Details	? Yes		
Expand into multiple lines	? Yes		
Show Ledger Current Balances	? Yes		
Show Balances as on Voucher Date	? No		

Fig. 5.17 Setting Voucher Entry Configuration

Accounting Vouchers

Skip Date field in Creation Mode (faster entry!)

By default, the Cursor skips the Date field during Voucher creation. If you do not want to skip the date field then set this option to No.

Use Single Entry Mode for Pymt/Rcpt/Contra

By default, Tally.ERP 9 displays single entry mode for payment/receipt/contra entry. If you want to display it in double entry mode, then set this option to No.

Use Payment / Receipt as contra

By enabling this option, you can enter contra in payment as well as receipt voucher.

Use Cr/Dr instead of To/By during Entry

By enabling this option, you can change To/By to Cr/Dr in the Voucher Entry screen.

Warn on Negative Cash Balance

By Default, Tally.ERP 9 displays a Negative Cash balance warning Message. If you set it to No, this error message will not be displayed.

Pre-Allocate Bills for Payment/Receipt

By enabling this option, you can pre-allocate the bills before specifying the Ledger amount.

Allow Cash Accounts in Journal

By enabling this option, you can select cash and also bank account in Journal.

Allow Expenses / Fixed Assets in Purchase Voucher

By enabling this option, you can select the expenses and also Fixed Asset ledger in Purchase Voucher Entry.

Allow income accounts in Sales Voucher

By enabling this option, you can select the income ledger in sales voucher entry.

Show inventory Details

By default, Tally.ERP 9 displays inventory details in the voucher entry screen. If you set it to No, the inventory details will not be displayed.

Show Table of Bill details for selection

By default, Tally.ERP 9 displays Pending Bills list of a ledger account in the voucher entry screen. If you set it to No, the pending bills list will not be displayed.

Show Bill-wise Details

By default, Bill-wise details of a ledger account are displayed in the Voucher entry screen. If you set it to No, Bill wise details will not be displayed.

Expand into Multiple Lines

This is a sub-option of the Show bill-wise Details option. When you enter credit days in the Bill-wise Details screen, Tally.ERP 9 displays the due date below the credit days. By default, it displays both credit days and Due date in the voucher entry screen. If you set it to No, it will display only credit days.

Show ledger current balance

By default, Tally.ERP 9 displays the ledger current balance up to last voucher entry date. If you set it to No, the ledger current balance will not be displayed.

Show balance as on voucher date

By default, Tally.ERP 9 displays the ledger current balance up to Last voucher entry date. If you set it to Yes, it will display the ledger balance up to current voucher entry date.

Inventory Vouchers

Use Reference number in Stock Journal

By enabling this option, you can add the voucher reference field in stock journal also.

Warn on Negative stock balance

By default, Tally.ERP 9 displays a warning message for negative stock balance. If you set it to No, the error message will not be displayed.

Honor Expiry Dates usage for Batches

By default, Tally.ERP 9 displays expiry batches in the List of Active batches during Voucher Entry. If you set it to No, expiry batches will not be displayed in the List of Active batches.

Show Balances as on Voucher Date

By default, Tally.ERP 9 displays the Stock Item balance up to the Last voucher entry date. If you set it to Yes, it will display the Stock Item balance up to current voucher entry date.

Show Godown-wise Details

This option is used only in the case of Rejection in and Rejection out vouchers. By default, Tally.ERP 9 displays the Godown details in Rejection in/out vouchers. If you set it to No, the godown details will not be displayed in Rejection in/out vouchers.

Show Batch-Wise Details

This option is used to display batch information pertaining to Stock Items during Voucher Entry. If you set it to No, the Batch-Wise details will not be displayed.

Invoice / Orders Entry

`Go to Gateway of Tally > F12: Configure > Invoice/Orders Entry`

By default 15 configuration settings are displayed in the Invoice/Order Entry configuration screen,. You can change the options as per your requirement.

Note: Depending upon the Company Features, options get added in Invoice/order Entry configuration. For instance, if you enable VAT option in F11 Statutory Features, Allow selection of VAT/TAX Class during entry, Warn on Mismatch in VAT Rates and Activate E1 or E2 Transaction option gets added in Invoice/Order entry configuration.

Invoice / Delivery Note / Order Configuration

General		Inventory	
Accept Supplementary Details *(Address Details, Despatch Details etc.)*	? Yes	Warn on Negative Stock Balance	? Yes
		Honor Expiry Dates usage for Batches	? Yes
		Complete Accounting Allocations in Order/Delivery Note	? Yes
Allow Separate Buyer and Consignee Names	? No	**Statutory**	
Allow modification of ALL fields during entry	? No		
Use Common Ledger A/c for Item Allocation	? No	Calculate Tax on current Sub-Total *(else calculations are on Inventory Total only)*	? No
Use Defaults for Bill Allocations	? No		
Use Additional Description(s) for Item Name	? No		
Use Additional Description(s) for Ledger Name *(for Accounting Invoice.)*	? No		
Show turnover achieved with Customer	? No		
Exporters' Options			
Specify Export Shipping details	? No		
Specify Marks & Nos./Container No.	? No		
Specify No. and Kind of Packages	? No		

Fig. 5.18 Invoice/Order Entry Configuration

General Options

Accept Supplementary Details

By default, this option is set to YES.

Tally.ERP 9 displays an additional screen to feed in the delivery note details, order details, Terms of payment, party address details, etc., after selecting the required Party ledger account.

Print Default Name & Address of Party

By default, Print Default Name & Address of Party is not visible in the Invoice Entry configuration Screen. This option is available only if Accept Supplementary Details in F12 Configure is set to No.

On setting this option to Yes, Tally.ERP 9 Prints the Party Ledger's Mailing Name and address details given in the Ledger master – in the Invoice. On setting this option to No – the invoice printout will display only the Party Ledger's Name without address details.

Allow Separate Buyer and Consignee Names

By default, this option is set to No.

If set to Yes – Tally.ERP 9 provides an option to enter consignee Name and address in the Supplementary details screen.

Allow Modification of ALL Fields During Entry

Default order/delivery note entries appearing in the invoice can be changed during invoice entry. Set this to Yes to permit modification of all fields.

Use Common Ledger A/c for Item Allocation

By default, this option is set to Yes.

This automates the updation process of the Sales and Purchase accounts for all the items selected in the invoice. In case this option is Set to No – Tally.ERP 9 prompts for sales or purchase accounting allocations after every item.

Use Defaults for Bill Allocations

By default, this option is set to Yes. In this case, Tally.ERP 9 automatically takes the invoice number as the bill reference name and the credit period given in the Party ledger master as the credit period – both as part of the bill-wise details. This enables faster data entry.

Note: In a purchase invoice, Tally.ERP 9 automatically takes the invoice reference number as Bill reference. If invoice reference number is empty then it will take invoice number as Bill reference.

However, if this option is set to No – Tally.ERP 9 prompts the user for bill-wise details at the end of the entry.

Use Additional Description(s) for Item Name

By default, this option is set to No.

If it is set to Yes – Tally.ERP 9 automatically allows you to specify description for each item selected in the invoice.

Use Additional Descriptions(s) for Ledger Name

By default, this option is set to No.

If it is set to Yes – Tally.ERP 9 automatically allows you to specify the description for each Ledger selected in the Accounting invoice entries.

Note: This options are provided to specify any additional description for sales ledger selected in the Accounting Invoice mode not in the Item invoice mode.

Show turnover achieved with Customer

By default, this option is set to No.

If you want to view the turnover achieved till date with a particular customer, set this option to Yes.

Exporter's Options

Specify Export Shipping Details

By default, this option is set to No.

If set to Yes, Tally.ERP 9 provides an option to enter export details for the invoice in the Supplementary details screen.

You can enter the following details:

- Place of Receipt
- Vessel / Flight No. (the transport used to send the goods)
- Port of Loading (from where the goods are despatched)
- Port of Discharge (where the goods will be finally offloaded)
- Country To (to which country the goods are being sent).

Specify Marks & Nos. / Container No.

By default, this option is set to No. If set to Yes – Tally.ERP 9 allows you to specify Marks details for every item selected in the invoice.

Specify No. and Kind of packages

By default, this option is set to No.

If set to Yes – Tally.ERP 9 allows to you to specify Num. Packages for every item selected in the invoice.

Inventory

Warn on Negative Stock Balance

By default, this option is set to Yes.

This is similar to the option available in the Voucher Entry Configuration screen. You can configure Tally.ERP 9 to warn in case the item selected reaches a negative balance.

Honor Expiry Dates usage for Batches

By default, this option is set to YES.

This is similar to the option available in the Voucher Entry Configuration Screen. You can configure Tally.ERP 9 NOT to include expired batches in the list of batches displayed at the time of entry.

Complete Accounting Allocations in Order / Delivery Note

By default, this option is set to Yes.

This means that in the Sales / Purchase Order and Delivery / Receipt Note entries, you can allocate a sales / Purchase ledger. This enables faster data entry at the time of entering sales / purchase invoices against the Delivery / Receipt notes.

Statutory

Calculate Tax on Current Sub-Total

By default, this option is set to No.

For example:

	Qty	Rate	Amount
Item A	10 No.	100 / No.	1000
Item B	10 No.	200 / No.	2000
		Total Item value	3000
Discount		-10%	-300

If you add another line, Tax 1%, it will calculate 1% on 3000 (on Total Item value) giving 30 as Tax value. However, if you opt for calculating on the current sub-total, Tax value will be calculated on 2700 [3000-300] giving 27 as Tax value.

Printing

The printing option allows you to configure the printing parameters of a Voucher, Invoice and Statement layouts before final printing.

```
Go to Gateway of Tally > F12: Configure > Printing
```

General

This configuration is applicable for all print reports.

In Printing General Configuration, by default the following configurations are available.

Print Date & Time of Report

Setting this option to YES, Tally.ERP prints system date and time on Report printing. After enabling this option, (on all pages of report) sub-option gets display. This sub-option is used for to decide whether to print system date and time in all pages or in first page only.

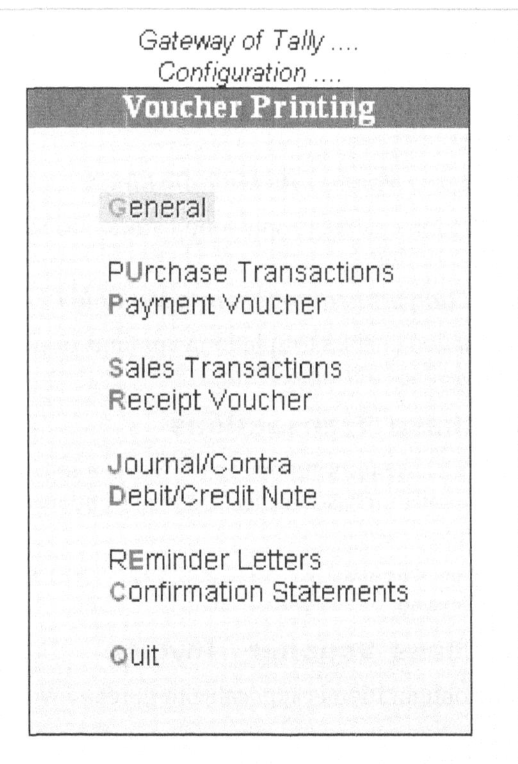

Print Date & Time of Voucher Printing

Setting this option to YES, Tally.ERP prints system date and time on Voucher printing. After enabling this option, (on all pages of voucher) sub-option gets display. This sub-option is used for to decide whether to print system date and time in all pages or in first page only.

Print State and Pin Code with Address

Setting this option to YES, Tally.ERP prints state and pin code with address of company in Reports and vouchers printing.

Note: This option also effect in invoice Entry. During Invoice Entry, Party's state and pincode is captured in supplementary details below the address line.

Stop printing Vertical Lines/Borders

Setting this option to YES, Tally.ERP will not print the vertical lines for reports and voucher printing. This enables faster printing in dot matrix printers.

Standard Space on Top of pages (Inches):

This option is used for to set Top margin for reports and voucher printing.

By default, this field is set to 0.5 inch. However, you can change it as per your requirement.

Configuration

Print Date & Time of Report	? **No**
Print Date & Time of Voucher Printing	? **No**
Print State and PIN Code with Address	? **No**
Stop printing Vertical Lines/Borders *(for faster printing on dot-matrix printers)*	? **No**
Standard Space on Top of pages (inches)	: **0.50**

Settings for 'Quick Format'

Split long names into multiple lines	? **No**
Split long amts/numbers into multiple lines	? **No**

Settings for "Quick Format"

Tally.ERP prints in two formats – Neat and Quick. Neat printing takes advantage of fonts of the printer and is the default. It also compresses long data like long names and amounts and auto-fits them according to space.

Quick printing is suitable for Dot Matrix printers where speed is an issue. Hence, quick printing does not print fancy fonts. The auto-fit facility is, thus, not possible in quick printing.

Therefore, it will truncate data longer than the allotted space. To prevent this, Tally.ERP provides two options:

Split Long Names into Multiple Lines

This option enables to split long names into multiple lines during printing.

Split Long amts/numbers into Multiple Lines

This option enables to split long amounts or numbers into multiple lines during printing.

Purchase Transactions

The Purchase printing option allows you to configure the printing of Purchase Invoice, Purchase Orders and Receipt Note.

```
Go to Gateway of Tally > F12: Configure >
Printing > Purchase Transactions
```

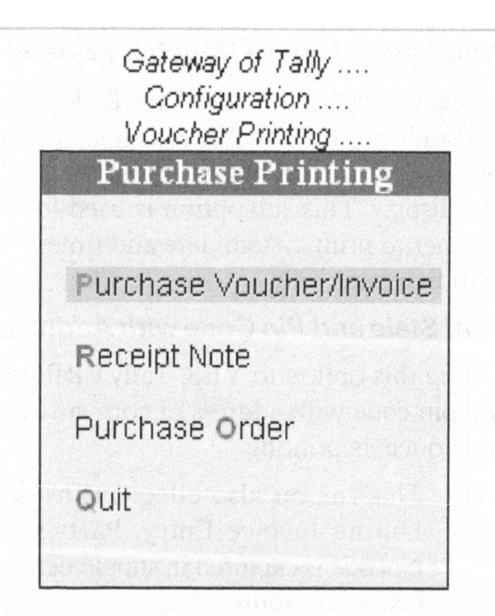

Purchase Voucher / Invoice

This configuration is applicable to purchase voucher type.

Purchase Printing Configuration

Title of Document	: INVOICE		
(for Optional Voucher)	: INVOICE		
Sub Title (if any)	:		
Height of Normal Invoice (inches)	: 10	Simple/Voucher :	10
Width of Normal Invoice (inches)	: 7.50	Simple/Voucher :	7.50
Space to leave on top (default 0.25)	: 0.25	Simple/Voucher :	0.25
Space to leave on left (default 0.5)	: 0.50	Simple/Voucher :	0.50

Number of Copies to Print	: 1	Print Quantity Column	? Yes
Print in Simple Format	? No	Print Actual Quantity Column	? No
Print in Voucher Format	? No	Print Rate Column	? Yes
Print Cost Allocations in Voucher Format	? No	Print Batch Details	? Yes
Print Voucher Reference	? Yes	Print Rate of Duty with Items	? No
Print Order Details	? No	Print Sub-Totals after each line	? No
Print Company's Tax Regn. Numbers	? Yes	Print Narration	? No
Print Supplier's Tax Regn. Numbers	? Yes	Print Narration for each entry	? No

Method to use for Stock Item Name	: Name Only
Jurisdiction	:

Fig. 5.19 Purchase Printing Configuration

Title of Document

By default, Title of Purchase Invoice will be displayed as INVOICE. However, you can change the Title as per your requirement.

Note: You can also set the Title for Optional Purchase Invoices.

Sub Title (if any)

By default, sub-title of purchase invoice is set as blank. However, you can set the sub title as per your requirement.

Voucher/ Invoice Print Page Setup

Page setup contains Height, width, Top margin and left margin. By default, Height is set as 10 inch, width is set as 7.50 inch, Top margin is set as 0.25 inch and Left margin is set as 0.50 inch.

Number of copies

By Default, number of copies is set as 1. However you can increase the number of copies as per your requirement.

Formats

By default, Tally.ERP 9 prints a purchase invoice in the Invoice format. However you can print the Purchase Invoice in two other formats: Simple format and Voucher format.

Print Cost Allocation in Voucher format

By default, this option is set to NO.

If set to YES – Tally.ERP 9 prints cost allocation details in purchase voucher format printing.

Print Voucher reference

By default, this option is set to YES. Tally.ERP 9 prints the purchase voucher reference number in the purchase document.

Print Order Details

By default, this option is set to NO.

If set to YES – Tally.ERP 9 prints the purchase order number and date in the purchase document.

Note: In purchase vouche, format printing, order details will not be printed.

Print Company's Tax Regn. Numbers

By default, this option is set to YES. Tally.ERP 9 prints the company's Tax registration number as mentioned in statutory features.

Print Supplier's Tax Regn. Numbers

By default, this option is set to YES. Tally.ERP 9 prints the Suppliers Tax registration number as mentioned in the supplier's Ledger master.

Print Quantity Column

By default, this option is set to YES. Tally.ERP 9 prints the Item Billed quantity in the purchase document.

Print Actual Quantity Column

By default, this option is set to NO. Tally.ERP 9 prints the Item Shipped (Actual) quantity in the purchase Invoice when printed in the simple format.

Print Rate Column

By default, this option is set to YES. Tally.ERP 9 prints the Item Rate in purchase printing.

Print Batch Details

By default, this option is set to YES. Tally.ERP 9 prints Item Batch details including Batch number, manufacturing date and expiry date.

Print Rate of Duty with Items

By default, this option is set to NO. Tally.ERP 9 prints the Item Rate of duty in the purchase invoice format.

Print Sub-Totals for each Line

By default, this option is set to NO. Tally.ERP 9 prints lines for each sub-total in purchase invoice/ simple format printing.

Print Narration

By default, this option is set to NO. Tally.ERP 9 prints Narration details in the Remarks field in purchase Invoice / Simple format printing.

Print Narration for each Entry

By default, this option is set to NO. Tally.ERP 9 prints the Narration for each entry in purchase voucher format printing.

Method to use stock Item Name

This list of options displays the different printing methods for displaying Stock Item Name in purchase Invoice/Simple printing.

Jurisdiction

By default, jurisdiction is set as blank. You can set the jurisdiction as per your requirement. In the Invoice format, it prints in the bottom portion. In the simple format, it prints in the Top portion.

Note: Depending upon the Company Features, options get added in the Purchase Printing configuration. For instance, if you enable VAT option in F11 Statutory Features, Print VAT Analysis of Items, Print Vat% Column option gets added in Purchase Printing Configuration.

Receipt Note

This configuration is applicable to Receipt Note voucher type.

Receipt Note Printing Configuration

Title of Document	: Receipt Note		
(for Optional Voucher)	: *Receipt Note*		
Sub Title (if any)	:		
Height of Normal Invoice (inches)	: 10	Simple: 10	
Width of Normal Invoice (inches)	: 7.50	Simple: 7.50	
Space to leave on top (default 0.25)	: 0.25	Simple: 0.25	
Space to leave on left (default 0.5)	: 0.50	Simple: 0.50	
Number of Copies to Print	: 1	Print Quantity Column	? Yes
Print in Simple Format	? No	Print Actual Quantity Column	? No
Print Voucher Reference	? Yes	Print Rate Column	? Yes
Print Order Details	? No	Print Amount Column	? Yes
Print Company's Tax Regn. Numbers	? Yes	Print Batch Details	? Yes
Print Supplier's Tax Regn. Numbers	? Yes	Print Rate of Duty with Items	? No
		Print Sub-Totals after each line	? No
		Print Narration	? No
Method to use for Stock Item Name	: Name Only		
Jurisdiction	:		

Fig. 5.20 Receipt Note Printing Configuration

Purchase Order

This configuration is applicable to Purchase Order voucher type.

Some of the printing configurations have already been explained under purchase printing Configuration.

Print Terms of Payment and Delivery

By default, Tally.ERP prints the Terms of Payment and Delivery entered in the Supplementary details under Purchase Order Entry. If you set this to NO, in supplementary details, Order details option will not appear in Purchase order Printing.

Print details of Despatch

By default, Tally.ERP prints Details of Despatch which includes Despatch through and Destination in purchase order printing. If you set this to NO, in supplementary details, Receipt details option will not appear in Purchase order printing.

Purchase Order Printing Configuration

Title of Document	: PURCHASE ORDER		
(for Optional Voucher)	: PURCHASE ORDER		
Sub Title (if any)	:		
Height of Normal Purchase Order (inches)	: 10	Simple: 10	
Width of Normal Purchase Order (inches)	: 7.50	Simple: 7.50	
Space to leave on top (default 0.25)	: 0.25	Simple: 0.25	
Space to leave on left (default 0.5)	: 0.50	Simple: 0.50	

Number of Copies to Print	: 1	Print Quantity Column	? Yes
Print in Simple Format	? No	Print Actual Quantity Column	? No
Print Voucher Reference	? Yes	Print Rate Column	? Yes
Print Terms of Payment and Delivery	? Yes	Print Delivery Date / Batch Details	? Yes
Print details of Despatch	? Yes	Print Rate of Duty with Items	? No
Print Company's Tax Regn. Numbers	? Yes	Print Sub-Totals after each line	? No
		Print Narration	? No

Method to use for Stock Item Name	: Name Only
Jurisdiction	:

Fig. 5.21 Purchase Order Printing Configuration

Print Delivery Date / Batch Details

By default, this option is set to NO.

If set to YES – Tally.ERP prints Order due on Date and Item batch Details in purchase order printing.

Payment Voucher

This configuration is applicable to Payment voucher type.

Voucher Print Page Setup

Voucher Print Page setup contains Height, width, Top margin and left margin. By default, Height is set as 7 inch, width is set as 5 inch, Top margin is set as 0.25 inch and Left margin is set as 0.50 inch.

Payment Mode on Top of Voucher

By default, this option is set to NO.

If set to Yes – Tally.ERP 9 prints the Cash / Bank Ledger name at the top of the Voucher.

Print Bill-wise Details

By default, Tally.ERP 9 prints bill-wise details during payment voucher printing.

Print Inventory Details

By default, this option is set to NO.

If set to Yes – Tally.ERP 9 prints the inventory item details during payment voucher printing.

Space for Checked/Verified initials

By default, this option is set to NO.

If set to Yes – Tally.ERP 9 prints Checked and Verified by at the bottom of the payment voucher.

Payment Printing Configuration

Height of Voucher (inches)	: 7
Width of Voucher (inches)	: 5
Space to leave on top (default 0.25)	: 0.25
Space to leave on left (default 0.75)	: 0.75
Payment Mode on Top of Voucher	? No
Print Bill-wise Details	? Yes
Print Inventory Details	? No
Space for Checked/Verified initials	? No
Print Foreign Currency Symbol on Cheque	? No
Print Narration	? Yes
Print Narration for each entry	? Yes

Print Foreign Currency symbol on Cheque

By default, this option is set to NO.

If set to Yes – Tally.ERP 9 prints the Foreign Currency symbol on the Cheque.

Print Narration

By default, Tally.ERP 9 prints the narration during payment voucher printing..

Print Narration for each entry

By default, Tally.ERP 9 prints the narration for each entry during payment voucher printing.

Sales Transactions

The Sales printing option allows you to configure the printing of Sales Invoice, POS Invoice, Delivery Note, Sales Order and Quotation.

```
Go to Gateway of Tally > F12: Configure > Printing >Sales Transactions
```

Sales Invoice

This configuration is applicable to Sales voucher type.

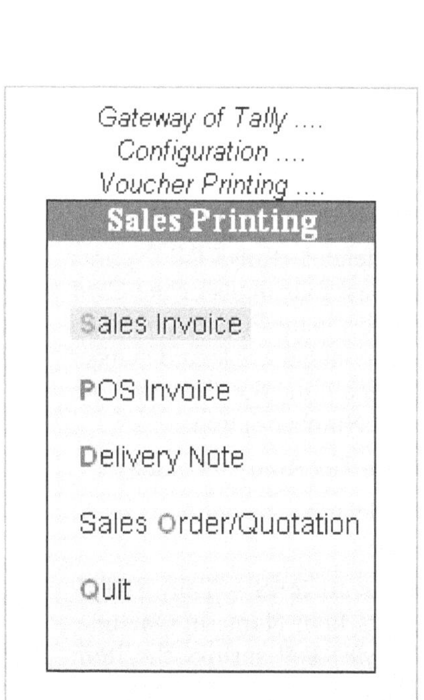

Some of the printing configurations have already explained under purchase printing Configuration.

Print Tax Analysis of Items

By default, this option is set to NO.

If set to YES – Tally.ERP 9 prints Tax analysis in the Invoice.

Print Declaration

By default, Tally.ERP 9 prints the declaration for Sales Invoice. You can set the declaration in the Sales voucher type.

Print Serial No.

By default, Tally prints the serial number for each item in Sales Invoice printing.

Note: Depending on the Company Features, options get added in Purchase Printing configuration. For instance, if you enable VAT option in F11: Statutory Features, then the option Print VAT Analysis of Items, Print Vat% Column gets added in Purchase Printing Configuration.

Invoice Printing Configuration

Title of Document	: INVOICE_		
(for Optional Voucher)	: *PROFORMA INVOICE*		
Sub Title (if any)	:		
Height of Normal Invoice (inches)	: 10	Simple:	10
Width of Normal Invoice (inches)	: 7.50	Simple:	7.50
Space to leave on top (default 0.25)	: 0.25	Simple:	0.25
Space to leave on left (default 0.5)	: 0.50	Simple:	0.50

Number of Copies to Print	: 1	Print Serial No.	? Yes
Print in Simple Format	? No	Print Quantity Column	? Yes
Print Voucher Reference	? Yes	Print Actual Quantity Column	? No
Print Order Details	? Yes	Print Rate Column	? Yes
Print Terms of Payment and Delivery	? Yes	Print Batch Details	? Yes
Print details of Despatch	? Yes	Print Rate of Duty with Items	? No
Print Tax Analysis of Items	? No	Print Sub-Totals after each line	? No
Print Company's Tax Regn. Numbers	? Yes	Print Narration	? No
Print Buyer's Tax Regn. Number	? Yes		

Method to use for Stock Item Name	: Name Only
Jurisdiction	:

Fig. 5.22 Invoice Printing Configuration

POS Invoice

This configuration is applicable to Sales voucher type having the POS option enabled.

Some of the configurations have already explained in the Purchase printing configuration.

POS Invoice Printing Configuration

Title of Document	: INVOICE_
Method to use for Stock Item Name	: Name Only
Print Item Name in one line	? No
Print Serial No.	? Yes
Print Rate Column	? Yes
Print Additional Description(s) for Item Name	? No
Print Card / Cheque No.	? Yes
Print whole Card Number	? No
Print Tax Analysis of Items	? No
Print Narration	? No
Print Default Name & Address of Party	? Yes

Print Card / Cheque No.

By default, Tally.ERP 9 prints the last four digits of the Card number in the POS Bill. You can also print the whole card number by enabling the Print Whole card Number option.

Print Tax Analysis of Items

By default, this option is set to NO.

If set to YES – Tally.ERP 9 prints Item Name in One line. Tally.ERP 9 shrinks the Item Name to fit it in one line.

Print Additional Description(s) for Item Name

By default, this option is set to NO.

If set to YES – Tally.ERP 9 prints additional description for each item in the POS bill.

Print Default Name & Address of Party

By default, Tally.ERP 9 prints Party's Name and Address (if selected in POS Entry) in the POS Bill.

Delivery Note

This configuration is applicable to Delivery Note voucher type.

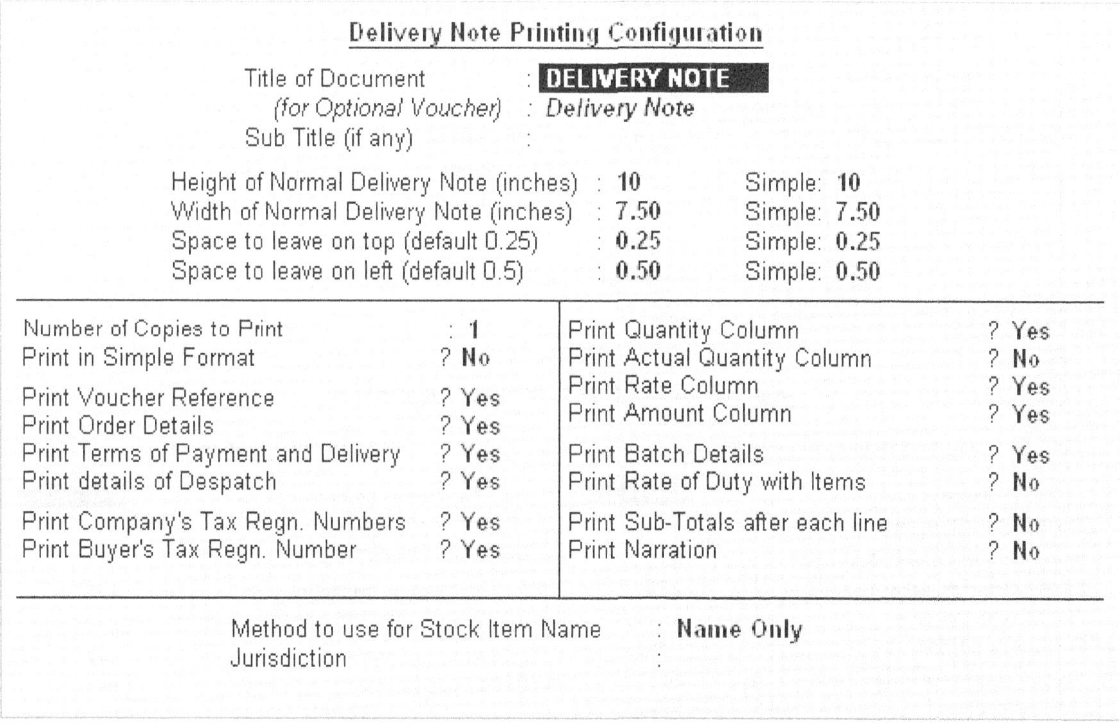

Delivery Note Printing Configuration

Title of Document : DELIVERY NOTE
(for Optional Voucher) : *Delivery Note*
Sub Title (if any) :

Height of Normal Delivery Note (inches)	: 10	Simple:	10
Width of Normal Delivery Note (inches)	: 7.50	Simple:	7.50
Space to leave on top (default 0.25)	: 0.25	Simple:	0.25
Space to leave on left (default 0.5)	: 0.50	Simple:	0.50

Number of Copies to Print	: 1	Print Quantity Column	? Yes
Print in Simple Format	? No	Print Actual Quantity Column	? No
Print Voucher Reference	? Yes	Print Rate Column	? Yes
Print Order Details	? Yes	Print Amount Column	? Yes
Print Terms of Payment and Delivery	? Yes	Print Batch Details	? Yes
Print details of Despatch	? Yes	Print Rate of Duty with Items	? No
Print Company's Tax Regn. Numbers	? Yes	Print Sub-Totals after each line	? No
Print Buyer's Tax Regn. Number	? Yes	Print Narration	? No

Method to use for Stock Item Name : Name Only
Jurisdiction :

Fig. 5.23 Delivery Note Printing Configuration

Sales Order/Quotation

This configuration is applicable to Sales Order voucher type.

Receipt Voucher

This configuration is applicable to Receipt voucher type.

Receipt printing configuration has already been explained in the payment voucher printing Configuration.

You can also set the Formal Receipt configuration in the above configuration setup.

Journal/Contra

This configuration is applicable to Journal voucher type.

Sales Order Printing Configuration

Title of Document	: SALES ORDER		
(for Optional Voucher)	: QUOTATION		
Sub Title (if any)	:		
Height of Normal Sales Order (inches)	: 10	Simple:	10
Width of Normal Sales Order (inches)	: 7.50	Simple:	7.50
Space to leave on top (default 0.25)	: 0.25	Simple:	0.25
Space to leave on left (default 0.5)	: 0.50	Simple:	0.50

Number of Copies to Print	: 1	Print Quantity Column	? Yes
Print in Simple Format	? No	Print Actual Quantity Column	? No
Print Voucher Reference	? Yes	Print Rate Column	? Yes
Print Terms of Payment and Delivery	? Yes	Print Delivery Date / Batch Details	? Yes
Print details of Despatch	? Yes	Print Rate of Duty with Items	? No
Print Company's Tax Regn. Numbers	? Yes	Print Sub-Totals after each line	? No
		Print Narration	? No

Method to use for Stock Item Name	: Name Only
Jurisdiction	:

Fig. 5.24 Sales Orderr Printing Configuration

Journal Printing Configuration

Height of Voucher (inches)	: 7
Width of Voucher (inches)	: 5
Space to leave on top (default 0.25)	: 0.25
Space to leave on left (default 0.75)	: 0.75
Print Bill-wise Details	? Yes
Print Inventory Details	? No
Space for Checked/Verified initials	? No
Print Narration	? Yes
Print Narration for each entry	? Yes

Receipt Printing Configuration

Height of Voucher (inches)	: 7
Width of Voucher (inches)	: 5
Space to leave on top (default 0.25)	: 0.25
Space to leave on left (default 0.75)	: 0.25
Receipt Mode on Top of Voucher	? No
Print Bill-wise Details	? Yes
Print Inventory Details	? No
Space for Checked/Verified initials	? No

Formal Receipt Printing Configuration

Height of Receipt (inches)	: 6
Width of Receipt (inches)	: 5
Space to leave on top (default 0.25)	: 0.25
Print Narration	? Yes
Print Narration for each entry	? Yes

Debit/Credit Note

This configuration is applicable to Debit / Credit note voucher type.

Debit / Credit note printing configuration has already been explained in the payment voucher printing Configuration.

Print full Ledger Details

By default, this option is set to NO.

If set to Yes – Tally.ERP 9 displays Print Inventory Details, Print with narrations, Print narration for each entry and Print Bill-wise Details options in the printing configuration.

Reminder Letters

The Reminder Letters feature in Tally.ERP 9 is used to send the outstanding Aging report to a customer in the form of Letter. You can also configure the letter in the Reminder Letter Configuration settings.

Go to Gateway of Tally > F12 Configuration > Printing > Reminder Letters

Debit/Credit Note Printing Configuration

Height of Voucher (inches)	: 6
Width of Voucher (inches)	: 5
Space to leave on top (default 0.25)	: 0.25
Space to leave on left (default 0.75)	: 0.75
Print full Ledger details	? No
Print Inventory details	? No
Print with Narrations	? No
Print Narration for each entry	? No
Print Bill-wise Details	? No
Space for Checked/Verified initials	? No

Space to leave at the top (default 0.5 inch) and Space to leave on the left (default 0.5 inch) : by default these fields are set to 0.5 inch. However, you can change it as per your requirement.

Reminder Letter Configuration

Space to leave on top (default 0.5 inch)	: 0.50
Space to leave on left (default 0.5 inch)	: 0.50
Information in First Paragraph	: Given below is the detail of amounts outstanding against your name in our books till today.
Information in Second Paragraph	: We request you to take immediate steps for settling the overdue bills and oblige.

Information in First Paragraph and Information in Second Paragraph: The information provided in these two fields can be edited as per your requirement.

Confirmation Statements

Confirmation Statements is used to send confirmation of account balance to customers, suppliers, lenders and borrowers.

You can configure the Confirmation Statement as per your requirement.

Go to Gateway of Tally > F12 Configuration > Printing > Reminder Letters

Confirmation of A/cs' Configuration

Space to leave on top (default 0.5 inch)	: 0.50
Titling for 'Subject' in Letter	: Confirmation of Accounts
Information in First Paragraph	: Given below is the details of your Accounts as standing in my/our Books of Accounts for the above mentioned period.
Information in Second Paragraph	: Kindly return 3 copies stating your I.T. Permanent A/c No., duly signed and sealed, in confirmation of the same. Please note that if no reply is received from you within a fortnight, it will be assumed that you have accepted the balance shown below.
Sign-off used for the Letter	: I/We hereby confirm the above

Space to leave on top (default 0.5 inch): By default this field is set to 0.5 inch. However, you can change it as per your requirement.

Titling for 'Subject' in Letter: The default text is Confirmation of Accounts. You have the option of changing it as per your requirement.

Information in First Paragraph and Information in Second Paragraph: The information provided in these two fields can be edited as per your requirement.

Sign-off used for the Letter: The default text can be changed in this field also.

Data Configuration

Tally.ERP 9 allows the user to add or modify the path where the Language, Data and Configuration files reside. To change the required configurations, execute the following steps.

Go to Gateway of Tally or Company Info menu

- Press F12:Configure
- Select Data Configuration.

The Data Configuration screen is displayed.

- By default C:\Tally.ERP9\Lang appears in Location of Language Files field. Specify the required path, if the language files reside in another folder.
- By default C:\Tally.ERP9 appears in Location of Tally Configuration Files field. Specify the required path, if the configuration file resides in another folder.
- By default C:\Tally.ERP9\Data appears in Location of Data Files field. Specify the required path, if you want to change the data folder.
- By default Load Companies on Startup is enabled,
- Select the required companies from the List of Companies.

Note: In case you do not want Tally.ERP 9 to load companies on startup, set Load Companies on Startup to No.

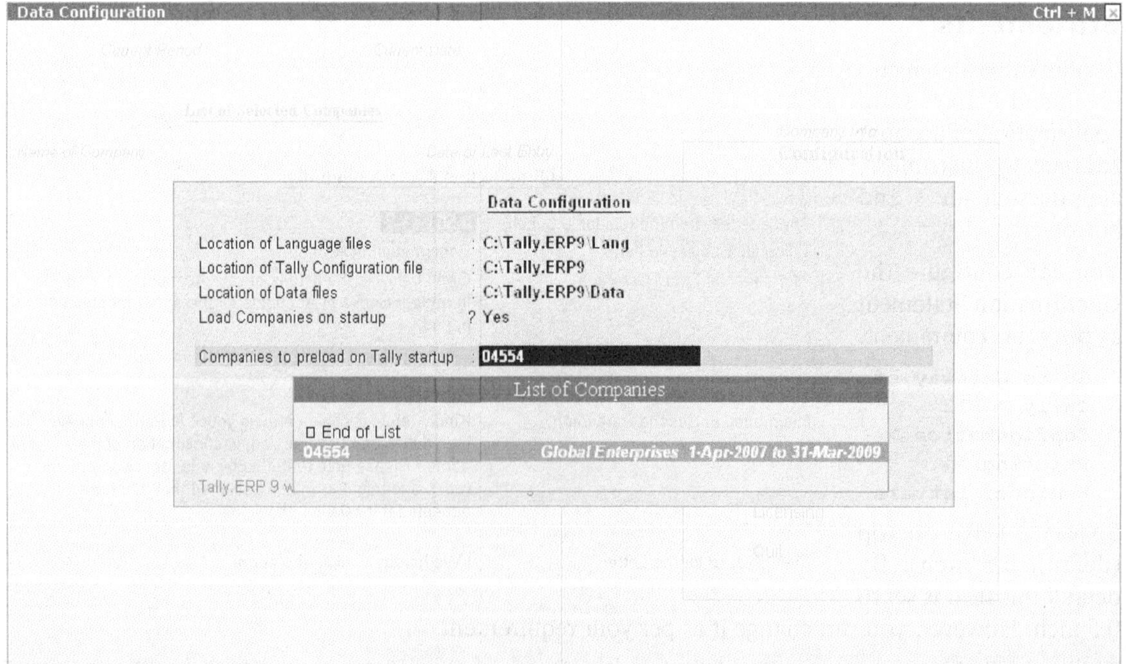

Fig. 5.25 Data Configuration

- Select End of List.
- Accept to save the data configurations.
- Tally.ERP 9 displays a message Do you want to restart Tally.ERP 9 for the changes to have effect?
- Press Y or click Yes to effect changes and restart Tally.ERP 9.

TDL Configuration

The TDL Configuration screen shows the details about the TDLs that are active and their origin. In Tally.ERP 9 with the availability of remote access the application can get TDLs from the following locations:

- Remote Server
- The Owner Account and
- Locally available TDLs.

The TDLs are categorized as Local TDLs, Account TDLs and Remote TDLs.

Select the option F12: Configure >TDL Configuration. Nexr screen is displayed.

Press F1: Detailed to view the details of the Files in each section.

Local TDLs

Displays the TDLs that are available and their Status as Active, Not Allowed and Error. Select the button F4: Local TDLs, it displays the following screen:

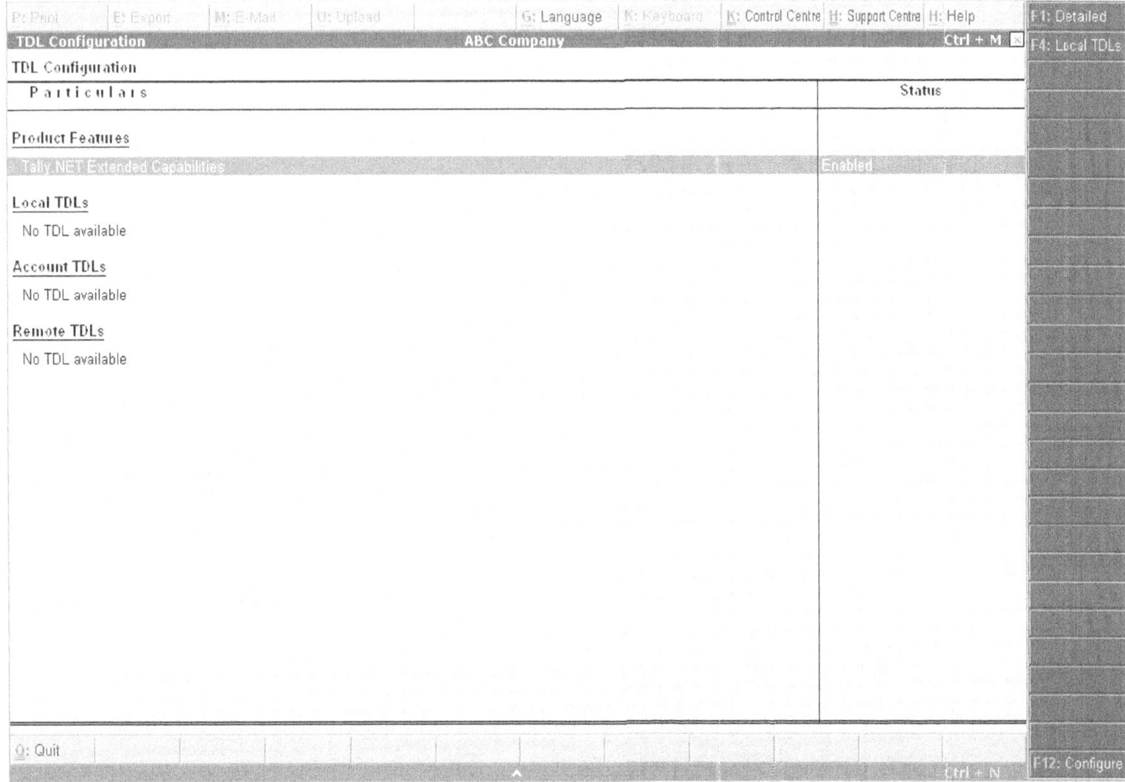

Fig. 5.26 TDL Configuration

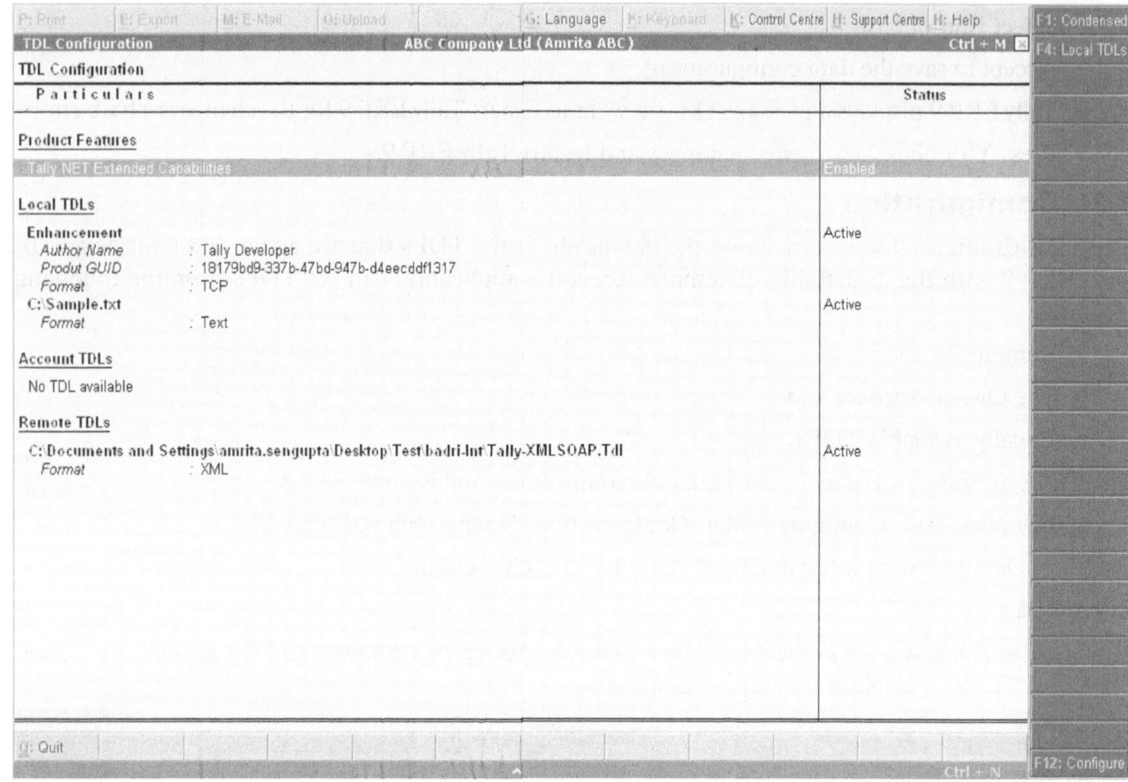

Fig. 5.27 TDL Configuration Screen

Multiple TDL files can be specified in this TDL configuration screen as shown:

Once the TDLs are attached, the screen also displays the status of each file.

When the TDLs are loaded successfully its status is displayed as Active.

If there is any problem in loading the TDL file then its status is shown as Error. On drill down it displays the details about the error that had occurred.

A TDL file can be disabled by prefixing the file name with '#' symbol.

The status of the disabled file is then shown as TDL Config screen.gif.

Account TDLs

The list of TDLs are received from the account are displayed under the section Account TDLs.

Following screen shows that no TDLs are received from the account:

Remote TDLs

When a user selects the option to "Login as Remote User", then the TDLs that are attached on the remote server are also available for the client.

TDLs received from the remote server are listed under the heading "Remote TDLs" as shown:

The List of all the active TDLs on the remote is displayed.

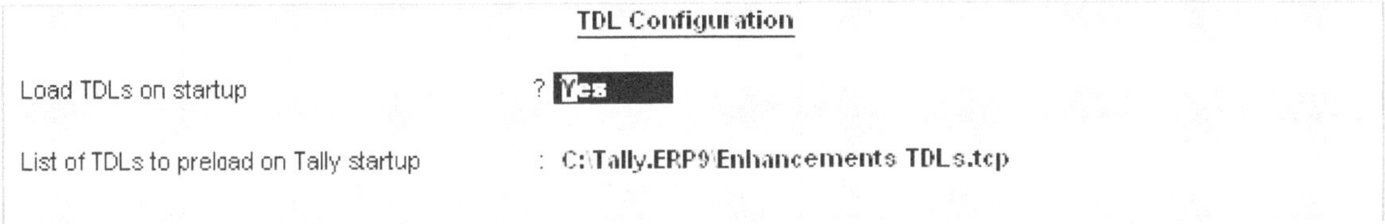

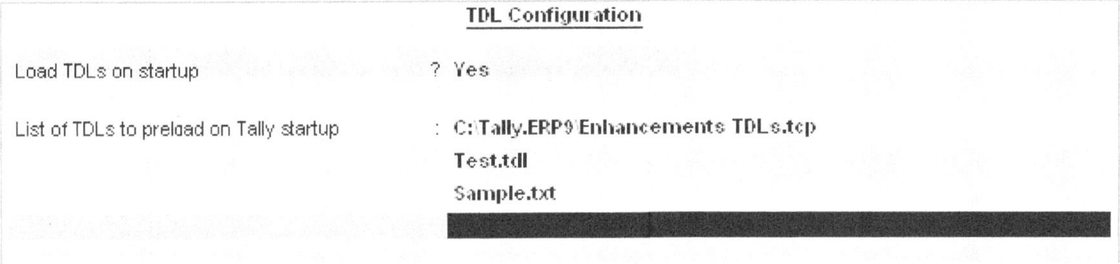

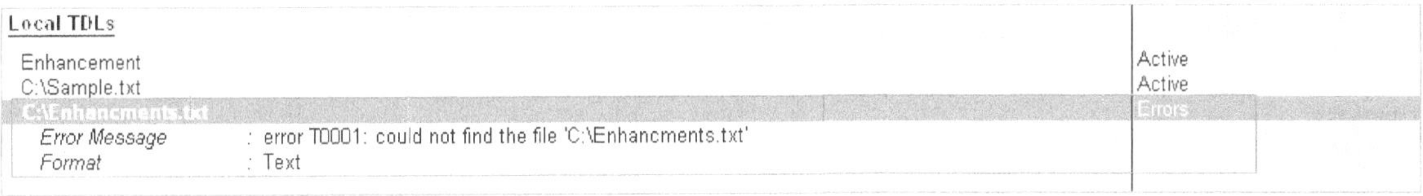

TDL Configuration

Load TDLs on startup ? Yes

List of TDLs to preload on Tally startup : C:\Tally.ERP9\Enhancements TDLs.tcp

TDL Configuration

Load TDLs on startup ? Yes

List of TDLs to preload on Tally startup : C:\Tally.ERP9\Enhancements TDLs.tcp
Test.tdl
Sample.txt

Local TDLs	
Enhancement	Active
C:\Sample.txt	Active
C:\Enhancments.txt	Errors

Local TDLs	
Enhancement	Active
C:\Sample.txt	Active
C:\Enhancments.txt	Errors
Error Message : error T0001: could not find the file 'C:\Enhancments.txt'	
Format : Text	

Advanced Configuration

The user can add or modify the required parameters required for Synchronization and ODBC. To change the required configurations follow the steps shown:

Go to Gateway of Tally or Company Info menu

- Press F12:Configure
- Select Advanced Configuration

The Client/Server Configuration screen is displayed.

- In Tally is acting as field select the required type from the list of Client /Server.
- Enter the required port number in the Port field.
- Ignore Client's modified Voucher Type Masters should be set to No, so that modifications made on the Client to Voucher Type Masters are updated on the Server.
- Ignore Server modified Voucher type Master should be set to No, so that modifications made on the Server to Voucher Type Masters are updated on the Client.
- Enable Sync Logging should be set to Yes, to generate a Log file which contains synchronized vouchers and is saved in the Tally folder.
- By default Use HTTP Proxy Server is set to No. In case you are using a proxy server set this option to Yes.
- Enter the required address in the URL field.

TDL Configuration

Load TDLs on startup ? Yes

List of TDLs to preload on Tally startup : #C:\Tally.ERP9\Enhancements TDLs.tcp
C:\Sample.txt
C:\Enhancments.txt

Local TDLs	
C:\Tally.ERP9\Enhancements TDLs.tcp	Not Allowed
C:\Sample.txt	Active
C:\Enhancments.txt	Errors

Account TDLs	
No TDL available	

Remote TDLs	
.\Sample.txt	Active

Remote TDLs	
.\Sample.txt	Active
./ToolTip.txt	Active

- To authenticate before connecting, set Authentication Required to Yes.
- Provide the required username and password in the User Name and Password fields respectively.
- Accept to save the configurations.
- Tally.ERP 9 displays a message Do you want to restart Tally.ERP 9 for the changes to have effect?
- Press Y or click Yes to effect changes and restart Tally.ERP 9.

Client/Server Configuration

Tally is acting as : Both
Enable ODBC Server ? Yes
Port : 9000

Tally Sync Configuration

Ignore Client's modified Voucher Type Masters ? No
Ignore Server's modified Voucher Type Masters ? No
Enable Sync Logging (SockReq.log) ? No

Proxy Configuration

Use HTTP Proxy Server ? Yes
URL :
Authentication Required ? Yes
User Name : sanjay
Password : *****

Accept ?

Yes or No

F11: Company Features in Tally.ERP 9

Different features of a company can be selected or modified by using the F11: Features button. This button is available in almost all the screens of Tally.ERP 9 enabling the user to modify it as and when your requirements change.

Unlike F12: Configure, F11: Company Features is specific to the current company only. Therefore, each company may have different active features. Configuration options, on the other hand, affect all companies maintained in the same Tally.ERP 9 directory and setting the configuration for one company will affect the configuration of other companies in that particular data directory.

Note: Certain features like multi-currency and multi-locations, once set to Yes, cannot be modified if the feature has been used. However, other features like Bill-wise details, Reversing Journals & Optional vouchers, etc., can be modified even if they are used.

```
Go to Gateway of Tally > F11: Features
```

The F11: Features menu is displayed as shown.

F11: Accounting Features

This feature enables you to set the various Accounting Features required for transaction entries.

```
Go to Gateway of Tally > F11: Features > F1: Accounts
```

General

Integrate Accounts and Inventory

This option has a significant effect on the Balance Sheet and Profit & Loss Account. If set to Yes, it extracts the stock/inventory balance figures from the inventory records and provides a drill down to the Stock registers from the Balance Sheet.

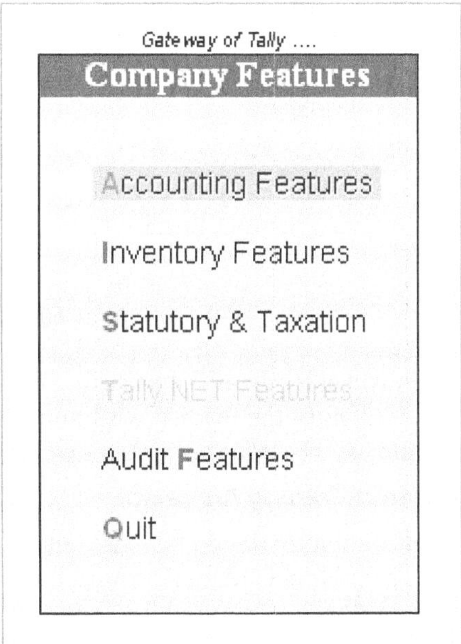

If set to No, it ignores the inventory books figures and picks up manually entered closing stock balances from the ledger account created. This facilitates the maintaining of accounts and inventory separately.

Stock records often contain compensating errors caused by wrong allocation to items. This feature enables finalisation of financial books without waiting for the reconciliation of stocks.

Income/Expense Statement Instead of P & L

By Default, this option is set to NO.

If set to Yes – Tally.ERP 9 displays Income & Expenses A/c instead of Profit & Loss A/c in the Gateway of Tally.ERP 9 Menu. Income and Expenditure statement generally used for Non-Trading accounts and Profit & Loss a/c are used for trading accounts.

Allow Multi-Currency

By Default, this option is NO.

Set this option to Yes, if you want to create multiple currencies and the Menu Currencies is displayed in Gateway of Tally > Accounts Info. menu.

Outstandings Management

Maintain Bill wise Details

The Bill-wise facility is made functional by setting this option to Yes. By activating the Billwise feature, the ledger masters under Sundry Debtors and Sundry Creditors automatically displays an additional option called Maintain balances bill-by-bill. On setting this option to Yes, an additional option Default Credit Period is displayed.

Company: ABC Company

Accounting Features

General		Invoicing	
Integrate Accounts and Inventory	? Yes	Allow Invoicing	? Yes
Income/Expense Statement instead of P & L	? No	Enter Purchases in Invoice Format	? Yes
Allow Multi-Currency	? No	Use Debit/Credit Notes	? No
		Use Invoice mode for Credit Notes	? No
		Use Invoice mode for Debit Notes	? No
Outstandings Management		**Budgets & Scenario Management**	
Maintain Bill-wise Details	? Yes	Maintain Budgets and Controls	? No
(for Non-Trading A/cs also)	? No	Use Reversing Journals & Optional Vouchers	? No
Activate Interest Calculation	? No		
(use advanced parameters)	? No		
Cost/Profit Centres Management		**Other Features**	
Maintain Payroll	? No	Enable Cheque Printing	? No
Maintain Cost Centres	? No	Set/Alter Cheque Printing Configuration	? No
Use Cost Centre for Job Costing	? No	Allow Zero valued entries	? No
More than ONE Payroll / Cost Category	? No		
Use Pre-defined Cost Centre Allocations during Entry	? No		

F1: Accounts F2: Inventory F3: Statutory F5: Audit

Fig. 5.28 Accounting Features Screen

When you enter details of sales and purchases with the Bill-wise option activated, Tally.ERP 9 prompts you to identify the invoice with an appropriate reference number. The reference can then be used to allocate payments to the correct invoice to maintain an accurate account of outstanding.

(For Non-Trading A/cs also)

If you want to maintain bill wise details for Non-Trading Accounts also, set this option to Yes. Bill wise Details for Non-Trading Accounts is useful in those cases where one needs to track either an installment to be paid or a loan amount to be received over a certain period of time.

Activate Interest calculation

Set this option to Yes to enable Tally.ERP 9 to calculate interest automatically based on the interest rate and style of calculation specified. Enabling this option allows interest calculation on outstanding balances for any ledger account or on each invoice for the period it is outstanding completely or partly.

Use advanced parameters

The advanced parameters are useful when interest rates change from time to time. Set this option to Yes to enable this function.

Cost/Profit Centres Management

Maintain Payroll

Set this option to Yes if you want to maintain Payroll information on Tally.ERP 9 for the selected company.

Maintain Cost Centres

A Cost Centre can be defined as a unit of an organization to which transactions can be posted. When only costs or expenses are allocated to these units, they are referred to as Cost Centres. The Cost Centre feature is activated by setting this option to Yes.

Use Cost Center for Job Costing

Set this option to Yes to track all income and expenses for a Job/Project.

More than ONE Payroll/Cost category

Set this option to Yes to create more than one Payroll or Cost Category.

Use Pre-defined Cost Centre Allocations during Entry

Set this option to Yes to define Cost Centre Allocations.

Invoicing

Allow Invoicing

Set this option to Yes, to create Sales and Purchase vouchers in the invoice format. The advantage of using the invoice format for sales invoice entry is that it enables automatic calculations of Duties and Taxes accounts.

Enter Purchases in Invoice Format

Set this option to Yes, to enable voucher class option in purchase voucher type.

Use Debit/Credit Notes

The Debit Note and Credit Note voucher types are made available only if this feature is set to Yes.

Use Invoice Mode for Credit Notes

Set this option to Yes to create Credit Notes in Invoice Mode.

Use Invoice Mode for Debit Notes

Set this option to Yes to create Debit Notes in Invoice Mode.

Budgets & Scenario Management

Maintain Budgets and Controls

Set this option to Yes, to create multiple budgets. The Budgets menu option is displayed in Gateway of Tally > Masters Info. > Accounts Info. menu.

Use Reversing Journals & Optional Vouchers

Setting this option to Yes displays the Scenario option in Accounts Info menu. You will now be able to create and alter Scenarios. You can enter the Reversing Journal and make it Optional, so that the entries do not to affect the books.

Other Features

Enable Cheque Printing

Set this option to Yes, to enable Cheque Printing. Refer Cheque Printing for details.

Set/Alter Cheque Printing Configuration

If this option is set to Yes, Tally.ERP 9 will allow you to alter the Cheque Printing Configuration.

Allow Zero Valued Entries in Vouchers

Set this option to Yes, to allow Zero valued entries in vouchers.

Note: You can toggle between the Accounts, Inventory and the Statutory features screen using F1, F2 and F3 keys or by using the options on the Button Bar respectively.

F11: Inventory Features

This feature enables you to set the Inventory Features required for the transactions.

```
Go to Gateway of Tally > F11: Features > F2: Inventory
```

General

Integrate Accounts and Inventory

This field performs the same function as explained in Accounting Features.

Allow Zero Valued Entries in Vouchers

Set this option to Yes, to allow zero valued entries in Inventory vouchers.

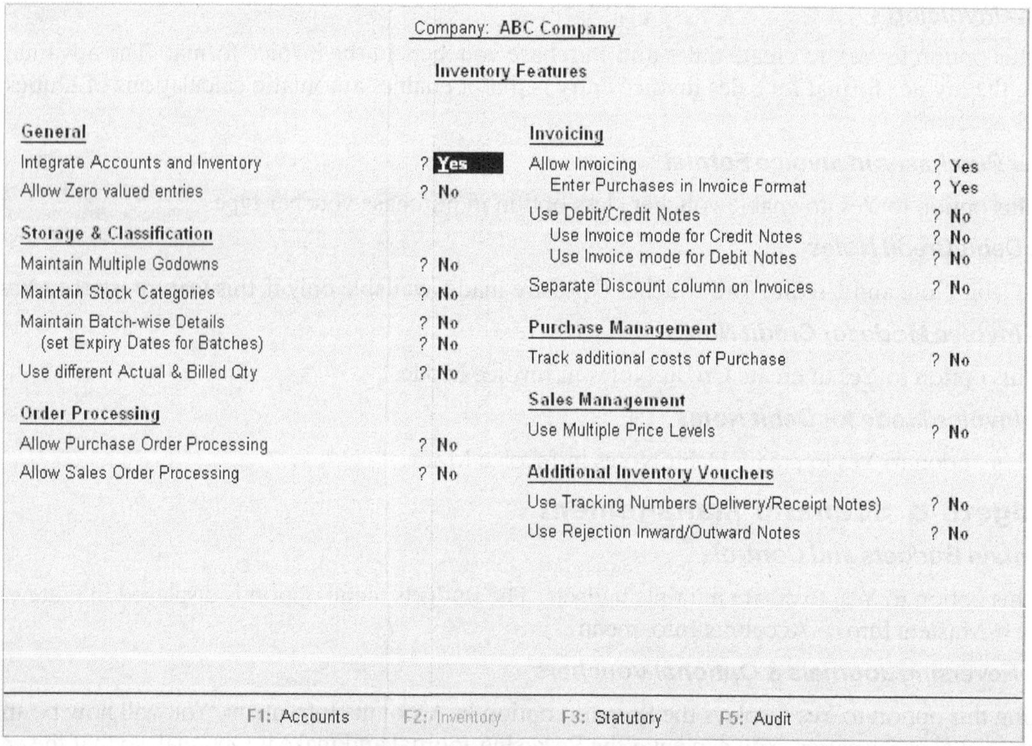

Company: ABC Company

Inventory Features

General		Invoicing	
Integrate Accounts and Inventory	? Yes	Allow Invoicing	? Yes
Allow Zero valued entries	? No	Enter Purchases in Invoice Format	? Yes
Storage & Classification		Use Debit/Credit Notes	? No
Maintain Multiple Godowns	? No	Use Invoice mode for Credit Notes	? No
Maintain Stock Categories	? No	Use Invoice mode for Debit Notes	? No
Maintain Batch-wise Details	? No	Separate Discount column on Invoices	? No
(set Expiry Dates for Batches)	? No	**Purchase Management**	
Use different Actual & Billed Qty	? No	Track additional costs of Purchase	? No
Order Processing		**Sales Management**	
Allow Purchase Order Processing	? No	Use Multiple Price Levels	? No
Allow Sales Order Processing	? No	**Additional Inventory Vouchers**	
		Use Tracking Numbers (Delivery/Receipt Notes)	? No
		Use Rejection Inward/Outward Notes	? No

F1: Accounts F2: Inventory F3: Statutory F5: Audit

Fig. 5.29 Inventory Features Screen

Storage & Classification

Maintain Multiple Godowns

Set this option to Yes, if you have more than one stock point/storage Locations/ Godowns, and you want to track stock movement across these Locations. You can create any number of Stock Locations/ Godowns. The Godowns/Locations option is displayed in Gateway of Tally > Inventory Info. menu only if you set this option to Yes. You will be able to identify your stocks at each location as well as assign stock movement to one or more locations during voucher entry.

Maintain Stock Categories

Set this option to Yes, if you wish to create and maintain Stock Categories. This creates a new field Category in the Stock Item Creation screen.

Maintain Batch-Wise Details

Set this option to Yes, to maintain batch information pertaining to Stock Items. A new field Maintain in Batches is displayed in the Stock Item Creation screen.

Set Expiry Dates for Batches

Set this option to Yes, if you want to set expiry dates for the batches. This displays an additional field Use Expiry Dates in the Stock Item Creation screen.

This is useful for businesses that deal in goods that have expiry dates like medicines, food and other perishables. During voucher entry, by default the date of the voucher is considered as the date of manufacture of the product. This date can be changed, but not to a date later than the voucher date. At the same time, the Expiry date cannot be a date prior to the voucher date.

Use different Actual & Billed Quantity

Set this option to Yes, if you want to specify quantities, that are different from those delivered/ received, when invoicing.

Order Processing

Allow Purchase Order Processing

Set this option to Yes, to create Purchase Orders.

Allow Sales Order Processing

Set this option to Yes, to create Sales Orders.

Invoicing

Allow Invoicing

This field performs the same function as explained in Accounting Features.

- Enter Purchases in Invoice Format

This field performs the same function as explained in Accounting Features.

Use Debit/Credit Notes

This field performs the same function as explained in Accounting Features.

- Use Invoice Mode for Credit Notes

This field performs the same function as explained in Accounting Features.

- Use Invoice Mode for Debit Notes

This field performs the same function as explained in Accounting Features.

Separate Discount Column on Invoices

This option is active only if Allow invoicing is set to Yes. Set this option to Yes, if you want a separate column for discounts in invoices.

Purchase Management

Track Additional Costs of Purchase

Set this option to Yes, to obtain a break-up of purchase costs, without the need to separately debit ledger accounts for expenses.

Sales Management

Use Multiple Price Levels

Set this option to Yes to create Multiple Price Levels. Refer Enable and Create Price Lists for more details.

Additional Inventory Vouchers

Use Tracking Numbers (Delivery/Receipt Notes)

Set this option to Yes, if you want to use tracking numbers to maintain the relation between delivery notes and invoices/bills. This is available for both purchases and sales.

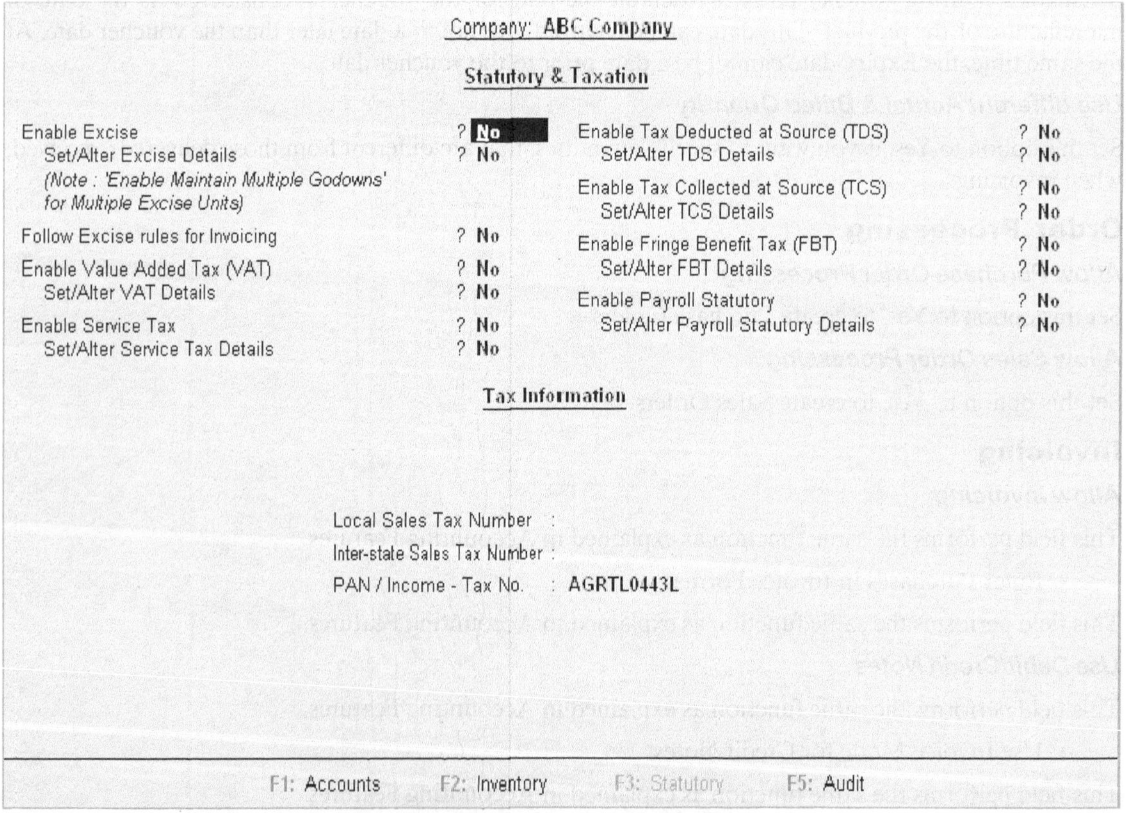

Company: ABC Company

Statutory & Taxation

Enable Excise ? No
Set/Alter Excise Details ? No
(Note : 'Enable Maintain Multiple Godowns' for Multiple Excise Units)
Follow Excise rules for Invoicing ? No
Enable Value Added Tax (VAT) ? No
Set/Alter VAT Details ? No
Enable Service Tax ? No
Set/Alter Service Tax Details ? No

Enable Tax Deducted at Source (TDS) ? No
Set/Alter TDS Details ? No
Enable Tax Collected at Source (TCS) ? No
Set/Alter TCS Details ? No
Enable Fringe Benefit Tax (FBT) ? No
Set/Alter FBT Details ? No
Enable Payroll Statutory ? No
Set/Alter Payroll Statutory Details ? No

Tax Information

Local Sales Tax Number :
Inter-state Sales Tax Number :
PAN / Income - Tax No. : AGRTL0443L

F1: Accounts F2: Inventory F3: Statutory F5: Audit

Fig. 5.30 Statutory & Taxation Screen

Use Rejection Inward/Outward Notes

Set this option to Yes, if you wish to record rejection of goods separately and not through a common Debit Note or Credit Note.

F3 : Statutory & Taxation

This feature enables you to set the Statutory Features required for the transactions.

`Go to Gateway of Tally > F11: Features > F2: Statutory & Taxation`

F4: Tally.NET Features

To Configure Tally.NET Features in Tally.ERP 9, execute the following steps:

`Go to Gateway of Tally > F11: Features > F4: Tally.NET Features`

The Tally.NET Features screen is displayed as shown.

Under Registration Details

- Connect Name: The user can enter a Connect Name for the Company to be connected as per his requirements or retain the company name mentioned in the Company Master.
- Contact Person Name: Specify the Name of the Contact Person.
- Contact Number: Specify the Contact Number.

Fig. 5.31 Tally.NET Features

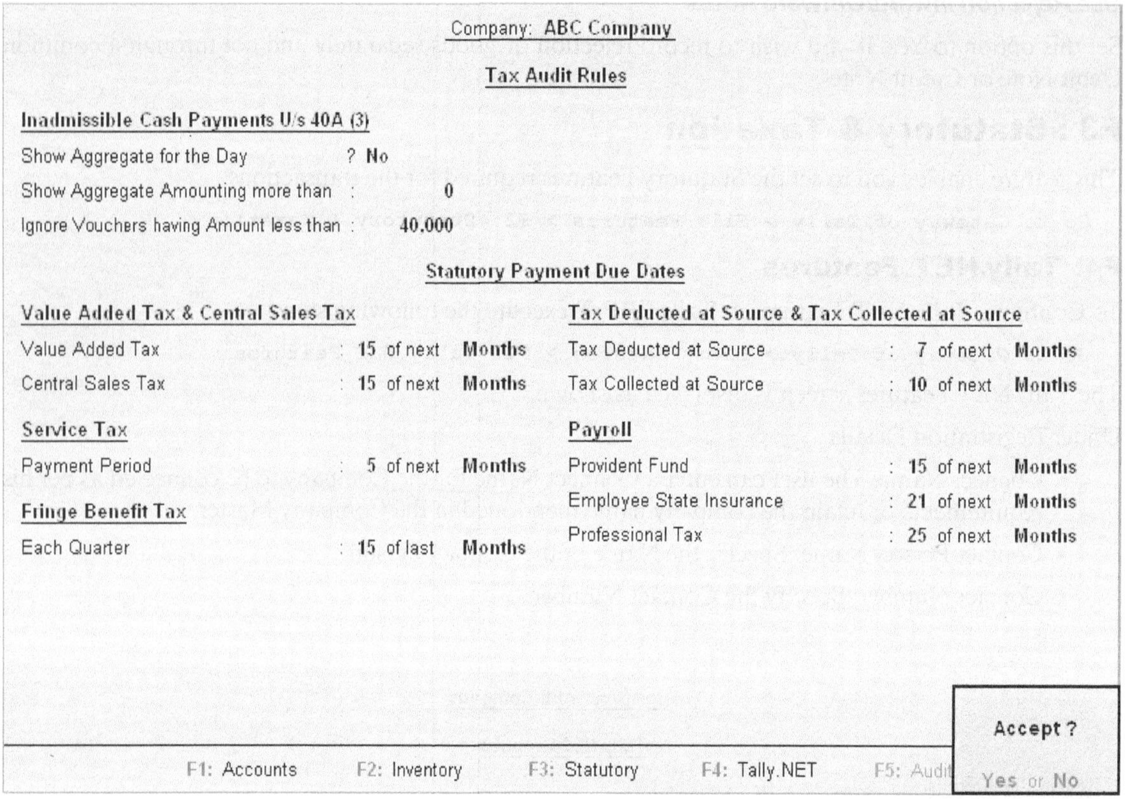

Company: ABC Company
Tax Audit Rules
Inadmissible Cash Payments U/s 40A (3)
Show Aggregate for the Day ? No
Show Aggregate Amounting more than : 0
Ignore Vouchers having Amount less than : 40,000
Statutory Payment Due Dates
Value Added Tax & Central Sales Tax
Value Added Tax : 15 of next Months
Central Sales Tax : 15 of next Months
Service Tax
Payment Period : 5 of next Months
Fringe Benefit Tax
Each Quarter : 15 of last Months
Tax Deducted at Source & Tax Collected at Source
Tax Deducted at Source : 7 of next Months
Tax Collected at Source : 10 of next Months
Payroll
Provident Fund : 15 of next Months
Employee State Insurance : 21 of next Months
Professional Tax : 25 of next Months
Accept ?
Yes or No
F1: Accounts
F2: Inventory
F3: Statutory
F4: Tally.NET
F5: Audit

Fig. 5.32 Tax Audit Rules

Under Connect for Remote Access

- Allow to Connect Company: Set this option to Yes, when the user needs to establish a connection with the Tally.NET server.
- Connect on Load: Set this option to Yes, when the user requires the company to be connected to Tally.NET server on loading the data.
- Press Enter to accept.

F5: Audit Features

This feature enables you to set the Tax Audit Rules and Statutory Payment Due dates for Tax Audit and Statutory Compliance tools.

```
Go to Gateway of Tally > F11: Features
> F5: Audit Features
```

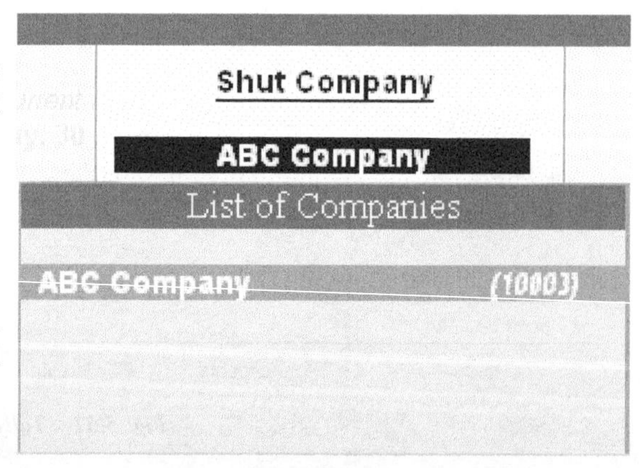

Shut a Company

Shut Company
ABC Company
List of Companies
ABC Company
(10003)

Shut a Company is to unload it. It does not mean that you have deleted it. Simply select it again to load and work on it again.

You can shut a company in two ways – either using

the button F1: Shut Cmp (Alt + F1) or pressing Enter on Shut Company menu option on the Company Info. Menu.

The screen appears as shown below:

Select the company to be shut from the List of Primary Companies.

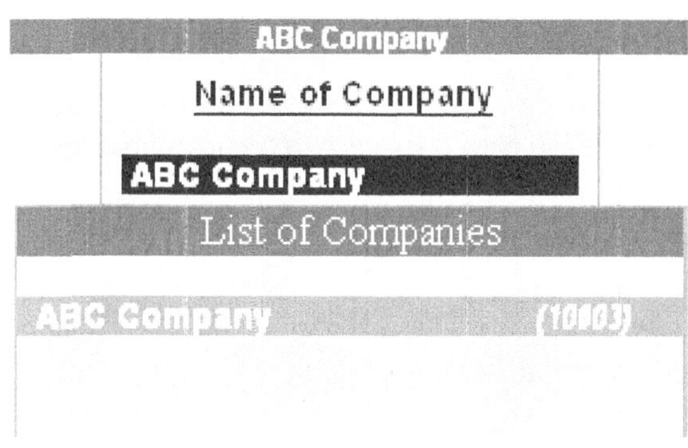

Alter a Company

You can modify any information at any time that is set while creating a company.

Go to Gateway of Tally

Select F3: Cmp Info. (ALT+F3) from the button bar

Select Alter and press Enter and the screen appears as shown here:

Make the necessary changes in the required fields. To change the password if Use Security Control is set to Yes:

1. Enter the Name of Administrator.
2. Enter the new password.
3. Re-enter the password in the Repeat field to confirm.
4. Enter the Old Password and Accept the screen to alter the company.

Security Control

Disallow opening in Educational mode ? No
Use Security Control ? Yes
(Enable Security to avail Tally.NET Features)
Name of Administrator : Admin
Password : *****
Repeat Password : *****
Old Password : *****
Use Tally Audit Features ? Yes

Delete a Company

To delete a company, you have to load the company first.

1. Select F3: Cmp Info. (ALT+F3) from the Gateway of Tally to proceed to the Company Information menu.
2. Select Alter and press Enter.
3. Select the company to be deleted. The Company Alteration screen is displayed.
4. Use Alt + D to delete. Tally.ERP 9 will prompt for a confirmation on deleting the company.
5. Press enter to delete the company.

Maintaining Group Company in Tally.ERP 9

The books of Account of different companies belonging to the same management or owners are required to be consolidated to present the financial position of the group of companies as a whole. This is mandatory in many developed countries and currently shareholders would rather know the performance of the group as a whole and not the performance of individual constituent companies.

Tally.ERP 9 simplifies the task of consolidation of accounts. You can consolidate the accounts of any number of companies as well as keep them separate.

The first step is to create a Group Company, which is simply a name and identity given to the merged accounts of constituent (member) companies of the group. A group company may also include other group companies.

Creating a Group Company

A Group Company can be created only for companies that have already been loaded. Hence, you must first load the companies whose accounts are to be grouped. Select the companies using F1:Select Cmp button.

Tally.ERP 9 now displays two company names in the Gateway of Tally.

Note: The Company which is in bold, is the active company. Here, Company A is the active company.

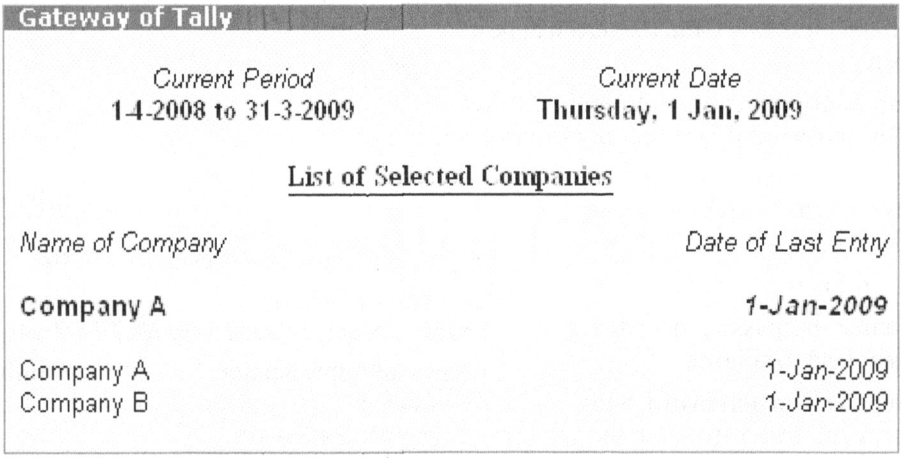

Gateway of Tally

Current Period	Current Date
1-4-2008 to 31-3-2009	Thursday, 1 Jan, 2009

List of Selected Companies

Name of Company	Date of Last Entry
Company A	***1-Jan-2009***
Company A	1-Jan-2009
Company B	1-Jan-2009

Use Alt+F3 to get the company info Menu in which there is an additional option Create Group Company (this is available only when two or more companies are loaded).

Press Enter on Create Group Company. The Group Company Creation screen is displayed.

All the loaded companies are displayed under List of companies. Select the member companies from the List of companies and accept to Create the Group Company.

At the Gateway of Tally, Tally.ERP 9 displays AB Group company and the member companies. You can close the member companies by pressing Alt+F1, so that only the Group Company is displayed in the Gateway of Tally.

Note:

1. Entering a Transaction is not possible in Group Company, that is, in AB Group company. [You have to enter the transaction in a member company only, that is, Company A or Company B].
2. The Group company will give the summary (report) level consolidation and NOT transaction (voucher) level consolidation (that is, NO Merging of vouchers)
3. The member companies of a Group Company should have the same Base Currency Symbol and Formal Name (you cannot group a company with $ as symbol with another company having Rs. as the currency symbol).

Directory : C:\Tally.ERP9\Data
Name : AB Group
Mailing Name : AB Group
Address : No.9, AB Complex
Hosur Road
Bangalore

Country : India
State : Karnataka
PIN Code : 560072
Telephone No. : 080-57845814
E-Mail : sales@abgroup.com

Members : Company A

List of Companies

Company B (10021)

Altering a Group Company

You can alter a Group company by editing the details or adding or removing the member companies.

Load the Group Company and from

Gateway of Tally > Press Alt+F3 > Select Alter > Press [Enter]

Gateway of Tally

Current Period	Current Date
1-4-2008 to 31-3-2009	Thursday, 1 Jan, 2009

List of Selected Companies

Name of Company	Date of Last Entry
AB Group	
AB Group	
Company A	1-Jan-2009
Company B	1-Jan-2009
Company A	1-Jan-2009
Company B	1-Jan-2009

Select Group Company [Group companies are marked with an asterisk].

The Group Company alteration screen is displayed as shown:

Company A
Name of Company
Company A
List of Companies
AB Group (10001) *
Company A (10019)
Company B (10021)

Any modifications made will come into effect only on shutting the group company and then reloading it.

Points to remember:

- The Group Company must contain at least two members.
- It is possible to combine accounts of different companies.
- Create as many Group companies as you need.
- A constituent company can be a member of more than one group.
- A group company can also be a constituent of another group company.

Notes

- It is advisable not to delete the member company, which belongs to Group Company.
- If the member company has a password then without entering the password the Group Company cannot be opened.

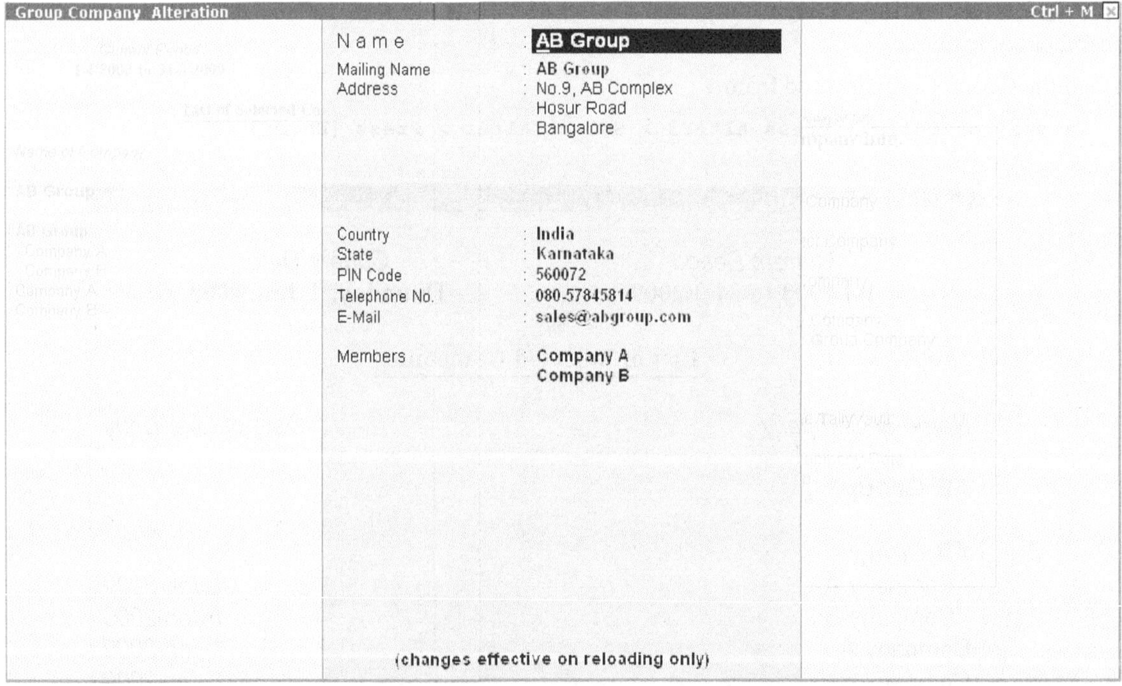

Fig. 5.33 Group Company Alteration Screen

6 Advance Features of Tally.ERP 9

Advanced Accounting Features in Tally.ERP 9

Cost Centres

A Cost Centre is any unit of an organisation to which transactions (generally, revenue) can be allocated. When only costs or expenses are allocated to these units, they are referred to as Cost Centres. When profits are also allocated to these units, they become Profit Centres. You can now obtain a Profit and Loss account of each such Profit Centre.

Cost Centre in Tally.ERP 9 allows an additional dimension to a transaction where a Ledger account indicates the nature of the transaction. It does not readily disclose, except in the narration field, which part of the organisation was involved in the transaction.

With the help of Cost Centres, a transaction can be allocated to it, which would then enable accumulation of the all transactions for that particular Cost Centre. Tally.ERP 9 gives you the Cost Centre break-up of each transaction as well as details of transactions for each Cost Centre.

Some examples of Cost Centres are:

- Departments of an organisation - Finance, Manufacturing, Marketing, and so on.
- Products of a company.
- Individuals such as Salesman A, Salesman B.

Use of Cost Centres

You can classify Cost Centres, just as how you classify Group/Ledger accounts. You can have Primary Cost Centres and several levels of Cost Centres under each Primary Cost Centre.

Consider the following example.

Primary Cost Centres - Finance, Manufacturing, Marketing.

Under Marketing, classify the company's sales executives as Cost Centres. This will help you track a sales executive's performance, in terms of cost and revenue generated.

You will then have the following Cost Centre structure.

Primary Cost Centre - Marketing

Under Marketing:

- Salesman A
- Salesman B
- Salesman C.

Allocate expenditure incurred on sales by the salesmen, as well as the sales generated by them, directly to their Cost Centres. The allocation is done at the time of voucher entry. This prevents allocation errors at the end of the period.

By allocating expenses and sales transactions to the salesmen, you are setting up a valuable information system that tracks the performance of your salesmen.

Creating a Single Cost Centre

To create a Cost Centre, set Maintain Cost Centres to Yes in F11: Accounting Features. For parallel allocation of Cost, you can set More than ONE Payroll/ Cost Category to Yes.

By default, Tally.ERP 9 activates the Cost Centre feature for Ledger accounts under Sales Accounts, Purchase Accounts, Expense and Income groups.

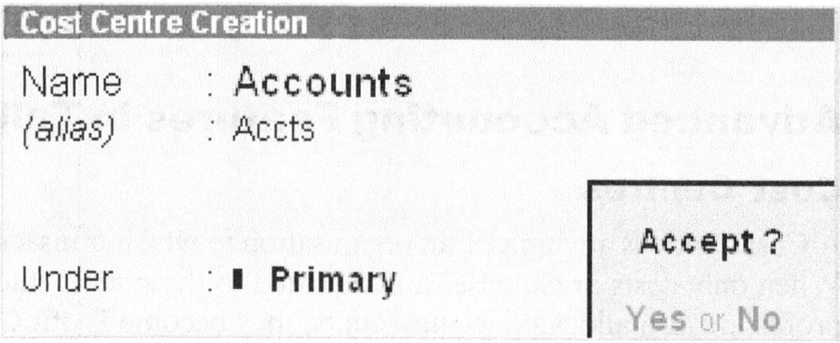

Cost Centre Creation

Name : Accounts
(alias) : Accts

Under : Primary

Accept ?
Yes or No

```
Go to Gateway of Tally> Accounts Info.> Cost Centres> Create (Single Cost Centre)
```

The Cost Centre Creation screen is displayed as shown.

A brief explanation on each of the fields in the Cost Centre Creation screen follows.

Name

Enter the name of the Cost Centre in this field. For example, Name, function, activity, department, task and so on.

alias

Enter an alternative name, if required. For example, a short name or a code number

Under

Select the parent Cost Centre under which the Cost Centre is grouped or created from the List of Cost Centres. If you want the Cost Centre to be a Primary Cost Centre, select Primary from the list.

Note: Unlike Groups, you can allocate transactions to Primary Cost Centres. However, you should do so when you do not have Sub Cost Centres under the Primary Cost Centre.

Displaying a Single Cost Centre

To display the details of Cost Centre masters

```
Go to Gateway of Tally > Accounts Info. > Cost Centres > Display (under Single Cost Centre)
```

The Cost Centre Display screen appears. It is not possible to make any modifications to the Cost Centre master in the Display mode. You can only view the details in this mode.

Altering a Cost Centre

To alter an existing Cost Centre

```
Go to Gateway of Tally> Accounts Info.> Cost Centres> Alter (under Single Cost Centre)
```

The Cost Centre Alteration displays,

Make the necessary changes and Accept to save.

Fig. 6.1 Cost Centre Alteration

Deleting a Cost Centre

You can delete a Cost Centre from the Cost Centre Alteration screen by pressing ALT+D.

You can delete a Cost Centre only if

- It does not have any Cost Centres created under it.
- It is not used in any transactions.

Explanation of Buttons for Cost Centres in Single Mode

Groups, Ledgers, Voucher Types

It enables you to switch to these areas without having to quit from the current screen.

F11: Features

To change company features.

F12: Configure

To change the configuration of master information.

Note: F12: Configuration changes affect all companies in the data directory, whereas F11: Features changes affect the current company only.

Creating Multiple Cost Centres

You can create multiple Cost Centres in this mode.

```
Go to Gateway of Tally> Accounts Info.> Cost Centres> Create (under Multiple Ledgers)
```

The Multi Cost Centre Creation screen is displayed as shown.

Multi Cost Centre Creation — ABC Company — Ctrl + M

Under Cost Centre : All Items

S.No.	Name of Cost Centre	Under
1.	Marketing	Primary
2.	Sales	Primary
3.	Accounts	Primary

Accept ?

Yes or No

Fig. 6.2 Multi Cost Centre Creation

A brief explanation on each of the fields in the Multi Cost Centre Creation screen follows.

Under Cost Centre

Select a particular Cost Centre as the parent Cost Centre, to create cost centres under it. If you wish to create cost centres under different Cost Centres, select All Items and specify the relevant cost centres in the Under field.

Name of Cost Centre

Enter the name of the Cost Centre to be created.

Under

The Parent Cost Centre selected in the Under Cost Centre field displays automatically in the Under field for Cost Centres created newly. If All Items is selected in the Under Cost Centre field, you have the option of selecting the Cost Centre from the List of Cost Centres.

Displaying Cost Centres in Multiple Mode

You can display the details of multiple Cost Centres at a time in this mode.

```
Go to Gateway of Tally> Accounts Info.> Cost Centres> Display (under Multiple
Cost Centres)
```

Select a Cost Centre or All Items to display the details of all the Cost Centres under it. Alteration of Cost Centres will not be possible in Display mode.

Note: The alias option will not be available in Multiple Cost Centre Creation mode. However, you can specify aliases to Cost Centres by selecting each cost centre.

Altering Cost Centres in Multiple Mode

You can alter multiple Cost Centres at a time in this mode.

```
Go to Gateway of Tally > Accounts Info.> Cost Centres > Alter (under Multiple
Cost Centres)
```

Use <backspace> to move back to the field Under Cost Centre or use the button F4: Parent to change parent Cost Centre. Make the necessary changes in the respective fields and Accept to save.

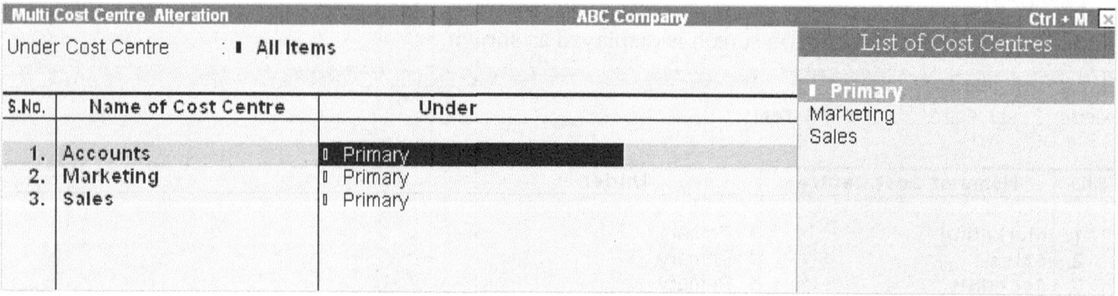

Multi Cost Centre Alteration ABC Company Ctrl + M

Under Cost Centre : All Items

S.No.	Name of Cost Centre	Under
1.	Accounts	Primary
2.	Marketing	Primary
3.	Sales	Primary

List of Cost Centres

Primary
Marketing
Sales

Fig. 6.3 Multi Cost Centre Alteration

Note: You cannot delete a Cost Centre in multiple mode.

Explanation on Buttons in Multiple Mode.

F4: Parent

It is used to move the cursor to the field Under Cost Centre.

Ctrl + F4: New Parent

It is used to bring up the list of Cost Centres, to select a new parent Cost Centre.

F6: Skip Name/Edit Name

It is used for faster data entry when you need to alter only the Category and the Parent Cost Centre, but not the names. While skipping names, you might change the Category or the parent Cost Centre to one, which belongs to another Category, in such instances Tally.ERP 9 displays an error message at the time of accepting the screen.

F7: Skip Parent/Edit Parent

It is used for quicker data entry, when you do not need to alter the parent Cost Centres but only the name of the Cost Centre. While skipping Parent Cost Centres, you might change the Category or the Cost Centres names, in such instances Tally.ERP 9 displays an error message at the time of accepting the screen.

Groups, Ledgers, Cst Cat:

It enables you to switch to these areas without having to quit from the current screen.

F11: Features:

To change Company features.

Cost Categories

Cost Categories are useful for organisations that require allocation of Revenue and Non-Revenue Items to parallel sets of Cost Centres. Cost categories facilitate third dimensional reporting of Expenditure and revenue. Some of the examples of Cost Categories can be Regionwise or geographywise, Gradewise, Departmentwise and so on.

Use of Cost Categories

By using Cost Categories you may allocate, in parallel, a transaction to more than one set of Cost Centres. The following example illustrates the use of Cost Categories.

The Cost Centres such as Marketing, Finance and Manufacturing can now belong to a category - Departments.

The Salesmen A, B and C can be Cost Centres under a Category - Executives.

Similarly, you can create a new Cost Category Projects under which Cost Centres such as Airport construction, Road construction and Buildings may be created. The classification appears as following:

Cost Categories	*Departments*	*Executives*	*Projects*
Cost Centres	Marketing	Salesman A	Airport Construction
	Manufacturing	Salesman B	Road Construction
	Finance	Salesman C	Buildings

Specify a Cost Category to allow allocation of only revenue items or items of both revenue and capital (Non-Revenue) nature. Here in this instance, enable Revenue Items and Non-Revenue Items to Yes for Departments and Projects Categories and only Allow Revenue Items for Executives.

By allocating expenses to parallel Cost Centres under different categories, you are simply assigning the amounts to them; the amount does not increase. Tally.ERP 9 performs an automatic reconciliation on real-time basis, saving you the effort of reconciling Ledgers and Cost Centres.

Note: Transactions are not allocated to Cost Categories but to Cost Centres only.

Creating a Single Cost Category

To create a Cost Category, set Maintain Cost Centres to Yes in F11: Accounting Features and then set More than ONE Payroll/ Cost Category to Yes.

Cost/Profit Centres Management

Maintain Payroll ? No
Maintain Cost Centres ? Yes
Use Cost Centre for Job Costing ? No
More than ONE Payroll / Cost Category ? Yes
Use Pre-defined Cost Centre Allocations during Entry ? No

This option is by default, set to No. When this option is set to Yes, Tally.ERP 9 creates a single Cost Category called Primary Cost Category automatically and allows creation of Cost Centres under the Primary Cost Category. However, you may also create new Cost Categories or alter existing Cost Categories.

To create a Cost Category

```
Go to Gateway of Tally > Accounts Info. > Cost Categories > Create (under Single
Cost Category)
```

The Cost Category Creation screen is displayed as shown.

A brief description on each of the fields in the Cost Category Creation screen follows.

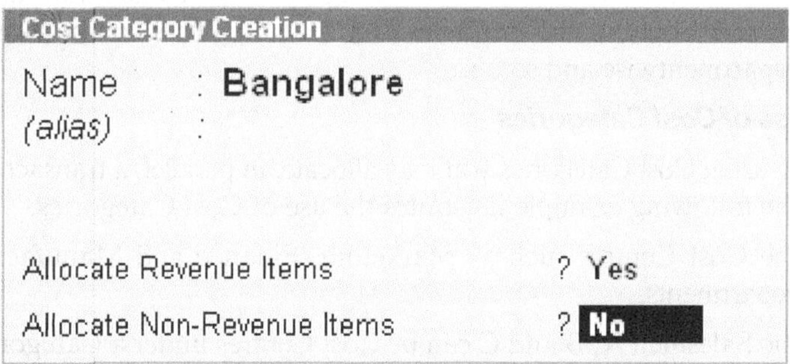

Name

Enter the name of the Cost Category.

Note: There is no sub-classification of Cost Categories and hence you do not find an Under option. Though, there is a Primary Cost Category, it is not a parent of other categories.

(alias)

Enter an alias, if you wish to call the Category by another name or even by a code number. This field displays only if you set Allow ADVANCED entries in Masters in Gateway of Tally >F12: Configure> Accts/Inv Info. to Yes.

Allocate Revenue Items

Set this option to Yes, to allocate all sales, purchase, expenses and income related transactions to Cost Centres created under this Cost Category. However, if you wish to allocate only capital/non-revenue items to Cost Centres created under this Cost Category, set this option to No.

Allocate Non-Revenue Items

Set this option to Yes, to allocate transactions related to capital or non-revenue nature to Cost Centres created under this Cost Category. By default, this option is set to No.

Note: Enable either Revenue or Non-Revenue items, or both. Do not disable both. Tally.ERP 9 sets Yes, by default, for Revenue items and No for Non-Revenue items.

Displaying a Single Cost Category

To view the details of the selected Cost Category masters from this mode

```
Go to Gateway of Tally> Accounts Info.> Cost Categories> Display (under Single
Cost Category)
```

- Select a Cost Category from the List of Categories. The Cost Category Display screen is displayed.

You cannot make any changes to the fields in the Display mode.

Altering a Cost Category

To alter an existing Cost Category

```
Go to Gateway of Tally> Accounts Info.> Cost Categories> Alter (under Single
Cost Category)
```

Select the Cost Category from the List of Categories. The Cost Category Alteration screen displays. Make the changes in the required fields and Accept to save.

Deleting a Cost Category

You may delete a Cost Category that does not have any cost centre under it from the Cost Category Alteration screen. Use ALT+D to delete it. Tally.ERP 9 does not allow deletion of a Cost Category that has Cost Centres.

Buttons in Single Cost Category screens

Groups, Ledgers, Cst Ctr, Vch Types

It enables you to switch to these areas without having to quit from the current screen.

F11: Features

To change company features. A detailed explanation on features has been given in the earlier section under Gateway of Tally.

Note: F12: Configuration changes affect all companies, whereas F11: Features changes affect only the current company

Creating Multiple Cost Categories

You can create multiple Cost Categories at a time using the multiple mode.

```
Go to Gateway of Tally > Accounts Info. > Cost Categories > Create (under
Multiple Cost categories)
```

The Multi Cost Category Creation screen is displayed as shown:

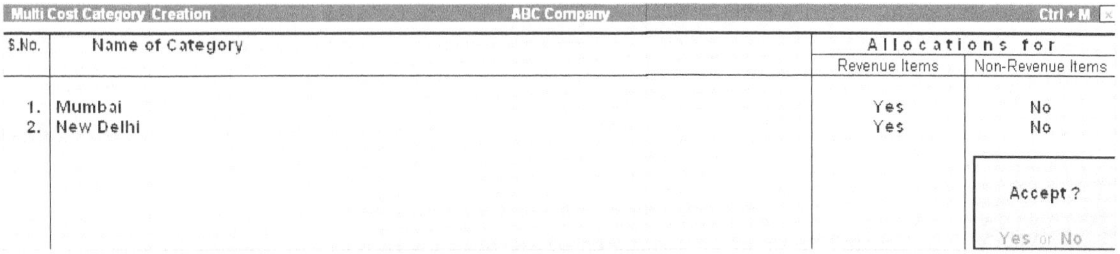

Multi Cost Category Creation ABC Company Ctrl + M

S.No.	Name of Category	Allocations for	
		Revenue Items	Non-Revenue Items
1.	Mumbai	Yes	No
2.	New Delhi	Yes	No

Accept ?

Yes or No

Fig. 6.4 Multi Cost Category Creation

An explanation on each of the fields in Multi Cost Category Creation screen follows.

S. No.

This is an auto-generated serial number.

Name of Category

Enter the name of the Cost Category.

Allocations for

The Allocations for column is divided into two options, Revenue Items and Non-Revenue Items.

Revenue Items

This is set to Yes, by default. However, you have the option of altering it. This denotes whether you want to allocate revenue items to Cost Centres created under the Cost Category.

Non-revenue Items

This option is set to No, by default. You can set it to Yes, if you wish to allocate Non-Revenue or Capital items to Cost Centres created under the Cost Category.

Note: There is no Under field as you cannot sub-classify Cost Categories. Cost Categories have Cost Centres as their sub-classification.

Displaying Cost Categories in Multiple Mode

You can display multiple Cost Categories at a time in this mode. To display Cost Categories in the multiple mode

```
Go to Gateway of Tally> Accounts Info.> Cost Categories > Display (under
Multiple Cost Categories)
```

The Multi Cost Category Display screen is displayed. View the details of all the Cost Categories created. It is not possible to make any changes in display mode.

Altering Cost Categories in Multiple Mode

You can alter multiple Cost Categories at a time in this mode. To alter Cost Categories in the multiple mode

```
Go to Gateway of Tally> Accounts Info.> Cost Categories > Alter (under Multiple
Cost Categories)
```

The Multi Cost Category Alteration screen displays. Make the necessary changes and Accept to save.

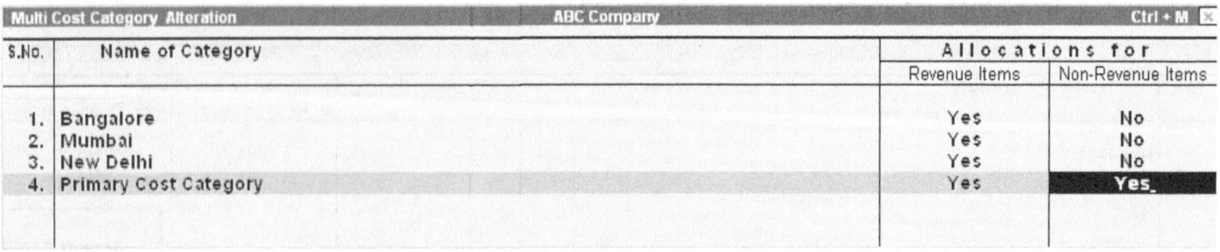

Multi Cost Category Alteration | ABC Company | Ctrl + M

S.No.	Name of Category	Allocations for	
		Revenue Items	Non-Revenue Items
1.	Bangalore	Yes	No
2.	Mumbai	Yes	No
3.	New Delhi	Yes	No
4.	Primary Cost Category	Yes	Yes_

Fig. 6.5 Multi Cost Category Alteration

Note: You will not be able to delete a Cost Category in multiple mode.

Buttons in Single Multiple Cost Category screens

F6: Skip names

It is used for quicker data entry when you need to alter only the Allocation details and not the names of the Cost Categories.

F8: Skip Details

It is used for faster data entry when you do not need to alter the Allocation (Revenue and Non- revenue) details. You need to give only the names and the default allocations of Yes for Revenue and No for Non-revenue display automatically when you are creating Cost Categories. If you are in Alter mode, the allocations that you opted for when creating the Categories are retained.

Groups, Ledgers, Cst Ctr

It enables you to switch to these areas, without having to quit from the current screen.

F11: Features

It is used to change company features.

Note: F12: Configuration changes affect all companies, whereas F11: Features changes affect only the current company.

Creating Cost Centres under Cost Categories

To create a Cost Centre under a Cost Category, set More than ONE Payroll/Cost Category to Yes in F11: Accounting Features.

```
Go to Gateway of Tally > Accounts Info. > Cost Centre > Create (under Single
Cost Centres)
```

Category

This field appears only when you have opted for More than ONE Payroll/ Cost Category in F11: Features. Else, Tally.ERP 9 automatically creates a Primary Cost Category to which all cost centres are assigned.

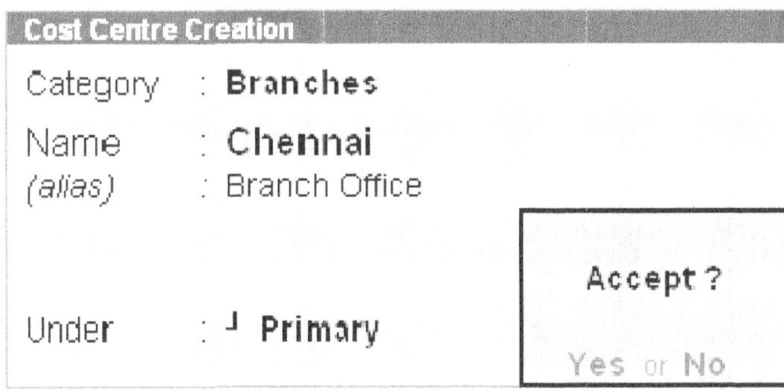

Displaying and Altering Cost Centres under Cost Categories in Single mode is similar to Displaying and Altering Cost Centres in Single mode explained previously. The only additional field is Category.

Creating Multiple Cost Centres under Cost Categories

```
Go to Gateway of Tally> Accounts Info.> Cost Centres> Create (under Multiple
Cost Centres)
```

This is a quick way to create multiple cost centres under a single Cost Category at a time.

Under Cost Centre

Select a particular Cost Centre as the parent cost center, if you wish to create multiple cost centres under it.

Category

Select the Category under which the Cost Centre will be created from the List of Categories or create a new category by pressing [Alt+C].

Name of Cost Centre

Enter the name of the new cost centre. The alias facility is not available in this mode. Select single alter to give aliases to Cost Centres created in multiple mode.

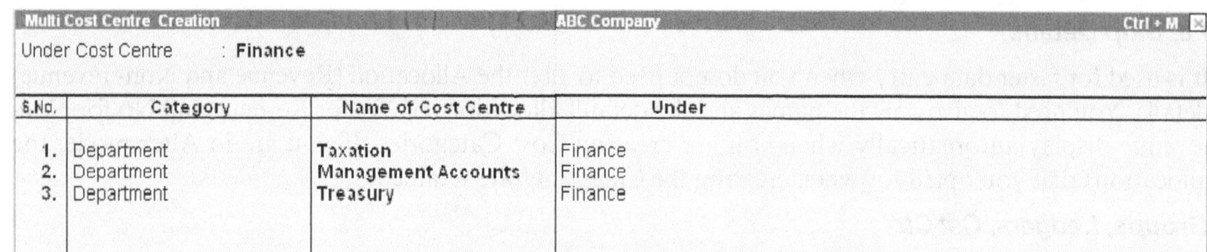

Multi Cost Centre Creation | ABC Company | Ctrl + M

Under Cost Centre : **Finance**

S.No.	Category	Name of Cost Centre	Under
1.	Department	**Taxation**	Finance
2.	Department	**Management Accounts**	Finance
3.	Department	**Treasury**	Finance

Fig. 6.6 Multi Cost Centre Creation

Under

Select the parent Cost Centre from the List of Cost Centres. The list displays only the Cost Centres that belong to the selected Category.

Multi Cost Centre Creation | ABC Company | Ctrl + M

Under Cost Centre : ┘ **All Items**

S.No.	Category	Name of Cost Centre	Under
1.	Branches	**New Delhi**	┘ Primary
2.	Department	**Human Resourse**	┘ Primary
3.			

List of Categories

┘ End of List
Branches
Department
Machines
Primary Cost Category
Processes
Products

Fig. 6.7 Selecting Category

Displaying and Altering Cost Centres under Cost Categories in Multiple mode is similar to Displaying and Altering Cost Centres in Multiple mode explained in the respective chapters. The only additional field is Category.

Error in Categorisation of Cost Centres:

PARENT BELONGS TO ANOTHER CATEGORY!

This error occurs when you try to assign a cost centre to a parent cost centre belonging to a different category. In most places, Tally.ERP 9 prevents you from making this error, by not displaying a cost centre belonging to a different category.

However, this action is not possible when you are altering a cost centre in multiple mode, selecting All Items in Under Cost Centre field. (You may have chosen to skip either or both).

You would have changed the Category without changing the name and the parent. However, Tally.ERP 9 will prompt for this error only at the time of accepting the screen.

Budgets

A budget is a plan prepared for the flow of funds in an organisation. It contains financial guidelines for the future plan of action for a selected period of time.

A budget helps to refine goals and use funds efficiently. It provides accurate information for evaluation of financial activities, aids in decision making and provides a reference for future planning.

Multiple budgets can be created for specific purposes in Tally.ERP 9. Budgets for Banks, Head offices, Departmental budgets like Marketing Budgets, Finance Budgets, and so on, can also be created. The Budgeted figures in Tally.ERP 9 can be compared with Actual figures and variance report can be generated.

In Tally.ERP 9, you can create, alter and delete a budget.

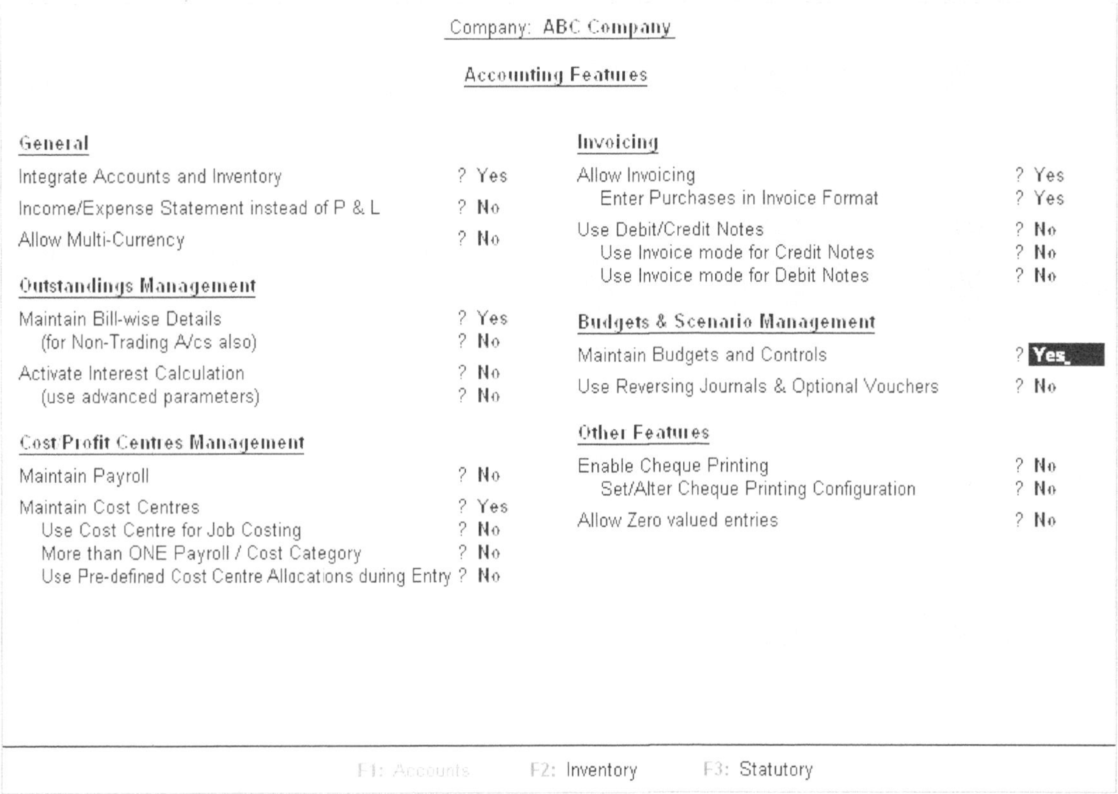

Company: ABC Company

Accounting Features

General		Invoicing	
Integrate Accounts and Inventory	? Yes	Allow Invoicing	? Yes
Income/Expense Statement instead of P & L	? No	Enter Purchases in Invoice Format	? Yes
Allow Multi-Currency	? No	Use Debit/Credit Notes	? No
		Use Invoice mode for Credit Notes	? No
		Use Invoice mode for Debit Notes	? No
Outstandings Management		**Budgets & Scenario Management**	
Maintain Bill-wise Details	? Yes	Maintain Budgets and Controls	? Yes
(for Non-Trading A/cs also)	? No	Use Reversing Journals & Optional Vouchers	? No
Activate Interest Calculation	? No		
(use advanced parameters)	? No		
Cost/Profit Centres Management		**Other Features**	
Maintain Payroll	? No	Enable Cheque Printing	? No
Maintain Cost Centres	? Yes	Set/Alter Cheque Printing Configuration	? No
Use Cost Centre for Job Costing	? No	Allow Zero valued entries	? No
More than ONE Payroll / Cost Category	? No		
Use Pre-defined Cost Centre Allocations during Entry	? No		

F1: Accounts F2: Inventory F3: Statutory

Fig. 6.8 Setting Budgets in Accounting Features

Activating Budgets Feature

To activate the Budgets feature in Tally.ERP 9:

1. Select F11: Features > F1: Accounting Features.
2. Set Maintain Budgets and Controls? to Yes.
3. Accept to save.

Creating a Budget

To create a Budget in Tally.ERP 9

Go to Gateway of Tally > Accounts Info > Budgets > Create

1. In the Budget Creation screen enter a Name for your budget.
2. Select from the List of Budgets for Under field. You can have a hierarchical setup for budgets. In the List of Budgets, Primary is at the top of the hierarchy and you can create more primary budgets. Sub-budgets can be created under Primary budgets.
3. Enter the period of the budget in the From and To fields. The period entered can be a month, a year or any other period.
4. In Set/Alter Budgets of, select

- Groups - To create a budget for a Group of ledger accounts.

- Ledgers - To create a budget for Ledgers.
- Cost Centres - To create a budget for Cost Centres.

5. Accept to save.

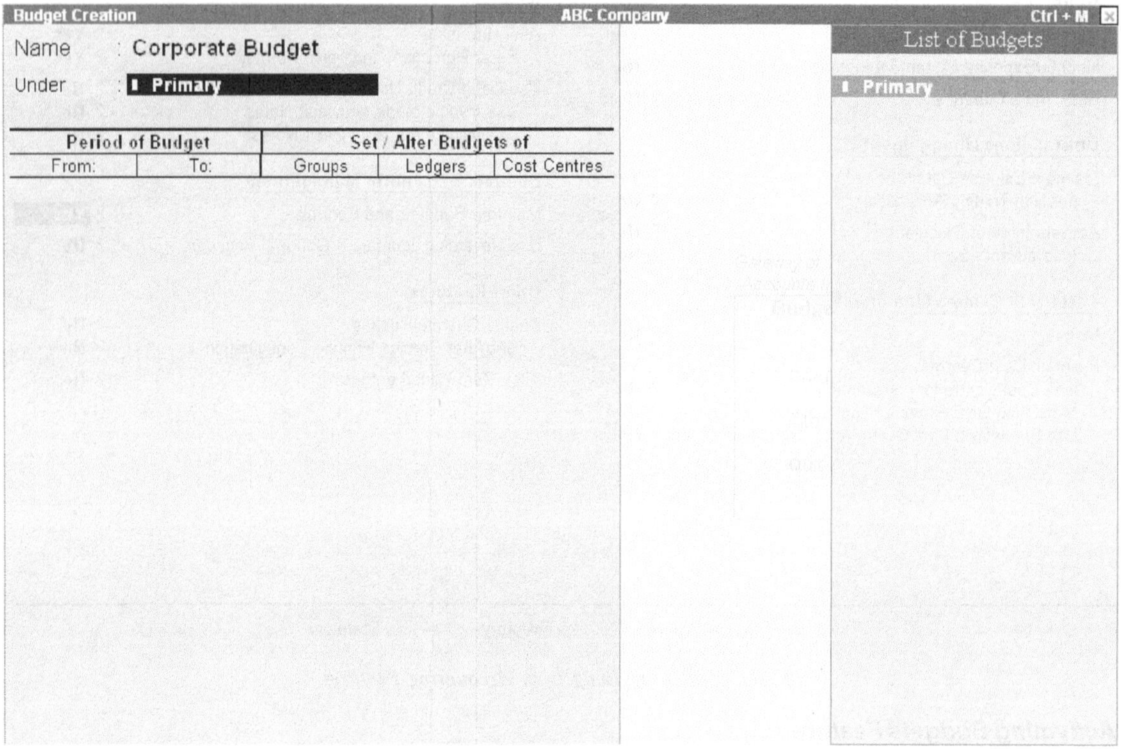

Budget Creation ABC Company Ctrl + M

Name : Corporate Budget

Under : Primary

Period of Budget		Set / Alter Budgets of		
From:	To:	Groups	Ledgers	Cost Centres

List of Budgets

Primary

Fig. 6.9 Budget Creation

Altering a Budget

You can modify a budget, using the alter option.

Go to Gateway of Tally > Accounts Info > Budgets > Alter

1. In the Budget Alteration screen, modify the fields as required. Change the period or change budgets of Groups, Ledgers and Cost Centres.

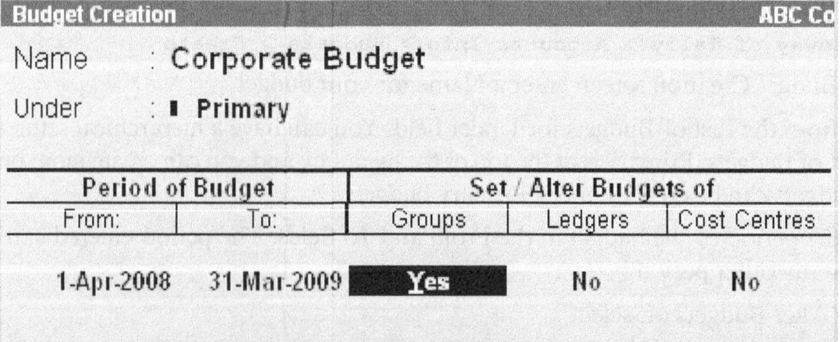

Fig. 6.10 Altering a Budget

Note: By default, Set/Alter Budgets is set to No. Set this option to Yes to alter.

Deleting a Budget

To delete a budget:

```
Go to Gateway of Tally > Accounts Info > Budgets > Alter
```

- Press Alt+D.

Creating Budget for Groups

In the Budget Creation/Alteration screen, set Yes in the Groups field, to set budgets for a group or group of ledgers.

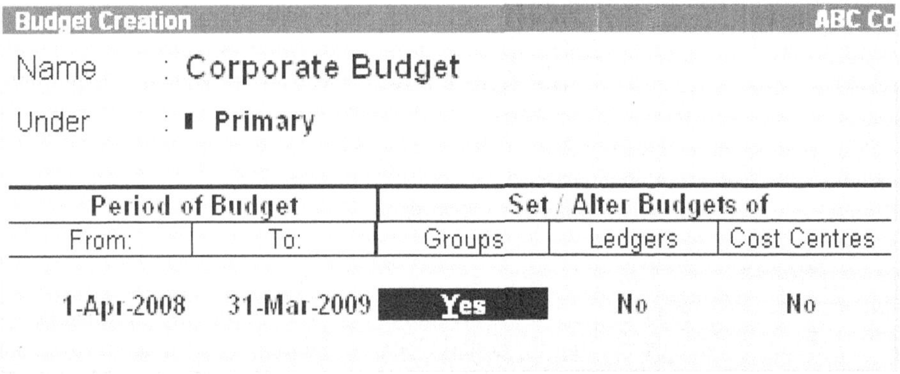

Budget Creation ABC Co

Name : Corporate Budget

Under : Primary

Period of Budget		Set / Alter Budgets of		
From:	To:	Groups	Ledgers	Cost Centres
1-Apr-2008	31-Mar-2009	Yes	No	No

Fig. 6.11 Creating Budgets for Groups

In the Group Budget screen, select a Group from the List of Groups and enter Account Name.

Enter the cost centre for a group in Cost Centres field, select Not Applicable, if the budget is not for a particular cost center.

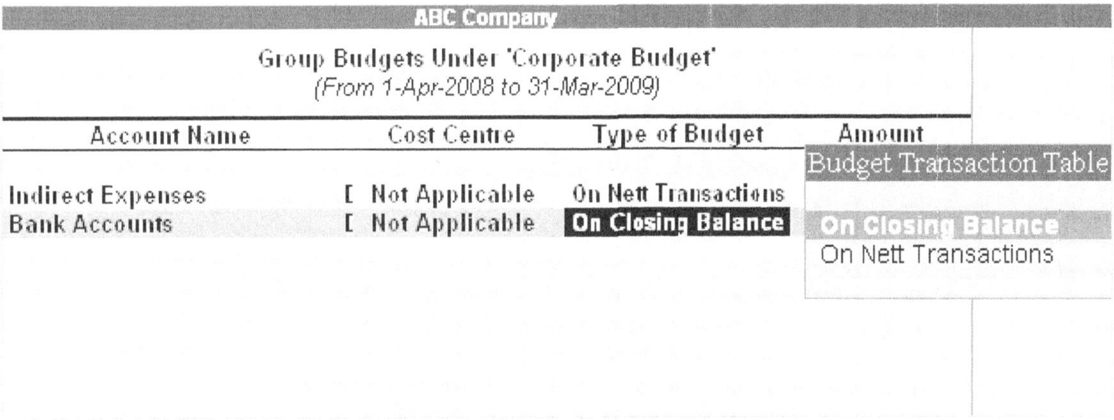

ABC Company

Group Budgets Under 'Corporate Budget'
(From 1-Apr-2008 to 31-Mar-2009)

Account Name	Cost Centre	Type of Budget	Amount
Indirect Expenses	Not Applicable	On Nett Transactions	
Bank Accounts	Not Applicable	On Closing Balance	

Budget Transaction Table
On Closing Balance
On Nett Transactions

Fig. 6.12 Selecting Budget Transaction Table

In Type of Budget, select from the following two types.

1. On Nett Transactions

Select this option to monitor the transaction amounts and not the balances. Nett is net of debits and credits for the specified period. Nett transactions Budgets specified for a period automatically gets apportioned over the period. *i.e.*, When On Nett transactions Budgets are defined, the debit amount for the specified period after reducing the credits for the same period is considered without taking into account opening and closing balances. For example to compare transactions against budgets, especially revenue income and expenses On Nett Transactions can be selected.

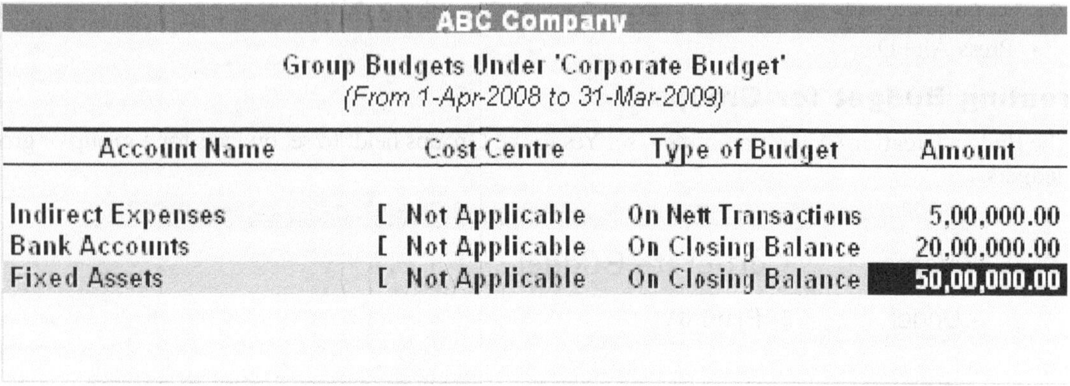

ABC Company			
Group Budgets Under 'Corporate Budget' (From 1-Apr-2008 to 31-Mar-2009)			
Account Name	Cost Centre	Type of Budget	Amount
Indirect Expenses	[Not Applicable	On Nett Transactions	5,00,000.00
Bank Accounts	[Not Applicable	On Closing Balance	20,00,000.00
Fixed Assets	[Not Applicable	On Closing Balance	50,00,000.00

Fig. 6.13 Nett Transactions

2. On Closing Balance

Select this option to monitor the balances of the Accounts and the not the transactions. *i.e.*, each month will have the same budget value except that the actual Opening Balance is also taken into account. Budgets on Closing balances can be set for Bank Account Ledgers, Debtors Ledger balances and so on. For example to compare closing balance figures in final statements, especially Balance Sheet items like assets and liabilities, select Closing Balances.

Enter the budget amount in the Amount field.

Note: Group Budgets do not get apportioned whereas Ledger Budgets get apportioned for each month.

Creating Budget for Ledger Accounts

In the Budget Creation/Alteration screen, set Yes in the Ledgers field, to set budgets for ledgers.

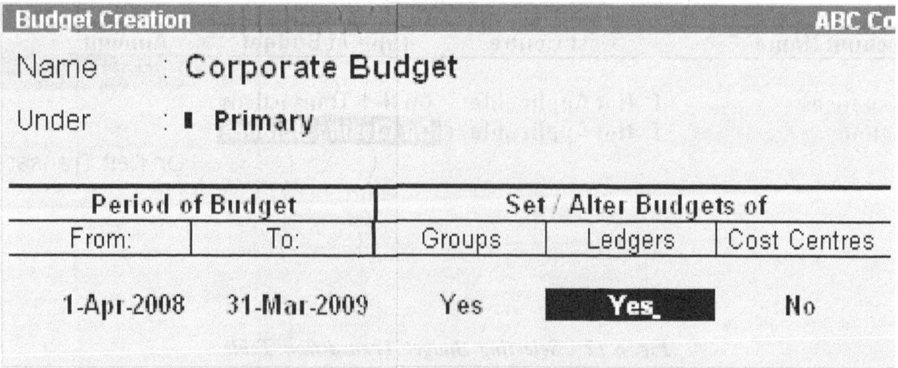

Budget Creation — ABC Co

Name : Corporate Budget

Under : ▪ Primary

Period of Budget		Set / Alter Budgets of		
From:	To:	Groups	Ledgers	Cost Centres
1-Apr-2008	31-Mar-2009	Yes	Yes_	No

Fig. 6.14 Creating Budgets for Ledger Accounts

In the Ledger Budget screen, select a Ledger from the List of Ledgers and enter Account Name.

Budgets can also be defined for Cost Centres pertaining to Ledger Accounts wherein you can repeat the same ledger with another Cost Centre.

Enter the cost centre for the Ledger Account in the Cost Centre field. Select Not Applicable if the budget is not for a particular cost centre, but for the company.

ABC Company

Ledger Budgets Under 'Corporate Budget'
(From 1-Apr-2008 to 31-Mar-2009)

Account Name	Cost Centre	Type of Budget	Amou
Advertisement	Marketing Department	On Nett Transactions	5.00.
Printing & Stationery	Financial Department	On Closing Balance	

Ctrl + M

List of Cost Centres

- Not Applicable
- Financial Department
- Marketing Department
- Sales Man A
- Sales Man B

Fig. 6.15 Selecting the Cost Centre

In Type of Budget, select from the following two types.

1. On Nett Transactions

Select this option to monitor the transaction amounts and not the balances. Nett is net of debits and credits for the specified period. Nett transactions Budgets specified for a period automatically gets apportioned over the period, *i.e.*, when On Nett transactions Budgets are defined, the debit amount for the specified period after reducing the credits for the same period is considered without taking into account opening and closing balances. For example to compare transactions against budgets, especially revenue income and expenses On Nett Transactions can be selected.

2. On Closing Balance

Select this option to monitor the balances of the Accounts and the not the transactions. i.e., each month will have the same budget value except that the actual Opening Balance is also taken into account. Budgets on Closing balances can be set for Bank Account Ledgers, Debtors Ledger balances and so on. For example to compare closing balance figures in final statements, especially Balance Sheet items like assets and liabilities, select Closing Balances.

Enter the budget amount in the Amount field.

ABC Company

Ledger Budgets Under 'Corporate Budget'
(From 1-Apr-2008 to 31-Mar-2009)

Account Name	Cost Centre	Type of Budget	Amount
Advertisement	Marketing Department	On Nett Transactions	5,00,000.00
Printing & Stationery	Financial Department	On Nett Transactions	50,000.00

Fig. 6.16 Entering the Budget Amount

Note: Ledger Budgets get apportioned for each month.

Creating Budgets for Cost Centres

The purpose of a budget is to control expenditure. You can create multiple budgets in Tally.ERP 9, each for a specific purpose such as for the Bank, for the Head Office, Marketing budgets, Finance budgets, and so on.

1. In the Cost Centres field in the Budget Creation/Alteration screen, set Yes to set budgets for cost centres.

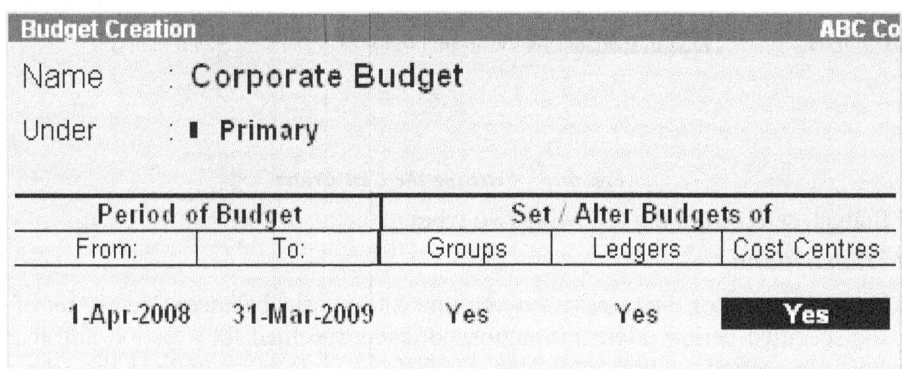

Fig. 6.17 Creating Budget for Cost Centres

2. In the Cost Centre Budget screen, select a Cost Centre from the List of Cost Centres and enter Cost Centre.
3. Enter a budget figure in Expenses for the cost centre.
4. Enter a budget figure in Income for the cost centre.
5. Enter Closing Balance.
6. Accept to save.

ABC Company

Cost Centre Budgets Under 'Corporate Budget'
(From 1-Apr-2008 to 3-Apr-2008)

Cost Centre	Expenses	Income	Closing Balance
Financial Department	15,000.00	5,000.00	10,000.00
Marketing Department	25,000.00	4,000.00	21,000.00

Fig. 6.18 Entering Budgets for Cost Centres

Viewing Budget Variance

Budget Variance report can be viewed from Trial Balance, Group Summary, monthly summary etc. The Budget Variance button (Alt+B) is active, if Budgets feature is enabled and at least one budget created. Budget Variance displays Budgets, Actuals with percentage and Variance from the budget with percentage.

1. Budget Variance can be accessed from:

- Gateway of Tally > Display > Trial Balance to display the Trial Balance screen.
- Gateway of Tally > Display > Account Books > Group Summary and select a group from List of Groups to display the Group Summary screen.

2. Click on Budget Variance (Alt+B) from the toolbar to display the Budget Analysis screen.
3. Select from the List of Budgets for Budgets/Scenario.
4. Three columns display Budget, Actuals and Budget Variance, respectively.

Note: Use Column functionality to add/ remove columns for Multi-period or Multi-budget Comparative Variance report.

Corporate budget Column displays the values of the Budget, which is defined.

Actuals Column displays the value of Actual Expenditure incurred.

Corporate Budget Variance displays the values of the Variance of the Actuals and Budgets. *i.e.*, Budgets – Actuals = Variance .

Note: If the Budget Variance shows the negative value, then the actual expenditure value has exceeded the Budgeted values.

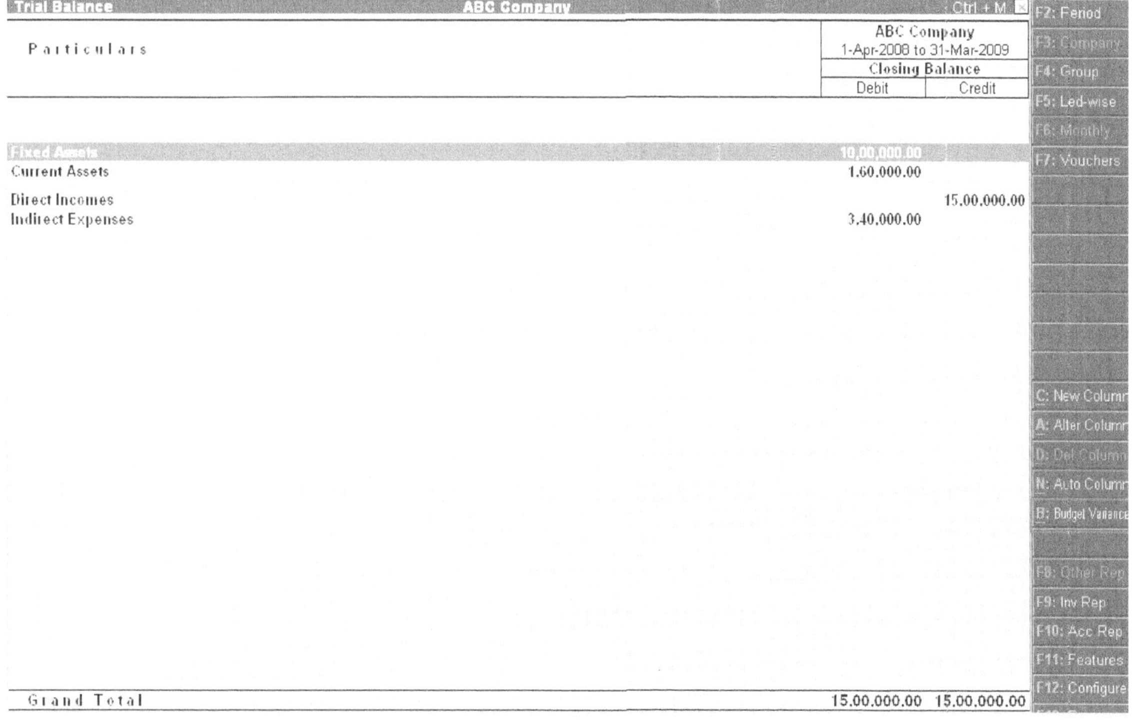

Fig. 6.19 Seeing Budget Variance in Trial Balance

Interest Calculation in Tally.ERP 9

Tally.ERP 9 allows you to obtain reports on interest calculated by Tally.ERP 9 based on the instructions you furnish. Interest figures are typically desired in the following situations:

1. On outstanding balance amounts

Trial Balance	ABC Company					Ctrl + M
Particulars	ABC Company 1-Apr-2008 to 31-Mar-2009 *Corporate Budget*		ABC Company *1-Apr-2008 to 31-Mar-2009* Actuals		ABC Company 1-Apr-2008 to 31-Mar-2009 *Corporate Budget Variance*	
	Closing Balance		Closing Balance		Closing Balance	
	Debit	Credit	Debit	Credit	Debit	Credit
Fixed Assets	**50,00,000.00**		*10,00,000.00 20.00%*		**40,00,000.00** 80%	
Building			10,00,000.00			
Current Assets	**20,00,000.00**		*1,60,000.00 8.00%*		**18,40,000.00** 92%	
Bank Accounts	20,00,000.00		*1,60,000.00 8.00%*		18,40,000.00 92%	
Direct Incomes				*15,00,000.00*		
Income Received				15,00,000.00		
Indirect Expenses	**5,00,000.00**		*3,40,000.00 68.00%*		**1,60,000.00** 32%	
Advertisement			3,00,000.00			
Printing & Stationery			40,000.00			
Profit & Loss A/c		5,00,000.00				(-)5,00,000.00 *(-)100%*
Grand Total	75,00,000.00	5,00,000.00	15,00,000.00 *20.00%*	15,00,000.00 *300.00%*	60,00,000.00	(-)5,00,000.00

Fig. 6.20 Seeing Budget Variance in Trial Balance with Percentage

2. On outstanding bills/invoices/transactions (Receivable and payable)

Tally.ERP 9 gives you an tremendous capability to obtain interest implications on both.

Activate Interest Calculations

Interest is a legitimate return on money invested and chargeable in the business world on loans and also on delayed payments. Interest can be calculated on the basis of Simple or Compound Interest.

The Activate Interest Calculation field is displayed in the Ledger Creation screen only, if Activate Interest Calculations is set to Yes in F11: Features.

Set this field to Yes for each specific ledger account for which interest is to be calculated.

Interest Calculation in Simple Mode

To calculate Interest in the Simple Mode:

1. Go to Gateway of Tally> F11: Features> Accounting Features > Set Activate Interest Calculation to Yes. > Set Use Advanced Parameters to No.
2. In the Ledger Creation screen set Activate Interest Calculation to Yes.
3. The Interest Parameters sub screen is displayed. Enter the Rate and select the interest style from the list.

Interest calculations on outstanding balances

Enter Interest details in Vouchers (only in case of transaction by transaction/Bill-by-bill) and view Interest reports.

You will have to alter existing ledger accounts to permit interest calculations on them. The same operation will apply when creating a new ledger account.

Interest calculation on outstanding balances is allowed for any ledger account. You simply specify the interest rate and style of calculation. Nothing is required to be done for interest during voucher entry.

Let's take an example: Interest calculated on Outstanding Balances.

Go to Gateway of Tally> Accounts Info.> Ledgers> Alter (Single)> XY Bank (bank account)

1. Set Activate interest Calculation to Yes.
2. On activation, the Interest Parameters must be set. It is the basis on which interest will be calculated for this Ledger account.
3. Rate: This is the rate at which the interest has to be calculated. In this case, specify 15%.
4. Interest Style: It is the basis on which the rate is applied. Of the four options, select 365-Day Year.
5. Accept the screen.
6. You can now view the amount of interest that could be charged by the Bank.

Report on Interest Calculated on outstanding balances

The Interest Calculations Report can be displayed and printed.

Go to Gateway of Tally> Display> Statements of Accounts> Interest Calculations> Ledger> XY Bank (Bank Account)

Interest calculation transaction by transaction

Activate and specify interest calculations in ledger masters.

Transaction by transaction or Bill-by-Bill interest calculation is permitted for 'Party' accounts like accounts falling under the groups Sundry Debtors and Sundry Creditors. For example:

1. Alter a Customer account (under the group Sundry Debtors or one of its sub-groups).
2. Set Activate Interest Calculation to Yes. In the Interest Parameters now you have three lines to answer.
3. Set Calculate Interest Transaction-by-transaction to Yes.
4. Set Over-ride Parameters for each transaction to No.

If set to No, you are not allowed to change interest parameters in voucher/invoice entry. If set to Yes, you can change the interest parameters during entry.

Report on Interest Calculated on outstanding transactions/bills

To view the Interest calculated

Go to Gateway of Tally> Display> Statements of Accounts> Interest Calculations> Ledger> CP Ltd

The report is similar to the Bill-wise Outstanding Statement. The last column gives the interest amount on the transaction. Select the line to be viewed in detail for its calculations.

Interest Calculation in Advance Mode

The advanced parameters are particularly useful where interest rates change from time to time.

- Go to Gateway of Tally> F11: Features > Accounting Features > Set Activate Interest Calculation to Yes. > Set Use Advanced Parameters to Yes.
- The Interest Parameters sub-screen is displayed

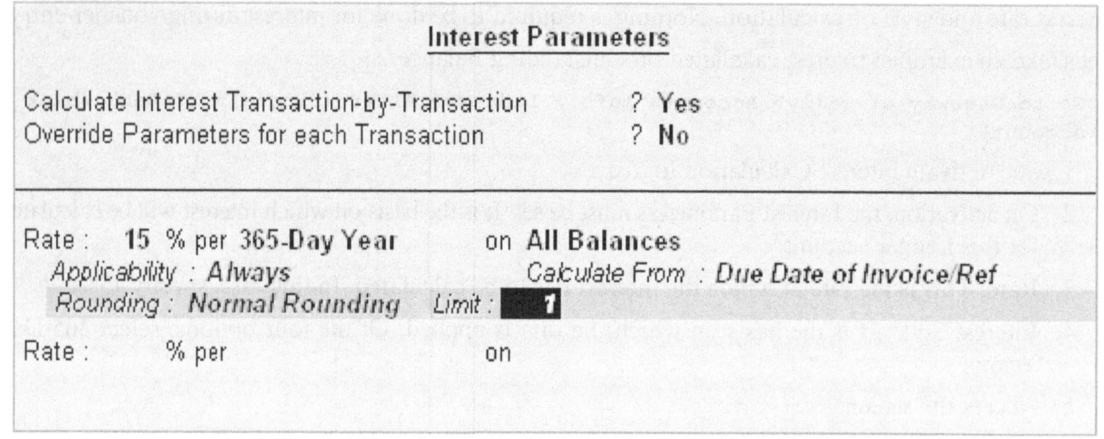

Fig. 6.21 Interest Calculations in Advanced Mode

For Ledgers created under the Group Sundry Debtors/Sundry Creditors, the Interest Parameters sub-screen is displayed as shown below:

- Set Calculate Interest Transaction-by-Transaction to Yes, if you want to calculate interest for each transaction.
- Set Override Parameters for each Transaction to Yes, if you want to override the interest rates and parameters set here during voucher entry.
- Enter the interest rate in the Rate field.
- Select the interest rate calculation period from the Interest Style list in the Per field.
- Select the choice of balances for which the interest has to be calculated from the Interest Balances list in the On field. The balances are All Balances, Credit Balances only and Debit balances only. Interest can be calculated on all outstanding balances, whether debit or credit. You would like to select only credit balances in case of accounts like Bank accounts, if you want to know the interest that the bank might charge on overdrawn balances.
- Select the rounding method applicable from the Rounding Methods list. The amount can be rounded off normally or upward or downward. If you do not want any rounding method, select Not Applicable.

For Ledgers created under the Group Bank Accounts, or if the option Calculate Interest Transaction by Transaction is set to No, then the Interest Parameters sub-screen is displayed as shown below.

Enter the interest rate in the Rate field.

- Select the interest rate calculation period from the Interest Style list in the Per field.
- Select the choice of balances for which the interest has to be calculated from the Interest Balances

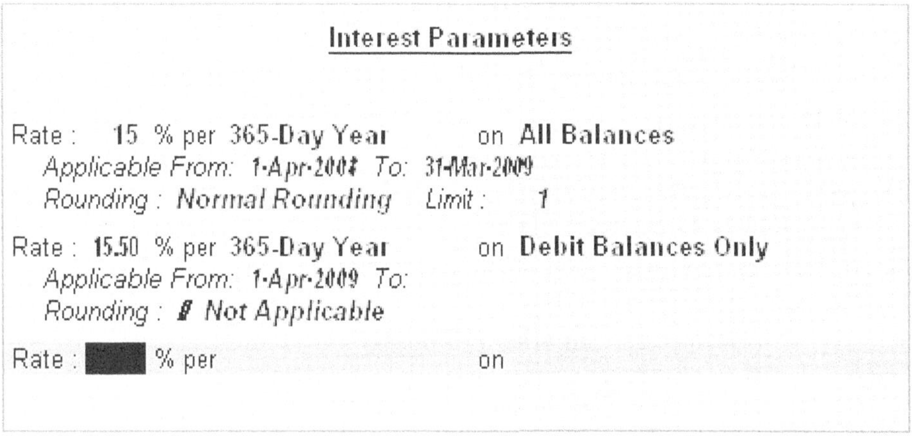

Interest Parameters

Rate : 15 % per 365-Day Year on All Balances
Applicable From: 1-Apr-2008 To: 31-Mar-2009
Rounding : Normal Rounding Limit : 1

Rate : 15.50 % per 365-Day Year on Debit Balances Only
Applicable From: 1-Apr-2009 To:
Rounding : Not Applicable

Rate : % per on

Fig. 6.22 Interest Calculations on Balances

list in the On field. The balances are All Balances, Credit Balances only and Debit balances only. Interest can be calculated on all outstanding balances, whether debit or credit. You would like to select only credit balances in case of accounts like Bank accounts, if you want to know the interest that the bank might charge on overdrawn balances.

- Specify the interest rate applicable period from the Applicable From: and To: fields.
- Select the rounding method applicable from the Rounding Methods list. The amount can be rounded off normally or upward or downward. If you do not want any rounding method, select Not Applicable.

Display Report – Interest on Outstanding Balances

To view the report on Outstanding balances:

```
Go to Gateway of Tally> Display> Statements of Accounts.> Interest Calculations>
Ledgers> XY Bank
```

Advanced Parameters - Interest calculation transaction by transaction

Activate and specify interest calculations in ledger masters.

The following extra options now become available:

- You can now have Multiple Rates of Interest.

Ledger Interest — ABC Company

Ledger : XY Bank — 1-Apr-2008 to 2-Apr-2008

Balance	From:	To:	Total Days	Rate %	Interest
20,00,000.00 Dr	31-Mar-2008	2-Apr-2008	2 days	15 %	1,644.00 Dr
20,00,000.00 Dr	31-Mar-2008	2-Apr-2008	2 days	15.50 %	1,698.63 Dr
				Grand Total	3,342.63 Dr

Fig. 6.23 Ledger Interest Calculations

- You can Override Advanced Parameters during voucher entry. Hence, each entry could have different parameters.
- Choice of Balances – All Balances, Credit Balances only, Debit Balances only.
- Applicability - This actually applies to the viewing of the statement and not the levy of interest.
- Calculate from - You can decide whether interest is to be levied from the Due Date or from the Effective Date of the transaction (or the voucher date if effective date is not activated) or even Date ranges specified during Voucher Entry.
- Choice of methods for Rounding off of interest amounts.

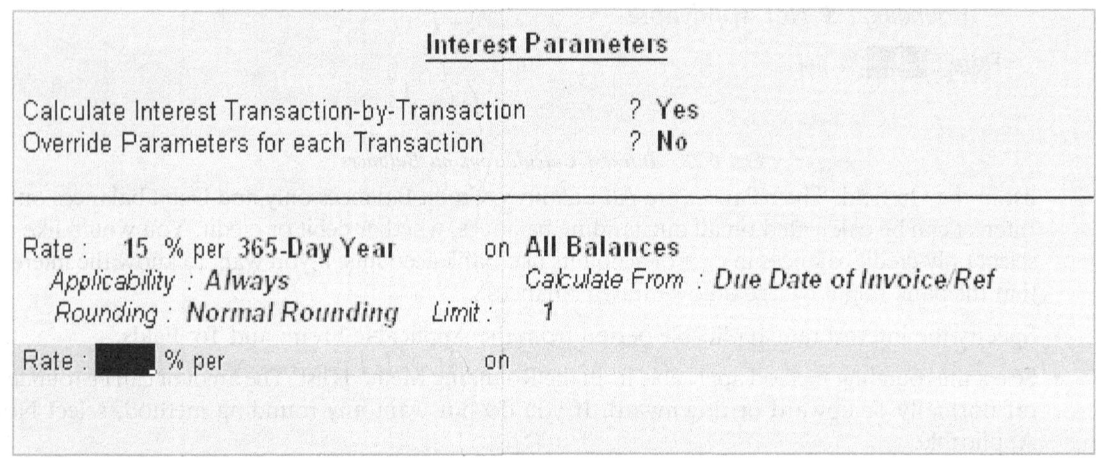

Fig. 6.24 Setting Parameters

Note: To obtain the option Calculate from Date Specified during Entry, you must have Override advanced parameters set to Yes. The option is required if you want to specify interest to be calculated at different rates for different periods. If you choose to override parameters then information would be asked during voucher/invoice entry. The interest information is required after the bill-wise details have been entered.

Report on Interest Calculated on Outstanding Transactions/Bills

```
Go to Gateway of Tally> Display> Statements of Accounts> Interest Calculations>
Ledger> CP Ltd.
```

Press the button F1: Detailed on the Button bar to see the calculation and the period. Previous transactions are calculated from Effective date of Transaction as default. Date Specified during Entry has not been used.

Note: Part monies received have been accounted for and interest calculated on the balance.

A look at Calculate From Dates Specified during Voucher Entry.

You have set up the Interest Parameters for CP Ltd to calculate on Dates specified during Voucher Entry.

We will take one invoice and put in the interest information.

To view the interest amount:

```
Go to Gateway of Tally> Display> Statements of Accounts> Interest Calculations>
Ledger> CP Ltd.
```

Ledger Interest — ABC Company — Ctrl + M

Ledger : CP Ltd — 1-Apr-2008 to 1-Dec-2008

Date	Ref. No.		Opening Amount	Pending Amount	Interest
2-Apr-2008	CP/00043325		44,000.00 Dr		1,085.00 Dr
		44,000.00 Dr 1-Jun-2008 31-Jul-2008 60 days 15 % 1,085.00 Dr			
2-Apr-2008	CP/00489		1,20,000.00 Dr		2,022.00 Dr
		1,20,000.00 Dr 2-May-2008 2-Jun-2008 31 days 15 % 1,529.00 Dr			
		40,000.00 Dr 2-Jun-2008 2-Jul-2008 30 days 15 % 493.00 Dr			
2-Apr-2008	CP/00466993		40,000.00 Dr	27,565.00 Dr	2,565.00 Dr
		40,000.00 Dr 2-May-2008 2-Jul-2008 61 days 15 % 1,003.00 Dr			
		25,000.00 Dr 2-Jul-2008 1-Dec-2008 152 days 15 % 1,562.00 Dr			
2-May-2008	CP/005662		27,000.00 Dr	27,000.00 Dr	2,031.00 Dr
		27,000.00 Dr 1-Jun-2008 1-Dec-2008 183 days 15 % 2,031.00 Dr			
			2,31,000.00 Dr	54,565.00 Dr	7,703.00 Dr

Fig. 6.25 Ledger with Interest

Book Entries and adjustment of interest

We have seen the reports on interest amounts calculated in different ways but these have not been brought into books! They simply give you the interest implications. You must book them now.

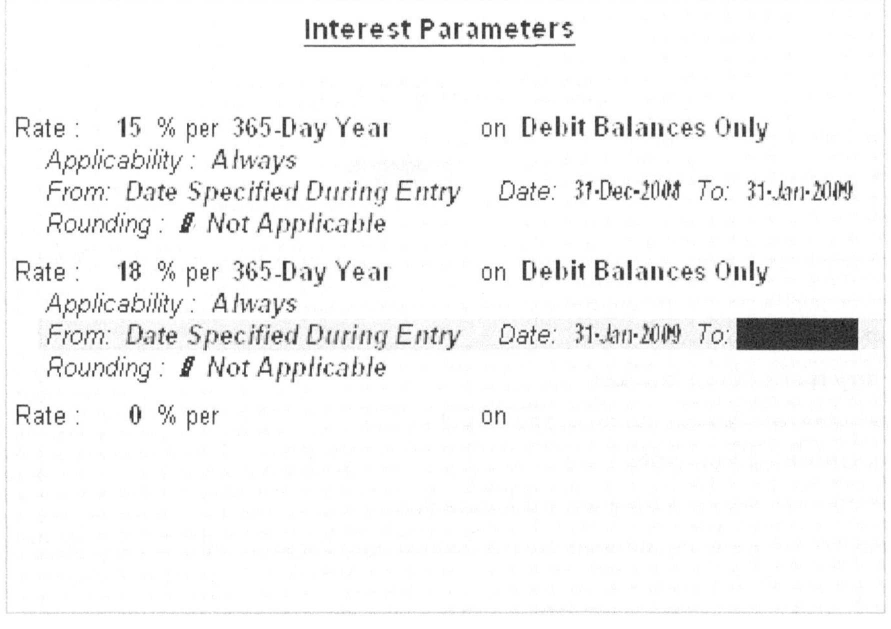

Fig. 6.26 Setting Interest Parameters

How to enter the calculated interest amounts?

Use Debit Notes and Credit Notes with Voucher Classes

Use Debit notes for Interest receivable and Credit Notes for Interest Payable. Interest is calculated on Simple or Compound basis and separate classes should be used for them.

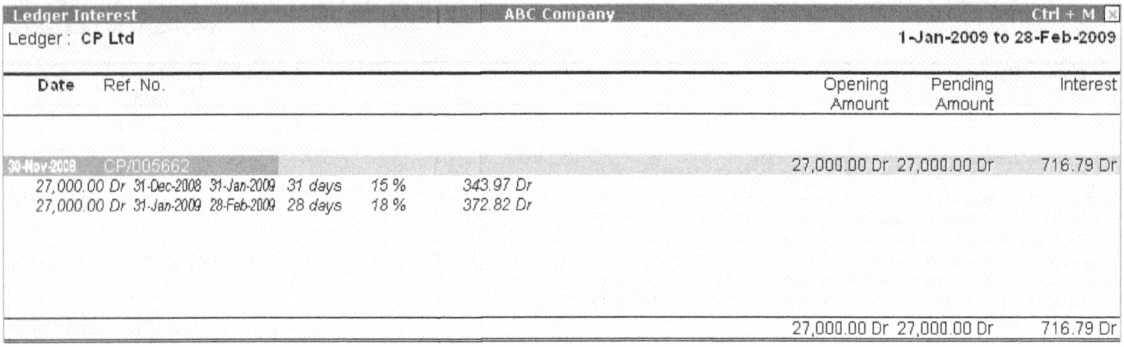

Ledger Interest	ABC Company							Ctrl + M
Ledger : CP Ltd								1-Jan-2009 to 28-Feb-2009
Date	Ref. No.					Opening Amount	Pending Amount	Interest
30-Nov-2008	CP/005662					27,000.00 Dr	27,000.00 Dr	716.79 Dr
27,000.00 Dr	31-Dec-2008	31-Jan-2009	31 days	15 %	343.97 Dr			
27,000.00 Dr	31-Jan-2009	28-Feb-2009	28 days	18 %	372.82 Dr			
						27,000.00 Dr	27,000.00 Dr	716.79 Dr

Fig. 6.27 Ledger with Interest

Set-up Debit/Credit Note Classes for interest entries

Set up Debit Notes. Credit Notes will behave the same way.

Go to Gateway of Tally> Accounts Info.> Voucher Types> Create/Alter

- Alter the Voucher Type Debit Note.
- Tab down to the field Class.
- Type the name of the Class.
- Type Interest - Simple

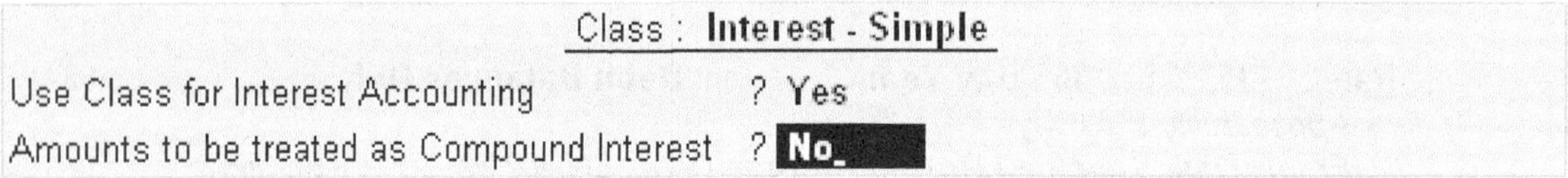

Class : **Interest - Simple**	
Use Class for Interest Accounting	? Yes
Amounts to be treated as Compound Interest	? No

Likewise, create a Class – Compound Interest and set Yes to Amounts to be treated as Compound Interest.

Accept the Voucher Type and return to the Gateway of Tally. Create a ledger account Interest Received under Group Indirect Income.

Voucher Entry for booking Interest

Go to Gateway of Tally> Accounting Voucher

1. Select Ctrl+F9: Debit Note.
2. There are two situations for interest adjustment:-

- Simple Interest – Interest amounts are not debited onto the same bills. Create a fresh reference for it.
- Compound Interest – Amounts are auto-debited to the selected bills. Bill-wise details will not appear in this case.
- Interest on balances only.

Bill-wise interest entry

- Debit CP Ltd.
- Credit Interest Received.

When you debit the party account, a list of bills for which interest is applicable pops up. Select the bills to adjust. Note that even cleared bills appear.

Select the respective interest bills from the list . The debit amount is filled up with the total. Select New Ref in the bill-wise allocation. In the interest sub-screen, ensure that the rate of interest is 0. Now, Credit Interest Received. The amount is already filled in.

Interest Details for : CP Ltd

Name

List of Interest Bills

CP/0043325	2-Apr-2008	(120 days)	*Cleared*	*Intr.* 2,170.00 Dr
CP/00466993	1-Dec-2008	(89 days)	Balance27,565.00 Dr	*Intr.* 1,008.00 Dr
CP/00489	2-Apr-2008	(91 days)	*Cleared*	*Intr.* 3,501.00 Dr
CP/005662	31-Dec-[illegible]	(31 days)	Balance27,[illegible] Dr	*Intr.* 716.79 Dr

Your voucher will resemble the one below:

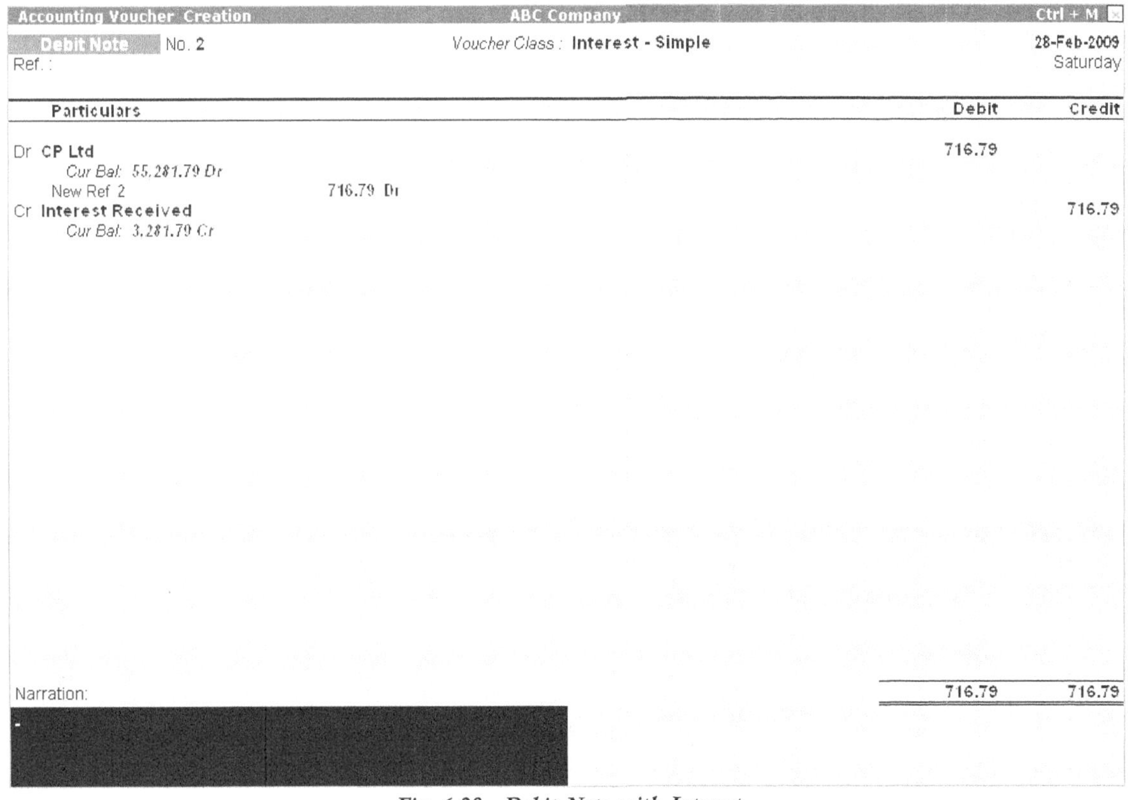

Fig. 6.28 Debit Note with Interest

Entries for compound interest are exactly the same as for Simple Interest where all you do is select the Voucher Class Compound Interest. Also the Bill-wise details popup sub-screen does not come up as the amounts are added onto the bills.

Select the required bill from the list and complete a Debit Note.

Now display Outstandings for CP Ltd.

The Bill reference CP/00466993 is the invoice onto which interest has been compounded.

A new Reference no 2 has been created for Simple Interest due from CP Ltd.

Entries for Interest on Balances only

Again, the issues are Simple and Compound Interest:

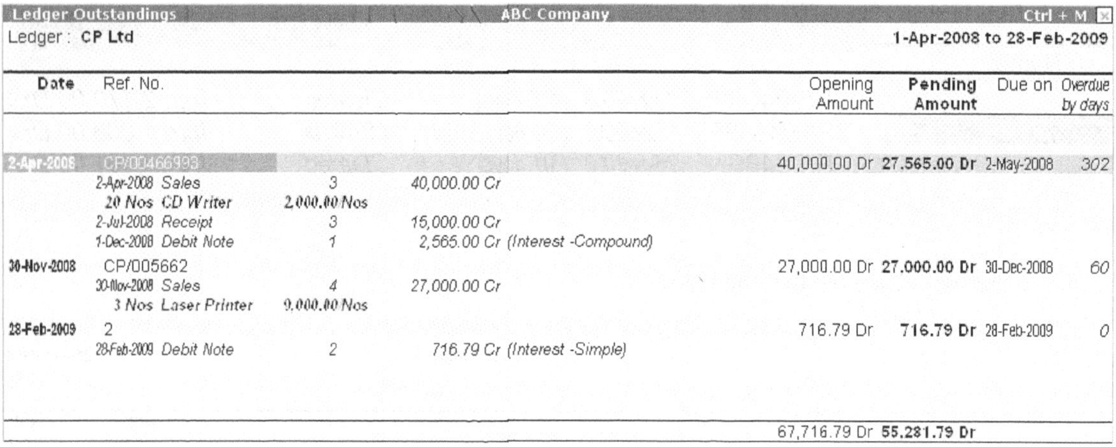

Ledger Outstandings		ABC Company					Ctrl + M
Ledger : **CP Ltd**							1-Apr-2008 to 28-Feb-2009
Date	Ref. No.			Opening Amount	**Pending Amount**	Due on	Overdue by days
2-Apr-2008	CP/00466993			40,000.00 Dr	**27,565.00 Dr**	2-May-2008	302
	2-Apr-2008 Sales	3	40,000.00 Cr				
	20 Nos CD Writer	2,000.00/Nos					
	2-Jul-2008 Receipt	3	15,000.00 Cr				
	1-Dec-2008 Debit Note	1	2,565.00 Cr (Interest -Compound)				
30-Nov-2008	CP/005662			27,000.00 Dr	**27,000.00 Dr**	30-Dec-2008	60
	30-Nov-2008 Sales	4	27,000.00 Cr				
	3 Nos Laser Printer	9,000.00/Nos					
28-Feb-2009	2			716.79 Dr	**716.79 Dr**	28-Feb-2009	0
	28-Feb-2009 Debit Note	2	716.79 Cr (Interest -Simple)				
				67,716.79 Dr	**55,281.79 Dr**		

Fig. 6.29 Ledger Outstanding with Interest

Compound Interest

Make the following entries in a Debit note with Compound Interest Voucher Class.

- Debit Bank Ltd (the amount is automatically filled up with the calculated interest).
- Credit Interest Received.

And nothing needs to be done! The Bank Account has been increased by the amount of interest due and the Income account of Interest Received also credited.

Simple Interest

Make the same entry as above.

However, since it has the effect of increasing the Bank Ltd account with the amount due (compound effect), you must make a journal entry to reverse it. The reversal entry would be something like this:

- Debit Interest Receivable (a current asset account).
- Credit Bank Ltd.

Use a normal Journal voucher for this entry.

We have to necessary go this route to take advantage of the auto filling of the interest amount which can appear only when we use the Bank Ltd account in Debit Note in the first place.

Interest Calculation Reports

Interest Calculation reports are automatically produced if the feature is activated In F11: F1: Accounting Features and the parameters are set for individual ledger accounts.

There are two types of reports, one pertaining to interest on balances of accounts like loans, and the other interest on overdue invoices.

Interest reports are available for individual ledger accounts as well as for Groups.

Interest Calculation on Group

The Group Interest Calculation statement is a list of all accounts and sub-groups belonging to the selected group that displays the current balance in each account or sub-group and the total interest.

```
Go to Gateway of Tally> Display > Statements of Accounts > Interest Calculations
> Group
```

Select a Group, *e.g.*, Loans (Liability)

The Cr in the interest amount should not be confused to mean an Income. It only means that it is payable and is a liability.

To ease interest recording, Tally.ERP 9 has an interest template, a special voucher class in Debit Note and Credit Notes.

Drill down to the Ledger level Interest report.

Group Interest Calculations ABC Company Ctrl + M

Particulars	Loans (Liability) ABC Company 1-Apr-2008 to 31-Mar-2009	
	Interest Calculation	
	Cl. Balance	Interest
Bank Loan Account	4,80,000.00 Cr	65,023.23 Cr
Grand Total	4,80,000.00 Cr	65,023.23 Cr

Fig. 6.30 Group Interest Calculations

Interest Calculation on Ledger Balances

You can get a report on the Ledger balances for the interest calculated.

```
Go to Gateway of Tally> Display> Statements of Accounts> Interest Calculations>
Ledger
```

Select Account *e.g.*, Bank Loan Account.

Interest is re-calculated with every change in balance outstanding. The Cr in the interest amount should not be confused to resemble an Income. It only means that it is payable and is a Liability.

To ease interest recording, Tally.ERP 9 has an interest template, a special voucher class in Debit Note and Credit Notes.

The interest screen will appear similar to the one below:

Ledger Interest — ABC Company

Ledger : **Bank Loan Account** — **1-Apr-2008 to 28-Feb-2009**

Balance	From:	To:	Total Days	Rate %	Interest
50,000.00 Cr	31-Mar-2008	18-Apr-2008	18 days	12 %	295.89 Cr
41,500.00 Cr	18-Apr-2008	1-Oct-2008	166 days	12 %	2,264.88 Cr
30,000.00 Cr	1-Oct-2008	31-Dec-2008	91 days	13.50 %	1,009.73 Cr
30,000.00 Cr	31-Dec-2008	28-Feb-2009	59 days	20 %	969.86 Cr
				Grand Total	4,540.36 Cr

Fig. 6.31 Ledger Interest Calculations

Interest calculation on Bank Loan account.

Statement of Interest Due on Invoices

You can calculate interest on each invoice for the period it is outstanding, wholly or partly. Transaction by transaction or bill-by-bill interest calculation is permitted for 'Party' accounts like accounts falling under the groups Sundry Debtors and Sundry Creditors. Bill-wise details should be active for the company and the party.

The report is similar to the Bill-wise Outstandings Statement. The last column gives the interest amount on the transaction. Press F1: Detailed to see the calculation.

```
Go to Gateway of Tally > Display > Statements of Accounts > Interest
Calculations > Ledger
```

Select the ledger Account XYZ Agency.

Interest is re-calculated with every change in balance outstanding. The Cr in the interest amount should not be confused to mean an Income. It only means that it is payable and is a liability. The figure is illustrative only and you will need to account for the interest expense and liability through a journal entry.

To ease interest recording, Tally.ERP 9 has an interest template, a special voucher class in Debit Note and Credit Notes.

Cheque Printing in Tally.ERP 9

You can choose to print Cheques in Tally.ERP 9 at the time of making payments to Creditors/ parties during Voucher Entry i.e., directly from the Payment Voucher.

Enabling Cheque Printing

To enable Cheque Printing in Tally.ERP 9,

Ledger Interest — ABC Company — Ctrl + M

Ledger : XYZ Agency — 1-Apr-2008 to 30-Sep-2008

Date	Ref. No.							Opening Amount	Pending Amount	Interest
2-Apr-2008	PUR/01							1,30,000.00 Cr	1,30,000.00 Cr	4,840.27 Cr
		1,30,000.00 Cr	2-May-2008	30-Sep-2008	151 days	9 %	4,840.27 Cr			
5-May-2008	PUR/02							88,000.00 Cr	88,000.00 Cr	1,909.48 Cr
		88,000.00 Cr	4-Jul-2008	30-Sep-2008	88 days	9 %	1,909.48 Cr			
6-Jun-2008	PUR/03							36,000.00 Cr	36,000.00 Cr	674.63 Cr
		36,000.00 Cr	16-Jul-2008	30-Sep-2008	76 days	9 %	674.63 Cr			
7-Jul-2008	PUR/04							70,000.00 Cr	70,000.00 Cr	604.11 Cr
		70,000.00 Cr	26-Aug-2008	30-Sep-2008	35 days	9 %	604.11 Cr			
								3,24,000.00 Cr	3,24,000.00 Cr	8,028.49 Cr

Fig. 6.32 Ledger Interest Calculations

`Go to Gateway of Tally > F11: Accounting Features`

1. Set Enable Cheque Printing to Yes.
2. Set/Alter Cheque Printing Configuration to Yes.
3. The screen appears as shown.

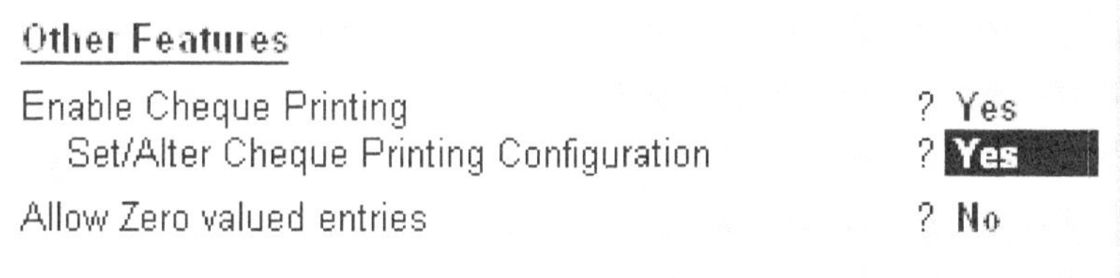

Once the option Set/Alter Cheque Printing Configuration is activated to Yes, you will get the below screen.

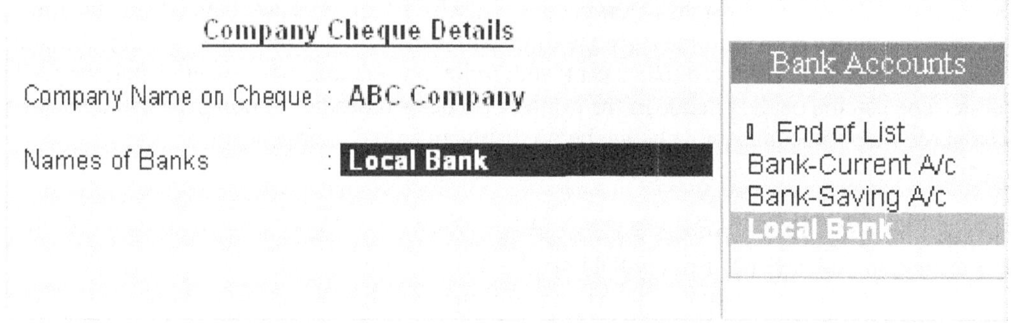

Fig. 6.33 Selecting Bank Account

Company Name on Cheque:

To print the company name on the cheque for signature purposes, mention the name of the Company (for example, ABC Company). If you do not want Tally.ERP 9 to print the name, you can leave it blank. Many banks issue cheques with your company name printed.

Cheque Printing Configuration

(All Dimensions in mm only)

Width of Cheque	: 158
Height of Cheque	: 76
Distance of Date Line from Top Edge	: 23
Starting Location of Date from Left Edge	: 116
Distance of Party's Name Line from Top Edge	: 31
Starting Location of Name from Left Edge	: 10
Width of Name area	: 94
Distance of 2nd Amt-in-words Line from Top Edge	: 50
Height (gap) of Amt-in-words Line	: 5
Starting Location of Amt-in-words from Left Edge	: 10
Width of Amt-in-words area	: 99
Distance of Amt-in-figures Line from Top Edge	: 55
Starting Location of Amt-in-figures from Left Edge	: 110
Width of Amt-in-figures area	: 41
Distance of Company Signature Bottom Line from Top Edge	: 59
Starting Location of Signature from Left Edge	: 120
* Width of Signature area	: 35
* Height of Signature area	: 14
*(* mandatory to save configuration)*	
Salutation of 1st Signatory (if 2 signatories)	: Managing Director
Salutation of 2nd or Single Signatory	: Secretary

Fig. 6.34 Selecting Cheque Printing Options

Name of Banks

Select the Bank from the Bank accounts list.

You will have to fill in the dimensions of the cheque. Tally.ERP 9 accepts user defined cheque dimensions. Take the bank's cheque book and measure the dimensions of a cheque leaf carefully in millimeters and fill in the above form. You may need to correct it after trying out a couple of cheques so that the positioning is accurate. The placing of the cheque in the printer also determines the printing. To avoid mistakes trial could be made on photocopies of a cheque before using an actual cheque leaf.

Note:

1. Salutation fields are for signatures and naturally follow the Company name (for example, Director)
2. Ensure that you have not left any field blank other than the salutation fields. Trial and error is the only way to get the printing in the right positions. Change the set-up a couple of times to set it right. This is necessary to enable printing on Cheques correctly on different sizes of Cheques used by different banks.

For ABC & Company

Managing Director

Note: All dimensions must be more than 0 for cheques to be successfully printed.

If your cheque has two signatories, both can be specified. Both could be the same salutation or different. For example, one could be Managing Director; the other could be Director etc.

Give details of whatever you are using currently. Many banks will pre-print both the company name and the salutation in their cheques, in which case you can leave them blank.

You are now ready to print the cheque. Remember that this option is available only for the banks for which you have Ledger account.

Printing Cheques

To print the cheque after making the required settings,

`Go to Gateway of Tally > Voucher Entry > F5: Payment`

Name on Cheque

Debit the Party Ledger and give the bill reference details if any. Credit the bank for which the cheque printing is enabled. The name of the Debited party account appears next to the field Name on the cheque by default. You can change the name on the cheque if necessary.

Cross Cheque using

This is filled in by the most common words used - Account payee. You may change it if required.

Note: Cheque Printing feature is available only from the Payment voucher.

- Enter the Cheque Number (Ch. No.) and save the Voucher. Then, you will get the Cheque Printing sub-screen appears as shown below:

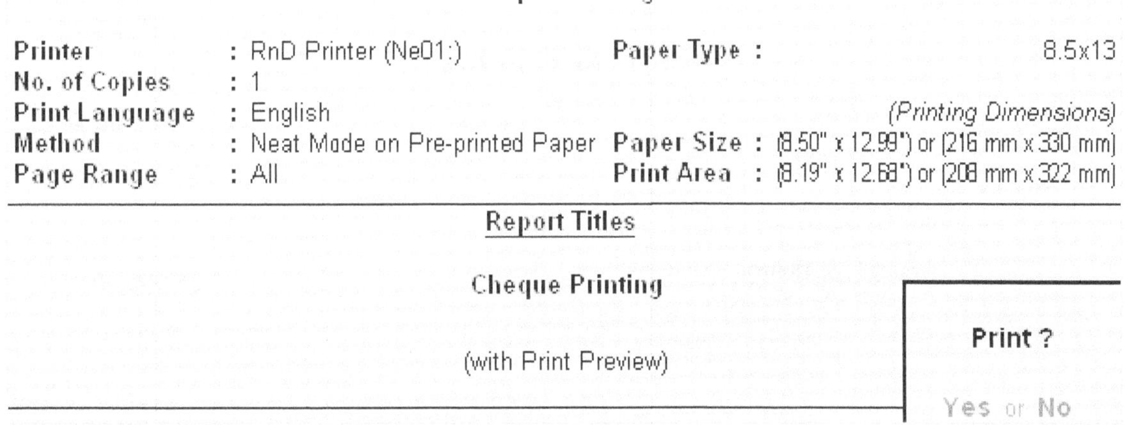

Fig. 6.35 Selecting Cheque Printing Printer Options

Select Yes to print the cheque.

The printed Cheque appears as shown :

Multi-Currency in Tally.ERP 9

Many Organizations have transactions in more than one currency. Such transactions have to be recorded either in the base (home) currency or in the foreign currency. If the transactions are recorded in home currency, the rate at which the foreign currency is exchanged should be recorded as well. At times you

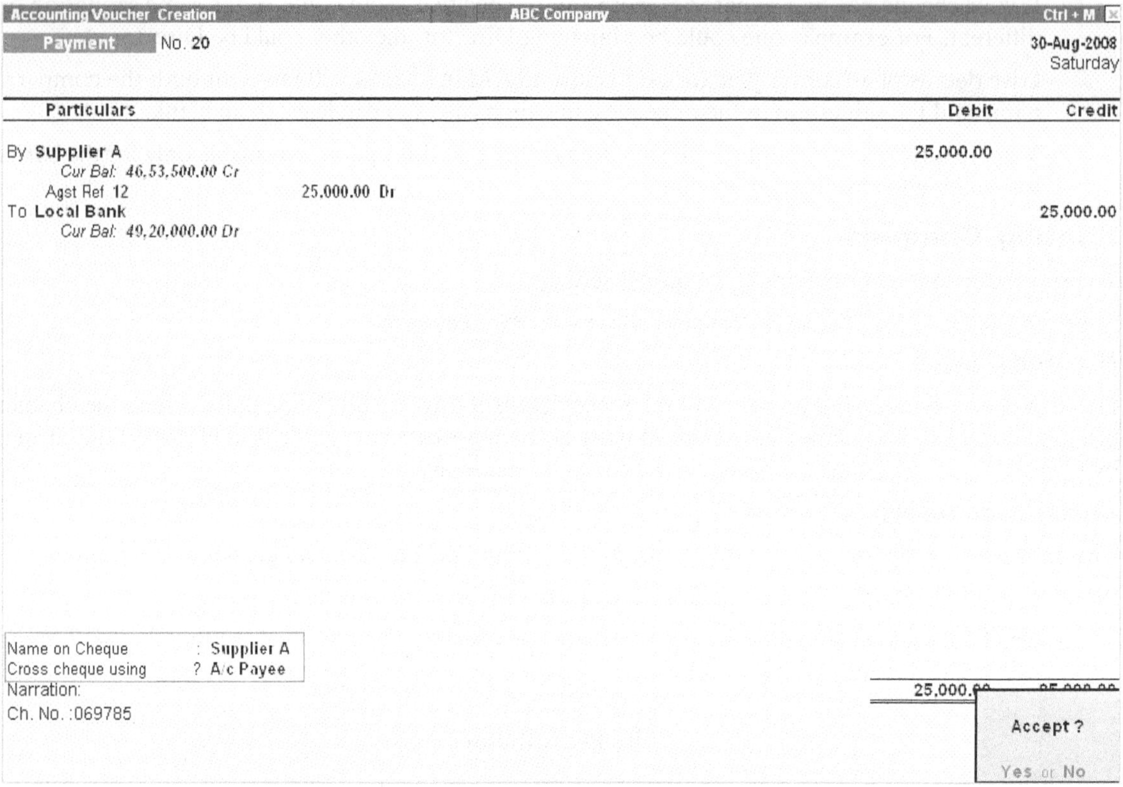

Accounting Voucher Creation   ABC Company   Ctrl + M

Payment No. 20   30-Aug-2008 Saturday

Particulars		Debit	Credit
By **Supplier A**		25,000.00	
Cur Bal: 46,53,500.00 Cr			
Agst Ref 12	25,000.00 Dr		
To **Local Bank**			25,000.00
Cur Bal: 49,20,000.00 Dr			
		25,000.00	25,000.00

Name on Cheque : Supplier A
Cross cheque using ? A/c Payee
Narration:
Ch. No. :069785

Accept ?
Yes or No

Fig. 6.36 Say Yes for Printing

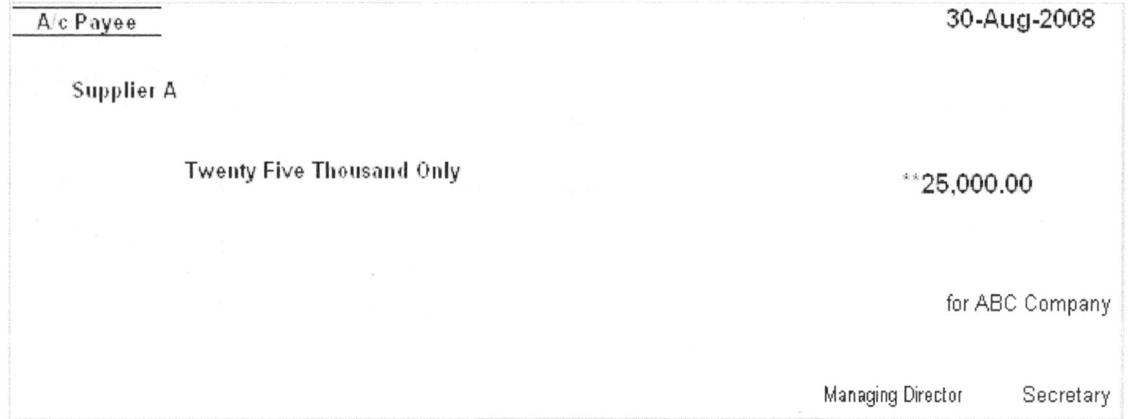

Fig. 6.37 Printed Cheque

need to record the transaction in the foreign currency itself when you maintain the balance of the concerned account in foreign currency.

Tally.ERP 9 uses the term base currency for the currency in which your account books are kept. Foreign Exchange is used interchangeably with foreign currency. The base currency is specified while creating the company.

Tally.ERP 9 makes it easy to manage multiple currencies, automatic calculations of exchange rates, automatic conversion of any currency used to record a transaction to the currency of the account, etc.

The Balance Sheet and Profit & Loss Account of the company is maintained in the base currency. Conversion of foreign currency account balances is done as per rules set by you.

```
Go to Company Info. > Create Company
```

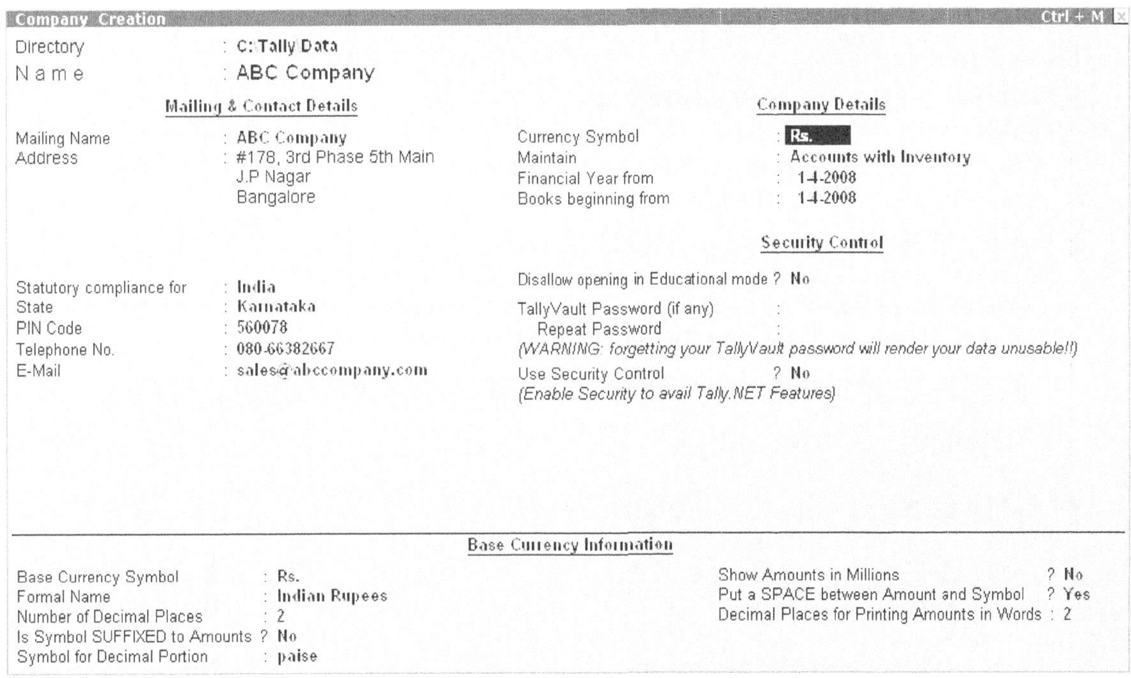

Fig. 6.38 Selecting the Currency Symbol

Note: At time of installing Tally.ERP 9, if the Country Selection is opted as India/Saarc, the Currency Symbol is defaulted as Rs. in the Company master otherwise if the Country Selection is opted as International (Others), the Currency Symbol is defaulted as £ in the Company master.

Enabling Multi-Currency

Enable Multi-Currency feature to view and enter transactions in multiple currencies.

- Go to Gateway of Tally
- Select F11: Accounting Features
- Set Allow Multi-Currency to Yes
- Accept to Save.

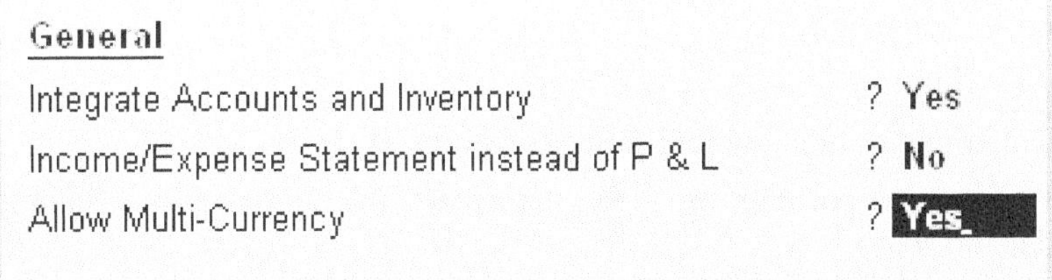

Multi Currency feature is now enabled.

Currencies menu

Once the Multi-Currency feature is enabled in F11: Accounting Features, you can view the Currencies menu from Gateway of Tally > Accounts Info > Currencies.

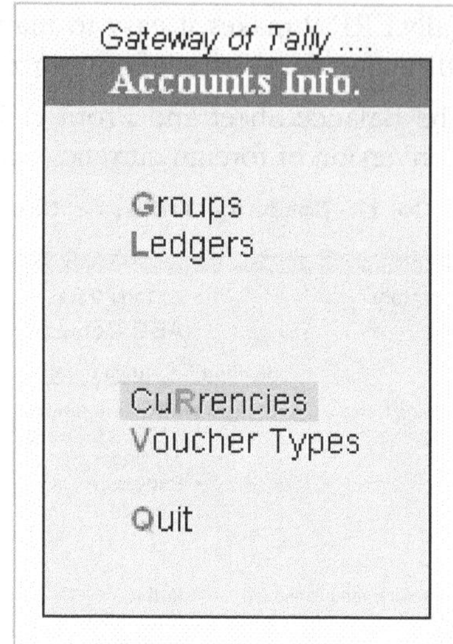

Creating a Currency

To create a foreign currency

Go to Gateway of Tally > Accounts Info. > Currencies > Create

1. Enter the currency symbol in Symbol field. This symbol appears in your reports, wherever applicable.
2. Use ASCII Special Characters with [Alt] key combination, if your keyboard does not have the symbol. Utilities like Character Map (Start > All Programs > Accessories > System Tools) in Windows, shows the key combination for most symbols. This might be different on some notebook computers, refer to the computer's user manual or the vendor.

Currency Creation ABC Cor

Symbol : $

Formal Name : Dollar

Number of Decimal Places : 2
Show Amounts in Millions ? No

Is Symbol SUFFIXED to Amounts ? No
Put a SPACE between Amount and Symbol ? No

Symbol for Decimal Portion of Amount :
Decimal Places for Printing Amounts in Words : 2

Fig. 6.39 Selecting the Currency Symbol

3. You cannot assign a duplicate currency symbol for a company in Tally.ERP 9.
4. The Key combinations for a few currency symbols are given below:
   - Alt + 156 –Pound Sterling - £
   - Alt + 0165 – Japanese Yen - ¥
   - Alt + 0128 – Euro - €
   - Use the Dollar and the Rs. Symbol from the keyboard
5. Enter the name of the currency in Formal Name, *e.g.*, US Dollars, Pound Sterling, Indian Rupees, Omani Rial and so on.

6. A formal name is required to distinguish different currencies with the same symbols. For e.g. Assume you have created two companies (ABC & XYZ) in Tally.ERP 9. ABC and XYZ have different set of currencies. ABC uses symbol $ for Australian Dollars and XYZ uses the symbol $ for U.S. Dollars. The formal name distinguishes two different currencies with the same symbol, when you compare Books of Accounts of the two companies.
7. The company that is loaded first retains the original symbol for display purposes. The other company's currency symbol will be prefixed with the first letter/first few letters (to make it unique) of the formal name. Here, if ABC is loaded first then the symbol $ is for Australian Dollars and in XYZ (loaded next) the symbol $ is prefixed with the letter U (first letter of its formal name).

Note: You cannot assign a duplicate Formal Name for a currency in Tally.ERP 9.

8. Enter the number of decimal places for the currency in Number of Decimal Places. For example, Currencies with 2 decimal places like paisa and currencies with three decimal places like dinar. There are currencies that do not have decimal places, *e.g.*, Vietnamese Dong.

   Tally.ERP 9 has two formats for displaying an amount, viz., in millions and in lakhs. 1000000 (one followed by six zeroes) in millions format would appear as 1,000,000 and lakhs would appear as 10,00,000.

   Select the required parameter in Show Amounts in Millions field. If you select No, the amounts will appear in Lakhs, by default.

Note: You can always specify the appearance of numbers in specific reports, e.g. In Profit & Loss Account display, press F12: Configure to change scale factors for values.

9. Set Is Symbol SUFFIXED to Amounts to Yes for the symbol to appear after the amount. Set it to No, for the symbol to be prefixed to the amount.

   Set Put a SPACE between Amounts and symbol? to Yes to apply a space between amounts and symbol.
10. Enter the Symbol for Decimal portion of currency in Symbol for Decimal Portion of Amount field. For example, Ps. for Paise.
11. Enter the number of decimal places for printing the amounts in words in Decimal Places for Printing Amounts in Words field. This number should be equal to or lesser than the number specified in Number of Decimal Places field.

Note: The Currency cannot be translated or transliterated but will appear in the Language created.

Buttons available in the Currency creation/alteration screen:

Buttons	*Keys*	*Description and usage*
G: Groups	Ctrl+G	User is allowed to create Accounting Group from the Currency Creation/Alteration screen.
L: Ledgers	Ctrl+L	User is allowed to create Accounting Ledgers from the Currency Creation/Alteration screen.
S: Cst Cat	Ctrl+S	User is allowed to create Cost Category from the Currency Creation/Alteration screen.
C: Cst Ctr	Ctrl+C	User is allowed to create Cost Centre from the Currency Creation/Alteration screen.

B: Budget	Ctrl+B	User is allowed to create Budget from the Currency Creation/Alteration Screen.
V: Vch Types	Ctrl+V	User is allowed to create Voucher Type from the Currency Creation/Alteration screen.

Altering a Currency

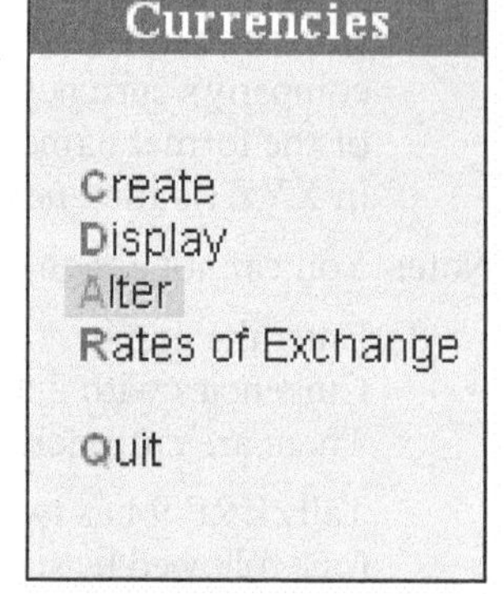

You can modify or delete a currency master using the Alter option. Rates of Exchange can also be altered from here.

To alter a currency master:

Go to Gateway of Tally > Accounts Info. > Currencies > Alter

1. Select a Currency from the Currencies list (displayed if there is more than 1 currency)
2. In the Currency Alteration screen, alter details as required.

Displaying a Currency

The Currency Display screen displays the details and rates of exchange for a selected currency.

To display the Currency screen:

1. Go to Gateway of Tally > Accounts Info. > Currencies > Display
2. Select a Currency from Currencies list (displayed, if there is more than 1 currency)
3. Enter to view the details.

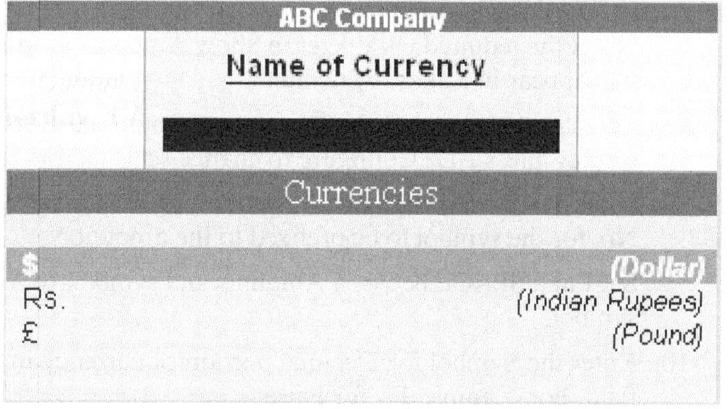

Currency Alteration ABC Company Ctrl + M

Symbol : $

Formal Name : Dollar

Number of Decimal Places	: 2	Show Amounts in Millions	? No
Decimal Places for Printing Amounts in Words	: 2	Put a SPACE between Amount and Symbol	? No
Is Symbol SUFFIXED to Amounts	? No		
Symbol for Decimal Portion of Amount	:		

Rates of Exchange

Standard		Selling			Buying		
Date	Specified Rate	Date	Last Voucher Rate	Specified Rate	Date	Last Voucher Rate	Specified Rate

Fig. 6.40 Displaying the Currency

Deleting a Currency

To delete a Currency:

1. Go to Gateway of Tally > Accounts Info. > Currencies > Alter
2. Select a currency from the Currencies list (displayed, if there is more than 1 currency)

3. Press Alt + D in the Currency Alteration screen to delete.

Note: You cannot delete a Currency, if it is used in any transaction.

Defining Rates of Exchange

In the Rates of Exchange menu, you can specify the rate of foreign currency for a specific date. Foreign exchange variations occur every day with different selling and buying rates. Rates of Exchange feature helps you record rate of Currency for particular date and apply in your transactions.

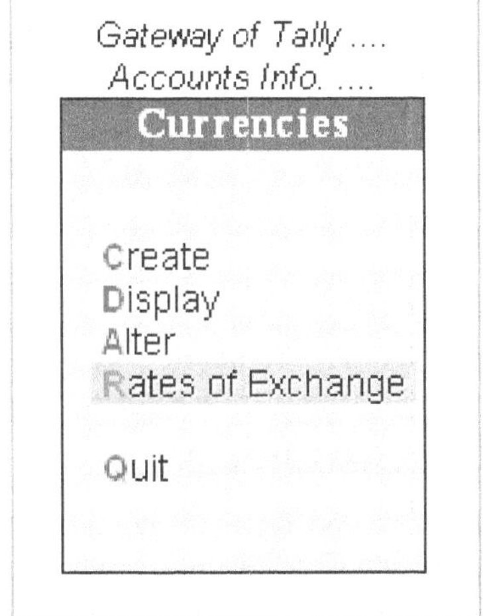

To Display/Alter Rates of Exchange:

```
Go to Gateway of Tally > Accounts Info > Currencies
> Rates of Exchange
```

Enter to view the Multi Currency Alteration screen as shown :

1. Enter the date for which the exchange rate is applicable
2. Enter the Standard Rate (optional) which is used to calculate variances from the actual transaction rates
3. Enter the Selling Rate (your selling rate)
4. Enter the Buying Rate (your buying rate)
5. Accept to Save.

Multi Currency Alteration ABC Company Ctrl + M

Date for Rate of Exchange : 1-Apr-2008

S.No.	Currency	Std. Rate	Selling Rate		Buying Rate	
			Last Voucher Rate	Specified Rate	Last Voucher Rate	Specified Rate
1.	$ (Dollar)			Rs. 600/$		Rs. 500/$
2.	A$ (Australian Dollar)	Rs. 100/A$		Rs. 250/A$		Rs. 200/A$
3.	¥ (Yen)	Rs. 160/¥		Rs. 400/¥		Rs. 250/¥

Fig. 6.41 Altering the Currency

Note: Last Voucher Rate is displayed, if any voucher has been entered earlier.

Selling Rate – Specified Rate

Selling rate is your selling rate (as opposed to bank's selling rate) used for receipt voucher entry where you receive foreign exchange.

This is the rate obtained from your banker or also available in the daily newspaper. Once the Selling Rate is specified in the Rates of Exchange menu, while entering a foreign exchange transaction, the rates are defaulted automatically. However, you can alter the rate as required.

The actual rate at which the currency was last used is displayed and cannot be changed.

The specified rate is used for calculating foreign exchange variances only in case where there is no standard rate.

Buying Rate – Specified Rate

Buying Rate is your buying rate (as opposed to bank's buying rate) used in payment vouchers.

The actual rate at which the currency was last used is displayed and cannot be changed.

The specified rate is used for calculating foreign exchange variances only in case where there is no standard rate.

Note: Tally.ERP 9 automatically calculates Forex Gain or Loss for foreign exchange transactions using the standard rates, specified rates and actual transaction rates specified in the Rates of Exchange menu.

Buttons available in the Rates of Exchange screen:

Buttons	*Keys*	*Description and usage*
G :Groups	Ctrl+G	User is allowed to create Accounting Group from the Rates of Exchange screen.
L: Ledgers	Ctrl+L	User is allowed to create Accounting Ledgers from the Rates of Exchange screen.
S: Cst Cat	Ctrl+S	User is allowed to create Cost Category from the Rates of Exchange screen.
C: Cst Ctr	Ctrl+C	User is allowed to create Cost Centre from the Rates of Exchange screen.

Credit Limits

Credit Limit refers to the monetary limit agreed upon mutually by the seller and the buyer for trading purposes. Credit Limits can be specified for any Ledger account falling under the groups Sundry Debtors and Sundry Creditors. Ledger Accounts created under Sundry Creditors are also allowed for defining Credit Limits for the reason that there may be two-way trade between the parties i.e., you may sell to a Sundry Creditor and buy from a Sundry Debtor Accounts.

Setting Credit Limits

You can set credit limits for ledgers accounts grouped under Sundry Debtors and Sundry Creditors at the time of ledger creation or from the alteration screen or also at the time of invoicing. To activate Credit Limits feature in Tally.ERP 9,

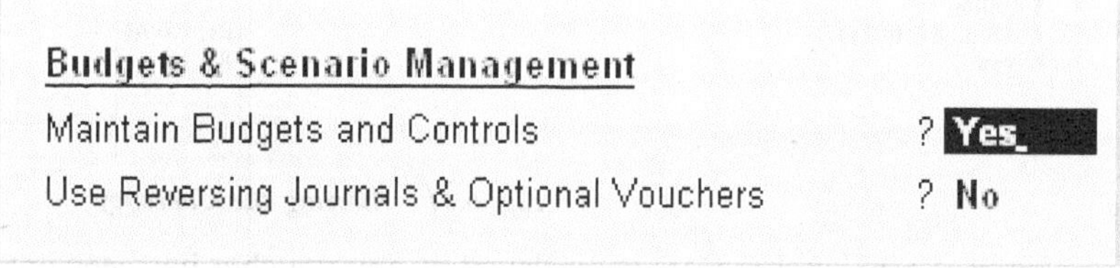

Budgets & Scenario Management

Maintain Budgets and Controls ? Yes

Use Reversing Journals & Optional Vouchers ? No

`Go to F11 Features > Accounting Features > Set Maintain Budgets and Controls to Yes`

To set Credit Limits for Single Ledger Account, follow the steps given below:

`Go to Gateway of Tally> Accounts Info> Ledgers> Create / Alter (under Single Ledger)`

Select the required party ledger from the List of ledgers to set credit terms. The single Ledger Alteration screen is displayed. You can set credit limits for both amount and period here.

To set credit limits for multiple ledgers:

`Go to Gateway of Tally> Accounts Info> Ledgers> Credit Limits (under Multiple Ledgers)`

Select the required group of ledgers from the List of Groups to set credit terms. The Multi Ledger Limit Alteration screen is displayed. The list of ledger accounts under the selected group is displayed. You can now set credit limits for both amounts and periods here.

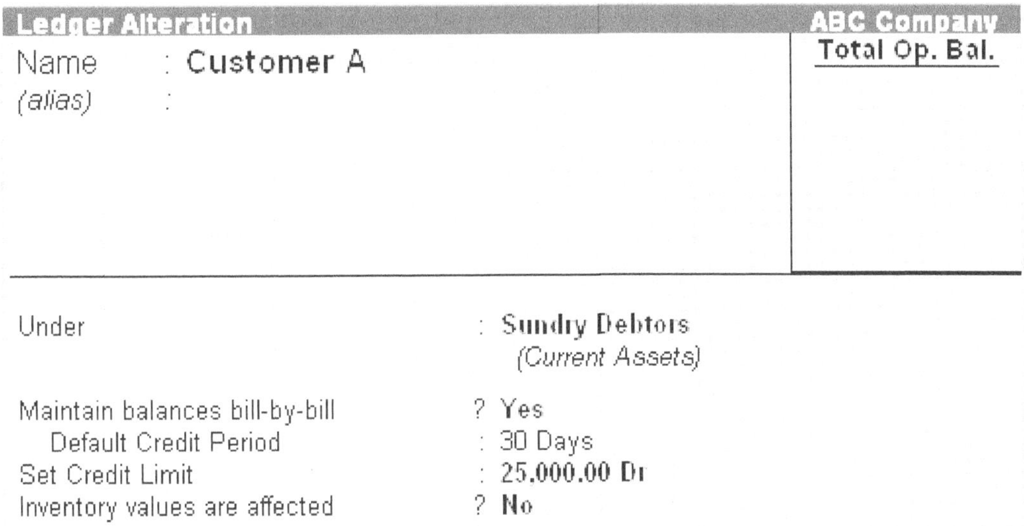

Ledger Alteration ABC Company

Name : Customer A
(alias) :

Total Op. Bal.

Under : Sundry Debtors
(Current Assets)

Maintain balances bill-by-bill ? Yes
Default Credit Period : 30 Days
Set Credit Limit : 25,000.00 Dr
Inventory values are affected ? No

Fig. 6.42 Seeting Credit Limit in Ledger

Credit Limit

Specify the amount of credit limit against the ledger account in this field. You can set the amount limits in foreign currency if required, for ledgers involving forex transactions.

Credit Period

Credit period can be either specified in No. of days or the due date (for eg., 31.10.09) and are calculated from the Voucher date or Invoice date or the effective date, as applicable i.e., if only Voucher Date exists, it is considered as the effective date for calculation for Credit Days otherwise if effective date is specified in the Voucher, it is considered for calculation for due date.

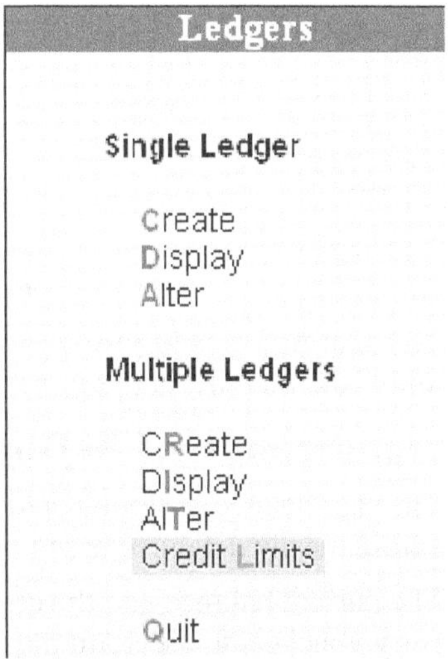

Ledgers

Single Ledger

Create
Display
Alter

Multiple Ledgers

CReate
DIsplay
AlTer
Credit Limits

Quit

Exceeding Credit Limits

During invoice or order entry, if the credit amount limit is exceeded, at the accepting the voucher, Tally.ERP 9 prompts an error message displaying the amount exceeding the credit limit specified. You can however,

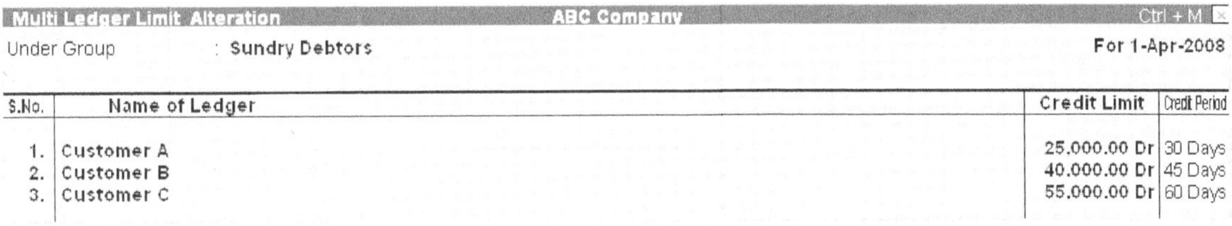

Multi Ledger Limit Alteration ABC Company Ctrl + M

Under Group : Sundry Debtors For 1-Apr-2008

S.No.	Name of Ledger	Credit Limit	Credit Period
1.	Customer A	25,000.00 Dr	30 Days
2.	Customer B	40,000.00 Dr	45 Days
3.	Customer C	55,000.00 Dr	60 Days

Fig. 6.42a Credit Limit with Credit Period

Enter a lower value (within the prescribed credit limit) to complete the entry ; or

Abandon the current entry and obtain authorization to increase the credit amount limit in the Multi Ledger Limit Alteration screen.

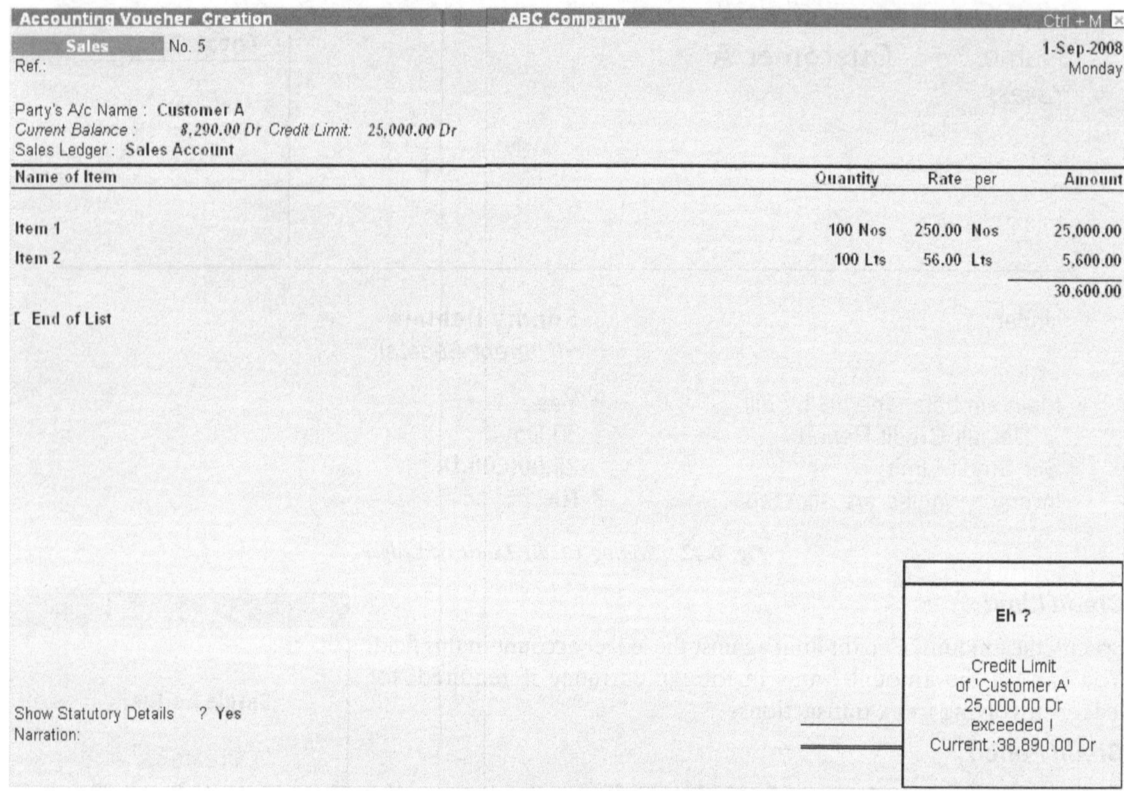

Accounting Voucher Creation | ABC Company | Ctrl + M

Sales No. 5 — 1-Sep-2008, Monday

Ref.:

Party's A/c Name : Customer A

Current Balance : 8,290.00 Dr Credit Limit: 25,000.00 Dr

Sales Ledger : Sales Account

Name of Item	Quantity	Rate per	Amount
Item 1	100 Nos	250.00 Nos	25,000.00
Item 2	100 Lts	56.00 Lts	5,600.00
			30,600.00

[End of List

Show Statutory Details ? Yes

Narration:

Fig. 6.43 Sales Voucher Displaying Credit Limit

This feature helps in restricting Invoicing for the customers or parties exceeding the prescribed credit limits and thereby facilitating better and effective control of the outstandings.

Significance of Setting Credit Limits

The significance of setting credit limits is that during voucher entry (or invoicing), the credit terms are automatically defaulted based on the configuration made in the ledger master.

The current balance and the credit limit of the Ledger accounts are displayed in the Order and Invoice entry vouchers to ascertain the amount permitted or acceptable

Accounting Voucher Creation | ABC Company | Ctrl + M

Sales No. 5 — 1-Sep-2008, Monday

Ref.:

Party's A/c Name : Customer A

Current Balance : 8,290.00 Dr Credit Limit: 25,000.00 Dr

Sales Ledger : Sales Account

Name of Item	Quantity	Rate per	Amount
Item 1	100 Nos	250.00 Nos	25,000.00

Fig. 6.44 Sales Voucher Displaying Credit Limit

Advanced Inventory Features in Tally.ERP 9

Besides, the basic Inventory capabilities, Tally.ERP 9 also comprises of advanced features for better management and generation of advanced and MIS Reports. Some of advanced Inventory features in Tally.ERP 9 features include:

- Re-Order Levels & Re-Order Quantity
- Price Levels & Price Lists
- Point of Sales (POS)
- Job Costing.

Reorder Levels and Reorder Quantity

Reorder Level signifies the quantity of a Stock Item in hand, after reaching which you must place orders for your supplies. The importance of Reorder Level arises from the need to have sufficient stocks to service customer orders and, at the same time, not to unnecessarily accumulate stock.

Therefore, the points to be considered while deciding the reorder levels are as follows:

- The lead-time for suppliers to deliver the stock.
- The delivery time specified by the customer.
- The stock-in-hand to satisfy orders in the meantime.

In simple mode, Tally.ERP 9 accepts the quantities that you specify. In advanced mode, it considers the past consumption patterns to suggest reorder levels. You can however, choose to define your own reorder levels. You may also specify the minimum quantity of the item to be ordered, either in simple or advanced mode.

The purpose of specifying reorder levels is to obtain a report that indicates the quantity of a Stock Item that you must order.

Note: The option Reorder Levels is displayed in the Inventory Info. menu only if Allow Purchase Order Processing is enabled in F11: Inventory Features

Specifying Reorder Levels

Tally.ERP 9 allows you to specify Reorder levels and minimum Order Quantity for each stock item with simple and advanced parameters.

Specifying Simple Reorder Level and Minimum Quantity

When you select the Stock Group under the Reorder Levels menu, the Simple Reorder Levels screen will be available, by default.

```
Go to Gateway of Tally > Inventory Info. > Reorder Levels
```

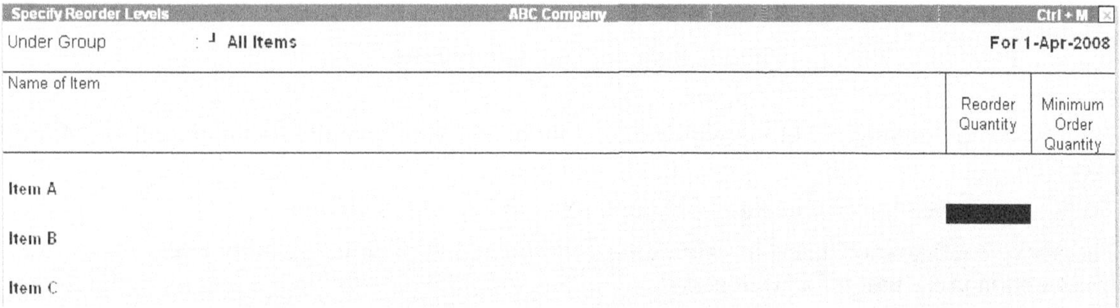

Specify Reorder Levels | ABC Company | Ctrl + M

Under Group : All Items | For 1-Apr-2008

Name of Item	Reorder Quantity	Minimum Order Quantity
Item A		
Item B		
Item C		

Fig. 6.45 Reorder Levels

Select a group of Stock Items from the List of Groups, to specify Reorder Levels for the Stock Items in the Specify Reorder Levels screen. For each item in stock, you can define a Reorder Level and the Minimum Order Quantity.

The Simple Reorder Levels screen appears as follows:

- Enter the level/quantity in the Reorder quantity field.

In Simple Reorder Levels screen, the consumption alternatives will not be available and hence you have to input the only the quantities, *i.e.*, the options that you have in the above mode are to define Reorder Quantity and Minimum Order Quantity.

If you have used Advanced Reorder options earlier, click Simple Reorder button, to specify simple reorder levels.

The options available in the Reorder Levels screen are as follows :

`R : Adv Reorder`

Press Alt+R to toggle to Advanced Reorder Levels screen.

`M : Adv Min Qty`

Press Alt+M to toggle to Advanced Minimum Order Quantity screen.

Specifying Advanced Reorder Levels and Minimum Quantities

To specify advanced Reorder Levels,

`Go to Gateway of Tally > Inventory Info. > Reorder Levels`

When you select the Stock Group under the Reorder Levels menu, the Simple Reorder Levels screen will be available, by default. To view Advanced Reorder Levels screen, press Alt+R or click on R: Adv Reorder from the Button Bar.

The Advanced Reorder Levels screen appears as follows:

Specify Reorder Levels | ABC Company | Ctrl + M

Under Group : All Items | For 1-Apr-2008

Name of Item	Reorder Quantity		Advance Parameter for Reorder Level (Consumption for the last)		Minimum Order Quantity
			Period	Criteria	
Item A	500 Nos	or	15 Days	Higher	450 Nos
Item B	750 Nos	or	2 Weeks	Higher	600 Nos
Item C	800 Nos	or	1 Months	Higher	750 Nos

Fig. 6.45a Advance Reorder Levels

In the same way, press Alt+M to view Advanced Minimum Order Quantity screen, or click on M: Adv Min Qty.

The Reorder Levels screen with advanced parameters will appear as shown:

The above configuration helps in calculation of Reorder Level/Order quantity based on the total consumption in the past for a given period.

Specify Reorder Levels | ABC Company | Ctrl + M

Under Group : All Items | For 1-Apr-2008

Name of Item	Reorder Quantity	Advance Parameter for Reorder Level (Consumption for the last)		Minimum Order Quantity	Advance Parameter for Minimum Order (Consumption for the last)	
		Period	Criteria		Period	Criteria
Item A	500 Nos or	15 Days	Higher	450 Nos or	10 Days	Higher
Item B	750 Nos or	2 Weeks	Higher	600 Nos or	1 Weeks	Higher
Item C	800 Nos or	1 Months	Higher	750 Nos or	3 Weeks	Higher

Fig. 6.46 Displaying Reorder Levels

Advanced Parameters in Advanced Reorder Levels

Period

You can select consumption for various periods viz., Days, Weeks, Months & Years. Here, in this case, it not the average consumption for a period but the total consumption. Enter 0 (Zero), if you do not wish to calculate the reorder level based on the consumption in the past.

Criteria

You can choose, whether the consumption is higher or lower i.e., input /calculated level/quantity.

Advanced Parameters for Minimum Order

Minimum Order Quantity

Specify the minimum order quantity required.

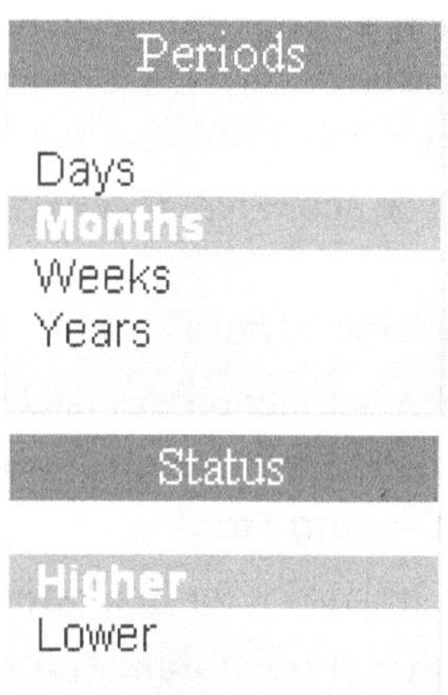

Period

You can select consumption for various periods viz., Days, Weeks, Months & Years. Here, in this case, it not the average consumption for a period but the total consumption. Enter 0 (Zero), if you do not wish to calculate the reorder level based on the consumption in the past.

Criteria

You can choose, whether the consumption is higher or lower, *i.e.*, input / calculated level/quantity.

The options available in the Advanced Reorder Levels screen are as follows:

`R : Simple Reorder`

Press Alt+R to toggle to Simple Reorder Levels screen.

`M : Simple Min Qty`

Press Alt+M to toggle to Simple Minimum Order Quantity screen.

Altering Reorder Levels and Minimum Quantities

There are two ways of altering the Reorder Levels and the Minimum Order Quantities defined earlier.

1. Go to Gateway of Tally > Inventory Info > Reorder Levels

   Select the Group of the Stock Items from the List of Groups to display the Specify Reorder Levels screen. Make the necessary changes and accept to save.

OR

2. Go to Gateway of Tally > Display > Statements of Inventory > Reorder Status

   Select the Group of the Stock Items for which you want to make changes to display the Inventory Reorder Status screen. Drill down the fields Reorder Level/Minimum Order Quantity to display the Specify Reorder Levels screen. Make the necessary changes and accept to save.

Reorder Status and Quantities to Order

Go to Gateway of Tally > Display > Statements of Inventory > Reorder Status

- Select a Group of Stock Items from the List of Groups.

The Inventory Reorder Status screen displays:

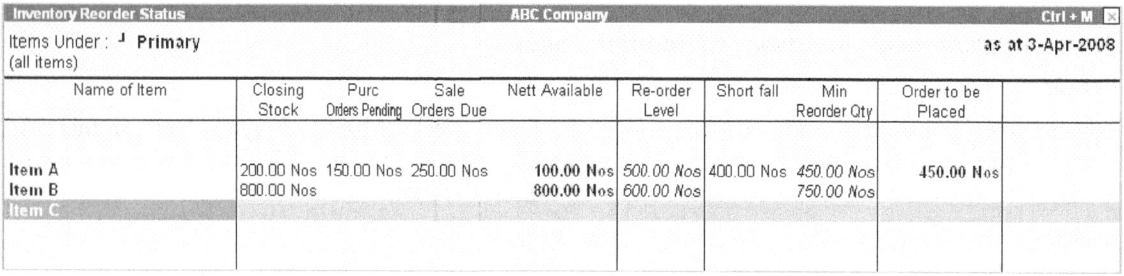

Inventory Reorder Status — ABC Company — Ctrl + M

Items Under : Primary (all items) — as at 3-Apr-2008

Name of Item	Closing Stock	Purc Orders Pending	Sale Orders Due	Nett Available	Re-order Level	Short fall	Min Reorder Qty	Order to be Placed
Item A	200.00 Nos	150.00 Nos	250.00 Nos	**100.00 Nos**	*500.00 Nos*	400.00 Nos	*450.00 Nos*	**450.00 Nos**
Item B	800.00 Nos			**800.00 Nos**	*600.00 Nos*		*750.00 Nos*	
Item C								

Fig. 6.47 Reorder Levels and Quantity to Order

This report gives you the reorder status of Stock Items grouped under the selected Stock Group. When Primary group is selected in Items Under field, the report displays Reorder Status of all the Stock Items.

Click the button A: Reorder Only to remove those items for which there are no orders to be placed For instance, In the above screen, Item C does not have any quantity for Reorder status and hence you may select A: Reorder Only to eliminate the same from the list.

The above report besides indicating the quantity to be ordered, also allows drill down from the fields for more information.

Name of Item

Press Enter on this field for information on suppliers of this Stock Item and the details of their previous supplies.

Closing Stock

Drill down for Item Monthly Summary (Inwards and Outwards) and other details.

Purchase Orders Pending

Press Enter on this field for details on the pending purchase orders.

Sales Orders Due

Drill down to know the details on the sales orders, which are due, *i.e.*, free stock available for sale.

Reorder Level

Drill down by pressing Enter to display the Reorder Level Specification screen for the Stock Item.

Short Fall

Tally.ERP 9 calculates this value based on the Nett Available Stock and Re-Order Level.

Min Reorder Quantity

Drill down by pressing Enter to display the Reorder Level Specification screen for the Stock Item.

Order to be Placed

Tally.ERP 9 calculates this value based on the re-order definition.

Price Levels

In Tally.ERP 9, you can create different Price Levels and assign different Price Lists to these Price Levels. For example, you can create Wholesaler, Distributor and Customer as Price Levels and assign applicable Price Lists to these Price levels, as per your requirements, so that only the relevant prices and discount rates are used during entry of orders and invoices. Before you start creating Price Lists, you may decide to create Price Levels as required.

Creating Price Levels

Ensure that whether the Company is enabled for Accounts with Inventory in the Company Master screen.

To enable Price Levels, Set the following fields to Yes in F11: Features > F2: Inventory Features screen.

Sales Management

Use Multiple Price Levels ? Yes

1. Allow Invoicing (If you do not set this option to Yes, the options for Price Lists will not be available.)
2. Set Use Multiple Price Levels to Yes.
3. Type the name of the price levels to be created, in the Company Price Levels screen.
4. Press Ctrl + A to accept the screen and return to the F11: Inventory Features screen. Set the other options as required and accept Yes to save.

Company Price Levels

1. Wholesale
2. Retail
3. Customer
4.

Altering Price Levels

To alter a Price Level,

Go to Gateway of Tally > F11: Features > F2: Inventory Features screen.

1. Tab down to Use Multiple Price Levels field and press Enter to go to Company Price Levels screen.

Price Lists

Price Lists are useful for orders and invoices. An up-to-date price list helps in decision-making even at the lower levels of the organization and quickens the sales process. Tally.ERP 9 assists in creating quantity based pricing with complex discount structure. Price Lists are available only for inventory items and hence the feature is available only if inventory and invoicing are activated for the company.

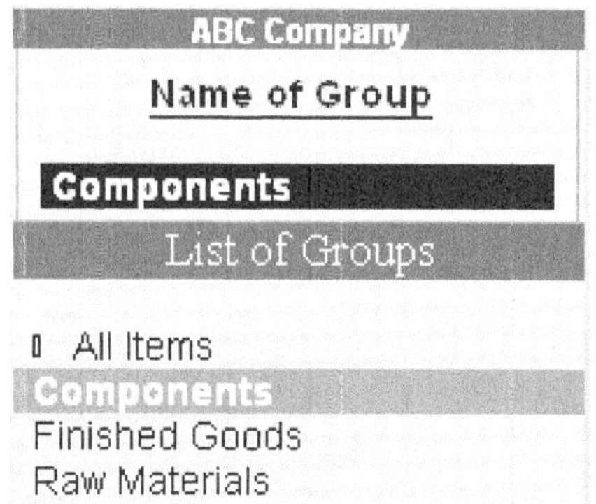

You can have one or more price lists. You may require more

than one price list, when you have different price structures/levels for different purposes viz., different groups of customers requiring different discounts or dealing in different products.

Creating a Price List

Once you have created Price Levels, the Price List option appears in the Inventory Info. menu

`Go to Gateway of Tally > Inventory Info. > Price List`

- Select a group from the List of Groups.
- If you want to create a Price List consisting of all stock Items falling under different Stock Groups, select All Items in the Under Group field.
- Select the Price Levels from the list.

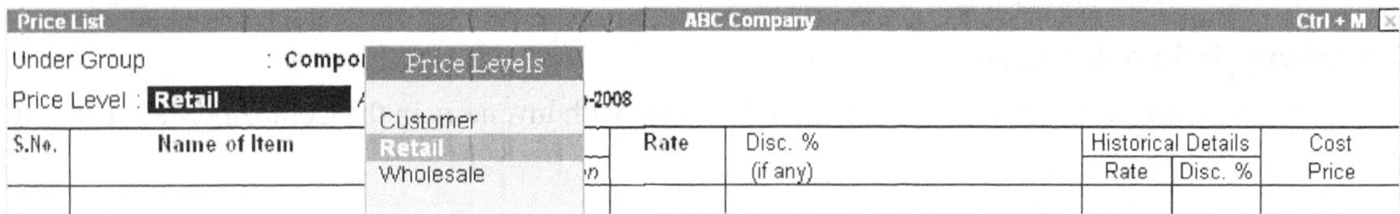

Fig. 6.48 Selecting the Price Level

- Type the applicable rates for the stock items for the selected Price Levels

Price List — ABC Company — Ctrl + M

Under Group : **Components**

Price Level : **Retail** Applicable From: **1-Sep-2008**

S.No.	Name of Item	Quantities From:	Quantities Less than	Rate	Disc. % (if any)	Historical Details Rate	Historical Details Disc. %	Cost Price
1.	240 GB Hard Disk Drive							
			10 Nos	3,200.00/Nos				2,594.12/Nos
		10 Nos	20 Nos	3,200.00/Nos	2 %			
		20 Nos		3,200.00/Nos	5 %			
2.	2 GB RAM Sticks							
			20 Nos	1,600.00/Nos				1,302.96/Nos
		20 Nos	40 Nos	1,600.00/Nos				
		40 Nos		1,600.00/Nos	2 %			
3.	Colour Monitor 17"							
			5 Nos	27,500.00/Nos				25,677.50/Nos
		5 Nos	10 Nos	27,500.00/Nos	3 %			
		10 Nos		27,500.00/Nos	5 %			
4.	CPU Cabinet							
			40 Nos	540.00/Nos				483.33/Nos
		40 Nos	80 Nos	540.00/Nos	5 %			
		80 Nos		540.00/Nos	10 %			
5.	CPU Fan							
			50 Nos	135.00/Nos				109.57/Nos
		50 Nos	100 Nos	135.00/Nos	5 %			
		100 Nos		135.00/Nos	10 %			
6.	Dual Core Processor							
			10 Nos	4,100.00/Nos				3,502.29/Nos
		10 Nos	20 Nos	4,100.00/Nos	3 %			
		20 Nos		4,100.00/Nos	6 %			

Accept ?

Yes or No

Fig. 6.49 Price Level of Stock Items

- Accept to save

Under Group

This is the stock group of the Stock Item, for which you want to define the Price Lists.

Price Level

This is the Price Level under which the Price List needs to be created.

Applicable From

Specify the date from when the Price List will be applicable.

The columns you see are as follows.

Sl. No

This column is auto-generated serial numbers to track the number of items in the Price List.

Name of Item

This column contains the Name of the Stock Items under the selected Stock group. You can define the Price List for each item.

Quantities - From & Less Than

These fields are repeated for an item and begin with a blank for 0 items and end with a blank for any number of items (i.e., upto 50 Nos you can have a certain pricing if someone buys more than 50Nos you can specify a different rate). This is useful for quantity based pricing and discounts. You can create a staggered quantity price structure, if required.

If you do not require quantity based pricing, leave From and Less Than fields blank.

Rate & Discount (if any)

Under this column, you can specify Rate and discount for each Quantity band or you may also choose to maintain the same price for all bands, but define different discounts.

Historical Details (Rate and Disc%)

This column displays the last Price List specified for such Stock Group.

Cost Price

This Column displays the cost price (based on the Costing Method set in the Stock Item Master) of the item to help fixing of prices.

Configuration in Price Lists Screen

F4: New Parent

Select this option to change the Stock Group in the Under Group field.

Print/Export/E-mail/Upload Price Lists

Select the relevant buttons while the price list is displayed for it to be printed / sent by e-mail or published.

Altering a Price List

To alter a Price List,

```
Go to Gateway of Tally > Inventory Info. > Price List
```

1. Select the required Stock Group from the List of Groups drop down.
2. Change the Applicable From date, as required.

Follow the same procedure as discussed in Creating a Price List, to alter the Price Lists.

Assigning Price Levels to Ledger Accounts

Once the Price Levels are created in Tally.ERP 9, a new option appears in Ledgers grouped under Sundry Debtors and Sundry Creditors, with the help of which you can assign a specific Price Level to the ledger account.

```
Go to Gateway of Tally > Accounting Info > Ledgers > Create
```

You can choose the Price Level that you want to assign to the Ledger, by selecting the Price Level from the Price Levels list in the Pricing Level Applicable field. Select Not Applicable, if you do not want to assign any Price Levels to the Ledger.

If you want to assign Price Levels to ledgers created earlier, alter the ledger account, tab down to Pricing Level Applicable field and select the applicable price level from the list.

Note: For a Ledger, you can only assign / tag only one Price Level at a time, however you can change the Price Level selection depending upon your requirement in alteration mode or during Voucher Entry.

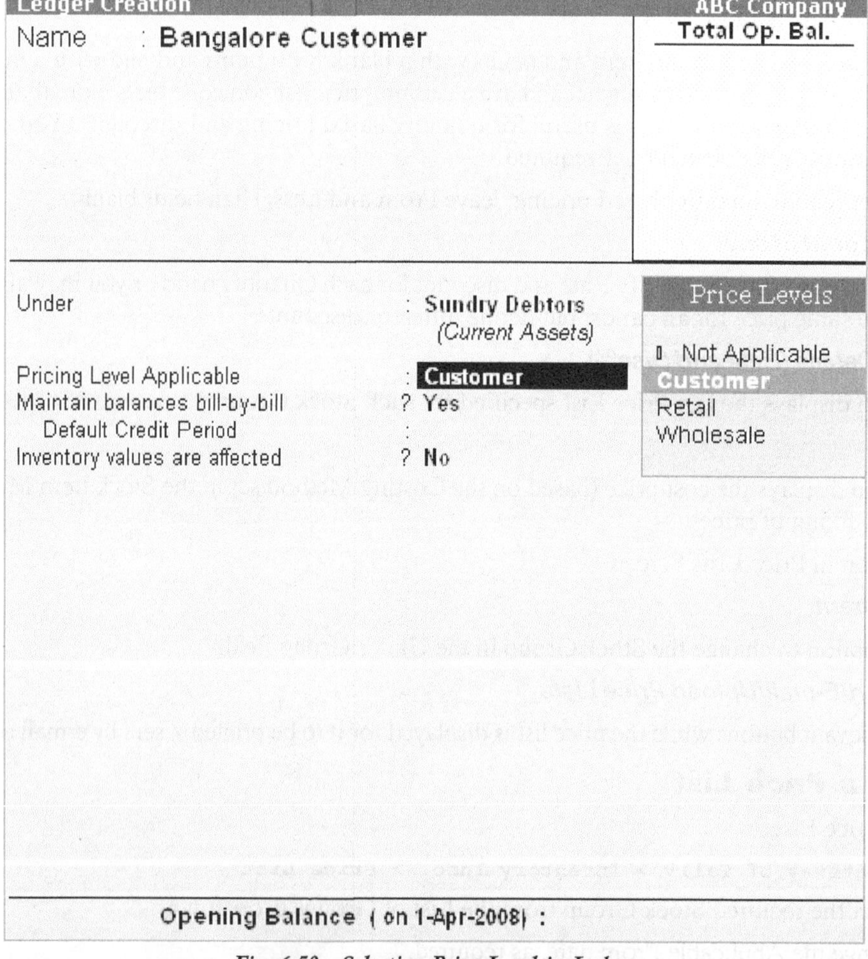

Fig. 6.50 Selecting Price Level in Ledger

Using Price Levels during Invoicing (Voucher Entry)

The price levels created and assigned to Ledger Accounts automates Stock Item Prices and helps minimizing errors during Invoicing.

`Go to Gateway of Tally > Accounting Vouchers > F8: Sales`

1. Select As Invoice.
2. Accept to save.

During Invoicing, there is an additional field Price Level enabled once Price Levels feature is activated and is prefilled with the Price Level which are specified for the selected Party ledger and the cursor skips this field.

You may change the Price Level during Invoicing by pressing F12: Configure and setting Yes to Allow modification of ALL fields during entry.

`Go to Gateway of Tally > F12: Configure > Invoice/Orders Entry`

Set Allow modification of ALL fields during entry to No to prevent changes made to prices. If you set it to Yes, you can override the prices already defined.

`Go to Gateway of Tally > Accounting Vouchers > F8: Sales`

1. Select As Invoice.

Once the above configuration is enabled in F12: Configure, you will now be allowed to modify the Price Levels for the selected Party Ledger during Invoicing.

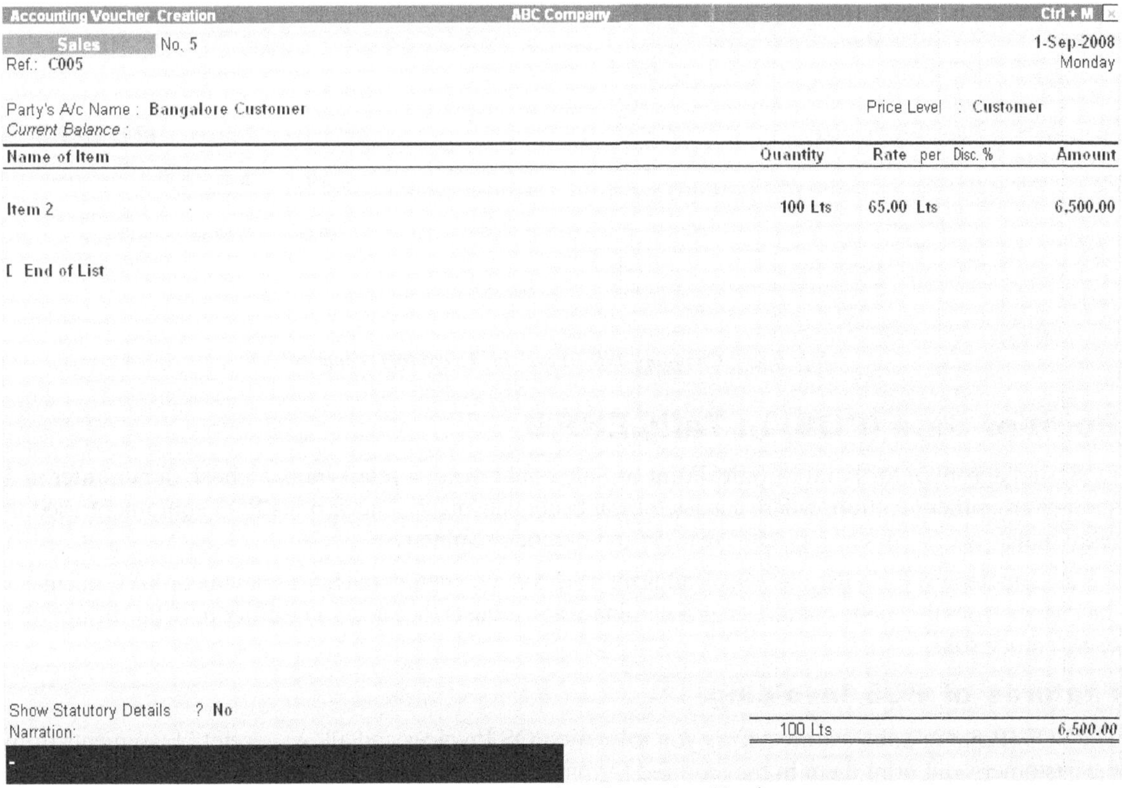

Accounting Voucher Creation ABC Company Ctrl + M

Sales No. 5 1-Sep-2008
Ref.: C005 Monday

Party's A/c Name : Bangalore Customer Price Level : Customer
Current Balance :

Name of Item	Quantity	Rate	per	Disc. %	Amount
Item 2	100 Lts	65.00	Lts		6,500.00
[End of List					

Show Statutory Details ? No
Narration: 100 Lts 6,500.00

Fig. 6.51 Price Level in Accounting Voucher

Invoice / Delivery Note / Order Configuration

General

Accept Supplementary Details (Address Details, Despatch Details etc.)	? No
Print Default Name & Address of Party	? Yes
Allow Separate Buyer and Consignee Names	? No
Allow modification of ALL fields during entry	? No
Use Common Ledger A/c for Item Allocation	? Yes
Use Defaults for Bill Allocations	? Yes
Use Additional Description(s) for Item Name	? No
Use Additional Description(s) for Ledger Name (for Accounting Invoice.)	? No
Show turnover achieved with Customer	? No

Exporters' Options

Specify Export Shipping details	? No
Specify Marks & Nos./Container No.	? No
Specify No. and Kind of Packages	? No

Inventory

Warn on Negative Stock Balance	? Yes
Honor Expiry Dates usage for Batches	? Yes
Complete Accounting Allocations in Order/Delivery Note	? Yes

Statutory

Calculate Tax on current Sub-Total (else calculations are on Inventory Total only)	? No
Allow selection of VAT/Tax Class during entry	? No
Warn on Mismatch in VAT Rates	? No
Activate 'E1' or 'E2' Transaction (VAT)	? No

POS

Skip Qty field during POS Invoicing (faster entry!)	? Yes
Allow modification of Rate field during POS Invoicing	? No
Allow Party Details in POS Invoice	? Yes

Fig. 6.52 Setting Options for Invoice/Delivery Note

Accounting Voucher Creation — ABC Company — Ctrl + M

Sales No. 5 — 1-Sep-2008, Monday

Ref.: C005

Party's A/c Name : Bangalore Customer — Price Level : Retail

Current Balance :

Name of Item	Quantity	Rate	per
Item 2	100 Lts	65.00	Lts
End of List			

Price Levels: Not Applicable, Customer, Retail, Wholesale

Fig. 6.53 Changing Price Level in Accounting Voucher

Point of Sale (POS) in Tally.ERP 9

POS is an acronym for Point of Sale. Point of Sale could mean a retail shop, a check-out counter in a shop or any other location, where a sales transaction takes place. The various POS equipment used in retail outlets are Cash registers, card readers and barcode scanners.

It is a computerized Cash Register which adds the sales total, computes the State sales tax or VAT, calculates the change from the money tendered and automatically adjusts the store's inventory to debit the amount of inventory sold.

Features of POS Invoicing

The POS (Point-of-Sale) feature allows you to create POS Invoices and allows receipt of payments from the customers and print them in the required formats.

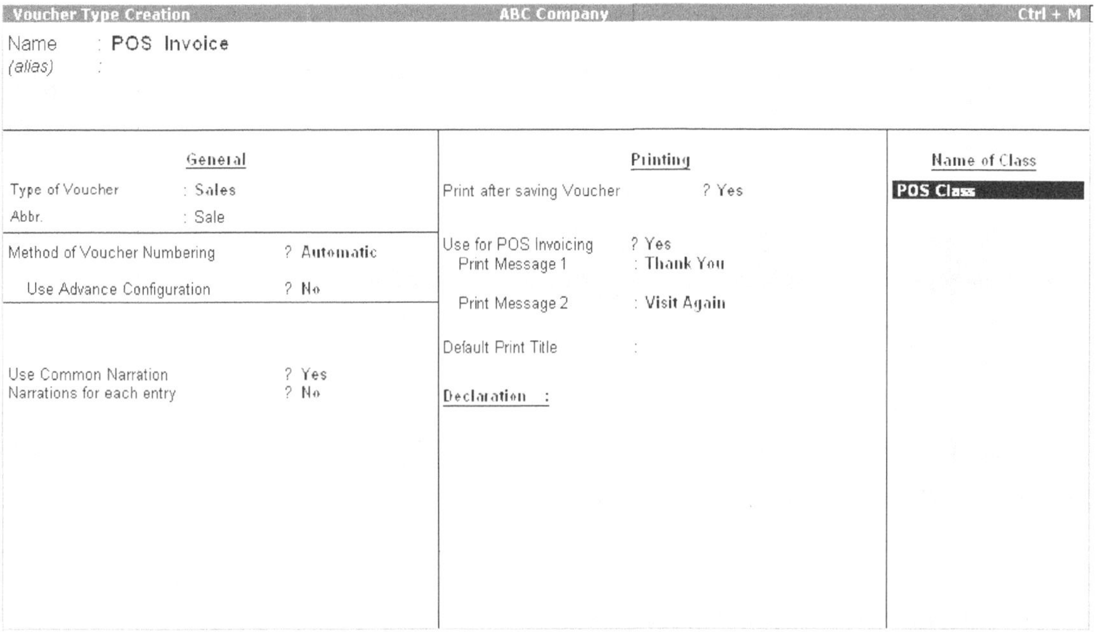

Voucher Type Creation — ABC Company — Ctrl + M

Name : POS Invoice
(alias) :

General

Type of Voucher	: Sales
Abbr.	: Sale
Method of Voucher Numbering	? Automatic
Use Advance Configuration	? No
Use Common Narration	? Yes
Narrations for each entry	? No

Printing

Print after saving Voucher	? Yes
Use for POS Invoicing	? Yes
Print Message 1	: Thank You
Print Message 2	: Visit Again
Default Print Title	:
Declaration :	

Name of Class

POS Class

Fig. 6.54 Point of Sales in Accounting Voucher

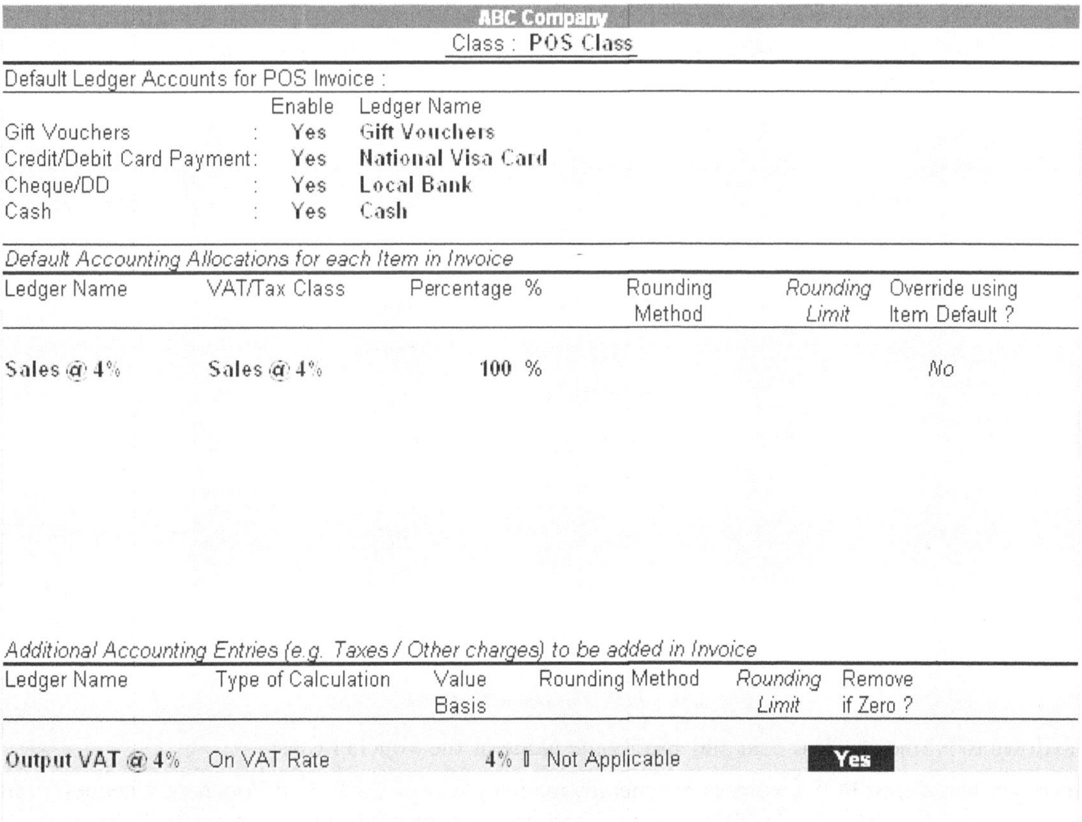

ABC Company

Class : POS Class

Default Ledger Accounts for POS Invoice :

	Enable	Ledger Name
Gift Vouchers :	Yes	Gift Vouchers
Credit/Debit Card Payment:	Yes	National Visa Card
Cheque/DD :	Yes	Local Bank
Cash :	Yes	Cash

Default Accounting Allocations for each Item in Invoice

Ledger Name	VAT/Tax Class	Percentage %	Rounding Method	Rounding Limit	Override using Item Default ?
Sales @ 4%	Sales @ 4%	100 %			No

Additional Accounting Entries (e.g. Taxes / Other charges) to be added in Invoice

Ledger Name	Type of Calculation	Value Basis	Rounding Method	Rounding Limit	Remove if Zero ?
Output VAT @ 4%	On VAT Rate	4%	Not Applicable		Yes

Fig. 6.55 Setting the Point of Sales Options

Features of POS Invoicing in Tally.ERP 9.

The POS Invoicing functionality in Tally.ERP 9 is:

- Simple and user friendly
- Quick and easy to setup and use
- Facilitates faster data entry and calculations
- Helps you to calculate sales and sale proceeds
- Manages inventory and facilitates bar code scanner operations
- Offers a flexible and simple way of querying your inventory and sales information
- Helps you to track the movement of items and how much you are spending on them
- Tracks and records the date and time of every sale made at the store
- Helps faster printing of Invoices.

Creating POS Voucher Type with Voucher Class

To create a POS Invoice Voucher Type with Voucher Class, you may create a new POS Invoice Voucher Type or alter an existing Sales Voucher Type with Use for POS Invoicing option set to Yes.

To create POS Voucher Type with Voucher Class,

`Go to Gateway of Tally > Accounts Info > Voucher Type > Create`

Voucher Type Creation ABC Company Ctrl + M

Name : POS Invoice
(alias) :

General		Printing		Name of Class
Type of Voucher	: Sales	Print after saving Voucher	? Yes	
Abbr.	: Sale			
Method of Voucher Numbering	? Automatic	Use for POS Invoicing	? Yes	
		Print Message 1	: Thank You	
Use Advance Configuration	? No	Print Message 2	: Visit Again	
		Default Print Title	:	
Use Common Narration	? Yes	Declaration :		
Narrations for each entry	? No			

Accept ?
Yes or No

Fig. 6.56 POS Voucher with Voucher Class

Tab down to Name of Class field and specify the name of the Voucher Class

The payments against POS Invoices are generally made by way of Cash, Gift Vouchers, Cheques/Drafts or through Credit/Debit Cards. To account for receipt of payments from customers by different modes, set the required option to Yes and select the required ledger in the respective fields.

1. Set Yes in Gift Vouchers field to enable the option during POS Invoice Entry and select the Gift Vouchers under Ledger Name field (if does not exist, create using Alt+C. The Gift Vouchers ledger should be created under Sundry Debtors group).
2. Set Yes in Credit/Debit Card Payment field to enable the option during POS Invoice Entry and select the required Bank Ledger under Ledger Name field.
3. Set Yes in Cheque/DD field to enable the option during POS Invoice Entry and select the required Bank Ledger under Ledger Name field.
4. Set Yes in Cash field to enable the option during POS Invoice Entry and select the required Cash Account under Ledger Name field.

Note:

- For Gift Vouchers, the ledgers should be created under Sundry Debtors Group.
- For Credit/Debit Cards, the respective Bank Ledger should be created under Bank account or Bank OD/OCC.
- For Payment through Cheque/DD, the respective Bank Ledger should be created under the group Bank Accounts or Bank OD/OCC.
- For Cash, the Ledger should be under group Cash-in-Hand.

Creating a POS Voucher Type without Voucher Class

To enable POS Invoicing in Tally.ERP 9. create a POS Invoice Voucher Type. You may also alter an existing Sales voucher type for this feature to be enabled.

`Go to Gateway of Tally > Accounts Info > Voucher Type > Create`

Name: Enter the name of the Voucher type (For example, POS Invoice).

Type of Voucher: Select the type of Voucher as Sales from the predefined Voucher Types.

Abbreviation: By default, Sales text will appear in the abbreviation field. However, you can enter the abbreviation as per your requirements.

Used for POS Invoicing? On selecting the Sales voucher type from the list, Used for POS Invoicing? Option appears, set this option to Yes

Print Message 1 and Print Message 2: These two additional fields for messages appear on enabling the above POS feature, which can used for custom messages viz., *Thank You* or *Visit Again* and so on as per your requirements. The same will be printed at the bottom of the POS invoice.

Default Print Title: You can specify the printing title of the POS Invoice and the same will be printed in the Invoice.

Note:

1. Once Use POS for Invoicing option is set to Yes in voucher type, you will not be entitled to set this field to No, if you have passed any POS Invoice.
2. To know about advanced configurations refer detailed information on Use Advance Configuration usage.

Creating a POS Invoice

To enter a simple transaction using a POS Invoice with single payment mode:

`Go to Gateway of Tally > Accounting Vouchers > Select F8: Sales`

1. Select the POS Invoice as the Voucher type from the list of Voucher types.
2. Select the Godown, Sales Ledger and VAT/Tax Class as applicable.
3. Select the Item using the Bar code reader to scan the bar code or select the Item from the list.
4. The Rates of the Item is picked up from Set Standard Rates screen (Stock Item Creation screen) or from the Price List screen.
5. Select VAT/Tax Ledger from the list of Ledger Accounts.
6. By default for the first time, the POS Invoice screen will appear in Single Mode Payment.

The screen will appear as below with the Cash and Cash tendered fields:

Accounting Voucher Creation — ABC Company — Ctrl + M

POS Invoice No. 5 — Voucher Class : POS Class — 1-Sep-2008 Monday

Godown : Godown A

Party's A/c Name : Customer A

Name of Item	Quantity	Rate	per	Disc %	Amount
Item 1	10 Nos	55.00	Nos		550.00
Output VAT @ 4%		4%			22.00
	10 Nos				572.00

Cash : Cash 572.00 Cash Tendered : 600.00 Balance : 28.00

Narration: Sale of Item 1

Accept ? Yes or No

Fig. 6.57 POS Voucher with Voucher Class

Accept to save.

Configurations in POS Invoice:

1. Allow Party Details in POS Invoice: By setting this option to Yes, you are able to select the Customer's Ledger. If you do not want to create a separate Ledger for the Buyer and still would like to print the customer's name in the Invoice print, select Not Applicable from the List of Ledger Accounts and specify the Buyer's name and address details in the Buyer's details.
2. Skip Qty field during POS Invoicing (faster entry): By default, the same will be set to Yes so that while passing the Invoice, the cursor will skip the Quantity field. The user may set this option to No, to specify the required number of quantity.

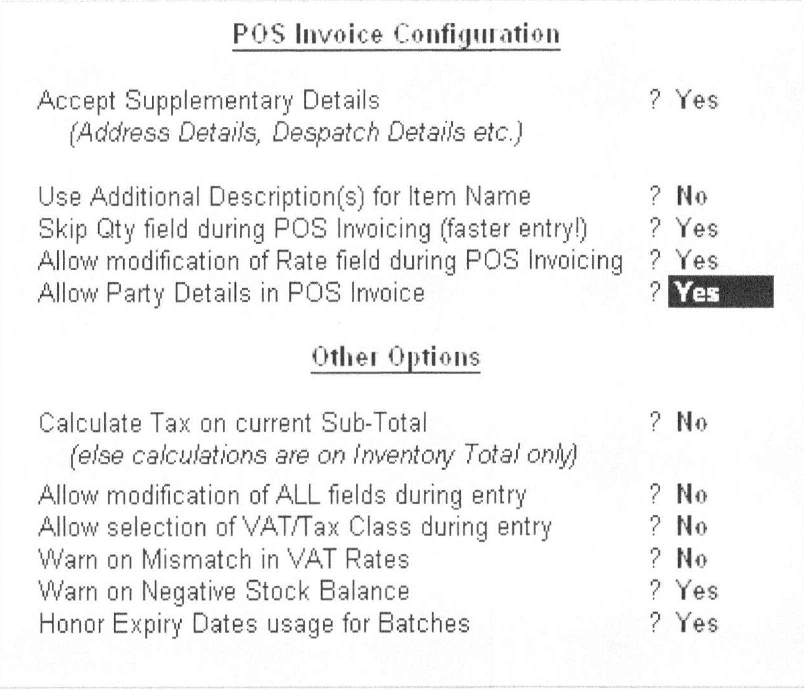

POS Invoice Configuration

Accept Supplementary Details *(Address Details, Despatch Details etc.)*	? Yes
Use Additional Description(s) for Item Name	? No
Skip Qty field during POS Invoicing (faster entry!)	? Yes
Allow modification of Rate field during POS Invoicing	? Yes
Allow Party Details in POS Invoice	? Yes

Other Options

Calculate Tax on current Sub-Total *(else calculations are on Inventory Total only)*	? No
Allow modification of ALL fields during entry	? No
Allow selection of VAT/Tax Class during entry	? No
Warn on Mismatch in VAT Rates	? No
Warn on Negative Stock Balance	? Yes
Honor Expiry Dates usage for Batches	? Yes

Fig. 6.58 Setting POS Invoice Configuration

3. Allow modification of Rate field during POS Invoicing: The rates are automatically picked as per the Standard rates defined in the Stock Item master or from the Price List. However, you can change the rate during entry, by setting this option to Yes.

Creating a POS Invoice with Multi-Mode Payment

To create a POS Invoice with Multi Mode Payment, click on the Multi Mode Pymt button in the Button bar, to account for receipt of payments through other modes like Gift vouchers, Credit card/Debit Card or by cheque/DD etc.

To enter POS Invoice with Multi Mode Payment:

`Go to Gateway of Tally > Accounting Vouchers > Select F8: Sales`

1. Select the POS Invoice as the Voucher type from the list of Voucher types.
2. Select Multi Mode Pymt option from the Button Bar or press Ctrl+P.
3. Select the Godown, Sales Ledger and VAT/Tax Class if applicable.
4. Select the Item using the Bar code reader to scan the bar code or select the Item from the list.
5. The Rates of the Item is picked up from Set Standard Rates screen (Stock Item master) or from the Price List screen.
6. Select VAT/Tax Ledger from the list of Ledger Accounts.
7. Allocate the Bill amount to the relevant modes of payment.
8. Select Gift voucher from the list and enter the amount OR Select Credit/Debit Card Payment and enter the amount and the card number OR Select the Cheque and enter the amount, Bank Name and Cheque Number OR Select Cash ledger from the list and enter the amount to be paid.

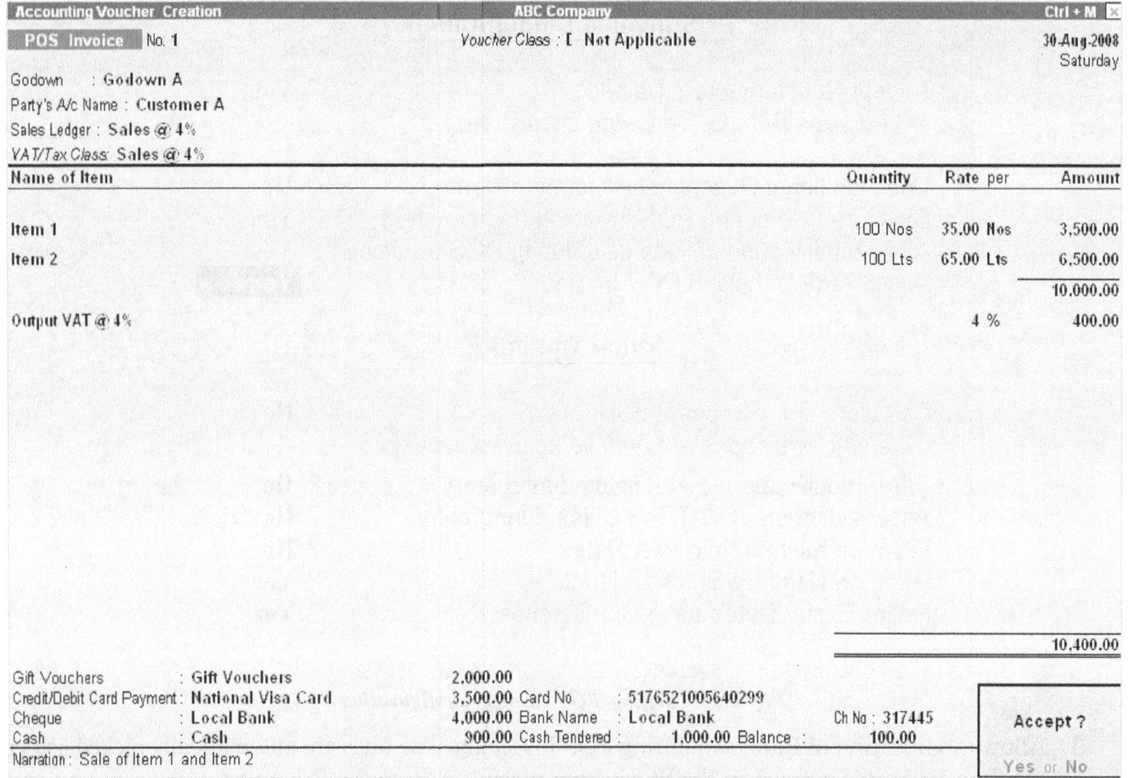

Fig. 6.59 POS Invoice

9. Accept the POS Sales Invoice screen.

Note:

- Though Maintain Multiple Godown feature is set to Yes in F11: Inventory Features, you can select only one Godown, while passing a POS Invoice.
- Single Mode/ Multi Mode Pymt: You can toggle between single and multi mode payments by clicking on the Single Mode Pymt button. In Multi Mode the customer can choose to make his payment by Credit/Debit cards, Gift Vouchers, Cheque or Cash and have all details available on his invoice. In Single Mode only Cash field will be available in the Invoice.
- If Use Multiple Price level for Invoicing is enabled for the Item then the rates of the Item is picked up from the price levels. Else, you can set the price of the Item in the Stock Item creation screen using the Set Standard Rates to Yes. Enter the standard selling price of the Item (Press F12: Configure button in the Stock Item creation screen and set Allow Std. Rates for Stock Items to Yes).
- If you have set the rate for an Item both in Price Levels and in Set Standard Rates (in Stock Item Creation screen), the rate is picked up from the Price List and not from the Set Standard Rates in Stock Item creation screen.

POS Invoicing with Advance Configurations

- Set Maintain Batch-wise Details and Set Expiry Dates for Batches to Yes in the F11: Inventory

Features screen.

- Set Use different Actual & Billed Qty. to Yes in F11: Inventory Features screen to specify the free items.
- Set Separate Discount column on Invoices to Yes to specify the discount on any items while making a POS sales invoice.
- Create Stock Items. Place the cursor in the alias field and use the Bar Code Reader to scan and read the bar code of the Item. This code will automatically get displayed in the alias field. Select the Unit of measure and Set Maintain in Batches to Yes. On setting this option you will get Track Date of Mfg and Use expiry dates set these two fields to Yes.
- Set Standard Rates to Yes and enter the standard selling price of the Item (Press F12: Configure button in the Stock Item creation screen and Set Allow Std. Rates for Stock Items to Yes). If you have specified the rates in the price level then you can skip this field.
- Set Use Security Control to Yes in Company Creation/Alteration screen and create the user login name using the security feature in Tally.ERP 9. The user who logs in to Tally.ERP 9 with the name of the user and password can print the POS Invoice with the user name.

Creating a POS Invoice using Voucher Class

To create a POS Invoice using Voucher Class:

`Go to Gateway of Tally > Accounting Vouchers > Select F8: Sales`

1. Select the POS Invoice as the Voucher type from the list of Voucher types.
2. Select POS Class from the Voucher Class List.
3. Select Multi Mode Pymt option from the Button Bar or press Ctrl+P.
4. Select the Godown and Party's A/c Name.
5. Select the Item select the Item from the list or using the Bar code scanner or
6. The Rates of the Item is picked up from Standard Rates (Stock Item Creation screen) or from the Price List screen.
7. The Item will be allocated to the Sales Ledger as defined and Tax will also get calculated automatically.
8. Allocate the Bill amount to the relevant modes of payment.

Cash Tendered Field: When the payment is made by way of cash and once the user specifies the Cash tendered value, the balance will be calculated automatically.

In the above example: the Cash tendered by the buyer is Rs. 500 and payable amount was Rs. 360 and hence the balance to be paid back is Rs. 140.

Creating a POS Invoice with Batchwise Details

`Go to Gateway of Tally > Accounting Vouchers > Select F8: Sales`

1. Select the POS Voucher Type.
2. Select Godown, Party A/c Name, Sales Ledger and VAT/Tax Class (if applicable) from the list.
3. Select the Item from the list or use the scanner to read the bar code of the item. On selecting the Item from the list or by scanning, you will be prompted to enter the Batch Name in the New Number screen. Enter the Batch Name of the Item.

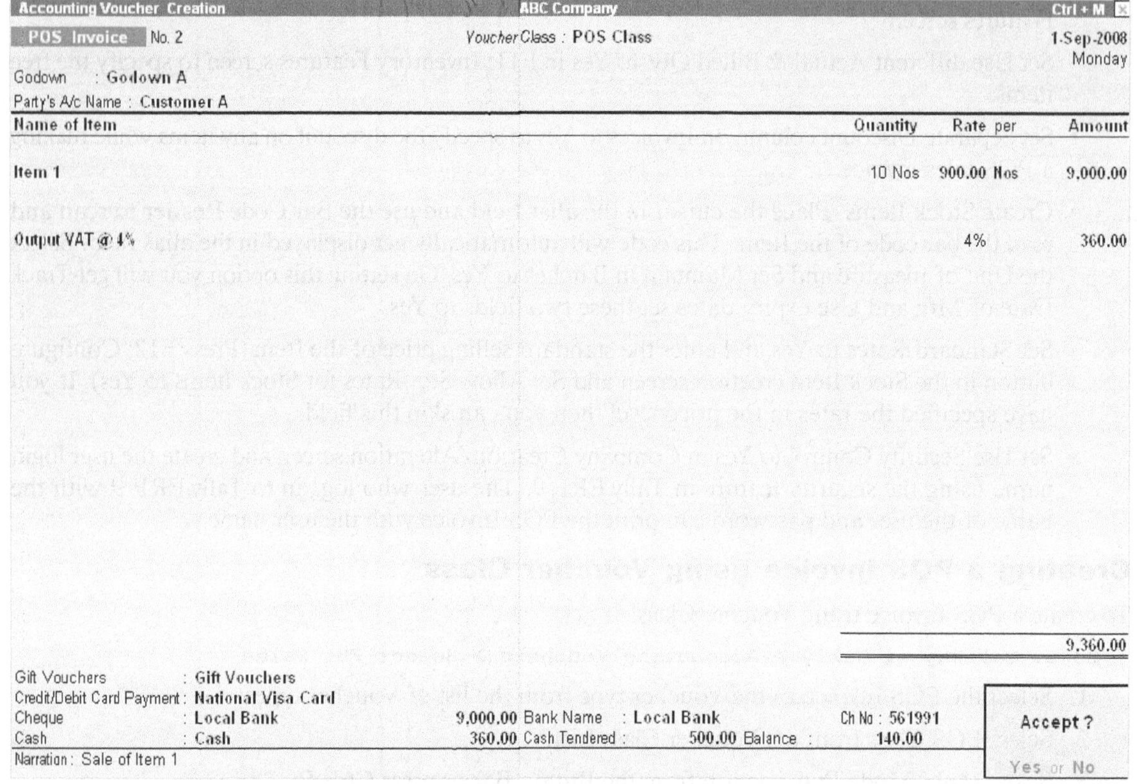

Fig. 6.60 POS Invoice using Voucher Class

4. Tally.ERP 9 prompts you to enter the Manufacturing Date and the Expiry Date as below:
5. The rate of the Item entered in the Set Standard Rates (in Stock Item creation master) or in Price List screen will get prefilled in the Rate field.
6. Now, you can print POS Invoice with Batch details. All other configurations are similar to creating a POS Invoice. For more information refer Creating a POS Invoice.

   Example:

   If you buy 2 shirts and get 1 shirt free with it, while entering POS Invoice, enter 3 shirts in the Actual Column and 2 shirts in the Billed Column. While printing the Invoice, the difference in the actual and billed quantity will be shown as Free in the Rate Column.

   In the example below, for 100 nos. of purchase, 10 quantity is given free.
7. Select VAT/Tax from the list.
8. Select Gift voucher from the list OR Select Credit/Debit Card Payment and the card number and enter the amount OR Select the Cheque and enter the amount, Bank Name and Cheque Number.
9. Select the Cash account and enter the cash paid by the customer at the counter. The balance amount, which has to be paid to the customer, will be calculated automatically.
10. Accept the POS Sales Invoice screen to save the transaction.
11. Extra Features available from a POS Invoice screen are:

New Number ABC Company Ctrl + M

New Number

Fig. 6.61 Setting the New Number

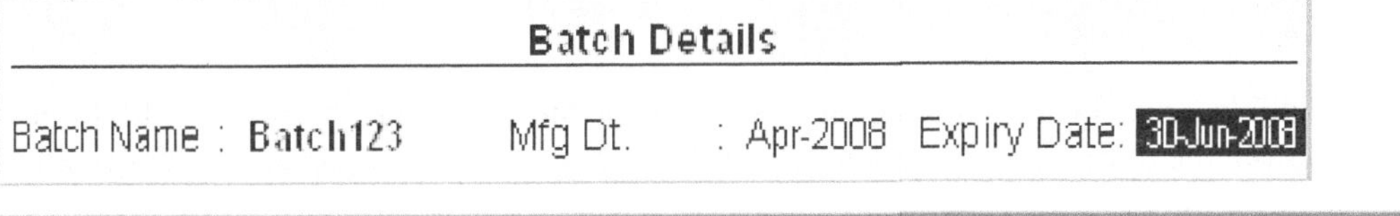

Accounting Voucher Creation ABC Company Ctrl + M

POS Invoice No. 3 Voucher Class : [Not Applicable 1-Sep-2008 Monday

Godown : Godown A
Party's A/c Name : Customer B
Sales Ledger : Sales @ 4%
VAT/Tax Class: Sales @ 4%

Name of Item	Quantity		Rate	per	Disc %	Amount
	Actual	Billed				
Item 1	110 Nos	100 Nos	55.00	Nos	10 %	4,950.00

Fig. 6.62 POS Invoice

12. Single Mode/ Multi Mode Pymt: You can toggle between single and multi mode payments by clicking on the Single Mode Pymt button. In Multi Mode the customer can choose to make his payment by Credit/Debit cards, Gift Vouchers, Cheque or Cash and have all details available on his invoice. In Single Mode only the Cash transaction fields will be printed on the invoice.

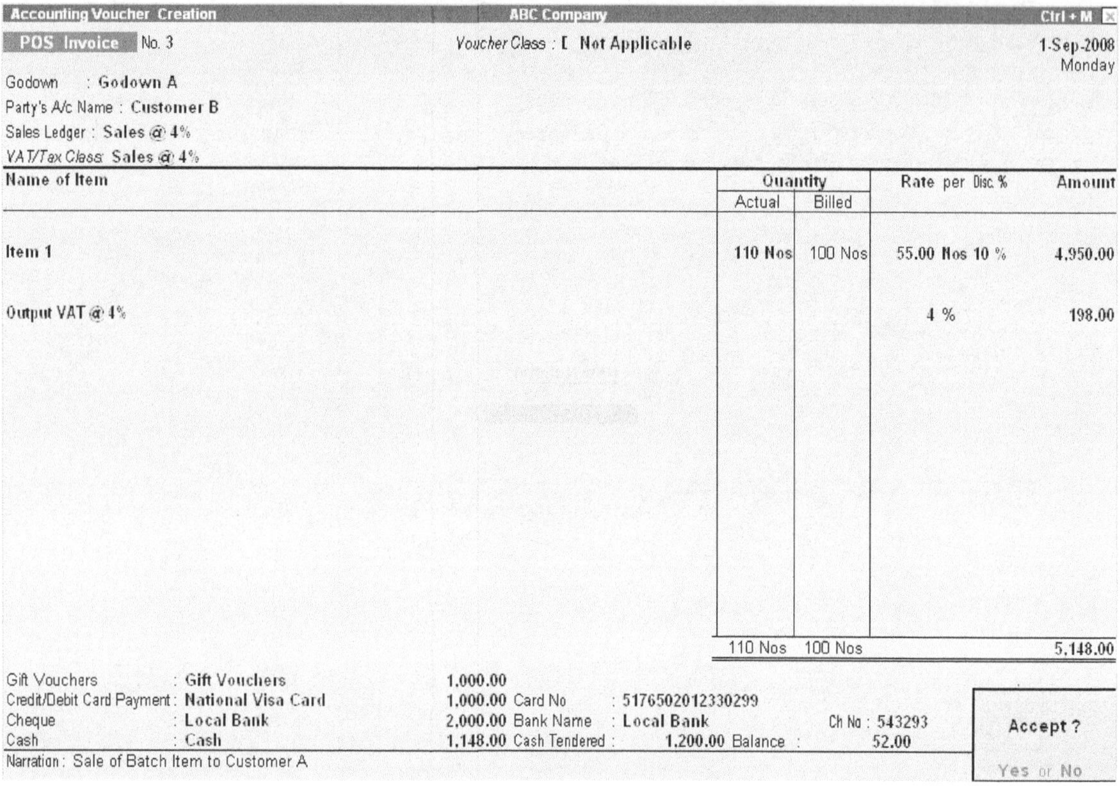

Accounting Voucher Creation	ABC Company	Ctrl + M
POS Invoice No. 3	Voucher Class : Not Applicable	1-Sep-2008 Monday

Godown : Godown A
Party's A/c Name : Customer B
Sales Ledger : Sales @ 4%
VAT/Tax Class: Sales @ 4%

Name of Item	Quantity Actual	Quantity Billed	Rate per Disc. %	Amount
Item 1	110 Nos	100 Nos	55.00 Nos 10 %	4,950.00
Output VAT @ 4%			4 %	198.00
	110 Nos	100 Nos		5,148.00

Gift Vouchers	: Gift Vouchers	1,000.00		
Credit/Debit Card Payment	: National Visa Card	1,000.00	Card No : 5176502012330299	
Cheque	: Local Bank	2,000.00	Bank Name : Local Bank	Ch No : 543293
Cash	: Cash	1,148.00	Cash Tendered : 1,200.00	Balance : 52.00

Narration : Sale of Batch Item to Customer A

Accept ? Yes or No

Fig. 6.63 Accepting the POS Invoice

Note:

- If Use Multiple Price level for Invoicing is enabled for the Item then the rates of the Item is picked up from the price levels. Else, you can set the price of the Item in the Stock Item creation screen using the Set Standard Rates to Yes. Enter the standard selling price of the Item (Press F12: Configure button in the Stock Item creation screen and set Allow Std. Rates for Stock Items to Yes).
- If you have set the rate for an Item both in Price Levels and in Set Standard Rates (in Stock Item Creation screen), the rate is picked up from the Price List and not from the Set Standard Rates in Stock Item creation screen.

13. Set Use Security Control to Yes in Company Creation/Alteration screen and create the user login name using the security feature in Tally.ERP 9. The user who logs in to Tally.ERP 9 with the name of the user and password can print the POS Invoice with the user name.

Creating a POS Invoice with different Actual & Billed Qty

`Go to Gateway of Tally > Accounting Vouchers > Select F8: Sales`

1. Select the POS Voucher Type.
2. Select Godown, Party A/c Name, Sales Ledger and VAT/Tax Class (if applicable) from the list.
3. Select the Item from the list or use the scanner to read the bar code of the item. On selecting the Item from the list or by scanning, you will be prompted to enter the Actual Qty and Billed Qty.

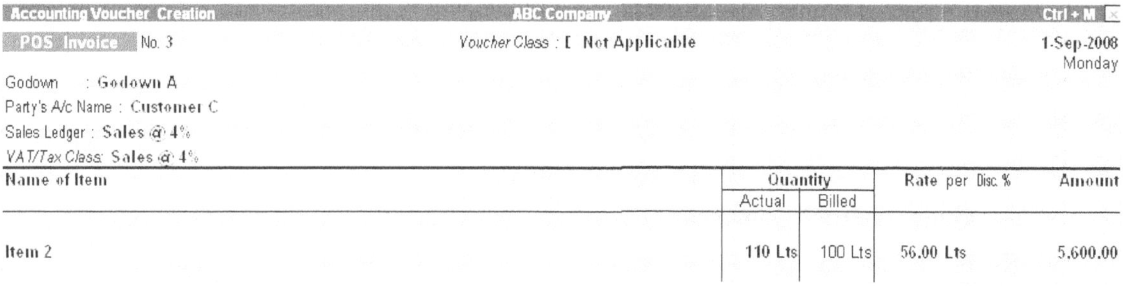

Accounting Voucher Creation ABC Company Ctrl + M

POS Invoice No. 3 Voucher Class : [Not Applicable 1-Sep-2008 Monday

Godown : Godown A
Party's A/c Name : Customer C
Sales Ledger : Sales @ 4%
VAT/Tax Class: Sales @ 4%

Name of Item	Quantity		Rate	per	Disc %	Amount
	Actual	Billed				
Item 2	110 Lts	100 Lts	56.00	Lts		5,600.00

Fig. 6.64 POS Invoice with different Actual and Billed Quantity

4. Select Gift voucher from the list OR Select Credit/Debit Card Payment and the card number and enter the amount OR Select the Cheque and enter the amount, Bank Name and Cheque Number.
5. Select the Cash account and enter the cash paid by the customer at the counter. The balance amount, which has to be paid to the customer, will be calculated automatically.
6. Accept the POS Sales Invoice screen to save the transaction.

Now, you can print POS Invoice with different Actual and Billed Quantities. All other configurations are similar to creating a POS Invoice.

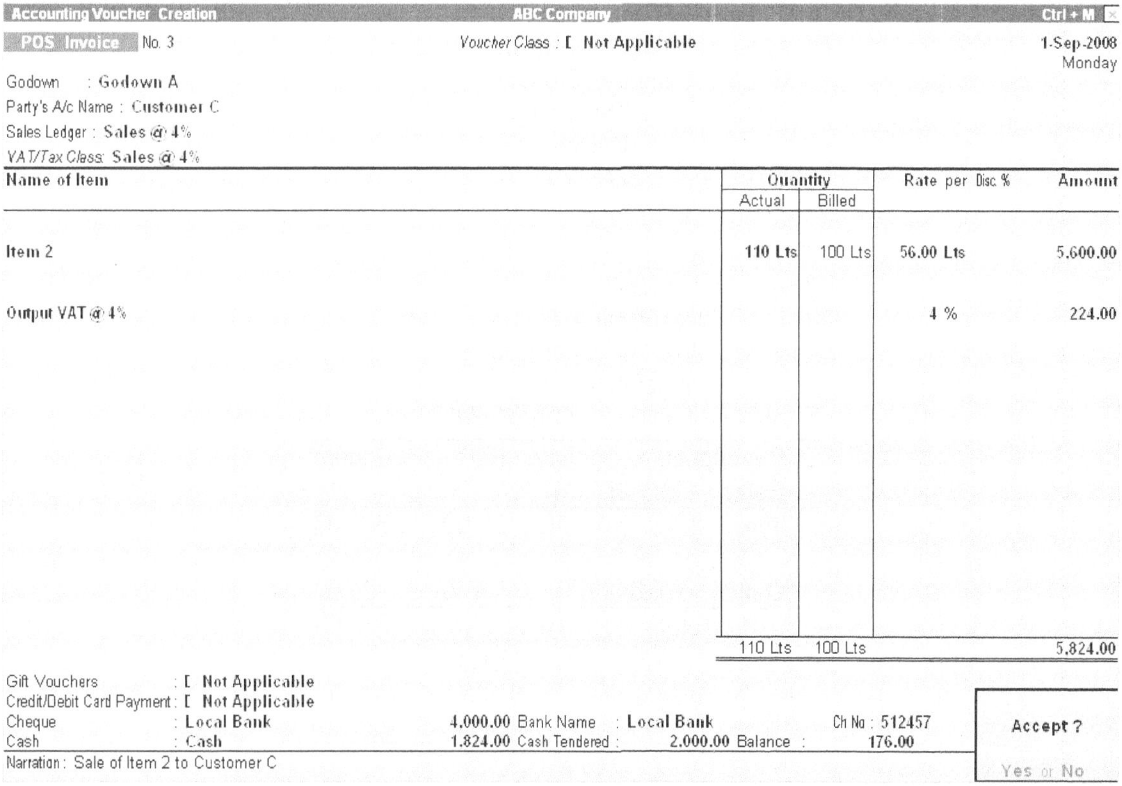

Accounting Voucher Creation ABC Company Ctrl + M

POS Invoice No. 3 Voucher Class : [Not Applicable 1-Sep-2008 Monday

Godown : Godown A
Party's A/c Name : Customer C
Sales Ledger : Sales @ 4%
VAT/Tax Class: Sales @ 4%

Name of Item	Quantity		Rate	per	Disc %	Amount
	Actual	Billed				
Item 2	110 Lts	100 Lts	56.00	Lts		5,600.00
Output VAT @ 4%			4	%		224.00
	110 Lts	100 Lts				5,824.00

Gift Vouchers : [Not Applicable
Credit/Debit Card Payment : [Not Applicable
Cheque : Local Bank 4,000.00 Bank Name : Local Bank Ch No : 512457
Cash : Cash 1,824.00 Cash Tendered : 2,000.00 Balance : 176.00
Narration : Sale of Item 2 to Customer C

Accept ?

Yes or No

Fig. 6.65 Accepting the POS Invoice with Different Quantities

Printing a POS Invoice

On accepting the POS Sales Invoice screen, press ALT+P or click on Print button, Tally.ERP 9 prompts you to print. Press ALT+S or click on the Select Printer button and select the printer from the list. Currently, Tally.ERP 9 support STAR TSP 600 Compatible, Epson TM T88iii Compatible and Epson TM U220 Compatible printers.

Press ALT+F or click on the Print Format to select the print mode. You can either select the Neat Mode or Quick /Draft. In Neat Mode format you will be able to preview the POS Invoice where as in Quick/ Draft mode you cannot preview the POS Invoice.

1. Printing a POS Invoice in Single Mode Payment

The POS Invoice in preview mode

ABC Company
No. 225, 9th Cross,
AMC Road
Bangalore
VAT TIN : 72451285236

Bill No. : 6 Time : 17:24 hrs
Date : 1-9-2008 User : A
Party : Customer A
Address : 482, Ali Asker Road,
Hyderabad
Buyer's VAT TIN : 32567845231

Sl Description Batch Mfg Dt.	Qty	Rate	Amount
1 Item 1	10	55.00	550.00
Output VAT @ 4%		4 %	22.00
Total	10		572.00

Cash : 572.00
Cash Tendered : *600.00*
Balance : *28.00*

Thank You
Visit Again

2. Printing a POS Invoice in Multiple Mode Payment with batch-wise details

The POS Invoice in preview mode

ABC Company
No. 225, 9th Cross,
AMC Road
Bangalore
VAT TIN : 72451285236

Bill No. : 3 Time : 17:08 hrs
Date : 1-9-2008 User : A
Party : Customer A
Address : 301 Regency Buildings,
2134 Colaba Seaface, Mumbai
Buyer's VAT TIN : 32567845231

Sl	Description Batch Mfg Dt.	Qty	Rate Exp Dt.	Amount
1	Item 1	10	900.00	9000.00
	Batch123 1-4-2008		*30-6-2008*	
	Output VAT @ 4%		4 %	360.00
	Total	10		9360.00

Gift Voucher : 1000.00
Cr/Dr Card : 2000.00
Card No : xxxx xxxx xxxx 0299
Cheque : 4000.00
Cheque No. : 561991, Local Bank
Cash : 2360.00
Cash Tendered : 2500.00
Balance : 140.00

Thank You
Visit Again

3. Print Configurations in POS Invoice

Press F12 or click on F12: Configure button and set the required options:

1. Set Print Item Name in One Line to Yes to print the Item details in a single line. If print format is set to Neat Mode then Tally.ERP 9 will compress the name of the Item and prints in one single line. However, if the print format is set to Quick Draft Mode then Tally.ERP 9 truncates the text and prints in multiple lines.
2. Set Print Serial No. to Yes to print the serial number.
3. Set Print Rate Column to Yes to print the rate column.

4. Print Batch Details is set to No by default, set this option to Yes, if you wish to print the Manufacturing Date and Expiry Date.
5. Set Print Card/Cheque No. to Yes to print the Card/Cheque number.
6. Print whole Card Number is set to No by default, which will print only last 4 digit of card number. Set this option to Yes to print the 16 digit card number on the POS Invoice.
7. Set Print VAT Analysis of Item to Yes to print the VAT Analysis on POS Invoice.

POS Invoice Printing Configuration

Title of Document	: POS Invoice
Method to use for Stock Item Name	: Name Only
Print Item Name in one line	? Yes
Print Serial No.	? Yes
Print Rate Column	? Yes
Print Additional Description(s) for Item Name	? No
Print Batch Details	? Yes
Print Mfg Date	? Yes
Print Expiry Date	? Yes
Print Card / Cheque No.	? Yes
Print whole Card Number	? Yes
Print VAT Analysis of Items	? Yes
Print Narration	? Yes
Print Default Name & Address of Party	? Yes

8. Set Print Narration to Yes to print the Narration on POS Invoice.
9. Set Print Default Name & Address of Party to Yes to print the Narration on POS Invoice.
10. Accept the Print screen to view the POS Invoice in preview mode (Only for Neat Mode format).

The Invoice displays the company name and address, TIN, CST, Bill number, time, date, user name, serial number, description, quantity, rate, amount, Batch number, Expiry date, Manufacturing date, Free Item (if any), discount (if any) Vat analysis, payment mode details, balance to be paid to the customer and the print message.

Displaying POS Register

POS Register lists all transactions made over a particular day and by default displays the last invoice entry date of a POS invoice. Each POS Invoice is further drilled down to obtain the lowest level of information.

It could also be set to list all the transactions made over a period. Press F2: Period on the button bar or press the keys Alt+F2.

To view the list of POS Invoice Statement:

```
Go to Gateway of Tally > Display > Accounts Books > POS Register
```

POS Register — ABC Company — Ctrl + M

List of All POS Vouchers — 1-Apr-2008 to 1-Sep-2008

Date	Vch Type	Vch No.	Gift Vouchers	Credit/Debit Card Payment	Cheque	Cash	Total
15-4-2008	POS Invoice	1			2,000.00	860.00	2,860.00
15-4-2008	POS Invoice	2				1,164.80	1.164.80
30-8-2008	POS Invoice	3	2,000.00	3,500.00	4,000.00	900.00	10.400.00
1-9-2008	POS Invoice	4	1,000.00	2,000.00	4,000.00	2,360.00	9.360.00
1-9-2008	POS Invoice	5	1,000.00	2,000.00	5,000.00	424.00	8.424.00
		Total:	4,000.00	7,500.00	15,000.00	5,708.80	32.208.80

Fig. 6.66 POS Register

Note: POS Register option will appear, only if the option Use for POS Invoicing is activated in Voucher Type and at least one entry is made.

Press ALT+F1 or click on F1: Detailed button to view the POS Invoice in detailed format with all the tax details.

Press F12 key or click on F12: Configure button.

Set Show Inventory Details also to Yes and view the List of All POS Vouchers with Inventory details.

F5: Columnar: This button allows you to select different columns for the report. For additional information refer to Columnar Sales Register.

F6: Extract: Provides you with a break down of the POS Invoice vouchers and groups them to provide totals for each group and ledger used in all POS Invoice for that particular date.

Click on the Print button or press ALT+P to view the POS Register in print preview mode. Press ALT+Z to zoom the print preview screen.

ABC Company
No. 225, 9th Cross,
AMC Road
Bangalore

VAT TIN : 72451285236

POS Invoice

Bill No.	: 3	Time	: 16:26 hrs
Date	: 1-9-2008	User	: A
Party	: Customer C		
Address	: 102 Amar Buildings, 480 Ferguson College Road, Pune		

Buyer's VAT TIN : 3698521472

Sl	Description Batch	Mfg Dt.	Qty	Rate Exp Dt.	Amount
1	Item 1		10	900.00	9000.00
	Batch123	*1-4-2008*		*30-6-2008*	
	Discount				(-)900.00
	Item 1		1	Free	--
		Output VAT @ 4%		4 %	324.00
		Total	11		8424.00

VAT @	4 %	on	8100.00	324.00
			Total Tax	324.00

Gift Voucher	:	1000.00
Cr/Dr Card	:	2000.00
Card No	: *5176213255220299*	
Cheque	:	5000.00
Cheque No.	: *321456, Local Bank*	
Cash	:	424.00
Cash Tendered	:	*500.00*
Balance	:	*76.00*

Sale of Item 1 to Customer C

Thank You
Visit Again

Fig. 6.67 POS Invoice

POS Register — ABC Company — Ctrl + M

List of All POS Vouchers — 1-Apr-2008 to 1-Sep-2008

Date	Vch Type	Vch No.	Gift Vouchers	Credit/Debit Card Payment	Cheque	Cash	Total
15-4-2008	POS Invoice	1			2,000.00	860.00	2,860.00
	Output VAT @ 4%	110.00					
	Sales @ 4%	2,750.00					
15-4-2008	POS Invoice	2				1,164.80	1,164.80
	Output VAT @ 4%	44.80					
	Sales @ 4%	1,120.00					
30-8-2008	POS Invoice	3	2,000.00	3,500.00	4,000.00	900.00	10,400.00
	Sales @ 4%	10,000.00					
	Output VAT @ 4%	400.00					
1-9-2008	POS Invoice	4	1,000.00	2,000.00	4,000.00	2,360.00	9,360.00
	Sales @ 4%	9,000.00					
	Output VAT @ 4%	360.00					
1-9-2008	POS Invoice	5	1,000.00	2,000.00	5,000.00	424.00	8,424.00
	Sales @ 4%	8,100.00					
	Output VAT @ 4%	324.00					
		Total:	4,000.00	7,500.00	15,000.00	5,708.80	32,208.80

Fig. 6.68 POS Register

Configuration

Show Extract of Register	? **No**
Show Columnar Register	? **No**
Show Gross Profit estimates	? **No**
Format	: **Detailed**
Show Inventory Details also	? **Yes**
Show Entered/Altered By	? **No**
Show Forex Transactions	? **No**
Appearance of Names	: **Name Only**
Sorting Method	: **Default**

Job Costing in Tally.ERP 9

Job costing is a form of specific order costing, which applies to a job undertaken according to customer requirements and specifications. Tally.ERP 9 enables the tracking of cost and revenue information down to the smallest detail. With a view to ascertaining the actual costs incurred for each job, each job is assigned a job number or Job name. Job costing systems then accumulate costs separately for each product or service, based on the jobs undertaken, for each product or service.

Some of the examples of Job Costing are Interior Decoratoration, Construction, Architecture, Printing etc.,

Use of Job Costing

- To determine the true cost for each job broken down by locations.
- To determine the revenue and expenditure and therefore the profit associated with each job.

POS Register — ABC Company — Ctrl + M

List of All POS Vouchers — 1-Apr-2008 to 1-Sep-2008

Date	Vch Type	Vch No.		Gift Vouchers	Credit Debit Card Payment	Cheque	Cash	Total
15-4-2008	POS Invoice	1				2,000.00	860.00	2,860.00
	Output VAT @ 4%	110.00						
	Sales @ 4%	2,750.00						
	Item 2	50 Lts	2,750.00					
15-4-2008	POS Invoice	2					1,164.80	1.164.80
	Output VAT @ 4%	44.80						
	Sales @ 4%	1.120.00						
	Item 2	20 Lts	1,120.00					
30-8-2008	POS Invoice	3		2,000.00	3,500.00	4,000.00	900.00	10.400.00
	Sales @ 4%	10.000.00						
	Item 1	10 Nos	10,000.00					
	Output VAT @ 4%	400.00						
1-9-2008	POS Invoice	4		1,000.00	2,000.00	4,000.00	2,360.00	9.360.00
	Sales @ 4%	9.000.00						
	Item 1	10 Nos	9,000.00					
	Output VAT @ 4%	360.00						
1-9-2008	POS Invoice	5		1,000.00	2,000.00	5,000.00	424.00	8.424.00
	Sales @ 4%	8.100.00						
	Item 1	10 Nos	8,100.00					
	Output VAT @ 4%	324.00						
		Total:		4,000.00	7,500.00	15,000.00	5,708.80	32.208.80

Fig. 6.69 POS Register showing all POS invoices

- To track overhead costs by allocating them for each job.
- To identify loss on projects at an early stage.

Features of Job Costing

- It helps in accumulating Cost and Revenue for a particular Job / Project.
- It allows tracking transfers of materials from one godown to another.
- It allows tracking of consumption of materials at different locations.
- It ascertains profitability i.e., Net Profit / Loss for a particular Job / Project.
- It provides summary of inventory movements (Opening, Inwards, Outwards , Transfer, Consumption etc.)
- Allows comparison of each element of cost, selling price and profit with other jobs in single screen.
- Allows drill down till voucher level for any kind of alteration or reference.

Enabling Job Costing

The Job Costing feature in Tally.ERP 9 is used to track all the incomes and expenses for a project. Each project or job is created as a Cost Centre. The Cost Centres and Inventory Options (Maintain Multiple Godowns) are integrated in Tally.ERP 9 to enable Job Costing, if the company maintains Accounts with Inventory features. For companies that maintain Accounts Only, the Job Costing feature will not be available.

To enable Job Costing:

`Go to Gateway of Tally > F11: Company Features ( F1: Accounting features)`

1. Set Maintain Cost Centres and Use Cost Centre for Job Costing to Yes.
2. Set Maintain Multiple Godowns to Yes in F11: Company Features (F2: Inventory Features).
3. Click Accept to save.

Note: For companies, that Maintain Accounts only, the Job Costing feature will not be available.

Creating Masters for Job Costing

Creating masters for Job Costing is similar to creation of other ledgers. The masters for job work analysis are:

1. Cost Centres for Job Costing.
2. Godowns dedicated to specific jobs.
3. Stock Items.
4. Customer and Supplier ledgers.
5. Sales and Purchase ledger accounts.
6. Expenses and Income Accounts.
7. Stock Journal Voucher class.
    - Transfer voucher class
    - Consumption voucher class.

Company: ABC Company

Accounting Features

General		Invoicing	
Integrate Accounts and Inventory	? Yes	Allow Invoicing	? Yes
Income/Expense Statement instead of P & L	? No	Enter Purchases in Invoice Format	? Yes
Allow Multi-Currency	? No	Use Debit/Credit Notes	? No
		Use Invoice mode for Credit Notes	? No
Outstandings Management		Use Invoice mode for Debit Notes	? No
Maintain Bill-wise Details	? Yes	**Budgets & Scenario Management**	
(for Non-Trading A/cs also)	? No	Maintain Budgets and Controls	? No
Activate Interest Calculation	? No	Use Reversing Journals & Optional Vouchers	? No
(use advanced parameters)	? No		
Cost/Profit Centres Management		**Other Features**	
Maintain Payroll	? No	Enable Cheque Printing	? No
Maintain Cost Centres	? Yes	Set/Alter Cheque Printing Configuration	? No
Use Cost Centre for Job Costing	? Yes	Allow Zero valued entries	? No
More than ONE Payroll / Cost Category	? No		
Use Pre-defined Cost Centre Allocations during Entry	? No		

F1: Accounts F2: Inventory F3: Statutory F4: Tally.NET

Fig. 6.70 Job Costing option in Accounting Features

Creating Cost Centres for Job Costing

Creating Cost Centres for Job Costing is similar to creation of other Cost Centres. Refer Cost Centres for additional Information.

Company: ABC Company

Inventory Features

General		Invoicing	
Integrate Accounts and Inventory	? Yes	Allow Invoicing	? Yes
Allow Zero valued entries	? No	Enter Purchases in Invoice Format	? Yes
Storage & Classification		Use Debit/Credit Notes	? No
Maintain Multiple Godowns	? Yes	Use Invoice mode for Credit Notes	? No
Maintain Stock Categories	? No	Use Invoice mode for Debit Notes	? No
Maintain Batch-wise Details	? No	Separate Discount column on Invoices	? No
(set Expiry Dates for Batches)	? No	**Purchase Management**	
Use different Actual & Billed Qty	? No	Track additional costs of Purchase	? No
Order Processing		**Sales Management**	
Allow Purchase Order Processing	? No	Use Multiple Price Levels	? No
Allow Sales Order Processing	? No	**Additional Inventory Vouchers**	
		Use Tracking Numbers (Delivery/Receipt Notes)	? No
		Use Rejection Inward/Outward Notes	? No

F1: Accounts F2: Inventory F3: Statutory F4: Tally.NET

Fig. 6.71 Job Costing Cost Centers in Inventory Features

```
Go to Gateway of Tally > Accounts Info > Cost Centres > Create
```

1. Enter the name of the Cost Centre in the Name field, *e.g.*, Project 1.
2. In the Under field select Primary from the List of Options.
3. Set the option Use for Job Costing to Yes. This cost centre will then be available in the drop down for the Job Work Analysis report.
4. Click Accept to save the settings.

Creating Godowns for Job Costing

For creating Project / Job Location use Godown Creation.

Once Godown is allocated to the Job/ Project, it is taken into account that all the materials issued or received for that particular Job/Project and will reflect in the reports. It is always advised to create separate godowns for each Job/Project.

```
Go to Gateway of Tally>
Inventory Info > Godowns >
Create
```

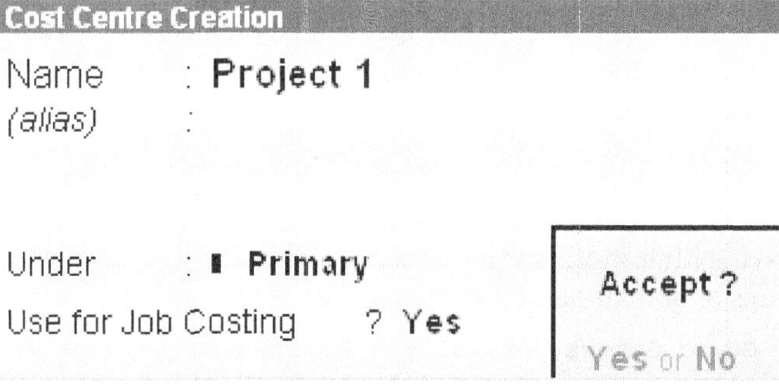

1. In the Godown Creation screen, Allow Storage of Materials is automatically set to Yes. Ex: Bangalore.
2. An additional field Set Job/Project Name for Job Costing is displayed. Press the spacebar in the field and the list of Cost Centres for which Use for Job Costing was set to yes is displayed in the List of Cost Centres sub-screen.
3. Select the Cost Centre to which the Godown is associated.
4. Click Yes to Save.

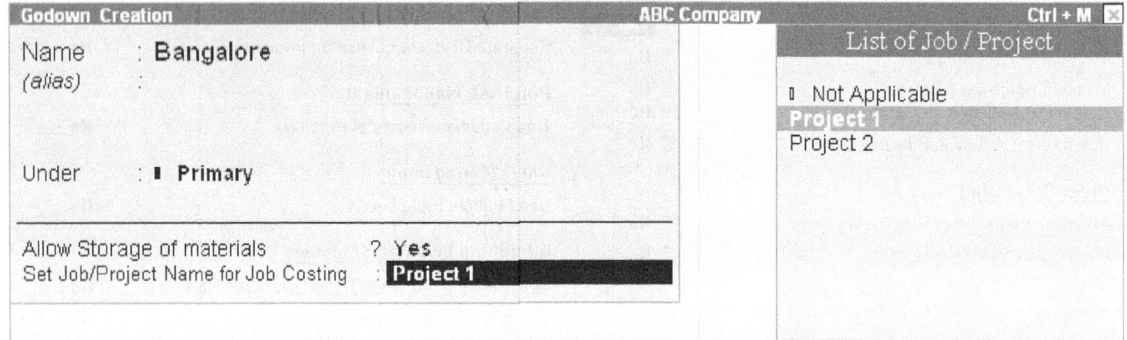

Fig. 6.72 Godown Creation

Creating Ledgers for Job Costing

Creating Ledgers for Job Costing is similar to that of other Ledgers. Refer Ledgers for additional information.

Creating Job Costing Party Ledgers

Create party accounts for our Customers under Sundry Debtors. For example, you can create a Ledger for a Bangalore customer and one for a Chennai customer. Similarly create your Suppliers under Sundry Creditors.

Creating Sales and Purchases Ledgers

Create Sales Ledgers under Sales Accounts and Purchase Ledgers under Purchase Accounts. Ensure that the field Cost Centres are applicable? is Yes for the Ledgers you want to include in Job Costing.

Creating Income and Expenses Ledgers

Create Income Ledgers such as Project Inspection Charges etc. under Direct Income. Expense ledgers such as Transportation Charges, Project Site Rent, and so on can be created under Direct Expenses. Staff Welfare, Telephone Charges etc. can be created under Indirect Expenses as required by your project. Ensure that the field Cost Centres are applicable? is Yes for all the Ledger Accounts you want to include in Job Costing.

Creating Stock Journal Voucher class

Stock Journal classes allow you to handle transfers from one location (Godown) to another, for companies having Multi-Location Inventory and at least two locations/Godowns created. It also allows you to track transfer of materials for consumption.

```
Go to Gateway of Tally > Accounting Info or Inventory Info > Voucher Types >
Alter > Stock Journal > under 'Name of Class' give the name as 'Transfer':
```

Class : Transfer	
Use Class for Inter- Godown Transfers	? Yes
Use Class for Job Costing Consumption	? No

1. Below 'Transfer - Name of Class' give the name as 'Consumption'.

Class : Consumption	
Use Class for Inter- Godown Transfers	? No
Use Class for Job Costing Consumption	? Yes

The Stock Journal Voucher screen, which contains both Transfer and Consumption voucher class is displayed as shown.

Creating Purchase Vouchers

If you would like to allocate the Cost Centers, then enter purchase voucher in As Voucher mode as the Cost Allocation sub-screen does not appear in the As Invoice mode, else enter purchase voucher in As Invoice. In the purchase entry it is not necessary to allocate to Job Costing for Job Cost reporting.

`Go to Gateway of Tally > Accounting Vouchers`

1. In the Voucher Creation screen select F9: Purchase.
2. Select As Invoice.
3. Enter the current date and reference.
4. Select the Party to be credited from the List of Ledger Accounts in Party's A/c name.

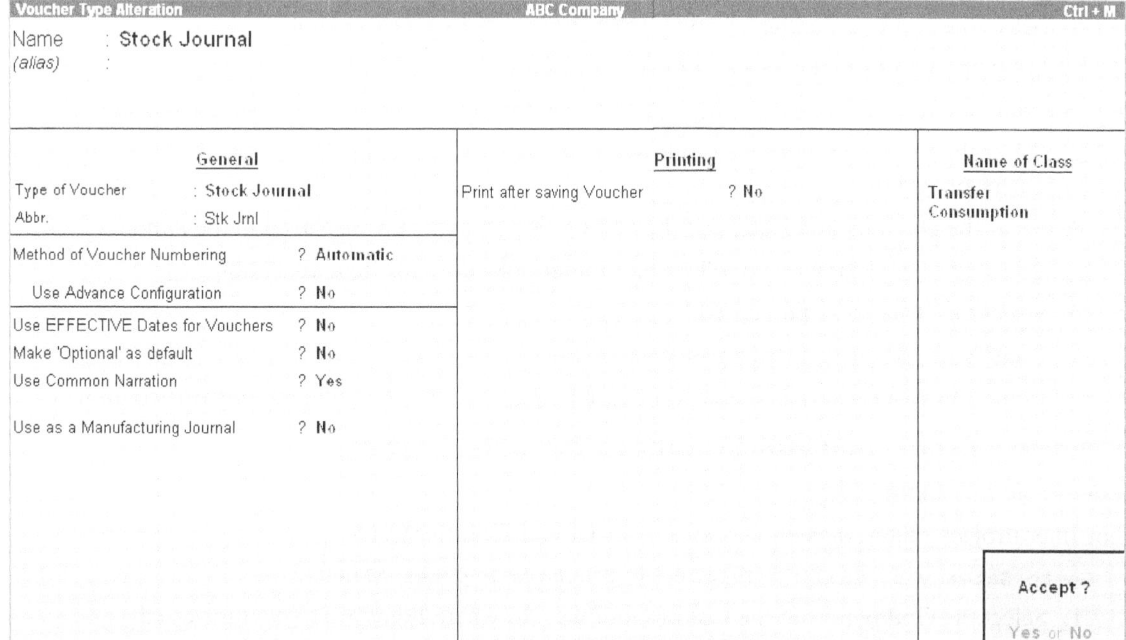

Fig. 6.73 Stock Jorunal

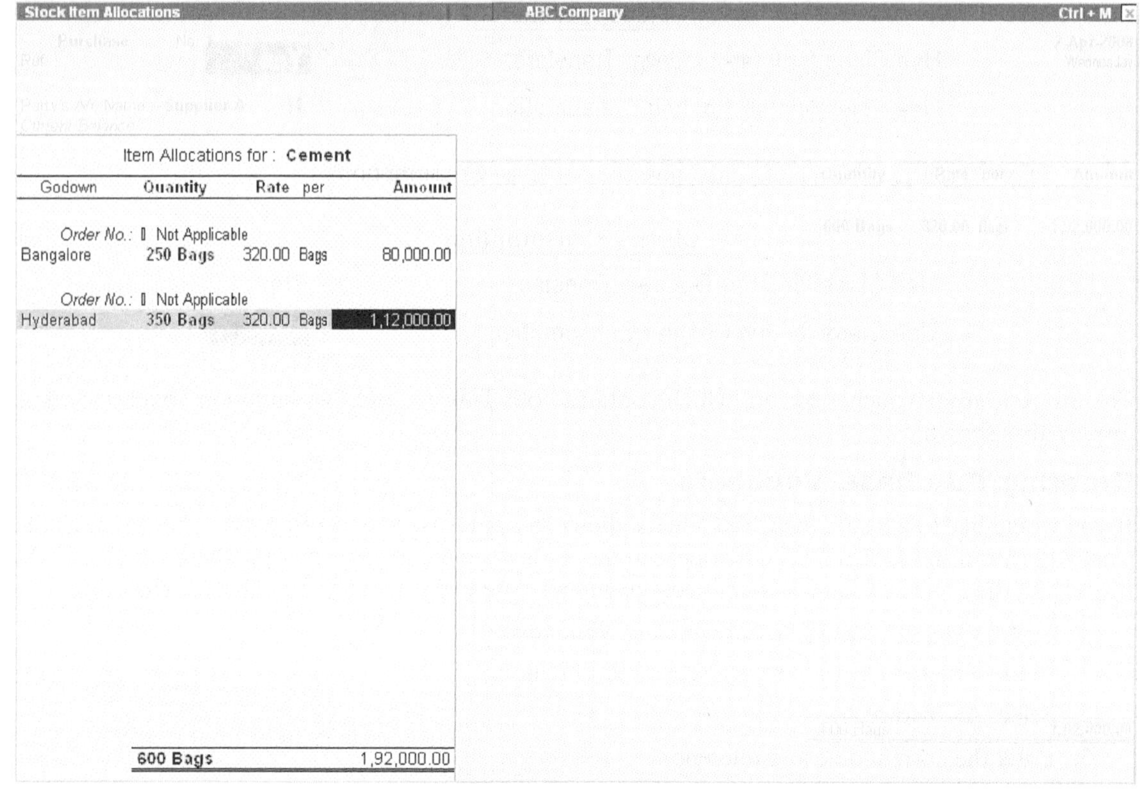

Fig. 6.74 Stock Item Allocations

5. Select the required Purchase Ledger from the List of Ledger Accounts.
6. Select an item from the Stock Items List of Items.

On selecting the Item, an Item Allocations sub screen for the selected Item is displayed as shown.

7. Select the Godown under the Godown field and specify the quantity to be allocated under the Quantity field.
8. Enter the Quantity and Rate, and the amount is automatically displayed in the Amount field.
9. Select another Godown and follow the similar procedure for Item allocation.
10. Select the Items to be purchased.
11. Enter Narration if required and accept to save.

Note: In the Job Work Analysis report, purchase amount will be shown in the inwards column.

Creating Stock Journal Vouchers for Job Costing

Inter Project Transfer Entry:

For Inter Project / Site Transfer, use Stock Journal with Transfer Class.

`Go to Gateway of Tally > Inventory Vouchers > press Alt+F7`

1. Select the Godown from the List of Godowns, to where Items are to be transferred.
2. Select the item from the List of Items.

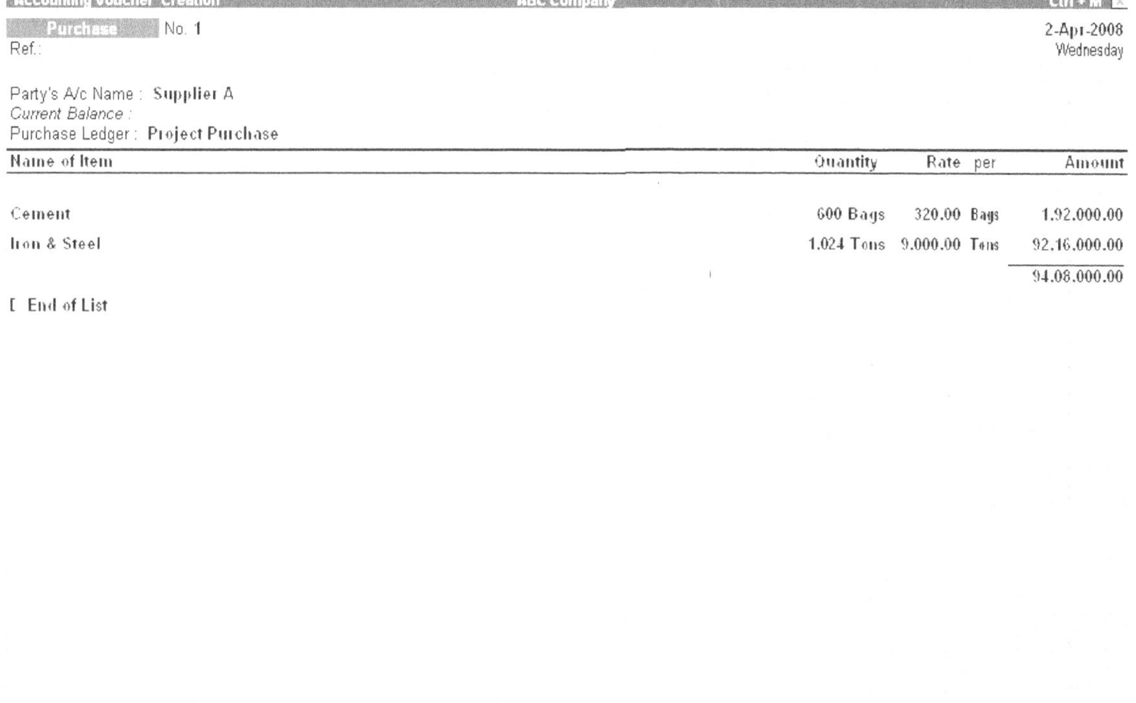

Fig. 6.75 Purchase Voucher with Stock Item

3. Select the Godown from the List of Godowns, from where goods are transferred.

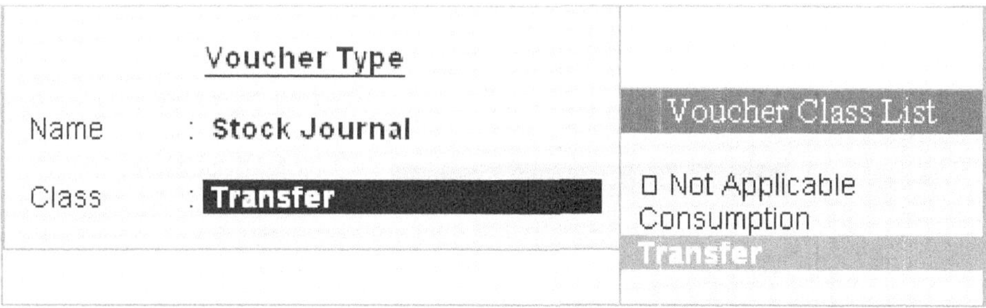

4. Enter the Quantity and Rate, Amount will be displayed automatically.
5. Enter the Narration, if required.

Consumption Entry

For consumption of material, use Stock journal voucher with Consumption Class.

```
Go to Gateway of Tally > Inventory info > press Alt+F7 > select Consumption
under Class.
```

1. Enter the Date as current date or as required.

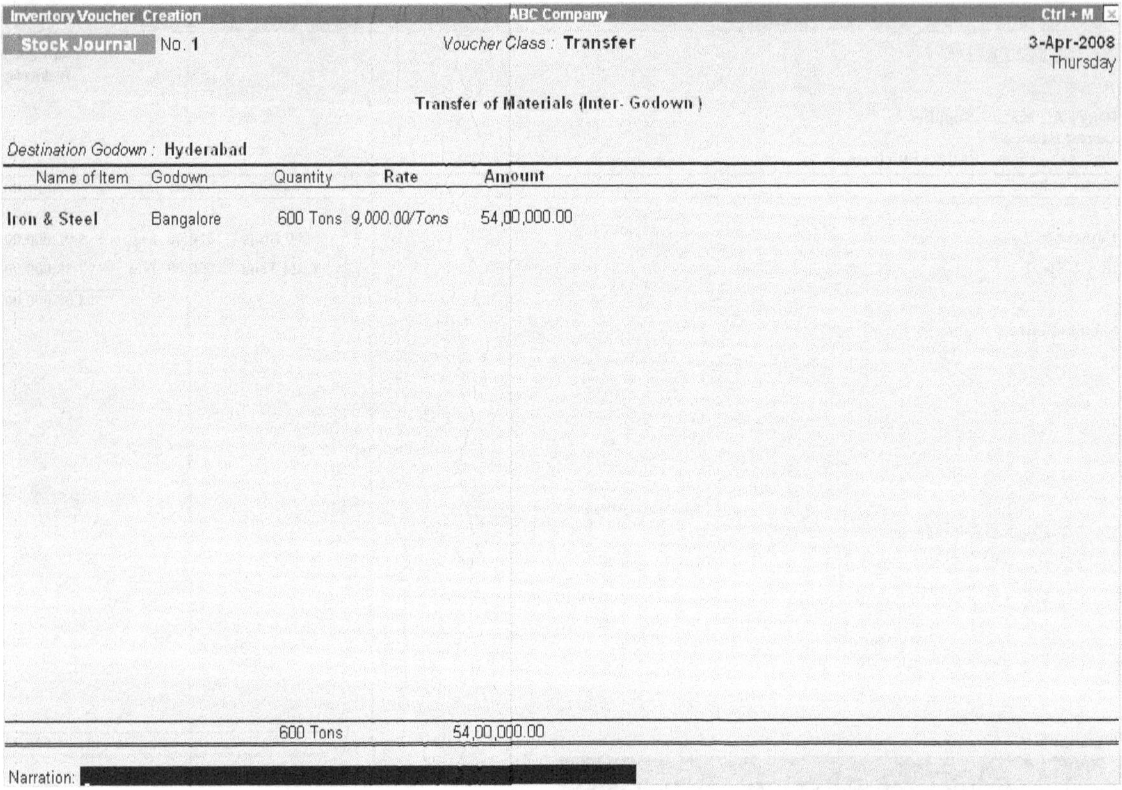

Inventory Voucher Creation
ABC Company
Ctrl + M
Stock Journal No. 1
Voucher Class : Transfer
3-Apr-2008
Thursday
Transfer of Materials (Inter- Godown)
Destination Godown : Hyderabad
Name of Item Godown Quantity Rate Amount
Iron & Steel Bangalore 600 Tons 9,000.00/Tons 54,00,000.00
600 Tons 54,00,000.00
Narration:

Fig. 6.76 Stock Journal Voucher

2. Select the stock Items from the 'List of Items' screen.

Voucher Type
Name : Stock Journal
Class : Consumption
Voucher Class List
Not Applicable
Consumption
Transfer

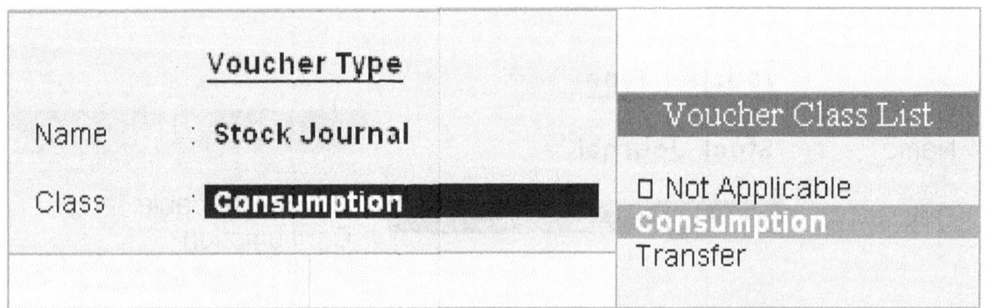

3. Select the Godown from which the items are to be consumed.
4. Enter the Quantity and Rate. The amount is automatically displayed in the Amount field.
5. Enter the Narration if required.

Note: This Consumption Amount will be shown under 'consumption' column in the Job Work Analysis Report.

Other Transfers:

When materials are transferred from one godown to another (Godown tagged to the Job Costing) without

Inventory Voucher Creation				ABC Company					Ctrl + M
Stock Journal No. 2				Voucher Class : Consumption					4-Apr-2008 Friday
				Transfer of Materials					
Source (Consumption)					Destination (Production)				
Name of Item	Godown	Quantity	Rate	Amount	Name of Item	Godown	Quantity	Rate	Amount
Cement	Hyderabad	200 Bags	320.00/Bags	64,000.00	▪ End of List				
Iron & Steel	Hyderabad	500 Tons	9,000.00/Tons	45,00,000.00					
				45,64,000.00					

Narration:

Fig. 6.77 Stock Journal Inventory Voucher

selecting the voucher class (Classes created for 'Transfer' and 'Consumption'), it will be taken under 'Other Transfers' in the Job Work Analysis report.

Creating Manufacturing Journal for Job Costing

Job Work Analysis report will also take into consideration of a product produced by passing Manufacturing Journal voucher.

Creating Manufacturing Voucher Type

`Go to Gateway of Tally > Accounts Info or Inventory Info > Voucher Types > Create`

1. Under Name type Manufacturing Journal.
2. Under Type of Voucher select Stock Journal.
3. Set Use as a Manufacturing Journal to Yes.

Creating Bill of Materials:

In the item master creation screen (Building), press F12: Configure (Stock Item Configuration) and set Allow component list details (Bill of Materials) to Yes.

Accept to save the screen.

Now In the Item master creation screen, set Set Components (BoM) to Yes, then the BoM Components screen will be displayed.

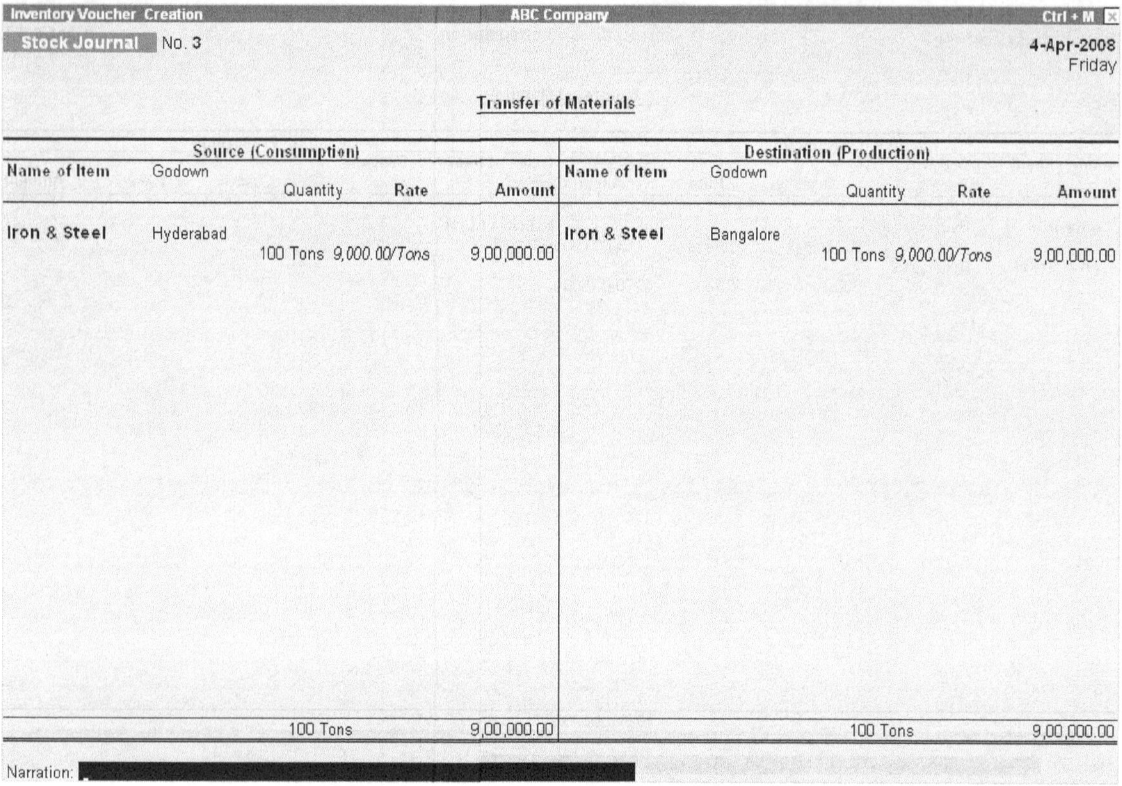

Inventory Voucher Creation					ABC Company					Ctrl + M
Stock Journal No. 3										4-Apr-2008 Friday
					Transfer of Materials					
Source (Consumption)					Destination (Production)					
Name of Item	Godown	Quantity	Rate	Amount	Name of Item	Godown	Quantity	Rate	Amount	
Iron & Steel	Hyderabad	100 Tons	9,000.00/Tons	9,00,000.00	Iron & Steel	Bangalore	100 Tons	9,000.00/Tons	9,00,000.00	
		100 Tons		9,00,000.00			100 Tons		9,00,000.00	

Narration:

Fig. 6.78 Stock Journal Inventory Voucher Creation

Voucher Type Creation	ABC Company	Ctrl + M
Name : Manufacturing Journal		
General	**Printing**	**Name of Class**
Type of Voucher : Stock Journal Abbr. : Stk Jrnl	Print after saving Voucher ? No	
Method of Voucher Numbering ? Automatic Use Advance Configuration ? No		
Use EFFECTIVE Dates for Vouchers ? No Make 'Optional' as default ? No Use Common Narration ? Yes Use as a Manufacturing Journal ? Yes		

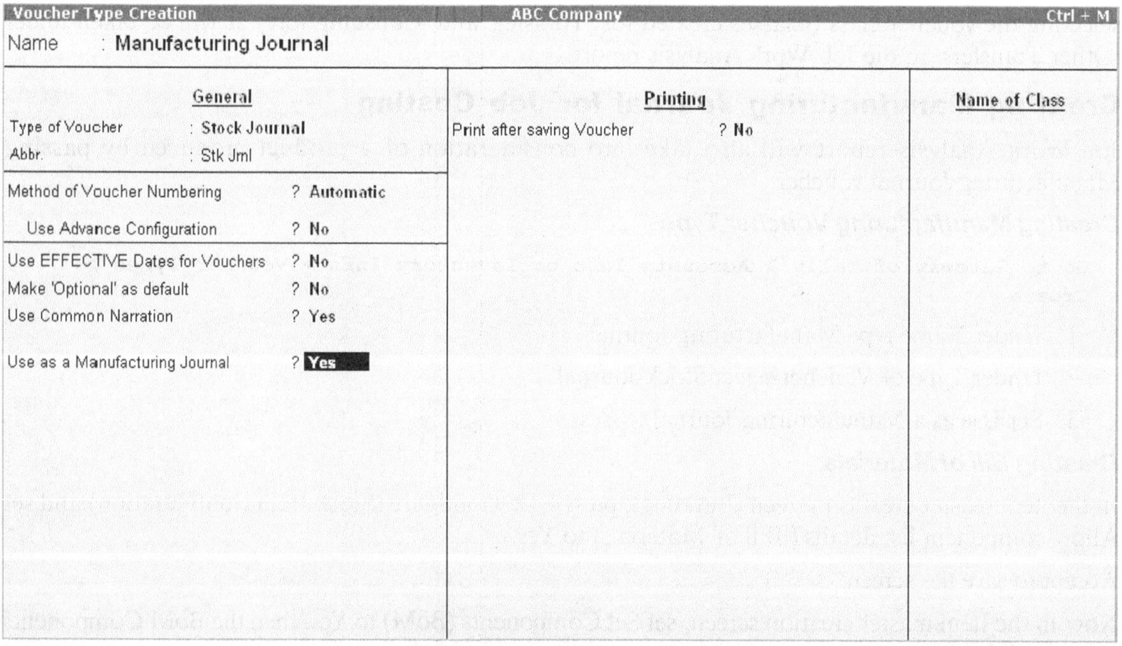

Fig. 6.79 Manufacturing Journal

```
Go to Gateway of Tally >Inventory Vouchers > press Alt+F7 > select
'Manufacturing Journal' under Voucher Type.
```

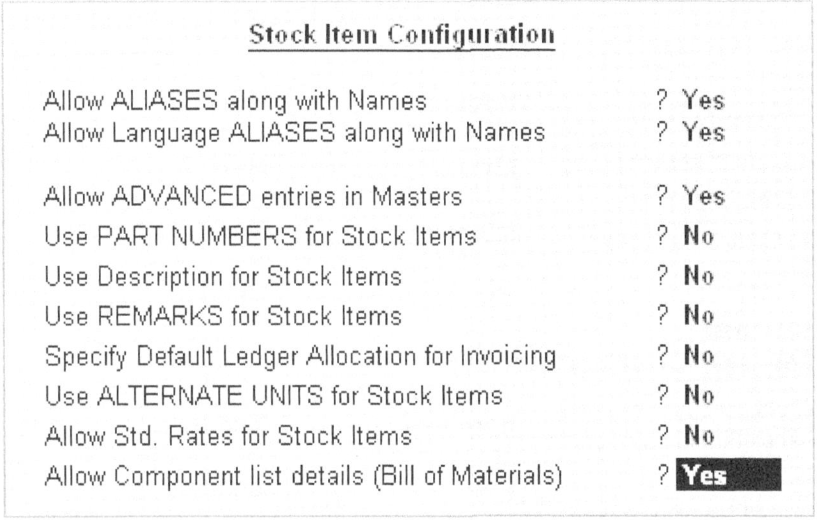

Stock Item Configuration

Allow ALIASES along with Names	? Yes
Allow Language ALIASES along with Names	? Yes
Allow ADVANCED entries in Masters	? Yes
Use PART NUMBERS for Stock Items	? No
Use Description for Stock Items	? No
Use REMARKS for Stock Items	? No
Specify Default Ledger Allocation for Invoicing	? No
Use ALTERNATE UNITS for Stock Items	? No
Allow Std. Rates for Stock Items	? No
Allow Component list details (Bill of Materials)	? Yes

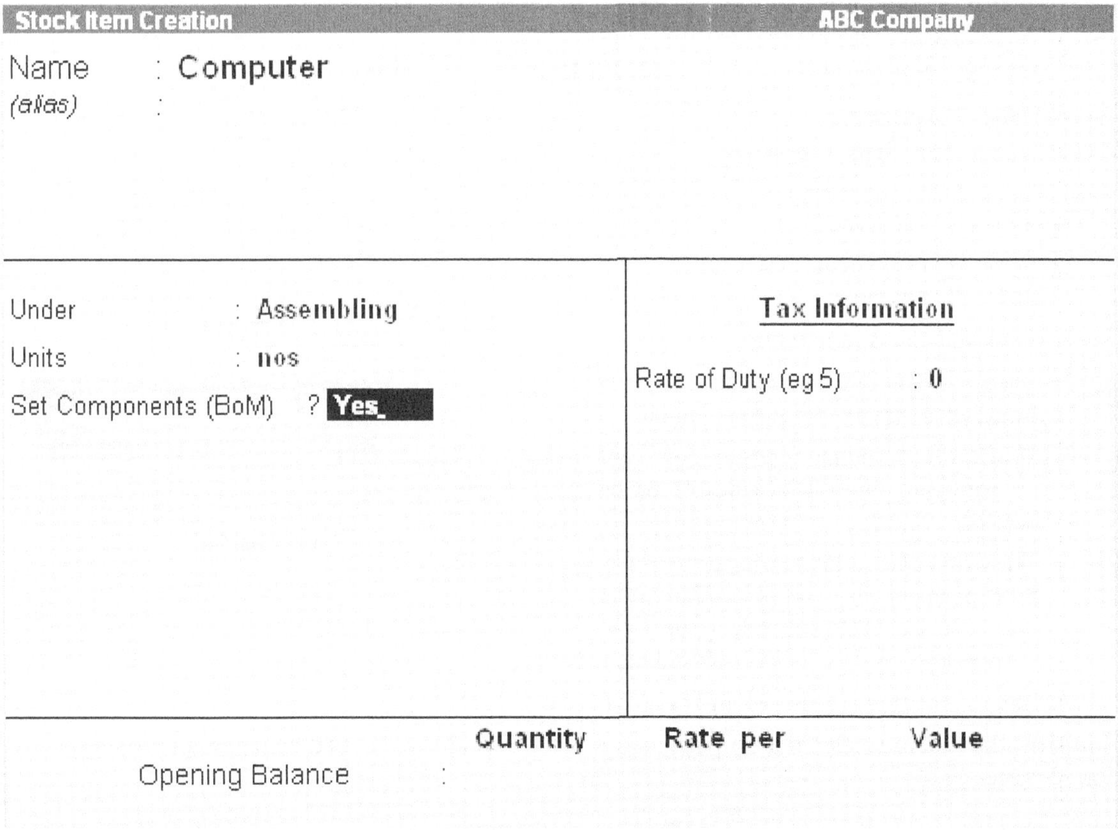

Stock Item Creation ABC Company

Name : Computer
(alias) :

Under : Assembling
Units : nos
Set Components (BoM) ? Yes_

Tax Information

Rate of Duty (eg 5) : 0

	Quantity	Rate per	Value
Opening Balance :			

Fig. 6.80 Stock Item Creation

Passing Manufacturing Journal

1. Select the Product under Name of Product.
2. Select the appropriate Godown (Job/Project).
3. Enter the quantity.
4. Sub-Component items will be displayed automatically.
5. Enter the Addl.cost, if any.
6. Enter the Narration.

Components of : Computer
Unit of manufacture : 1 nos

Item	Godown	Quantity
Keyboard	Mumbai	1 nos
Mouse	Mumbai	1 nos
Monitor	Mumbai	1 nos
Micro Processor	Mumbai	1 nos
Cabinet	Mumbai	1 nos
Hard Disk	Mumbai	1 nos
DVD Drive	Mumbai	1 nos
Memory Stick	Mumbai	1 nos
SMPS Unit	Mumbai	1 nos

Creating Journal Vouchers for Job Costing

Even Journal Vouchers could be used to allocate the receipts and payments for Job/Projects.

Note: In the Journal Voucher screen, enable the option Allow Cash Accounts in Journals in F12: Configuration screen.

Creating Payment Vouchers for Job Costing

`Go to Gateway of Tally > Accounting Vouchers`

1. In the Voucher Creation screen select F5: Payment.
2. Enter the date and reference.
3. Select the Bank Account or Cash Account from where payment has to be made.
4. Select the Expense Ledger Account created and enter the amount to be debited.
5. The Cost Allocations sub-screen appears. If the payment has to be allocated to more than one Cost Centre, select the Cost Centres and allocate the corresponding amount.
6. Enter Narration if required and accept to save.

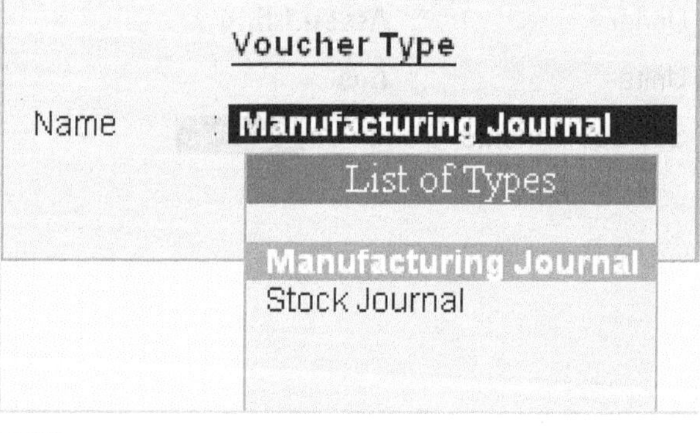

Similarly, the expenses related for a particular project could be accounted by tagging to the respective Job/Projects.

Inventory Voucher Creation ABC Company Ctrl + M

Manufacturing Journal No. 1 15-Apr-2008 Tuesday

Manufacture of Materials

Name of Product : Computer Godown: Mumbai Qty 10 nos

Components (Consumption)				
Name of Item	Godown	Quantity	Rate	Amount
Keyboard	Mumbai	10 nos	1,250.00/nos	12,500.00
Mouse	Mumbai	10 nos	650.00/nos	6,500.00
Monitor	Mumbai	10 nos	17,500.00/nos	1,75,000.00
Micro Processor	Mumbai	10 nos	3,500.00/nos	35,000.00
Cabinet	Mumbai	10 nos	250.00/nos	2,500.00
Hard Disk	Mumbai	10 nos	5,500.00/nos	55,000.00
DVD Drive	Mumbai	10 nos	2,200.00/nos	22,000.00
Memory Stick	Mumbai	10 nos	1,800.00/nos	18,000.00
SMPS Unit	Mumbai	10 nos	1,100.00/nos	11,000.00
		90 nos		3,37,500.00

Cost of Components :		33,750.00/nos	3,37,500.00
Type of Addl. Cost	%-age		
Labour Charges			2,000.00
Total Addl. cost	:		2,000.00
Effective Cost	:		3,39,500.00
Effective Rate	:		33,950.00/nos

Narration:

Fig. 6.81 Manufacturing Journal

Accounting Voucher Creation ABC Company Ctrl + M

Journal No. 1 10-Apr-2008 Thursday

Particulars	Debit	Credit
Dr Labour Charges	1,50,000.00	
Cur Bal: 1,50,000.00 Dr		
Project 1 75,000.00 Dr		
Project 2 75,000.00 Dr		
Cr Bank Account		1,50,000.00
Cur Bal: 45,000.00 Dr		

Narration: 1,50,000.00 1,50,000.00

Accept ?

Yes or No

Fig. 6.82 Journal Voucher Creation

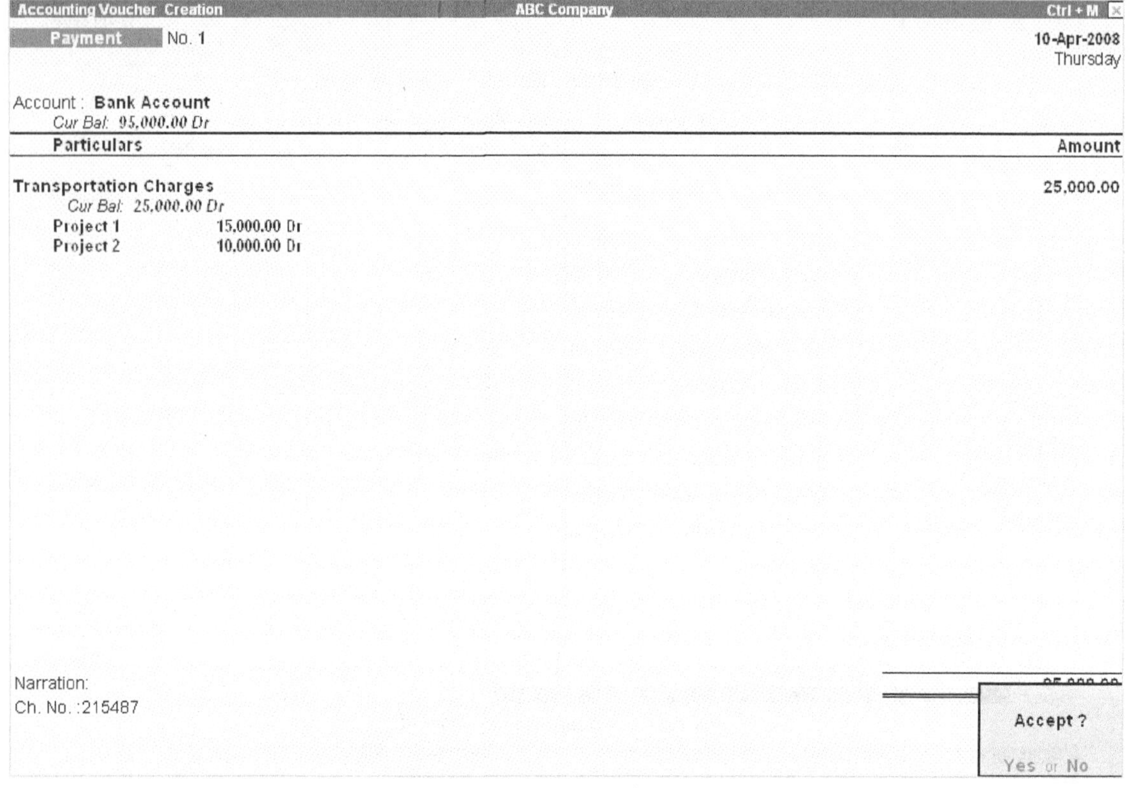

Fig. 6.83 Payment Voucher Creation

Creating Sales Voucher for Job Costing

Go to Gateway of Tally > Accounting Vouchers

1. In the Voucher Creation screen, select F8: Sales.
2. Select As Voucher.

Note: You can create an Item Invoice or an Account Invoice and allocate appropriate Cost Centers or Job/Project and also sales can be created - As Voucher or As Invoice.

3. Enter the date and reference.
4. Select the appropriate Customer in the Party's A/c Name.
5. Enter the amount in the Amount field.
6. Select the Sales ledger from the List of Ledger Accounts.
7. In the Cost Allocations sub screen, select the Cost Centre from the List of Cost Centres under the field Name of Cost Centre and enter the amount to be allocated to that Cost Centre.
8. Enter Narration if required and accept to save.

Note: When sales is created as Item Invoice, this details is available under Cost of Sales in the Job Work Analysis - Consumption report.

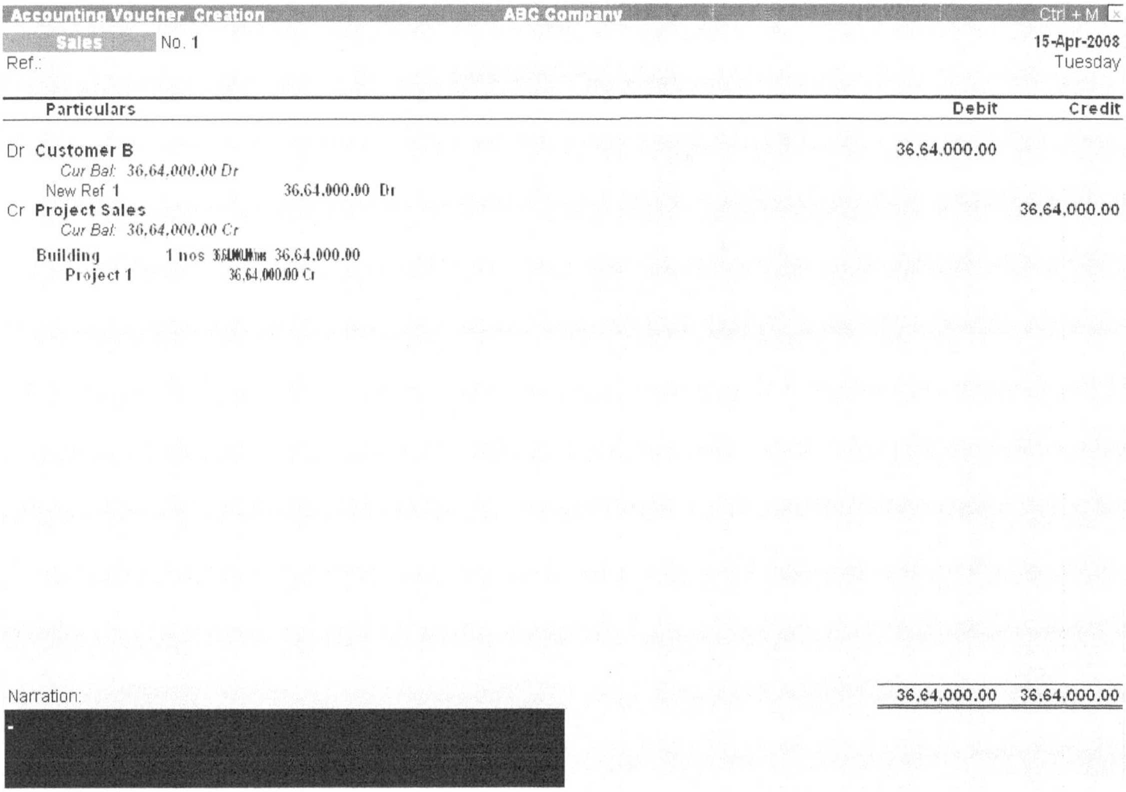

Accounting Voucher Creation
ABC Company
Ctrl + M
Sales No. 1
15-Apr-2008
Ref.:
Tuesday
Particulars
Debit
Credit
Dr Customer B
36,64,000.00
Cur Bal: 36,64,000.00 Dr
New Ref 1 36,64,000.00 Dr
Cr Project Sales
36,64,000.00
Cur Bal: 36,64,000.00 Cr
Building 1 nos 36,64,000.00
Project 1 36,64,000.00 Cr
Narration:
36,64,000.00 36,64,000.00

Fig. 6.84 Sales Voucher Creation

Job Costing Reports

Job costing report enables the user to know the Net Profit/Loss for the selected re the reports available in Job Work Analysis.

The following reports are available for Job Costing :

- Job Work Analysis
- Material Consumption Summary
- Comparative Job Work Analysis report.

Job Work Analysis Report

```
Go to Gateway of Tally > Display > Statement of Inventory > Job Work Analysis
```

Job Work Analysis report is displayed as shown:

Detailed view

Press Alt+F1 in the Job Work Analysis report, to view a detailed report.

Detailed view with percentage

Press F12 in the Job Work Analysis report, and set Show Percentage to Yes.

Configuration
Format : Condensed
Show Percentages ? Yes
Appearance of Names : Name Only
Scale Factor for Values : Default

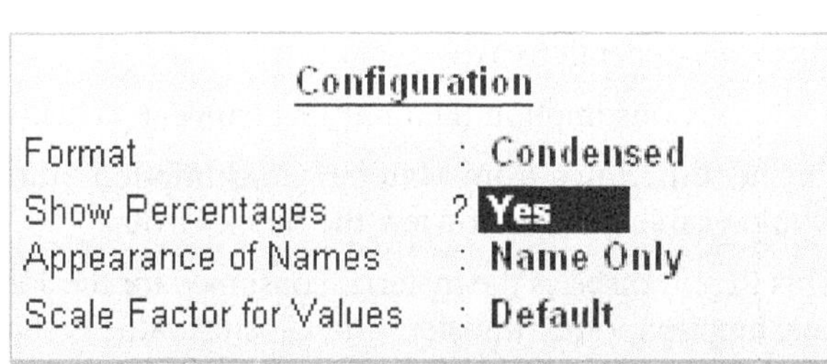

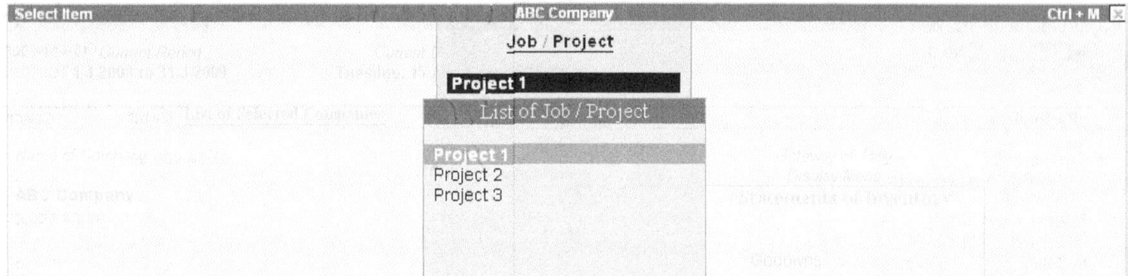

Fig. 6.85 Selecting the Project

Job Work Analysis — ABC Company — Ctrl + M

Particulars		Project 1 ABC Company 1-Apr-2008 to 15-Apr-2008
A. Revenue (Income) :		
Sales Accounts		15,45,000.00
Indirect Incomes		1,10,000.00
		16,55,000.00
B. Cost (Expenses) :		
Consumption		6,17,000.00
Opening Stock	67,000.00	
Add: Inwards	23,64,500.00	
Less: Outwards	32,000.00	
Less: Closing Stock	17,82,500.00	
Direct Expenses		75,000.00
Indirect Expenses		15,000.00
		7,07,000.00
Nett Profit: (A - B)		9,48,000.00

Fig. 6.86 Job Work Analysis

Materials Consumption Summary Report

To view the Material Consumption Summary report, scroll down to the line Consumption in Job Work Analysis Report and press Enter.

The Material Consumption Summary report is displayed.

Here it will display Opening Value, Inward Value, Consumption, Other Transfers and Closing Value.

It will display the Godown of the particular Job/Project:

Detailed view of Inward Value, Consumption and Other Transfers:

Press F12 and set Show goods inwards in detail, Show goods Consumption in detail and Show goods outwards in detail to Yes.

Material Consumption Summary will appear as below:

Further drill down from Material Consumption Summary to Material Consumption Stock Summary, would enable the user to view the Stock Group.

This Report displays the material consumed for the Job/Project. Details of Opening value, Inward Value, consumption, other transfers and Closing value is shown – Drill down.

Job Work Analysis ABC Company Ctrl + M

Particulars			Project 1 ABC Company 1-Apr-2008 to 15-Apr-2008
A. Revenue (Income) :			
Sales Accounts			15,45,000.00
Project Sales		15,45,000.00	
Indirect Incomes			1,10,000.00
Commission & Brokerage		1,10,000.00	
			16,55,000.00
B. Cost (Expenses) :			
Consumption			6,17,000.00
Cost of Sales			
Job Consumption	5,000.00		
Opening Stock		67,000.00	
Add: Inwards		23,64,500.00	
Purchase	22,72,000.00		
Manufacturing Journal			
Inter Project Transfer	76,500.00		
Other Transfer	16,000.00		
Less: Outwards		32,000.00	
Manufacturing Journal			
Inter Project Transfer	32,000.00		
Other Transfer			
Less: Closing Stock		17,82,500.00	
Direct Expenses			75,000.00
Labour Charges		75,000.00	
Indirect Expenses			15,000.00
Transportation Charges		15,000.00	
			7,07,000.00
Nett Profit: (A - B)			9,48,000.00

Fig. 6.87 Job Work Analysis 1/2

Job Work Analysis ABC Company Ctrl + M

Particulars			Project 1 ABC Company 1-Apr-2008 to 15-Apr-2008	
A. Revenue (Income) :				
Sales Accounts			15,45,000.00	93.35 %
Project Sales		15,45,000.00		
Indirect Incomes			1,10,000.00	6.65 %
Commission & Brokerage		1,10,000.00		
			16,55,000.00	100 %
B. Cost (Expenses) :				
Consumption			6,17,000.00	37.28 %
Cost of Sales				
Job Consumption	5,000.00			
Opening Stock		67,000.00		
Add: Inwards		23,64,500.00		
Purchase	22,72,000.00			
Manufacturing Journal				
Inter Project Transfer	76,500.00			
Other Transfer	16,000.00			
Less: Outwards		32,000.00		
Manufacturing Journal				
Inter Project Transfer	32,000.00			
Other Transfer				
Less: Closing Stock		17,82,500.00		
Direct Expenses			75,000.00	4.53 %
Labour Charges		75,000.00		
Indirect Expenses			15,000.00	0.91 %
Transportation Charges		15,000.00		
			7,07,000.00	42.72 %
Nett Profit: (A - B)			9,48,000.00	57.28 %

Fig. 6.88 Job Work Analysis 2/2

Job Work Analysis	ABC Company		Ctrl + M
Particulars		Project 3 ABC Company 1-Apr-2008 to 15-Apr-2008	
A. Revenue (Income) :			
Sales Accounts			17,60,000.00
Project Sales		17,60,000.00	
			17,60,000.00
B. Cost (Expenses) :			
Consumption			14,06,200.00
Cost of Sales	11,30,456.25		
Job Consumption	55,000.00		
Opening Stock		38,500.00	
Add: Inwards		32,55,331.25	
Purchase	16,87,500.00		
Manufacturing Journal	11,98,968.75		
Inter Project Transfer	41,600.00		
Other Transfer	19,700.00		
Less: Outwards		15,42,850.00	
Manufacturing Journal	11,81,250.00		
Inter Project Transfer	41,600.00		
Other Transfer	17,500.00		
Less: Closing Stock		3,44,781.25	
			14,06,200.00
Nett Profit: (A - B)			3,53,800.00

Fig. 6.89 Job Work Analysis

Material Consumption Summary	ABC Company				Ctrl + M
Particulars	Project 3 ABC Company 1-Apr-2008 to 15-Apr-2008				
	Opening Value	Inward Value	Consumption	Other Transfers	Closing Value
Finished Goods		15,65,631.25	13,72,450.00		1,93,181.25
Raw Material	38,500.00	16,89,700.00	33,750.00	15,42,850.00	1,51,600.00
Grand Total	38,500.00	32,55,331.25	14,06,200.00	15,42,850.00	3,44,781.25

Fig. 6.90 Material Consumption Summary

Opening Value: Opening Balance of the items which are tagged to the Godowns (Job/Project) is displayed here.

Configuration	
Show Opening Balance	? Yes
Show goods inwards	? Yes
Show goods inwards in details	? Yes
Show Consumption	? Yes
Show goods Consumption in details	? Yes
Show goods outwards	? Yes
Show goods outwards in details	? Yes
Show Closing Balance	? Yes
Appearance of Names	: Name Only
Scale Factor for Values	: Default

Inwards:

- Purchase: The value of the materials which are purchased for the project is displayed here.
- Manufacturing Journal: The value of the materials which are produced by passing Manufacturing Journal voucher tagging to the appropriate godown, is displayed here under Inwards.

Material Consumption Summary — ABC Company — Ctrl + M

Project 3
ABC Company
1-Apr-2008 to 15-Apr-2008

Particulars	Opening Value	Inwards				Consumption		Outwards			Closing Value
		Purchase	Manufacturing Journal	Inter Project Transfer	Other Transfers	Cost of Sales	Job Consumption	Manufacturing Journal	Inter Project Transfer	Other Transfers	
Finished Goods			15,41,531.25	6,600.00	17,500.00	13,70,250.00	2,200.00				1,93,181.25
Raw Material	38,500.00	16,87,500.00			2,200.00		33,750.00	15,18,750.00	6,600.00	17,500.00	1,51,600.00
Grand Total	38,500.00	16,87,500.00	15,41,531.25	6,600.00	19,700.00	13,70,250.00	35,950.00	15,18,750.00	6,600.00	17,500.00	3,44,781.25

Fig. 6.91 Material Consumption Summary

Material Consumption Stock Summary — ABC Company — Ctrl + M

Godown : Finished Goods
Project 3
ABC Company
1-Apr-2008 to 15-Apr-2008

Particulars	Opening Value	Inwards				Consumption		Outwards			Closing Value
		Purchase	Manufacturing Journal	Inter Project Transfer	Other Transfers	Cost of Sales	Job Consumption	Manufacturing Journal	Inter Project Transfer	Other Transfers	
Assembling	38,500.00		15,41,531.25			13,73,940.22					2,06,091.03
Parts				6,600.00	17,500.00		2,200.00				21,900.00
Grand Total	38,500.00		15,41,531.25	6,600.00	17,500.00	13,73,940.22	2,200.00				2,27,991.03

Fig. 6.92 Material Consumption Stock Summary

- Inter Project Transfer: The value of the transfer entry which is made by using 'Class' created for 'Stock Journal' and tagging to the appropriate godown is displayed here.
- Other Transfers: Transfer of materials which are done by NOT using the 'Transfer Class' created for Stock Journal would appear here.

Consumption:

- Cost of Sales: The Value of Cost of Sales will be displayed here. Cost of Sales is nothing but Number of quantities (Sold) x Cost of Purchase. Sales which is made by using Item invoice will appear here.
- Job Consumption: The value of the entries which are made using 'Consumption Class' create for Stock Journal is displayed here.

Outwards:

- Manufacturing Journal: The value of the materials which are used\ consumed for a Job/Project in the manufacturing journal voucher entry is displayed here.
- Inter Project Transfer: The value of the transfer entry which is made by using 'Class' created for 'Stock Journal' and tagging to the appropriate godown is displayed here.
- Other Transfers: Transfer of materials which are done by NOT using the 'Transfer Class' created for Stock Journal would appear here.

Closing Value:

Closing value of an item will be determined based on costing method.

```
Closing value = Opening Value + Inwards - Consumption - Other Transfers
```

Drill down from the above report, will display the Stock items used for Job/Project.

Material Consumption Stock Summary — ABC Company — Ctrl + M

Godown : Finished Goods
Project 3
ABC Company
1-Apr-2008 to 15-Apr-2008

Particulars	Opening Value	Inwards				Consumption		Outwards			Closing Value
		Purchase	Manufacturing Journal	Inter Project Transfer	Other Transfers	Cost of Sales	Job Consumption	Manufacturing Journal	Inter Project Transfer	Other Transfers	
Computer	38,500.00		15,41,531.25			13,73,940.22					2,06,091.03
Grand Total	38,500.00		15,41,531.25			13,73,940.22					2,06,091.03

Fig. 6.93 Material Consumption Stock Summary

Drill down further to display the Godown Voucher screens.

Godown Vouchers — ABC Company — Ctrl + M

Stock Item: **Computer**
Godown : **Finished Goods**
1-Apr-2008 to 15-Apr-2008

Date	Particulars	Vch Type	Vch No.	Inwards Quantity	Inwards Value	Outwards Quantity	Outwards Value	Closing Quantity	Closing Value
1-4-2008	Opening Balance			1 nos	38,500.00			1 nos	38,500.00
15-4-2008	Keyboard	[illegible]	1	45 nos	15,41,531.25				
15-4-2008	Customer A	Sales	3			40 nos	17,60,000.00	6 nos	2,06,091.03
	Totals :			46 nos	15,80,031.25	40 nos	17,60,000.00	6 nos	2,06,091.03

Fig. 6.94 Godown Vouchers

It displays the report godown wise - Inwards, Outwards and Closing Balance.

To view total material consumption of all the Job/Projects.

The button Auto Column is available to view all the Job/Projects material consumption report in one sheet. Press Alt+N.

Auto Repeat Columns

Repeat Using : **Job / Project**
Show Total Column ? **Yes**

Material Consumption Summary — ABC Company — Ctrl + M

Particulars	Total				
	Opening Value	Inward Value	Consumption	Other Transfers	Closing Value
					3 more ...
Bangalore	67,000.00				17,82,500.00
Finished Goods	38,500.00				2,27,991.03
Hyderabad	69,500.00				9,65,000.00
Raw Material					1,13,100.00
Grand Total	1,75,000.00				30,88,591.03

Fig. 6.95 Material Consumption Summary

For comparison of one Job/Project material consumption with other Job/Project.

The button New Column is also available in the report to view the period for a particular period that can be selected from the list – Press Atl+C.

ABC Company — Ctrl + M

Column Details

From (blank for beginning) : 1-4-2008
To (blank for end) : 15-4-2008
Currency : ▮ Base Currency
Name of Cost Centre : Project 2

List of Job / Project

Project 1
Project 2
Project 3

Fig. 6.96 Selecting the Project

Material Consumption Summary — ABC Company — Ctrl + M

Particulars	Project 2 ABC Company 1-Apr-2008 to 15-Apr-2008				
	Opening Value	Inward Value	Consumption	Other Transfers	Closing Value
Hyderabad	69,500.00	18,52,000.00	8,64,000.00	92,500.00	9,65,000.00
Grand Total	69,500.00	18,52,000.00	8,64,000.00	92,500.00	9,65,000.00

Fig. 6.97 Material Consumption Summary

Viewing other Job/project from the screen on one Job/Project:

The button Alter Column is also available in the report to view the other job or Project. Press Alt+A

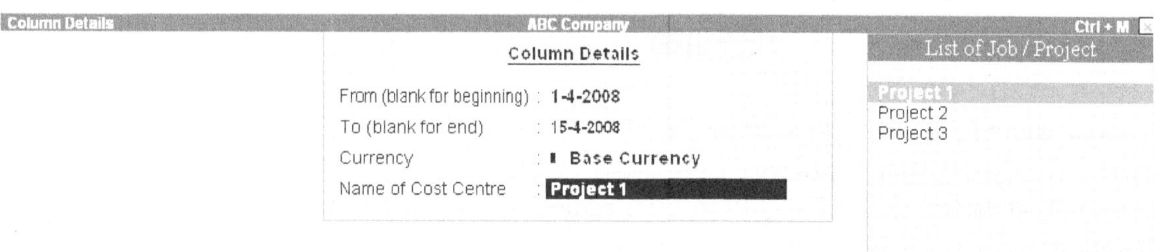

Fig. 6.98 Selecting an Alternate Project

F4 button:

Click this button to select the other Job/Project from the list.

Material Consumption Summary — ABC Company — Ctrl + M

Particulars	Project 1 ABC Company 1-Apr-2008 to 15-Apr-2008				
	Opening Value	Inward Value	Consumption	Other Transfers	Closing Value
Bangalore	67,000.00	23,64,500.00	6,17,000.00	32,000.00	17,82,500.00
Grand Total	67,000.00	23,64,500.00	6,17,000.00	32,000.00	17,82,500.00

Fig. 6.99 Material Consumption Summary

Material Consumption Stock Summary ABC Company Ctrl + M

Particulars	Godown : Finished Goods Project 3 ABC Company 1-Apr-2008 to 15-Apr-2008							
	Opening Value	Inwards	Consumption				Outwards	Closing Value
			Cost of Sales	Gross Profit	Perc %	Job Consumption		
Assembling	38,500.00	15,41,531.25	13,73,940.22	3,86,059.78	21.94 %			2,06,091.03
Parts		24,100.00				2,200.00		21,900.00
Grand Total	38,500.00	15,65,631.25	13,73,940.22	3,86,059.78		2,200.00		2,27,991.03

Fig. 6.100 Material Consumption Stock Summary

F7: Button or Show:

Profit button is available in the Material Consumption Stock Summary report, to view the Gross Profit with Percentage for a particular Job/Project.

Comparative Job Work Analysis Report

To view multiple Job/Projects

The Job Work Analysis report supports details of Multiple Jobs in a single report. All these details are viewed as different columns with the help of New Column button. Alt+N

Comparative Job Work Analysis report will be displayed as shown:

Auto Repeat Columns

Repeat Using : **Job / Project**

Show Total Column ? **Yes**

Comparison of one Job with another Job:

The button Auto Column is available in the report to view the period for a particular period that can be selected from the list. Refer Modify Reports for adding, deleting and altering columns. Press Alt+C.

Job Work Analysis report will appear as below:

Job Work Analysis ABC Company Ctrl + M Ctrl + M

Particulars	Total		Project 1 ABC Company 1-Apr-2008 to 15-Apr-2008		Project 2 ABC Company 1-Apr-2008 to 15-Apr-2008	
A. Revenue (Income) :						
Sales Accounts		46,35,000.00		15,45,000.00		15,45,000.00
Indirect Incomes		3,30,000.00		1,10,000.00		1,10,000.00
		49,65,000.00		16,55,000.00		16,55,000.00
B. Cost (Expenses) :						
Consumption		28,90,890.22		6,17,000.00		8,64,000.00
Opening Stock	1,75,000.00		67,000.00		69,500.00	
Add: Inwards	74,71,831.25		23,64,500.00		18,52,000.00	
Less: Outwards	16,67,350.00		32,000.00		92,500.00	
Less: Closing Stock	30,88,591.03		17,82,500.00		9,65,000.00	
Direct Expenses		1,50,000.00		75,000.00		75,000.00
Indirect Expenses		25,000.00		15,000.00		10,000.00
		30,65,890.22		7,07,000.00		9,49,000.00
Nett Profit: (A - B)		18,99,109.78		9,48,000.00		7,06,000.00

Fig. 6.101 Job Work Analysis

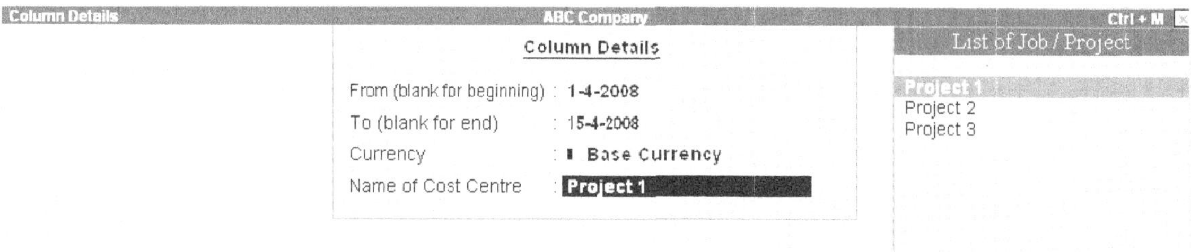

Fig. 6.102 Selecting the Cost Centre

Job Work Analysis — ABC Company — Ctrl + M

Particulars	Project 1 ABC Company 1-Apr-2008 to 31-Mar-2009		Project 2 ABC Company 1-Apr-2008 to 31-Mar-2009	
A. Revenue (Income) :				
Sales Accounts		15,45,000.00		13,90,000.00
Indirect Incomes		1,10,000.00		1,15,000.00
		16,55,000.00		15,05,000.00
B. Cost (Expenses) :				
Consumption				
Opening Stock	67,000.00		69,500.00	
Add: Inwards				
Less: Outwards				
Less: Closing Stock	12,33,900.00		5,11,600.00	
Direct Expenses		75,000.00		75,000.00
Indirect Expenses		15,000.00		10,000.00
		90,000.00		85,000.00
Nett Profit: (A - B)		15,65,000.00		14,20,000.00

Fig. 6.103 Job Work Analysis

ABC Company — Ctrl + M

Column Details

From (blank for beginning) : 1-4-2008

To (blank for end) : 31-3-2009

Currency : Base Currency

Name of Cost Centre : Project 2

List of Job / Project

Project 1

Project 2

Project 3

Fig. 6.104 Changing the Cost Centre

Viewing any other Project/Job from the existing project Job Work Analysis report:

The button Alter Column is also available in the report to view the other job or Project Alt+A

Job Work Analysis report will appear as shown:

Press F4 button, to select the other Job/Project from the list.

It allows the user to drill down from Job Work Analysis report to voucher entry, to view a break up of Job/Project.

Job Work Analysis	ABC Company			Ctrl + M
Particulars	Project 1 ABC Company 1-Apr-2008 to 15-Apr-2008		Project 2 ABC Company 1-Apr-2008 to 31-Mar-2009	
A. Revenue (Income) :				
Sales Accounts		15,45,000.00		13,90,000.00
Indirect Incomes		1,10,000.00		1,15,000.00
		16,55,000.00		15,05,000.00
B. Cost (Expenses) :				
Consumption		6,17,000.00		
Opening Stock	67,000.00		69,500.00	
Add: Inwards	23,64,500.00			
Less: Outwards	32,000.00			
Less: Closing Stock	17,82,500.00		9,65,000.00	
Direct Expenses		75,000.00		75,000.00
Indirect Expenses		15,000.00		10,000.00
		7,07,000.00		85,000.00
Nett Profit: (A - B)		9,48,000.00		14,20,000.00

Fig. 6.105 Job Work Analysis of two Cost Centres

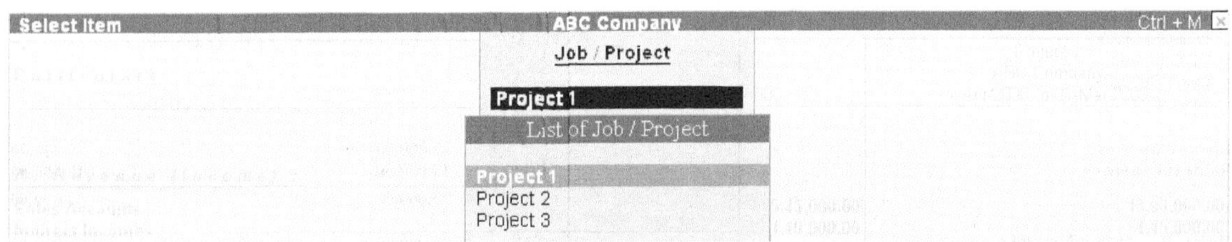

Fig. 6.106 Selecting a Project

7 Accounting Reports of Tally.ERP 9

Tally.ERP 9 Reports

Tally's Display of information is designed to allow a user get the maximum benefit of the data that is entered. A user gets a holistic picture of the data and is also able to present information using different options. The purpose of compiling data is to present it in comprehensible accounting reports. On entering the vouchers, Tally.ERP 9 uses the same data and provides you with the management control reports in addition to all books and statements.

The display screens of Tally.ERP 9 are dynamic and interactive. They are not spooled print files but are specially designed for the screen. Whatever you see on the screen can be printed as well depending upon your printer's capabilities.

To view the Display Menu:

```
Go to Gateway of Tally > Display
```

The Display Menu screen is displayed as shown:

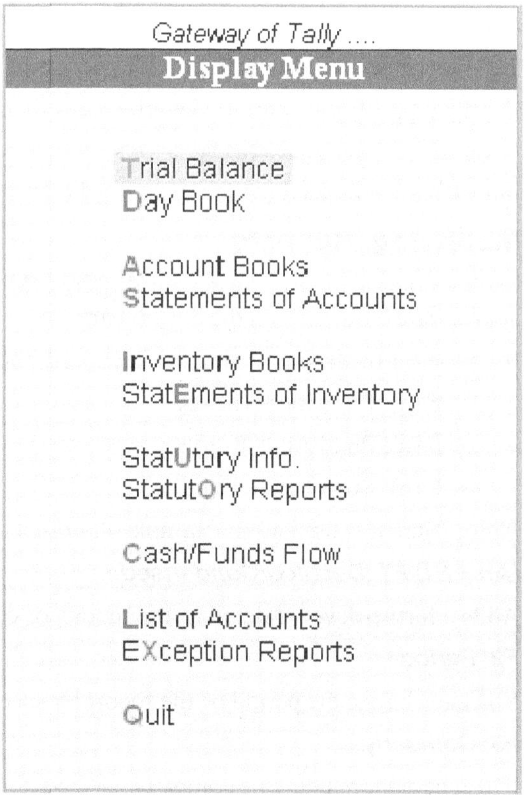

Gateway of Tally ....

Display Menu

Trial Balance
Day Book

Account Books
Statements of Accounts

Inventory Books
StatEments of Inventory

StatUtory Info.
StatutOry Reports

Cash/Funds Flow

List of Accounts
EXception Reports

Quit

Gateway of Tally displays only the Balance Sheet and Profit & Loss Account directly as these statements are considered the most important. All the other Tally.ERP 9 reports are classified into two broad categories, namely. Accounting reports and Inventory reports conforming to the two major areas of operations. Each area is further grouped into books and statements.

The Cash Flow and Funds Flow display too has not been grouped under Statements of Accounts.

Trial Balance provides you a report on the account balances sorted by groups, for all the accounts of the selected company. In other words, the Trial balance displays a collection of main groups and their closing balances.

The Stock Summary is a statement of stock-in-hand on a particular date and gets updated every transaction so as to provide the current stock position.

The Ratio Analysis Statement is a single sheet report indicating the company's performance based on values and key indicators, over a selected period. This report gives a manager an idea of the company's financial condition and where it is going in the short-term.

The Day Book contains all vouchers for the day, including inventory vouchers. Its purpose is to show you a day's transactions, though you can display a report for any period using Change period option.

The List of Accounts gives the tree structure of all your masters, namely, Groups, Ledgers, Stock items, Cost Centers, Currencies, etc.

Exception Reports are those reports that track unusual transactions or balances.

Basic Features of Displaying Reports

Tally.ERP 9 creates the books of accounts and the financial statements based on the vouchers entered till date. You can then customise the appearance of reports as required.

For example, you can compare different companies, periods of the financial year, groups and ledgers.

Press Enter after highlighting the item in a report, to navigate to the next level of detail till you reach an individual voucher. Similarly, you can navigate back to higher levels by pressing Esc. The special features available for a displayed report are indicated on the button bar, which can be operated by a single- click of the mouse.

Accessing reports

The Gateway of Tally menu provides access to all the financial reports listed in the Display Menu.

For example, if you want to view the Sales Register,

```
Go to Gateway of Tally > Display > Account Books > Sales Register.
```

Tally.ERP 9 will display the report for the currently selected period.

Modifying Reports

On selecting a report, the screen displays. Modify the display to suit your requirements using the appropriate buttons from the button bar.

If you select the buttons using the keyboard, the conventions are:

- F (n): Press the F (n) key
- F (n): Press Alt + F (n)
- F (n): Press Ctrl + F (n)

Note: Here n is used as an example of a function key (Eg: F1,F2 and so on).

(Alt + F1) F1 :Detailed/Condensed

Adds a further level of detail to the report, or condenses the report.

F2: Period

You can change the period of the report by specifying From/To dates.

Change Period	
From	: 1-4-2008
To	: 31-03-2009

F3: Company

If you have more than one company selected, this button enables you to switch among them to display the new company data in the current screen format.

F4: to F10:

The functions performed by these buttons vary from report to report.

F11: Company Features

This button is not related to displaying reports but to setting the options that affect the voucher entry.

F12: Configure

This button is very relevant to displaying reports and enables you to define the report-specific options.

For example, depending on the report displayed you can specify whether it should be in horizontal or vertical format, show percentages, show gross profit, show opening and/or closing balances, change the periodicity, change the sorting method, and so on.

For instance, if you want to view graphs with monthly reports:

1. Select the F12: Configure Button while in the Gateway of Tally screen and you will be taken to the Configuration menu.
2. Select General and by default Show Monthly Reports with Graphs under Other Options is set to Yes. If this option is No set it to Yes.

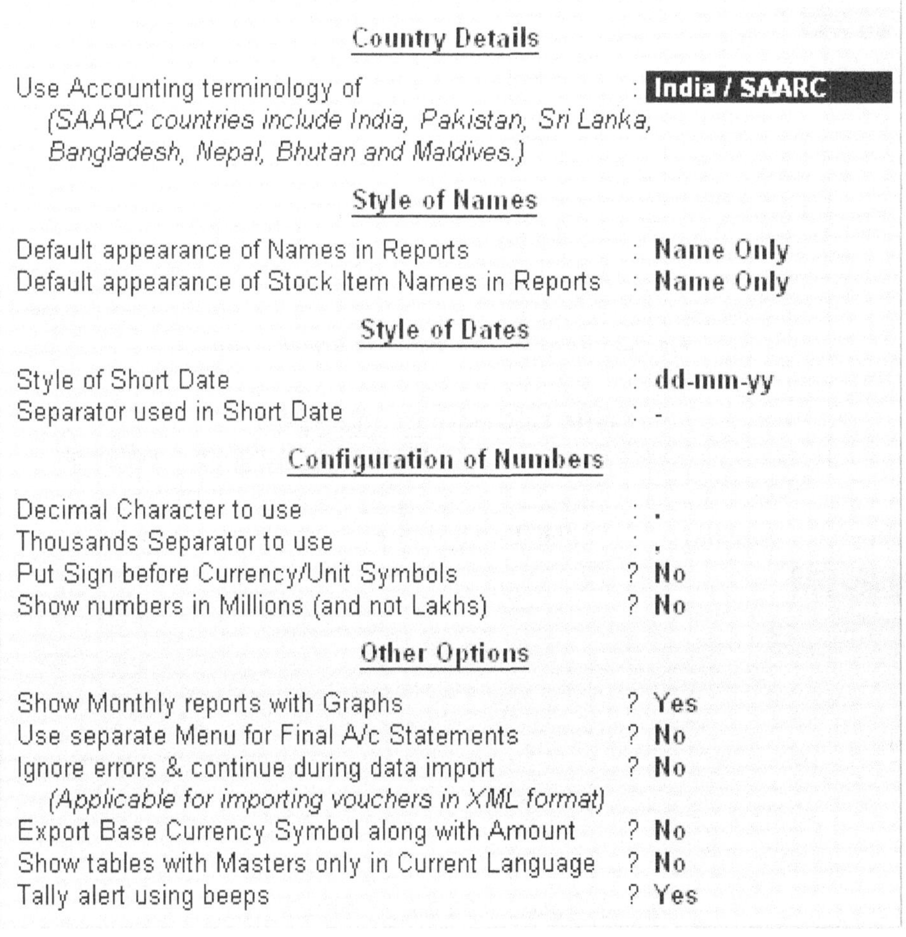

Fig. 7.1 Selecing Country in Country Details

(Alt + F12) F12: Range

This button enables you to filter the information displayed based on monetary values.

For example, you can specify that you want Tally to display only Vouchers having Batch Names greater than $5,000 in a Day Book.

(Ctrl + F12) F12: Value

This button enables you to filter vouchers.

For example, you can specify that you want vouchers having Employee-Attendance Entries with their Designation containing all the details about the employee.

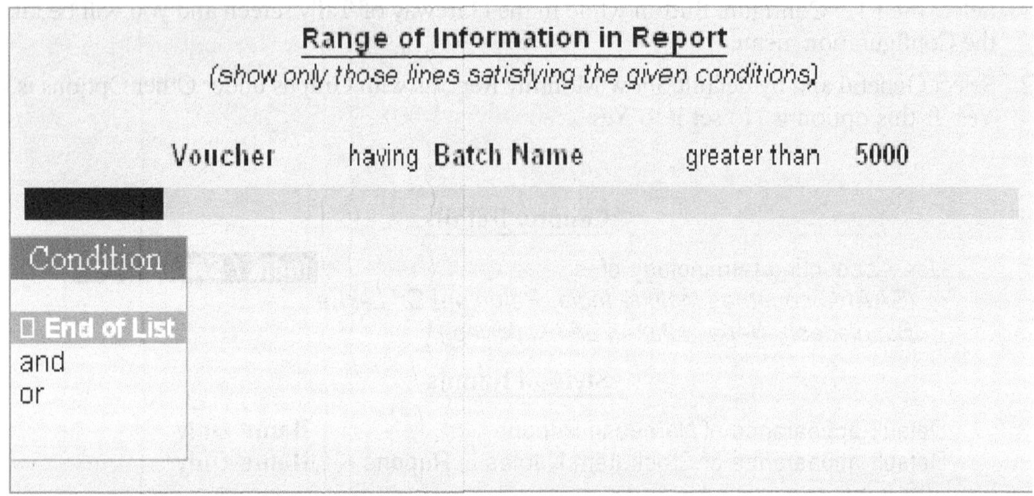

Fig. 7.2 Range of Information in Report Screen

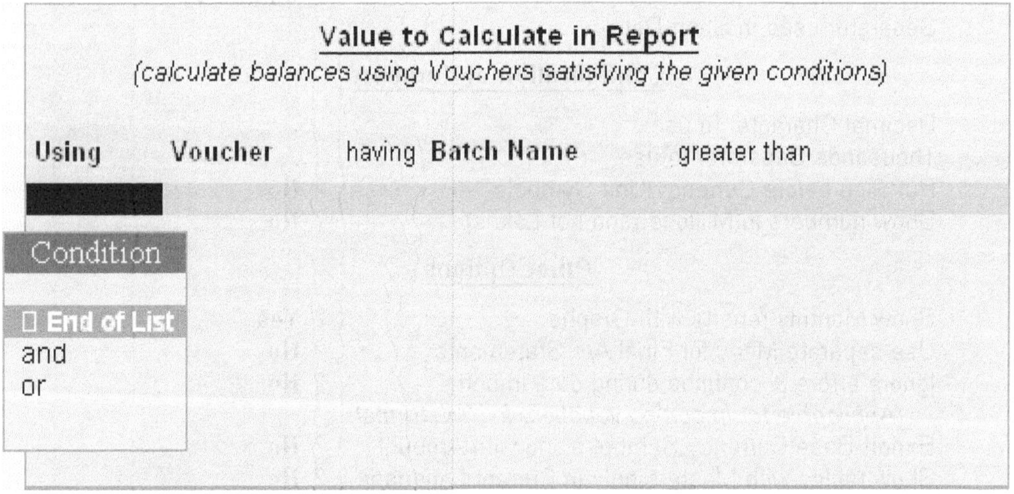

Fig. 7.3 Value to Calculate in Report Screen

New Column (Alt + c)

This button enables you to add and display another column in the report to compare information.

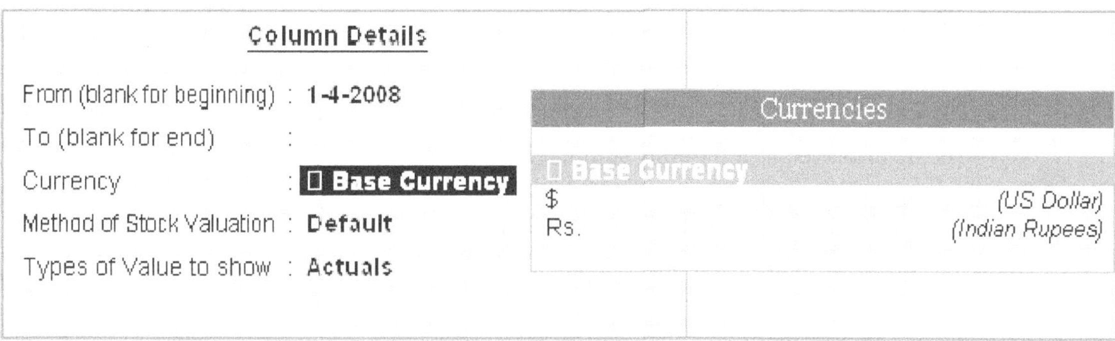

Fig. 7.4 Selecing the Basic Currency

Alter Column (Alt + a)

This button enables you to alter the details of a new column added previously, for example, the date range. Select the column to be altered by positioning the cursor on it.

Del Column (Alt + d)

Use this button to delete the columns, which you no longer wish to have in the report.

Auto Column (Alt + n)

Use this button to add multiple columns to a report.

For example, add columns for each month, or to accommodate other companies if more than one company has been selected. You can also have a total column.

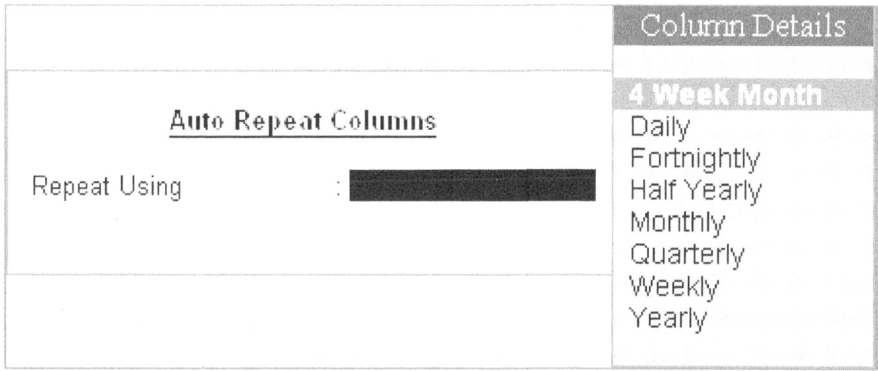

Fig. 7.5 Selecing the Column Details

Report Specific Options

Report specific options, if any are displayed at the bottom-half of the screen and can be amended as per requirements.

Financial Statements

Financial Statements summarises the individual transactions to show totals, ratios and statistics required by the users to analyze the company's financial data in in a wide variety of ways. Broadly, Financial statements are classified into following three major statements, which form part of the statutory requirements in most countries.

- Balance Sheet
- Profit & Loss A/c
- Trial Balance

1. All books are displayed as a monthly summary with opening and closing balances.
2. Select a month and press Enter to display all transactions for the month. The opening and closing balances as well as the total of all transactions are displayed.
3. Select a transaction to bring up the voucher. The voucher displays either in alteration mode or simply displays depending on your access rights.

Display Balance Sheet

A Balance Sheet is a financial statement that reports a firm's financial position at a specific time. The term balance sheet implies that a report shows the balance between two figures. It shows a balance between the assets and liabilities of a firm and the owner's funds. The fundamental accounting equation applicable is therefore, Assets = Liabilities + Owner's Equity.

To view the Balance Sheet:

`Go to Gateway of Tally > Balance Sheet`

Press F12: Configuration and set the required parameters to display the Balance Sheet according to your preferences.

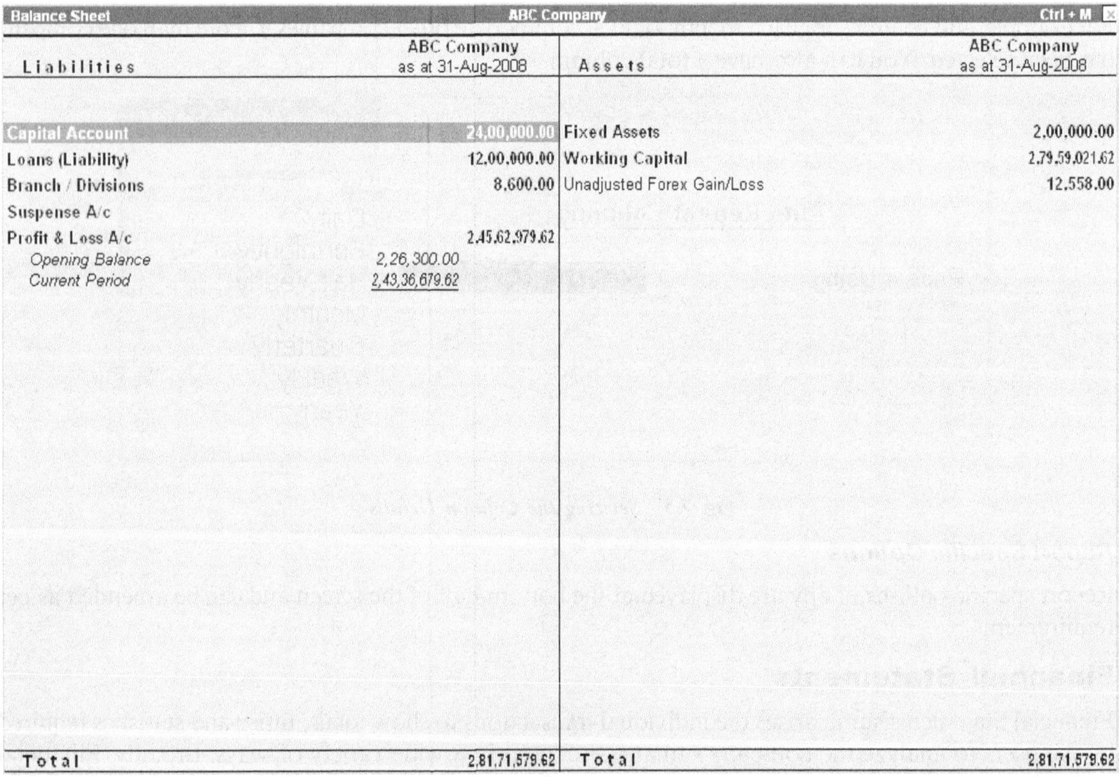

Balance Sheet | ABC Company | Ctrl + M

Liabilities		ABC Company as at 31-Aug-2008	Assets	ABC Company as at 31-Aug-2008
Capital Account		24,00,000.00	Fixed Assets	2,00,000.00
Loans (Liability)		12,00,000.00	Working Capital	2,79,59,021.62
Branch / Divisions		8,600.00	Unadjusted Forex Gain/Loss	12,558.00
Suspense A/c				
Profit & Loss A/c		2,45,62,979.62		
Opening Balance	*2,26,300.00*			
Current Period	*2,43,36,679.62*			
Total		2,81,71,579.62	Total	2,81,71,579.62

Fig. 7.6 Balance Sheet According to your Preferences

Note: Balance Sheet gets updated instantly with every transaction voucher that is entered and saved. You can view additional information or toggle to another report using the options available in the Button Bar.

Some of the Button Bar options are

- Select F1:Detailed/Condensed to explode the summarized information.
- Change the date of the Balance Sheet using F2: Period.
- View different effect of different Stock Valuations on the Balance Sheet.
- Add up new columns to
  - Display the Balance Sheet for a different date to compare with current one
  - Display the Balance Sheet in a different currency
  - Display the Budget figures and analyze the variances.

Configuring the Balance Sheet

To view additional information in the Balance Sheet, you may configure the Balance Sheet in the manner as shown :

```
Go to Gateway of Tally > F12: Configuration > General
```

Set Use accounting terminology of to India/SAARC or International under the Country Details to Yes.

If you have activated India/SAARC, the Balance Sheet will display Sources of Funds and Application of Funds. And if you have activated International the Balance Sheet will display Assets and Liabilities

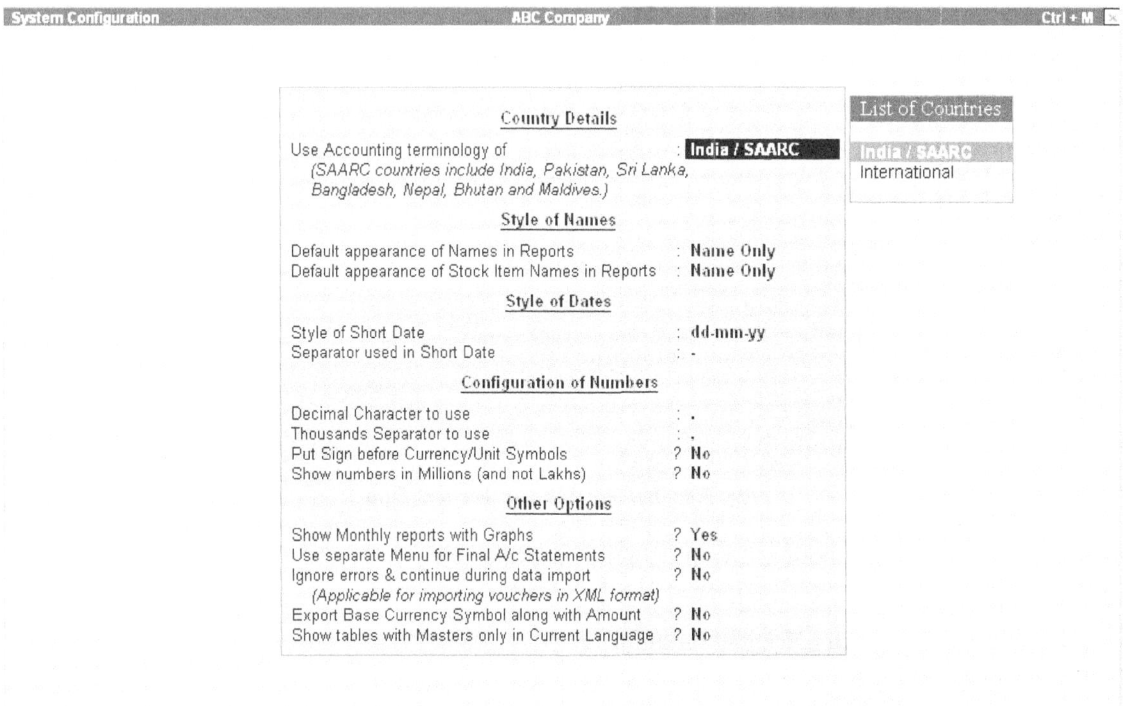

Fig. 7.7 Selecting Country in Accounting Terminology

Show Vertical Balance Sheet

By default, the Balance Sheet screen is displayed in the Horizontal form. However, you may configure the Balance Sheet to appear in Vertical form, by pressing F12: Configure and set Show Vertical Balance Sheet to Yes.

Accept to Save.

The Balance Sheet in Vertical form appears as shown :

Configuration

Show Vertical Balance Sheet	? Yes
Show Percentages	? No
Show Working Capital figures	? Yes
Method of showing Balance Sheet	? Liabilities / Assets
Appearance of Names	: Name Only
Scale Factor for Values	: Default

Profit or Loss, both as Liability?

Set this to No, to move the Profit & Loss Account to the Asset side of the Balance Sheet.

Balance Sheet — ABC Company — Ctrl + M

		ABC Company as at 31-Mar-2009
Sources of Funds :		
Capital Account		24,00,000.00
Loans (Liability)		12,00,000.00
Branch / Divisions		8,600.00
Suspense A/c		
Profit & Loss A/c		3,92,87,104.00
Opening Balance	2,26,300.00	
Current Period	3,90,60,804.00	
Total		4,28,95,704.00
Application of Funds :		
Fixed Assets		2,00,000.00
Working Capital		4,26,83,146.00
Unadjusted Forex Gain/Loss		12,558.00
Total		4,28,95,704.00

Fig. 7.8 Balance Sheet in Vertical form

Note: The Profit or Loss, both as Liability option is available in horizontal form.

Show Percentages?

To view balance sheet with percentage column

- Set Show Percentages to Yes in the balance sheet configuration screen.
- Press Alt+F1 to view the detailed Balance Sheet.

The resultant balance sheet is displayed as shown.

Balance Sheet		ABC Company				Ctrl + M	
Liabilities		ABC Company as at 31-Mar-2009		Assets		ABC Company as at 31-Mar-2009	
Capital Account		24,00,000.00	3.63%	Fixed Assets		2,00,000.00	0.30%
Capital Account	*24,00,000.00*			*Capital Goods*	*2,00,000.00*		
Loans (Liability)		12,00,000.00	1.81%	Current Assets		6,59,65,112.25	99.68%
Loan From Bank	*12,00,000.00*			Closing Stock	*2,51,66,005.25*		
Current Liabilities		2,32,81,966.25	35.18%	Loans & Advances (Asset)	65,000.00		
Duties & Taxes	*1,34,586.75*			Sundry Debtors	*3,07,23,732.00*		
Sundry Creditors	*2,31,22,704.50*			Cash-in-Hand	*74,53,050.00*		
CST Deferred Account	*3,200.00*			Bank Accounts	*25,52,825.00*		
Interest Payable Account	*16,275.00*			*CST Refund Granted Ac*	*2,000.00*		
Tax Deferred A/c	*5,200.00*			*Entry Tax*	*3,500.00*		
Branch / Divisions		8,600.00	0.01%	Unadjusted Forex Gain/Loss		12,558.00	0.02%
Branch/ Division	*8,600.00*						
Suspense A/c							
Refund Claim on Exports							
Profit & Loss A/c		3,92,87,104.00	59.37%				
Opening Balance	*2,26,300.00*						
Current Period	*3,90,60,804.00*						
Total		6,61,77,670.25	100%	Total		6,61,77,670.25	100%

Fig. 7.9 Balance Sheet Showing Percentages

Each line is expressed as a percentage of the total in the Balance Sheet.

Show Working Capital figures?

Using this option, you can set Balance Sheet to show working capital values. Working capital is the difference between current assets and current liabilities.

Set Show Working Capital figures to Yes, to display Current Assets, less Current Liabilities as shown:

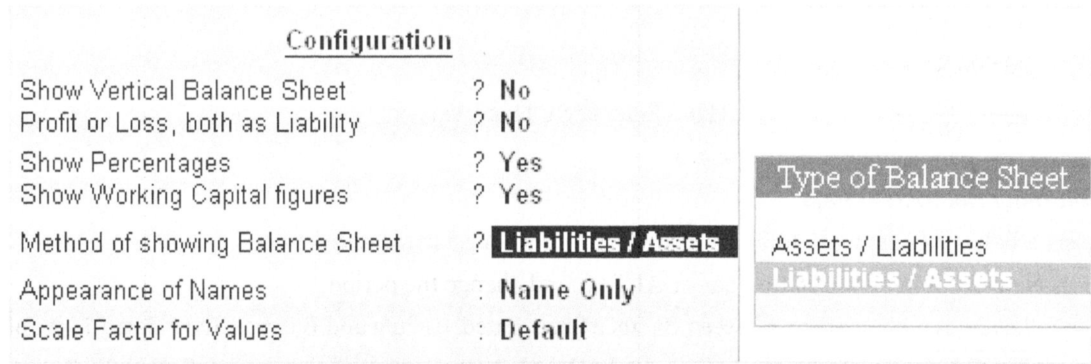

Fig. 7.10 Setting method of showing Balance Sheet

- Select F1: Detailed from the button bar or press the keys Alt + F1.

The Balance Sheet with working capital figures is displayed as shown:

Balance Sheet		ABC Company			Ctrl + M
Liabilities		**ABC Company** as at 31-Mar-2009	**Assets**		**ABC Company** as at 31-Mar-2009
Capital Account		24,00,000.00	**Fixed Assets**		2,00,000.00
Capital Account	24,00,000.00		*Capital Goods*	2,00,000.00	
Loans (Liability)		12,00,000.00	**Working Capital**		4,26,83,146.00
Loan From Bank	12,00,000.00		**Current Assets**		
Branch / Divisions		8,600.00	Closing Stock	2,51,65,005.25	
Branch/ Division	8,600.00		Loans & Advances (Asset)	65,000.00	
Suspense A/c			Sundry Debtors	3,07,23,732.00	
Refund Claim on Exports			Cash-in-Hand	74,53,050.00	
Profit & Loss A/c		3,92,87,104.00	Bank Accounts	25,52,825.00	
Opening Balance	2,26,300.00		*CST Refund Granted Ac*	2,000.00	
Current Period	3,90,60,804.00		*Entry Tax*	3,500.00	
				6,59,65,112.25	
			Less: **Current Liabilities**		
			Duties & Taxes	1,34,586.75	
			Sundry Creditors	2,31,22,704.50	
			CST Deferred Account	3,200.00	
			Interest Payable Account	16,275.00	
			Tax Deferred A/c	5,200.00	
				2,32,81,966.25	
			Unadjusted Forex Gain/Loss		12,558.00
Total		4,28,95,704.00	**Total**		4,28,95,704.00

Fig. 7.11 Balance Sheet with Working Capital

Method of Showing the Balance Sheet

The options are:

- Liabilities/Assets
- Assets/Liabilities.

Format of the Balance Sheet

For Horizontal Balance Sheet: Left Hand Side/Right Hand Side

For Vertical Balance Sheet: Top/Bottom.

Columnar Balance Sheets

Select a Balance Sheet for a different date to compare alongside the current one.

Press New Column on the Button bar or ALT+C and change the period.

The following is a comparison between Balance Sheet dated 1st July and Balance Sheet dated 15th July.

Press New Column on the button bars or ALT+C and change only the currency to display the Balance Sheet with figures in a different currency.

ABC Company

Column Details

From (blank for beginning) : 15-7-2008
To (blank for end) : 15-7-2008
Currency : Base Currency
Method of Stock Valuation : Default

Fig. 7.12 Setting Column Details for Period

Balance Sheet ABC Company Ctrl + M

	ABC Company as at 1-Jul-2008		ABC Company as at 15-Jul-2008	
Sources of Funds :				
Capital Account		24,00,000.00		24,00,000.00
Capital Account	24,00,000.00		24,00,000.00	
Loans (Liability)		12,00,000.00		12,00,000.00
Loan From Bank	12,00,000.00		12,00,000.00	
Branch / Divisions		8,600.00		8,600.00
Branch/ Division	8,600.00		8,600.00	
Suspense A/c				
Refund Claim on Exports				
Profit & Loss A/c		1,73,93,617.70		2,07,02,475.20
Opening Balance	1,45,59,497.70		2,07,02,475.20	
Current Period	28,34,120.00			
Less: Transferred				
Total		2,10,02,217.70		2,43,11,075.20
Application of Funds :				
Fixed Assets		2,00,000.00		2,00,000.00
Capital Goods	2,00,000.00		2,00,000.00	
Working Capital		2,08,02,217.70		2,40,98,517.20
Current Assets				
Closing Stock	78,46,531.45		1,24,15,388.95	
Loans & Advances (Asset)			65,000.00	
Sundry Debtors	1,54,02,790.00		1,53,90,232.00	
Cash-in-Hand	11,16,350.00		11,16,350.00	
Bank Accounts	39,17,625.00		25,62,625.00	
CST Refund Granted Ac	2,000.00		2,000.00	
				11 more ...

Fig. 7.13 Balance Sheet after Changing the Currency

The following is a comparison of the Balance Sheet dated 15th July based on different currency.

Show Quarterly Balance Sheet

To view a Quarterly Balance Sheet

- Press Auto-column on the button bar or use the key ALT+N.
- Select Quarterly from the list of periods.

The quarterly balance sheet will be displayed as shown.

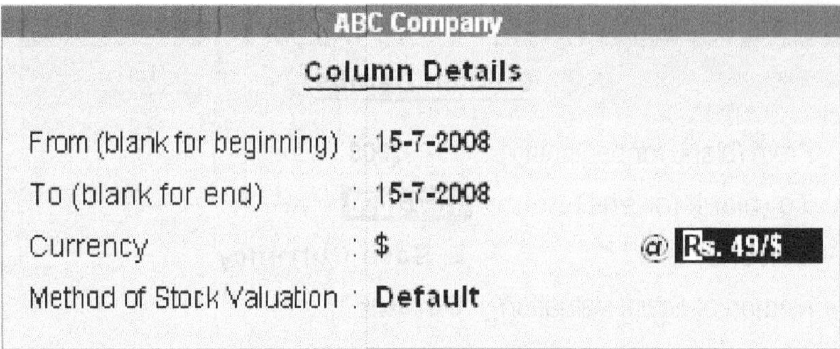

ABC Company

Column Details

From (blank for beginning) : 15-7-2008
To (blank for end) : 15-7-2008
Currency : $ @ Rs. 49/$
Method of Stock Valuation : Default

Fig. 7.14 Setting the Currency Rate

Balance Sheet — ABC Company — Ctrl + M

	ABC Company (in Indian Rupees) as at 15-Jul-2008		ABC Company (in Dollar @ Rs. 49/$) as at 15-Jul-2008	
Sources of Funds :				
Capital Account		**24,00,000.00**		***48,979.59***
Capital Account	*24,00,000.00*		48,979.59	
Loans (Liability)		**12,00,000.00**		***24,489.80***
Loan From Bank	*12,00,000.00*		24,489.80	
Branch / Divisions		**8,600.00**		***175.51***
Branch/ Division	*8,600.00*		175.51	
Suspense A/c				
Refund Claim on Exports				
Profit & Loss A/c		**2,07,02,475.20**		***4,22,499.49***
Opening Balance	*2,07,02,475.20*		4,22,499.49	
Current Period				
Total		**2,43,11,075.20**		***4,96,144.39***
Application of Funds :				
Fixed Assets		**2,00,000.00**		***4,081.63***
Capital Goods	*2,00,000.00*		4,081.63	
Working Capital		**2,40,98,517.20**		***4,91,806.47***
Current Assets				
Closing Stock	*1,24,15,388.95*		2,53,375.28	
Loans & Advances (Asset)	*65,000.00*		1,326.53	
Sundry Debtors	*1,53,90,232.00*		3,14,086.37	
Cash-in-Hand	*11,16,350.00*		22,782.65	
Bank Accounts	*25,62,625.00*		52,298.47	
CST Refund Granted Ac	*2,000.00*		40.82	

11 more ...

Fig. 7.15 Balance Sheet after Changing the Currency Rate

Integrate Accounts with Inventory

Effect on Balance Sheet and Profit & Loss Account:

Integrate Accounts with Inventory in F11: Features (F1: Accounting Features) has a significant effect on the Balance Sheet and Profit & Loss Account.

- If Accounts with Inventory is set to Yes in F11: Accounting Features/ Inventory Features, the stock/inventory balance figures are automatically updated from the inventory records. You may also drill down to Stock Register from the Balance Sheet.

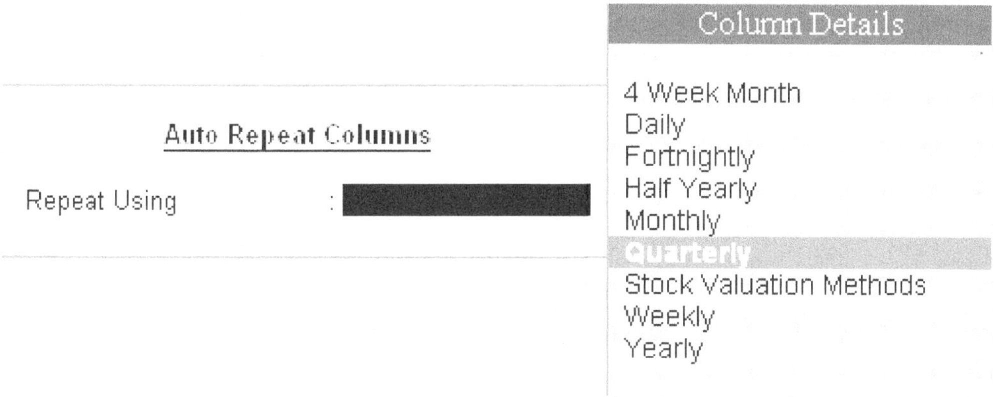

Column Details

4 Week Month
Daily
Fortnightly
Half Yearly
Monthly
Quarterly
Stock Valuation Methods
Weekly
Yearly

Auto Repeat Columns

Repeat Using :

Fig. 7.16 Setting the Column Period

Balance Sheet — ABC Company — Ctrl + M

	ABC Company as at 30-Jun-2008	ABC Company as at 30-Sep-2008	ABC Company as at 31-Dec-2008	ABC Company as at 31-Mar-2009
Sources of Funds :				
Capital Account	9.00.000.00	24.00.000.00	24.00.000.00	24.00.000.00
Loans (Liability)	12.00.000.00	12.00.000.00	12.00.000.00	12.00.000.00
Branch / Divisions	8.600.00	8.600.00	8.600.00	8.600.00
Suspense A/c				
Profit & Loss A/c	1.45.59.497.70	2.57.40.079.44	3.32.29.472.83	3.92.87.104.00
Opening Balance	2,26,300.00	1,45,59,497.70	2,57,40,079.44	3,32,29,472.83
Current Period	1,43,33,197.70	1,11,80,581.74	74,89,393.39	60,57,631.17
Total	1.66.68.097.70	2.93.48.679.44	3.68.38.072.83	4.28.95.704.00
Application of Funds :				
Fixed Assets	2.00.000.00	2.00.000.00	2.00.000.00	2.00.000.00
Working Capital	1.64.68.097.70	2.91.36.121.44	3.66.25.514.83	4.26.83.146.00
Unadjusted Forex Gain/Loss		12.558.00	12.558.00	12.558.00
Total	1.66.68.097.70	2.93.48.679.44	3.68.38.072.83	4.28.95.704.00

Fig. 7.17 Balance Sheet after Changing the Period

- If the option Accounts with Inventory is set to No in F11: Accounting Features/ Inventory Features, the inventory values are ignored and closing stock balances are entered manually.

Note: Sometimes, Stock records may contain compensating errors which are caused by incorrect allocations to the Stock Items. This feature of Tally enables the finalisation of financial books without considering such errors.

Setting Closing Stock Manually in the Balance Sheet

In Tally.ERP 9, the value of closing stock displayed in the Balance Sheet is based on the Costing Method defined for each Stock Item in the Stock Item Master. The general principle of accounting is to value the stock at purchase cost or market value, whichever is lower. Tally.ERP 9 allows you to enter the closing stock value manually.

For example, consider that the market value of stock on 31-12-2008 is Rs.25,000. To show this amount as the closing stock value,

- Set Integrate Accounts and Inventory to No in F11: Features (F1:Accounting Features).

Balance Sheet — ABC Company — Ctrl + M

Liabilities		ABC Company as at 31-Mar-2009	Assets		ABC Company as at 31-Mar-2009
Capital Account		**24,00,000.00**	**Fixed Assets**		**2,00,000.00**
Capital Account	24,00,000.00		*Capital Goods*	2,00,000.00	
Loans (Liability)		**12,00,000.00**	**Working Capital**		1,37,37,640.75
Loan From Bank	12,00,000.00		**Current Assets**		
Branch / Divisions		**8,600.00**	Closing Stock	40,000.00	
Branch/ Division	8,600.00		Loans & Advances (Asset)	65,000.00	
Suspense A/c			Sundry Debtors	3,06,11,232.00	
Refund Claim on Exports			Cash-in-Hand	74,53,050.00	
Profit & Loss A/c		1,03,73,248.75	Bank Accounts	25,52,825.00	
Opening Balance	2,26,300.00		*CST Refund Granted Ac*	2,000.00	
Current Period	1,01,46,948.75		*Entry Tax*	3,500.00	
				4,07,27,607.00	
			Less: **Current Liabilities**		
			Duties & Taxes	1,34,586.75	
			Sundry Creditors	2,68,30,704.50	
			CST Deferred Account	3,200.00	
			Interest Payable Account	16,275.00	
			Tax Deferred A/c	5,200.00	
				2,69,89,966.25	
			Unadjusted Forex Gain/Loss		12,558.00
			Diff. in Opening Balances		31,650.00
Total		1,39,81,848.75	**Total**		1,39,81,848.75

Fig. 7.17a Balance Sheet with Closing Stock

- Create a ledger Stock (under Stock-in-Hand).
  - In Closing Balance of Balance Sheet, specify date as 31/12/08 and value as 40,000.

The balance sheet is displayed as shown.

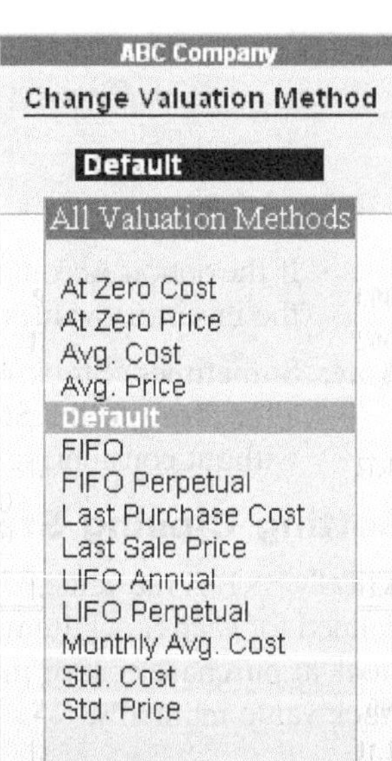

When the balances are carried forward to the next year, the opening value of stock would be taken as 25,000, if Integrate Account and Inventory option is set to No in F11: Features (F1:Accounting Features).

If this feature is set to Yes, the manual entry is not considered and the value is calculated automatically based on the Inventory values. Tally.ERP 9 allows the flexibility to toggle the option Integrate Accounts with Inventory to Yes or No.

Displaying Balance Sheet with Different Stock Valuation Methods

You can select the method of valuation for the inventories in the balance sheet. Tally.ERP 9 provides you with different valuation methods for different items, from which you can select the appropriate valuation method, as per your requirements. *i.e.*, you can view different valuation methods like (FIFO, LIFO, Avg Cost, Avg Price, Std. Cost, Std. Price , etc) for the Inventories in the Balance Sheet.

The various Stock Valuation Methods available in Tally.ERP 9 are:

To view Stock valuations under each of the Stock Valuation Methods in separate columns in the same Balance Sheet, press Alt+N to display the Auto columns.

Select Stock Valuation Methods in Repeat Using field. The columnar report will display valuation based on each valuation method.

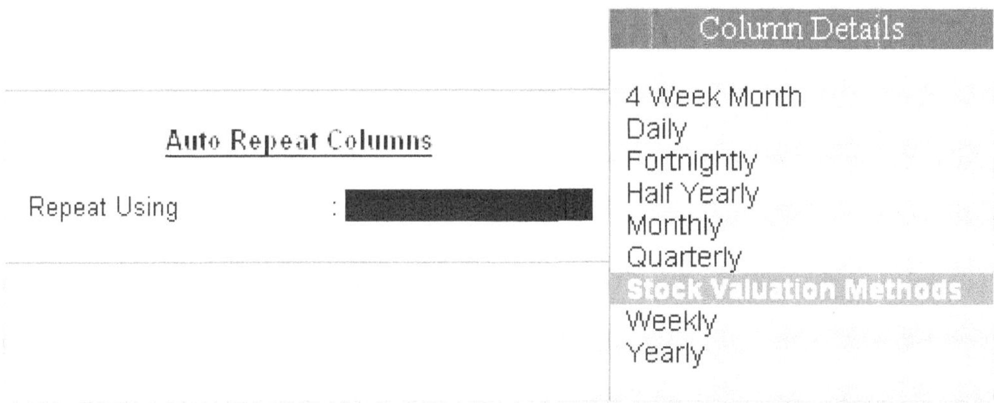

Fig. 7.18 Setting the Details as Stock Valuation Methods

The Balance Sheet with all the valuation methods is displayed as shown:

Balance Sheet	ABC Company							Ctrl + M
	ABC Company *Default* as at 31-Mar-2009		ABC Company FIFO *as at 31-Mar-2009*		ABC Company *LIFO Perpetual* as at 31-Mar-2009		ABC Company LIFO Annual *as at 31-Mar-2009*	
								7 more ...
Sources of Funds :								
Capital Account		24,00,000.00		24,00,000.00		24,00,000.00		24,00,000.00
Loans (Liability)		12,00,000.00		12,00,000.00		12,00,000.00		12,00,000.00
Branch / Divisions		8,600.00		8,600.00		8,600.00		8,600.00
Suspense A/c								
Profit & Loss A/c		3,92,87,104.00		4,53,08,201.98		4,43,26,731.90		4,43,26,731.90
Opening Balance	2,26,300.00		2,26,300.00		2,26,300.00		2,26,300.00	
Current Period	3,90,60,804.00		4,50,81,901.98		4,41,00,431.90		4,41,00,431.90	
Total		4,28,95,704.00		4,89,16,801.98		4,79,35,331.90		4,79,15,331.90
Application of Funds :								
Fixed Assets		2,00,000.00		2,00,000.00		2,00,000.00		2,00,000.00
Working Capital		4,26,83,146.00		4,87,04,243.98		4,77,22,773.90		4,77,12,773.90
Unadjusted Forex Gain/Loss		12,558.00		12,558.00		12,558.00		12,558.00
Total		4,28,95,704.00		4,89,16,801.98		4,79,35,331.90		4,79,15,331.90

Fig. 7.19 Balance Sheet with Valuation Methods

Display Profit & Loss Account

Profit and Loss Account or Income Statement is a periodic statement, which shows the net result of business operations for a specified period. All the expenses incurred and incomes earned during the reporting period are recorded in the Profit and Loss account or Income and Expenditure account.

The profit and loss account in Tally.ERP 9 displays the information based on the default primary groups. It is updated instantly with every transaction/ voucher that is entered and saved. No special processing is required to produce a profit and loss account in Tally.ERP 9.

To view the Profit & Loss Account of ABC Company,

`Go to Gateway of Tally > Profit & Loss A/c`

- Click F1: Detailed, to view the Profit & Loss Account in detailed format.

The Profit & Loss Account is displayed as shown:

Profit & Loss A/c | ABC Company | Ctrl + M

Particulars	ABC Company 1-Apr-2008 to 31-Mar -2009	Particulars	ABC Company 1-Apr-2008 to 31-Mar -2009
Opening Stock	56,650.00	Sales Accounts	3,90,55,008.75
Purchase Accounts	2,47,70,497.50	Closing Stock	2,51,65,005.25
Direct Expenses	2,62,587.50		
Indirect Expenses	69,475.00		
Nett Profit	3,90,60,804.00		
Total	6,42,20,014.00	Total	6,42,20,014.00

Fig. 7.20 Profit and Loss A/c

The Profit & Loss account is generated and updated immediately from the date of opening of books till the date of last entry.

Press F2: Period to change the period as required.

Note: The Profit & Loss Account is displayed according to the configuration set up in the F12: Configure.

Horizontal Form of Profit & Loss Account

The Profit & Loss A/c, by default in horizontal form. However, you may configure the same to view in

Vertical form by pressing it in F12: Configure. You can view additional information or toggle to another report using the options available in the Button Bar.

Some of the Button Bar options are:

- Select F1: - Detailed/Condensed to display more information or condense.
- Change the date of the Profit & Loss Account using F2: Period.
- Add new columns to:
    - Display the Profit & Loss Account for a different period to compare with the current one.
    - Display the Profit & Loss Account in a different currency.
    - Display a column with Budget figures and analyse variances.
    - See the effect of different Stock Valuations on the Profit/Loss account.
    - Select and compare Profit & Loss of different companies.

Configuring Profit & Loss Account

To configure Profit Loss Account, Press F12: Configure

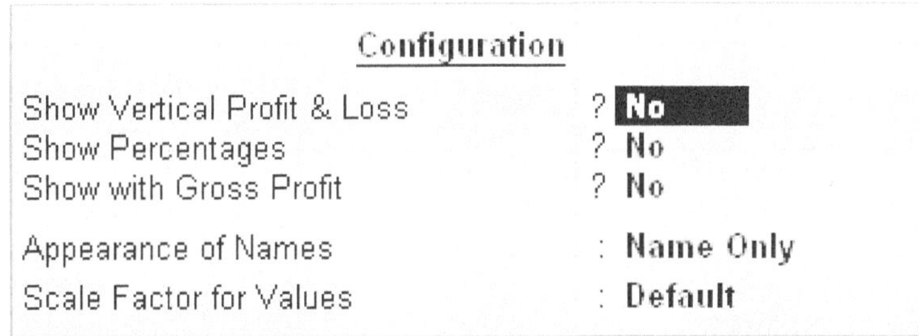

Show Vertical Profit & Loss?

The Profit and Loss Account will be displayed in the Horizontal (default) form if you set the option Show Vertical Profit & Loss? to No.

- Set the option to Yes to display Profit & Loss Account in the Vertical form.

Profit & Loss A/c — ABC Company — Ctrl + M

Particulars	ABC Company 1-Apr-2008 to 31-Mar -2009	
Trading Account :		
Sales Accounts		3,89,42,508.75
Cost of Sales :		2,87,26,085.00
Opening Stock	25,000.00	
Add: Purchase Accounts	2,84,78,497.50	
Less: Closing Stock	40,000.00	
	2,84,63,497.50	
Direct Expenses	2,62,587.50	
Gross Profit :		1,02,16,423.75
Income Statement :		
Indirect Expenses		69,475.00
Nett Profit :		1,01,46,948.75

Fig. 7.21 Profit and Loss A/c in Vertical Form

The Vertical Form shows the Trading Account and the Income Statements separately.

Show Percentages

Each line is expressed as a percentage of Sales Accounts, *i.e.*, if you consider Sales Accounts to be 100%, the rest of the lines would be a percentage of Sales Accounts.

Show With Gross Profit

If the option Show With Gross Profit is set to Yes, the Profit & Loss Statement is split to show Trading Profit, which considers only the Cost of Sales and Direct Expenses. Indirect Expenses are deducted from the Gross Profit to show the Nett Profit.

Note: This field is applicable only to Horizontal Form of Profit and Loss Account.

Columnar Profit & Loss Account: Some Examples

- Select a column to display the Profit & Loss Account in a different currency.
- Press New Column on the button bar or the keys ALT+C, change only the Currency and give the closing Exchange Rate.

The Profit & Loss Account figures are converted at this rate.

Profit & Loss A/c — ABC Company — Ctrl + M

Particulars	ABC Company (in Indian Rupees) 1-Apr-2008 to 31-Mar-2009		ABC Company (in Dollar @ Rs. 47/$) 1-Apr-2008 to 31-Mar-2009	
Trading Account :				
Sales Accounts		3,89,42,508.75		8,28,564.02
Cost of Sales :		2,87,26,085.00		6,11,193.30
Opening Stock	25,000.00		531.91	
Add: Purchase Accounts	2,84,78,497.50		6,05,925.48	
Less: Closing Stock	40,000.00		851.06	
	2,84,63,497.50		6,05,606.33	
Direct Expenses	2,62,587.50		5,586.97	
Gross Profit :		1,02,16,423.75		2,17,370.72
Income Statement :				
Indirect Expenses		69,475.00		1,478.19
Nett Profit :		1,01,46,948.75		2,15,892.53

Fig. 7.22 Profit and Loss A/c after Changing Currency and Rate

- Select a column to display the Profit & Loss Account with a different stock valuation method.
- Press New Column on the button bar or the keys ALT+C and change only the Stock Valuation Method to LIFO Annual.

The Profit and Loss screen will be displayed as shown.

Show Quarterly Profit & Loss Account

- Press Auto Column on the button bar or the keys ALT+N.
- Select Quarterly from the list of periods.

The Profit and Loss screen will be displayed as shown:

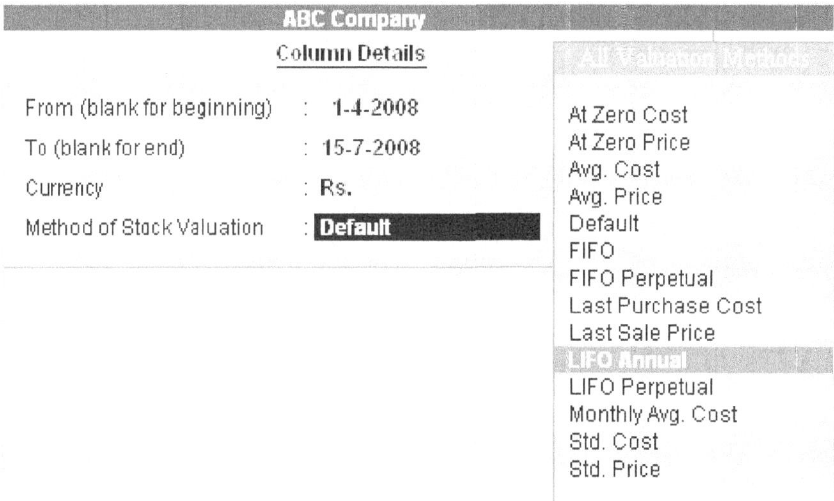

Fig. 7.23 Setting up the Method of Stock Valuation

Profit & Loss A/c — ABC Company — Ctrl + M

Particulars	ABC Company Default (in Indian Rupees) 1-Apr-2008 to 15-Jul-2008		ABC Company LIFO Annual (in Indian Rupees) 1-Apr-2008 to 15-Jul-2008	
Trading Account :				
Sales Accounts		1,45,15,508.75		1,45,15,508.75
Cost of Sales :		26,43,569.52		26,43,569.52
Opening Stock	350.00		350.00	
Add: Purchase Accounts	74,46,097.50		74,46,097.50	
Less: Closing Stock	48,04,177.98		48,04,177.98	
	26,42,269.52		26,42,269.52	
Direct Expenses	1,300.00		1,300.00	
Gross Profit :		1,18,71,939.23		1,52,27,927.00
Income Statement :				
Indirect Expenses		59,675.00		59,675.00
Nett Profit :		1,18,12,264.23		1,51,68,252.00

Fig. 7.24 Profit and Loss A/c after Changing Stock Valuation

Income/Expense Statement instead of P&L

Account statements for Non-Trading Organisations

Income / Expense Statements are appropriate for Non-Trading Organisations, which generally are not engaged in trading of goods or services and thus the books of accounts comprises of only the sources of Income and expenditure earned/incurred during a given period. This is useful for non-profit organizations such as Trusts, Educational Institutions, NGOs, and Hospitals etc.

You can toggle between Income / Expenditure Statement & Profit & Loss A/c, by pressing F11 feature and set Income/Expense Stmt instead of P & L to Yes or No.

Reports

Balance Sheet
Income & Expense A/c
Stock Summary
Ratio Analysis

Display
Multi Account Printing

Quit

The report menu will display Income & Expenditure A/c instead of Profit & Loss A/c.

The Income & Expenditure Statement is displayed as shown.

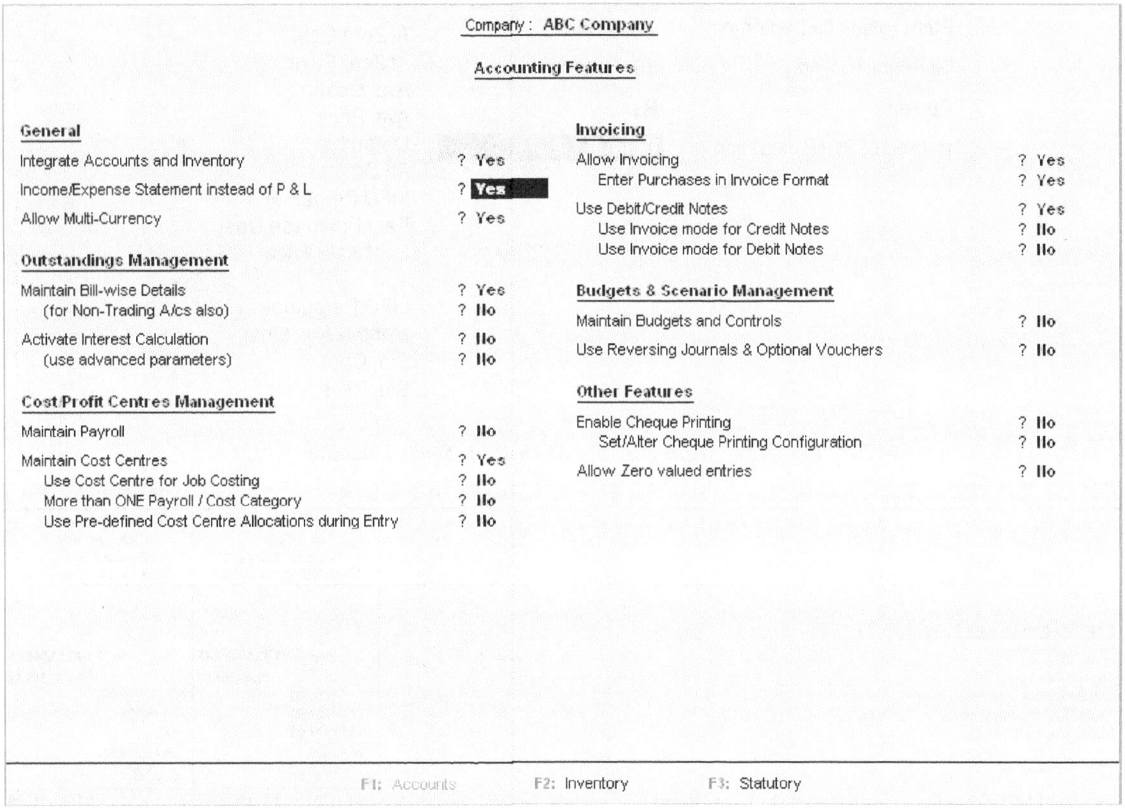

Company : ABC Company

Accounting Features

General		Invoicing	
Integrate Accounts and Inventory	? Yes	Allow Invoicing	? Yes
Income/Expense Statement instead of P & L	? Yes	Enter Purchases in Invoice Format	? Yes
Allow Multi-Currency	? Yes	Use Debit/Credit Notes	? Yes
		Use Invoice mode for Credit Notes	? No
Outstandings Management		Use Invoice mode for Debit Notes	? No
Maintain Bill-wise Details	? Yes	**Budgets & Scenario Management**	
(for Non-Trading A/cs also)	? No	Maintain Budgets and Controls	? No
Activate Interest Calculation	? No	Use Reversing Journals & Optional Vouchers	? No
(use advanced parameters)	? No		
Cost/Profit Centres Management		**Other Features**	
Maintain Payroll	? No	Enable Cheque Printing	? No
		Set/Alter Cheque Printing Configuration	? No
Maintain Cost Centres	? Yes	Allow Zero valued entries	? No
Use Cost Centre for Job Costing	? No		
More than ONE Payroll / Cost Category	? No		
Use Pre-defined Cost Centre Allocations during Entry	? No		

F1: Accounts F2: Inventory F3: Statutory

Fig. 7.25 Setting for Income/Expense Statement Instead of Profit and Loss A/c

Display Trial Balance

A Trial Balance is a summary of all ledger balances to check whether the figures are correct and balanced. Considering that the journal entries are error-free and posted correctly to the general ledger, the total of all debit balances should equal the total of all the credit balances.

In Tally.ERP 9, the matching of the Trial Balance is a foregone conclusion since all voucher entries are in Debit - Credit format and must balance at the entry point.

To view the Trial Balance

```
Go to Gateway of Tally > Display>Trial Balance
```

Note: As per accounting principles, the Trial Balance does not list Closing Stock.

Tally.ERP 9 shows group wise Trial Balance. Next level detail for a group can be exploded by pressing Shift+Enter. Details of all groups can also be obtained through configuration, except for groups behaving like sub-ledgers.

Select F1: Detailed to break down the grouped information or simply drill down a Group for further detail.

Income & Expenditure Statement	ABC Company		Ctrl + M
Particulars	ABC Company 1-Apr-2008 to 10-Jan-2009	Particulars	ABC Company 1-Apr-2008 to 10-Jan-2009
Opening Stock	390.00	Sales Accounts	1,50,96,758.75
Purchase Accounts	85,85,947.50	Closing Stock	64,97,512.77
Direct Expenses	7,475.00		
Gross Profit c/o	*1,30,00,499.02*		
	2,15,94,271.52		2,15,94,271.52
Indirect Expenses	69,475.00	*Gross Profit b/f*	*1,30,00,499.02*
Excess of Income over Expenditure	*1,29,31,024.02*		
Total	1,30,00,499.02	Total	1,30,00,499.02

Fig. 7.26 Income/Expense Statement

Trial Balance	ABC Company	Ctrl + M
Particulars	ABC Company 1-Apr-2008 to 31-Mar-2009 Closing Balance	
	Debit	Credit
Capital Account		24,00,000.00
Loans (Liability)		12,00,000.00
Current Liabilities	5,45,257.50	2,38,27,223.75
Fixed Assets	2,00,000.00	
Current Assets	4,08,56,757.00	
Branch / Divisions		8,600.00
Sales Accounts		3,90,55,008.75
Purchase Accounts	2,47,70,497.50	
Direct Expenses	2,62,587.50	
Indirect Expenses	69,475.00	
Profit & Loss A/c		2,26,300.00
Unadjusted Forex Gain/Loss	12,558.00	
Grand Total	6,67,17,132.50	6,67,17,132.50

Fig. 7.27 Trial Balance

The screen is displayed as shown:

Trial Balance	ABC Company	Ctrl + M
Particulars	ABC Company 1-Apr-2008 to 31-Mar-2009 Closing Balance Debit	 Credit
Capital Account		**24,00,000.00**
Capital Account		*24,00,000.00*
Loans (Liability)		**12,00,000.00**
Loan From Bank		*12,00,000.00*
Current Liabilities	**5,45,257.50**	**2,38,27,223.75**
Duties & Taxes	1,15,982.50	2,50,569.25
Sundry Creditors	4,29,275.00	2,35,51,979.50
CST Deferred Account		*3,200.00*
Interest Payable Account		*16,275.00*
Tax Deferred A/c		*5,200.00*
Fixed Assets	**2,00,000.00**	
Capital Goods	*2,00,000.00*	
Current Assets	**4,08,56,757.00**	
Opening Stock	56,650.00	
Loans & Advances (Asset)	65,000.00	
Sundry Debtors	3,07,23,732.00	
Cash-in-Hand	74,53,050.00	
Bank Accounts	25,52,825.00	
CST Refund Granted Ac	*2,000.00*	
Entry Tax	*3,500.00*	
Branch / Divisions		**8,600.00**
Branch/ Division		*8,600.00*
Sales Accounts		**3,90,55,008.75**
Sales Bills to Make	1,12,500.00	
Branch Transfer - Outwards		*7,92,000.00*
		51 more ...
Grand Total	**6,67,17,132.50**	**6,67,17,132.50**

Fig. 7.28 Trial Balance with Accounts

Select F5: Led-wise to list all ledgers and their closing balances. The screen is displayed as shown on the next page.

Select New Column to bring up the closing balances for another date. The screen is displayed as shown on the next page.

F12: Configuration in Trial Balance

This report shows the flow of the accounts from Opening Balance to the effect of transactions on Closing Balance.

- Select F12: Configure and set the parameters as shown.

A Trial Balance can be shown with opening balance, transactions and closing balance or any one of these. Choosing transactions will give further liberty to restrict Net transaction (Net of Dr and Cr). Net transactions will be useful while viewing group summary for Expenditure groups / Income Groups.

The Trial Balance after configurations made is displayed as shown.

Books and Registers

In Tally.ERP 9, as soon as the transactions are entered they are immediately posted to the respective ledgers, books and registers thereby facilitating instant reporting and faster decision making.

Trial Balance ABC Company Ctrl + M

Particulars	ABC Company 1-Apr-2008 to 31-Mar-2009 Closing Balance	
	Debit	Credit
Opening Stock	56,650.00	
A/C Repair	7,400.00	
Bank-Current A/c	1,20,000.00	
Bank-Saving A/c	23,59,000.00	
Blue Nile Stationeries	3,57,275.00	
Branch/ Division		8,600.00
Branch Transfer - Outwards		7,92,000.00
Bright Industries		13,05,100.00
Capital Account		24,00,000.00
Capital Goods	2,00,000.00	
Cash	74,53,050.00	
City Dealer	72,000.00	
Commission		11,520.00
CST@2%		12,600.00
CST @2% Lower Rate		1,680.00
CST @ 3%	15,670.00	
CST@5%		9,420.00
CST Deferred Account		3,200.00
Cst New		1,49,401.00
CST Refund Granted Ac	2,000.00	
Customer A	12,46,130.00	
Customer B	11,48,664.00	
Customer C	1,67,75,363.00	
Discount	2,62,587.50	
Entry Tax	3,500.00	
Entry Tax Payable		1,000.00
Equipment Sales Corporation		16,75,000.00
		72 more ...
Grand Total	7,03,12,632.50	7,03,12,632.50

Fig. 7.29 Trial Balance with Ledgers and Closing Balances

Trial Balance ABC Company Ctrl + M

Particulars	ABC Company 1-Apr-2008 to 31-Mar -2009 Closing Balance		*ABC Company 1-Apr-2008 to 31-Aug -2008* Closing Balance	
	Debit	Credit	Debit	Credit
Opening Stock	**56,650.00**		***56,650.00***	
A/C Repair	7,400.00		3,900.00	
Bank-Current A/c	1,20,000.00		1,20,000.00	
Bank-Saving A/c	23,59,000.00		23,59,000.00	
Blue Nile Stationeries	3,57,275.00		3,57,275.00	
Branch/ Division		8,600.00		8,600.00
Branch Transfer - Outwards		7,92,000.00		7,92,000.00
Bright Industries		13,05,100.00		13,05,100.00
Capital Account		24,00,000.00		24,00,000.00
Capital Goods	2,00,000.00		2,00,000.00	
Cash	74,53,050.00		11,76,800.00	
City Dealer	72,000.00		72,000.00	
Commission		11,520.00		11,520.00
CST@2%		12,600.00		12,600.00
CST @2% Lower Rate		1,680.00		1,680.00
CST @ 3%	15,670.00		15,670.00	
CST@5%		9,420.00		9,420.00
CST Deferred Account		3,200.00		3,200.00
Cst New		1,49,401.00		1,49,401.00
CST Refund Granted Ac	2,000.00		2,000.00	
Customer A	12,46,130.00		12,46,130.00	
Customer B	11,48,664.00		11,48,664.00	
Customer C	1,67,75,363.00		84,45,363.00	
Discount	2,62,587.50		40,450.00	
Entry Tax	3,500.00		3,500.00	
Entry Tax Payable		1,000.00		1,000.00
Equipment Sales Corporation		16,75,000.00		16,75,000.00
				72 more ...
Grand Total	7,03,12,632.50	7,03,12,632.50	3,83,88,245.00	3,83,88,245.00

Fig. 7.30 Trial Balance with Ledgers and Closing Balances on two Dates

Configuration

Show Opening Balances	? Yes
Show transactions	? Yes
Nett transactions only	? No
Show Closing Balances	? Yes
Show Percentages	? No
Appearance of Names	: Name Only
Scale Factor for Values	: Default
Sorting Method	: Default
Expand all levels in Detailed Format	? No

Fig. 7.31 Setting the Levels of Detailed Formats

Trial Balance — ABC Company — Ctrl + M

Particulars	ABC Company 1-Apr-2008 to 31-Mar-2009			
	Opening Balance	Transactions Debit	Transactions Credit	Closing Balance
Capital Account	**1,00,000.00 Cr**		*23,00,000.00*	**24,00,000.00 Cr**
Capital Account	*1,00,000.00 Cr*		23,00,000.00	*24,00,000.00 Cr*
Loans (Liability)			*12,00,000.00*	**12,00,000.00 Cr**
Loan From Bank			12,00,000.00	*12,00,000.00 Cr*
Current Liabilities	**3,00,700.00 Cr**	*12,57,639.25*	*2,42,38,905.50*	**2,32,81,966.25 Cr**
Duties & Taxes	16,000.00 Dr	6,47,456.25	7,98,043.00	1,34,586.75 Cr
Sundry Creditors	3,16,700.00 Cr	6,10,183.00	2,34,16,187.50	2,31,22,704.50 Cr
CST Deferred Account			3,200.00	*3,200.00 Cr*
Interest Payable Account			16,275.00	*16,275.00 Cr*
Tax Deferred A/c			5,200.00	*5,200.00 Cr*
Fixed Assets		*2,00,000.00*		**2,00,000.00 Dr**
Capital Goods		2,00,000.00		*2,00,000.00 Dr*
Current Assets	**13,30,100.00 Dr**	*4,31,55,996.00*	*36,29,339.00*	**4,08,56,757.00 Dr**
Opening Stock	56,650.00 Dr			56,650.00 Dr
Loans & Advances (Asset)		65,000.00		65,000.00 Dr
Sundry Debtors	1,55,600.00 Dr	3,19,61,021.00	13,92,889.00	3,07,23,732.00 Dr
Cash-in-Hand	2,17,850.00 Dr	79,75,000.00	7,39,800.00	74,53,050.00 Dr
Bank Accounts	9,00,000.00 Dr	31,49,000.00	14,96,175.00	25,52,825.00 Dr
CST Refund Granted Ac		2,000.00		*2,000.00 Dr*
Entry Tax		3,975.00	475.00	*3,500.00 Dr*
Branch / Divisions	**8,600.00 Cr**			**8,600.00 Cr**
Branch/ Division	*8,600.00 Cr*			*8,600.00 Cr*
Sales Accounts	**6,97,000.00 Cr**	*5,90,256.25*	*3,89,48,265.00*	**3,90,55,008.75 Cr**
Sales Bills to Make		1,12,500.00		1,12,500.00 Dr
Branch Transfer - Outwards	*6,97,000.00 Cr*		95,000.00	*7,92,000.00 Cr*
Exports			2,80,000.00	*2,80,000.00 Cr*
				51 more ...
Grand Total		**7,05,17,709.50**	**7,05,17,709.50**	

Fig. 7.32 Trial Balance with Details

Books of account

Books of account record the transaction details as entered. Although items are posted too many different ledgers, Tally.ERP 9 brings all the transactions of a particular category together into a book of account for viewing and printing. For example, Cash Book records all the transactions affecting cash and the Sales Book records all sales transactions.

Let us see some typical examples of how to display the books of account and registers. You will then be able to experiment with other Books for yourself.

Sales Register (Sales Day Book)

Sales Register displays the monthly summary of sales transactions and closing balances. The list of transactions pertaining to each month can be viewed by selecting that month and viewing its details. Tally.ERP 9 permits you to change the display according to the information required.

The period of the report and the content details can be modified. Columnar periodic reports can be generated using Alt+N: Auto Column button for different periods as shown by the columnar details list. Tally.ERP 9 also allows you to compare similar data of two or more companies stored in the same data directory.

Uses of Sales Register

- The periodic turnover can be analysed using the F2: Period button.
- The periodic taxes on such turnovers can be easily computed.
- Errors made while recording the transactions can be easily traced.
- Sales returns during the year can be analysed and timely action can be taken to remove the undesirable causes.
- Performance analysis of godown, salesperson, sales area etc. can be done with the help of cost centre and cost category report.

Sales register displays the monthly summary of sales made during the selected period.

To view Sales Register,

```
Go to Gateway of Tally > Display >Account books > Sales Register
```

The Sales Register screen is displayed as shown on the next page.

By default, all registers display Monthly Summary with transactions and closing balances.

Drill down into each month to view the sales voucher register for that month, which finally takes the user to the accounting voucher alteration (secondary) screen.

Select a month and press Enter to see the Sales Voucher Register, as shown on the next month.

A list of all sales vouchers pertaining to the month you selected is displayed. You can use the options in the button bar to change the display according to your preferences. You can change the period of the report as well as the depth of information.

Use F12: Configure to see the report with some or all of the following information, namely Narrations, Bill-wise details, Cost Centre details and Inventory details.

Click on F1: Detailed to view the reports in detailed format from within the Sales Voucher Register screen.

Display Columnar Sales Register

Tally.ERP 9 provides you the capability to generate columnar reports for different periods. Select the option F5: Columnar from the button bar, in the Sales Voucher Register screen.

The following screen is displayed.

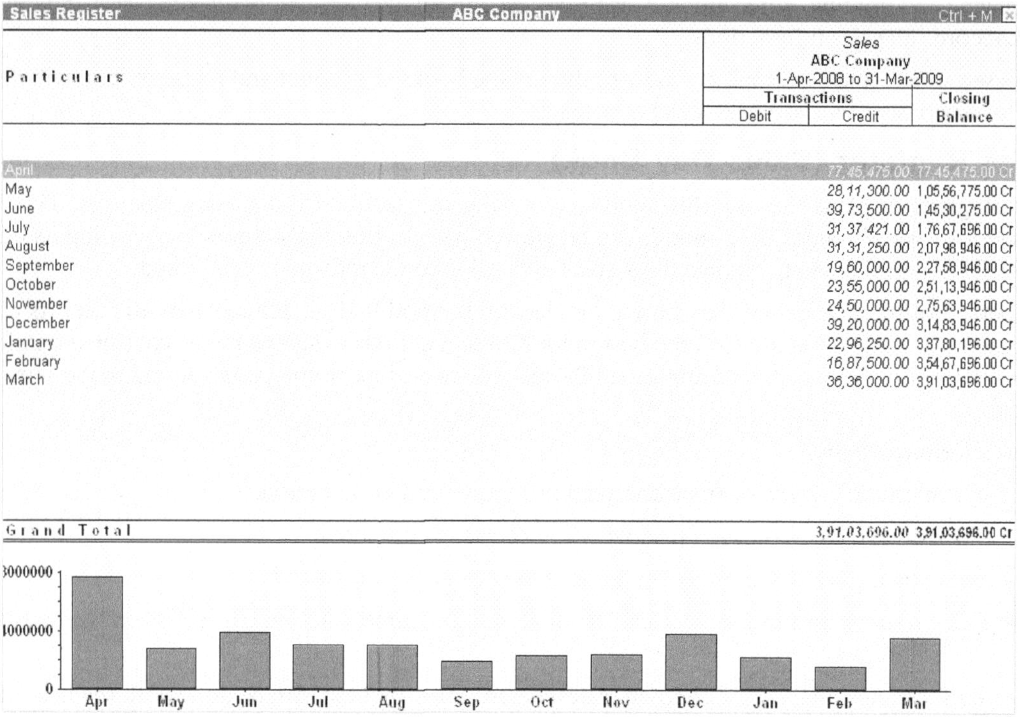

Sales Register — ABC Company — Ctrl + M

Particulars	Sales ABC Company 1-Apr-2008 to 31-Mar-2009		
	Transactions		Closing Balance
	Debit	Credit	
April		77,45,475.00	77,45,475.00 Cr
May		28,11,300.00	1,05,56,775.00 Cr
June		39,73,500.00	1,45,30,275.00 Cr
July		31,37,421.00	1,76,67,696.00 Cr
August		31,31,250.00	2,07,98,946.00 Cr
September		19,60,000.00	2,27,58,946.00 Cr
October		23,55,000.00	2,51,13,946.00 Cr
November		24,50,000.00	2,75,63,946.00 Cr
December		39,20,000.00	3,14,83,946.00 Cr
January		22,96,250.00	3,37,80,196.00 Cr
February		16,87,500.00	3,54,67,696.00 Cr
March		36,36,000.00	3,91,03,696.00 Cr
Grand Total		3,91,03,696.00	3,91,03,696.00 Cr

Fig. 7.33 Sales Register Monthwise

Voucher Register — ABC Company — Ctrl + M

List of All Sales Vouchers — 1-Apr-2008 to 30-Apr-2008

Date	Particulars	Vch Type	Vch No.	Debit Amount	Credit Amount
1-4-2008	Customer A	Retail Invoice	1	61,000.00	
2-4-2008	Customer C	Retail Invoice	2	18,750.00	
3-4-2008	Customer B	Tax Invoice	1	4,16,000.00	
4-4-2008	Customer B	Tax Invoice	2	88,400.00	
5-4-2008	Customer A	Retail Invoice	3	5,25,000.00	
5-4-2008	Customer A	Retail Invoice	4	2,57,250.00	
6-4-2008	Global Computech Pvt Ltd.,	Retail Invoice	5	2,10,000.00	
7-4-2008	Customer A	Retail Invoice	6	6,69,500.00	
18-4-2008	Bank-Saving A/c	Tax Invoice	3	54,000.00	
19-4-2008	Customer A	Retail Invoice	7	3,50,200.00	
22-4-2008	City Dealer	Tax Invoice	4	72,000.00	
24-4-2008	Customer B	Retail Invoice	8	6,30,000.00	
28-4-2008	Silverline Trading Corporation	Tax Invoice	5	65,000.00	
29-4-2008	Manchester Computers	Tax Invoice	6	3,42,000.00	
29-4-2008	Platinum Rectifiers	Tax Invoice	7	36,36,000.00	
30-4-2008	Patel Chemicals Pvt Ltd.,	Retail Invoice	9	20,000.00	
30-4-2008	Blue Nile Stationeries	Retail Invoice	10	1,70,000.00	
30-4-2008	Customer C	Retail Invoice	11	96,000.00	
30-4-2008	Blue Nile Stationeries	Retail Invoice	12	64,375.00	
			Total:	77,45,475.00	

Fig. 7.34 Voucher Register

Set the options listed to Yes or No, depending on how you want the Sales Register to be displayed.

Configuration

Show Extract of Register	? No
Show Columnar Register	? No
Show Gross Profit estimates	? No
Format	: Condensed
Show Narrations also	? No
Show Billwise Details also	? No
Show Cost Centre Details also	? No
Show Inventory Details also	? No
Show Forex Transactions	? No
Appearance of Names	: Name Only
Sorting Method	: Default

Type of Column

Select the type of column from the screen.

If you select Ledger or Group as Type of Column, you will be provided with one more list for choosing the ledger/group. Your choice will be displayed under Name of Account.

All Items (automatic columns)

If this option is selected, every ledger account will be displayed in separate column.

All Item (in one col.)

If this option is selected, all the ledger accounts are displayed in one single column.

Voucher Register ABC Company Ctrl + M

List of All Sales Vouchers 1-Apr-2008 to 30-Apr-2008

Date	Particulars		Vch Type	Vch No.	Debit Amount	Credit Amount
1-4-2008	Customer A		Retail Invoice	1	61,000.00	
	Sales - Zero Rated	61,000.00 Cr				
2-4-2008	Customer C		Retail Invoice	2	18,750.00	
	Sales - Tax Free	18,750.00 Cr				
3-4-2008	Customer B		Tax Invoice	1	4,16,000.00	
	Sales @ 4%	4,00,000.00 Cr				
	Output VAT @ 4%	16,000.00 Cr				
4-4-2008	Customer B		Tax Invoice	2	88,400.00	
	Sales @ 4%	85,000.00 Cr				
	Output VAT @ 4%	3,400.00 Cr				
5-4-2008	Customer A		Retail Invoice	3	5,25,000.00	
	Sales - Exports	5,25,000.00 Cr				
5-4-2008	Customer A		Retail Invoice	4	2,57,250.00	
	$5,250.00 @ Rs. 49/$					
	Sales - Exports	2,57,250.00 Cr				
	$5,250.00 @ Rs. 49/$					
6-4-2008	Global Computech Pvt Ltd..		Retail Invoice	5	2,10,000.00	
	Sales - Deemed Export	2,10,000.00 Cr				
7-4-2008	Customer A		Retail Invoice	6	6,69,500.00	
	Sales - Interstate	6,50,000.00 Cr				
	CST @ 3%	19,500.00 Cr				
18-4-2008	Bank-Saving A/c		Tax Invoice	3	54,000.00	
	Sales @ 12.5%	48,000.00 Cr				
	Output VAT @ 12.5%	6,000.00 Cr				
19-4-2008	Customer A		Retail Invoice	7	3,50,200.00	
	Sales - Interstate	3,40,000.00 Cr				
	CST @ 3%	10,200.00 Cr				
						24 more ...
				Total:	77,45,475.00	

Fig. 7.35 Voucher Register Columnwise

Group

You can also select a group of ledger accounts to be displayed together in one column, e.g., Sales accounts. For other columns, you can use the additional options, namely Related accounts (automatic columns) or Related Items (in one col.).

Type of Column

- End of List
- All Items (automatic columns)
- All Items (in one col.)
- Group
- Ledger

Columnar Register Alteration

Company: **ABC Company**

for: **Sales**

Show Voucher Type	? Yes
Show Voucher Number	? Yes
Show Voucher Ref.	? No
Show Partys' Tax Regn. No.	? No
Show Service Tax Regn. No.	? No
Show Voucher Narration	? No
Show Quantity Details	? Yes
Show Rate Details	? Yes

Type of Column Name of Account

The following screen is displayed.

Voucher Register ABC Company Ctrl + M

List of All Sales Vouchers 1-Apr-2008 to 30-Apr-2008

Date	Particulars	Voucher Type	Vch No.	Quantity	Rate	Gross Total	Sales - Zero Rated	Sales - Tax Free	Sales @ 4%	Output VAT @ 4%
										14 more ...
1-Apr-2008	Customer A	Retail Invoice	1	1,000 Lts	61.00/Lts	61,000.00	61,000.00			
2-Apr-2008	Customer C	Retail Invoice	2	50 Nos	375.00/Nos	18,750.00		18,750.00		
3-Apr-2008	Customer B	Tax Invoice	1	50 Nos	8,000.00/Nos	4,16,000.00			4,00,000.00	16,000.00
4-Apr-2008	Customer B	Tax Invoice	2	50 Nos	1,700.00/Nos	88,400.00			85,000.00	3,400.00
5-Apr-2008	Customer A	Retail Invoice	3	30 Nos	17,500.00/Nos	5,25,000.00				
5-Apr-2008	Customer A	Retail Invoice	4	30 Nos	$175.00/Nos	2,57,250.00				
6-Apr-2008	Global Computech Pvt Ltd.,	Retail Invoice	5	12 Nos	17,500.00/Nos	2,10,000.00				
7-Apr-2008	Customer A	Retail Invoice	6	250 Nos	2,600.00/Nos	6,69,500.00				
18-Apr-2008	Bank-Saving A/c	Tax Invoice	3	300 Nos	160.00/Nos	54,000.00				
19-Apr-2008	Customer A	Retail Invoice	7	20 Nos	17,000.00/Nos	3,50,200.00				
22-Apr-2008	City Dealer	Tax Invoice	4	150 Lts	400.00/Lts	72,000.00				
24-Apr-2008	Customer B	Retail Invoice	8	75 Nos	8,400.00/Nos	6,30,000.00			6,05,745.00	24,255.00
28-Apr-2008	Silverline Trading Corporation	Tax Invoice	5	50 Nos	1,250.00/Nos	65,000.00			62,500.00	2,500.00
29-Apr-2008	Manchester Computers	Tax Invoice	6	30 Nos	9,500.00/Nos	3,42,000.00				
29-Apr-2008	Platinum Rectifiers	Tax Invoice	7	900 Nos	4,000.00/Nos	36,36,000.00				
30-Apr-2008	Patel Chemicals Pvt Ltd.,	Retail Invoice	9			20,000.00				
30-Apr-2008	Blue Nile Stationeries	Retail Invoice	10	10 Nos	17,000.00/Nos	1,70,000.00				
30-Apr-2008	Customer C	Retail Invoice	11	30 Nos	3,200.00/Nos	96,000.00				
30-Apr-2008	Blue Nile Stationeries	Retail Invoice	12	50 Nos	1,250.00/Nos	64,375.00				
	Grand Total					77,45,475.00	61,000.00	18,750.00	11,53,245.00	46,155.00

Fig. 7.36 Voucher Register with Details

Related Items (automatic columns or in one column)

Related items means all the ledger accounts used in a voucher. Hence, the report will be similar to All Items (automatic columns). This option is helpful when used in conjunction with a Group or a specific ledger account in the first column.

The following screen is displayed.

Voucher Register ABC Company Ctrl + M

List of All Sales Vouchers 1-Apr-2008 to 30-Apr-2008

Date	Particulars	Voucher Type	Vch No.	Quantity	Rate	Gross Total	All Items
1-Apr-2008	Customer A	Retail Invoice	1	1,000 Lts	61.00/Lts	61,000.00	61,000.00
2-Apr-2008	Customer C	Retail Invoice	2	50 Nos	375.00/Nos	18,750.00	18,750.00
3-Apr-2008	Customer B	Tax Invoice	1	50 Nos	8,000.00/Nos	4,16,000.00	4,16,000.00
4-Apr-2008	Customer B	Tax Invoice	2	50 Nos	1,700.00/Nos	88,400.00	88,400.00
5-Apr-2008	Customer A	Retail Invoice	3	30 Nos	17,500.00/Nos	5,25,000.00	5,25,000.00
5-Apr-2008	Customer A	Retail Invoice	4	30 Nos	$175.00/Nos	2,57,250.00	2,57,250.00
6-Apr-2008	Global Computech Pvt Ltd.,	Retail Invoice	5	12 Nos	17,500.00/Nos	2,10,000.00	2,10,000.00
7-Apr-2008	Customer A	Retail Invoice	6	250 Nos	2,600.00/Nos	6,69,500.00	6,69,500.00
18-Apr-2008	Bank-Saving A/c	Tax Invoice	3	300 Nos	160.00/Nos	54,000.00	54,000.00
19-Apr-2008	Customer A	Retail Invoice	7	20 Nos	17,000.00/Nos	3,50,200.00	3,50,200.00
22-Apr-2008	City Dealer	Tax Invoice	4	150 Lts	400.00/Lts	72,000.00	72,000.00
24-Apr-2008	Customer B	Retail Invoice	8	75 Nos	8,400.00/Nos	6,30,000.00	6,30,000.00
28-Apr-2008	Silverline Trading Corporation	Tax Invoice	5	50 Nos	1,250.00/Nos	65,000.00	65,000.00
29-Apr-2008	Manchester Computers	Tax Invoice	6	30 Nos	9,500.00/Nos	3,42,000.00	3,42,000.00
29-Apr-2008	Platinum Rectifiers	Tax Invoice	7	900 Nos	4,000.00/Nos	36,36,000.00	36,36,000.00
30-Apr-2008	Blue Nile Stationeries	Retail Invoice	10	10 Nos	17,000.00/Nos	1,70,000.00	1,70,000.00
30-Apr-2008	Customer C	Retail Invoice	11	30 Nos	3,200.00/Nos	96,000.00	96,000.00
30-Apr-2008	Blue Nile Stationeries	Retail Invoice	12	50 Nos	1,250.00/Nos	64,375.00	64,375.00
	Grand Total					77,25,475.00	77,25,475.00

Fig. 7.37 Voucher Register Groupwise

Ledger

Select a specific ledger account e.g., VAT/Sales Tax. All other accounts can be put in one or more columns.

The following screen is displayed.

Change Voucher Types

Use this button to view a different register from within an existing register. For example, If you are in Sales Register and want to view the Payment register, press F4: Chg Vch and select Payment.

Payment Register

The screen is displayed.

Display Monthly Sales Summary

The monthly summary shows each month's total transactions and closing balance.

Group Monthly Summary

When drilling down from a statement into any Group, Ledger, Stock item or Cost centre, the Monthly summary screen is displayed first. Monthly Summary can also be accessed from a voucher level screen with the help of the monthly button. The monthly summary shows the opening balance for the year, and then lists each month's total transactions, inclusive of both debit (inwards for stocks) and credit (outwards for stocks) and finally each month's closing balance.

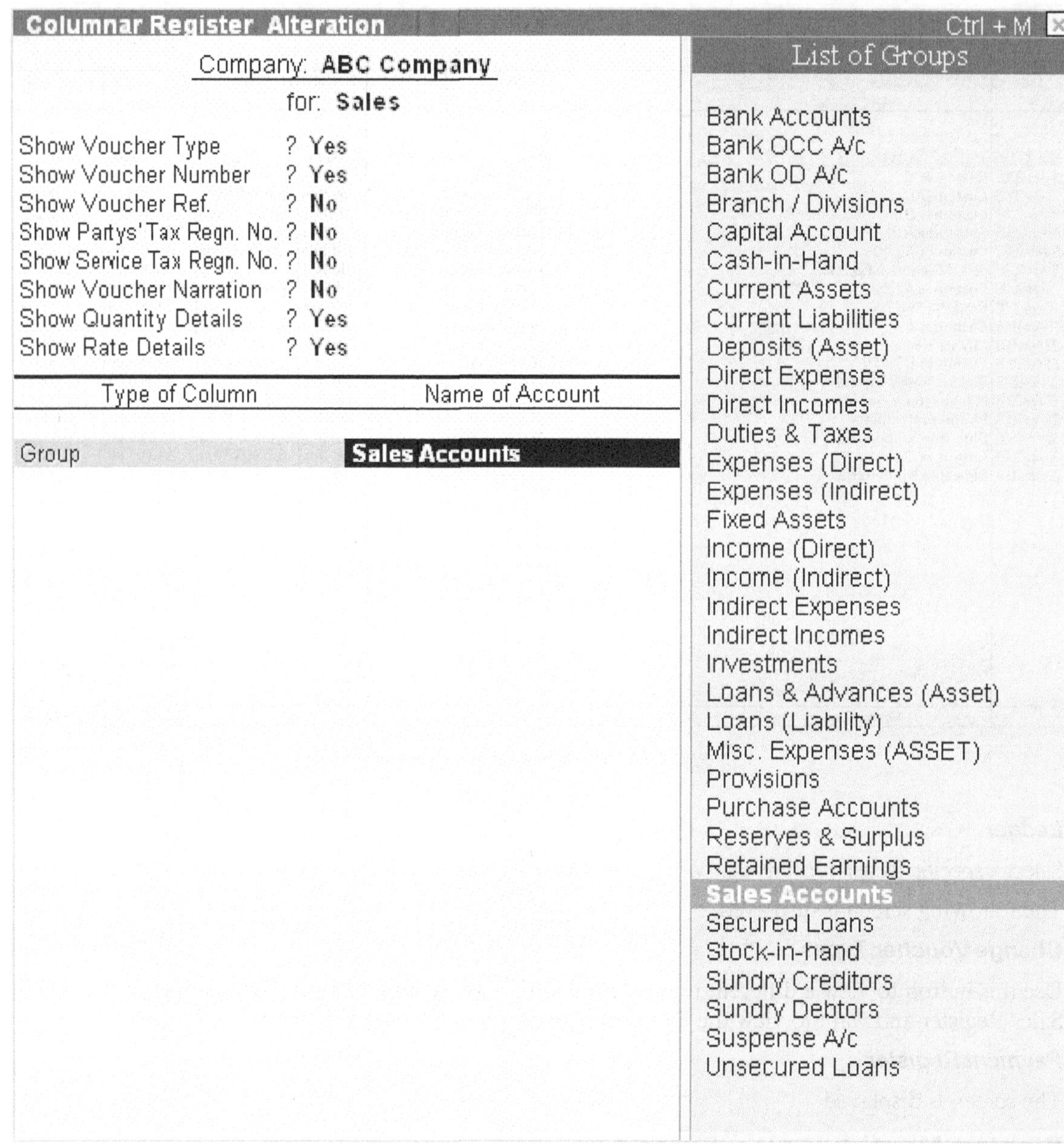

Fig. 7.38 Voucher Register Groupwise

To view Group monthly summary,

`Go to Gateway of Tally > Display > Accounts Books > Group Vouchers`

- Select Sales Accounts from the list of Groups
- Press F6:Monthly.

The Group Monthly summary screen is displayed as shown.

Use F12: Configure to display the monthly summary according to your requirements.

Voucher Register ABC Company Ctrl + M

List of All Sales Vouchers 1-Apr-2008 to 30-Apr-2008

Date	Particulars	Voucher Type	Vch No.	Quantity	Rate	Gross Total	Sales Accounts
1-Apr-2008	Customer A	Retail Invoice	1	1,000 Lts	61.00/Lts	61,000.00	61,000.00
2-Apr-2008	Customer C	Retail Invoice	2	50 Nos	375.00/Nos	18,750.00	18,750.00
3-Apr-2008	Customer B	Tax Invoice	1	50 Nos	8,000.00/Nos	4.00,000.00	4,00,000.00
4-Apr-2008	Customer B	Tax Invoice	2	50 Nos	1,700.00/Nos	85,000.00	85,000.00
5-Apr-2008	Customer A	Retail Invoice	3	30 Nos	17,500.00/Nos	5.25,000.00	5,25,000.00
5-Apr-2008	Customer A	Retail Invoice	4	30 Nos	$175.00/Nos	2.57,250.00	2,57,250.00
6-Apr-2008	Global Computech Pvt Ltd..	Retail Invoice	5	12 Nos	17,500.00/Nos	2.10,000.00	2,10,000.00
7-Apr-2008	Customer A	Retail Invoice	6	250 Nos	2,600.00/Nos	6.50,000.00	6,50,000.00
18-Apr-2008	Bank-Saving A/c	Tax Invoice	3	300 Nos	160.00/Nos	48,000.00	48,000.00
19-Apr-2008	Customer A	Retail Invoice	7	20 Nos	17,000.00/Nos	3.40,000.00	3,40,000.00
22-Apr-2008	City Dealer	Tax Invoice	4	150 Lts	400.00/Lts	60,000.00	60,000.00
24-Apr-2008	Customer B	Retail Invoice	8	75 Nos	8,400.00/Nos	6.05,745.00	6,05,745.00
28-Apr-2008	Silverline Trading Corporation	Tax Invoice	5	50 Nos	1,250.00/Nos	62,500.00	62,500.00
29-Apr-2008	Manchester Computers	Tax Invoice	6	30 Nos	9,500.00/Nos	2.85,000.00	2,85,000.00
29-Apr-2008	Platinum Rectifiers	Tax Invoice	7	900 Nos	4,000.00/Nos	36.00,000.00	36,00,000.00
30-Apr-2008	Blue Nile Stationeries	Retail Invoice	10	10 Nos	17,000.00/Nos	1.70,000.00	1,70,000.00
30-Apr-2008	Customer C	Retail Invoice	11	30 Nos	3,200.00/Nos	96,000.00	96,000.00
30-Apr-2008	Blue Nile Stationeries	Retail Invoice	12	50 Nos	1,250.00/Nos	62,500.00	62,500.00
	Grand Total					75,36,745.00	75,36,745.00

Fig. 7.39 Voucher Register Groupwise

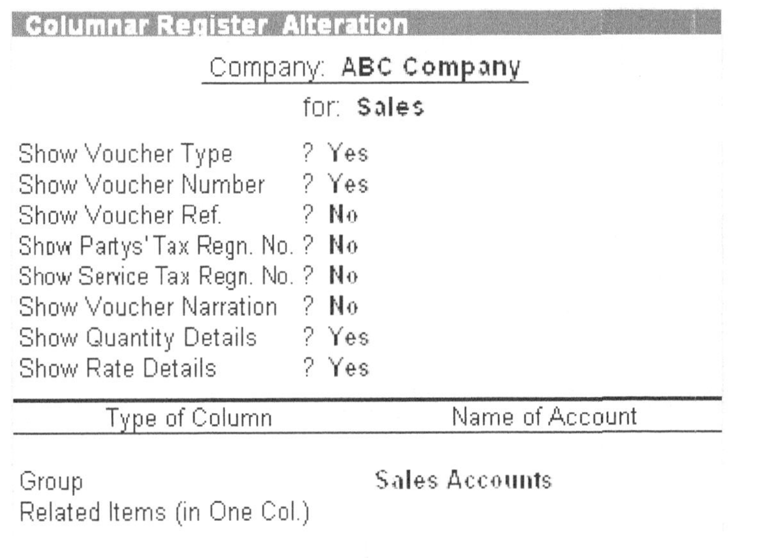

Columnar Register Alteration

Company: **ABC Company**

for: **Sales**

Show Voucher Type ? Yes
Show Voucher Number ? Yes
Show Voucher Ref. ? No
Show Partys' Tax Regn. No. ? No
Show Service Tax Regn. No. ? No
Show Voucher Narration ? No
Show Quantity Details ? Yes
Show Rate Details ? Yes

Type of Column	Name of Account
Group	Sales Accounts
Related Items (in One Col.)	

Accept ?

Yes or No

Fig. 7.40 Column Alteration Register

Voucher Register **ABC Company** Ctrl + M

List of All Sales Vouchers 1-Apr-2008 to 30-Apr-2008

Date	Particulars	Voucher Type	Vch No.	Quantity	Rate	Gross Total	Sales Accounts	Related Items
1-Apr-2008	Customer A	Retail Invoice	1	1,000 Lts	61.00/Lts	61,000.00	61,000.00	
2-Apr-2008	Customer C	Retail Invoice	2	50 Nos	375.00/Nos	18,750.00	18,750.00	
3-Apr-2008	Customer B	Tax Invoice	1	50 Nos	8,000.00/Nos	4,16,000.00	4,00,000.00	16,000.00
4-Apr-2008	Customer B	Tax Invoice	2	50 Nos	1,700.00/Nos	88,400.00	85,000.00	3,400.00
5-Apr-2008	Customer A	Retail Invoice	3	30 Nos	17,500.00/Nos	5,25,000.00	5,25,000.00	
5-Apr-2008	Customer A	Retail Invoice	4	30 Nos	$175.00/Nos	2,57,250.00	2,57,250.00	
6-Apr-2008	Global Comptech Pvt Ltd.,	Retail Invoice	5	12 Nos	17,500.00/Nos	2,10,000.00	2,10,000.00	
7-Apr-2008	Customer A	Retail Invoice	6	250 Nos	2,600.00/Nos	6,69,500.00	6,50,000.00	19,500.00
18-Apr-2008	Bank-Saving A/c	Tax Invoice	3	300 Nos	160.00/Nos	54,000.00	48,000.00	6,000.00
19-Apr-2008	Customer A	Retail Invoice	7	20 Nos	17,000.00/Nos	3,50,200.00	3,40,000.00	10,200.00
22-Apr-2008	City Dealer	Tax Invoice	4	150 Lts	400.00/Lts	72,000.00	60,000.00	12,000.00
24-Apr-2008	Customer B	Retail Invoice	8	75 Nos	8,400.00/Nos	6,30,000.00	6,05,745.00	24,255.00
28-Apr-2008	Silverline Trading Corporation	Tax Invoice	5	50 Nos	1,250.00/Nos	65,000.00	62,500.00	2,500.00
29-Apr-2008	Manchester Computers	Tax Invoice	6	30 Nos	9,500.00/Nos	3,42,000.00	2,85,000.00	57,000.00
29-Apr-2008	Platinum Rectifiers	Tax Invoice	7	900 Nos	4,000.00/Nos	36,36,000.00	36,00,000.00	36,000.00
30-Apr-2008	Blue Nile Stationeries	Retail Invoice	10	10 Nos	17,000.00/Nos	1,70,000.00	1,70,000.00	
30-Apr-2008	Customer C	Retail Invoice	11	30 Nos	3,200.00/Nos	96,000.00	96,000.00	
30-Apr-2008	Blue Nile Stationeries	Retail Invoice	12	50 Nos	1,250.00/Nos	64,375.00	62,500.00	1,875.00
	Grand Total					77,25,475.00	75,36,745.00	1,88,730.00

Fig. 7.41 List of all Sales Vouchers

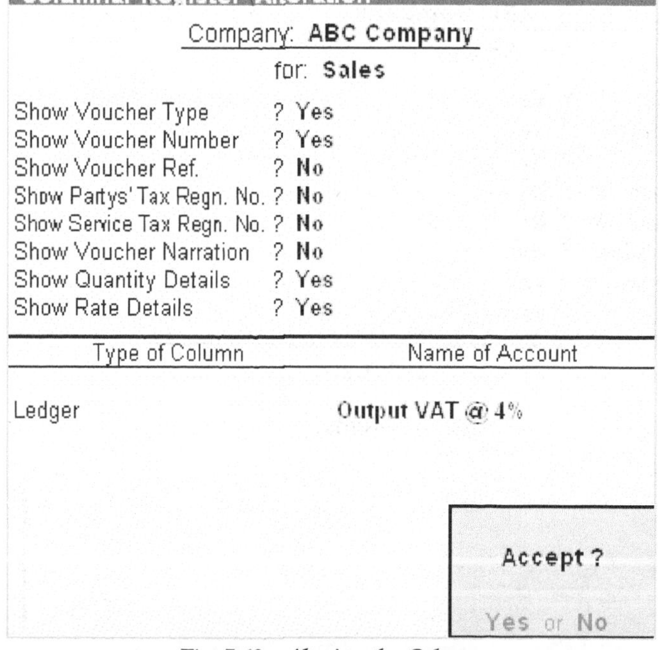

Columnar Register Alteration

Company: **ABC Company**

for: **Sales**

Show Voucher Type ? **Yes**
Show Voucher Number ? **Yes**
Show Voucher Ref. ? **No**
Show Partys' Tax Regn. No. ? **No**
Show Service Tax Regn. No. ? **No**
Show Voucher Narration ? **No**
Show Quantity Details ? **Yes**
Show Rate Details ? **Yes**

Type of Column	Name of Account
Ledger	**Output VAT @ 4%**

Accept ?

Yes or No

Fig. 7.42 Altering the Columns

Voucher Register | ABC Company | Ctrl + M

List of All Sales Vouchers | 1-Apr-2008 to 30-Apr-2008

Date	Particulars	Voucher Type	Vch No.	Quantity	Rate	Gross Total	Output VAT @ 4%
1-Apr-2008	Customer A	Retail Invoice	1	1,000 Lts	61.00/Lts		
2-Apr-2008	Customer C	Retail Invoice	2	50 Nos	375.00/Nos		
3-Apr-2008	Customer B	Tax Invoice	1	50 Nos	8,000.00/Nos	16.000.00	16,000.00
4-Apr-2008	Customer B	Tax Invoice	2	50 Nos	1,700.00/Nos	3.400.00	3,400.00
5-Apr-2008	Customer A	Retail Invoice	3	30 Nos	17,500.00/Nos		
5-Apr-2008	Customer A	Retail Invoice	4	30 Nos	$175.00/Nos		
6-Apr-2008	Global Computech Pvt Ltd..	Retail Invoice	5	12 Nos	17,500.00/Nos		
7-Apr-2008	Customer A	Retail Invoice	6	250 Nos	2,600.00/Nos		
18-Apr-2008	Bank-Saving A/c	Tax Invoice	3	300 Nos	160.00/Nos		
19-Apr-2008	Customer A	Retail Invoice	7	20 Nos	17,000.00/Nos		
22-Apr-2008	City Dealer	Tax Invoice	4	150 Lts	400.00/Lts		
24-Apr-2008	Customer B	Retail Invoice	8	75 Nos	8,400.00/Nos	24.255.00	24,255.00
28-Apr-2008	Silverline Trading Corporation	Tax Invoice	5	50 Nos	1,250.00/Nos	2.500.00	2,500.00
29-Apr-2008	Manchester Computers	Tax Invoice	6	30 Nos	9,500.00/Nos		
29-Apr-2008	Platinum Rectifiers	Tax Invoice	7	900 Nos	4,000.00/Nos		
30-Apr-2008	Blue Nile Stationeries	Retail Invoice	10	10 Nos	17,000.00/Nos		
30-Apr-2008	Customer C	Retail Invoice	11	30 Nos	3,200.00/Nos		
30-Apr-2008	Blue Nile Stationeries	Retail Invoice	12	50 Nos	1,250.00/Nos		
	Grand Total					46.155.00	46,155.00

Fig. 7.43 Columnwise Sales Vouchers

Press the button F5: Quarterly, to view the summarized quarterly figures.

Use the options in F12: Configure to view the details of percentages, averages and so on.

Below the monthly summary, is a bar chart showing the movement of account.

Display Extract of Sales Register

To view an extract of all sales vouchers for a particular month,

```
Go to Gateway of Tally > Display >
Account books > Sales Register
```

1. Select month (For example, select June and press Enter to view the sales voucher register for June 2008)
2. Press F6: Extract
3. Click on F1: Detailed.

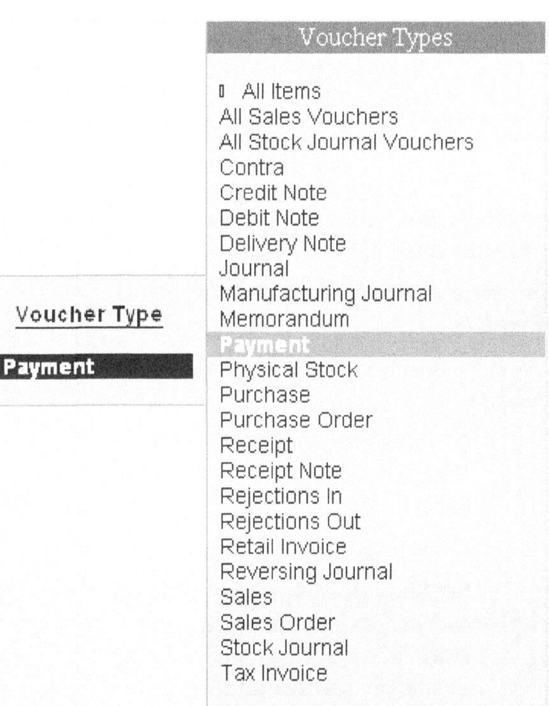

The sales voucher register is displayed as shown.

The extract gives a break-down of the sales

Voucher Register		ABC Company			Ctrl + M
List of Payment Vouchers				1-Apr-2008 to 30-Apr-2008	
Date	**Particulars**	**Vch Type**	**Vch No.**	**Debit Amount**	**Credit Amount**
1-4-2008	Office Expenses	Payment	1	1,550.00	
10-4-2008	Entry Tax	Payment	2	475.00	
15-4-2008	General Expenses	Payment	3	1,600.00	
30-4-2008	Staff Welfare	Payment	4	20,000.00	
30-4-2008	A/C Repair	Payment	5	2,500.00	

Fig. 7.44 Voucher Register

Group Monthly Summary	ABC Company		Ctrl + M
	Sales Accounts ABC Company 1-Apr-2008 to 31-Mar-2009		
	Transactions		Closing
Particulars	Debit	Credit	Balance
Opening Balance			6,97,000.00 Cr
April	2,05,756.25	76,32,045.00	81,23,288.75 Cr
May		26,61,300.00	1,07,84,588.75 Cr
June	3,84,500.00	39,69,400.00	1,43,69,488.75 Cr
July		29,88,020.00	1,73,57,508.75 Cr
August		34,28,750.00	2,07,86,258.75 Cr
September		19,60,000.00	2,27,46,258.75 Cr
October		23,55,000.00	2,51,01,258.75 Cr
November		24,50,000.00	2,75,51,258.75 Cr
December		39,20,000.00	3,14,71,258.75 Cr
January		22,96,250.00	3,37,67,508.75 Cr
February		16,87,500.00	3,54,55,008.75 Cr
March		36,00,000.00	3,90,55,008.75 Cr
Grand Total	5,90,256.25	3,89,48,265.00	3,90,55,008.75 Cr

Fig. 7.45 Group Monthly Summary

vouchers and ledger used to record all sales vouchers for the period. The extract also groups them to show the totals for each group.

Inventory-wise Extract of Sales Register

To view Inventory-wise extract of sales register,

- In the Sales Voucher Register, select F6: Extract from the button bar
- Go to F12: Configure
- Set Show Inventory-wise Extract to Yes to view the report of the stock items sold along with the details on quantity and value.

Configuration		
Nett transactions only	?	No
Show Closing Balances	?	Yes
Show Percentages	?	No
Appearance of Names	:	Name Only
Scale Factor for Values	:	Default
Periodicity to use	:	Monthly
Show Average Details	?	No
Graphs		
Show with Graph	?	Yes

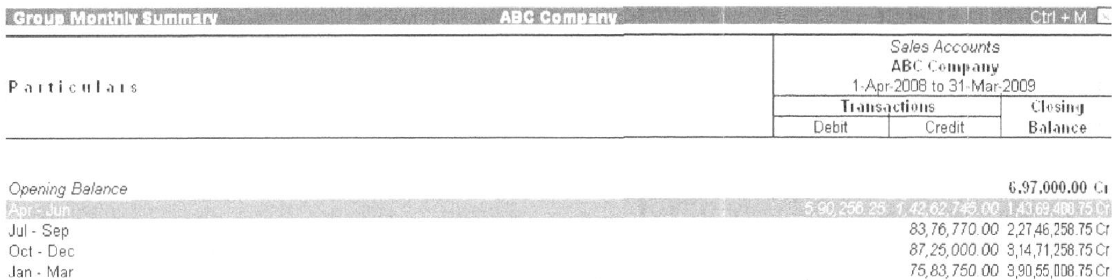

Group Monthly Summary | ABC Company | Ctrl + M

Particulars	Sales Accounts ABC Company 1-Apr-2008 to 31-Mar-2009 Transactions Debit	 Credit	 Closing Balance
Opening Balance			6,97,000.00 Cr
Apr - Jun	5,90,256.25	1,42,62,745.00	1,43,69,488.75 Cr
Jul - Sep		83,76,770.00	2,27,46,258.75 Cr
Oct - Dec		87,25,000.00	3,14,71,258.75 Cr
Jan - Mar		75,83,750.00	3,90,55,008.75 Cr
Grand Total	5,90,256.25	3,89,48,265.00	3,90,55,008.75 Cr

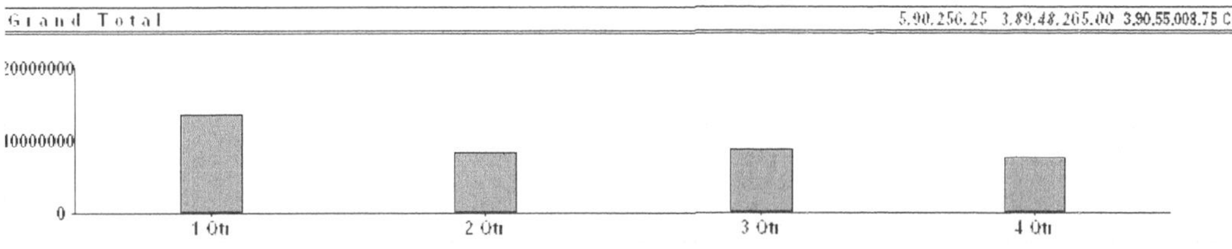

Fig. 7.46 Group Monthly Summary

Group Monthly Summary | ABC Company | Ctrl + M

Particulars	Sales Accounts ABC Company 1-Apr-2008 to 31-Mar-2009 Transactions Debit		 Credit		 Closing Balance
Opening Balance					6,97,000.00 Cr
Apr - Jun	5,90,256.25	100.00%	1,42,62,745.00	36.62%	1,43,69,488.75 Cr
Jul - Sep			83,76,770.00	21.51%	2,27,46,258.75 Cr
Oct - Dec			87,25,000.00	22.40%	3,14,71,258.75 Cr
Jan - Mar			75,83,750.00	19.47%	3,90,55,008.75 Cr
Grand Total	5,90,256.25	100.00%	3,89,48,265.00	100.00%	3,90,55,008.75 Cr

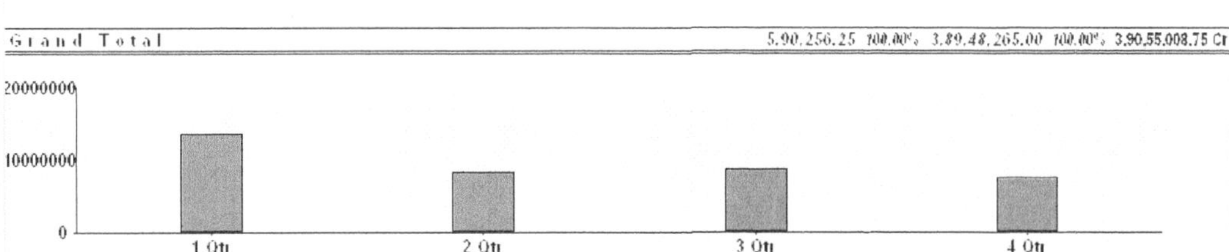

Fig. 7.47 Group Monthly Summary

The sales voucher register with inventory details is displayed as shown:

Voucher Register — ABC Company — Ctrl + M

Extract of All Sales Vouchers — 1-Jun-2008 to 30-Jun-2008

Particulars	Inwards Qty	Rate	Amount	Outwards Qty	Rate	Amount
Computer Spares				1,412 Nos	2,758.07	38,94,400.00
240 GB Hard Disk Drive				*20 Nos*	*9,620.00*	*1,92,400.00*
2 GB RAM Sticks				*250 Nos*	*3,200.00*	*8,00,000.00*
2 GB USB Drive				*1,110 Nos*	*2,285.59*	*25,37,000.00*
Colour Monitor 17"				*2 Nos*	*17,500.00*	*35,000.00*
Dual Core Processor				*30 Nos*	*11,000.00*	*3,30,000.00*
Cooling Equipment				1 Nos	55,000.00	55,000.00
Grand Total :				1,413 Nos	2,795.05	39,49,400.00

Fig. 7.48 Extract of Sales Vouchers

Display Sales Register with Profitability

Tally.ERP 9 provides product-wise and invoice-wise profitability. It calculates gross profits for each invoice based on the Transaction Value and Cost. Gross profit is the difference between sales value and Cost.

To display invoice-wise profitability:

1. Display the Sales Voucher Register for a particular period by drilling down a month and change the period if required.

Voucher Register — ABC Company — Ctrl + M

List of All Sales Vouchers — 1-Apr-2008 to 30-Apr-2008

Date	Particulars	Vch Type	Vch No.			Debit Amount	Credit Amount	
1-4-2008	Customer A	Retail Invoice	1	61,000.00	61,000.00		61,000.00	100.00 %
2-4-2008	Customer C	Retail Invoice	2	18,750.00	18,750.00		18,750.00	100.00 %
3-4-2008	Customer B	Tax Invoice	1	4,16,000.00	4,00,000.00	1,75,000.00	2,25,000.00	56.25 %
4-4-2008	Customer B	Tax Invoice	2	88,400.00	85,000.00	45,336.00	39,664.00	46.66 %
5-4-2008	Customer A	Retail Invoice	3	5,25,000.00	5,25,000.00		5,25,000.00	100.00 %
5-4-2008	Customer A	Retail Invoice	4	2,57,250.00	2,57,250.00		2,57,250.00	100.00 %
6-4-2008	Global Computech Pvt Ltd..	Retail Invoice	5	2,10,000.00	2,10,000.00		2,10,000.00	100.00 %
7-4-2008	Customer A	Retail Invoice	6	6,69,500.00	6,50,000.00	5,06,862.50	1,43,137.50	22.02 %
18-4-2008	Bank-Saving A/c	Tax Invoice	3	54,000.00	48,000.00	51,786.00	(-)3,786.00	(-)7.89 %
19-4-2008	Customer A	Retail Invoice	7	3,50,200.00	3,40,000.00		3,40,000.00	100.00 %
24-4-2008	Customer B	Retail Invoice	8	6,30,000.00	6,05,745.00	50,493.75	5,55,251.25	91.66 %
28-4-2008	Silverline Trading Corporation	Tax Invoice	5	65,000.00	62,500.00	38,928.50	23,571.50	37.71 %
29-4-2008	Manchester Computers	Tax Invoice	6	3,42,000.00	2,85,000.00	1,05,000.00	1,80,000.00	63.16 %
29-4-2008	Platinum Rectifiers	Tax Invoice	7	36,36,000.00	36,00,000.00	81,000.00	35,19,000.00	97.75 %
30-4-2008	Patel Chemicals Pvt Ltd..	Retail Invoice	9	20,000.00	20,000.00		20,000.00	100.00 %
30-4-2008	Blue Nile Stationeries	Retail Invoice	10	1,70,000.00	1,70,000.00	10,000.00	1,60,000.00	94.12 %
30-4-2008	Customer C	Retail Invoice	11	96,000.00	96,000.00	60,592.50	35,407.50	36.88 %
30-4-2008	Blue Nile Stationeries	Retail Invoice	12	64,375.00	62,500.00	43,422.00	19,078.00	30.52 %

Fig. 7.49 Sales Register with Profitability

2. Select F7: Show Profit or activate the option Show Gross profit estimates to Yes in F12: Configure

The report now displays each invoice with:

- Transaction Value - Invoice value including taxes
- Gross Revenue – Actual sale value minus taxes
- Cost – Book cost of the product
- Gross Profit – Amount of profit or loss on the sale.

Display Comparative Sales Register

Comparative Sales reports can be generated using Alt + C: New Column button for different periods as shown in the Columnar details list. You can also compare similar data of two or more companies stored in the same data directory.

Using New Column button:

Use the New Column button to bring up the Monthly Summary of another ledger or the same ledger in another company.

Press New Column on the Button bar or ALT+C and change the Name of Voucher Type.

The columnar report is displayed as shown:

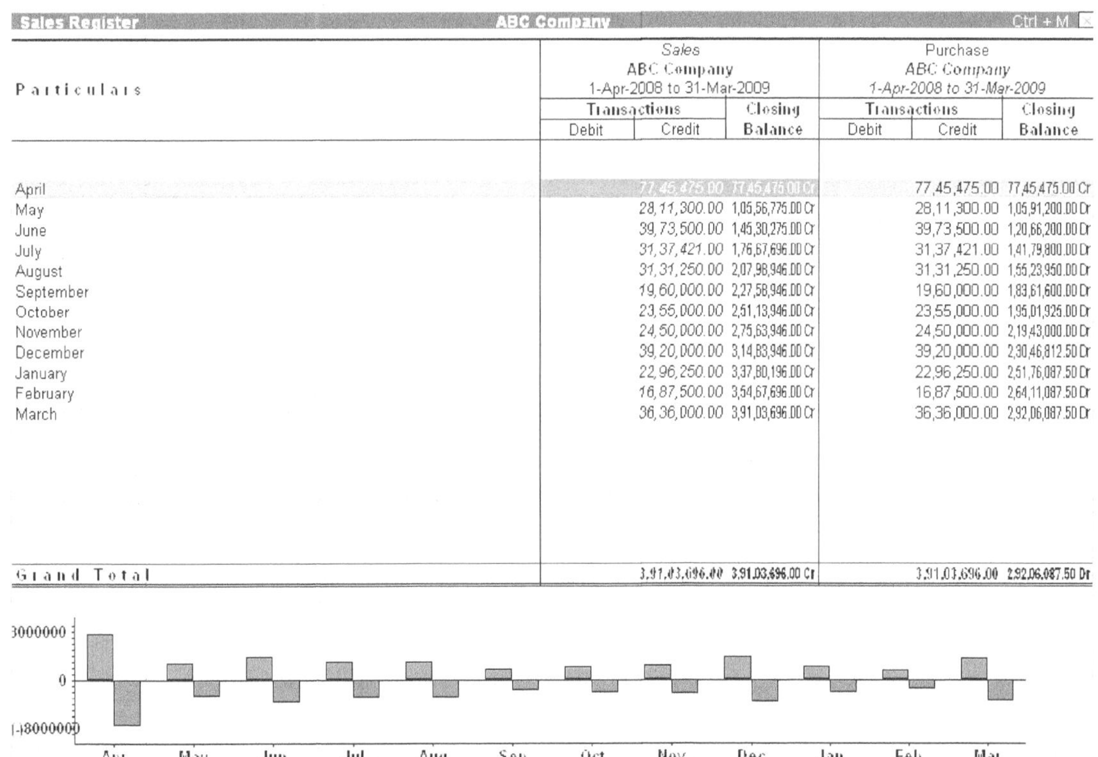

Sales Register | ABC Company | Ctrl + M

Particulars	Sales ABC Company 1-Apr-2008 to 31-Mar-2009 Transactions			Purchase ABC Company 1-Apr-2008 to 31-Mar-2009 Transactions		
	Debit	Credit	Closing Balance	Debit	Credit	Closing Balance
April		77,45,475.00	77,45,475.00 Cr		77,45,475.00	77,45,475.00 Cr
May		28,11,300.00	1,05,56,775.00 Cr		28,11,300.00	1,05,91,200.00 Dr
June		39,73,500.00	1,45,30,275.00 Cr		39,73,500.00	1,20,66,200.00 Dr
July		31,37,421.00	1,76,67,696.00 Cr		31,37,421.00	1,41,79,800.00 Dr
August		31,31,250.00	2,07,98,946.00 Cr		31,31,250.00	1,55,23,950.00 Dr
September		19,60,000.00	2,27,58,946.00 Cr		19,60,000.00	1,83,61,600.00 Dr
October		23,55,000.00	2,51,13,946.00 Cr		23,55,000.00	1,95,01,925.00 Dr
November		24,50,000.00	2,75,63,946.00 Cr		24,50,000.00	2,19,43,000.00 Dr
December		39,20,000.00	3,14,83,946.00 Cr		39,20,000.00	2,30,46,812.50 Dr
January		22,96,250.00	3,37,80,196.00 Cr		22,96,250.00	2,51,76,087.50 Dr
February		16,87,500.00	3,54,67,696.00 Cr		16,87,500.00	2,64,11,087.50 Dr
March		36,36,000.00	3,91,03,696.00 Cr		36,36,000.00	2,92,06,087.50 Dr
Grand Total		3,91,03,696.00	3,91,03,696.00 Cr		3,91,03,696.00	2,92,06,087.50 Dr

Fig. 7.50 Sales Register Monthwise

Using Alter Column button:

Use the Alter Column button to Alter the column in the report which can be viewed in columnar format

Press Alter Column on the Button bar or ALT+A and change the period.

You can alter the information of the existing or newly added column like Name of company, Date range, Currency and Name of Voucher Type.

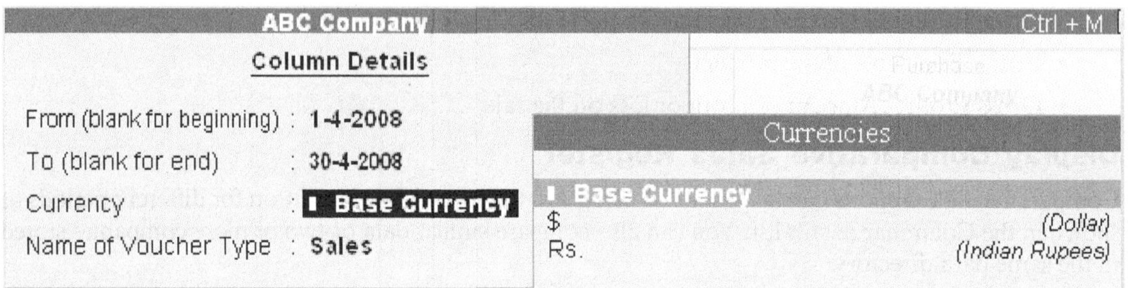

Using Auto Column button:

Use the Auto Column button to Auto Repeat columns in the report based on the options selected.

- Press Auto Column on the Button bar or ALT+N
- Select Daily as Repeat using option in Auto Repeat Columns screen.

Auto Repeat Columns

Repeat Using : Daily

Show Total Column ? Yes

The following screen displays Daily Sales:

Sales Register — ABC Company — Ctrl + M

Particulars	Total			Sales ABC Company 1-Apr-2008 to 31-Mar-2009		
	Transactions		Closing Balance	Transactions		Closing Balance
	Debit	Credit		Debit	Credit	
						29 more ...
1-Apr		61,000.00	61,000.00 Cr		61,000.00	61,000.00 Cr
2-Apr		37,500.00	98,500.00 Cr		18,750.00	79,750.00 Cr
3-Apr		8,32,000.00	9,11,750.00 Cr		4,16,000.00	4,95,750.00 Cr
4-Apr		1,76,800.00	6,72,550.00 Cr		88,400.00	5,84,150.00 Cr
5-Apr		15,64,500.00	21,48,650.00 Cr		7,82,250.00	13,66,400.00 Cr
6-Apr		4,20,000.00	17,86,400.00 Cr		2,10,000.00	15,76,400.00 Cr
7-Apr		13,39,000.00	29,15,400.00 Cr		6,69,500.00	22,45,900.00 Cr
8-Apr			22,45,900.00 Cr			22,45,900.00 Cr
9-Apr			22,45,900.00 Cr			22,45,900.00 Cr
10-Apr			22,45,900.00 Cr			22,45,900.00 Cr
11-Apr			22,45,900.00 Cr			22,45,900.00 Cr
12-Apr			22,45,900.00 Cr			22,45,900.00 Cr
13-Apr			22,45,900.00 Cr			22,45,900.00 Cr
14-Apr			22,45,900.00 Cr			22,45,900.00 Cr
15-Apr			22,45,900.00 Cr			22,45,900.00 Cr
16-Apr			22,45,900.00 Cr			22,45,900.00 Cr
17-Apr			22,45,900.00 Cr			22,45,900.00 Cr
						348 more ...
Grand Total		4,67,88,171.00	4,67,88,171.00 Cr		3,91,03,696.00	3,91,03,696.00 Cr

Fig. 7.51 Daily Sales Register

Display Purchase Register

A Purchase Register displays the information on the periodic purchases of a business concern. Purchase register helps in analyzing the details of movement of purchased goods to various godowns, on the basis of which the stock movement at each godown is determined.

```
Go to Gateway of Tally > Display >Account books > Purchase Register
```

The following screen is displayed.

Purchase returns made during a year can also be traced. The parties to whom the purchase returns have been made and the causes thereof can be analysed to draw conclusions on the supplier and the quality of purchases made.

Purchase Register — ABC Company — Ctrl + M

Particulars	Purchase, ABC Company, 1-Apr-2008 to 31-Mar-2009		
	Transactions		Closing Balance
	Debit	Credit	
April	91,74,900.00		91,74,900.00 Dr
May	14,16,300.00		1,05,91,200.00 Dr
June	14,75,000.00		1,20,66,200.00 Dr
July	21,13,600.00		1,41,79,800.00 Dr
August	13,44,150.00		1,55,23,950.00 Dr
September	28,37,650.00		1,83,61,600.00 Dr
October	11,40,325.00		1,95,01,925.00 Dr
November	24,41,075.00		2,19,43,000.00 Dr
December	11,03,812.50		2,30,46,812.50 Dr
January	21,29,275.00		2,51,76,087.50 Dr
February	12,35,000.00		2,64,11,087.50 Dr
March	27,95,000.00		2,92,06,087.50 Dr
Grand Total	2,92,06,087.50		2,92,06,087.50 Dr

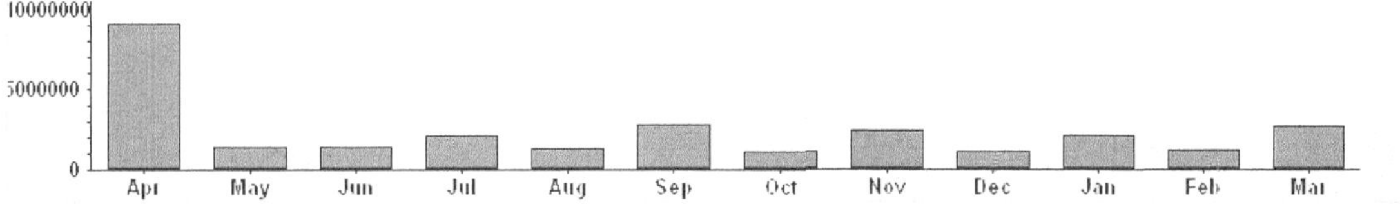

Fig. 7.52 Purchase Register

A Purchase Register can be configured using the Ctrl+F12: Value button to view the following information.

- Actual Quantity
- Billed Quantity
- Date
- Bill Name
- Cost Centre
- Cost Category
- Voucher Number
- Narration

- Stock item
- Godown Name.

Note: All reports and configurations for Purchase Register are similar to as explained in for Sales Register.

Display Cash Book

Account Books record individual transaction details that have been entered. Though the items are posted to different ledgers, Tally.ERP 9 brings together all the transactions of one category into books of account for viewing and printing. For example, the cash book records all transactions that affect cash.

Cash/Bank Summary

To display the cash/bank summary

`Go to Gateway of Tally > Display > Account Books > Cash/Bank Book(s)`

The Cash/Bank Summary is displayed as shown:

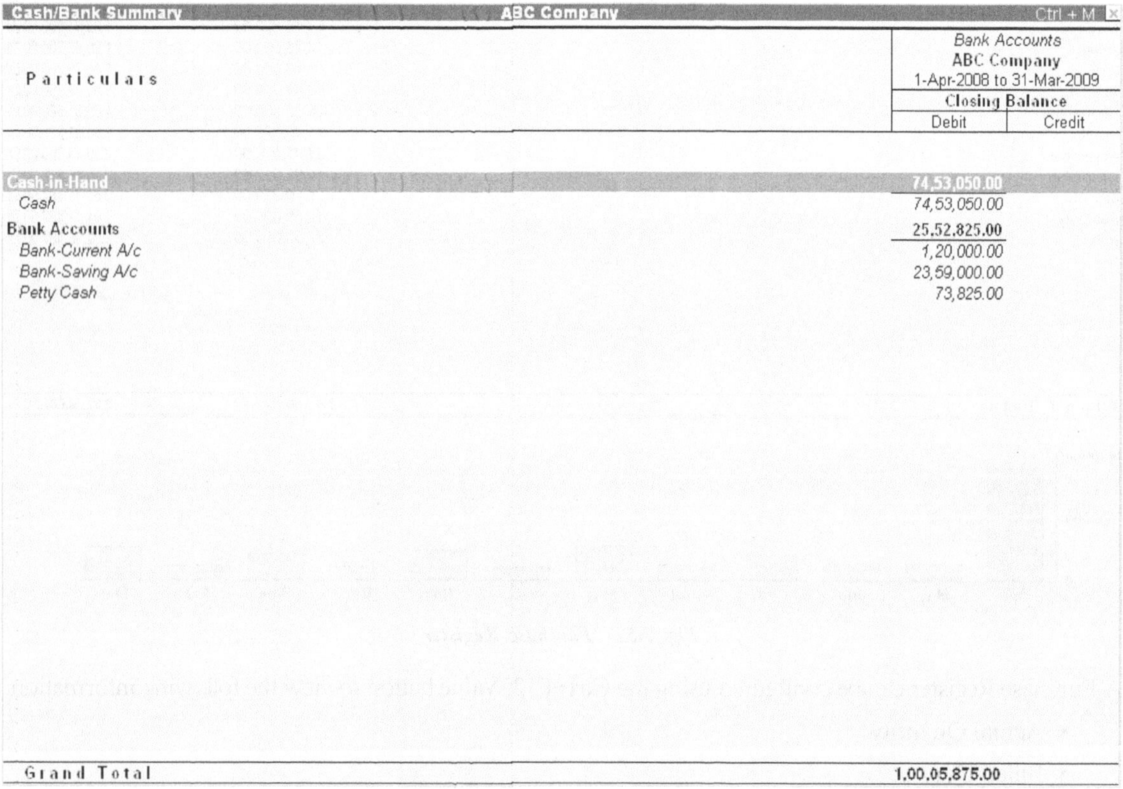

Cash/Bank Summary | ABC Company | Ctrl + M

Particulars	Bank Accounts ABC Company 1-Apr-2008 to 31-Mar-2009 Closing Balance Debit	Credit
Cash-in-Hand	**74,53,050.00**	
Cash	*74,53,050.00*	
Bank Accounts	**25,52,825.00**	
Bank-Current A/c	*1,20,000.00*	
Bank-Saving A/c	*23,59,000.00*	
Petty Cash	*73,825.00*	
Grand Total	**1,00,05,875.00**	

Fig. 7.53 Cash/Bank Summary

Place the highlight bar over the figures for the month of May, press Enter to display the Ledger Vouchers screen. Note that all the vouchers for May are listed. Press Alt + F2 to view the vouchers for the months of May and July.

The Ledger Vouchers screen is displayed as shown next.

The Cash ledger account screen displays the debit and credit amounts of all the vouchers for the period specified.

Ledger Vouchers — ABC Company — Ctrl + M

Ledger: Cash — 1-May-2008 to 31-Jul-2008

Date	Particulars	Vch Type	Vch No.	Debit	Credit
31-5-2008	Customer A	Receipt	4	5,25,000.00	
5-6-2008	Sales Account	Retail Invoice	24	1,25,000.00	
1-7-2008	Customer A	Receipt	7	1,25,000.00	
30-7-2008	Frieght Charges	Payment	17		800.00
		Opening Balance :		3,41,350.00	
		Current Total :		7,75,000.00	800.00
		Closing Balance :		11,15,550.00	

Fig. 7.54 Ledger Voucher Screen

Accessing F12: Configure - here you can view the highest or lowest cash balance on a particular date.

The Ledger Monthly Summary screen is displayed as shown:

Configuration

Nett transactions only	? No
Show Closing Balances	? Yes
Show Percentages	? No
Appearance of Names	: Name Only
Scale Factor for Values	: Default
Periodicity to use	: Monthly
Show Average Details	? No
Show High/Low Details	? Yes

Graphs

Show with Graph	? No

Display Multi-Column Cash Book

To display Multi-Column Cash Book, you need to select multiple ledgers and use Alt+C. By default the Multi-Columnar Cash Book is displayed for the current period. Press F2 button (Change Period) to display the multi-column cash book for a selected period.

Ledger Monthly Summary — ABC Company — Ctrl + M

Cash — ABC Company — 1-Apr-2008 to 31-Mar-2009

Particulars	Transactions Debit	Transactions Credit	Closing Balance
Opening Balance			2,17,850.00 Dr
April	8,00,000.00	6,76,500.00	3,41,350.00 Dr
May	5,25,000.00		8,66,350.00 Dr
June	1,25,000.00		9,91,350.00 Dr
July	1,25,000.00	800.00	11,15,550.00 Dr
August	61,250.00		11,76,800.00 Dr
September			11,76,800.00 Dr
October	23,55,000.00	18,750.00	35,13,050.00 Dr
November			35,13,050.00 Dr
December			35,13,050.00 Dr
January	22,96,250.00	43,750.00	57,65,550.00 Dr
February	16,87,500.00		74,53,050.00 Dr
March			74,53,050.00 Dr
Grand Total	79,75,000.00	7,39,800.00	74,53,050.00 Dr
Highest Balance	(dt. 10-Oct-2008) 23,55,000.00	(dt. 10-Oct-2008) 5,32,500.00	(dt. 10-Oct-2008) 74,53,050.00 Dr
Lowest Balance	(dt. 1-Aug-2008) 15,000.00	(dt. 30-Jul-2008) 800.00	(dt. 1-Apr-2008) 3,14,650.00 Cr

Fig. 7.55 Ledger Monthly Summary

Use the New Column button to bring up the Petty Cash book Monthly Summary along with the discount column monthly summary.

Press New Column on the Button bar or ALT+C and change the Name of Ledger.

The columnar report is displayed as shown:

Ledger Monthly Summary | ABC Company | Ctrl + M

Particulars	Cash ABC Company 1-Apr-2008 to 31-Mar-2009			Petty Cash ABC Company 1-Apr-2008 to 31-Mar-2009		
	Transactions		Closing Balance	Transactions		Closing Balance
	Debit	Credit		Debit	Credit	
Opening Balance			**2,17,850.00 Dr**			**1,00,000.00 Dr**
April	8,00,000.00	6,76,500.00	3,41,350.00 Dr		6,125.00	93,875.00 Dr
May	5,25,000.00		8,66,350.00 Dr		3,050.00	90,825.00 Dr
June	1,25,000.00		9,91,350.00 Dr		5,300.00	85,525.00 Dr
July	1,25,000.00	800.00	11,15,550.00 Dr		3,300.00	82,225.00 Dr
August	61,250.00		11,76,800.00 Dr			82,225.00 Dr
September			11,76,800.00 Dr			82,225.00 Dr
October	23,55,000.00	18,750.00	35,13,050.00 Dr		3,700.00	78,525.00 Dr
November			35,13,050.00 Dr			78,525.00 Dr
December			35,13,050.00 Dr			78,525.00 Dr
January	22,96,250.00	43,750.00	57,65,550.00 Dr		4,700.00	73,825.00 Dr
February	16,87,500.00		74,53,050.00 Dr			73,825.00 Dr
March			74,53,050.00 Dr			73,825.00 Dr
Grand Total	79,75,000.00	7,39,800.00	74,53,050.00 Dr		26,175.00	73,825.00 Dr

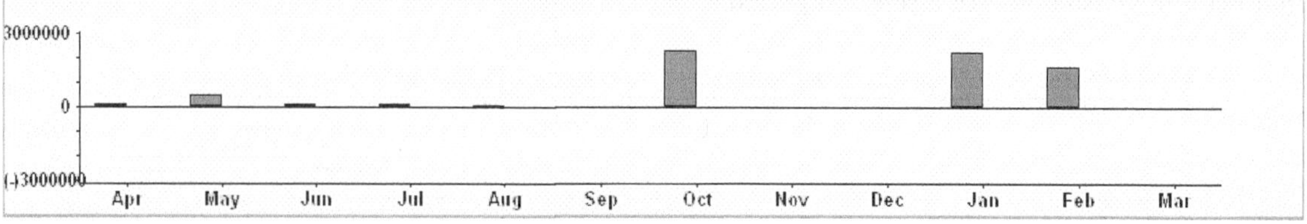

3000000
0
(-)3000000
Apr May Jun Jul Aug Sep Oct Nov Dec Jan Feb Mar

Fig. 7.56 Columnar Report

Note: Comparison of data using multi-columnar reporting is useful when you want to display multiple ledgers along with their opening or closing balances.

Display Bank Book

To view the Bank Book Summary

```
Go to Gateway of Tally > Display > Account Books > Cash/Bank Book(s)
```

If you have more than one bank account, select the required Bank account and press Enter to display the Ledger Monthly Summary.

Display Multi-Column Bank Book

Tally.ERP 9 allows the facility to compare bank book with cash book or two or more banks by using the multi-columnar reporting facility. You can compare the information for multiple periods (year, month, or user defined period) for two or more banks on the same screen, instead of toggling between different periods / ledgers.

Cash/Bank Summary — ABC Company — Ctrl + M

Particulars	Bank Accounts ABC Company 1-Apr-2008 to 31-Mar-2009 Closing Balance	
	Debit	Credit
Cash-in-Hand	74,53,050.00	
Cash	74,53,050.00	
Bank Accounts	25,52,825.00	
Bank-Current A/c	1,20,000.00	
Bank-Saving A/c	23,59,000.00	
Petty Cash	73,825.00	
Grand Total	1,00,05,875.00	

Fig. 7.57 Cash/Bank Summary

Ledger Monthly Summary — ABC Company — Ctrl + M

Particulars	Bank-Saving A/c ABC Company 1-Apr-2008 to 31-Jul-2008 Transactions		Closing Balance
	Debit	Credit	
Opening Balance			8,00,000.00 Dr
April	79,000.00	20,000.00	8,59,000.00 Dr
May	12,00,000.00	70,000.00	19,89,000.00 Dr
June	2,50,000.00	25,000.00	22,14,000.00 Dr
July	15,00,000.00	13,55,000.00	23,59,000.00 Dr
Grand Total	30,29,000.00	14,70,000.00	23,59,000.00 Dr

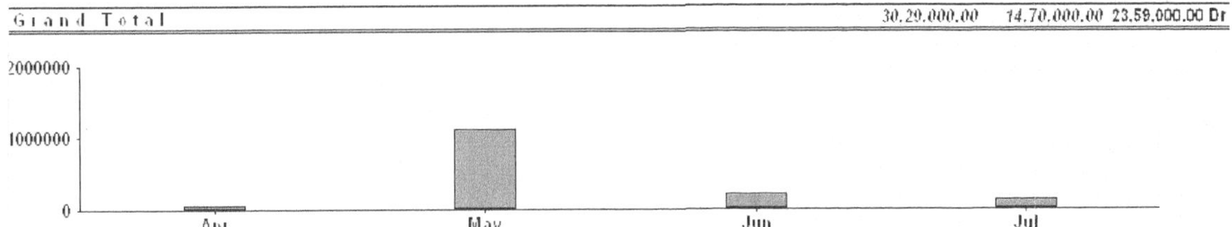

Fig. 7.58 Multi Column Bank Book

Use the New Column button to bring up the Cash book Monthly Summary.

Press New Column on the Button bar or ALT+C and change the Name of Ledger.

Based on the option selected in Tally.ERP 9 now displays comparisons as shown:

Daily Balances & Transactions Value

Tally.ERP 9 provides a facility of viewing Cash/Bank books in daily breakup basis. You can view information for total transaction value as well as closing balances for all days. In the same report the you can also get daily average details as well as high and low details for the month.

Select Display > Accounts Books > Cash/Bank Books > Drill down from the Bank Ledger and select a particular month and press Enter.

```
Press F6 (Daily Break Up) then select F12 (Configuration) and Activate Show
Average Details and Show High / Low Details.
```

The Daily Breakup of Ledger screen is displayed as shown:

Note: Tally.ERP 9 displays Average details for the month with High and Low details as well. You may also drill down to voucher level.

Ledger Monthly Summary — ABC Company — Ctrl + M

Particulars	Bank-Saving A/c, ABC Company, 1-Apr-2008 to 31-Jul-2008			Cash, ABC Company, 1-Apr-2008 to 31-Jul-2008		
	Transactions		Closing Balance	Transactions		Closing Balance
	Debit	Credit		Debit	Credit	
Opening Balance			8,00,000.00 Dr			2,17,850.00 Dr
April	79,000.00	20,000.00	8,59,000.00 Dr	8,00,000.00	6,76,500.00	3,41,350.00 Dr
May	12,00,000.00	70,000.00	19,89,000.00 Dr	5,25,000.00		8,66,350.00 Dr
June	2,50,000.00	25,000.00	22,14,000.00 Dr	1,25,000.00		9,91,350.00 Dr
July	15,00,000.00	13,55,000.00	23,59,000.00 Dr	1,25,000.00	800.00	11,15,550.00 Dr
Grand Total	30,29,000.00	14,70,000.00	23,59,000.00 Dr	15,75,000.00	6,77,300.00	11,15,550.00 Dr

Fig. 7.60 Ledger Monthly Summary

Ledger Vouchers — ABC Company — Ctrl + M

Ledger: **Bank-Saving A/c** — **1-Apr-2008 to 30-Apr-2008**

Date	Particulars	Vch Type	Vch No.	Debit	Credit
5-4-2008	Customer C	Receipt	1	25,000.00	
18-4-2008	Sales @ 12.5%	Tax Invoice	3	54,000.00	
30-4-2008	Staff Welfare	Payment	4		20,000.00
		Opening Balance :		8,00,000.00	
		Current Total :		79,000.00	20,000.00
		Closing Balance :		8,59,000.00	

Fig. 7.61 Ledger Vouchers Summary

Bank Reconciliation

Reconciling the company's bank books with the banker's statement is a regular task of accounting. In Tally.ERP 9, Reconciliation of Bank Books facilitates the following:

Ability to check back the correctness of reconciliation

Tally.ERP 9 uses Bank Date to mark the voucher. For instance, if you issue a cheque on 8th April and your bank clears it on 19th April, you would set the Bank Date for the voucher as 19th April. This means that when you need to check back later, whether the entry made by you is correct, you will only need to verify the bank statement of the 19th.

Recovering the reconciliation of any date

This is of crucial importance in Auditing. The Bank Reconciliation is one of the pre-requisites of auditing and verification of the correctness of accounts at the year end. However, it is not a real-time task, meaning auditors do not do it on the first day of the next year.

Note: For example, a reconciliation made on 31st March, should be viewable even in August, by when almost all the cheques would have subsequently been marked Reconciled. Tally.ERP 9 provides you with a facility of achieving this also.

Bank accounts may have a different Starting Date for reconciliation purposes. When you create a bank account, you are prompted to give an Effective Date for Reconciliation. Normally, this would be the Books Beginning from date itself.

Daily Breakup of Ledger | ABC Company | Ctrl + M

Particulars	Bank-Saving A/c ABC Company 1-Apr-2008 to 30-Apr-2008		
	Transactions		Closing Balance
	Debit	Credit	
Opening Balance			8,00,000.00 Dr
1-Apr			8,00,000.00 Dr
2-Apr			8,00,000.00 Dr
3-Apr			8,00,000.00 Dr
4-Apr			8,00,000.00 Dr
5-Apr	25,000.00		8,25,000.00 Dr
6-Apr			8,25,000.00 Dr
7-Apr			8,25,000.00 Dr
8-Apr			8,25,000.00 Dr
9-Apr			8,25,000.00 Dr
10-Apr			8,25,000.00 Dr
11-Apr			8,25,000.00 Dr
12-Apr			8,25,000.00 Dr
13-Apr			8,25,000.00 Dr
14-Apr			8,25,000.00 Dr
15-Apr			8,25,000.00 Dr
16-Apr			8,25,000.00 Dr
17-Apr			8,25,000.00 Dr
18-Apr	54,000.00		8,79,000.00 Dr
19-Apr			8,79,000.00 Dr
20-Apr			8,79,000.00 Dr
			10 more ...
Grand Total	79,000.00	20,000.00	8,59,000.00 Dr
Average	2,633.33	666.67	8,44,400.00 Dr
Highest Balance	(dt. 18-Apr-2008) 54,000.00	(dt. 18-Apr-2008) 20,000.00	(dt. 18-Apr-2008) 8,79,000.00 Dr
Lowest Balance	(dt. 5-Apr-2008) 25,000.00	(dt. 30-Apr-2008) 20,000.00	(dt. 31-Mar-2008) 8,00,000.00 Dr

Fig. 7.62 Ledger Datewise

However, you could have imported data from a previous version of Tally or from any other system (where the reconciliation process was not available or was different). In that case, you may not want to reconcile the bank account with your bank statements from the very beginning. Give the date from which you want the reconciliation to be done. Once you do this, entries made earlier than this date would not appear for reconciliation, but would be shown as a reconciled Opening Balance.

A quick experiment with Reconciliation will show you what it all means. Here is how you go about it:

1. Bring up the monthly summary of any bank book.

   (You can choose a bank book from any of the following: Balance Sheet, Trial Balance or Display > Account Books > Cash/Bank Books)

2. Bring the cursor to the first month (typically April), and press Enter. This brings up the vouchers for the month of April. Since this is a bank account, there is an additional button F5: Reconcile on the button bar, press to the right. Press F5 to reconcile.

Bank Reconciliation | ABC Company | Ctrl + M

Ledger: Bank-Saving A/c | (Reconciliation) | 1-Apr-2008 to 30-Apr-2008

Date	Particulars	Vch Type	Bank Date	Debit	Credit
5-4-2008	Customer C	Receipt	1-5-2008	25,000.00	
18-4-2008	Sales @ 12.5%	Tax Invoice	5-5-2008	54,000.00	
30-4-2008	Staff Welfare	Payment	15-5-2008		20,000.00
			Balance as per Company Books :	8,59,000.00	
			Amounts not reflected in Bank :	79,000.00	20,000.00
			Balance as per Bank :	8,00,000.00	

Fig. 7.63 Bank Reconciliation

3. The display goes to the Reconciliation mode, which can be edited. The primary component of the current screen is the column for Bankers Date.

4. The Reconciliation found at the bottom of the screen shows:
   - Balance as per Company Books
   - Amounts not reflected in Bank
   - Balance as per Bank

The Balance as per Company Books reflects the balance as on the last date (in the example, it is 30th April).

The Amounts not reflected in Bank are the debit and credit sums of all those vouchers, whose Bank Date is either BLANK, or LATER than 30-Apr (*i.e.*, these vouchers have not yet been reflected in the bank statement).

The Balance as per Bank is the net effect of the Book Balance offset by the amounts not reflected in the Bank – which must be equal to the balance in the bank statement.

Note: Some discrepancies may persist due to entries made

Configuration

Select vouchers to show	:	All Vouchers
Format	:	Condensed
Show Narrations also	?	No
Show Forex details also	?	No
Show Forex Transactions only	?	No
Include Opening Balances	?	Yes
(set as 'no' to remove from filtered reports)		
Show Reconciled Vouchers also	?	Yes
Allow back dated Reconciliation	?	No
Appearance of Names	:	Name Only

in the bank statement, which you have not yet entered in your books. You would reconcile these manually, and print your reconciliation.

As you mark the individual vouchers by setting the Bank Date, you will notice that the Reconciliation at the bottom of the screen keeps updating the changes. Once this process is complete, press Ctrl + A or Enter as many times as necessary to skip over the unmarked vouchers and accept the screen.

Gateway of Tally ....
Display Menu ....
Account Books ....

Journal Register

Journal Register
Debit Note Register
Credit Note Register
Quit

The next time you opt for reconciliation, the screen displays only those vouchers that remain un-reconciled. You can also display vouchers that are already marked as reconciled, in case you need to edit the marking, by using F12: Configure.

Set Show Reconciled Vouchers also to Yes to see the reconciled vouchers.

Note: It is not possible to reconcile opening balance and can be done only with available physical transactions.

Set Allow back dated Reconciliation to Yes to enter bank dates which are lesser than the Voucher date.

Press Alt+P or click on the Print button to print your reconciliation report.

The print preview screen is displayed as shown on next page.

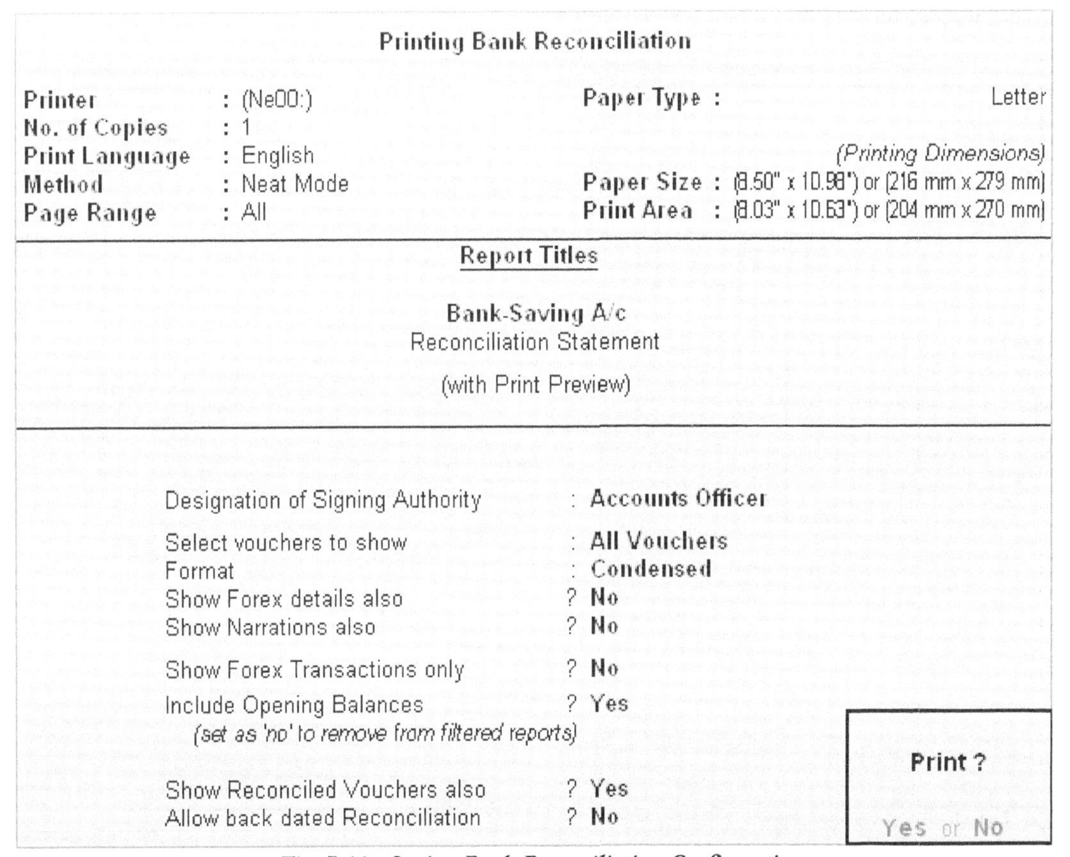

Printing Bank Reconciliation

Printer : (Ne00:)
No. of Copies : 1
Print Language : English
Method : Neat Mode
Page Range : All

Paper Type : Letter
(Printing Dimensions)
Paper Size : (8.50" x 10.98") or (216 mm x 279 mm)
Print Area : (8.03" x 10.63") or (204 mm x 270 mm)

Report Titles

Bank-Saving A/c
Reconciliation Statement
(with Print Preview)

Designation of Signing Authority : **Accounts Officer**
Select vouchers to show : **All Vouchers**
Format : **Condensed**
Show Forex details also ? **No**
Show Narrations also ? **No**
Show Forex Transactions only ? **No**
Include Opening Balances ? **Yes**
(set as 'no' to remove from filtered reports)
Show Reconciled Vouchers also ? **Yes**
Allow back dated Reconciliation ? **No**

Print ?
Yes or No

Fig. 7.64 Setting Bank Reconciliation Configuration

ABC Company

Bank-Saving A/c

Reconciliation Statement

1-Apr-2008 to 30-Apr-2008

Page 1

Date	Particulars	Vch Type	Bank Date	Debit	Credit
5-4-2008	Customer C	Receipt	1-5-2008	25,000.00	
18-4-2008	Sales @ 12.5%	Tax Invoice	5-5-2008	54,000.00	
30-4-2008	Staff Welfare	Payment	15-5-2008		20,000.00
		Balance as per Company Books :		8,59,000.00	
		Amounts not reflected in Bank :		79,000.00	20,000.00
		Balance as per Bank :		8,00,000.00	

Fig. 7.65 Print Preview

Display Journal Register

Journal register report displays all the journal vouchers that have been passed.

To view journal register details

Go to Gateway of Tally > Display > Account Books > Journal Register.

The Journal Register screen is displayed as shown:

Journal Register ABC Company Ctrl + M

Particulars	Journal ABC Company 1-Apr-2008 to 31-Mar-2009 Transactions Total Vouchers	(cancelled)
April	18	
May	0	
June	6	
July	1	
August	0	
September	0	
October	0	
November	0	
December	0	
January	0	
February	0	
March	0	
Grand Total		

Fig. 7.66 Journal Register

You can also view transactions related to other voucher types like sales or purchases in this screen.

To change voucher type Press F4 at the journal register screen which will then display the details of the selected voucher type.

Display Day Book

The Day Book lists all transactions made in a particular day and by default displays the last voucher entry date of a regular voucher. It could also be set up to list all the transactions made over a certain period. Transactions include all financial vouchers, reversing and memorandum journals as well as inventory vouchers.

In Tally.ERP 9, the Day Book is by default displayed for the current date (as on the last date of voucher entry). However, you may specify the required period, as per your requirements.

To view the Day Book,

```
Go to Gateway of Tally > Display > Daybook
```

- Press F2: Period on the button bar or press the key Alt+F2
- Specify the required period.

The Day Book for a specified period will display as shown :

Day Book — ABC Company — Ctrl + M

Day Book — 1-Apr-2008 to 31-Mar-2009

Date	Particulars	Vch Type	Vch No.	Debit Amount / Inwards Qty	Credit Amount / Outwards Qty
1-4-2008	Office Expenses	Payment	1	1,550.00	
1-4-2008	Customer A	Retail Invoice	1	61,000.00	
1-4-2008	Bright Industries	Purchase	1		47,500.00
1-4-2008	Unisys Global Systems	Purchase	2		90,900.00
1-4-2008	Supplier C	Purchase	3		18,36,000.00
1-4-2008	Cash	Purchase	4		5,32,500.00
1-4-2008	2 GB RAM Sticks	Physical Stock	1	1,300 Nos	
1-4-2008	Cooling Equipment	Stock Journal	1	2 Nos	
2-4-2008	Customer C	Retail Invoice	2	18,750.00	
2-4-2008	Global Traders	Purchase	5		28,125.00
2-4-2008	Cooling Equipment	Stock Journal	2	2 Nos	
3-4-2008	Customer B	Tax Invoice	1	4,16,000.00	
3-4-2008	Cooling Equipment	Stock Journal	3	2 Nos	
4-4-2008	Customer B	Tax Invoice	2	88,400.00	
5-4-2008	Customer C	Receipt	1		25,000.00
5-4-2008	Customer C	Credit Note	1		12,000.00
5-4-2008	Customer A	Retail Invoice	3	5,25,000.00	
5-4-2008	Customer A	Retail Invoice	4	2,57,250.00	
5-4-2008	Supplier A	Purchase	6		10,12,000.00
5-4-2008	Equipment Sales Corporation	Purchase	7		7,80,000.00
6-4-2008	Global Computech Pvt Ltd..	Retail Invoice	5	2,10,000.00	
7-4-2008	Customer A	Retail Invoice	6	6,69,500.00	
9-4-2008	Supplier A	Purchase	8		1,10,000.00
10-4-2008	Entry Tax	Payment	2	475.00	
10-4-2008	Customer C	Credit Note	2		1,875.00
10-4-2008	Supplier A	Purchase	9		6,02,000.00
15-4-2008	General Expenses	Payment	3	1,600.00	
15-4-2008	Capital Account	Receipt	2		8,00,000.00
15-4-2008	Cash	Purchase	10		1,44,000.00
15-4-2008	2 GB RAM Sticks	Physical Stock	2	1,300 Nos	
17-4-2008	Customer B	Credit Note	3		55,936.00

172 more ...

Fig. 7.67 Day Book for a Specified Period

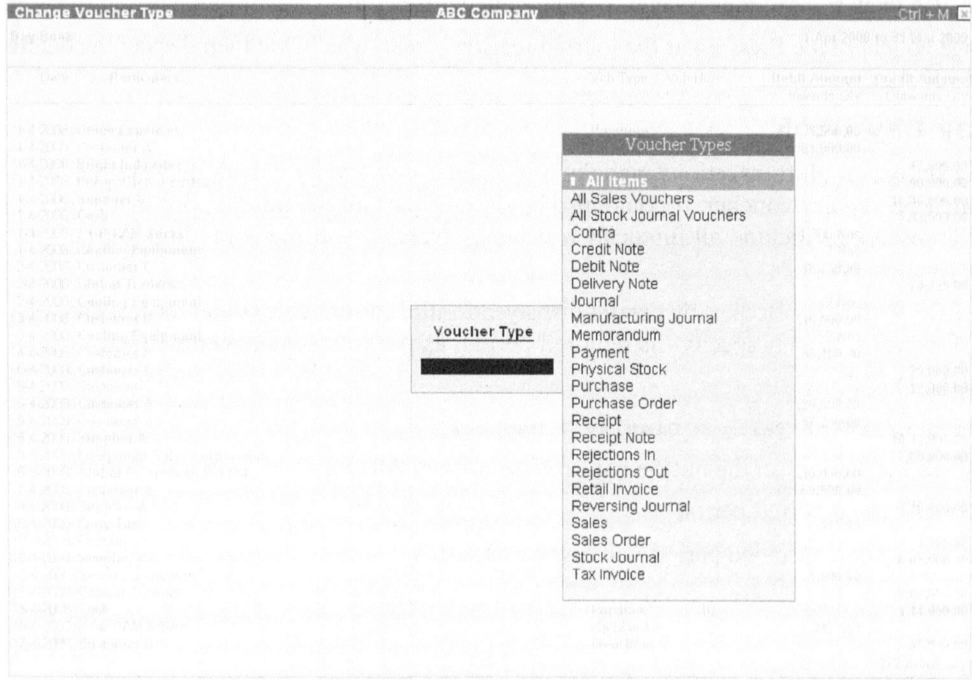

Fig. 7.68 Changing Voucher Type

To view Day Book for a particular voucher type, you can press F4: Chg Vch button from the button bar Select the required Voucher Type to display. The screen is displayed as shown:

Day Book | **ABC Company** | Ctrl + M

List of Retail Invoice Vouchers — **1-Apr-2008 to 31-Mar-2009**

Date	Particulars	Vch Type	Vch No.	Debit Amount	Credit Amount
1-4-2008	Customer A	Retail Invoice	1	61,000.00	
2-4-2008	Customer C	Retail Invoice	2	18,750.00	
5-4-2008	Customer A	Retail Invoice	3	5,25,000.00	
5-4-2008	Customer A	Retail Invoice	4	2,57,250.00	
6-4-2008	Global Computech Pvt Ltd..	Retail Invoice	5	2,10,000.00	
7-4-2008	Customer A	Retail Invoice	6	6,69,500.00	
19-4-2008	Customer A	Retail Invoice	7	3,50,200.00	
24-4-2008	Customer B	Retail Invoice	8	6,30,000.00	
30-4-2008	Blue Nile Stationeries	Retail Invoice	10	1,70,000.00	
30-4-2008	Customer C	Retail Invoice	11	96,000.00	
30-4-2008	Blue Nile Stationeries	Retail Invoice	12	64,375.00	
1-5-2008	Global Computech Pvt Ltd..	Retail Invoice	13	1,75,000.00	
1-5-2008	Global Computech Pvt Ltd..	Retail Invoice	14	7,45,000.00	
1-5-2008	Customer A	Retail Invoice	15	56,000.00	
1-5-2008	Customer A	Retail Invoice	16	56,000.00	
1-5-2008	UN Diplomatic Mission	Retail Invoice	17	17,50,000.00	
1-5-2008	Customer A	Retail Invoice	18	16,800.00	
30-5-2008	Innovative Solutions Pvt Ltd	Retail Invoice	19	12,500.00	
1-6-2008	Silverline Trading Corporation	Retail Invoice	20	95,000.00	
2-6-2008	Blue Nile Stationeries	Retail Invoice	21	1,25,000.00	
3-6-2008	Silverline Trading Corporation	Retail Invoice	22	2,50,000.00	
4-6-2008	Bank-Saving A/c	Retail Invoice	23	2,50,000.00	
5-6-2008	Cash	Retail Invoice	24	1,25,000.00	
6-6-2008	Customer A	Retail Invoice	25	1,25,000.00	
7-6-2008	Unisys Global Systems	Retail Invoice	26	1,10,000.00	
8-6-2008	Customer C	Retail Invoice	27	8,56,800.00	
9-6-2008	Innovative Solutions Pvt Ltd	Retail Invoice	28	55,000.00	
10-6-2008	Innovative Solutions Pvt Ltd	Retail Invoice	29	1,10,000.00	
11-6-2008	Customer C	Retail Invoice	30	66,000.00	
					8 more ...
			Total:	96,04,055.00	

Fig. 7.69 Day Book of Retail Invoices

Statements and Reports

The Statements of Accounts are derived from individual transactions but are not statutory requirements. Financial Statements though derived from individual transactions tend to show summary totals, ratios and statistics, analyzing a company's financial data in a wide variety of ways. Financial statements include Balance Sheet, Profit & Loss A/c,and Cash Flow Analysis and form part of the statutory requirements in most countries.

1. All books are displayed as a monthly summary with opening and closing balances.
2. Select a month and press Enter to display all transactions for the month. The opening and closing balances as well as the total of all transactions are displayed.
3. Select a transaction to bring up the voucher. The voucher displays either in alteration mode or simply displays depending on your access rights.

Let us see some typical examples of how to display the books of account and financial statements. You will then be able to experiment with other statements for yourself.

Display Group Summary

The group summary statement shows the closing balances of the accounts of a selected group for a specified period up to the current date. The default view is that of sub-groups within a group.

To view group summary,

```
Go to Gateway of Tally > Display > Account Books > Group Summary> Select a group
```

In this example, select group Indirect Expenses and press Enter.

The Group Summary screen is displayed as shown:

Group Summary — ABC Company — Ctrl + M

Particulars	Indirect Expenses ABC Company 1-Apr-2008 to 31-Mar-2009 Closing Balance	
	Debit	Credit
A/C Repair	7,400.00	
General Expenses	6,200.00	
Interest Account	16,275.00	
Office Expenses	12,100.00	
Staff Welfare	27,500.00	
Grand Total	69,475.00	

Fig. 7.70 Group Summary

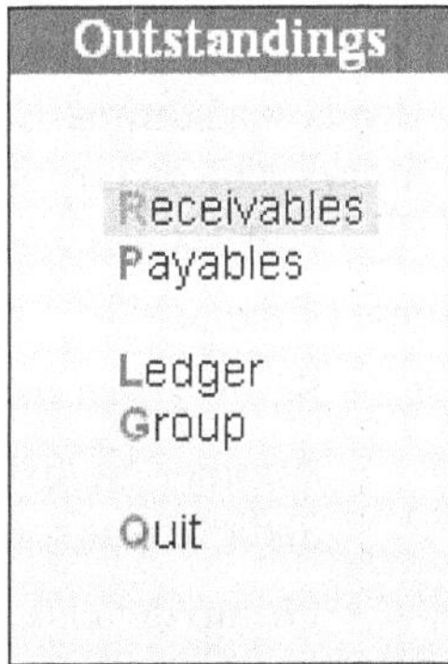

Statements of Accounts

Statements of Accounts are derived from the transactions recorded in the books of accounts. In Tally.ERP 9, they are generated for cost centres and outstanding accounts.

Outstandings

The Outstanding Statement in Tally.ERP 9 displays the status of receivables and payables of the business concern. These are the two important components of the working capital of every business entity. Receivables form a major component of current assets whereas payables form a component of current liabilities. Both determine the short-term liquidity and financial health of the company considerably. Therefore, effective control of the receivable and payable is a must for the financial soundness of a business concern.

The Outstanding Statement Display in Tally.ERP 9 can be any one of the following.

Receivables

This statement displays the sundry debtor's bill-wise balance till date. It is to be noted here that since this statement displays the information bill by bill, the same needs to be activated while recording the transactions in Tally.ERP 9. This statement provides the following information:

- The effective date of the invoice.
- The reference number given in the invoice while providing the bill-wise details.
- The party name and the outstanding balance of a particular invoice.

Payable

Payable outstanding displays the outstanding bill-wise balance of the sundry creditors. Again, this information can be viewed only on activating and entering the bill-wise details while recording the transactions. The information provided is similar to the receivables outstanding.

The uses of a payable outstanding statement are as follows:

- The pending party-wise bills and the number of days by which they are over-due can be viewed.
- The interest liability that is likely to arise can be estimated with the help of the number of days over-due.
- The credit period allowed by the party can be analysed and the need for arranging short-term funds can be evaluated.

Ledger

This summarises and displays the outstanding balance information with respect to each party. Thus, the bill status of a particular party account can be viewed with the help of this statement. Some of the uses of a ledger outstanding statement are:

- It displays information similar to the receivable and payable outstanding statements, but with respect to a particular party ledger. Thus, this statement can be put to a similar use as stated above.
- It facilitates the viewing of the address and contact details of the party selected, by using the Alt + C button.
- It can be used to generate reminder letters to be sent to the party specifying the details of outstanding bills. It is one of the very useful features in Tally.ERP 9 used with the Print Option.

Group

It displays a summarised view of the balances of all the ledgers under a particular group. For example, Sundry Debtors Group will display all the party ledgers with their account balances. It can further be drilled down to each account to show the bill-wise outstanding for that account.

Some of the uses of a group outstanding statement are as follows:

- Summarised information can be viewed and analysed for each group.
- Another group can be displayed in a column using the Alt+C: New Column button on the screen and comparisons can be made.
- Group details can be printed and submitted as a supporting schedule to the financial statements.

- The detailed break-up of parties under the chosen group and their pending balances can be viewed.

Display List of Vouchers

Vouchers or transactions of a similar nature or type entered over a period of time are collated and listed together to present meaningful information. There are different types of voucher lists, *e.g.*, Group Vouchers, Ledger Vouchers, Stock Vouchers, Godown/Location Vouchers, etc.

Display Group Vouchers

Group Vouchers is a list of all vouchers having at least one ledger account entry belonging to the selected group. This statement is useful when you want to list all transactions for a particular group.

To view the Group Vouchers

```
Go to Gateway of Tally > Display >Account Books > Group
Vouchers
```

Select the option Group Voucher and then Select Group Name, *e.g.*, Current Assets Press Enter.

Press F2: Period and change the period, if required.

The following screen is displayed as shown:

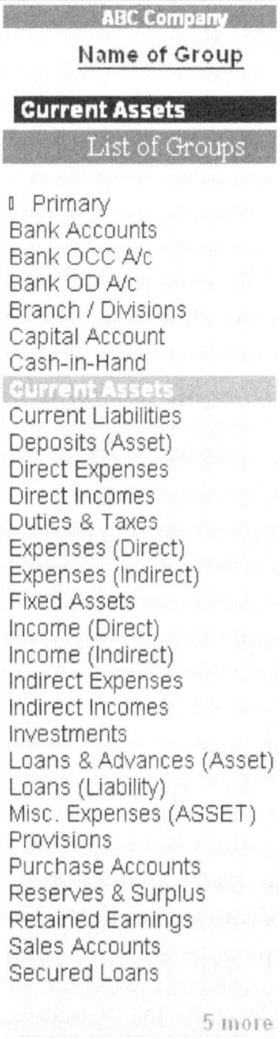

Group Vouchers ABC Company Ctrl + M

Group: Current Assets 1-Apr-2008 to 31-Mar-2009

Date	Particulars	Vch Type	Vch No.	Debit	Credit
1-4-2008	Sales - Zero Rated	Retail Invoice	1	61,000.00	
1-4-2008	Office Expenses	Payment	1		1,550.00
1-4-2008	Purchase @ 1%	Purchase	2		90,900.00
1-4-2008	Purchase	Purchase	4		5,32,500.00
2-4-2008	Sales - Tax Free	Retail Invoice	2	18,750.00	
3-4-2008	Sales @ 4%	Tax Invoice	1	4,16,000.00	
4-4-2008	Sales @ 4%	Tax Invoice	2	88,400.00	
5-4-2008	Sales @ 12.5%	Credit Note	1		12,000.00
5-4-2008	Bank-Saving A/c	Receipt	1	25,000.00	25,000.00
5-4-2008	Sales - Exports	Retail Invoice	3	5,25,000.00	
5-4-2008	Sales - Exports	Retail Invoice	4	2,57,250.00	
6-4-2008	Sales - Deemed Export	Retail Invoice	5	2,10,000.00	
7-4-2008	Sales - Interstate	Retail Invoice	6	6,69,500.00	
10-4-2008	Sales - Tax Free	Credit Note	2		1,875.00
10-4-2008	Petty Cash	Payment	2	475.00	475.00
15-4-2008	Purchase - Special Rate Goods	Purchase	10		1,44,000.00
15-4-2008	Capital Account	Receipt	2	8,00,000.00	
15-4-2008	General Expenses	Payment	3		1,600.00
17-4-2008	Sales @ 4%	Credit Note	3		55,936.00
18-4-2008	Sales @ 12.5%	Tax Invoice	3	54,000.00	
19-4-2008	Sales - Interstate	Retail Invoice	7	3,50,200.00	
24-4-2008	Sales @ 4%	Retail Invoice	8	6,30,000.00	
28-4-2008	Sales @ 4%	Tax Invoice	5	65,000.00	
29-4-2008	Sales Account	Tax Invoice	6	3,42,000.00	
29-4-2008	Sales @ 1%	Tax Invoice	7	36,36,000.00	
29-4-2008	Sales @ 12.5%	Credit Note	4		39,375.00
30-4-2008	Commission	Journal	10		475.00
30-4-2008	Commission	Journal	13	3,500.00	
30-4-2008	Sales- Resale of MRP Purchases	Retail Invoice	11	96,000.00	
30-4-2008	Sales @ 4%	Debit Note	2	5,200.00	
					74 more ...
		Opening Balance :		13,30,100.00	
		Current Total :		4,30,43,496.00	36,29,339.00
		Closing Balance :		4,07,44,257.00	

Fig. 7.71 Displaying Group Vouchers

Display Ledger Vouchers

To view the Ledger Vouchers,

```
Go to Gateway of Tally > Display > Account Books > Ledger >
Ledger account e.g. Commission account
```

Gateway of Tally ....
Display Menu ....
Account Books

Cash/Bank Book(s)

Ledger
Group Summary
Group Vouchers

Sales Register
Purchase Register

Journal Register

Quit

ABC Company
Name of Group

Current Assets

List of Groups

Primary
Bank Accounts
Bank OCC A/c
Bank OD A/c
Branch / Divisions
Capital Account
Cash-in-Hand
Current Assets
Current Liabilities
Deposits (Asset)
Direct Expenses
Direct Incomes
Duties & Taxes
Expenses (Direct)
Expenses (Indirect)
Fixed Assets
Income (Direct)
Income (Indirect)
Indirect Expenses
Indirect Incomes
Investments
Loans & Advances (Asset)
Loans (Liability)
Misc. Expenses (ASSET)
Provisions
Purchase Accounts
Reserves & Surplus
Retained Earnings
Sales Accounts
Secured Loans
5 more

Ledger Vouchers — ABC Company — Ctrl + M

Ledger: Commission — 1-Apr-2008 to 31-Mar-2009

Date	Particulars	Vch Type	Vch No.	Debit	Credit
1-4-2008	Supplier C	Purchase	3	36,000.00	
29-4-2008	Refund Claim	Journal	2	18,400.00	
30-4-2008	Supplier C	Debit Note	1		108.00
30-4-2008	Purchase @ 4%	Journal	7	1,000.00	
30-4-2008	Purchase @ 4%	Journal	9		23,000.00
30-4-2008	Entry Tax	Journal	10	475.00	
30-4-2008	CST @ 3%	Journal	11		19,500.00
30-4-2008	Special Incentive Scheme Output VAT	Journal	12	2,000.00	
30-4-2008	Entry Tax	Journal	13		2,500.00
30-4-2008	Special Incentive Scheme Output VAT	Journal	14		11,500.00
30-4-2008	Bright Industries	Debit Note	3		56,000.00
30-4-2008	Unisys Global Systems	Journal	15		5,000.00
30-4-2008	Output VAT @ 1%	Journal	17		42,787.00
1-5-2008	Bright Industries	Purchase	15	48,000.00	
10-7-2008	Bank-Saving A/c	Purchase	19	28,000.00	
		Opening Balance :		15,000.00	
		Current Total :		1,33,875.00	1,60,395.00
		Closing Balance :			11,520.00

Fig. 7.72 Displaying Ledger Vouchers

The list of vouchers for the current month is displayed. You can change the period using F2: Period button, as required. You may also access Ledger Vouchers by drilling down from different statements, such as Group Summary and Monthly Summary.

Buttons available in the Ledger Voucher screen:

Buttons	Shortcut Keys	Description and Use
F4	F4	To view the list of ledgers
F6	F6	To display daily balances
F7	F7	To view the monthly summary
F8	Alt + F8	To display columnar report which allows you to compare and analyse the data.
B	Alt + B	To display Bill wise detail for each transactions.

List of Accounts (Chart of Accounts)

Tally.ERP 9 gives you great flexibility in setting up your chart of accounts. It allows you to group your ledger accounts right at the time of creating your accounts chart. Your reports and statements reflect the desired classification at all times.

List of accounts displays the existing chart of accounts, listed as groups, in alphabetical order.

To view list of accounts:

`Go to Gateway of Tally > Display > List of Accounts`

You can Drill down to a ledger name to alter its details by pressing enter.

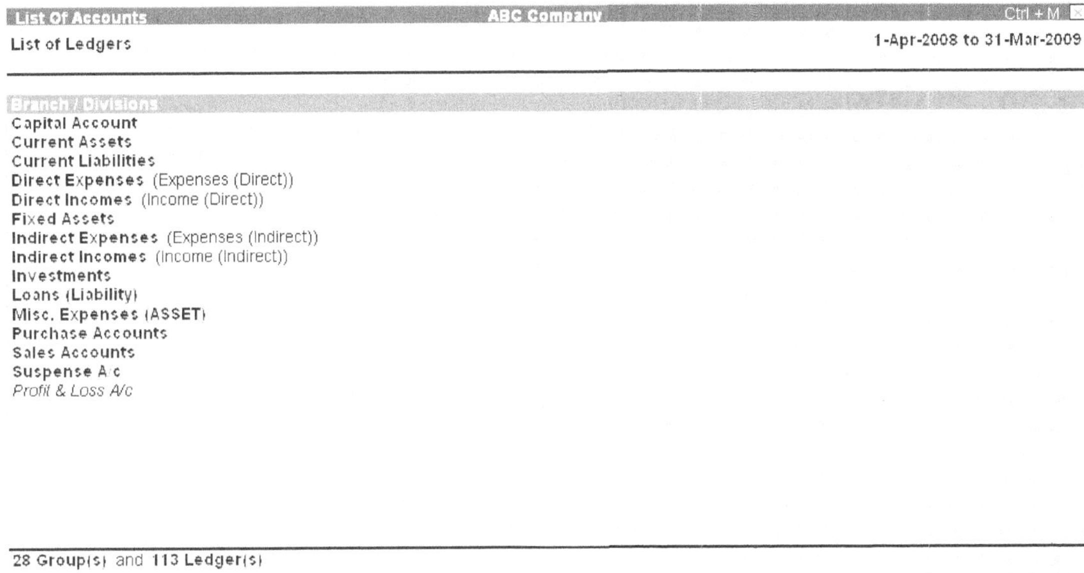
List Of Accounts | ABC Company | Ctrl + M

List of Ledgers | 1-Apr-2008 to 31-Mar-2009

Branch / Divisions

Capital Account
Current Assets
Current Liabilities
Direct Expenses (Expenses (Direct))
Direct Incomes (Income (Direct))
Fixed Assets
Indirect Expenses (Expenses (Indirect))
Indirect Incomes (Income (Indirect))
Investments
Loans (Liability)
Misc. Expenses (ASSET)
Purchase Accounts
Sales Accounts
Suspense A/c
Profit & Loss A/c

28 Group(s) and 113 Ledger(s)

Fig. 7.73 Chart of Accounts

At the highest level, accounts are classified into Capital or Revenue – and more specifically into Assets,

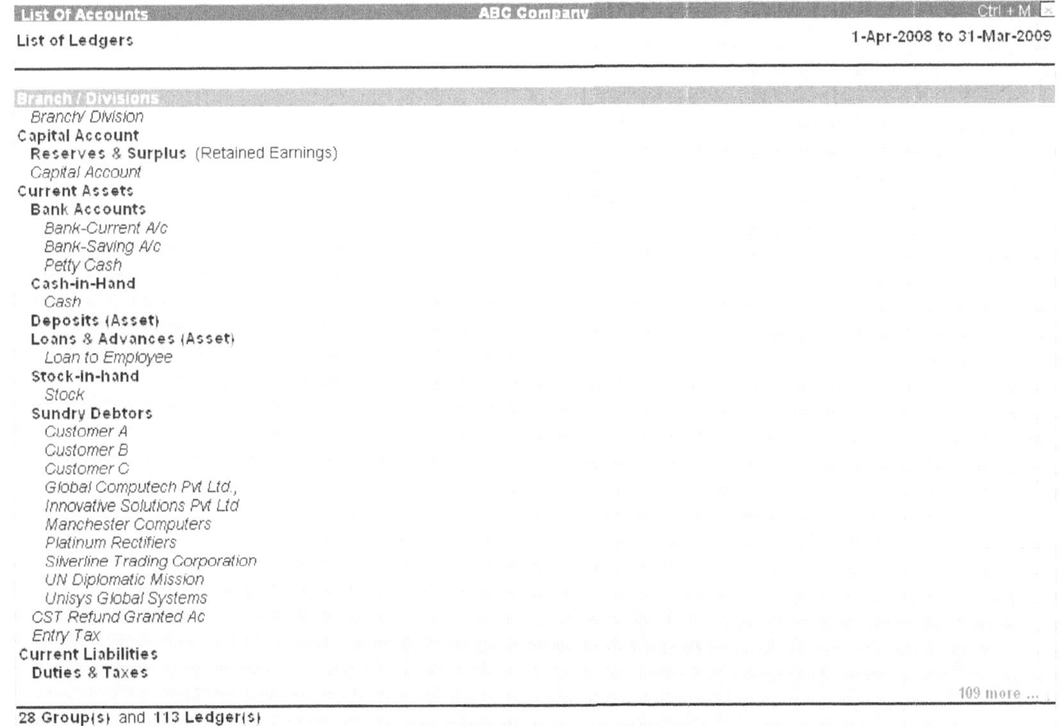
List Of Accounts | ABC Company | Ctrl + M

List of Ledgers | 1-Apr-2008 to 31-Mar-2009

Branch / Divisions

Branch/ Division
Capital Account
Reserves & Surplus (Retained Earnings)
Capital Account
Current Assets
Bank Accounts
Bank-Current A/c
Bank-Saving A/c
Petty Cash
Cash-in-Hand
Cash
Deposits (Asset)
Loans & Advances (Asset)
Loan to Employee
Stock-in-hand
Stock
Sundry Debtors
Customer A
Customer B
Customer C
Global Computech Pvt Ltd.,
Innovative Solutions Pvt Ltd
Manchester Computers
Platinum Rectifiers
Silverline Trading Corporation
UN Diplomatic Mission
Unisys Global Systems
CST Refund Granted Ac
Entry Tax
Current Liabilities
Duties & Taxes

109 more ...

28 Group(s) and 113 Ledger(s)

Fig. 7.74 List of Accounts

Liabilities, Income and Expenditure. Alternatively use the keys Shift+Enter from the group head to reduce the details. To record detailed transactions, you have to add further ledgers, groups and sub-groups of your choice. The ledgers in the Books of Accounts affect assets, liabilities, income or expenses. Tally.ERP 9 can generate a Profit & Loss account and a Balance Sheet immediately after a transaction has been entered. It can also generate a range of comprehensive financial statements and reports.

Display Statistics

The Statistics report displays the Masters created and the number of vouchers types entered. You can drill down to the transaction level from this report.

To view the Statistics report

Go to Gateway of Tally > Display > Statement of Accounts > Statistics

Registers from Statistics

To access the Voucher registers from the Statistics screen :

- Drill down a specific type of voucher to view the details. For example select Journal as Type of Vouchers and press enter.

Statistics — ABC Company — Ctrl + M

Types of Vouchers	ABC Company 1-Apr-2008 to 31-Mar-2009	Types of Accounts	ABC Company 1-Apr-2008 to 31-Mar-2009
Attendance	0	Groups	28
Contra	0	Ledgers	113
Credit Note	9	Cost Centres	2
Debit Note	3	Stock Groups	2
Delivery Note	4	Stock Categories	5
Journal	25	Stock Items	16
Manufacturing Journal	1	Godowns	3
Memorandum	0	Voucher Types	21
Payment	21	Units	2
Payroll	0	Currencies	2
Physical Stock	12 (1cancelled)		
Purchase	30		
Purchase Order	4		
Receipt	8		
Receipt Note	1		
Rejections In	1		
Rejections Out	1		
Retail Invoice	38		
Reversing Journal	0		
Sales	7		
Sales Order	6		
Stock Journal	12 (1cancelled)		
Tax Invoice	15		
Total	198 (2cancelled)		

The Voucher Monthly Register screen is displayed as shown:

Voucher Monthly Register — ABC Company — Ctrl + M

Particulars	Journal ABC Company 1-Apr-2008 to 31-Mar-2009 Transactions Total Vouchers (cancelled)
April	18
May	0
June	6
July	1
August	0
September	0
October	0
November	0
December	0
January	0
February	0
March	0

Fig. 7.74 Voucher Monthly Register

8 Inventory Reports of Tally.ERP 9

Display Inventory Reports & Statements

Inventory in Tally.ERP 9 operates in the same way as accounting with regard to displaying, modifying and printing reports. Tally.ERP 9 generates inventory reports based on the vouchers entered till date. You can use the customised reports to compare inventory data between different companies, periods of the financial year, and so on.

Highlight the item and press Enter to drill down to the next level of detail in a report. Repeat this process till you reach an individual voucher. Similarly, go back to higher levels by pressing Esc. The special features available for the currently displayed report are indicated on the button bar and can be selected with a single click of the mouse.

Displaying Stock Summary

Viewing Stock Summary

A Stock Summary is a statement of the stock-in-hand on a particular date. It is one of the primary inventory statements that is generated in Tally.ERP 9 and updates the stock record in real time as and when transactions are entered. Stock Summary provides information on stock groups and shows the quantity details, rate and closing value of the stock items under them.

The statement can be drilled-down, as with all Tally.ERP 9 reports, and configured to enable you to view different details, for instance, the total flow of stock can be viewed with a single report.

Tally.ERP 9 treats Stock Summary as one of the primary statements and makes it accessible directly from the Gateway of Tally.

To view Stock Summary

- Go to Gateway of Tally > Stock Summary
- By default Stock Group balances are displayed.
- Select Detailed to show another level of detail.

The detailed report which includes sub-groups or Stock Items (in cases where there are no sub-groups), is displayed as shown next.

The Stock Groups displays total quantities, as the unit of measure is the same for all the stock items added. A grand total is also available as there is a single unit of measure for all addable items. If there were different units of measure, then the grand total would not be calculated and displayed.

Configurations in Stock Summary

Stock Summary can be further configured to derive the following information.

1. Stock Flow: This can be viewed using the F12: Configure button on the Tally.ERP 9 screen. The flow of stock ranging from opening stock, goods inwards, goods outwards to the closing stock can

Particulars	ABC Company 1-Apr-2008 to 31-Mar-2009 Closing Balance Quantity	Rate	Value
Computer	5 Nos	1,69,114.37	8,45,571.85
Computer Spares	5,935 Nos	3,976.97	2,36,03,289.07
Cooling Equipment	6 Nos	450.00	2,700.00
CPU Fan	1,660 Nos	208.49	3,46,094.33
Hardware Manual	55 Nos	6,250.00	3,43,750.00
Rectified Spirit	200 Lts	400.00	80,000.00
Grand Total			2,52,21,405.25

Fig. 8.1 Stock Summary

be analyzed in terms of its quantity. It gives you an insight into the quantitative movement of each stock item. However, for reconciling the closing balance value, this report cannot be referred to, since the outward goods are valued at the sales price and not the cost price.

2. Profitability and Consumption: This can be viewed using the F7: Show Profit button on the screen. Stock Summary shows the profitability and consumption details for each stock item. This statement shows the quantity and value of the opening stock, inward goods, outward goods, closing stock and the value of consumption (using the cost method). This statement is used to reconcile the closing balance because here the closing value is derived by taking the consumption values instead of the outward goods at sales value.

Configuration	
Show Quantities	? Yes
Show Rates	? No
Show Values	? Yes
Show Opening Balance	? Yes
Show goods inwards	? Yes
Show goods outwards	? Yes
Show Closing Balance	? Yes
Show All Items (incl. zero balance)	? No
Show Consumption & Gross Profits	? No
Show using Alternate Units	? No
Show Tail Units of Compound Units	? No
Appearance of Stock Item Names	: Name Only
Appearance of Names	: Name Only
Scale Factor for Values	: Default
Sorting Method	: Alphabetical (Increasing)
Expand all levels in Detailed Format	? No

Stock Flow

You can configure the Stock Summary Statement to display the flow of goods.

- Select F12: Configure while on the Stock Summary screen.
- Set the configuration as shown.

The Stock Summary displays the flow of stock, *i.e.*, Opening Stock, Goods Inwards, Goods Outward and Closing Stock, as shown:

Stock Summary		ABC Company						Ctrl + M
Particulars	ABC Company 1-Apr-2008 to 31-Mar-2009							
	Opening Balance		Inwards		Outwards		Closing Balance	
	Quantity	Value	Quantity	Value	Quantity	Value	Quantity	Value
Computer			10 Nos	16,91,143.70	5 Nos	1,45,000.00	5 Nos	8,45,571.85
Computer Spares	41 Nos	55.000.00	9.100 Nos	2.77.66.284.30	3.206 Nos	3.09.47.451.95	5.935 Nos	2.36.03.289.07
Cooling Equipment	10 Nos	1,650.00	17 Nos	2,700.00	17 Nos	13,06,950.00	10 Nos	3,35,300.00
CPU Fan	25 Nos	3,125.00	2,920 Nos	4,91,642.00	1,260 Nos	2,83,050.00	1,685 Nos	3,49,666.95
Hardware Manual	35 Nos	21,000.00	100 Nos	6,25,000.00	45 Nos	16,875.00	90 Nos	3,64,750.00
Rectified Spirit	15 Lts	6,000.00	300 Lts	1,20,000.00	100 Lts	55,000.00	215 Lts	86,000.00
Grand Total		86.775.00		3.06.96.770.00		3.27.54.326.95		2.55.84.577.87

Fig. 8.2 Stock Summary with Opening, Closing Balances and other Details

The report is quantitatively reconciled, *i.e.*, Opening quantity + Inward Quantity – Outward Quantity = Closing Stock Quantity. However, this is incorrect for the values as the Outward Value displays Sale Values, not Cost. The Closing Stock Value is, however, based on Cost and the Cost Method adopted for each item. Value Reconciliation is possible if you are using Consumption figures instead of Sales Values.

Configuration	
Show Quantities	? Yes
Show Rates	? No
Show Values	? Yes
Show Opening Balance	? Yes
Show goods inwards	? Yes
Show goods outwards	? Yes
Show Closing Balance	? Yes
Show All Items (incl. zero balance)	? No
Show Consumption & Gross Profits	? Yes
Show using Alternate Units	? No
Show Tail Units of Compound Units	? No
Appearance of Stock Item Names	: Name Only
Appearance of Names	: Name Only
Scale Factor for Values	: Default
Sorting Method	: Alphabetical (Increasing)
Expand all levels in Detailed Format	? No

Profitability and Consumption

Stock Summary can also be expanded to show consumption and gross profits for each stock item.

- Select F7: Show Profits or F12: Configure while on the Stock Summary screen.
- Set Show Consumption and Gross Profits to Yes.

The Stock Summary report is displayed as shown.

Stock Summary		ABC Company									Ctrl + M
Particulars	ABC Company 1-Apr-2008 to 31-Mar-2009										
	Opening Balance		Inwards		Outwards					Closing Balance	
	Quantity	Value	Quantity	Value	Quantity	Value	Consumption	Gross Profit	Perc %	Quantity	Value
Computer			10 Nos	2,32,958.70	5 Nos	1,45,000.00	1,16,479.35	28,520.65	19.67 %	5 Nos	1,16,479.35
Computer Spares	41 Nos	55.000.00	9.100 Nos	2.77.66.284.30	3.211 Nos	3.09.58.701.95	42.29.245.23	2.67.29.456.72	86.34 %	5.930 Nos	2.35.92.039.07
Cooling Equipment	10 Nos	1,650.00	12 Nos	2,700.00	12 Nos	59,950.00	3,30,950.00	3,90,900.00	652.04 %	10 Nos	3,35,300.00
CPU Fan	25 Nos	3,125.00	2,920 Nos	4,91,642.00	1,260 Nos	2,83,050.00	1,45,100.05	1,37,949.95	48.74 %	1,685 Nos	3,49,666.95
Hardware Manual	35 Nos	21,000.00	200 Nos	65,000.00	30 Nos	12,300.00	10,978.72	1,321.28	10.74 %	205 Nos	75,021.28
Rectified Spirit	15 Lts	6,000.00	300 Lts	1,20,000.00	100 Lts	55,000.00	40,000.00	15,000.00	27.27 %	215 Lts	86,000.00
Grand Total		86.775.00		2.86.78.585.00		3,15,14,001.95	42,10,853.35	2,73,03,148.60	86.64 %		2,45,54,506.65

Fig. 8.3 Stock Summary with Consumption and Gross Profit

The Outward Column shows Cost of Goods Outwards termed as Consumption and Gross Profit value and percentage is displayed.

This statement is useful to analyze:

- Profitability Analysis of Sales (Outwards)
- Value Reconciliation of Stock.

Stock Valuation Methods

The Stock Summary report with stock valuation methods can be used to view the effects of different methods on the value of stock. Each stock item can be set up to have a different stock valuation method. In some instances, a particular method of valuation may be required, for example, to assess the replacement value or saleable value of stock. Tally.ERP 9 displays stocks in any or all the valuation methods dynamically and simultaneously, without any complicated procedure.

Suppose you want to use Last Purchase Cost method to assess the replacement value and the Last Sale Price method for realizable (saleable) value.

In the Stock Summary screen, select the New Column button on the button bar or press Alt+C. The screen appears as shown.

Select Last Sale Price from the Stock Valuation-Methods list.

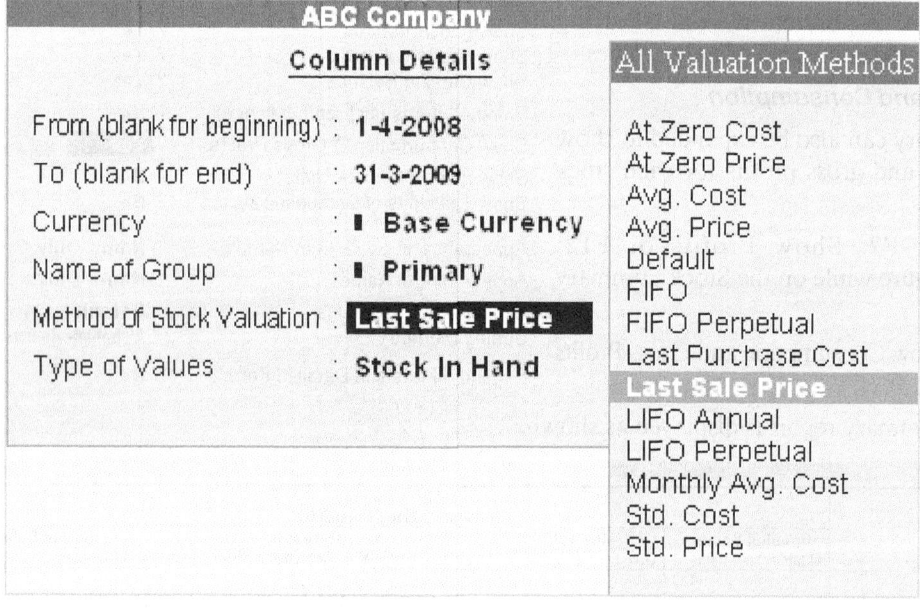

Fig. 8.4 Setting Last Sale Price

The Stock Summary report with Last Sale Price column is displayed as shown on next page.

Tally.ERP 9 allows you to view the effects of different stock valuation methods on the closing stock value. You can view simultaneous columnar display of different stock valuations by using the Alt + N: Auto Column button on the screen.

Stock Summary	ABC Company					Ctrl + M
Particulars	ABC Company 1-Apr-2008 to 31-Mar-2009			ABC Company 1-Apr-2008 to 31-Mar-2009 Last Sale Price		
	Closing Balance			Closing Balance		
	Quantity	Rate	Value	Quantity	Rate	Value
Computer	5 Nos	23,295.87	1,16,479.35	5 Nos	29,000.00	1,45,000.00
Computer Spares	5,930 Nos	3,978.42	2,35,92,039.07	5,930 Nos	5,622.60	3,33,42,000.00
Cooling Equipment	10 Nos	33,530.00	3,35,300.00	10 Nos	55,000.00	5,50,000.00
CPU Fan	1,685 Nos	207.52	3,49,666.95	1,685 Nos	185.00	3,11,725.00
Hardware Manual	205 Nos	365.96	75,021.28	205 Nos	410.00	84,050.00
Rectified Spirit	215 Lts	400.00	86,000.00	215 Lts	400.00	86,000.00
Grand Total			2,45,54,506.65			3,45,18,775.00

Fig. 8.5 Stock Summary with Last Sale Price

The screen is displayed as shown next.

Displaying Stock Items

Viewing Stock Items

1. Go to Gateway of Tally > Display > Inventory Books > Stock Item
2. Select an item from the List of Items.
3. Select F12: Configure. Set Show Graph by Values (not Qty)? to Yes and press Enter. This will display a graph showing Goods Inwards and Outwards (red for inwards, blue for outwards).

You can also use the Stock Summary to view Stock Items. Place the cursor on the item and press Enter.

Stock Summary	ABC Company								Ctrl + M
Particulars	ABC Company 1-Apr-2008 to 31-Mar-2009 Default			ABC Company 1-Apr-2008 to 31-Mar-2009 FIFO			ABC Company 1-Apr-2008 to 31-Mar-2009 LIFO Perpetual		
	Closing Balance			Closing Balance			Closing Balance		
	Quantity	Rate	Value	Quantity	Rate	Value	Quantity	Rate	Value
									8 more ...
Computer	5 Nos	23,295.87	1,16,479.35	5 Nos	21,353.74	1,06,768.70	5 Nos	25,238.00	1,26,190.00
Computer Spares	5,930 Nos	3,978.42	2,35,92,039.07	5,930 Nos	4,876.28	2,89,16,349.53	5,930 Nos	4,949.51	2,93,50,591.20
Cooling Equipment	10 Nos	33,530.00	3,35,300.00	10 Nos	336.00	3,360.00	10 Nos	336.00	3,360.00
CPU Fan	1,685 Nos	207.52	3,49,666.95	1,685 Nos	195.33	3,29,125.00	1,685 Nos	207.43	3,49,516.37
Hardware Manual	205 Nos	365.96	75,021.28	205 Nos	331.71	68,000.00	205 Nos	371.95	76,250.00
Rectified Spirit	215 Lts	400.00	86,000.00	215 Lts	400.00	86,000.00	215 Lts	400.00	86,000.00
Grand Total			2,45,54,506.65			2,95,09,603.23			2,99,91,907.57

Fig. 8.6 Stock Summary with Stock Valuations

Viewing Stock Item Vouchers

Stock Vouchers

1. Go to Gateway of Tally > Display > Inventory Books > Stock Items
2. Select a stock item from the list of items
3. Drill down from any month to display Stock Vouchers.

The list of stock vouchers for the current month is displayed as shown:

Stock Vouchers		ABC Company							Ctrl + M
Stock Item: 240 GB Hard Disk Drive									1-Jul-2008 to 31-Jul-2008
Date	Particulars	Vch Type	Vch No.	Inwards		Outwards		Closing	
				Quantity	Value	Quantity	Value	Quantity	Value
1-7-2008	Opening Balance			401 Nos	30,03,500.00			401 Nos	30,03,500.00
1-7-2008	Customer C	Tax Invoice	9			10 Nos	29,40,000.00		
1-7-2008	Customer C	Tax Invoice	10			10 Nos	48,020.00	381 Nos	28,53,500.00
4-7-2008	Physical Stock	Physical Stock	9	1,219 Nos				1,600 Nos	71,20,000.00
30-7-2008	Computer P-IV	Stock Journal	11			5 Nos	2,750.00	1,595 Nos	71,02,500.00
	Totals :			1,620 Nos	30,03,500.00	25 Nos	29,90,770.00	1,595 Nos	71,02,500.00

Fig. 8.7 Stock Summary with Stock Voucher Details

This list of vouchers for a stock item is the lowest level of collated data. If you drill-down any further, you can view the actual voucher.

You can also access Stock Vouchers by drilling-down from statements such as Stock Summary.

Stock Group Summary

This report is available when Integrate Accounts and Inventory is set to No in the Company Features screen.

It displays Opening and Closing Stock figures from the ledger account master, rather than the inventory records. Hence, it is possible that Stock Summary and the Stock Group Summary report display different figures.

To view Stock Group Summary:

Go to Gateway of Tally > Profit & Loss Account > Opening Stock (or Closing Stock)

Stock Group Summary	ABC Company			Ctrl + M
	Stock-in-hand ABC Company 1-Apr-2008 to 31-Mar-2009			
Particulars	Opening Balance		Closing Balance	
	Debit	Credit	Debit	Credit
Stock	25,000.00		40,000.00	
Grand Total	25,000.00		40,000.00	

Fig. 8.8 Stock Summary with Opening or Closing Stock

Drill-down from Stock Group Summary to view the Stock Ledger account where you can manually key in the closing balance for a given date. You can enter the closing stock figures for different dates.

The date for the closing balance is the beginning from date and till date. If there is no date that follows the last, then that Closing Balance continues. A blank against a date signifies zero balance.

Stock Category Summary

The Stock Category Summary lists the Closing Balances of all items belonging to the selected category.

To view Stock Category Summary:

- Go to Gateway of Tally > Display > Statements of Inventory > Categories
- Select a Category, Press Alt+F1 for Detailed report.
- You can Drill-down from stock category summary to display Item Monthly Summary and Stock Voucher list.
- Use Show Profit for profitability analysis for the Items in the Category.
- Press F7: Show Profits to expand the Outwards Column for Consumption and Profit figures:

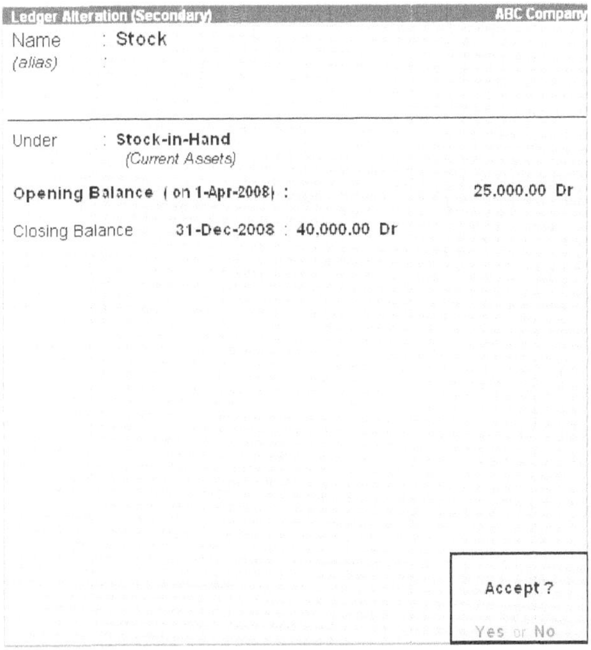

Ledger Alteration (Secondary) ABC Company

Name : Stock
(alias) :

Under : Stock-in-Hand
(Current Assets)

Opening Balance (on 1-Apr-2008) : 25,000.00 Dr

Closing Balance 31-Dec-2008 : 40,000.00 Dr

Accept ?
Yes or No

Stock Category Summary ABC Company Ctrl + M

Particulars	ABC Company 1-Apr-2008 to 31-Mar-2009 Closing Balance Quantity	Rate	Value
Cabinet	**20 Nos**	150.00	**3,000.00**
CPU Cabinet	*20 Nos*	150.00	*3,000.00*
Finished Goods	**5 Nos**	*23,295.87*	**1,16,479.35**
Computer P-IV	*5 Nos*	23,295.87	*1,16,479.35*
Manual	**205 Nos**	*365.96*	**75,021.28**
Hardware Manual	*205 Nos*	365.96	*75,021.28*
Memory	**5,860 Nos**	*3,866.65*	**2,26,58,549.04**
240 GB Hard Disk Drive	*1,550 Nos*	4,454.84	*69,05,000.00*
2 GB RAM Sticks	*3,615 Nos*	4,208.37	*1,52,13,265.23*
2 GB USB Drive	*695 Nos*	777.39	*5,40,283.81*
Motherboard	**30 Nos**	*12,776.87*	**3,83,306.20**
Cooling Equipment	*10 Nos*	33,530.00	*3,35,300.00*
Dual Core Processor	*20 Nos*	2,400.31	*48,006.20*
Grand Total	6,120 Nos		2,32,36,355.87

Fig. 8.9 Stock Category Summary

Stock Item Monthly Summary | ABC Company | Ctrl + M

Particulars	240 GB Hard Disk Drive ABC Company 1-Apr-2008 to 31-Mar-2009					
	Inwards		Outwards		Closing Balance	
	Quantity	Value	Quantity	Value	Quantity	Value
Opening Balance						3,500.00
April	500 Nos	37,50,000.00	80 Nos	6,85,000.00	421 Nos	31,53,500.00
May					421 Nos	31,53,500.00
June			20 Nos	1,92,400.00	401 Nos	30,03,500.00
July	1,219 Nos		25 Nos	29,90,770.00	1,595 Nos	71,02,500.00
August			15 Nos	29,42,750.00	1,580 Nos	70,10,000.00
September			10 Nos	19,60,000.00	1,570 Nos	69,75,000.00
October					1,570 Nos	69,75,000.00
November			10 Nos	24,50,000.00	1,560 Nos	69,40,000.00
December			10 Nos	39,20,000.00	1,550 Nos	69,05,000.00
January					1,550 Nos	69,05,000.00
February					1,550 Nos	69,05,000.00
March					1,550 Nos	69,05,000.00
Grand Total	**1,719 Nos**	**37,50,000.00**	**170 Nos**	**1,51,40,920.00**	**1,550 Nos**	**69,05,000.00**

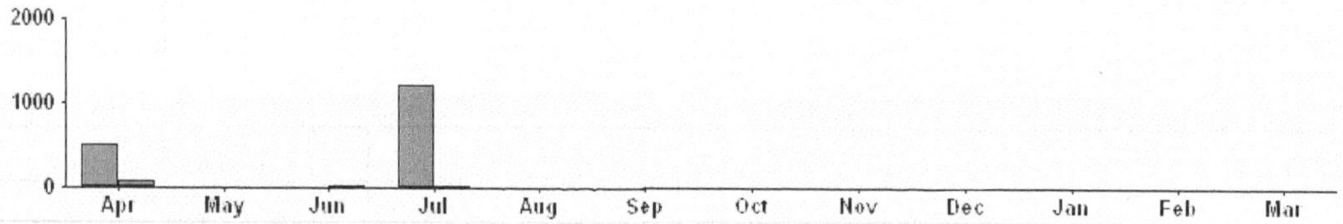

Fig. 8.10 Stock Item Monthly Summary

Stock Category Summary | ABC Company | Ctrl + M

Particulars	Memory ABC Company 1-Apr-2008 to 31-Mar-2009								
	Outwards						Closing Balance		
	Quantity	*Rate*	Value	Consumption	Gross Profit	Perc %	Quantity	*Rate*	Value
240 GB Hard Disk Drive	170 Nos	*89,064.24*	1,51,40,920.00	31,51,500.00	1,82,92,420.00	120.81 %	1,550 Nos	*4,454.84*	69,05,000.00
2 GB RAM Sticks	1,045 Nos	*2,113.49*	22,08,600.00	20,15,834.77	1,92,765.23	8.73 %	3,615 Nos	*4,208.37*	1,52,13,265.23
2 GB USB Drive	1,412 Nos	*1,627.73*	22,98,350.00	12,89,516.19	10,08,833.81	43.89 %	695 Nos	*777.39*	5,40,283.81
Grand Total	**2,627 Nos**		**1,96,47,870.00**	**(-)1,53,850.96**	**1,94,94,019.04**	**99.22 %**	**5,860 Nos**		**2,26,58,549.04**

Fig. 8.11 Stock Category Summary

Location / Godown Summary

The Godown/Location Summary statement shows the stock summary at different godowns/locations. While the main Stock Summary shows the stock position for the entire company on a given date, the Godown/Location Summary is a statement of stock-in-hand at each location on a particular date. As with all Tally.ERP 9 statements, it is updated with every transaction so that it provides current stock position for any godown/location at any time.

This statement can be drilled down and configured to view different details. It is also possible to view the total stock flow for each location in a single report.

To view the Godown/ Location Summary Report:

- Go to Gateway of Tally > Display > Statements of Inventory > Godowns > Primary
- Press Alt + F1 for a detailed view.

The Godown Summary screen is displayed as shown:

Godown Summary ABC Company Ctrl + M

Particulars	ABC Company 1-Apr-2008 to 31-Mar-2009 Closing Balance		
	Quantity	*Rate*	Value
Finished Goods Godown	131 Nos	6,498.26	8,51,271.85
Computer	5 Nos	1,69,114.37	8,45,571.85
Computer Spares	120 Nos	25.00	3,000.00
Cooling Equipment	6 Nos	450.00	2,700.00
Main Location			1,62,32,987.72
Aviation Turbine Fuel			
Computer			
Computer Spares	3,245 Nos	4,889.26	1,58,65,637.72
Cooling Equipment			
CPU Fan			
Hardware Manual	55 Nos	6,250.00	3,43,750.00
Rectified Spirit	200 Lts	400.00	80,000.00
Raw Material Godown	4,230 Nos	*1,910.34*	80,80,745.68
Computer Spares	2,570 Nos	3,009.59	77,34,651.35
Cooling Equipment			
CPU Fan	1,660 Nos	208.49	3,46,094.33
Grand Total	4,361 Nos		2,51,65,005.25

Fig. 8.12 Godown Summary

Godown / Location Stock Flow / Reconciliation

The reconciled flow of goods at each location is available.

Select F12:Configure while in the Godown/ Location Summary Screen.

The Godown Summary statement displays the flow of stock: Opening Stock, Goods Inwards, Goods Outward and Closing Stock, at each location.

The statement is quantitatively reconciled, not monetarily, *i.e.*, Opening quantity + Inward Quantity – Outward Quantity = Closing Stock Quantity.

However, this is not true of values because values do not add up in this manner. The Outwards value displays Sale Values, not Cost. The Closing Stock Value is, however, based on Cost and the Cost Method adopted for each item.

Configuration

Show Quantities	? **Yes**
Show Rates	? **No**
Show Values	? **Yes**
Show Opening Balance	? **Yes**
Show goods inwards	? **Yes**
Show goods outwards	? **Yes**
Show Closing Balance	? **Yes**
Show All Items (incl. zero balance)	? **No**
Show Consumption & Gross Profits	? **No**
Show using Alternate Units	? **No**
Show Tail Units of Compound Units	? **No**
Appearance of Stock Item Names	: **Name Only**
Appearance of Names	: **Name Only**
Scale Factor for Values	: **Default**
Sorting Method	: **Default**
Expand all levels in Detailed Format	? **No**

Value reconciliation is possible using Consumption figures, instead of Outward Values.

Godown Summary — ABC Company — Ctrl + M

Particulars	ABC Company 1-Apr-2008 to 31-Mar-2009							
	Opening Balance		Inwards		Outwards		Closing Balance	
	Quantity	Value	Quantity	Value	Quantity	Value	Quantity	Value
Finished Goods Godown			360 Nos	44,41,218.70	229 Nos	99,69,750.00	131 Nos	8,51,271.85
Computer			10 Nos	16,91,143.70	5 Nos	1,45,000.00	5 Nos	8,45,571.85
Computer Spares			344 Nos	27,47,375.00	224 Nos	98,24,750.00	120 Nos	3,000.00
Cooling Equipment			6 Nos	2,700.00			6 Nos	2,700.00
Main Location				2,50,84,542.00		2,09,13,445.00		1,62,32,987.72
Aviation Turbine Fuel			2,000 Lts	1,10,000.00	2,000 Lts	8,06,000.00		
Computer								
Computer Spares			5,817 Nos	2,31,44,900.00	2,572 Nos	1,24,87,520.00	3,245 Nos	1,58,65,637.72
Cooling Equipment			1 Nos	7,50,000.00	1 Nos	55,000.00		
CPU Fan			800 Nos	49,642.00	800 Nos	1,64,250.00		
Hardware Manual			100 Nos	6,25,000.00	45 Nos	16,875.00	55 Nos	3,43,750.00
Rectified Spirit			300 Lts	1,20,000.00	100 Lts	55,000.00	200 Lts	80,000.00
Raw Material Godown	51 Nos	56,650.00	5,065 Nos	(-)14,33,990.70	886 Nos	1,00,05,931.95	4,230 Nos	80,80,745.68
Computer Spares	41 Nos	55,000.00	2,939 Nos	18,74,009.30	410 Nos	86,35,181.95	2,570 Nos	77,34,651.35
Cooling Equipment	10 Nos	1,650.00	6 Nos	(-)37,50,000.00	16 Nos	12,51,950.00		
CPU Fan			2,120 Nos	4,42,000.00	460 Nos	1,18,800.00	1,660 Nos	3,46,094.33
Grand Total	51 Nos	56,650.00	5,425 Nos	2,80,91,770.00	1,115 Nos	4,08,89,126.95	4,361 Nos	2,51,65,005.25

Fig. 8.13 Godown Summary with Consumptions

Press F7: Show Profits to expand the Outwards Column for Consumption and Profit figures. Value Reconciliation is now possible using: Opening Value + Inward Value – Consumption Value = Closing Stock Value.

Columns

Use Columns to view stock balances of the Godowns/Locations on different dates/periods or other options listed in the Auto Columns options.

Even though you have selected a specific Godown/Location for display, you can still bring up information of the other godown(s)/location(s) in columns.

Select New Column or Auto-Column for such a display.

Godown Summary — ABC Company — Ctrl + M

Particulars	Raw Material Godown ABC Company 1-Apr-2008 to 31-Mar-2009 (in Indian Rupees)			Finished Goods Godown ABC Company 1-Apr-2008 to 31-Mar-2009 (in Indian Rupees)		
	Closing Balance			Closing Balance		
	Quantity	Rate	Value	Quantity	Rate	Value
Computer						
Computer Spares	2,570 Nos	3,009.59	77,34,651.35	120 Nos	25.00	3,000.00
Cooling Equipment				6 Nos	450.00	2,700.00
CPU Fan	1,660 Nos	208.49	3,46,094.33			
Grand Total	4,230 Nos		80,80,745.68	126 Nos		5,700.00

Fig. 8.14 Godown Summary with Columns

The above report is obtained by selecting:

New Column

Various reports are available from the Stock Item Monthly Summary, including different periodicity and Average stocks. Drill-down an item in the Stock or Godown/Location Summary level to the Item Monthly Summary and use F12: Configure options.

Godown / Location Vouchers

To list all the transactions of a particular Godown/ Location.

1. Go to Gateway of Tally > Display > Statements of Inventory > Godowns/ Locations
2. Select a Godown/Location.
3. Select an item from the List of Items and drill down to the voucher level.

Godown/Location Vouchers is a list of all vouchers for a particular item that are related to the selected Godown/Location during the period of display. The relationship could be stock inward/outward of the particular location.

Godown Vouchers ABC Company Ctrl + M

Stock Item: 2 GB RAM Sticks 1-Apr-2008 to 31-Mar-2009
Godown : Raw Material Godown

Date	Particulars	Vch Type	Vch No.	Inwards		Outwards		Closing	
				Quantity	Value	Quantity	Value	Quantity	Value
1-4-2008	Opening Balance			10 Nos	22,000.00			10 Nos	22,000.00
1-4-2008	Physical Stock	Physical Stock	1	1,290 Nos				1,300 Nos	28,60,000.00
10-4-2008	Supplier A	Purchase	9	300 Nos	6,00,000.00			1,600 Nos	32,20,645.15
15-4-2008	Physical Stock	Physical Stock	2			300 Nos		1,300 Nos	26,16,774.19
30-7-2008	Computer P-IV	Stock Journal	11			5 Nos	3,300.00	1,295 Nos	26,06,709.67
1-8-2008	Computer P-IV	Manufacturing Journal	1			5 Nos	3,300.00	1,290 Nos	25,96,645.15
	Totals :			1,600 Nos	6,22,000.00	310 Nos	6,600.00	1,290 Nos	25,96,645.15

Fig. 8.15 Godown Vouchers with inward/outward details

Stock Query

Stock Query is a statement which provides all the information related to a particular Stock Item such as

- Closing balance and its value.
- Cost price and Standard selling price of the product.
- Last purchase details such as date, party, quantity and rate.
- Information about last sales – date, quantity, rate, sales party etc.
- Warehouse details.
- Stock items under similar categories etc.

To view the Stock Query Report.

From Gateway of Tally> Display> Statements of Inventory> Stock Query> Select the Item from List of Items.

Press F12: Configure,

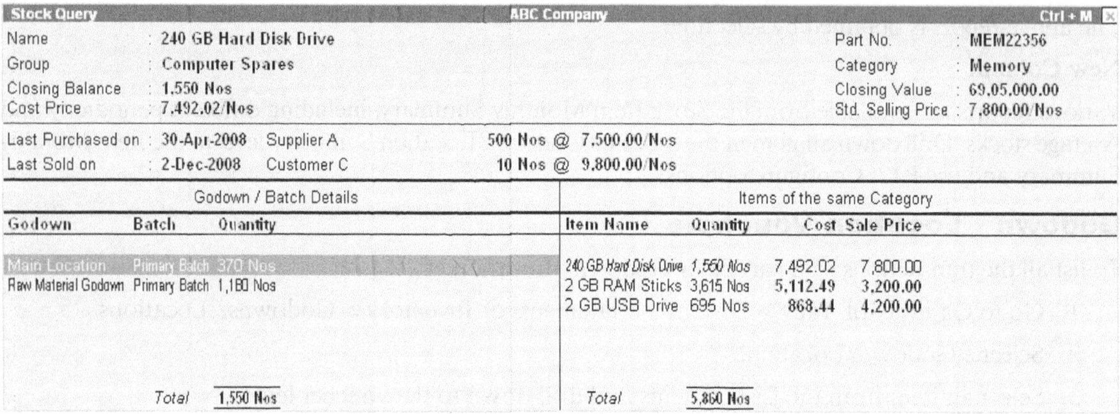

Stock Query — ABC Company — Ctrl + M

Name	: 240 GB Hard Disk Drive	Part No.	: MEM22356
Group	: Computer Spares	Category	: Memory
Closing Balance	: 1,550 Nos	Closing Value	: 69,05,000.00
Cost Price	: 7,492.02/Nos	Std. Selling Price	: 7,800.00/Nos

Last Purchased on : 30-Apr-2008 Supplier A 500 Nos @ 7,500.00/Nos
Last Sold on : 2-Dec-2008 Customer C 10 Nos @ 9,800.00/Nos

Godown / Batch Details

Godown	Batch	Quantity
Main Location	Primary Batch	370 Nos
Raw Material Godown	Primary Batch	1,180 Nos
Total		1,550 Nos

Items of the same Category

Item Name	Quantity	Cost	Sale Price
240 GB Hard Disk Drive	1,550 Nos	7,492.02	7,800.00
2 GB RAM Sticks	3,615 Nos	5,112.49	3,200.00
2 GB USB Drive	695 Nos	868.44	4,200.00
Total	5,860 Nos		

Fig. 8.16 Stock Query Screen

- Set Show related Items of same Stock Group to Yes, for displaying all items under the same Stock Group.
- Set Show Remarks of the Item to Yes, for displaying Remarks entered in the Stock Item master.

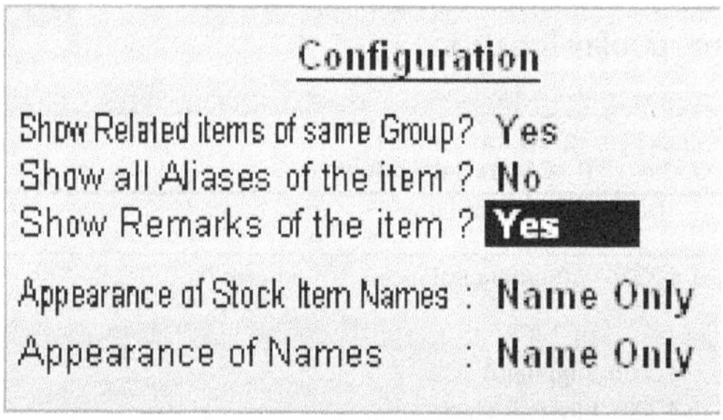

Configuration

Show Related items of same Group? Yes
Show all Aliases of the item ? No
Show Remarks of the item ? Yes

Appearance of Stock Item Names : Name Only
Appearance of Names : Name Only

The Stock query screen is displayed as shown:

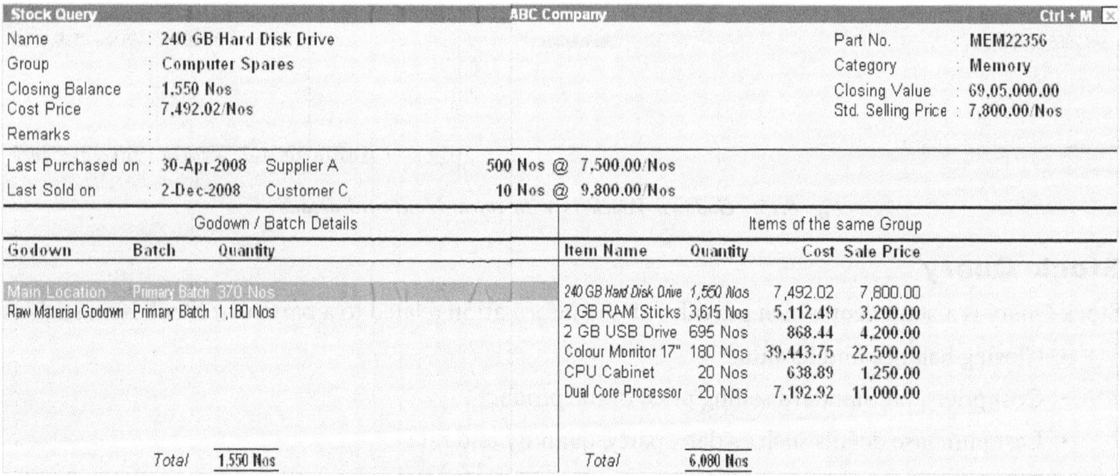

Stock Query — ABC Company — Ctrl + M

Name	: 240 GB Hard Disk Drive	Part No.	: MEM22356
Group	: Computer Spares	Category	: Memory
Closing Balance	: 1,550 Nos	Closing Value	: 69,05,000.00
Cost Price	: 7,492.02/Nos	Std. Selling Price	: 7,800.00/Nos
Remarks	:		

Last Purchased on : 30-Apr-2008 Supplier A 500 Nos @ 7,500.00/Nos
Last Sold on : 2-Dec-2008 Customer C 10 Nos @ 9,800.00/Nos

Godown / Batch Details

Godown	Batch	Quantity
Main Location	Primary Batch	370 Nos
Raw Material Godown	Primary Batch	1,180 Nos
Total		1,550 Nos

Items of the same Group

Item Name	Quantity	Cost	Sale Price
240 GB Hard Disk Drive	1,550 Nos	7,492.02	7,800.00
2 GB RAM Sticks	3,615 Nos	5,112.49	3,200.00
2 GB USB Drive	695 Nos	868.44	4,200.00
Colour Monitor 17"	180 Nos	39,443.75	22,500.00
CPU Cabinet	20 Nos	638.89	1,250.00
Dual Core Processor	20 Nos	7,192.92	11,000.00
Total	6,080 Nos		

Fig. 8.17 Stock Query Screen with Remarks

Stock query is the single stop for all information about a stock item. The stock position of a selected stock item at any point of time can be ascertained, information about the latest purchase can be quickly viewed and a godown where such stock is available can be easily located.

Stock Cost Estimation

Cost Estimation is a statement that gives the value of the cost incurred in the manufacturing of finished goods. To view the cost estimation of a particular finished product, select the relevant Stock Group which will display the stock consumption details and cost thereof for each of the stock items falling under that Group.

Cost estimation helps in fixing the selling price of the final product after charging appropriate overheads and allowing certain margin for profits. It also helps in Inventory Reports drawing conclusions regarding the cost of production and in determining the necessity to introduce cost reduction techniques in order to improve the manufacturing process.

To view Cost Estimation:

```
Go to Gateway of Tally > Display >
Statements of Inventory > Cost Estimation
```

The cost estimation screen is displayed as shown next.

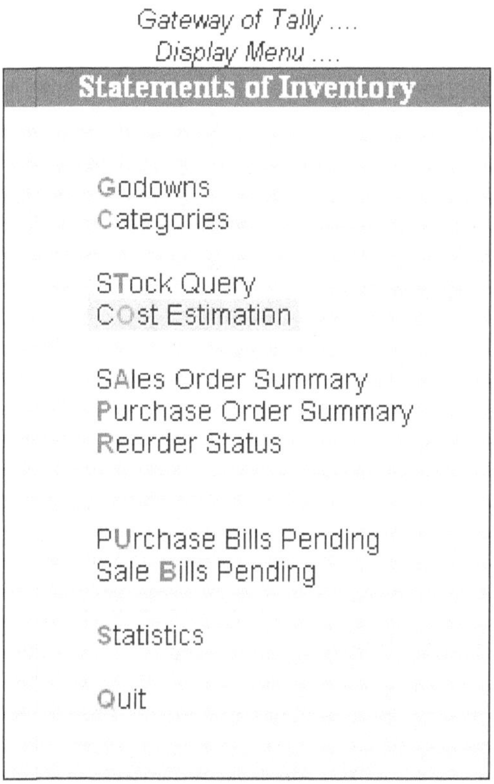

Gateway of Tally ....
Display Menu ....

Statements of Inventory

Godowns
Categories

STock Query
COst Estimation

SAles Order Summary
Purchase Order Summary
Reorder Status

PUrchase Bills Pending
Sale Bills Pending

Statistics

Quit

Sales Order Book

Sales Order is an order placed by a buyer for the purchase of goods. It consists of details of the items such as rate, terms and conditions, delivery schedule etc.

Sales Order Book displays a list of all Sales Orders.

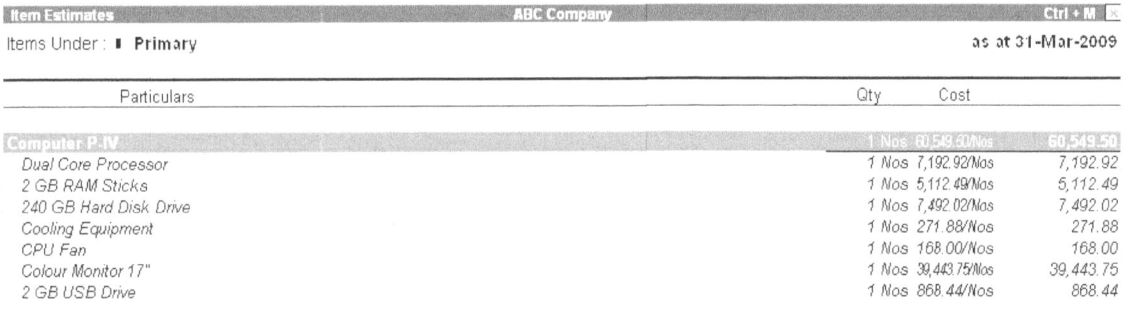

Item Estimates | ABC Company | Ctrl + M

Items Under : Primary | as at 31-Mar-2009

Particulars	Qty	Cost	
Computer P-IV	1 Nos	60,549.50/Nos	60,549.50
Dual Core Processor	1 Nos	7,192.92/Nos	7,192.92
2 GB RAM Sticks	1 Nos	5,112.49/Nos	5,112.49
240 GB Hard Disk Drive	1 Nos	7,492.02/Nos	7,492.02
Cooling Equipment	1 Nos	271.88/Nos	271.88
CPU Fan	1 Nos	168.00/Nos	168.00
Colour Monitor 17"	1 Nos	39,443.75/Nos	39,443.75
2 GB USB Drive	1 Nos	868.44/Nos	868.44

Fig. 8.18 Stock Item Estimates

```
From the Gateway of Tally> Display>Inventory Books>Sales Order Book
```

Sales Order Summary

Sales Order Summary statement gives detailed information on outstanding sales orders. The outstanding orders can be viewed Stock Item wise or Stock Group wise, using the toggle button F5.

Sales Order Summary is similar to Stock Summary, however by default it displays the status of the Sales Order Outstanding.

To view Sales Order Summary:

Sales Orders Book			ABC Company			Ctrl + M
List of All Sales Order Vouchers					1-Apr-2008 to 31-Mar-2009	
Date	Particulars		Vch Type	Vch No.	Debit Amount	Credit Amount
1-7-2008	Customer C		Sales Order	1	6,40,000.00	
	Sales Account	6,40,000.00 Cr				
30-7-2008	Customer B		Sales Order	2	87,500.00	
	Sales Account	87,500.00 Cr				
30-7-2008	Customer B		Sales Order	3	3,60,000.00	
	Sales Account	3,60,000.00 Cr				
30-7-2008	Customer C		Sales Order	4	8,25,000.00	
	Sales Account	8,25,000.00 Cr				
30-7-2008	Customer C		Sales Order	5	1,45,000.00	
	Sales Account	1,45,000.00 Cr				
15-8-2008	Customer A		Sales Order	6	3,50,000.00	
	Sales Account	3,50,000.00 Cr				
				Total:	24,07,500.00	

Fig. 8.19 Sales Order Book

Go to Gateway of Tally > Display > Statements of Inventory > Sales Order Summary

Sales Order Summary	ABC Company		Ctrl + M
Particulars	ABC Company 1-Apr-2008 to 31-Mar-2009 *Sales Orders Outstanding* On Order		
	Quantity	Rate	Value
Computer	15 Nos	33,666.67	5,05,000.00
Computer P-IV	*15 Nos*	*33,666.67*	*5,05,000.00*
Computer Spares	**10 Nos**	*17,500.00*	**1,75,000.00**
Colour Monitor 17"	*10 Nos*	*17,500.00*	*1,75,000.00*
Grand Total	25 Nos		6,80,000.00

Fig. 8.20 Sales Order Summary

Drilling down from a selected Stock Item displays the order detail screen which provides information on the order number, date of order, party, quantity, undelivered order, rate, value of ordered stock, due date for delivering the goods and the number of days overdue.

The order details will be displayed as shown:

Order Details		ABC Company					Ctrl + M
Item: Computer P-IV Sales Orders						1-Apr-2008 to 31-Mar-2009	
Date	Order Number	Name of Party	Ordered Quantity	Balance Quantity	Rate (*Disc %*)	Value	Due on (*overdue*)
Sales Orders Outstanding:							
30-Jul-2008	C002	Customer B	10 Nos	10 Nos	36,000.00	3,60,000.00	30-Aug-2008 (*213 days*)
30-Jul-2008	C004	Customer C	5 Nos	5 Nos	29,000.00	1,45,000.00	15-Aug-2008 (*228 days*)
			15 Nos	15 Nos		5,05,000.00	

Fig. 8.21 Order Details Summary

The order detail screen can be configured using the F12: Configure button.

It displays the other order details like cleared sales order, goods delivered without an order etc. as shown.

Tally.ERP 9 allows the user to switch over from the stock item order details screen to the party-wise order detail screen using the F5 button. Thus, Tally.ERP 9 allows the user to have multiple views and print such statements according to the requirements of the user.

Configuration

Show Outstanding Sales Orders	?	Yes
Show Cleared Sales Orders	?	Yes
Show Goods delivered but Orders not Recd.	?	Yes
Show Outstanding Purchase Orders	?	No
Show Cleared Purchase Orders	?	No
Show Goods received but Orders not sent	?	No
Show Batch/Location details	?	No
Appearance of Stock Item Names	:	Name Only
Appearance of Names	:	Name Only
Sorting Method	:	Default

Note: You will get the option for Sales/Purchase Order Summary only if you have activated the options for Orders under F11: Features.

Order Details ABC Company Ctrl + M

Item: Computer P-IV 1-Apr-2008 to 31-Mar-2009

Sales Orders

Date	Order Number	Name of Party	Ordered Quantity	Balance Quantity	Rate (Disc %)	Value	Due on (overdue)
Sales Orders Outstanding:							
30-Jul-2008	C002	Customer B	10 Nos	10 Nos	36,000.00	3,60,000.00	30-Aug-2008 (213 days)
30-Jul-2008	C004	Customer C	5 Nos	5 Nos	29,000.00	1,45,000.00	15-Aug-2008 (228 days)
			15 Nos	15 Nos		5,05,000.00	
Goods delivered but Orders not Recd. :							
15-Aug-2008	C004	Customer C	(-)5 Nos	(-)5 Nos	29,000.00	(-)1,45,000.00	15-Aug-2008 (228 days)
			(-)5 Nos	(-)5 Nos		(-)1,45,000.00	

Fig. 8.22 Order Details

Purchase Order Book

A Purchase order is raised when there is a request for material. Purchase Order Book displays the list of all Purchase Orders. You can view a summary of all the Purchase Orders till the date of last order entered.

From the Gateway of Tally> Display> Inventory Books>Purchase Order Book

The purchase order book is displayed as shown on next page.

Note: You will get this option only if you have activated Purchase Order processing under F11:Features (F2:Inventory)Purchase Order Summary

A Purchase Order Summary is a record of all the Purchase Orders pending on a particular date.

To view Purchase Order Summary:

Purchase Orders Book		ABC Company			Ctrl + M
List of All Purchase Order Vouchers					1-Apr-2008 to 31-Mar-2009
Date	Particulars	Vch Type	Vch No.	Debit Amount	Credit Amount
15-7-2008	Supplier C	Purchase Order	1		1,75,000.00
30-7-2008	Supplier A	Purchase Order	2		2,80,000.00
30-7-2008	Supplier B	Purchase Order	3		75,00,000.00
30-7-2008	Supplier B	Purchase Order	4		2,72,000.00
		Total:			82,27,000.00

Fig. 8.23 Purchase Order Book

Go to Gateway of Tally > Display > Statements of Inventory > Purchase Order Summary

The purchase order summary is displayed a shown:

Purchase Order Summary	ABC Company		Ctrl + M
Particulars	ABC Company 1-Apr-2008 to 31-Mar-2009 *Purchase Orders Outstanding*		
	On Order		
	Quantity	*Rate*	Value
Computer	**13 Nos**	*34,384.62*	**4,47,000.00**
Computer P-IV	*13 Nos*	34,384.62	*4,47,000.00*
Computer Spares	20 Nos	*14,000.00*	2,80,000.00
Colour Monitor 17"	*20 Nos*	14,000.00	*2,80,000.00*
Grand Total	33 Nos		7,27,000.00

Fig. 8.24 Purchase Order Summary

- Select Computer and Press Enter to view Order Details screen.
- Press Alt + F1 for detailed view.

The Order Details screen is displayed as shown:

Order Details		ABC Company					Ctrl + M
Item: Computer P-IV Purchase Orders							1-Apr-2008 to 30-Sep-2008
Date	Order Number	Name of Party	Ordered Quantity	Balance Quantity	Rate *(Disc %)*	Value	Due on *(overdue)*
Purchase Orders Outstanding:							
15-Jul-2008	S003	Supplier C	5 Nos	**5 Nos**	35,000.00	**1,75,000.00**	30-Aug-2008 *(31 days)*
	15-Jul-2008 Purchase Order 1	*5 Nos*					
30-Jul-2008	S004	Supplier B	8 Nos	**8 Nos**	34,000.00	**2,72,000.00**	*30-Sep-2008* *(0 days)*
	30-Jul-2008 Purchase Order 4	*8 Nos*					
			13 Nos	13 Nos		4,47,000.00	

Fig. 8.25 Order Details

A Purchase Order Summary is a statement of outstanding purchase orders. It gives information similar to the sales order summary such as date of order, supplier details, order number for reference, quantity ordered and undelivered ordered quantity, rate and value of pending orders, due-date and over-due days.

Information can also be retrieved for different reporting periods by using the F2: Period button on the screen.

Reorder Status

The Reorder Status gives you information on available stock, reorder level, minimum reorder quantity and accordingly the next order to be placed by the business concern.

This report will help you in taking the appropriate decision for timely Purchase of Materials and will readily provide all relevant information required for placement of a Purchase Order.

To display Inventory Reorder Status:

```
Go to Gateway of Tally > Display > Statement of Inventory > Reorder Status >
Select the Group
```

Inventory Reorder Status ABC Company Ctrl + M

Items Under : Computer Spares (all items) as at 30-Aug-2008

Name of Item	Closing Stock	Purc Orders Pending	Sale Orders Due	Nett Available	Re-order Level	Short fall	Min Reorder Qty	Order to be Placed
240 GB Hard Disk Drive	1,580 Nos			1,580 Nos	500 Nos		200 Nos	
2 GB RAM Sticks	2,615 Nos		200 Nos	2,415 Nos	1,000 Nos		250 Nos	
2 GB USB Drive	695 Nos			695 Nos	400 Nos		100 Nos	
Colour Monitor 17"	180 Nos	20 Nos		200 Nos	250 Nos	50 Nos	100 Nos	100 Nos
CPU Cabinet	20 Nos			20 Nos	200 Nos	180 Nos	50 Nos	180 Nos
Dual Core Processor	20 Nos			20 Nos	150 Nos	130 Nos	50 Nos	130 Nos

Fig. 8.26 Reorder Status Screen

The user can select the relevant column and drill down to get the detailed information on the same.

For instance, the re-order level column can be selected and drilled down further to analyse how the reorder level is specified in the master record. Similarly, an analysis can be done of the minimum reorder quantity, the net available quantity etc.

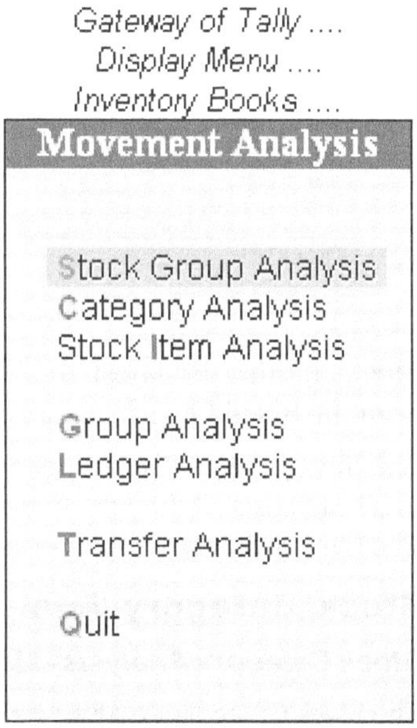

Movement Analysis

Movement analysis shows the analysis of only those inventory transactions which are integrated with the accounts, *i.e.*, inventories which are also recorded in the books of accounts. Inventory vouchers which affect the stock only in quantitative terms are not considered.

Movement analysis report is used for comparative studies. They give an insight into the flow characteristics of the stock in an organization. It also helps in finding out the slow moving items which cause blockages in the flow of the working capital of the organization.

```
Go to Gateway of Tally > Display > Inventory Books >
Movement Analysis
```

Gateway of Tally ....
Display Menu ....
Inventory Books ....

Movement Analysis

Stock Group Analysis
Category Analysis
Stock Item Analysis

Group Analysis
Ledger Analysis

Transfer Analysis

Quit

Movement Analysis Reports show only those inventory transactions for which accounting transactions have also been recorded. You can analyze stock movements by stock groups, categories, financial group or ledger.

Different types of movement analysis reports can be generated in Tally.ERP 9:

- Stock Group Analysis
- Stock Category Analysis
- Stock Item Analysis
- Group Analysis
- Ledger Analysis
- Transfer Analysis.

Stock Group Analysis

Movement Analysis (Stock Group Analysis)

This report shows the details of inward and outward transactions carried out for all the stock items in that group.

To view Item Movement Analysis for a specific stock group:

```
Go to Gateway of Tally > Display > Inventory Books > Movement Analysis > Stock
Group Analysis > Select Name of the group
```

Movement Analysis of a selected stock group displays the Total Inward and Outward movement of all the items in a selected Stock Group.

Movement Analysis | ABC Company | Ctrl + M

Computer Spares
ABC Company
1-Apr-2008 to 31-Mar-2009

Particulars	Inward			Outward		
	Quantity	*Eff. Rate*	Value	Quantity	*Eff. Rate*	Value
240 GB Hard Disk Drive	500 Nos	7,500.00	37,50,000.00	170 Nos	89,064.24	1,51,40,920.00
2 GB RAM Sticks	3,060 Nos	5,425.59	1,66,02,300.00	745 Nos	2,964.56	22,08,600.00
2 GB USB Drive	2,097 Nos	861.85	18,07,300.00	1,148 Nos	2,122.91	24,37,100.00
Colour Monitor 17"	100 Nos	39,443.75	39,44,375.00	229 Nos	42,924.67	98,29,750.00
CPU Cabinet	70 Nos	721.43	50,500.00	70 Nos	935.71	65,500.00
Dual Core Processor	140 Nos	7,192.92	10,07,009.30	120 Nos	9,609.02	11,53,081.95
Grand Total	5,967 Nos	4,551.95	2,71,61,484.30	2,482 Nos	12,423.43	3,08,34,951.95

Fig. 8.27 Movement Analysis

The quantities displayed are Actual Quantities of movement (which, in some cases, may be different from the Billed Qty in the transactions).

The Inward detail displays the Effective Rate or Final Landed Cost of the materials, after considering all overhead costs. If the Effective Rate varies from the Basic Invoice Rate of the materials, it is highlighted. The Outward detail displays the Basic Invoice Rate and Value of goods sold/transferred out.

Stock Category Analysis

Stock Category Analysis - Movement Analysis

The Stock Category Analysis statement displays the movement of Stock Items of a selected Stock Category.

To view Stock Category Analysis,

```
Go to Gateway of Tally > Display > Inventory Books > Movement Analysis >
Category Analysis
```

1. Select a category.
2. Change the period, if required.

Category Analysis | ABC Company | Ctrl + M

Particulars	Memory ABC Company 1-Apr-2008 to 31-Mar-2009					
	Inward			Outward		
	Quantity	Eff. Rate	Value	Quantity	Eff. Rate	Value
240 GB Hard Disk Drive	500 Nos	7,500.00	37,50,000.00	170 Nos	89,064.24	1,51,40,900.00
2 GB RAM Sticks	3,060 Nos	5,425.59	1,66,02,300.00	745 Nos	2,964.56	22,08,600.00
2 GB USB Drive	2,097 Nos	861.85	18,07,300.00	1,148 Nos	2,122.91	24,37,100.00
Grand Total	5,657 Nos	3,917.20	2,21,59,600.00	2,063 Nos	9,591.19	1,97,86,620.00

Fig. 8.28 Category Analysis

After selecting a Stock Category from List of Categories, the Category Analysis report displays information relating to Quantity, Effective Rate and Value under separate columns for Inward and Outward movement of goods.

The Inward and Outward movement of these items are summarised in the Summary. You can drill-down to display the Item Movement Analysis for the selected item.

Stock Item Analysis

Item Movement Analysis

Item Movement Analysis is the next level of information (press Enter on the Stock Item or Display > Inventory Books > Stock Item Analysis). This brings up the Party-wise/Transfer-wise detail of Movements. The Inward detail displays the Basic Invoice Rate and Effective Rate.

To view Stock Item Movement Analysis,

```
Go to Gateway of Tally > Display-Inventory Books > Movement Analysis > Stock
Item Analysis
```

This report will help you in comparing Purchase Costs across suppliers.

Press Enter on the Party Name or Stock Journal Name to display the transaction-level details on Date of goods received/sold, Quantities, Basic Rates, Addl. Costs, and Effective Rate for each transaction.

The default screen displays the Addl.Costs (if any), in a single column. To view the spread of costs, press F12: Configure and select to view Show Addl. Costs.

This brings up the bifurcation of all Additional Costs.

The report displays every purchase made during the period specified with break-down of Basic Value and Additional Cost.

Group Analysis

Group Analysis report contains information about Items transacted in Vouchers for the Ledgers created under the selected Group.

Item Movement Analysis	ABC Company			Ctrl + M
Particulars	2 GB RAM Sticks ABC Company 1-Apr-2008 to 31-Mar-2009 Movement Values			
	Quantity	Basic Rate	Effective Rate	Value
Movement Inward :				
Suppliers :				
Supplier A	500 Nos	2,000.00	2,024.00	10,12,000.00
Supplier B	2,150 Nos	6,868.60	6,868.60	1,47,67,500.00
Supplier C	410 Nos	2,000.00	2,013.66	8,25,600.00
	3,060 Nos		5,426.50	1,66,05,100.00
Movement Outward :				
Buyers :				
Customer A	230 Nos		2,547.83	5,86,000.00
Customer B	25 Nos		3,200.00	80,000.00
Customer C	480 Nos		3,200.00	15,36,000.00
	735 Nos		2,995.92	22,02,000.00
Transfers Outward (Consumption) :				
Manufacturing Journal	5 Nos		660.00	3,300.00
Stock Journal	5 Nos		660.00	3,300.00
	10 Nos		660.00	6,600.00
	745 Nos		2,964.56	22,08,600.00

Fig. 8.29 Item Movement Analysis

Item Voucher Analysis — ABC Company — Ctrl + M

Stock Item: 2 GB RAM Sticks — 1-Apr-2008 to 31-Mar-2009

InwardsUnder Ledger : Supplier A

Date	Particulars	Quantity	Basic Rate	Basic Value	Addl. Cost	Total Value	Eff. Rate
	Purchases						
5-Apr-2008	**Supplier A**	500 Nos	2,000.00/Nos	10,00,000.00	12,000.00	10,12,000.00	2,024.00/Nos
10-Apr-2008	Supplier A	300 Nos	2,000.00/Nos	6,00,000.00	2,000.00	6,02,000.00	2,006.67/Nos
	Total	800 Nos	2,000.00/Nos	16,00,000.00	14,000.00	16,14,000.00	2,017.50/Nos

Fig. 8.30 Item Voucher Analysis

Configuration	
Show Addl. Cost Column ?	Yes
Show full Addl. Cost Details ?	Yes
Format :	Condensed
Show Billed Qty Column ?	Yes
Show Base Rate Column ?	Yes
Show Base Value Column ?	Yes
Show Total Value Column ?	Yes
Show Eff. Rate Column ?	Yes

To view the movement analysis for any particular Account Group:

Go to Gateway of Tally > Display > Inventory Books > Group Analysis

After selecting an Account Group from List of Groups, information relating to Quantity, Effective Rate and Value under separate columns for Sales and Purchase is displayed.

Ledger Analysis

Ledger Analysis is similar to Group Movement Analysis, except that you can view movements of the items for the selected Ledger (Party). Thus, you get an analysis of all purchases made from a supplier, or all items sold to a customer. The next level of information brings up the transaction-level details.

Item Voucher Analysis		ABC Company					Ctrl + M
Stock Item: 2 GB RAM Sticks							1-Apr-2008 to 31-Mar-2009
InwardsUnder Ledger : Supplier A							
Date	**Particulars**	**Quantity**	**Basic Rate**	**Basic Value**	***CST on Purchase***	***Frieght Charges***	**Total Value**	**Eff. Rate**
	Purchases							
5-Apr-2008	Supplier A	500 Nos	2,000.00/Nos	10,00,000.00	*12,000.00*		10,12,000.00	2,024.00/Nos
10-Apr-2008	Supplier A	300 Nos	2,000.00/Nos	6,00,000.00		*2,000.00*	6,02,000.00	2,006.67/Nos
	Total	800 Nos	2,000.00/Nos	16,00,000.00	*12,000.00*	*2,000.00*	16,14,000.00	2,017.50/Nos

Fig. 8.31 Item Voucher Analysis with Full Details

To view the movement analysis for any particular Account Ledger:

Go to Gateway of Tally > Display > Inventory Books > Movement Analysis > Ledger Analysis

Group Analysis — ABC Company — Ctrl + M

Particulars	*Sundry Creditors* ABC Company 1-Apr-2008 to 31-Mar-2009					
	Purchases			Sales		
	Quantity	*Eff. Rate*	Value	Quantity	*Eff. Rate*	Value
240 GB Hard Disk Drive	500 Nos	*7,500.00*	37,50,000.00			
2 GB RAM Sticks	3,360 Nos	*5,121.16*	1,72,07,100.00			
2 GB USB Drive	2,147 Nos	*844.11*	18,12,300.00	150 Nos	*1,250.00*	1,87,500.00
Aviation Turbine Fuel	2,000 Lts	*55.00*	1,10,000.00			
Colour Monitor 17"			11,00,000.00	10 Nos	*17,000.00*	1,70,000.00
Cooling Equipment	1 Nos	*7,50,000.00*	7,50,000.00			
CPU Cabinet	50 Nos	*950.00*	47,500.00			
CPU Fan	600 Nos	*41.67*	25,000.00			
Dual Core Processor	110 Nos	*8,500.00*	9,35,000.00			
Hardware Manual	100 Nos	*6,250.00*	6,25,000.00			
Rectified Spirit				100 Lts	*550.00*	55,000.00
Grand Total			2,63,61,900.00			4,12,500.00

Fig. 8.32 Group Analysis

This report contains information about the Items which are transacted in Sales and Purchase Vouchers for the selected Ledgers. When you select an Account Ledger (Debtor/Creditor/Cash/Bank) for Ledger Analysis report, all the items which have some movement (sales/purchases) will be displayed in this report.

Ledger Analysis — ABC Company — Ctrl + M

Particulars	*Cash* ABC Company 1-Apr-2008 to 31-Mar-2009					
	Purchases			Sales		
	Quantity	*Eff. Rate*	Value	Quantity	*Eff. Rate*	Value
2 GB USB Drive				100 Nos	*1,250.00*	1,25,000.00
Colour Monitor 17"						61,87,500.00
CPU Fan	2,000 Nos	*200.00*	4,00,000.00	750 Nos	*263.33*	1,97,500.00
Fuel	2,500 Lts	*78.00*	1,95,000.00			
Rectified Spirit	300 Lts	*400.00*	1,20,000.00			
Grand Total			7,15,000.00	850 Nos	*7,658.82*	65,10,000.00

Fig. 8.33 Ledger Analysis

Transfer Analysis

When using different Stock Journals for each transaction, Transfer Analysis gives the movement details for each type of Stock Journal.

To view the Stock Transfer analysis for any Stock Journal Voucher Type:

Go to Gateway of Tally > Display > Inventory Books > Movement Analysis >Transfer Analysis

Transfer Analysis — ABC Company — Ctrl + M

Particulars	Stock Journal ABC Company 1-Apr-2008 to 31-Mar-2009					
	Goods In (Production)			Goods Out (Consumption)		
	Quantity	*Eff. Rate*	Value	Quantity	*Eff. Rate*	Value
240 GB Hard Disk Drive				5 Nos	*550.00*	2,750.00
2 GB RAM Sticks				5 Nos	*660.00*	3,300.00
2 GB USB Drive				5 Nos	*450.00*	2,250.00
Colour Monitor 17"	10 Nos	*1,58,437.50*	15,84,375.00	15 Nos	*13,833.33*	2,07,500.00
Computer P-IV	5 Nos	*25,238.00*	1,26,190.00			
Cooling Equipment	6 Nos	*450.00*	2,700.00	11 Nos	*450.00*	4,950.00
CPU Cabinet	20 Nos	*150.00*	3,000.00	20 Nos	*150.00*	3,000.00
CPU Fan	200 Nos	*123.21*	24,642.00	205 Nos	*345.37*	70,800.00
Dual Core Processor	30 Nos	*2,400.31*	72,009.30	35 Nos	*7,540.00*	2,63,900.00
Grand Total	271 Nos	*6,689.73*	18,12,916.30	301 Nos	*1,855.32*	5,58,450.00

Fig. 8.34 Transfer Analysis

This report displays information about the Items which are transacted in the Stock Journal Voucher. Generally in Stock Journal Voucher, Movement of goods, Manufacture of Goods or inter-Godown Transfer is recorded.

This is a very useful costing and waste analysis tool. In non-manufacturing set ups, which have Multiple Godowns, this report is a quick check to verify that all transfer entries have been entered correctly.

Stock Ageing Analysis

An Ageing Analysis Report in Tally.ERP 9 displays the age of the stock in hand. This report lists the age-wise break-up of Inventory to point out old stock. Tally.ERP 9 gives its users the flexibility to define their own ageing slabs.

Ageing Analysis lists out items batch wise that have already expired or may expire in the near future. This information will help you in keeping track of the age of stock and also quick moving inventory, since the older stock may depreciate in value or become obsolete and result in a loss.

To view Ageing Analysis Report.

Go to Gateway of Tally > Display > Inventory Books > Ageing Analysis > Select the group for which Ageing Analysis is required.

This report is displayed in a columnar format showing Item details, Quantity, value and age-wise break-up.

To get a report for all the Stock items, select Primary from List of Groups.

If you want to view only the Quantity of the Item, press the Hide Amount button or press Alt+A.

For getting the Item Monthly Summary report, press Enter in the Total Quantity Column of the Item.

For further drill down to Stock Journals of the Item, press Enter for the month you want the stock journal.

Stock Ageing Analysis — **ABC Company** — Ctrl + M

Items Under : **Primary** — as at 31-Aug-2008
All Batches (Aged by Date of Purchase) — *Valued based on Actual Purchase*

Particulars	Expiry Date	Total	(< 45 days)		45 to 90 days		90 to 180 days	
		Quantity	Quantity	Value	Quantity	Value	Quantity	Value
								2 more ...
240 GB Hard Disk Drive		**1,580 Nos**					**1,580 Nos**	**70,10,000.00**
Main Location		*370 Nos*					*370 Nos*	*27,75,000.00*
Raw Material Godown		*1,210 Nos*					*1,210 Nos*	*42,35,000.00*
2 GB RAM Sticks		**2,615 Nos**	**1,310 Nos**	**21,25,000.00**			**1,305 Nos**	**27,97,500.00**
Main Location		*1,325 Nos*	*1,310 Nos*	*21,25,000.00*			*15 Nos*	*19,500.00*
Raw Material Godown		*1,290 Nos*					*1,290 Nos*	*27,78,000.00*
2 GB USB Drive		**695 Nos**					**695 Nos**	**5,49,500.00**
Main Location		*550 Nos*					*550 Nos*	*5,35,000.00*
Raw Material Godown		*145 Nos*					*145 Nos*	*14,500.00*
Colour Monitor 17"		**180 Nos**			**90 Nos**	**12,60,000.00**	**90 Nos**	**25,44,375.00**
Finished Goods Godown		*100 Nos*			*90 Nos*	*12,60,000.00*	*10 Nos*	*15,84,375.00*
Raw Material Godown		*80 Nos*					*80 Nos*	*9,60,000.00*
Computer P-IV		**5 Nos**	**5 Nos**	**90,481.95**				
Finished Goods Godown		*5 Nos*	*5 Nos*	*90,481.95*				
Cooling Equipment		**10 Nos**					**10 Nos**	**3,360.00**
Finished Goods Godown		*6 Nos*					*6 Nos*	*2,700.00*
Raw Material Godown		*4 Nos*					*4 Nos*	*660.00*
CPU Cabinet		**20 Nos**			**20 Nos**	**3,000.00**		
Finished Goods Godown		*20 Nos*			*20 Nos*	*3,000.00*		
CPU Fan		**1,685 Nos**			**200 Nos**	**24,642.00**	**1,485 Nos**	**3,24,958.33**
Main Location		*250 Nos*			*200 Nos*	*24,642.00*	*50 Nos*	*2,083.33*
Raw Material Godown		*1,435 Nos*					*1,435 Nos*	*3,22,875.00*
Dual Core Processor		**20 Nos**	**20 Nos**	**48,006.20**				
Raw Material Godown		*20 Nos*	*20 Nos*	*48,006.20*				
Hardware Manual		**205 Nos**					**205 Nos**	**68,000.00**
Finished Goods Godown		*205 Nos*					*205 Nos*	*68,000.00*
								3 more ...
Grand Total			1,335 Nos	22,63,488.15	310 Nos	12,87,642.00		1,33,83,693.33

Fig. 8.35 Stock AgeingAnalysis with Date of Purchase

Stock Ageing Analysis — **ABC Company** — Ctrl + M

Items Under : **Primary** — as at 31-Aug-2008
All Batches (Aged by Date of Purchase) — *Valued based on Actual Purchase*

Particulars	Expiry Date	Total	(< 45 days)	45 to 90 days	90 to 180 days	(> 180 days)	Negative Stock
		Quantity	Quantity	Quantity	Quantity	Quantity	Quantity
240 GB Hard Disk Drive		**1,580 Nos**			**1,580 Nos**		
Main Location		*370 Nos*			*370 Nos*		
Raw Material Godown		*1,210 Nos*			*1,210 Nos*		
2 GB RAM Sticks		**2,615 Nos**	**1,310 Nos**		**1,305 Nos**		
Main Location		*1,325 Nos*	*1,310 Nos*		*15 Nos*		
Raw Material Godown		*1,290 Nos*			*1,290 Nos*		
2 GB USB Drive		**695 Nos**			**695 Nos**		
Main Location		*550 Nos*			*550 Nos*		
Raw Material Godown		*145 Nos*			*145 Nos*		
Colour Monitor 17"		**180 Nos**		**90 Nos**	**90 Nos**		
Finished Goods Godown		*100 Nos*		*90 Nos*	*10 Nos*		
Raw Material Godown		*80 Nos*			*80 Nos*		
Computer P-IV		**5 Nos**	**5 Nos**				
Finished Goods Godown		*5 Nos*	*5 Nos*				
Cooling Equipment		**10 Nos**			**10 Nos**		
Finished Goods Godown		*6 Nos*			*6 Nos*		
Raw Material Godown		*4 Nos*			*4 Nos*		
CPU Cabinet		**20 Nos**		**20 Nos**			
Finished Goods Godown		*20 Nos*		*20 Nos*			
CPU Fan		**1,685 Nos**		**200 Nos**	**1,485 Nos**		
Main Location		*250 Nos*		*200 Nos*	*50 Nos*		
Raw Material Godown		*1,435 Nos*			*1,435 Nos*		
Dual Core Processor		**20 Nos**	**20 Nos**				
Raw Material Godown		*20 Nos*	*20 Nos*				
Hardware Manual		**205 Nos**			**205 Nos**		
Finished Goods Godown		*205 Nos*			*205 Nos*		
							3 more ...
Grand Total			1,335 Nos	310 Nos			

Fig. 8.36 Stock Ageing Analysis Based on Actual Stocks

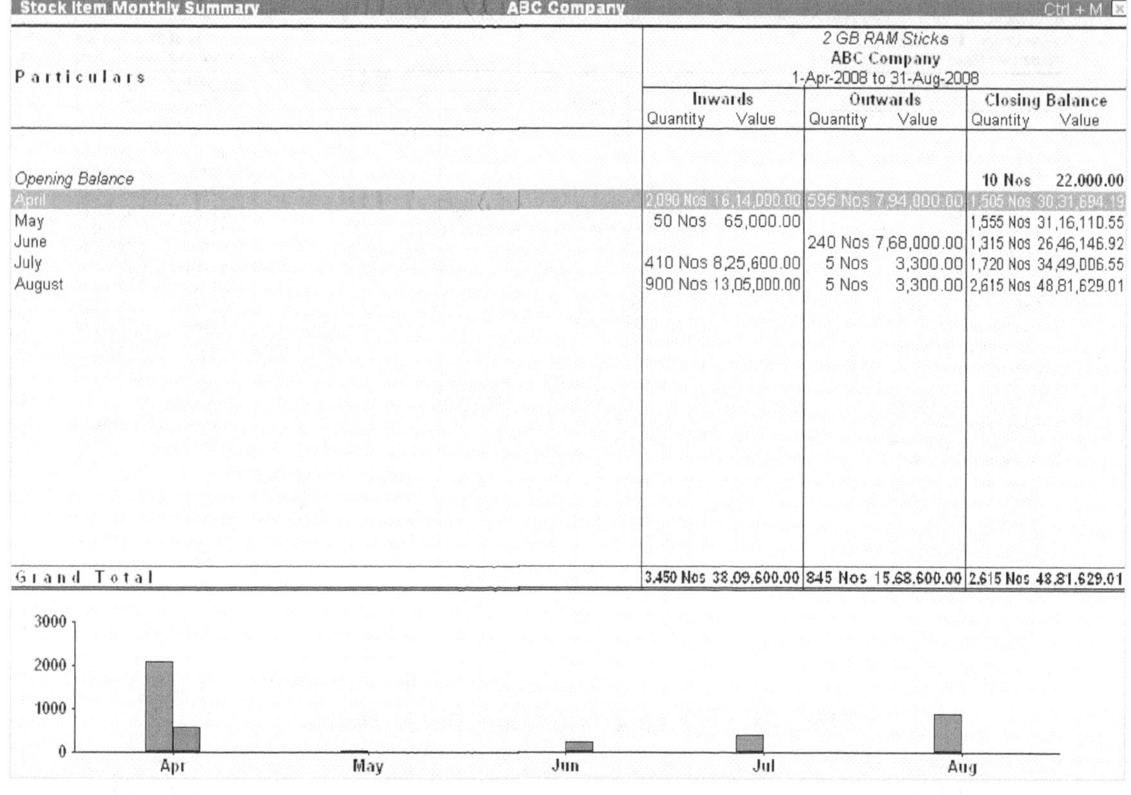

Stock Item Monthly Summary — ABC Company — Ctrl + M

2 GB RAM Sticks
ABC Company
1-Apr-2008 to 31-Aug-2008

Particulars	Inwards Quantity	Inwards Value	Outwards Quantity	Outwards Value	Closing Balance Quantity	Closing Balance Value
Opening Balance					10 Nos	22,000.00
April	2,090 Nos	16,14,000.00	595 Nos	7,94,000.00	1,505 Nos	30,31,694.19
May	50 Nos	65,000.00			1,555 Nos	31,16,110.55
June			240 Nos	7,68,000.00	1,315 Nos	26,46,146.92
July	410 Nos	8,25,600.00	5 Nos	3,300.00	1,720 Nos	34,49,006.55
August	900 Nos	13,05,000.00	5 Nos	3,300.00	2,615 Nos	48,81,629.01
Grand Total	3,450 Nos	38,09,600.00	845 Nos	15,68,600.00	2,615 Nos	48,81,629.01

Fig. 8.37 Stock item Monthly Summary

How to change default ageing period

The Ageing Analysis report produces a default ageing period of <45 days, 45-90 days, 90-180 days and >180 days. Depending on the requirement, you can also define the ageing slabs.

By default the items are aged from the date of purchase. You can change this by altering the configuration options.

To define the ageing slab press F6.

To get the value of the stock other than the default method, press F7 and select from All Valuation Method for example, Avg.Cost, Avg.Price,FIFO,etc.

Item details Valued using FIFO are displayed as shown next.

Stock Ageing Alteration

Company: **ABC Company**

From	: 0	To	: 30
From	: 30	To	: 60
From	: 60	To	: 90
From	: 90	To	: 0

Accept ?

Yes or No

How to change Ageing Style

Different ageing styles provided in Tally.ERP 9 include purchase date, expiry date, manufacturing date etc. These are activated using the Alt + S: Ageing Style button.

Stock Ageing Analysis — ABC Company — Ctrl + M

Items Under : Primary — as at 31-Aug-2008

All Batches (Aged by Date of Purchase) — *Valued using FIFO*

Particulars	Expiry Date	Total	(< 30 days)	30 to 60 days	60 to 90 days	(> 90 days)	Negative Stock
		Quantity	Quantity	Quantity	Quantity	Quantity	Quantity
240 GB Hard Disk Drive		**1,580 Nos**				**1,580 Nos**	
Main Location		*370 Nos*				*370 Nos*	
Raw Material Godown		*1,210 Nos*				*1,210 Nos*	
2 GB RAM Sticks		**2,615 Nos**	**900 Nos**	**410 Nos**		**1,305 Nos**	
Main Location		*1,325 Nos*	*900 Nos*	*410 Nos*		*15 Nos*	
Raw Material Godown		*1,290 Nos*				*1,290 Nos*	
2 GB USB Drive		**695 Nos**				**695 Nos**	
Main Location		*550 Nos*				*550 Nos*	
Raw Material Godown		*145 Nos*				*145 Nos*	
Colour Monitor 17"		**180 Nos**		**90 Nos**		**90 Nos**	
Finished Goods Godown		*100 Nos*		*90 Nos*		*10 Nos*	
Raw Material Godown		*80 Nos*				*80 Nos*	
Computer P-IV		**5 Nos**	**5 Nos**				
Finished Goods Godown		*5 Nos*	*5 Nos*				
Cooling Equipment		**10 Nos**				**10 Nos**	
Finished Goods Godown		*6 Nos*				*6 Nos*	
Raw Material Godown		*4 Nos*				*4 Nos*	
CPU Cabinet		**20 Nos**		**10 Nos**	**10 Nos**		
Finished Goods Godown		*20 Nos*		*10 Nos*	*10 Nos*		
CPU Fan		**1,685 Nos**			**200 Nos**	**1,485 Nos**	
Main Location		*250 Nos*			*200 Nos*	*50 Nos*	
Raw Material Godown		*1,435 Nos*				*1,435 Nos*	
Dual Core Processor		**20 Nos**	**20 Nos**				
Raw Material Godown		*20 Nos*	*20 Nos*				
Hardware Manual		**205 Nos**				**205 Nos**	
Finished Goods Godown		*205 Nos*				*205 Nos*	
							3 more ...
Grand Total			925 Nos	510 Nos	210 Nos		

Fig. 8.38 Stock Ageing Analysis with valued using FIFO

You may define Ageing Style in four different ways:

By Expiry Date	Displays age-wise break-up, based on Expiry Date of each batch.
To be Expired	Displays age-wise break-up for batches that will expire in future. It is very helpful to decide upon the batches to be disposed off first.
By Mfg. Date	Displays age-wise break-up taking into account the Mfg date of each Batch. It is helpful to identify the batches that have become old or nearing expiry.
By Date of Purchase	Displays age-wise break-up on the basis of Date of Purchase.

Press Alt+S to invoke the Ageing Style menu.

Select By Date of Purchase as Ageing Style, the following screen is displayed.

The Ageing Analysis report will help you find out which batches have already expired, which batches are going to expire or you can even list them as per Manufacturing or Purchase Date. It is very useful for industries dealing with perishable goods where goods past the expiry date are of no value.

Note: You will get the options Ageing Style and Expired Batches, only if you have activated Batch processing under F11:Features (F2:Inventory). Set Maintain Batchwise Details to Yes and set Expiry Date for Batches.

Item Inward Details

Age Analysis is done for stock-in-hand on the basis of it's purchase date. The Item Inwards details statement provides further information of aged stock such as date of purchase and supplier, and allows you to drill-down to the actual transaction voucher.

To view Item Inward Details,

Go to Gateway of Tally > Display > Inventory Books > Ageing Analysis

- Move the cursor to any of the age-wise columns (*i.e.*, < 45 days, 45 to 90 Days, > 180 Days) for an item and press Enter.

Stock Ageing Analysis — ABC Company — Ctrl + M

Items Under : **Primary** — **as at 31-Mar-2009**

All Batches (Aged by Date of Purchase) — *Valued based on Actual Purchase*

Particulars	Expiry Date	Total	(< 30 days)		30 to 60 days		60 to 90 days	
		Quantity	Quantity	Value	Quantity	Value	Quantity	Value
								2 more ...
240 GB Hard Disk Drive		**1,550 Nos**						
Main Location		*370 Nos*						
Raw Material Godown		*1,180 Nos*						
2 GB RAM Sticks		**3,615 Nos**	**50 Nos**	**27,95,000.00**	**50 Nos**	**12,35,000.00**	**50 Nos**	**20,15,000.00**
Main Location		*2,325 Nos*	*50 Nos*	*27,95,000.00*	*50 Nos*	*12,35,000.00*	*50 Nos*	*20,15,000.00*
Raw Material Godown		*1,290 Nos*						
2 GB USB Drive		**695 Nos**						
Main Location		*550 Nos*						
Raw Material Godown		*145 Nos*						
Colour Monitor 17"		**180 Nos**						
Finished Goods Godown		*100 Nos*						
Raw Material Godown		*80 Nos*						
Computer P-IV		**5 Nos**						
Finished Goods Godown		*5 Nos*						
Cooling Equipment		**10 Nos**						
Finished Goods Godown		*6 Nos*						
Raw Material Godown		*4 Nos*						
CPU Cabinet		**20 Nos**						
Finished Goods Godown		*20 Nos*						
CPU Fan		**1,685 Nos**					**350 Nos**	**43,750.00**
Raw Material Godown		*1,685 Nos*					*350 Nos*	*43,750.00*
Dual Core Processor		**20 Nos**						
Raw Material Godown		*20 Nos*						
Hardware Manual		**205 Nos**						
Finished Goods Godown		*205 Nos*						
Rectified Spirit		**215 Lts**						
								2 more ...
Grand Total			50 Nos	27,95,000.00	50 Nos	12,35,000.00	400 Nos	20,58,750.00

Fig. 8.38 Stock Ageing Analysis with Value Based on Date of Actual Purchase

Purchase Bills Pending

If you have entered a Receipt Note or Rejection Out with a New Tracking Number but have not entered Purchase or Debit Note linking the transaction, then although the inventory transactions have been recorded, relevant accounting entries are still pending.

If you want a list of bills for which Inventory transactions have been completed but the Accounting Transactions are not completed, then you can view them in the Purchase Bills Pending Report.

Item Inward Details | ABC Company | Ctrl + M

Stock Item: 2 GB RAM Sticks — 1-Apr-2008 to 31-Mar-2009

Date	Particulars	Vch Type	Vch No.	Inwards		
				Quantity	Rate	Value
1-4-2008	Opening Balance			10 Nos	2,200.00	22,000.00
1-4-2008	Physical Stock	Physical Stock	1	1,290 Nos		
5-4-2008	Supplier A	Purchase	7	500 Nos	2,024.00	10,12,000.00
10-4-2008	Supplier A	Purchase	10	300 Nos	2,006.67	6,02,000.00
15-4-2008	Physical Stock	Physical Stock	2			
30-4-2008	Customer A	Credit Note	5			
2-5-2008	Supplier B	Purchase	17	50 Nos	1,300.00	65,000.00
30-6-2008	Customer A	Credit Note	6			
30-7-2008	Supplier C	Purchase	20	410 Nos	2,013.66	8,25,600.00
2-8-2008	Supplier B	Purchase	21	900 Nos	1,450.00	13,05,000.00
3-9-2008	Supplier B	Purchase	22	900 Nos	3,061.11	27,55,000.00
10-10-2008	Supplier B	Purchase	23	50 Nos	22,100.00	11,05,000.00
3-11-2008	Supplier B	Purchase	25	50 Nos	48,100.00	24,05,000.00
10-12-2008	Supplier B	Purchase	26	50 Nos	21,750.00	10,87,500.00
10-1-2009	Supplier B	Purchase	27	50 Nos	40,300.00	20,15,000.00
14-2-2009	Supplier B	Purchase	29	50 Nos	24,700.00	12,35,000.00
29-3-2009	Supplier B	Purchase	30	50 Nos	55,900.00	27,95,000.00
	Totals :			4,660 Nos	3,697.23	1,72,29,100.00

Fig. 8.40 Item Inward Details

Similarly, if you have entered a Purchase Invoice or Debit Note with a New Tracking Number but have not entered Receipt Note or Rejection Out linking the transaction, this implies that although accounting transactions have been recorded, relevant inventory entries are still pending, this report will list all such transactions.

To view Purchase Bills Pending,

```
Go to Gateway of Tally > Display > Statements of Inventory > Purchase Bills
Pending
```

The default report is displayed as shown:

Purchase Bills Pending | ABC Company | Ctrl + M

Purchase Bills Pending — 1-Apr-2008 to 31-Mar-2009

Date	Tracking Number	Name of Item	Pending Quantity	Rate	Value
Goods Recd. but Bills not Recd. :					
1-May-2008	AR11245	CPU Fan *From:* Supplier A	120 Nos	350.00	42,000.00
1-May-2008	CE560	Cooling Equipment *From:* Supplier B	1 Nos	7,50,000.00	7,50,000.00
			119 Nos		(-)7,08,000.00

Fig. 8.41 Purchase Bills Pending

Note: Purchase Bills Pending Report is created when the option Tracking Numbers is set to Yes.

Sales Bills Pending

It lists all instances of incomplete sales, where goods may have been delivered but not invoiced. It also lists instances of invoices raised, but against which goods have not been delivered.

If you have entered a Delivery Notes or Rejection In with New Tracking Number but have not entered Sales Invoice (or Voucher) or Credit Note linking the transaction, it means that although inventory transactions have been recorded, relevant accounting entries are still pending. This report lists all such transactions.

Similarly, if you have entered certain Sales Invoice or Credit Note with New Tracking Number but have not entered Delivery Note or Rejection In linking the transaction, it implies that although accounting transactions have been recorded, relevant inventory entries are still pending. This report lists all such transactions.

```
Go to Gateway of Tally > Display > Statements of Inventory > Sales Bills Pending
```

The default report is displayed as shown:

Sales Bills Pending | ABC Company | Ctrl + M

Sales Bills Pending — 1-Apr-2008 to 31-Mar-2009

Date	Tracking Number	Name of Item	Pending Quantity	Rate	Value
Goods Delivered but Bills not Made :					
30-Aug-2008	3	Colour Monitor 17"	15 Nos	17,500.00	2,62,500.00
		Primary Batch Finished Goods Godown			
		To: Customer A			
	30-Aug-2008 Dely Note 3	*15 Nos @ 17,500.00*			
			15 Nos		2,62,500.00

Fig. 8.42 Sales Bills Pending

Click F12: Configure to view the Initial Quantity.

Click Detailed to view the transactions.

To drill down to voucher level, bring the cursor on the voucher detail line and press Enter.

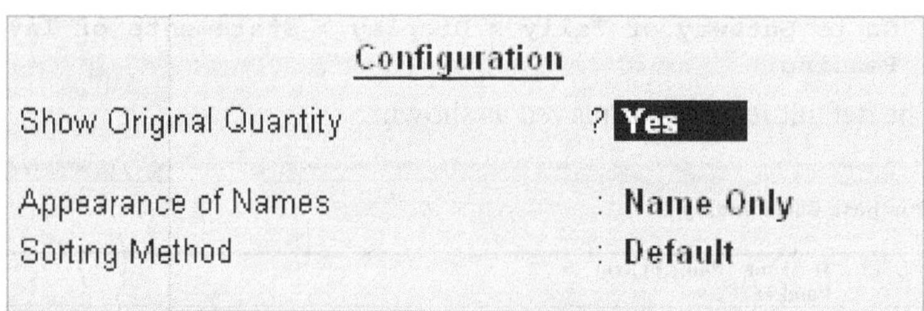

Note: Sales Bills Pending Report is generated when the option Tracking Numbers is set to Yes.

Stock Transfers Register

Stock Transfer displays the list of all the Stock Journal Vouchers used in Tally.ERP 9 to make stock adjustments. For example, to record any increase or decrease in stock due to shortage, wastage of stock or to record inter-godown transfers of stock, assembling or disassembling.

It is used to reflect the status of godown-wise stock. It is optional to enter the details of rate or amount in the stock journal. Additional cost incurred during stock transfer can also be tracked. This adds up to the value of the stock but does not get reflected in the accounts.

To view Stock Transfer Register:

```
Go to Gateway of Tally > Display > Inventory Books > Stock Transfers
```

Sales Bills Pending ABC Company Ctrl + M

Sales Bills Pending 1-Apr-2008 to 31-Mar-2009

Date	Tracking Number	Name of Item	Initial Quantity	Pending Quantity	Rate	Value
Goods Delivered but Bills not Made						
30-Aug-2008	3	Colour Monitor 17"	15 Nos	15 Nos	17,500.00	2,62,500.00
		Primary Batch Finished Goods Godown				
		To: Customer A				
		30-Aug-2008 Dely Note 3 15 Nos @ 17,500.00				
			15 Nos	15 Nos		2,62,500.00

Fig. 8.43 Sales Bills Pending with Original Quantity

The total number of vouchers and cancelled vouchers for each month of the Voucher Type - Stock Journal is shown in the default report.

Stock Journal Register ABC Company Ctrl + M

Particulars	Stock Journal ABC Company 1-Apr-2008 to 31-Mar-2009 Transactions Total Vouchers	(cancelled)
April	3	
May	2	
June	3	(1)
July	3	
August	2	
September	0	
October	0	
November	0	
December	0	
January	0	
February	0	
March	0	

Fig. 8.44 Stock Journal Register

To view the Stock Journal Vouchers for any month, press Enter on any month, all the vouchers of that month will be displayed.

Physical Stock Register

A Physical Stock Voucher is used to record the actual stock of a particular stock item. In the inventory books, the actual balance of stock in hand as on the date of voucher entry is shown and the difference in stock is automatically added as inwards or outwards as the case may be. The cause of discrepancy can be recorded in the narration field of the physical stock journal voucher.

This register summarises the stock adjustments made during the reporting period. An analysis of the stock recorded in the register gives us an insight into the causes of discrepancies to ensure that timely action is taken.

To view Physical Stock Register:

`Go to Gateway of Tally > Display > Inventory Books > Physical Stock Register`

Physical Stock Register	ABC Company	Ctrl + M
Particulars	Physical Stock ABC Company 1-Apr-2008 to 31-Mar-2009 Transactions Total Vouchers	(cancelled)
April	2	
May	2	
June	3	
July	4	(1)
August	1	
September	0	
October	0	
November	0	
December	0	
January	0	
February	0	
March	0	

Fig. 8.45 Physical Stock Register

Physical stock register displays a list, showing the number of vouchers in each month.

Statistics of Inventory Masters

The Statistics report displays the Masters created and the number of vouchers types entered. You can drill down to the transaction level from this report.

To view the Statistics report,

`Go to Gateway of Tally > Display > Statement of Inventory > Statistics`

You can Drill down to a specific type of voucher to view the details.

Types of Vouchers	ABC Company 1-Apr-2008 to 31-Mar-2009		Types of Accounts	ABC Company 1-Apr-2008 to 31-Mar-2009
Attendance	0		Groups	28
Contra	0		Ledgers	113
Credit Note	8		Cost Centres	2
Debit Note	3		Stock Groups	2
Delivery Note	4		Stock Categories	5
Journal	25		Stock Items	16
Manufacturing Journal	1		Godowns	3
Memorandum	0		Voucher Types	21
Payment	21		Units	2
Payroll	0		Currencies	2
Physical Stock	12	(1cancelled)	Budgets & Scenarios	0
Purchase	30			
Purchase Order	4			
Receipt	8			
Receipt Note	1			
Rejections In	1			
Rejections Out	1			
Retail Invoice	38			
Reversing Journal	0			
Sales	7			
Sales Order	6			
Stock Journal	12	(1cancelled)		
Tax Invoice	15			
Total	197	(2cancelled)		

Fig. 8.46 Statistics Screen

9 Other Reports of Tally.ERP 9

Management Information System (MIS) Reports

MIS Reports are reports required by the management to assess the performance of the organization and allow for faster decision-making.

Types of MIS Reports in Tally.ERP 9

- Accounting Reports: To obtain information on the financial position, operational performance and economic activities of the business.
- Financial Reports: To determine the financial condition of an organisation as required by shareholders, creditors and government units.
- Inventory Reports: To manage the Inventory effectively since the actual status of stock items is obtained.
- Management Control Reports: To utilise budgets, cost centre reports, scenario reports etc. for controlling activities.

Few of the Financial MIS reports are listed below:

- Receivables
- Payables
- Cost Centre Reports
- Ratio Analysis
- Cash Flow
- Funds Flow
- Exceptional Reports.

Display Receivables

Bills Receivable and Bills Payable

A bill of exchange can be treated as both bills receivable and bills payable. When the drawee accepts the bill and sends it back to the drawer, it becomes a bills receivable to the drawer as money is receivable on the bill. Therefore, it becomes an asset to him. On the other hand, it becomes a bills payable to the drawee if money is payable by him on the bill, in which case it is a liability for him.

The drawer can make use of the bill in one of the following ways:

1. Retain the bill till the date of maturity and collect the money from the drawee.
2. Endorse the bill to his creditor.
3. Discount the bill with the banker.

4. Send the bill to the banker for collection.

Display Receivable

Bills receivable is a bill of exchange on which payment is expected to be received at a later date.

To view the Receivables screen:

```
Go to Gateway of Tally > Display > Statements of Accounts > Outstandings >
Receivables
```

The Bills Receivable screen is displayed as shown:

Bills Outstanding | ABC Company | Ctrl + M

Bills Receivable | 1-Apr-2008 to 31-Mar-2009

Date	Ref. No.	Partys' Name	Pending Amount	Due on	Overdue by days
31-Mar-2007	Op Balance	Commission	15,000.00	31-Mar-2007	731
1-Apr-2008	3	Bright Industries	1,08,500.00	1-Apr-2008	364
1-Apr-2008	ATB/0032	Customer A	61,000.00	31-May-2008	304
3-Apr-2008	GI001	Customer B	4,16,000.00	3-Apr-2008	362
4-Apr-2008	GI002	Customer B	88,400.00	4-Apr-2008	361
5-Apr-2008	CA/5210	Customer A	5,25,000.00	5-Apr-2008	360
5-Apr-2008	FORX/2201	Customer A	2,46,750.00	5-Apr-2008	360
6-Apr-2008	GCPL/885	Global Computech Pvt Ltd..	2,10,000.00	6-Apr-2008	359
7-Apr-2008	CUST/1200	Customer A	6,69,500.00	7-Apr-2008	358
19-Apr-2008	CST/5562	Customer A	3,50,200.00	19-Apr-2008	346
24-Apr-2008	1524	Customer B	6,30,000.00	24-Apr-2008	341
28-Apr-2008	STC002	Silverline Trading Corporation	65,000.00	28-Apr-2008	337
29-Apr-2008	MC/225	Manchester Computers	3,42,000.00	29-Apr-2008	336
29-Apr-2008	PR/5520	Platinum Rectifiers	36,36,000.00	29-Apr-2008	336
30-Apr-2008	BNS/2205	Blue Nile Stationeries	1,70,000.00	30-Apr-2008	335
30-Apr-2008	13	Blue Nile Stationeries	64,375.00	30-Apr-2008	335
30-Apr-2008	2	Customer B	5,200.00	30-Apr-2008	335
30-Apr-2008	CCC/558	Customer C	96,000.00	30-Apr-2008	335
30-Apr-2008	10	Patel Chemicals Pvt Ltd..	20,000.00	30-Apr-2008	335
30-Apr-2008	1	Supplier C	2,808.00	30-Apr-2008	335
30-Apr-2008	U12	Unisys Global Systems	5,000.00	30-Apr-2008	335
1-May-2008	AAC/888	Customer A	56,000.00	30-Jun-2008	274
1-May-2008	CAA/885	Customer A	56,000.00	1-May-2008	334
1-May-2008	20	Customer A	16,800.00	30-Jul-2008	244
1-May-2008	GCC/887	Global Computech Pvt Ltd..	1,75,000.00	1-May-2008	334
1-May-2008	GCC/7778	Global Computech Pvt Ltd..	7,45,000.00	1-May-2008	334
1-May-2008	UN/445	UN Diplomatic Mission	17,50,000.00	1-May-2008	334
30-May-2008	IS004	Innovative Solutions Pvt Ltd	12,500.00	30-May-2008	305
1-Jun-2008	15	Silverline Trading Corporation	95,000.00	1-Jun-2008	303
				23 more ...	
			3,23,22,896.00		

Fig. 9.1 Bills Outstanding Screen

This report displays all outstanding receivables invoice by invoice till date. Remember that this report takes into consideration only those accounts that have Bill-by-Bill option activated.

Date

This is the Effective date of the invoice and not the actual date. Hence, if your invoice date is 15th November but the effective date is 30th November, and then 30-Nov-08 will be displayed here. Credit period is calculated from the effective date.

Reference Number

This is the Bill reference number that was entered in the Bill-wise Details.

Party's Name

The ledger name appears in this field.

Pending Amount

This is the outstanding balance on a particular invoice. To see the breakup, press SHIFT + ENTER.

If you want to see the breakup of all the bills, select the F1: Detailed button. This toggles with the button F1: Condensed.

Due On

This is the due date of the bill (with reference to the Effective date) specified during voucher entry.

Overdue by days

This is the period in days from the due date to the end date of the report. In the above example, the end date is 30-Aug-2008.

Drill-down

You can drill down any invoice for further details.

Configuration

Include Post-Dated Transactions	?	No
Show Bills in Foreign Exchange	?	No
Show Opening Amount	?	No
Show overdue using Bill Date	?	No
Range of Bills to show	:	Pending Bills
Show Qty Info in Detailed Format	?	Yes
Appearance of Names	:	Name Only
Sorting Method	:	Default

Buttons

Print the report or e-mail it or use other buttons to configure, make a query or change the format of the report.

F12: Configure Bill-wise Outstandings Report

The F12: Configuration screen for Bill-wise Outstanding Report is displayed as shown.

Include Post-Dated Transactions

Post-dated transactions are those, whose voucher dates are after the end date of the period of display.

If you set this option to Yes, you can have the post-dated transactions listed in the Outstandings report and see their effect.

In the above example, note that there is an additional column for Post-Dated Amount.

Show Bills in Foreign Exchange

If this option is set to Yes, the Bills Outstanding report will show only those bills raised in foreign currency. The bills raised in base currency will be excluded.

Show Over dues using Bill dates

Set this option to Yes if you want to use the invoice dates instead of due dates for calculating overdue days.

Ledger-wise Receivables Report

If you want to know the outstanding status of the bills of a particular party account, use the Ledger Outstanding Report.

Bills Outstanding		ABC Company			Ctrl + M
Bills Receivable				1-Apr-2008 to 31-Mar-2009	
Date	Ref. No.	Partys' Name	Pending Amount	Post-Dated Amount	Final Balance
31-Mar-2007	Op Balance	Commission	15,000.00		15,000.00 Dr
1-Apr-2008	3	Bright Industries	1,08,500.00		1,08,500.00 Dr
1-Apr-2008	ATB/0032	Customer A	61,000.00		61,000.00 Dr
3-Apr-2008	GI001	Customer B	4,16,000.00		4,16,000.00 Dr
4-Apr-2008	GI002	Customer B	88,400.00		88,400.00 Dr
5-Apr-2008	CA/5210	Customer A	5,25,000.00		5,25,000.00 Dr
5-Apr-2008	FORX/2201	Customer A	2,46,750.00		2,46,750.00 Dr
6-Apr-2008	GCPL/885	Global Computech Pvt Ltd..	2,10,000.00		2,10,000.00 Dr
7-Apr-2008	CUST/1200	Customer A	6,69,500.00		6,69,500.00 Dr
19-Apr-2008	CST/5562	Customer A	3,50,200.00		3,50,200.00 Dr
24-Apr-2008	1524	Customer B	6,30,000.00		6,30,000.00 Dr
28-Apr-2008	STC002	Silverline Trading Corporation	65,000.00		65,000.00 Dr
29-Apr-2008	MC/225	Manchester Computers	3,42,000.00		3,42,000.00 Dr
29-Apr-2008	PR/5520	Platinum Rectifiers	36,36,000.00		36,36,000.00 Dr
30-Apr-2008	BNS/2205	Blue Nile Stationeries	1,70,000.00		1,70,000.00 Dr
30-Apr-2008	13	Blue Nile Stationeries	64,375.00		64,375.00 Dr
30-Apr-2008	2	Customer B	5,200.00		5,200.00 Dr
30-Apr-2008	CCC/558	Customer C	96,000.00		96,000.00 Dr
30-Apr-2008	10	Patel Chemicals Pvt Ltd..	20,000.00		20,000.00 Dr
30-Apr-2008	1	Supplier C	2,808.00		2,808.00 Dr
30-Apr-2008	U12	Unisys Global Systems	5,000.00		5,000.00 Dr
1-May-2008	AAC/888	Customer A	56,000.00		56,000.00 Dr
1-May-2008	CAA/885	Customer A	56,000.00		56,000.00 Dr
1-May-2008	20	Customer A	16,800.00		16,800.00 Dr
1-May-2008	GCC/887	Global Computech Pvt Ltd..	1,75,000.00		1,75,000.00 Dr
1-May-2008	GCC/7778	Global Computech Pvt Ltd..	7,45,000.00		7,45,000.00 Dr
1-May-2008	UN/445	UN Diplomatic Mission	17,50,000.00		17,50,000.00 Dr
30-May-2008	IS004	Innovative Solutions Pvt Ltd	12,500.00		12,500.00 Dr
1-Jun-2008	15	Silverline Trading Corporation	95,000.00		95,000.00 Dr
					23 more ...
			3,23,22,896.00		3,23,22,896.00 Dr

Fig. 9.2 Bills Outstanding Screen with Post-dated Amount

Bills Outstanding		ABC Company			Ctrl + M
Bills Receivable				1-Apr-2008 to 31-Mar-2009	
Date	Ref. No.	Partys' Name	Pending Amount	Post-Dated Amount	Final Balance
5-Apr-2008	FORX/2201	Customer A	$5,250.00		$5,250.00 Dr
	5-Apr-2008 Retail Invoice 4	$5,250.00 Dr			
	30 Nos Colour Monitor 17" $175.00/Nos				
1-Jul-2008	CCC/5551	Customer C	$1,029.00		$1,029.00 Dr
	1-Jul-2008 Tax Invoice 10	$1,029.00 Dr			
	10 Nos 240 GB Hard Disk Drive $98.00/Nos				
			$6,279.00		$6,279.00 Dr

Fig. 9.3 Bills Outstanding Screen with Amount in Foreign Exchange

To view the Ledger-wise Receivable Report:

1. Go to Gateway of Tally > Display > Statements of accounts > Outstandings > Ledger
2. Select a ledger from the list.

Bills Outstanding | ABC Company | Ctrl + M

Bills Receivable | 1-Apr-2008 to 31-Mar-2009

Date	Ref. No.	Partys' Name	Pending Amount	*Post-Dated Amount*	Final Balance
31-Mar-2007	Op Balance	Commission	15,000.00		15,000.00 Dr
1-Apr-2008	3	Bright Industries	1,08,500.00		1,08,500.00 Dr
1-Apr-2008	ATB/0032	Customer A	61,000.00		61,000.00 Dr
3-Apr-2008	GI001	Customer B	4,16,000.00		4,16,000.00 Dr
4-Apr-2008	GI002	Customer B	88,400.00		88,400.00 Dr
5-Apr-2008	CA/5210	Customer A	5,25,000.00		5,25,000.00 Dr
5-Apr-2008	FORX/2201	Customer A	2,46,750.00		2,46,750.00 Dr
6-Apr-2008	GCPL/885	Global Computech Pvt Ltd..	2,10,000.00		2,10,000.00 Dr
7-Apr-2008	CUST/1200	Customer A	6,69,500.00		6,69,500.00 Dr
19-Apr-2008	CST/5562	Customer A	3,50,200.00		3,50,200.00 Dr
24-Apr-2008	1524	Customer B	6,30,000.00		6,30,000.00 Dr
28-Apr-2008	STC002	Silverline Trading Corporation	65,000.00		65,000.00 Dr
29-Apr-2008	MC/225	Manchester Computers	3,42,000.00		3,42,000.00 Dr
29-Apr-2008	PR/5520	Platinum Rectifiers	36,36,000.00		36,36,000.00 Dr
30-Apr-2008	BNS/2205	Blue Nile Stationeries	1,70,000.00		1,70,000.00 Dr
30-Apr-2008	13	Blue Nile Stationeries	64,375.00		64,375.00 Dr
30-Apr-2008	2	Customer B	5,200.00		5,200.00 Dr
30-Apr-2008	CCC/558	Customer C	96,000.00		96,000.00 Dr
30-Apr-2008	10	Patel Chemicals Pvt Ltd..	20,000.00		20,000.00 Dr
30-Apr-2008	1	Supplier C	2,808.00		2,808.00 Dr
30-Apr-2008	U12	Unisys Global Systems	5,000.00		5,000.00 Dr
1-May-2008	AAC/888	Customer A	56,000.00		56,000.00 Dr
1-May-2008	CAA/885	Customer A	56,000.00		56,000.00 Dr
1-May-2008	20	Customer A	16,800.00		16,800.00 Dr
1-May-2008	GCC/887	Global Computech Pvt Ltd..	1,75,000.00		1,75,000.00 Dr
1-May-2008	GCC/7778	Global Computech Pvt Ltd..	7,45,000.00		7,45,000.00 Dr
1-May-2008	UN/445	UN Diplomatic Mission	17,50,000.00		17,50,000.00 Dr
30-May-2008	IS004	Innovative Solutions Pvt Ltd	12,500.00		12,500.00 Dr
1-Jun-2008	15	Silverline Trading Corporation	95,000.00		95,000.00 Dr
					23 more ...
			3,23,22,896.00		3,23,22,896.00 Dr

Fig. 9.4 Bills Outstanding Screen with Amount Overdue

The Ledger Outstanding report is displayed as shown on the next page.

Detailed functionality available in this report, including F12: Configure and Age-wise Analysis is the same as that available in Receivables.

You can generate Reminder Letters from the ledger Outstanding report.

Use the Contact button on the button bar to view the address and other contact details.

Ageing Analysis Report

Ageing analysis of receivables is done to find out bills for which an amount is due for a long period of time. These bills can either be classified as bad debts or provisions can be made for such losses in the books of accounts depending on the results of ageing analysis.

Select F6: Age wise from the button bar in the Ledger Outstanding screen.

Select either the option Ageing by Bill Date or Ageing by Due Date for Methods of Ageing.

Set the age periods required for the report.

The Age of Bill in days column shows the age of the invoices in number of days.

Age-wise Analysis of a Single Ledger Account

1. Go to Gateway of Tally > Display > Statements of Accounts > Outstandings > Ledger

Ledger Outstandings — ABC Company — Ctrl + M

Ledger : **Customer A** — **1-Apr-2008 to 31-Aug-2008**

Date	Ref. No.	Opening Amount	Pending Amount	Due on	Overdue by days
1-Apr-2008	ATB/0032	61,000.00 Dr	61,000.00 Dr	31-May-2008	92
5-Apr-2008	CA/5210	5,25,000.00 Dr	5,25,000.00 Dr	5-Apr-2008	148
5-Apr-2008	FORX/2201	2,57,250.00 Dr	2,46,750.00 Dr	5-Apr-2008	148
7-Apr-2008	CUST/1200	6,69,500.00 Dr	6,69,500.00 Dr	7-Apr-2008	146
19-Apr-2008	CST/5562	3,50,200.00 Dr	3,50,200.00 Dr	19-Apr-2008	134
30-Apr-2008	4	32,960.00 Cr	32,960.00 Cr	30-Apr-2008	123
1-May-2008	AAC/888	56,000.00 Dr	56,000.00 Dr	30-Jun-2008	62
1-May-2008	CAA/885	56,000.00 Dr	56,000.00 Dr	1-May-2008	122
1-May-2008	20	16,800.00 Dr	16,800.00 Dr	30-Jul-2008	32
6-Jun-2008	CAF/774	1,25,000.00 Dr	1,25,000.00 Dr	6-Jul-2008	56
15-Jun-2008	2	35,000.00 Dr	35,000.00 Dr	14-Aug-2008	17
30-Jun-2008	6	32,960.00 Cr	2,47,160.00 Cr	30-Jun-2008	62
		20,85,830.00 Dr	18,61,130.00 Dr		

Fig. 9.5 Ledger Outstanding

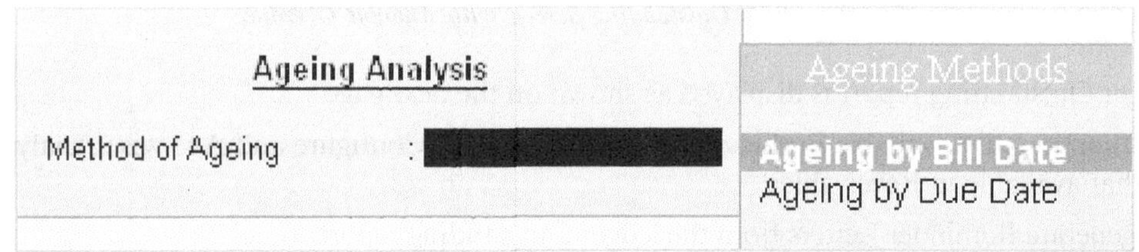

Ledger Outstandings — ABC Company — Ctrl + M

Ledger : Customer A — 1-Apr-2008 to 31-May-2008

Date	Ref. No.	Opening Amount	Pending Amount	(< 30 days)	30 to 60 days	60 to 120 days	(> 120 days)	On Account
1-Apr-2008	ATB/0032	61,000.00 Dr	61,000.00 Dr		61,000.00 Dr			
5-Apr-2008	CA/5210	5,25,000.00 Dr	5,25,000.00 Dr		5,25,000.00 Dr			
5-Apr-2008	FORX/2201	2,57,250.00 Dr	2,57,250.00 Dr		2,57,250.00 Dr			
7-Apr-2008	CUST/1200	6,69,500.00 Dr	6,69,500.00 Dr		6,69,500.00 Dr			
19-Apr-2008	CST/5562	3,50,200.00 Dr	3,50,200.00 Dr		3,50,200.00 Dr			
30-Apr-2008	4	32,960.00 Cr	32,960.00 Cr		32,960.00 Cr			
1-May-2008	AAC/888	56,000.00 Dr	56,000.00 Dr	56,000.00 Dr				
1-May-2008	CAA/885	56,000.00 Dr	56,000.00 Dr	56,000.00 Dr				
1-May-2008	20	16,800.00 Dr	16,800.00 Dr	16,800.00 Dr				
		19,58,790.00 Dr	19,58,790.00 Dr	1,28,800.00 Dr	18,29,990.00 Dr			

Fig. 9.6 Ledger Outstanding with Different Periods

2. Select the ledger account.
3. Select F6: Age-wise and one of the two methods of Ageing.
   - Ageing by Bill Date
   - Ageing by Due Date.
4. Set the age periods required for the report.

The aged bills report is generated accordingly. Drill down for more details on the individual invoices.

Ledger Outstandings — ABC Company — Ctrl + M

Ledger : Customer A — 1-Apr-2008 to 30-Jun-2008

Date	Ref. No.	Opening Amount	Pending Amount	(< 30 days)	30 to 60 days	60 to 120 days	(> 120 days)	On Account
1-Apr-2008	ATB/0032	61,000.00 Dr	61.000.00 Dr			61.000.00 Dr		
5-Apr-2008	CA/5210	5,25,000.00 Dr	5.25.000.00 Dr			5.25.000.00 Dr		
5-Apr-2008	FORX/2201	2,57,250.00 Dr	2.57.250.00 Dr			2.57.250.00 Dr		
7-Apr-2008	CUST/1200	6,69,500.00 Dr	6.69.500.00 Dr			6.69.500.00 Dr		
19-Apr-2008	CST/5562	3,50,200.00 Dr	3.50.200.00 Dr			3.50.200.00 Dr		
30-Apr-2008	4	32,960.00 Cr	32.960.00 Cr			32.960.00 Cr		
1-May-2008	AAC/888	56,000.00 Dr	56.000.00 Dr		56.000.00 Dr			
1-May-2008	CAA/885	56,000.00 Dr	56.000.00 Dr		56.000.00 Dr			
1-May-2008	20	16,800.00 Dr	16,800.00 Dr		16,800.00 Dr			
6-Jun-2008	CAF/774	1,25,000.00 Dr	1,25,000.00 Dr	1,25,000.00 Dr				
15-Jun-2008	2	35,000.00 Dr	35,000.00 Dr	35,000.00 Dr				
30-Jun-2008	6	32,960.00 Cr	2.47.160.00 Cr	2.47.160.00 Cr				
		20,85,830.00 Dr	18.71.630.00 Dr	87.160.00 Cr	1.28.800.00 Dr	18.29.990.00 Dr		

Fig. 9.7 Ledger Outstanding with Different Periods

Age-wise Analysis for a Group

1. Go to Gateway of Tally > Display > Statements of Accounts > Outstandings > Group
2. Select a group, *e.g.*, Sundry Debtors.
3. Click Age-wise and select one of the two Methods of Ageing: Ageing by Bill Date or Ageing by Due Date. Set the age periods required for the report.

Configuration

Range of Bills to show	:	Pending Bills
Show Nett Balances	?	Yes
Show Contact Details	?	No
Appearance of Names	:	Name Only
Scale Factor for Values	:	Default
Sorting Method	:	Default
Expand all levels in Detailed Format	?	No

4. The aged bills report is generated accordingly. You can drill down for further details on the individual invoices.
5. Set the appropriate parameter in F12: Configure to view the Nett Balances.

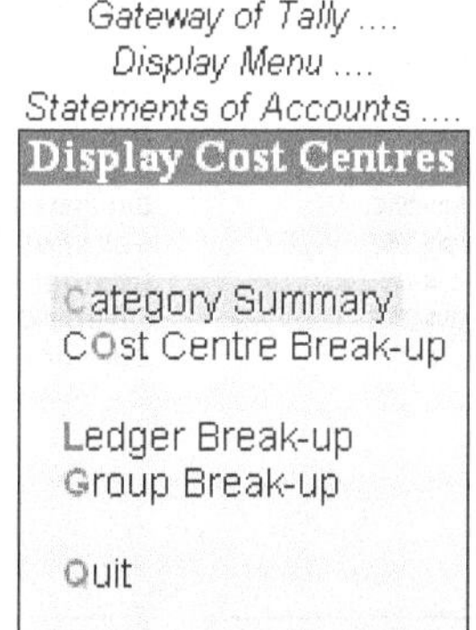

Age-wise Analysis for a Group will be displayed as shown on next page.

Note: You cannot print Reminder letters to a group from here. Use Multi-Account Printing available in Gateway of Tally.

Display Payables

Bills payable is a bill of exchange due for payment at a future date.

Group Outstandings ABC Company Ctrl + M

	Sundry Debtors ABC Company 1-Apr-2008 to 31-Mar -2009	Sundry Debtors ABC Company 1-Apr-2008 to 31-Mar -2009	Sundry Debtors ABC Company 1-Apr-2008 to 31-Mar -2009	Sundry Debtors ABC Company 1-Apr-2008 to 31-Mar -2009	Sundry Debtors ABC Company 1-Apr-2008 to 31-Mar -2009	Sundry Debtors ABC Company 1-Apr-2008 to 31-Mar -2009
	Pending Bills	(< 30 days)	30 to 60 days	60 to 120 days	(> 120 days)	On Account
Sales Bills to Make						
Customer A	18,61,130.00 Dr	18,61,130.00 Dr	18,61,130.00 Dr	18,61,130.00 Dr	18,61,130.00 Dr	18,61,130.00 Dr
Customer B	11,48,664.00 Dr	11,48,664.00 Dr	11,48,664.00 Dr	11,48,664.00 Dr	11,48,664.00 Dr	11,48,664.00 Dr
Customer C	1,67,75,363.00 Dr	1,67,75,363.00 Dr	1,67,75,363.00 Dr	1,67,75,363.00 Dr	1,67,75,363.00 Dr	1,67,75,363.00 Dr
Global Computech Pvt Ltd.,	11,35,600.00 Dr	11,35,600.00 Dr	11,35,600.00 Dr	11,35,600.00 Dr	11,35,600.00 Dr	11,35,600.00 Dr
Innovative Solutions Pvt Ltd	5,97,500.00 Dr	5,97,500.00 Dr	5,97,500.00 Dr	5,97,500.00 Dr	5,97,500.00 Dr	5,97,500.00 Dr
Manchester Computers	3,42,000.00 Dr	3,42,000.00 Dr	3,42,000.00 Dr	3,42,000.00 Dr	3,42,000.00 Dr	3,42,000.00 Dr
Platinum Rectifiers	72,72,000.00 Dr	72,72,000.00 Dr	72,72,000.00 Dr	72,72,000.00 Dr	72,72,000.00 Dr	72,72,000.00 Dr
Silverline Trading Corporation	3,19,875.00 Dr	3,19,875.00 Dr	3,19,875.00 Dr	3,19,875.00 Dr	3,19,875.00 Dr	3,19,875.00 Dr
UN Diplomatic Mission	17,50,000.00 Dr	17,50,000.00 Dr	17,50,000.00 Dr	17,50,000.00 Dr	17,50,000.00 Dr	17,50,000.00 Dr
Unisys Global Systems	24,100.00 Dr	24,100.00 Dr	24,100.00 Dr	24,100.00 Dr	24,100.00 Dr	24,100.00 Dr
	3,12,26,232.00 Dr	3,12,26,232.00 Dr	3,12,26,232.00 Dr	3,12,26,232.00 Dr	3,12,26,232.00 Dr	3,12,26,232.00 Dr

Fig. 9.8 Agewise Analysis for a Group

To view the Bills Payable screen,

Bills Outstanding ABC Company Ctrl + M

Bills Payable 1-Apr-2008 to 31-Mar-2009

Date	Ref. No.	Partys' Name	Pending Amount	Due on	Overdue by days
1-Apr-2008	154	Supplier C	18,36,000.00	1-Apr-2008	364
1-Apr-2008	2	Unisys Global Systems	90,900.00	1-Apr-2008	364
2-Apr-2008	3	Customer C	1,01,250.00	2-Apr-2008	363
2-Apr-2008	3	Global Traders	28,125.00	2-Apr-2008	363
5-Apr-2008	10	Customer C	37,000.00	5-Apr-2008	360
5-Apr-2008	721	Equipment Sales Corporation	7,80,000.00	5-Apr-2008	360
5-Apr-2008	6	Supplier A	10,12,000.00	5-Apr-2008	360
9-Apr-2008	12	Supplier A	1,10,000.00	9-Apr-2008	356
10-Apr-2008	2	Customer C	41,250.00	10-Apr-2008	355
10-Apr-2008	9	Supplier A	6,02,000.00	10-Apr-2008	355
17-Apr-2008	1	Customer B	55,936.00	17-Apr-2008	348
30-Apr-2008	4	Customer A	32,960.00	30-Apr-2008	335
30-Apr-2008	19	Equipment Sales Corporation	2,25,000.00	30-Apr-2008	335
30-Apr-2008	706	Patel Chemicals Pvt Ltd..	36,000.00	30-Apr-2008	335
30-Apr-2008	123	Supplier A	37,50,000.00	30-Apr-2008	335
30-Apr-2008	2	Supplier C	16,875.00	30-Apr-2008	335
1-May-2008	2	Bright Industries	1,02,000.00	1-May-2008	334
1-May-2008	0056	Bright Industries	12,48,000.00	1-May-2008	334
2-May-2008	5	Supplier B	1,50,30,087.50	2-May-2008	333
7-Jun-2008	18	Equipment Sales Corporation	6,25,000.00	7-Jun-2008	297
7-Jun-2008	58701	Supplier A	8,50,000.00	7-Jun-2008	297
30-Jun-2008	6	Customer A	2,47,160.00	30-Jun-2008	274
30-Jun-2008	7	Silverline Trading Corporation	90,125.00	30-Jun-2008	274
30-Jul-2008	18	Supplier C	8,25,600.00	30-Jul-2008	244
			2,77,73,268.50		

Fig. 9.9 Agewise Analysis with Number of Days

```
Go to Gateway of Tally > Display > Statements of Accounts > Outstandings >
Payables
```

F4: Payable in the Receivables screen helps you switch to the Bills Payable report.

Note: Payables are treated exactly the same way as Receivables.

Cost Centre Reports

For conceptual information on Cost Centres and Cost Categories, please look up the relevant chapters under Accounts Information.

Cost Centre Reports are primarily performance reports that give a different perspective to transactions. To access Cost Centre Reports:

```
Go to Gateway of Tally> Display > Statement of Accounts> Cost Centres
```

Note: Set Maintain Cost Centres to Yes in F11: Features.

Cost Category Summary

Cost Category Summary displays the information on all cost categories to which you have allocated the voucher transactions.

```
Go to Gateway of Tally > Display > Statements of Accounts > Cost centers >
Category Summary
```

Cost Category Summary ABC Company Ctrl + M

Particulars	ABC Company For 1-Apr-2008 Transactions Debit	Credit	Closing Balance
Department	35,000.00	65,000.00	**30,000.00 Cr**
Finance	25,000.00	55,000.00	*30,000.00 Cr*
Marketing	10,000.00	10,000.00	
Division	*30,000.00*	*30,000.00*	
Export	20,000.00	11,000.00	*9,000.00 Dr*
Retail	5,000.00	9,000.00	*4,000.00 Cr*
Wholesale	5,000.00	10,000.00	*5,000.00 Cr*
Primary Cost Category	*15,000.00*	*30,000.00*	**15,000.00 Cr**
Salesman A	4,000.00	15,000.00	*11,000.00 Cr*
Salesman B	6,000.00	10,000.00	*4,000.00 Cr*
Salesman C	5,000.00	5,000.00	

Fig. 9.10 Cost Category Summary

You can create any number of cost categories apart from the Primary one, which is the default category. Each Cost Category has cost centres listed under it. The names in italics are cost centres that do not have any sub-cost centres. The names that are in normal fonts are cost centres that have sub-cost centres under them.

The debit and credit transaction totals and the closing balance for each cost category are displayed together with their breakdown consisting of cost centre summaries.

Note: We can configure the report by selecting the required options in F12:Configure.

Cost Centre Vouchers

To display Cost Centre Vouchers,

1. From the Cost Category Summary, drill down into a cost centre for a monthly breakup of the figures.
2. Select a month to display the Cost Centre Vouchers pertaining to that month.
3. In the Cost Centre Vouchers use F2: Period to expand the date range if required.
4. To display more detailed cost centre vouchers, set the required options in F12: Configure.

The Cost Centre Vouchers screen is also accessible from all other Cost Centre Reports but the vouchers displayed are only those that relate to the currently selected cost centre.

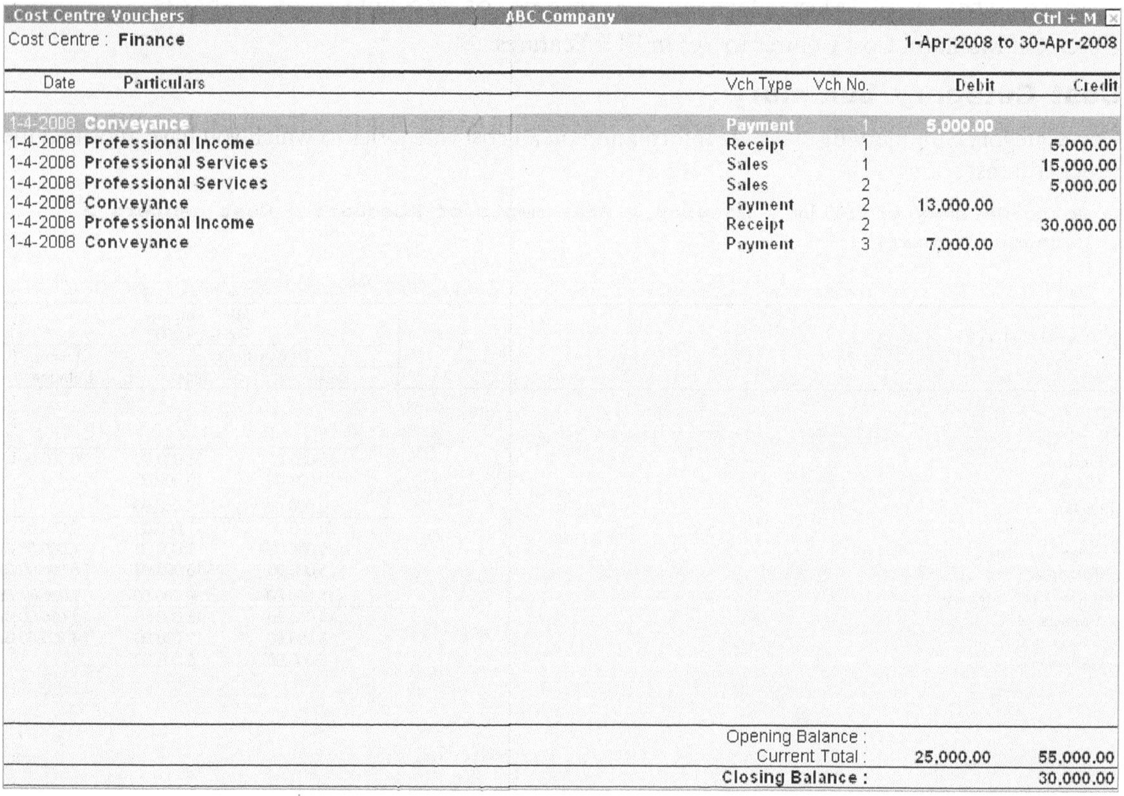

Cost Centre Vouchers ABC Company Ctrl + M

Cost Centre : **Finance** 1-Apr-2008 to 30-Apr-2008

Date	Particulars	Vch Type	Vch No.	Debit	Credit
1-4-2008	Conveyance	Payment	1	5,000.00	
1-4-2008	Professional Income	Receipt	1		5,000.00
1-4-2008	Professional Services	Sales	1		15,000.00
1-4-2008	Professional Services	Sales	2		5,000.00
1-4-2008	Conveyance	Payment	2	13,000.00	
1-4-2008	Professional Income	Receipt	2		30,000.00
1-4-2008	Conveyance	Payment	3	7,000.00	
		Opening Balance :			
		Current Total :		25,000.00	55,000.00
		Closing Balance :			30,000.00

Fig. 9.11 Cost Centre Vouchers

Cost Centre Break-up

Cost centre Break-up shows the ledger accounts that are used in vouchers, the cost centre they were allocated to, their total transaction values and the balance. If you consider only the revenue accounts, the Cost Centre break-up becomes the Profit or Loss statement of activities for the cost centre, and hence a powerful performance statement.

To access the Cost Centre Break-up screen,

1. Go to Gateway of Tally > Display > Statements of Accounts > Cost Centers > Cost Center Break-up

2. Select a cost centre, e.g. Finance
3. Click F1: Detailed to see the ledgers.

The Breakup of Cost Centre report will be displayed as shown.

Cost Breakup of Ledger — ABC Company — Ctrl + M

Particulars	Ledger: Conveyance ABC Company For 1-Apr-2008 Transactions Debit	Credit	Closing Balance
Department	35,000.00		35,000.00 Dr
Finance	25,000.00		*25,000.00 Dr*
Marketing	10,000.00		*10,000.00 Dr*
Division	*30,000.00*		**30,000.00 Dr**
Export	20,000.00		*20,000.00 Dr*
Retail	5,000.00		*5,000.00 Dr*
Wholesale	5,000.00		*5,000.00 Dr*
Primary Cost Category	*15,000.00*		**15,000.00 Dr**
Salesman A	4,000.00		*4,000.00 Dr*
Salesman B	6,000.00		*6,000.00 Dr*
Salesman C	5,000.00		*5,000.00 Dr*

Fig. 9.12 Cost Breakup of Ledgers

Use the button F5:Led-wise on the button bar to view the report in the alphabetic order of ledger accounts.

A columnar Cost-centre breakup enables comparison of two or more cost centres and assessment of their relative performance. Use New Column (Alt+C) to bring up the data of another cost centre for comparison alongside. Drill down for further details.

Breakup of Cost Centre — ABC Company — Ctrl + M

Particulars	Cost Centre: Finance ABC Company 1-Apr-2008 to 8-Apr-2008 Transactions Debit	Credit	Closing Balance	Cost Centre: Treasury ABC Company 1-Apr-2008 to 30-Apr-2008 Transactions Debit	Credit	Closing Balance
Conveyance	*13,000.00*		13,000.00 Dr	4,000.00		*4,000.00 Dr*
Professional Income		*15,000.00*	15,000.00 Cr			
Professional Services	*5,000.00*		5,000.00 Dr	5,000.00		5,000.00 Dr
Grand Total	*18,000.00*	*15,000.00*	3,000.00 Dr	9,000.00		*9,000.00 Dr*

Fig. 9.13 Two Cost Centres in Breakup Centres

Ledger Break-up of a Cost Centre

This provides you with another view of a cost centre report. It enables you to analyse the distribution of a ledger account across different cost centres.

If you want to know the Conveyance Expenses incurred by different cost centres, you need to view the Ledger wise break up of cost centres.

Go to Gateway of Tally > Display > Statement of Accounts > Cost Centers > Ledger Break-up

1. Select a ledger account, say for example, conveyance

The Ledger Break-up screen is displayed as shown:

Cost Breakup of Ledger | ABC Company | Ctrl + M

Particulars	Ledger: Conveyance ABC Company For 1-Apr-2008 Transactions Debit	Credit	Closing Balance
Department	35,000.00		35,000.00 Dr
Finance	25,000.00		25,000.00 Dr
Marketing	10,000.00		10,000.00 Dr
Division	30,000.00		30,000.00 Dr
Export	20,000.00		20,000.00 Dr
Retail	5,000.00		5,000.00 Dr
Wholesale	5,000.00		5,000.00 Dr
Primary Cost Category	15,000.00		15,000.00 Dr
Salesman A	4,000.00		4,000.00 Dr
Salesman B	6,000.00		6,000.00 Dr
Salesman C	5,000.00		5,000.00 Dr

Fig. 9.14 Cost Breakup of Ledger

The total Conveyance Expenses allocated to different Cost Centres under different Cost Categories are listed. If you have only one category, it lists out as per this category.

Use New Column to bring up another ledger account, say, Professional Services. You will be able to judge their relative performance or even compare the data with that of another company.

Cost Breakup of Ledger | ABC Company | Ctrl + M

Particulars	Ledger: Conveyance ABC Company For 1-Apr-2008 Transactions Debit	Credit	Closing Balance	Ledger: Professional Services ABC Company For 1-Apr-2008 Transactions Debit	Credit	Closing Balance
Department	35,000.00		35,000.00 Dr		30,000.00	30,000.00 Cr
Finance	25,000.00		25,000.00 Dr		20,000.00	20,000.00 Cr
Marketing	10,000.00		10,000.00 Dr		10,000.00	10,000.00 Cr
Division	30,000.00		30,000.00 Dr			
Export	20,000.00		20,000.00 Dr			
Retail	5,000.00		5,000.00 Dr			
Wholesale	5,000.00		5,000.00 Dr			
Primary Cost Category	15,000.00		15,000.00 Dr			
Salesman A	4,000.00		4,000.00 Dr			
Salesman B	6,000.00		6,000.00 Dr			
Salesman C	5,000.00		5,000.00 Dr			

Fig. 9.15 Cost Breakup of Ledger with two Ledgers

Note: Use F12: Configure option and enable the required options to display the report as per your requirement.

Group Break-up of a Cost Centre

The Group break-up of cost centre gives you another view of a cost centre report by enabling you to analyse the distribution of a group (of ledger accounts) across different cost centres.

This report helps to display the breakup of Indirect Expenses under each cost centre.

```
Go to Gateway of Tally > Display > Statements of Accounts > Cost Centers > Group
Break -up
```

1. Select a group account, say for example, Indirect Expenses.

The Group Break-up screen is displayed as shown:

Cost Breakup of Group — ABC Company — Ctrl + M

Particulars	Group: Indirect Expenses ABC Company 1-Apr-2008 to 8-Apr-2008		
	Transactions		Closing Balance
	Debit	Credit	
Branches	15,000.00		15,000.00 Dr
Bangalore	5,000.00		5,000.00 Dr
Mumbai	5,000.00		5,000.00 Dr
New Delhi	5,000.00		5,000.00 Dr
Department	15,000.00		15,000.00 Dr
Finance	13,000.00		13,000.00 Dr
Human Resource	2,000.00		2,000.00 Dr
Primary Cost Category	15,000.00		15,000.00 Dr
Marketing	15,000.00		15,000.00 Dr

Fig. 9.16 Cost Breakup of a Group

The total Indirect Expenses allocated to different Cost Centres under different Cost categories are given. If you have only one category, it will be listed under this category.

Use New Column to bring up another group of ledger account, say, Indirect Income. You will be able to judge their relative performance or even compare the data with that of another company.

Cost Breakup of Group — ABC Company — Ctrl + M

Particulars	Group: Indirect Expenses ABC Company 1-Apr-2008 to 8-Apr-2008			Group: Indirect Incomes ABC Company 1-Apr-2008 to 30-Apr-2008		
	Transactions		Closing Balance	Transactions		Closing Balance
	Debit	Credit		Debit	Credit	
Branches	15,000.00		15,000.00 Dr			
Bangalore	5,000.00		5,000.00 Dr			
Mumbai	5,000.00		5,000.00 Dr			
New Delhi	5,000.00		5,000.00 Dr			
Department	15,000.00		15,000.00 Dr		15,000.00	15,000.00 Cr
Finance	13,000.00		13,000.00 Dr		15,000.00	15,000.00 Cr
Human Resource	2,000.00		2,000.00 Dr			
Primary Cost Category	15,000.00		15,000.00 Dr			
Marketing	15,000.00		15,000.00 Dr			

Fig. 9.16a Cost Breakup of Two Groups

Note: Use F12: Configure option and enable the required options to display the report as per your requirement.

Display Cash Flow Statement

Cash Flow is the inflow and outflow of cash during an accounting period.

A cash flow statement concentrates on the transactions that have a direct impact on cash. It deals with the inflow and outflow of cash between two Balance Sheet dates. That is, it explains the changes in cash position between the two periods. Here the term cash stands for cash and bank balances.

Cash flow statements can also be used as receipts and payments statement. This is particularly useful for businesses such as Non Profit Organizations where receipts and payments statements need to be generated.

Cash Flow in Tally.ERP 9

To view Cash Flow:

1. Go to Gateway of Tally > Display > Cash/Funds Flow > Cash Flow
2. Press ALT+F2, change the period - From: 1-4-2008 to 30-9-2008.

The Cash flow statement is displayed as shown:

Cash Flow | ABC Company | Ctrl + M

Particulars	ABC Company 1-Apr-2008 to 30-Sep-2008		
	Cash Movement		Nett Flow
	Inflow	Outflow	
April	8,79,000.00	7,02,625.00	1,76,375.00
May	12,00,000.00	73,050.00	11,26,950.00
June	4,95,000.00	30,300.00	4,64,700.00
July	15,00,000.00	13,59,100.00	1,40,900.00
August	46,250.00		46,250.00
September			
Grand Total	41,20,250.00	21,65,075.00	19,55,175.00

Fig. 9.17 Cash Flow Screen

For Quarterly Cash Flow:

- Change Period by pressing F2: Period and set the period, e.g., 1-4-08 to 30-06-2008.
- Select the option Auto Column from the button bar.
- You can also select Quarterly (or Monthly or any other period) from the list

Columnar Cash Flow Statement is shown on the next page.

Display Fund Flow Statement

A Fund Flow statement is a report, which explains the movement of funds during an accounting period.

This statement consists of two parts.

- Sources of funds
- Application of funds.

The difference between the two shows the net change in the working capital during the period. Only those transactions that affect the net working capital of the firm, find place in this statement.

Cash Flow | ABC Company | Ctrl + M

Particulars	ABC Company 1-Apr-2008 to 30-Jun-2008			ABC Company 1-Jul-2008 to 30-Sep-2008		
	Cash Movement		Nett	Cash Movement		Nett
	Inflow	Outflow	Flow	Inflow	Outflow	Flow
Apr - Jun	25,74,000.00	8,05,975.00	17,68,025.00			
Jul - Sep				15,46,250.00	13,59,100.00	1,87,150.00
Grand Total	25,74,000.00	8,05,975.00	17,68,025.00	15,46,250.00	13,59,100.00	1,87,150.00

Fig. 9.18 Cash Flow Period Wise

The Fund Flow statement is a supplement to the two principal financial statements. While supplementing the position statement, it describes the sources from which additional fund were derived and for which these funds were used. The transactions, which increase working capital, are sources of funds and the transactions, which decrease working capital, are application of funds.

Fund Flow in Tally.ERP 9

To view Funds Flow,

`Go to Gateway of Tally > Display > Cash/Funds Flow > Funds Flow`

1. Press ALT+F2, change period - From: 1-04-2008 to 31-8-2008.

   The funds flow statement is displayed as shown:

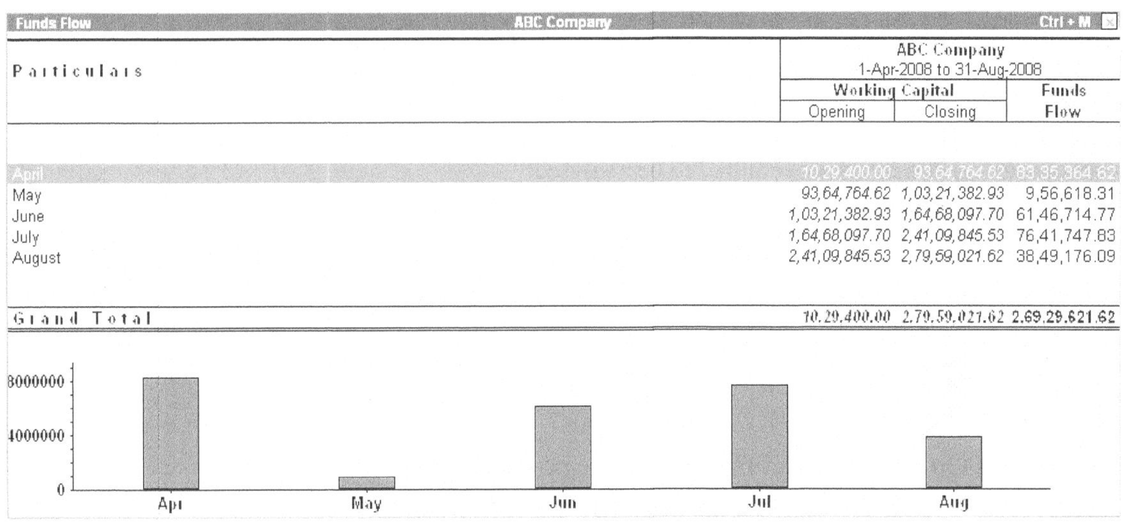

Funds Flow | ABC Company | Ctrl + M

Particulars	ABC Company 1-Apr-2008 to 31-Aug-2008		
	Working Capital		Funds
	Opening	Closing	Flow
April	10,29,400.00	93,64,764.62	83,35,364.62
May	93,64,764.62	1,03,21,382.93	9,56,618.31
June	1,03,21,382.93	1,64,68,097.70	61,46,714.77
July	1,64,68,097.70	2,41,09,845.53	76,41,747.83
August	2,41,09,845.53	2,79,59,021.62	38,49,176.09
Grand Total	10,29,400.00	2,79,59,021.62	2,69,29,621.62

Fig. 9.19 Fund Flow Statement

2. A Monthly Funds Flow Summary with the movement of working capital for each month is displayed. It shows the Opening and Closing Balances of each month with a column for Funds Flow.

3. Select a month and press Enter to drill down.
4. Select F1: Detailed to see the funds flow for the selected month.

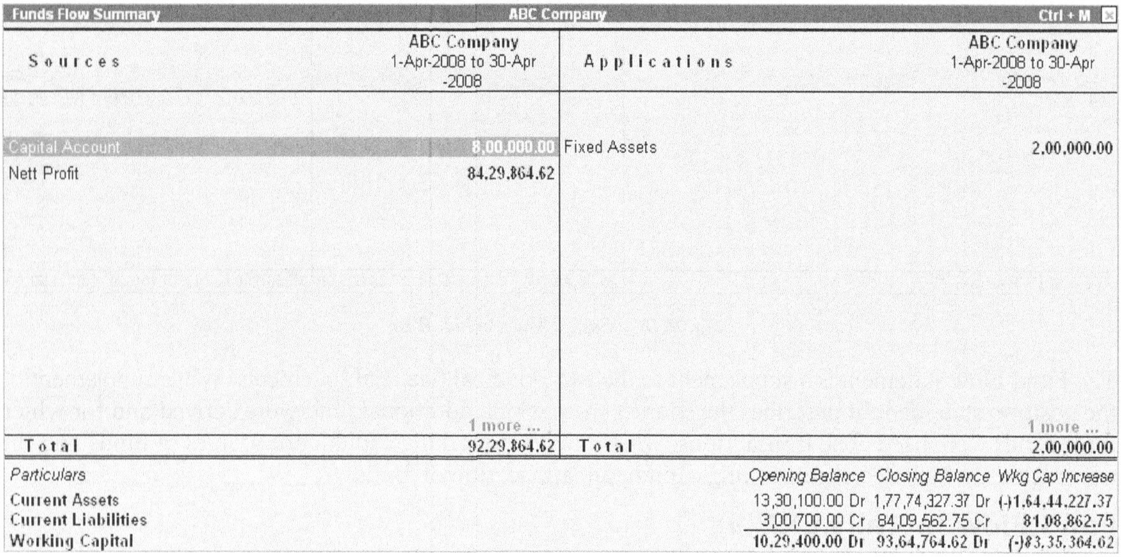

Funds Flow Summary — ABC Company — Ctrl + M

Sources	ABC Company 1-Apr-2008 to 30-Apr -2008	Applications	ABC Company 1-Apr-2008 to 30-Apr -2008
Capital Account	8,00,000.00	Fixed Assets	2,00,000.00
Nett Profit	84,29,864.62		
	1 more ...		1 more ...
Total	92,29,864.62	Total	2,00,000.00

Particulars	Opening Balance	Closing Balance	Wkg Cap Increase
Current Assets	13,30,100.00 Dr	1,77,74,327.37 Dr	(-)1,64,44,227.37
Current Liabilities	3,00,700.00 Cr	84,09,562.75 Cr	81,08,862.75
Working Capital	10,29,400.00 Dr	93,64,764.62 Dr	(-)83,35,364.62

Fig. 9.20 Fund Flow Statement for a Particular Month

Display Ratio Analysis Report

Ratio analysis is a powerful tool for financial analysis. A meaningful analysis of a financial statement is made possible by the use of ratios.

Ratios are a set of figures compared with another set. The comparison gives an understanding of the financial position of a business unit. There are a number of ratios which can be computed from a single set of financial statements. The ratios to be computed depend on the purpose for which these ratios are required. A single ratio may sometimes give some information, but to make a comprehensive analysis, a set of inter-related ratios are required to be analysed.

To view the Ratio Analysis.

```
Go to Gateway of Tally> Ratio Analysis
```

The Ratio Analysis screen is displayed as shown on the next page.

The screen is divided into two parts:

- Principal Groups
- Principal Ratios

The Principal Groups are the key figures that give perspective to the ratios.

Principal Ratios relate two pieces of financial data to obtain a comparison that is meaningful.

Principal Groups and Key Figures

Working Capital

The Net Working Capital is calculated by subtracting Current Liabilities from Current Assets. Financial

Ratio Analysis ABC Company Ctrl + M

Principal Groups	ABC Company 1-Apr-2008 to 31 -Mar-2009	Principal Ratios	ABC Company 1-Apr-2008 to 31 -Mar-2009
Working Capital	4,26,33,146.00 Dr	Current Ratio	2.83 : 1
(Current Assets-Current Liabilities)		(Current Assets : Current Liabilities)	
Cash-in-Hand	67,88,050.00 Dr	Quick Ratio	1.75 : 1
Bank Accounts	25,52,825.00 Dr	(Current Assets-Stock-in-hand : Current Liabilities)	
Bank OD A/c		Debt Equity Ratio	0.03 : 1
Sundry Debtors	3,13,38,732.00 Dr	(Loans (Liability) : Capital Account + Nett Profit)	
(due till today)	3,19,22,813.00 Dr	Gross Profit %	100.19 %
Sundry Creditors	2,31,22,704.50 Cr	Nett Profit %	100.01 %
(due till today)	2,73,93,387.50 Cr	Operating Cost %	(-)0.01 %
Sales Accounts	3,90,55,008.75 Cr	(as percentage of Sales Accounts)	
Purchase Accounts	2,47,70,497.50 Dr	Recv. Turnover in days	357.89 days
Stock-in-hand	2,51,65,005.25 Dr	(payment performance of Debtors)	
Nett Profit	3,90,60,804.00 Cr		
Wkg. Capital Turnover	0.92	Return on Investment %	94.21 %
(Sales Accounts / Working Capital)		(Nett Profit / Capital Account + Nett Profit)	
Inventory Turnover	1.55	Return on Wkg. Capital %	91.62 %
(Sales Accounts / Closing Stock)		(Nett Profit / Working Capital) %	

Fig. 9.21 Ratio Analysis Screen

Analysts often consider the total Current Assets as the Working Capital. This serves as a measure of how far the firm is protected from liquidity problems.

Cash in Hand and Bank Balances

This data presents another perspective on the liquidity position.

Sundry Debtors

(due till today)

The list of all the debtors and the total debts due as on the date of the statement, are displayed.

Sundry Creditors

(due till today)

The list of all the creditors and the total credits due as on the date of the statement are displayed.

Sales and Purchase Accounts

The Sales and Purchase Accounts, which collate the trading activity for the period, are displayed.

Stock in Hand

This field displays the stock in hand as on the date of the report and together with Cash and Bank Balances and Debtors, completes the Current Assets aspect of the Working Capital.

Net Profit

This is derived from the Profit & Loss Account and is the profit after direct and indirect expenses.

Wkg. Capital Turnover

(Sales Accounts/Working Capital)

This is an activity or efficiency ratio that shows the number of times the working capital has been rolled over during a particular period. It depicts how effectively the firm is using its working capital.

Inventory Turnover

(Sales Accounts/Closing Stock)

This is an activity or efficiency ratio that shows the number of times the stock has been rolled over during the period of the report. It depicts how effectively the firm is using its inventories.

Principal Ratios

You can compare Principal Ratios of your company over a certain period with industry averages as well as with ratios pertaining to other periods to assess current performance.

Current Ratio

(Current Assets: Current Liabilities)

This indicates the solvency position of the enterprise. The ideal ratio is 2 under normal business conditions.

Quick Ratio

(Current Assets – Stock in Hand : Current Liabilities)

This indicates the liquidity position of the enterprise. This ratio is useful in planning future cash requirements.

Debt Equity Ratio

(Loans (Liabilities) : Capital + Net Profit)

This indicates the level of exposure to external borrowings and is a useful tool in determining the options of raising additional capital internally or externally.

Gross profit %

(Gross Profit / total Turnover)

This indicates the percentage of profit earned from direct operations (manufacturing)., This ratio is useful, where an enterprise produces more than one product, in identifying the order of profitability and making decisions such as increasing production capacity, continuance of a product etc.

Net Profit %

(Net Profit/ Total Turnover)

This indicates the percentage of net profit earned by the enterprise after considering all expenses of the enterprise. This is useful in identifying the overall profitability of the enterprise.

Operating Cost %

(As percentage of Sales Accounts)

This is referred to as the percentage of operating cost with respect to the total turnover. This ratio is useful in making decisions in the areas of cost control, cost reduction etc.

Receivables Turnover in days

(Payment performance of Debtors)

This is an analysis of debtor wise payment performance and a useful tool in identifying the most preferred and least preferred customers or agents and planning the receivables collection process.

Return on Investment %

(Net Profit/Capital Account + Net Profit) %

This is a useful tool in measuring returns expected from the project/product and plan additional capital infusion, increase in production capacity (subject to market demand) etc.

Return on working capital

(Net Profit/Working Capital) %

This is referred to as the percentage of net profit to working capital (current assets – current liabilities).

Working capital turnover ratio

(Sales Account/Working Capital)

This indicates how effectively working capital is used in terms of turnover it can help to generate. It is a useful tool in identifying the level of deployment of funds with respect to sales.

Inventory turnover ratio

(Turnover / inventory)

This indicates the relationship of inventory with respect to sales. This is a useful tool in identifying the extent of investment in stock and indicates

- Stock control measures whether to be taken in case of change in demand
- Procurement planning

Payment Performance of Sundry Debtors

Payment Performance of Debtors (Receivable Turnover in days) is the average time the customers take to actually pay their bills irrespective of the outstanding balance on the statement date. It is quite possible that the receivable turnover is low and the payment performance is high, indicating that the customers cleared their outstanding, but took a long time doing it.

To get group level and customer level performance reports and a detailed position of debt collection, you have to drill down from the ratios. Use a customer statement that shows both the receivable turnover in days and the customer's actual payment performance.

The Ledger Payment Performance screen is displayed as shown:

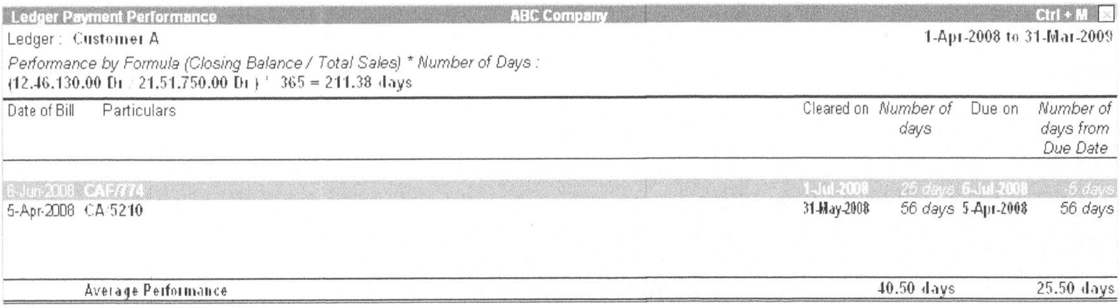

Ledger Payment Performance — ABC Company — Ctrl + M

Ledger : Customer A — 1-Apr-2008 to 31-Mar-2009

*Performance by Formula (Closing Balance / Total Sales) * Number of Days :*
(12,46,130.00 Dr / 21,51,750.00 Dr) * 365 = 211.38 days

Date of Bill	Particulars	Cleared on	*Number of days*	Due on	*Number of days from Due Date*
6-Jun-2008	CAF/774	1-Jul-2008	*25 days*	6-Jul-2008	*-5 days*
5-Apr-2008	CA/5210	31-May-2008	*56 days*	5-Apr-2008	*56 days*
	Average Performance		40.50 days		25.50 days

Fig. 9.22 Ledger Payment Performance Screen

The Ledger Payment Performance statement displays the receivable turnover in days. This is the balance outstanding in relation to the total sales made multiplied by the total number of days in the period. This ratio should be used in combination with the Average Performance of actual payments and the payment history of the customer to assess how long he might take to pay the outstanding balance.

The Actual payment history is given in the table for each invoice that was paid by the customer. It shows when the invoice was paid, how long it was due and what was the delay in payment. The customer's average performance is shown at the bottom of the screen.

Exception Reports

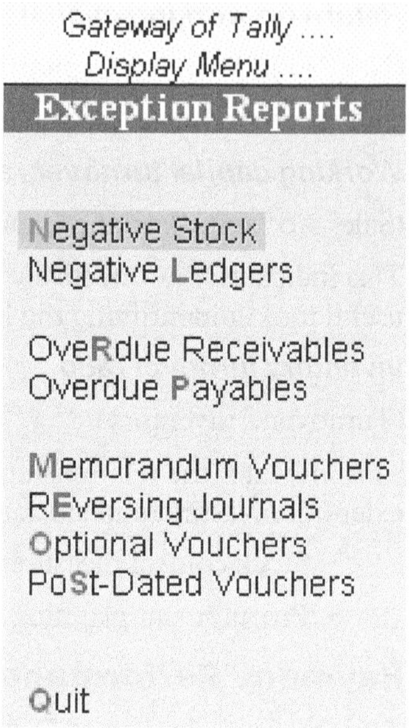

Exception Reports track unusual transactions or balances.

Go to Gateway of Tally > Display > Exception Reports

The different kinds of Exception Reports are:

Gateway of Tally ....
Display Menu ....
Exception Reports

Negative Stock
Negative Ledgers

OveRdue Receivables
Overdue Payables

Memorandum Vouchers
REversing Journals
Optional Vouchers
PoSt-Dated Vouchers

Quit

Negative Stock

Go to Gateway of Tally > Display > Exception Reports > Negative Stock

This report displays a list of all stock items that have a negative quantity (closing value) balance at the end of a specified period.

You can use the drill-down feature or view Stock Item display for further details.

Note: Once a Purchase entry is passed for the items which are shown in the Negative Stock reports, thereafter, these items will not be shown in the Negative Stock reports.

Negative Ledgers

This is a list of ledger accounts balances that is opposite to the nature of the account. For example, a creditor account with a debit balance and a Bank account with a credit balance.

Go to Gateway of Tally > Display > Exception Reports > Negative Ledgers

National Bank Account is a Bank account and is expected to have a debit balance. Supplier Account is a Creditor/Supplier account and should normally have a credit balance.

Overdue Receivables

This is a list of all sales invoices that are due as of the specified period.

Go to Gateway of Tally > Display > Exception Reports > Overdue Receivables

Date

The date of Invoice entry is displayed here.

Ref No.

Invoice number will be displayed here.

Party's Name

The name of the party from whom bills are due as of the specified period is displayed here.

Pending Amount

The amount which is pending/due as on period specified will be displayed.

Due on

The due date of receipt of the amount will be displayed.

Overdue by days

According to the period specified, Overdue by days will be displayed. By default it will calculate overdue days from the date of 'Due On'.

List of Negative Stock Items | ABC Company | Ctrl + M

Particulars	ABC Company For 1-Apr-2008		
	Closing Balance		
	Quantity	Rate	Value
Item A	(-)79.00 nos	900.00	(-)71,100.00
Item B	(-)218.00 nos	1,000.00	(-)2,18,000.00
Grand Total	(-)297.00 nos		(-)2,89,100.00

Fig. 9.23 List of Negative Stocks

List of Negative Ledger A/cs | ABC Company | Ctrl + M

Particulars	ABC Company 1-Apr-2008 to 30-Apr-2008	
	Closing Balance	
	Debit	Credit
Customer - Bangalore		1,500.00
National Bank Account		8,500.00
Supplier	10,000.00	
Grand Total	10,000.00	10,000.00

Fig. 9.24 List of Negative Stocks Ledgerwise

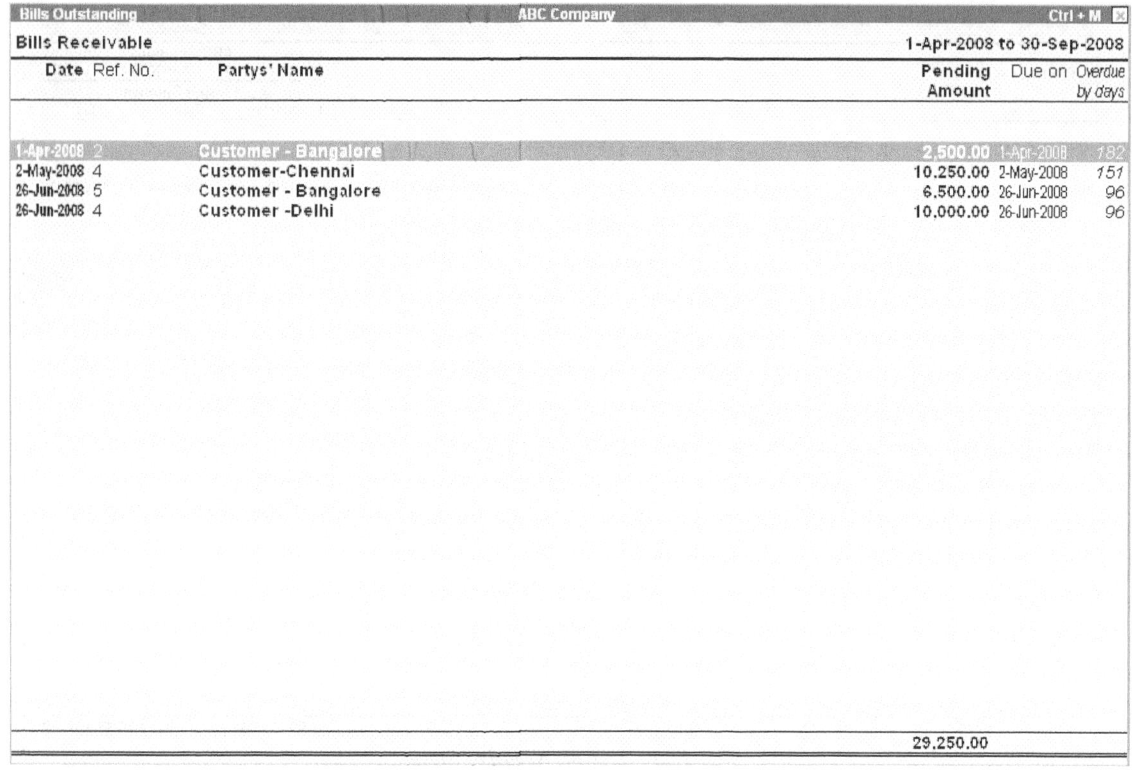

Bills Outstanding ABC Company Ctrl + M

Bills Receivable 1-Apr-2008 to 30-Sep-2008

Date	Ref. No.	Partys' Name	Pending Amount	Due on	Overdue by days
1-Apr-2008	2	Customer - Bangalore	2,500.00	1-Apr-2008	182
2-May-2008	4	Customer-Chennai	10,250.00	2-May-2008	151
26-Jun-2008	5	Customer - Bangalore	6,500.00	26-Jun-2008	96
26-Jun-2008	4	Customer -Delhi	10,000.00	26-Jun-2008	96
			29,250.00		

Fig. 9.25 Bills Outstanding

F12:Configuration in Overdue Receivables screen

Press F12: Configuration and set 'Include Post-Dated Transactions', 'Show Opening Amount' to Yes.

Configuration

Include Post-Dated Transactions	?	**Yes**
Show Opening Amount	?	**Yes**
Show overdue using Bill Date	?	**No**
Range of Bills to show	:	**Overdue Bills**
Show Qty Info in Detailed Format	?	**Yes**
Appearance of Names	:	**Name Only**
Sorting Method	:	**Default**

Opening Amount

The total amount of bills which are due against a party will be displayed here.

For ex: in the above screen, for customer-Bangalore, total Invoice amount is raised for Rs. 5,000/-.

Pending Amount

The amount which is due from the party will be displayed here. For ex: out of total amount of bill, *i.e.*, Rs. 5,000/-, if the party pays Rs. 1,000/-, then Rs. 4,000/- (5000-1000) will be displayed under pending amount.

Post-Dated Amount

In the above screen, the period is selected from 1st April 2008 to 30th September 2008. On 2nd May 2008, Customer-Chennai is having Pending Amount of Rs. 10,250/- but customer-Chennai has given the Post-Dated cheque for Rs. 2,000/-, *i.e.*, cheque dated after 30th September 2008. And if you wish to

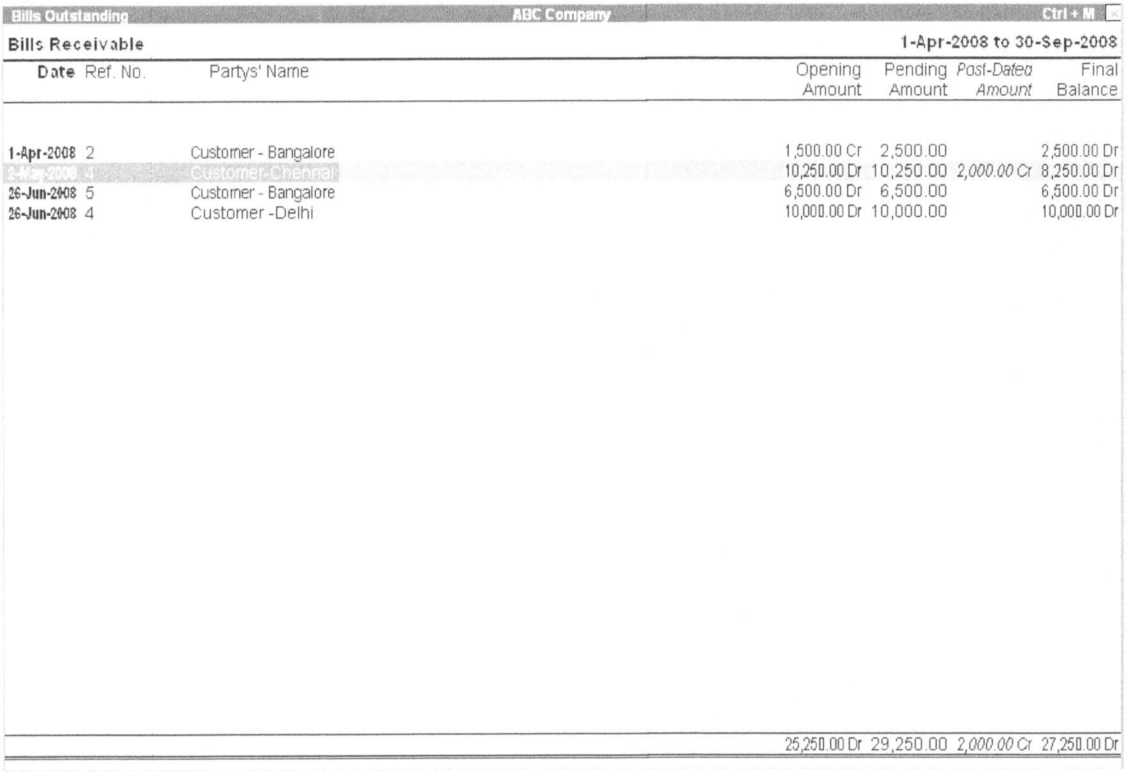

Bills Outstanding — ABC Company — Ctrl + M

Bills Receivable — 1-Apr-2008 to 30-Sep-2008

Date	Ref. No.	Partys' Name	Opening Amount	Pending Amount	Post-Dated Amount	Final Balance
1-Apr-2008	2	Customer - Bangalore	1,500.00 Cr	2,500.00		2,500.00 Dr
2-May-2008	4	Customer-Chennai	10,250.00 Dr	10,250.00	2,000.00 Cr	8,250.00 Dr
26-Jun-2008	5	Customer - Bangalore	6,500.00 Dr	6,500.00		6,500.00 Dr
26-Jun-2008	4	Customer -Delhi	10,000.00 Dr	10,000.00		10,000.00 Dr
			25,250.00 Dr	29,250.00	2,000.00 Cr	27,250.00 Dr

Fig. 9.26 Bills Outstanding Including Post Dated Transactions

view the details of this customer with Final Balance (Pending Amount – Post-Dated Amount) as on 30th September 2008, you need to enable 'Include Post-Dated Transactions' in F12: Configuration.

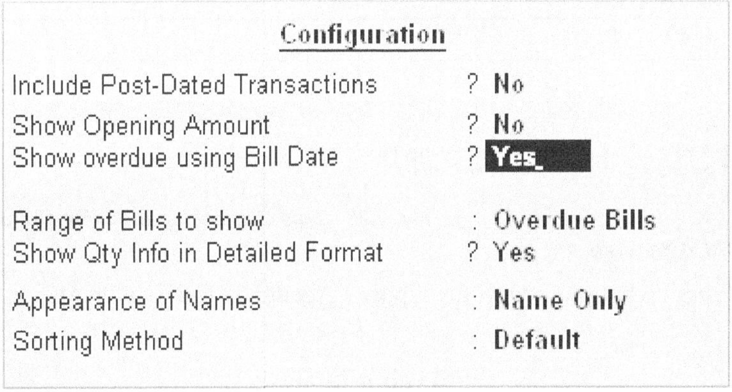

Configuration

Include Post-Dated Transactions	?	No
Show Opening Amount	?	No
Show overdue using Bill Date	?	Yes
Range of Bills to show	:	Overdue Bills
Show Qty Info in Detailed Format	?	Yes
Appearance of Names	:	Name Only
Sorting Method	:	Default

Show overdue using Bill Date

In F12: Configuration screen set Show overdue using Bill Date to Yes.

When you enable 'Show overdue using Bill Date', you can view the ageing days due by 'Bill date'.

For ex: in the above screen. Bill Date is on 01.04.2008 and Due on date is on 01.05.2008, when you set the option 'Show overdue using Bill Date' to Yes, it will calculate the 'Age of Bill in Days' from the date of Bill not from the due on date.

F4: Payable

This is the button to toggle to view the due of bills Payable and Receivable. If you wish to view the bills payable from this screen, then press F4: Payable button.

Bills Outstanding — ABC Company — Ctrl + M

Bills Receivable — 1-Apr-2008 to 30-Sep-2008

Date	Ref. No.	Partys' Name	Pending Amount	Due on	Age of Bill in Days
1-Apr-2008	2	Customer - Bangalore	2,500.00	1-Apr-2008	182
2-May-2008	4	Customer-Chennai	10,250.00	2-May-2008	151
26-Jun-2008	5	Customer - Bangalore	6,500.00	26-Jun-2008	96
26-Jun-2008	4	Customer -Delhi	10,000.00	26-Jun-2008	96
			29,250.00		

Fig. 9.27 Bills Outstanding Including Overdue

Bills Outstanding — ABC Company — Ctrl + M

Bills Receivable — 1-Apr-2008 to 30-Sep-2008

Date	Ref. No.	Partys' Name	Pending Amount	Due on	Age of Bill in Days
1-Apr-2008	2	Customer - Bangalore	2,500.00	1-Apr-2008	182
2-May-2008	4	Customer-Chennai	10,250.00	2-May-2008	151
26-Jun-2008	5	Customer - Bangalore	6,500.00	26-Jun-2008	96
26-Jun-2008	4	Customer -Delhi	10,000.00	26-Jun-2008	96

Fig. 9.28 Bills Outstanding Including Overdue Days

F6:Age wise

Press F6 button to view the report – Ageing by Bill date or Ageing by Due Date.

Overdue Payables

This is a list of all purchase bills that are overdue as of a specified period.

```
Go to Gateway of Tally > Display > Exception Reports > Overdue Payables
```

Bills Outstanding ABC Company Ctrl + M

Bills Payable 1-Apr-2008 to 30-Sep-2008

Date	Ref. No.	Partys' Name	Pending Amount	Due on	Overdue by days
1-Apr-2008	1	Bangalore Customer	20,500.00	1-Apr-2008	182
6-Jun-2008	5	Supplier-Bangalore	7,500.00	6-Jun-2008	116
6-Jun-2008	4	Supplier - Delhi	8,500.00	6-Jun-2008	116
5-Jul-2008	9	Supplier - Chennai	4,500.00	5-Jul-2008	87
			41,000.00		

Fig. 9.29 Bills Outstanding agewise

Date

The date of Invoice entry is displayed here.

Ref No.

Invoice number is displayed here.

Party's Name

The name of party to whom bills are due as of a specified period is displayed here.

Pending Amount

The amount which is pending/due as of a specified period is displayed here.

Configuration

Include Post-Dated Transactions ? Yes
Show Opening Amount ? Yes
Show overdue using Bill Date ? Yes
Range of Bills to show : Overdue Bills
Show Qty Info in Detailed Format ? Yes
Appearance of Names : Name Only
Sorting Method : Default

Due on

The due date of payment of the amount is displayed.

Overdue by days

According to the period specified, Overdue by days will be displayed. By default it will calculate overdue days from the date specified for 'Due On'.

Press F12:Configure in Overdue Payable screen:

Display Memorandum Vouchers

Memorandum Vouchers is a non-accounting voucher and the entries made using the memo voucher will not affect your accounts. In other words, Tally does not post these entries to ledgers but stores them in a separate Memorandum Register.

Uses of Memo Vouchers

- Making suspense payments

Consider a company gives its employee cash for Conveyance expenses, the exact nature and cost of which are unknown.

For the above transaction, you can enter a voucher for the petty cash advance. A voucher to record the actual expenditure details when they are known, and another voucher to record the return of surplus cash.

However, a simpler way of doing it is to enter a Memo voucher when the cash is advanced, and then turn it into a Payment voucher for the actual amount spent, when the actual details are known.

- Vouchers not verified at the time of entry

If you do not understand the details of a voucher you are entering, you can enter it as a Memo voucher and amend it later when the details are available.

- Items given on approval

Generally completed sales are entered into books. In case items are given on approval, use a Memo voucher to track and convert it into a proper Sales voucher. You can delete the memo voucher if the sale is not made.

Consider the following Example.

The Company pays its employee Rs.5000 as petty cash advance towards Conveyance Expenses.

The following entry has to be passed.

Debit - Conveyance Expenses A/c.

Credit – Cash A/c.

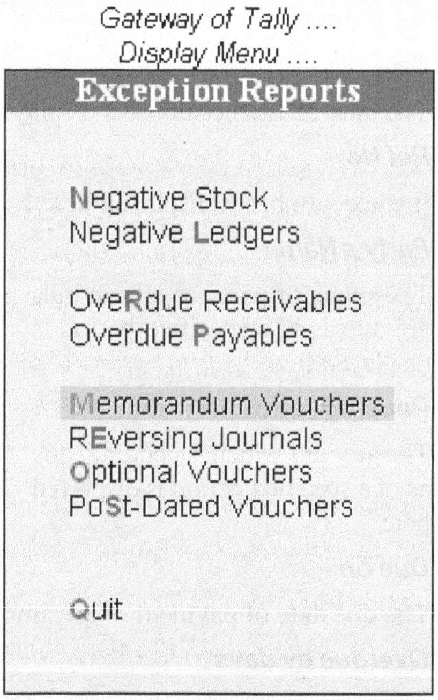

Activating Memo Vouchers:

Enable 'Use Reversing Journals & Optional Vouchers' in F11: Features: F1: Accounting Features.

```
Go to Gateway of Tally > Accounting Vouchers/
Inventory Vouchers > F10: Memos
```

Memorandum Voucher Register

To view all the memorandum vouchers:

```
Go to Gateway of Tally > Display > Exception
Reports > Memorandum Vouchers.
```

Note: You can also view memorandum vouchers from the Day Book.

Gateway of Tally ....
Display Menu ....

Exception Reports

Negative Stock
Negative Ledgers

OveRdue Receivables
Overdue Payables

Memorandum Vouchers
REversing Journals
Optional Vouchers
PoSt-Dated Vouchers

Quit

Company: ABC Company

Accounting Features

General

Integrate Accounts and Inventory	? Yes
Income/Expense Statement instead of P & L	? No
Allow Multi-Currency	? No

Outstandings Management

Maintain Bill-wise Details	? Yes
(for Non-Trading A/cs also)	? No
Activate Interest Calculation	? No
(use advanced parameters)	? No

Cost Profit Centres Management

Maintain Payroll	? No
Maintain Cost Centres	? No
Use Cost Centre for Job Costing	? No
More than ONE Payroll / Cost Category	? No
Use Pre-defined Cost Centre Allocations during Entry	? No

Invoicing

Allow Invoicing	? Yes
Enter Purchases in Invoice Format	? Yes
Use Debit/Credit Notes	? No
Use Invoice mode for Credit Notes	? No
Use Invoice mode for Debit Notes	? No

Budgets & Scenario Management

Maintain Budgets and Controls	? No
Use Reversing Journals & Optional Vouchers	? Yes

Other Features

Enable Cheque Printing	? No
Set/Alter Cheque Printing Configuration	? No
Allow Zero valued entries	? No

F1: Accounts F2: Inventory F3: Statutory F4: Tally.NET

Fig. 9.30 Setting the Features

Accounting Voucher Creation ABC Company Ctrl + M

Memorandum No. 1 1-Apr-2008 Tuesday

Particulars	Debit	Credit
Dr Conveyance Expenses	5,000.00	
Cur Bal: 5,000.00 Dr		
Cr Cash		5,000.00
Cur Bal: 45,000.00 Dr		
Narration:	5,000.00	5,000.00

Fig. 9.31 Memorendum Voucher Screen

You can alter and convert a Memo voucher into a regular voucher when you decide to consider the entry into your books.

Note: Use Scenarios to see the effect of Memo entries on reports and statements.

Display Reversing Journals

Reversing Journals are special journals that are automatically reversed after a specified date. They exist only till the specified date and are effective only when they are included in reports like the Balance Sheet. These are used in interim reporting in the course of the financial year where accruals are to be reported. These accruals are usually short term and are cleared in the subsequent period. However, to get a proper perspective, decision makers require the reports with the full impact of all aspects and transactions.

Activating Reversing Journals

To activate Reversing Journals

Enable 'Use Reversing Journals & Optional Vouchers' in F11: Features: F1: Accounting Features.

Company: ABC Company

Accounting Features

General		Invoicing	
Integrate Accounts and Inventory	? Yes	Allow Invoicing	? Yes
Income/Expense Statement instead of P & L	? No	Enter Purchases in Invoice Format	? Yes
Allow Multi-Currency	? No	Use Debit/Credit Notes	? No
		Use Invoice mode for Credit Notes	? No
Outstandings Management		Use Invoice mode for Debit Notes	? No
Maintain Bill-wise Details	? Yes	**Budgets & Scenario Management**	
(for Non-Trading A/cs also)	? No	Maintain Budgets and Controls	? No
Activate Interest Calculation	? No	Use Reversing Journals & Optional Vouchers	? Yes
(use advanced parameters)	? No	**Other Features**	
Cost/Profit Centres Management		Enable Cheque Printing	? No
Maintain Payroll	? No	Set/Alter Cheque Printing Configuration	? No
Maintain Cost Centres	? No	Allow Zero valued entries	? No
Use Cost Centre for Job Costing	? No		
More than ONE Payroll / Cost Category	? No		
Use Pre-defined Cost Centre Allocations during Entry	? No		

F1: Accounts F2: Inventory F3: Statutory F4: Tally.NET

Fig. 9.32 Setting the Accounting Vouchers Features

An example for Reversing Journal

- The provision for depreciation. Depreciation is usually provided for at the end of the year. However, including it for monthly reporting would give a more accurate status.

Another example:

- On 30th June you want to view the Balance Sheet as of today but June salaries are not paid until

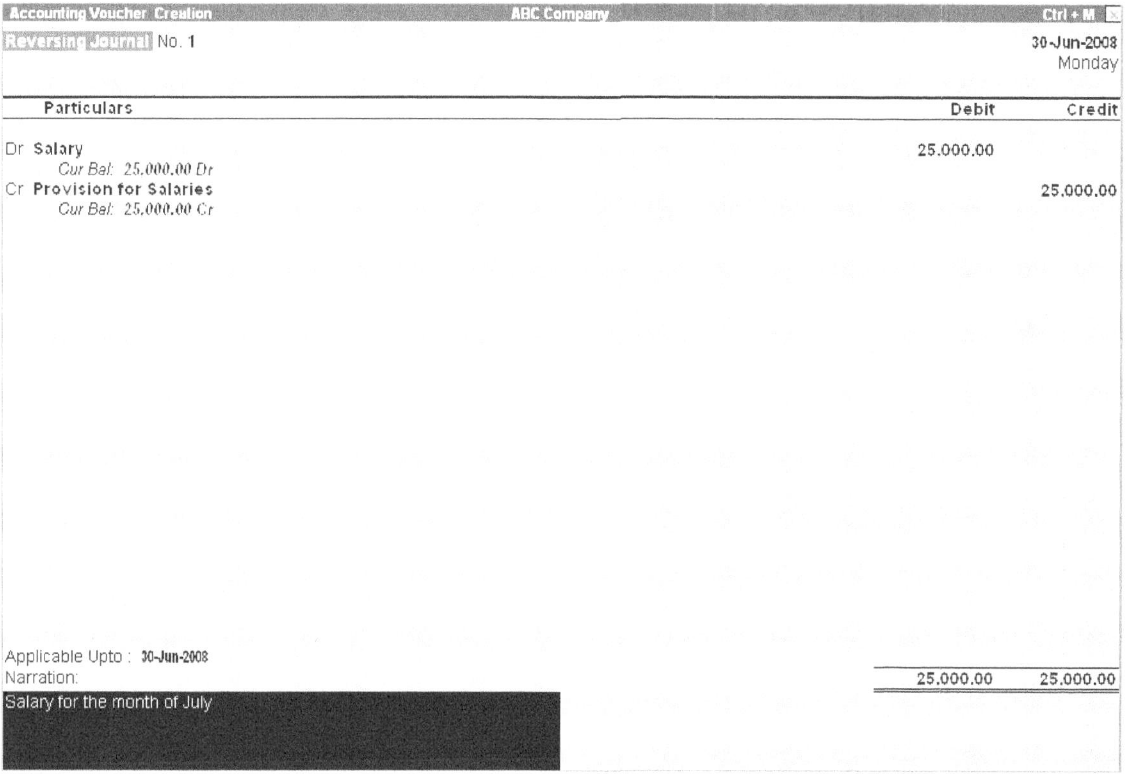

Accounting Voucher Creation | ABC Company | Ctrl + M

Reversing Journal No. 1 | 30-Jun-2008 Monday

Particulars	Debit	Credit
Dr Salary	25,000.00	
Cur Bal: 25,000.00 Dr		
Cr Provision for Salaries		25,000.00
Cur Bal: 25,000.00 Cr		
	25,000.00	25,000.00

Applicable Upto : 30-Jun-2008

Narration:

Salary for the month of July

Fig. 9.33 Reversing Journal Voucher

the first week of July. Thus, there is a large liability, which would not be reflected in the Balance Sheet. To overcome this, you enter a Reversing Journal Voucher dated 30th June, which would look like this:

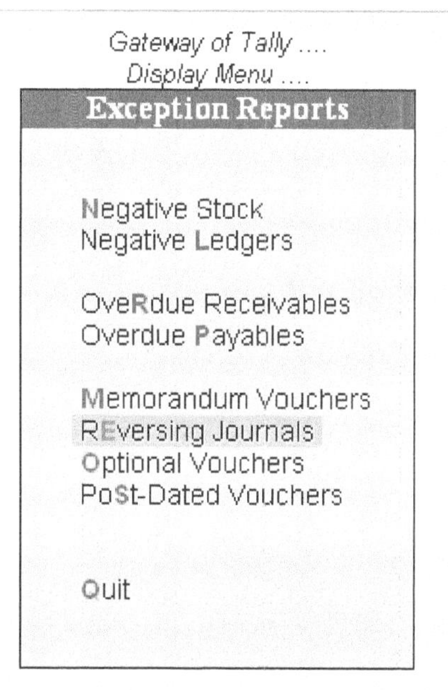

When you view the Balance Sheet, Tally.ERP 9 displays the report with the reversing journals included. The voucher affects the report only for that day, 30th June.

Applicable up to

This is the date up to which the Reversing Journal is available for inclusion in a scenario report. The Reversing Journal can be created as of a particular date and made Applicable up to a different date. For example the depreciation entry could be dated October 1, 2008 and applicable up to October 31, 2008. The journal will be available for inclusion in a scenario for any day from October 1, 2008 till October 31, 2008. It will not exist before 1st Oct and will be reversed automatically after 31st Oct and consequently unavailable.

Reversing Journal Register

All vouchers are maintained in a Reversing Journal Register.

These are not posted to any books of accounts and cannot be included in regular reports. They can only be seen through using a scenario.

```
Go to Gateway of Tally> Display> Exception Reports> Reversing Journals
```

Display Optional Vouchers

This is also a non-accounting voucher, but unlike a Memo voucher. This is not a separate voucher type. You can mark an existing voucher (for example, a payment voucher or a receipt voucher) as Optional. Press CTRL + L or click on Optional from the Button Bar. This button toggles with Regular. By marking a voucher Optional, the voucher does not get posted anywhere but remains in the Optional Register.

You can make a voucher type default to Optional if you need to create a new voucher type or alter an existing voucher type (Go to Gateway of Tally > Accounts Info > Voucher Types> select a Voucher Type> Set Make Optional as default to Yes).

Enabling Optional Vouchers

```
Go to Gateway of Tally > F11: Features: F2: Accounting Features > Set Use Rev.
Journals & Optional Vouchers? to Yes.
```

Use of Optional Vouchers

- If you do not want an incomplete transaction to affect the accounts, you can mark this as an Optional Voucher. Once the transaction is complete, modify the voucher and post it as a Regular Voucher. For example, Performa sales invoice. In fact, an optional sales invoice prints as a Performa Invoice.
- Optional Vouchers allow you to see the impact of transactions without actually posting them.

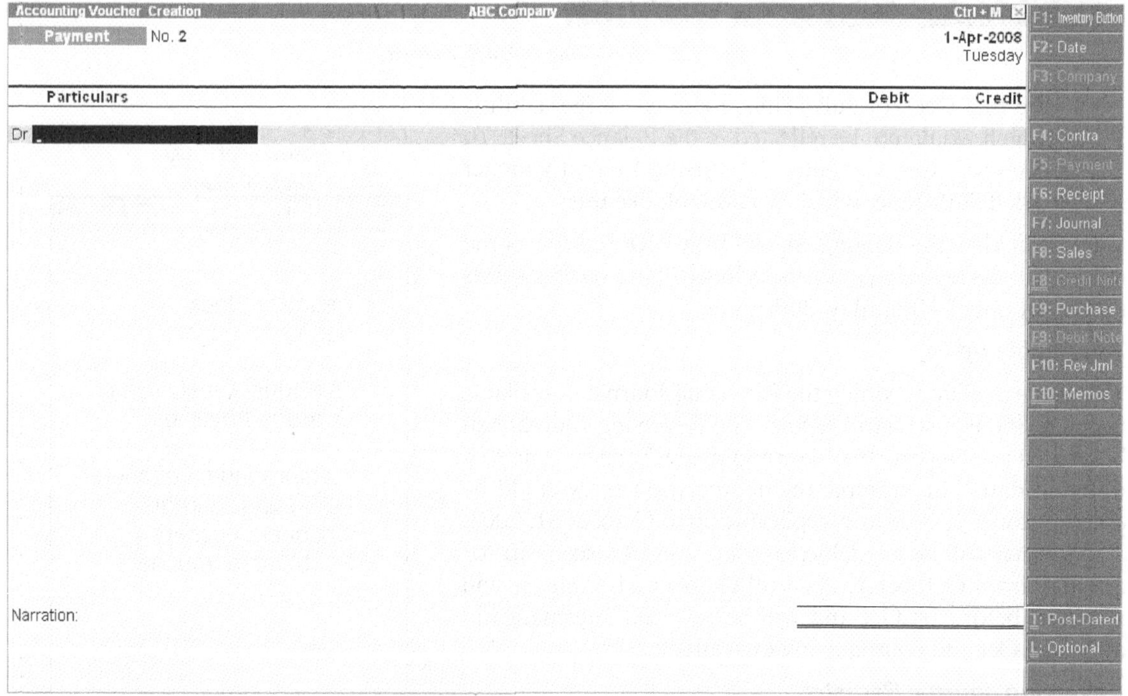

Fig. 9.34 Payment Journal Voucher

- Optional Vouchers can be used to forecast future sales. For example, create a New Voucher Type - Sales Forecast. Record future sales projections using this voucher type.

Let us consider the following example.

On 30th June you want to view the Balance Sheet as of that date, but June rent is not due for payment until the first week of July. This liability is not reflected in the Balance Sheet. To overcome this, enter an Optional Voucher dated 30th June. The above entry is made as shown:

Click on Optional or Ctrl+L to make the voucher as Optional Voucher.

Pass the entry as shown:

Debit – Rent Account

Credit – Cash/Bank Account.

In the Balance Sheet, Optional Vouchers can be viewed with the help of scenario. The Optional Voucher should be already defined as a Scenario (Refer section on Scenario Management for more details).

Note: Use Scenarios to see the effect of Optional voucher entries on reports and statements

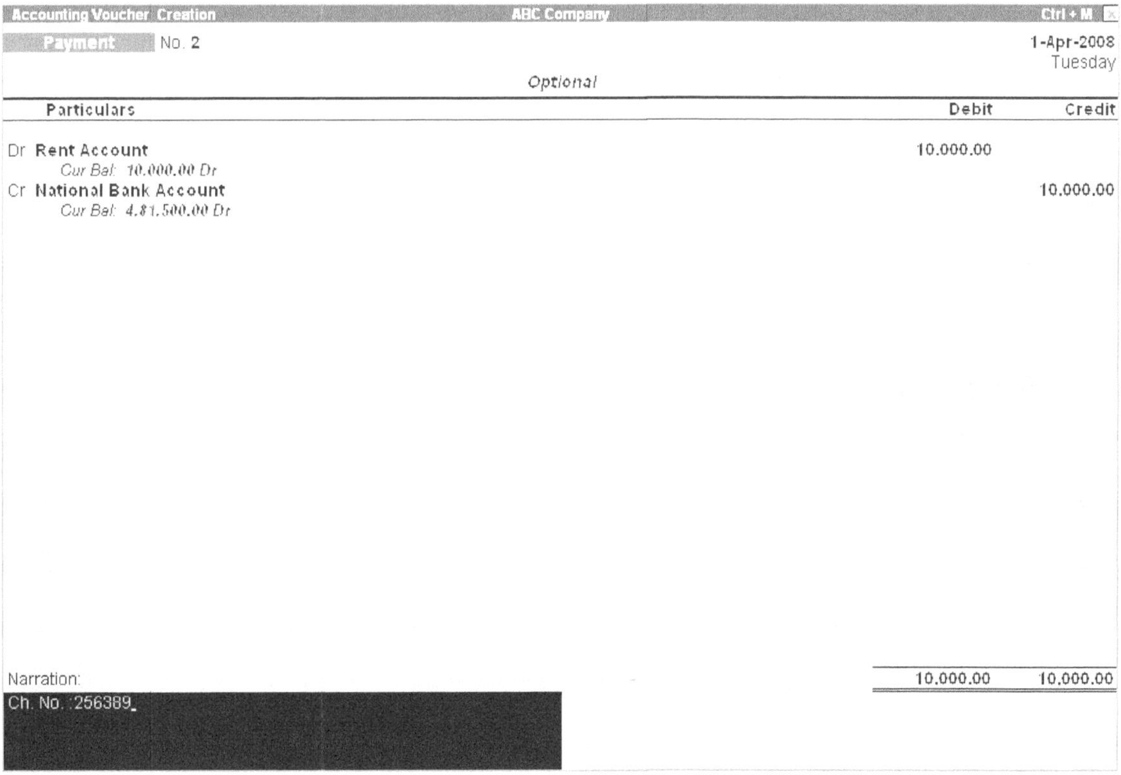

Accounting Voucher Creation ABC Company Ctrl + M

Payment No. 2 1-Apr-2008 Tuesday

Optional

Particulars	Debit	Credit
Dr Rent Account *Cur Bal: 10,000.00 Dr*	10,000.00	
Cr National Bank Account *Cur Bal: 4,81,500.00 Dr*		10,000.00
	10,000.00	10,000.00

Narration:
Ch. No. :256389

Fig. 9.35 Payment Accounting Voucher

Optional Vouchers Register

You can view all optional vouchers in the Optional Vouchers Register.

```
Go to Gateway of Tally > Display > Exception Reports > Optional Vouchers
```

Display Post Dated Vouchers

While entering vouchers, you can mark them as post dated. Tally.ERP 9 will not update the vouchers in ledgers until the specified date is approached. This is useful to enter transactions that take place on a regular basis. For example, if you pay for something by installments, you can set up the payments in advance, and Tally.ERP 9 will only enter them in the ledgers as they fall due.

Mark vouchers Post Dated by using CTRL+T or click on Post dated button from the Button Bar. This button toggles with Current.

Post Dated Payment Voucher entry is displayed as shown:

(Above entry will not appear in the ledger accounts, till 10th May)

Post-dated Vouchers Register

All Post-dated vouchers are maintained in a Post-dated voucher Register.

Go to Gateway of Tally> Display> Exception Reports> Post-Dated Vouchers

Difference in the treatment of Post-dated Vouchers and other Unconventional Vouchers

Gateway of Tally ....
Display Menu ....

Exception Reports

Negative Stock
Negative Ledgers

OveRdue Receivables
Overdue Payables

Memorandum Vouchers
REversing Journals
Optional Vouchers
PoSt-Dated Vouchers

Quit

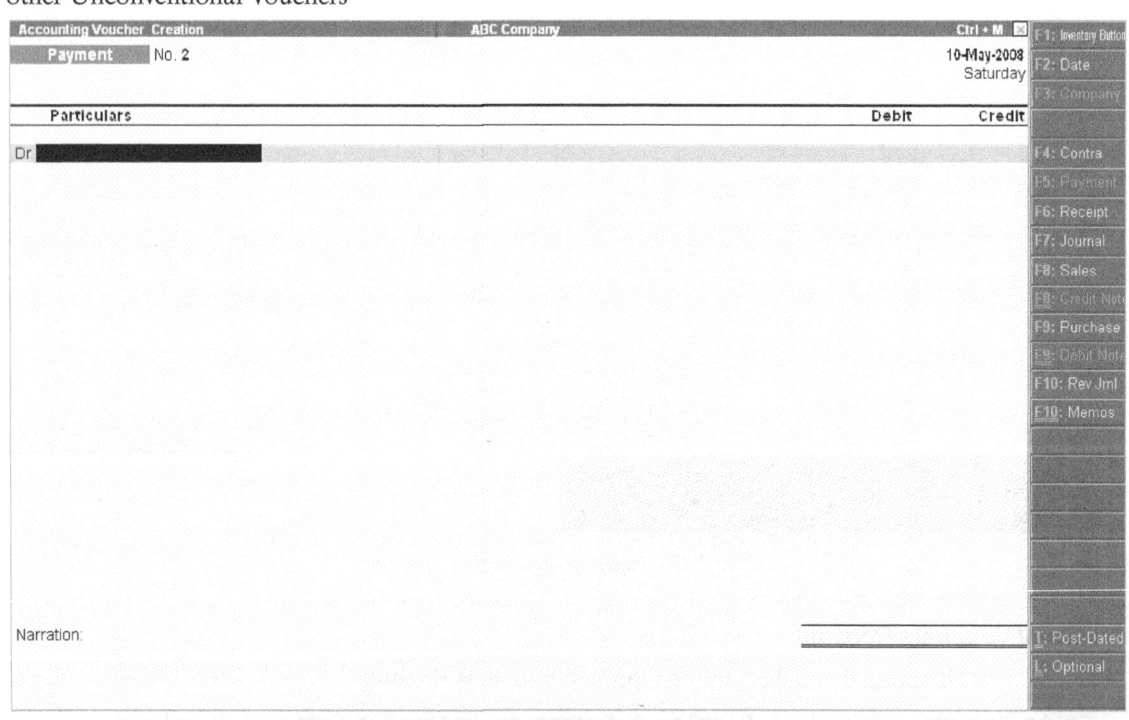

Fig. 9.36 Post Dated Payment Accounting Voucher

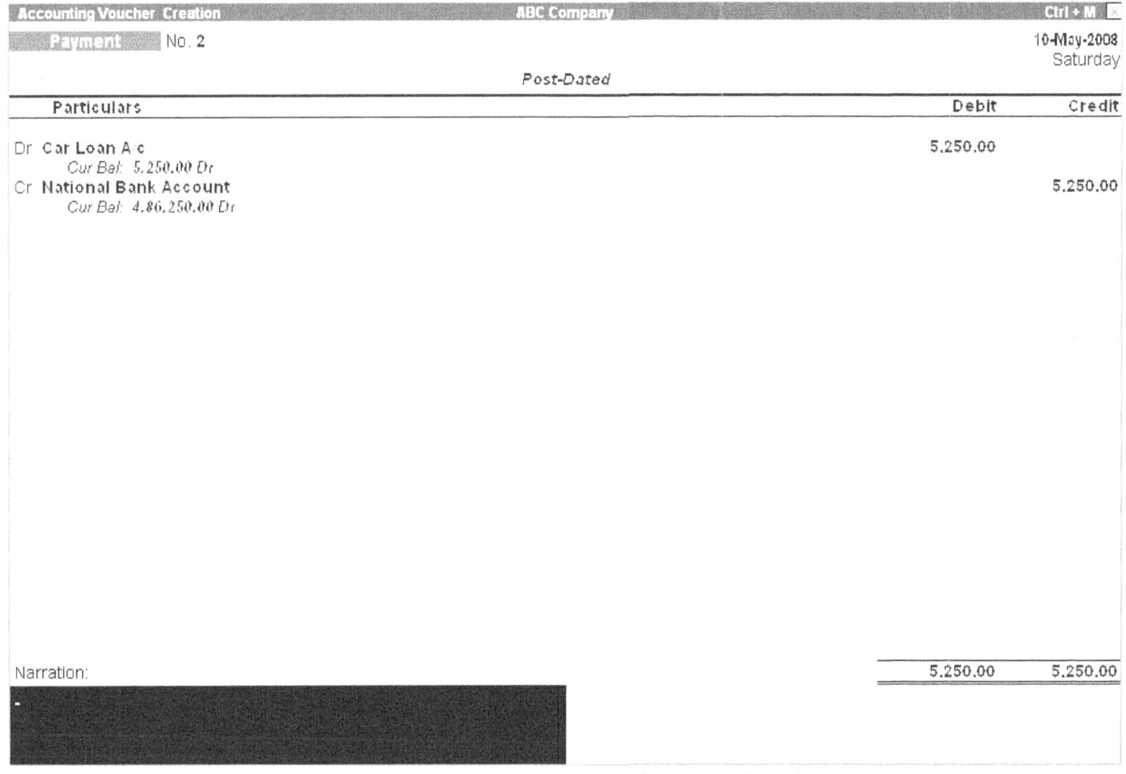

Fig. 9.37 Post Dated Payment Accounting Voucher

The major difference between post dated vouchers and other Unconventional vouchers are:

- Post dated Vouchers affect regular books of accounts on the date of the voucher
- Post-dated vouchers are not available for selection in Scenarios.

Gateway of Tally ....
Display Menu ....

Exception Reports

Negative Stock
Negative Ledgers

OveRdue Receivables
Overdue Payables

Memorandum Vouchers
REversing Journals
Optional Vouchers
PoSt-Dated Vouchers

Quit

Printing Reminder Letters

Reminder letters in Tally.ERP 9 can be configured to modify the text of the letter according to the preference of the user. The title of the subject, the first and the second paragraph of the letter and the sign-off style can be changed. This is one of the time saving utility of utilities available in Tally.ERP 9.

It is to be noted, that for this purpose, you have to activate the printing voucher configuration using the F12:Configuration in the Gateway of Tally screen.

Select Reminder Letters option from the Voucher Printing menu.

A sample of the printed reminder letter is displayed as shown.

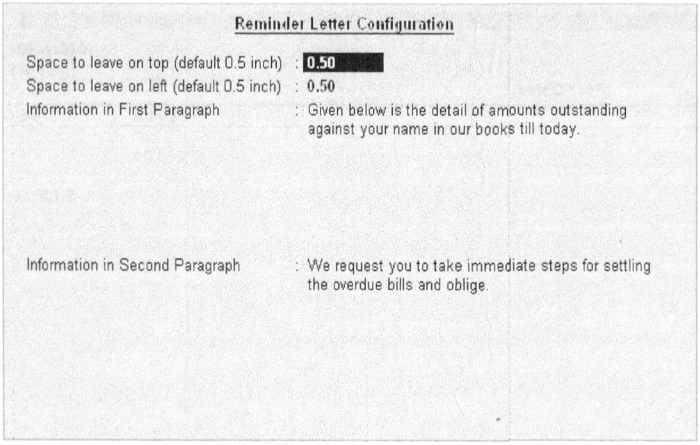

Reminder Letter Configuration

Space to leave on top (default 0.5 inch) : 0.50
Space to leave on left (default 0.5 inch) : 0.50
Information in First Paragraph : Given below is the detail of amounts outstanding against your name in our books till today.

Information in Second Paragraph : We request you to take immediate steps for settling the overdue bills and oblige.

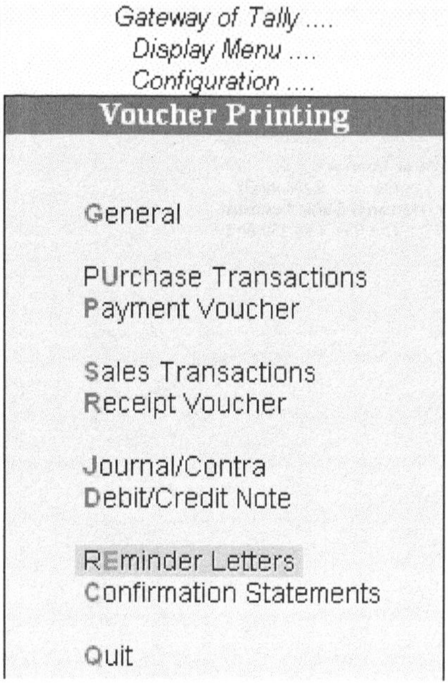

Gateway of Tally ....
Display Menu ....
Configuration ....

Voucher Printing

General

PUrchase Transactions
Payment Voucher

Sales Transactions
Receipt Voucher

Journal/Contra
Debit/Credit Note

REminder Letters
Confirmation Statements

Quit

Printing Reports

Reports and documents generated through Tally's extensive display capabilities can also be printed. The print options in Tally.ERP 9 are flexible and very easy to use.

Printing can be done in two ways.

- Using the Print (Alt+P) button.
- Using Multi-Account Printing option.

Both these methods yield the same output.

Using the Print (Alt+P) Button

You can obtain a printed version of the screen that is displayed by selecting Print from the button bar menu. This brings up new button bar options and the Print Configuration screen for the report, which displays Print? Yes or No. Select Yes to print the report using the options specified on the screen. Select No to change the print options before printing.

Multi-Account Printing

Multi-account printing is used to print the primary books of accounts like the Cash and Bank Books, Account Ledgers, Sales and Purchase Registers instead of selecting the accounts one at a time and pressing ALT+P. This facilitates to print one account at a time, all accounts or all accounts in a selected group. Before printing, the date range and other selections can also be set up.

Types of Print Configuration Options

Common Printing Options

Common printing options affect the printing of all reports and are changed by selecting the appropriate button from the button bar.

- With Preview: To view the report in print preview mode before actual printing.
- Titling: To change the title of the report.
- Page Nos: To specify the starting page number and page number range.
- Pre-Printed/ Plain Paper: Toggle to make the selection.

To : **Customer A** From: **ABC Company**
482, Ali Asker Road
Hyderabad

Dear Sir/Madam, Dated: **1-Apr-2009**

Sub : Outstandings

Given below is the detail of amounts outstanding against your name in our books till today.

We request you to take immediate steps for settling the overdue bills and oblige.

Date	Particulars	Due on	Overdue by	(< 30 days)	30 to 60 days	60 to 120 days	(> 120 days)
1-Apr-2008	ATB 0032	31-May-2008	(304 days)				61,000.00
5-Apr-2008	CA 5210	5-Apr-2008	(360 days)				5,25,000.00
5-Apr-2008	FORX 2201	5-Apr-2008	(360 days)				2,46,750.00
7-Apr-2008	CUST 1200	7-Apr-2008	(358 days)				6,69,500.00
19-Apr-2008	CST 5562	19-Apr-2008	(346 days)				3,50,200.00
1-May-2008	AAC 888	30-Jun-2008	(274 days)				56,000.00
1-May-2008	CAA 885	1-May-2008	(334 days)				56,000.00
1-May-2008	20	30-Jul-2008	(244 days)				16,800.00
6-Jun-2008	CAF 774	6-Jul-2008	(268 days)				1,25,000.00
15-Jun-2008	2	14-Aug-2008	(229 days)				35,000.00
							21,41,250.00

On Account 2,80,120.00 Cr

Total 18,61,130.00 Dr

Yours faithfully,

Sr. Accountant

Fig. 9.38 Print Preview

- Print Format: A pop-up list containing the printing formats available in Tally.ERP 9 is displayed. The formats provided are Dot-Matrix Format, Neat Format and Quick (Draft) Format.
- Copies: To specify the number of pages to be printed.
- Printer: To change the printer. This also displays the default paper size that is set for the printer.

Dynamic-Report Specific Options

If there are report specific options available for a report, they are displayed in a sub-screen when the print option is selected. You can change options before taking a final print.

Print Format

The user can specify print format settings as required. The print formats available in Tally.ERP 9 are Dot matrix format, Neat mode and Quick/ Draft.

The Print Format button appears on the Print screen (after you press Alt+P or on clicking the Print button). Click the Print Format button and Tally.ERP 9 displays a list of available Print formats as shown.

Dot matrix format allows you to print Tally.ERP 9 reports in text format using the dot matrix printers. As Tally.ERP 9 is a Windows-based software it uses a print format compatible with dot matrix printers.

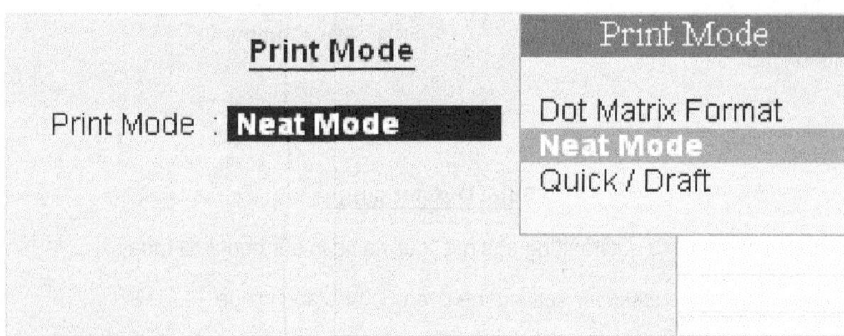

Usually Epson printer drivers are defined by default. Any dot matrix printer may be used, but only the Epson printer drivers (LQ and FX series) should be used for dot matrix format of Tally.ERP 9.

Select Dot Matrix Format. The screen is displayed as shown.

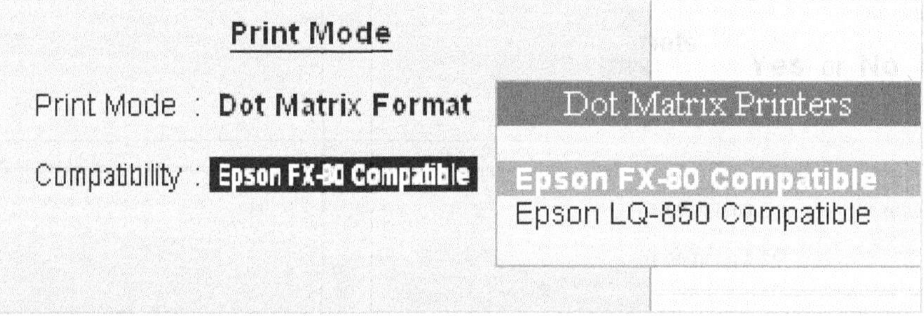

The neat mode and quick/ draft print modes are compatible with most of the printer drivers installed on the Windows Operating System. The default behaviour of Tally.ERP 9 is to print in neat mode. This can be altered by pressing ALT+F just before printing. All subsequent reports will be printed in quick/draft format until ALT+F is pressed again. Almost every report can be printed in quick/ draft mode (except for cheques).

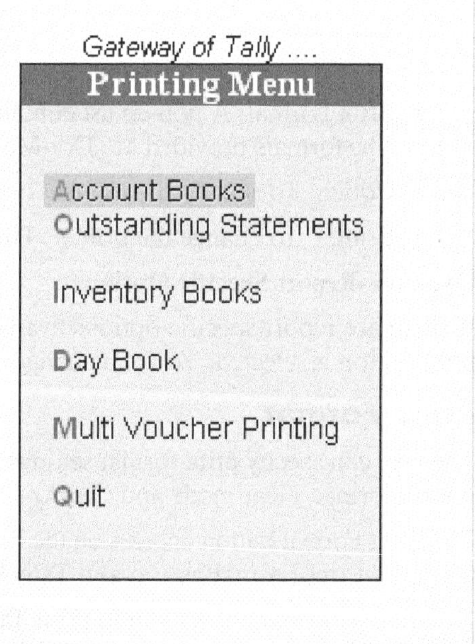

Multi - Account Printing

This option enables the printing of the primary Books of Accounts, like the Cash and Bank Books, Account Ledgers, Sales and Purchase Registers etc., without having to select the accounts one at a time and printing them.

Go to Gateway of Tally > Multi Account Printing.

Choose between the options – Account Books, Inventory Books, Day Book and Multi Voucher Printing.

You can select the date and other selections before printing the reports. Drill-down to Accounts Books,

Outstanding Statements and Inventory Books and select the appropriate reports to print.

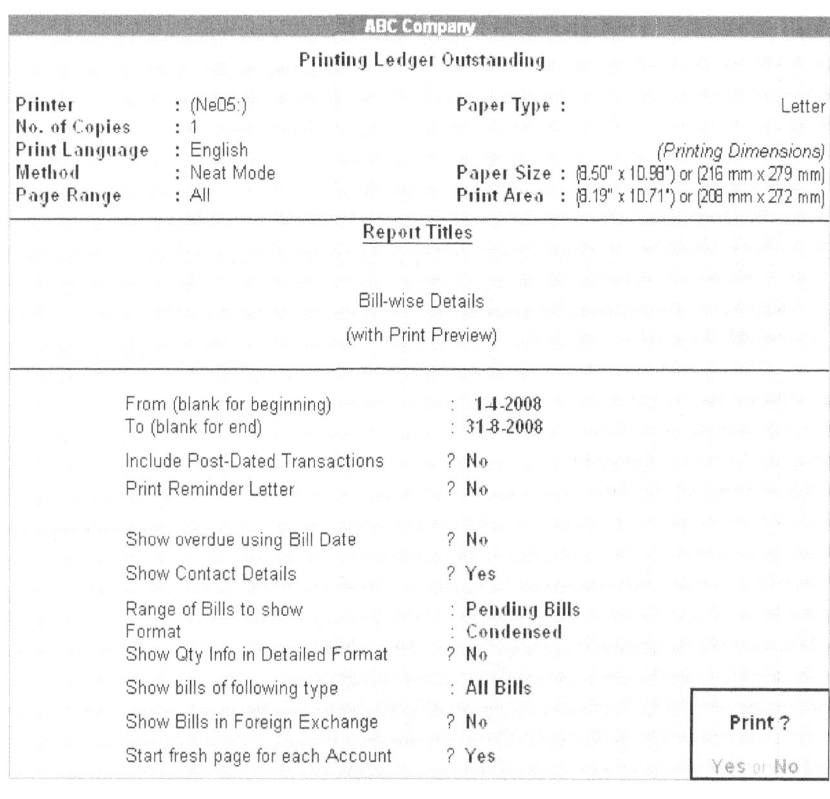

Change the common printing options by selecting the appropriate buttons on the right side of the screen. Tally.ERP 9 allows you to change and alter the following settings in the print configuration screen.

- **Printer** : Click Alt+S (Select Printer) to change printer settings. This also displays the default paper size set for the printer.
- **No. of Copies** : Click Alt+C (Copies) to specify the number of copies to be printed.
- **Print Language** : Click Alt+L (Print Language) to print in the language of your choice.
- **Method** : Click Alt+F (Print Format) to select the print format.

Printing All Accounts

```
Go to Gateway of Tally > Multi-Account Printing > Outstanding Statements >
Ledger > All Accounts
```

When Printing the Ledger Outstanding screen, if Show Contact Details is set to Yes, and Start Fresh Page for each Account is set to No, the Contact Person and the Tel. No. fields are displayed below each Ledger Account on the same page.

If Show Contact Details is set to Yes, and Start Fresh Page for each Account is also set to Yes, each Ledger Account is displayed on a fresh page, with the address appearing below the Ledger Name.

Note: For the Contact Person, Tel. No. and the address to be displayed, they should be entered in the Ledger Masters.

ABC Company

Customer B

Bill-wise Details

301 Regency Buildings
2134 Colaba Seaface
Mumbai

1-Apr-2008 to 31-Aug-2008

Page 5

Date	Ref. No.	Opening Amount	Pending Amount	Due on	Overdue by days
3-Apr-2008	GI001	4,16,000.00 Dr	**4,16,000.00 Dr**	3-Apr-2008	*150*
4-Apr-2008	GI002	88,400.00 Dr	**88,400.00 Dr**	4-Apr-2008	*149*
17-Apr-2008	1	55,936.00 Cr	**55,936.00 Cr**	17-Apr-2008	*136*
24-Apr-2008	1524	6,30,000.00 Dr	**6,30,000.00 Dr**	24-Apr-2008	*129*
30-Apr-2008	2	520.00 Dr	**5,200.00 Dr**	30-Apr-2008	*123*
	Sub Total	*10,78,984.00 Dr*	*10,83,664.00 Dr*		
31-Aug-2008	*On Account*	*65,000.00 Dr*	***65,000.00 Dr***		
		11,43,984.00 Dr	**11,48,664.00 Dr**		

Fig. 9.39 Print Preview

ABC Company

Bill-wise Details

1-Apr-2008 to 31-Aug-2008

Page 1

Date	Ref. No.	Opening Amount	Pending Amount	Due on	Overdue by days
	Customer A Contact Person : Mr A , Tel. No. : 9978532201				
31-Mar-2008	Opening Balance	50,000.00 Dr	**50,000.00 Dr**	31-Mar-2008	*153*
1-Apr-2008	ATB/0032	61,000.00 Dr	**61,000.00 Dr**	31-May-2008	*92*
5-Apr-2008	FORX/2201	2,57,250.00 Dr	**2,46,750.00 Dr**	5-Apr-2008	*148*
7-Apr-2008	CUST/1200	6,69,500.00 Dr	**6,69,500.00 Dr**	7-Apr-2008	*146*
19-Apr-2008	CST/5562	3,50,200.00 Dr	**3,50,200.00 Dr**	19-Apr-2008	*134*
30-Apr-2008	4	32,960.00 Cr	**32,960.00 Cr**	30-Apr-2008	*123*
1-May-2008	AAC/888	56,000.00 Dr	**56,000.00 Dr**	30-Jun-2008	*62*
1-May-2008	CAA/885	56,000.00 Dr	**56,000.00 Dr**	1-May-2008	*122*
1-May-2008	20	16,800.00 Dr	**1,800.00 Dr**	30-Jul-2008	*32*
15-Jun-2008	2	35,000.00 Dr	**35,000.00 Dr**	14-Aug-2008	*17*
30-Jun-2008	6	32,960.00 Cr	**2,47,160.00 Cr**	30-Jun-2008	*62*
		14,85,830.00 Dr	**12,46,130.00 Dr**		
	Customer B Contact Person : M. B , Tel. No. : 9825651832				
3-Apr-2008	GI001	4,16,000.00 Dr	**4,16,000.00 Dr**	3-Apr-2008	*150*
4-Apr-2008	GI002	88,400.00 Dr	**88,400.00 Dr**	4-Apr-2008	*149*
17-Apr-2008	1	55,936.00 Cr	**55,936.00 Cr**	17-Apr-2008	*136*
24-Apr-2008	1524	6,30,000.00 Dr	**6,30,000.00 Dr**	24-Apr-2008	*129*

Fig. 9.40 Print Preview

10 Tally.Net

Introduction

Tally.ERP 9 provides a new capability Tally.NET which is available by default. Tally.NET is a framework which works in the background and provides a broad range of services using the Internet.

Using Tally.NET the user can access the company's data from a remote location using another instance of Tally.ERP 9; similarly a practicing Chartered Accountant working with Tally.ERP 9 Auditor's License can scrutinize the client's Tally.ERP 9 data remotely from the office. The remote users can access or audit data belonging to one company at a time.

At the client's place the system administrator has to create remote users with the permission to access or audit data from a remote location and assign controls based on their security level for the required company only. The remote user accessing the company data acts as clients to Tally.NET.

Features of Tally.NET

Tally.NET is a default feature available in the product and provides a host of capabilities. Following is a list of capabilities available in Tally.ERP 9.

- Connect companies from Tally.ERP 9.
- Create and maintain Remote Users.
- Remote availability of Auditors' Edition of Tally.ERP 9 License.
- Synchronization of data (via Tally.NET).
- Remote access of data by any user (including BAP users).
- Use online help and support capability from within Tally or the browser.
- Support Centre to get instant access for support on functional and technical areas realted to the product.
- Control Centre to manage and centrally configure sites across locations.

Configuring Tally.NET Features

To Configure Tally.NET Features in Tally.ERP 9, execute the following steps:

`Go to Gateway of Tally > F11: Features > F4: Tally.NET Features`

The Tally.NET Features screen is displayed as shown.

Under Registration Details

- Connect Name: The user can enter a Connect Name for the Company to be connected as per his requirements or retain the company name mentioned in the Company Master.
- Contact Person Name: Specify the Name of the Contact Person.
- Contact Number: Specify the Contact Number.

Under Connect for Remote Access

- Allow to Connect Company: Set this option to Yes, when the user needs to establish a connection with the Tally.NET server.
- Connect on Load: Set this option to Yes, when the user requires the company to be connected to Tally.NET server on loading the data.

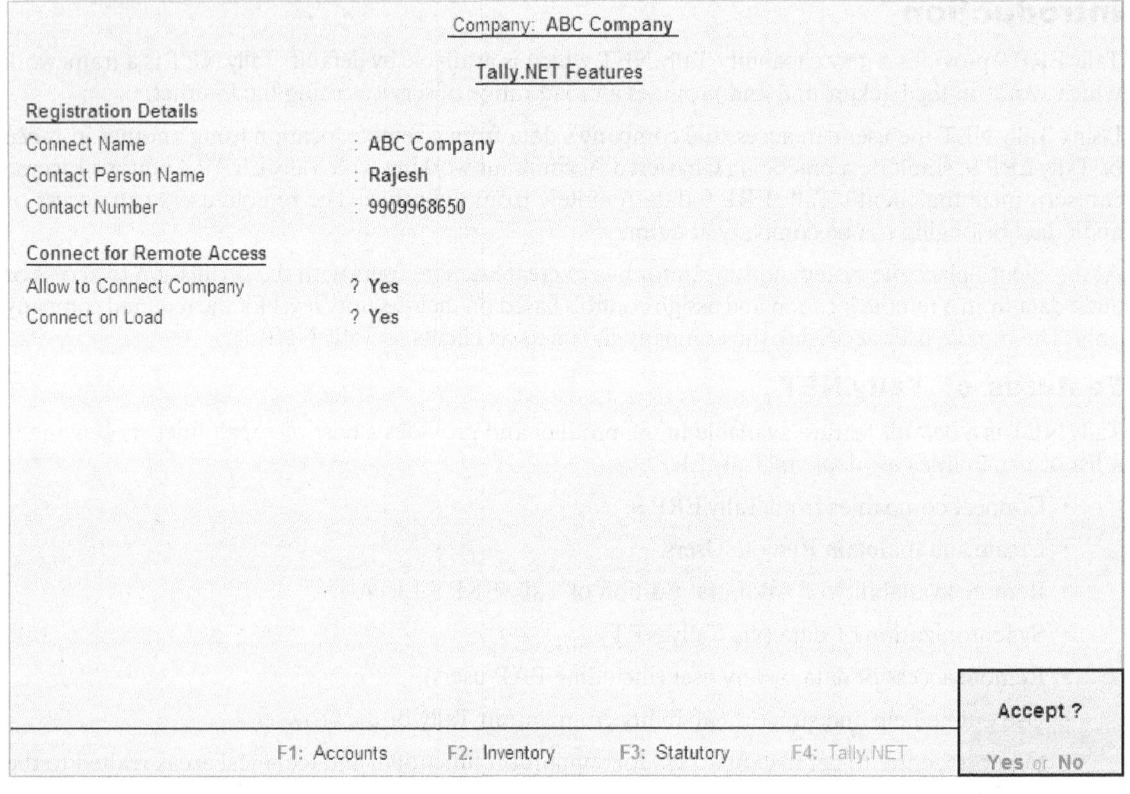

Fig. 10.1 Tally.Net Features

- Press Enter to accept.

Note: It is mandatory to enable Security Controls in the Company Creation master for Tally.NET features to be available in Tally. Incase the Security Controls feature is not enabled, go to Company Alteration (Alt+F3) screen and enable the same for proceeding further.

Creating Remote Users

Users classified under the security level Tally.NET User and Tally.NET Auditor should be created individually by the system administrator from Tally.ERP 9 or from www.tallysolutions.com.

Create Tally.NET User

To create a Tally.NET User execute the following steps:

`Go to Gateway of Tally`

1. Press Ctrl+K: Control Centre or press Ctrl + K.

2. The Remote Login screen is displayed.
3. Enter the required Account ID in the Your E-Mail ID field and Password in Your Tally.NET Password field. The password is sent by e-mail separately to the email address provided while activating Tally.ERP 9.

Login As Remote Tally.NET User

Your E-Mail ID : **tallyuser@tallysolutions.com**

Your Tally.NET Password : ********

(if you have forgotten your Tally.NET Password, please press F5:Reset Password. A new password will be sent to your E-Mail address, and you can then login).

4. Press Enter.

Note: The user can login ias an Account Administrator by providing the Account ID or as a Site Administrator by providing the Site E-Mail ID and providing the password.

The Control Centre screen appears as displayed.

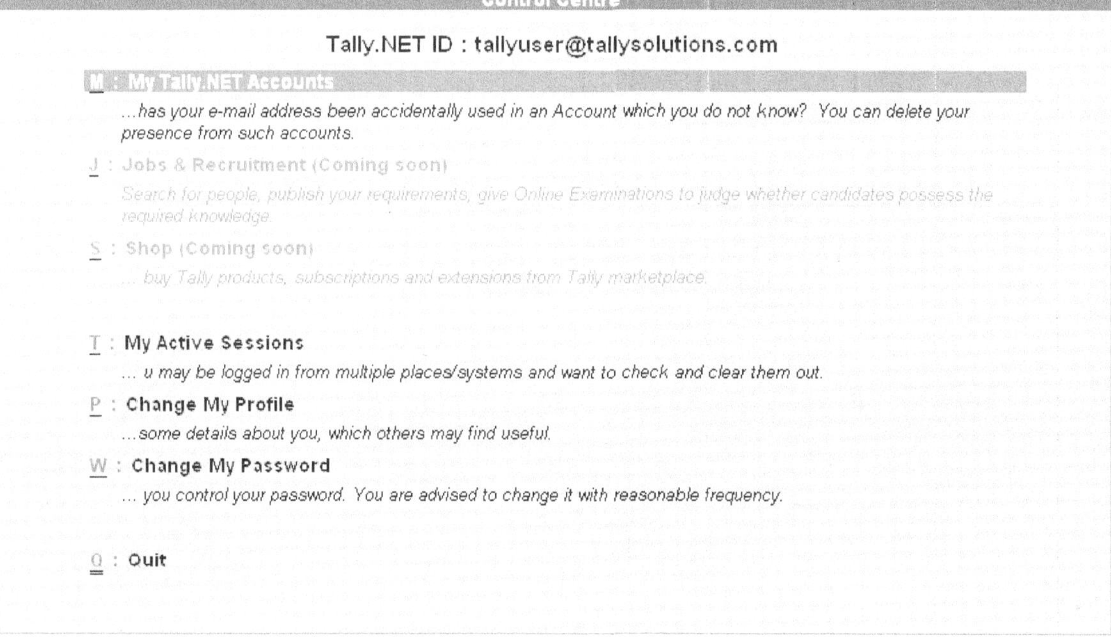

Fig. 10.2 Control Centre Screen

In the Control Centre Screen :

- Select My Tally.NET Accounts.
- The My Tally.NET Accounts screen is displayed.
- Select the required Account ID.

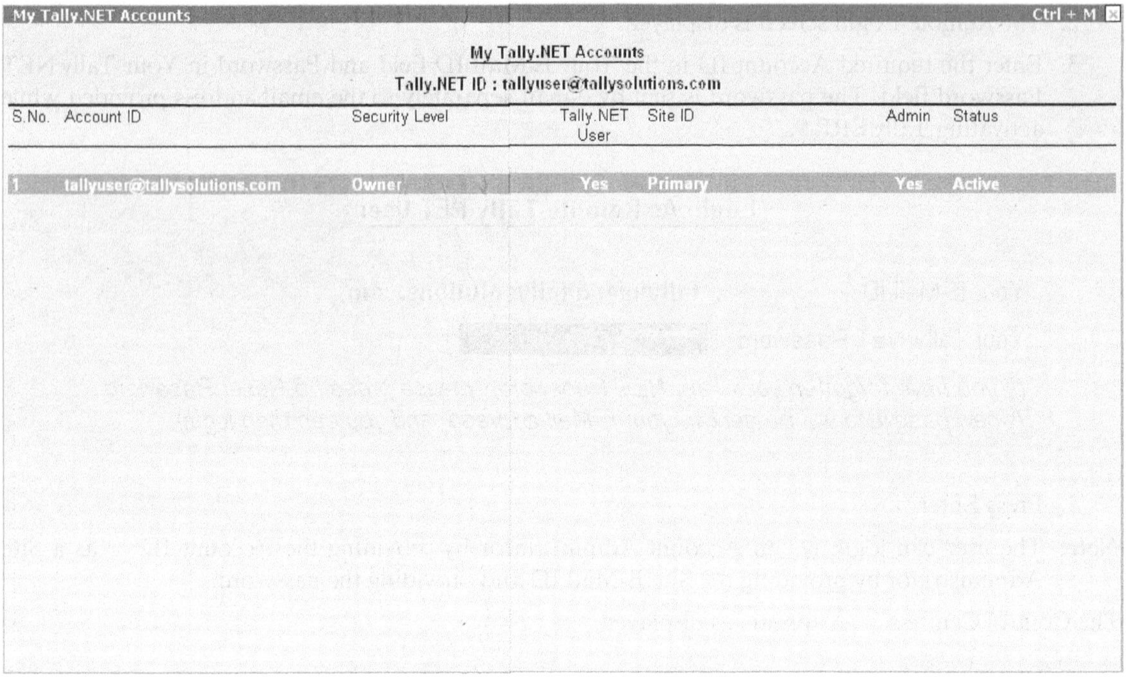

My Tally.NET Accounts Ctrl + M

My Tally.NET Accounts

Tally.NET ID : tallyuser@tallysolutions.com

S.No.	Account ID	Security Level	Tally.NET User	Site ID	Admin	Status
1	tallyuser@tallysolutions.com	Owner	Yes	Primary	Yes	Active

Fig. 10.3 Tally.Net Accounts

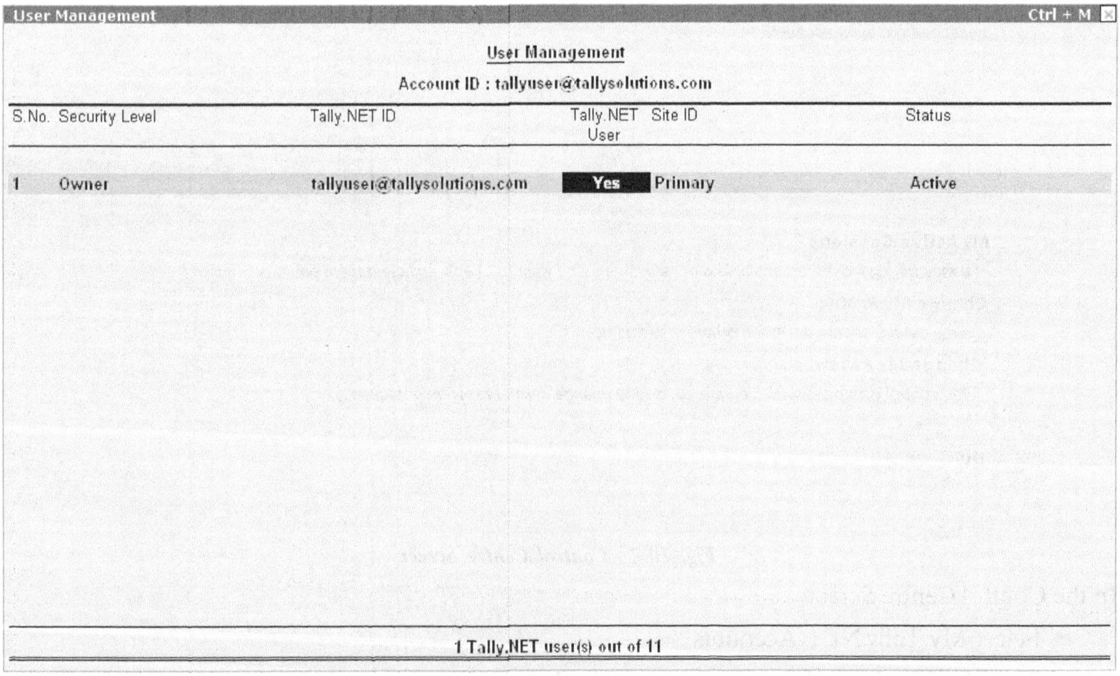

User Management Ctrl + M

User Management

Account ID : tallyuser@tallysolutions.com

S.No.	Security Level	Tally.NET ID	Tally.NET User	Site ID	Status
1	Owner	tallyuser@tallysolutions.com	Yes	Primary	Active

1 Tally.NET user(s) out of 11

Fig. 10.4 User Management Screen

- Press Enter.
- The Contol Centre screen is displayed.
- Select User Management and press Enter.
- The User Management is displayed, along with the details related of the Account ID.
- To create Tally.NET Users, execute the following steps:
    - Select Standard User from the list of Security Level.
    - Enter the required E-mail ID for the Remote Tally.NET User in Tally.NET ID field and press Enter.
    - Based on your requirement, select the status from the List of Status.
    - Select End of List.
    - Accept to save the new Tally.NET User that has been created.

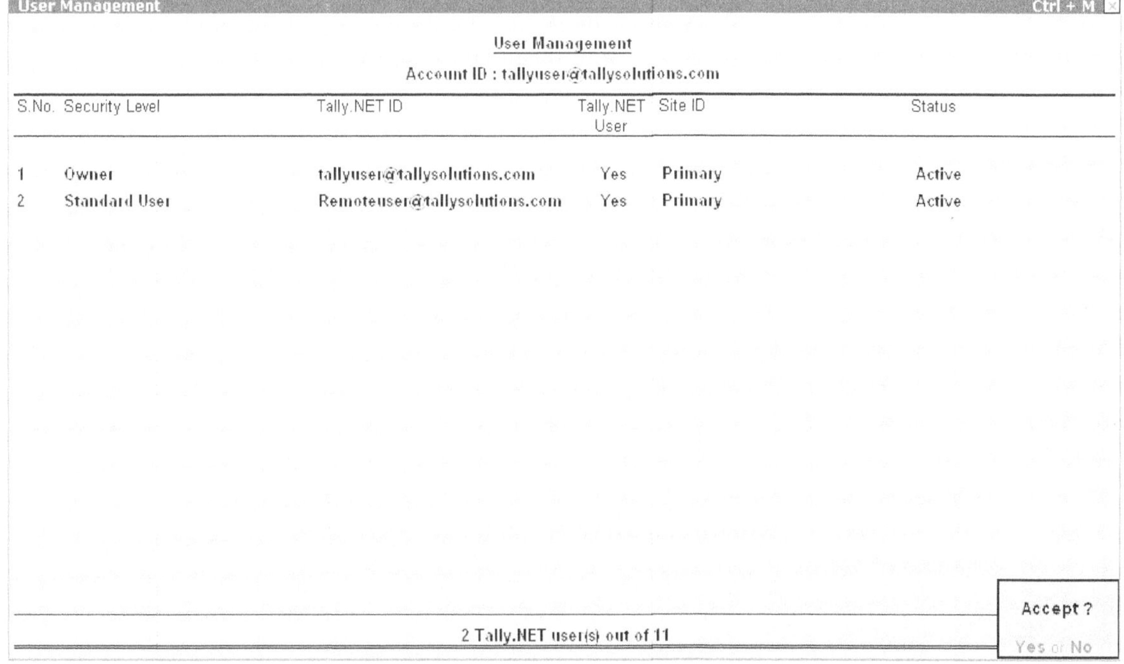

Fig. 10.5 User Management Showing More Than one User

Note: The company's system administrator should authorise the Tally.NET User ID and connect to Tally.NET and allow remote access.

Create Tally.NET Auditor

To create a Tally.NET Auditor (Remote Auditor) execute the following steps:

Go to Gateway of Tally

1. Press Ctrl+K: Control Centre or press Ctrl + K.
2. The Remote Login screen is displayed.

3. Enter the required Account ID in the Your E-Mail ID field and Password in Your Tally.NET Password field. The password is sent by e-mail separately to the email address provided while activating Tally.ERP 9.

Login As Remote Tally.NET User

Your E-Mail ID : **tallybapuser@tallysolutions.com**
Your Tally.NET Password : *********

(if you have forgotten your Tally.NET Password, please press F5:Reset Password. A new password will be sent to your E-Mail address, and you can then login).

4. Press Enter.

Note: The user can login ias an Account Administrator by providing the Account ID or as a Site Administrator by providing the Site E-Mail ID and providing the password.

The Control Centre screen appears as displayed.

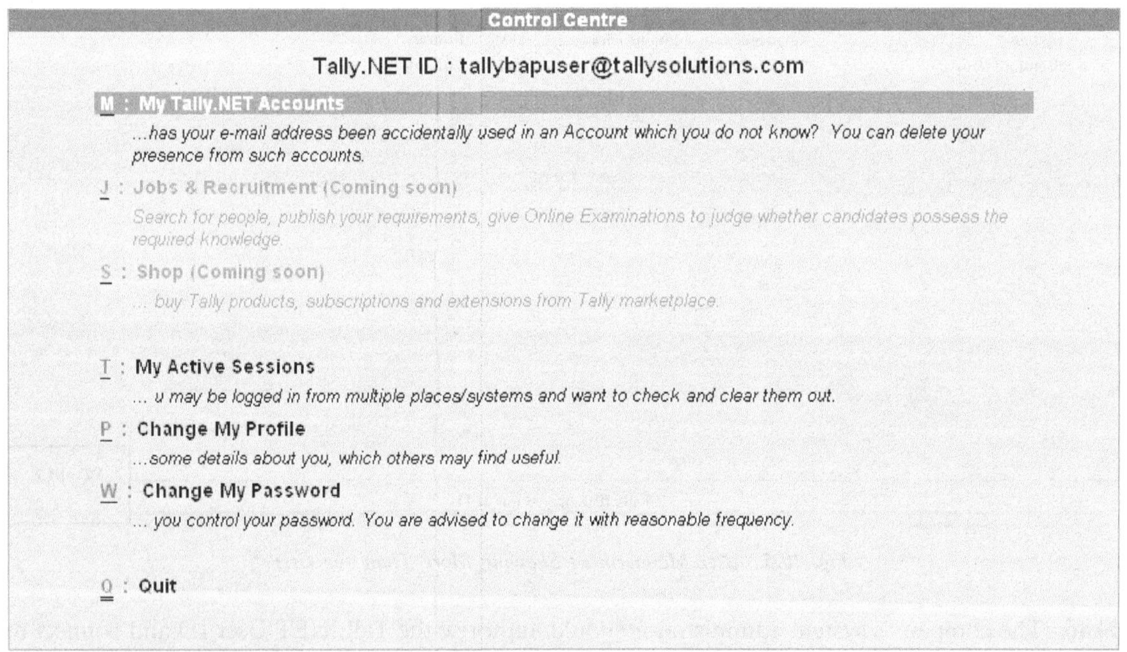

Fig. 10.6 Control Centre Screen

In the Control Centre Screen :

- Select My Tally.NET Accounts.
- The My Tally.NET Accounts screen is displayed.

Select the required Account ID.

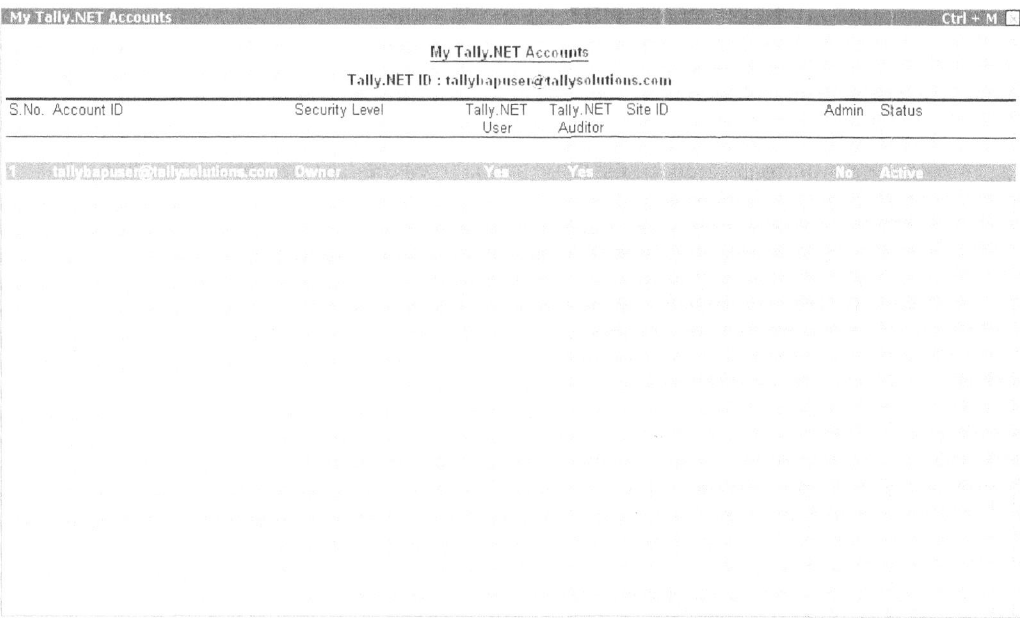

Fig. 10.7 Tally.Net Accounts

Press Enter.

The Contol Centre screen is displayed.

Select User Management and press Enter.

The User Management is displayed, along with the details related of the Account ID.

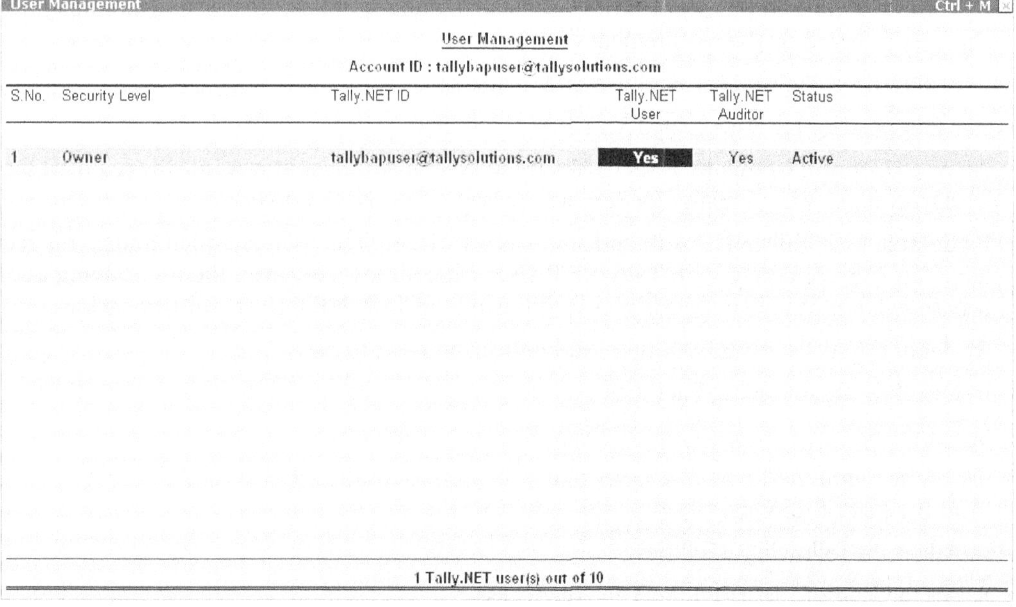

Fig. 10.8 User Management Screen

- To create Tally.NET Users, execute the following steps:
  - Select Standard User from the list of Security Level.
  - Enter the required E-mail ID for the Remote Tally.NET User in Tally.NET ID field and press Enter.
  - Based on your requirement, select the status from the List of Status.
  - Select End of List.
  - Accept to save the new Tally.NET User that has been created.

Note: The company's system administrator should authorise the Tally.NET User ID and connect to Tally.NET and allow remote access.

Creating Security Controls

By default, the Tally.NET User is authorised in the capacity of Data Entry operator, thereby having restricted access to the company data. Similarly the Tally.NET Auditor is authorised as Owner of the company and has full access to the company data. However, the system administrator can change the access controls of Tally.NET User or the Tally.NET Auditor based on the requirement. Any user created under these security levels require Tally.NET authentication to access data

Creating Security Controls to Tally.NET User

To create security controls for a Tally.NET User, execute the following steps:

`Go to Gateway of Tally > Alt+F3 > security Control > Types of Security`

1. In the Security Levels for company screen, select Tally.NET User.
2. In the Security Levels for Tally.NET User screen.
   - By default, Tally.NET User appears in the Name of Security Level field.
   - By default, Data Entry appears in the Use Basic Facilities of field, the system administrator can change this based on the requirement.
   - Type 0 in Days allowed for Back Dated vouchers.
   - The Cut-off date for Back Dated Vouchers is left blank.
   - Allow to Connect Company is set to Yes if the system administrator wants the required security level to connect the company for remote access to Tally.NET Server.
   - By default, Use Tally.NET Authentication is set to Yes. The user classified under this security level can login remotely with Tally.NET User capabilities. However, the user having auditor's license will not be able to perform an audit using the Tally.NET User Authentication.
   - By default, Use Tally.NET Auditor Authentication is set to No.
   - In Disallow the following Facilities.
   - Select the required Access Control from the Type of Access.
   - Select the required Report / Activity that you want to disallow based on the access control that from the List of Reports.
   - In Allow the following Facilities.
   - Select the End of List from the Type of Access.
3. Press Enter to save the access controls for Tally.NET User.

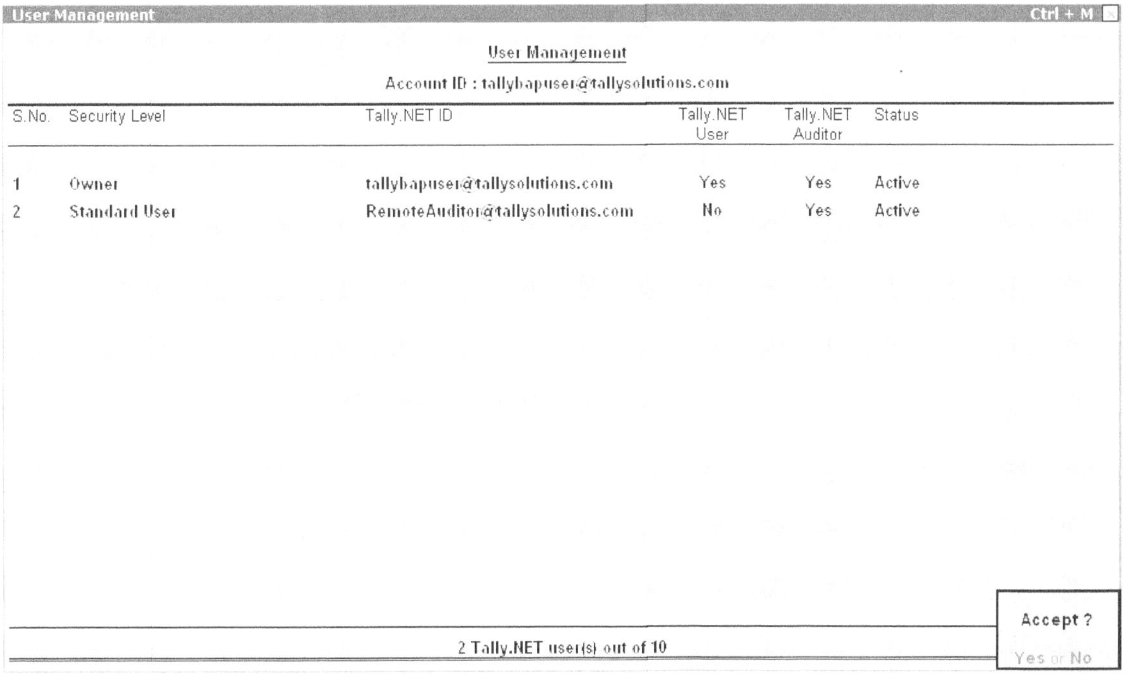

User Management Ctrl + M

User Management

Account ID : tallybapuser@tallysolutions.com

S.No.	Security Level	Tally.NET ID	Tally.NET User	Tally.NET Auditor	Status
1	Owner	tallybapuser@tallysolutions.com	Yes	Yes	Active
2	Standard User	RemoteAuditor@tallysolutions.com	No	Yes	Active

2 Tally.NET user(s) out of 10

Accept ?

Yes or No

Fig. 10.9 User Management Screen with two Users

Creating Security Controls to Tally.NET Auditor

To create security controls to Tally.NET Auditor, execute the following steps:

Go to Gateway of Tally > Alt+F3 > security Control > Types of Security

1. Select Tally.NET Auditor in the Types of Security.
2. The Security Levels for company screen is displayed.
3. By default, Tally.NET Auditor appears in the Name of Security Level field.
4. By default, Owner appears in the Use Basic Facilities of field, the system administrator can change this based on the requirement.
5. Type 0 in Days allowed for Back Dated vouchers.
6. The Cut-off date for Back Dated Vouchers is left blank.
7. Set Yes to Allow to Connect Company.
8. By default, Use Tally.NET Authentication is set to No.
9. Use Tally.NET Auditor Authentication is set to Yes, when the auditor wants to access the client's data and perform an audit. However, a user not having the auditor's license will not be able to perform an audit by setting Use Tally.NET Auditor Authentication to Yes.
10. In Disallow the following Facilities.
    - Select the End of List from the Type of Access.
11. In Allow the following Facilities.
    - Select Full Access from the Type of Access.

Security Levels — **ABC Company**

Name of Security Level : **Tally.NET User**

Use Basic Facilities of : **Data Entry**

Days allowed for Back Dated vouchers : **0**
Cut-off date for Back Dated vouchers :

Allow to Connect Company ? **No**
Use Tally.NET Authentication ? **Yes**
Use Tally.NET Auditor Authentication ? **No**

Disallow the following Facilities *(others will be allowed)*		Allow the following Facilities *(to re-enable disallowed facilities)*
Full Access	Accounts Masters	End of List
Full Access	Balance Sheet	
Full Access	Cash Flow	
Full Access	Company Features	
Full Access	Cost Centre Details	
Full Access	Funds Flow	
Full Access	Location-Wise Summary	
Full Access	Group Monthly Summary	
Full Access	Group Summary	
Full Access	Inventory Masters	
Full Access	Outstandings	
Full Access	Profit & Loss A/c	
Full Access	Stock Category Summary	
Full Access	Stock Summary	
Full Access	Trial Balance	
Full Access	Back Dated Vouchers	

Fig. 10.10 Various Security Levels

- Select Audit Listings from the List of Reports.

12. Press Enter to save the Security Controls for Tally.NET Auditor.

Connect Company on Tally.NET

Connect Company

In order to connect a company to Tally.NET for remote access, audit or synchronization, the user has to execute the following steps:

1. Click F4: Connect Cmp or press Alt + F4 from any menu in Tally.ERP 9.
2. The Connect Companies to Tally.NET screen is displayed.

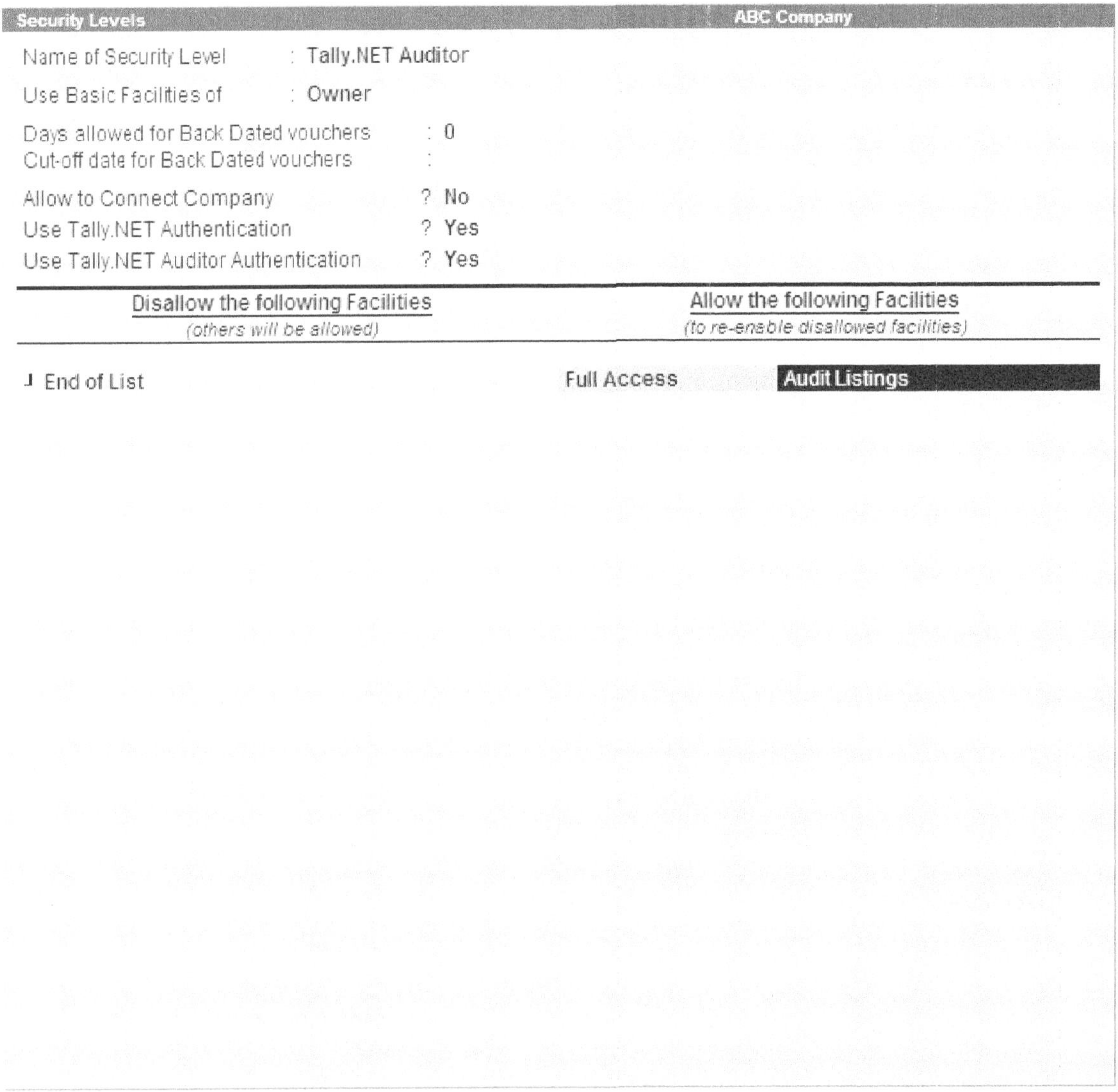

Security Levels ABC Company

Name of Security Level : Tally.NET Auditor

Use Basic Facilities of : Owner

Days allowed for Back Dated vouchers : 0
Cut-off date for Back Dated vouchers :

Allow to Connect Company ? No
Use Tally.NET Authentication ? Yes
Use Tally.NET Auditor Authentication ? Yes

Disallow the following Facilities (others will be allowed)		Allow the following Facilities (to re-enable disallowed facilities)
End of List	Full Access	Audit Listings

Fig. 10.11 Various Security Levels

3. Select the required companies from the List of Companies.

Note: When only one Company is Loaded, it will directly get connected to Tally.NET without showing the Connect Companies to Tally.NET screen.

1. The Company Name, Connect Company, Contact Person and Contact Number appear in Connect Companies to Tally.NET screen as shown:
2. Accept to connect company to Tally.NET.

The message indicating that the company is connected successfully is displayed in the calculator pane as shown:

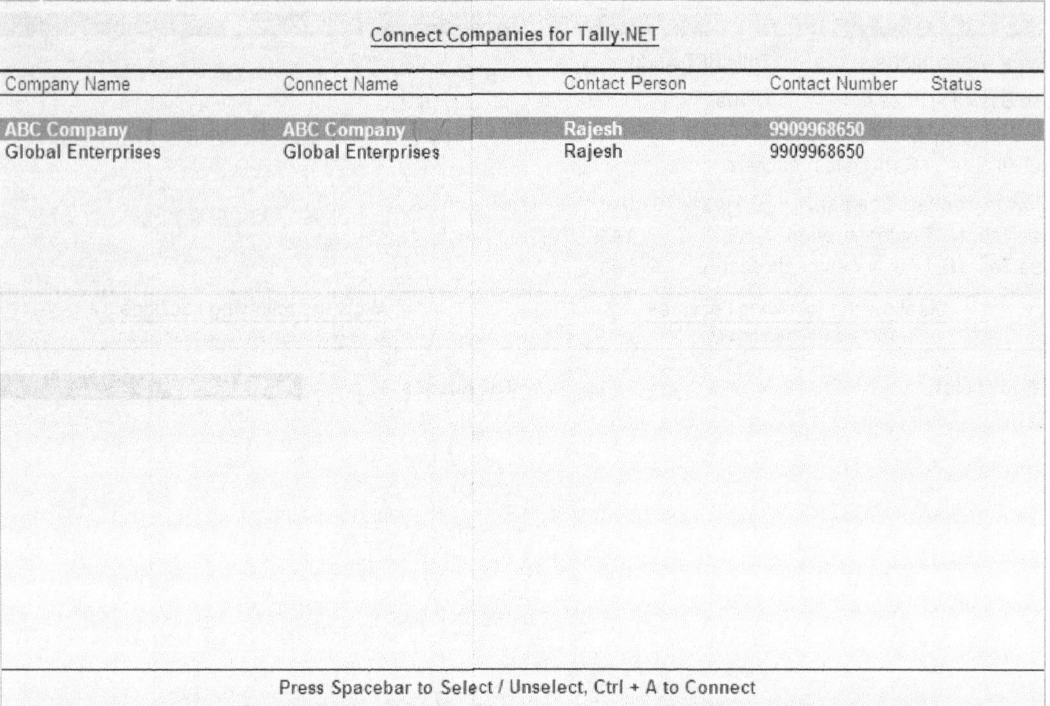

Fig. 10.12 Connected Connections

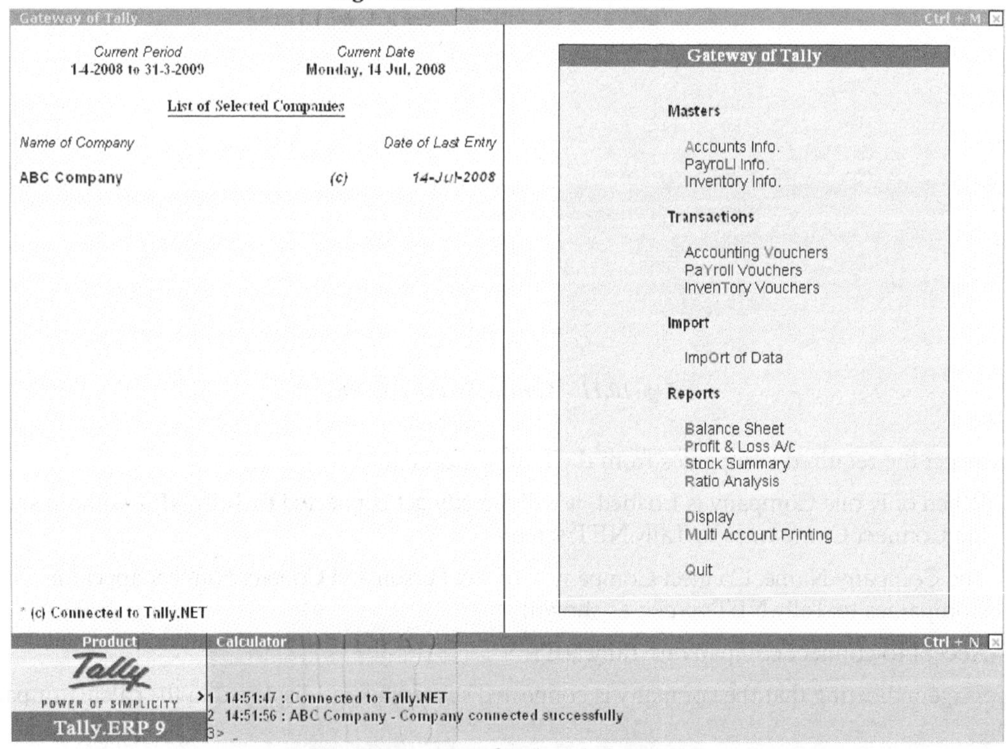

Fig. 10.13 List of Selected Companies

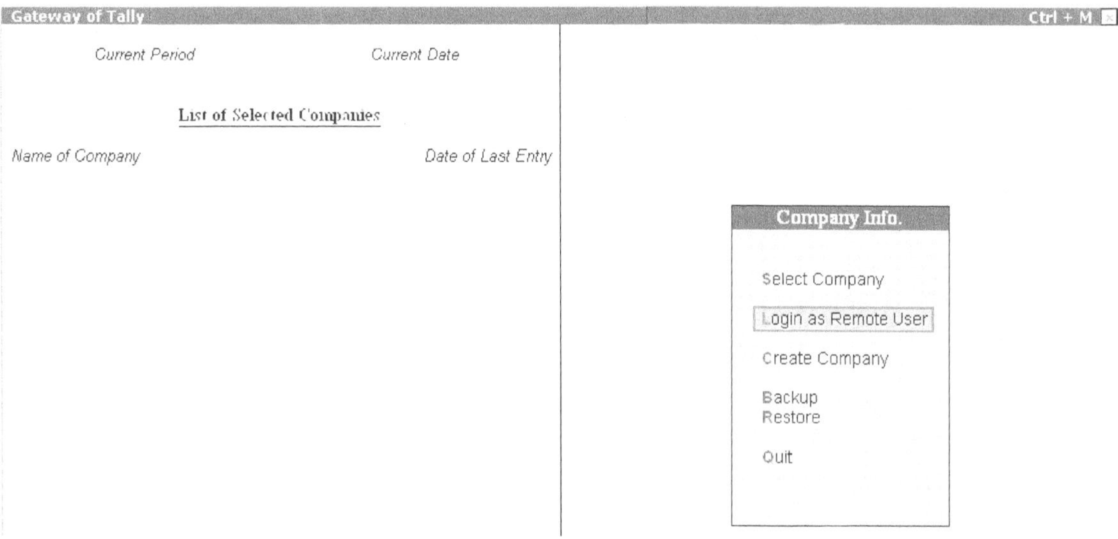

Fig. 10.14 Login as Remote User

Note: Changes made to the name of the Contact Person or the Contact Number will not be stored in the company masters.

Remote Login

The users classified under Tally.NET User or Tally.NET Auditor can access data from a remote location by providing the remote user Login Id and Password while Tally.ERP 9 is running in Licensed or Educational mode.

The user has to execute the following steps to login as a remote user:

1. Start Tally.ERP 9

   In the Company Info. menu or Startup screen

2. Select Login as Remote User
3. In the Login as Remote Tally.NET User screen.

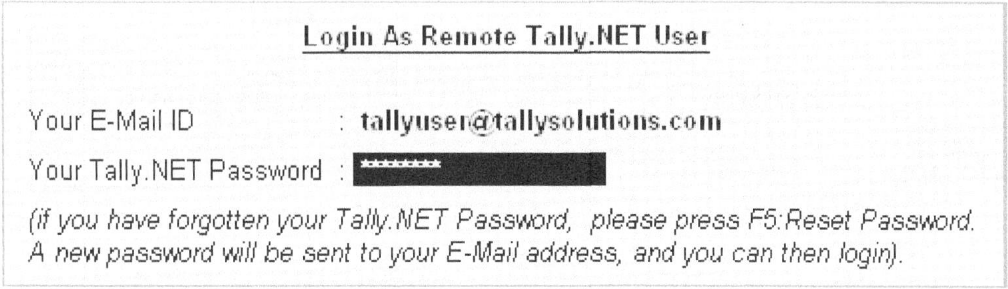

   a. Enter the required Tally.NET login id in the Your E-Mail Id field.

   b. Enter the required password in the Your Tally.NET Password field.

   On successful authentication, a remote session is created on Tally.NET which remains valid till

List of Remote Companies

Company Name	Account ID	Serial Number	Contact Person	Contact Number
Online Companies				
ABC Company	tally1@tallysolutions.com	702088209	Rajesh	
Spectrum Software Solutions Pvt. Ltd.	tally1@tallysolutions.com	702088209	Suresh	9909968555
Offline Companies				
Gobal Enterprises	tally1@tallysolutions.com	702088209	Rajesh	
Vetri - Tally.ERP 9 Demo Company	tally1@tallysolutions.com	702088209	Vetri	3216549870

Fig. 10.15 List of Remote Companies

the user logs out. A unique identification number is assigned to the remote session created. The remote user can work on one company only at a time.

4. In List of Remote Companies screen, select the required company from the List of Companies.

On successfully loading the selected company, the remote access license is displayed under the Edition tab as shown:

Depending on the additional license capabilities, the remote user can audit or access data.

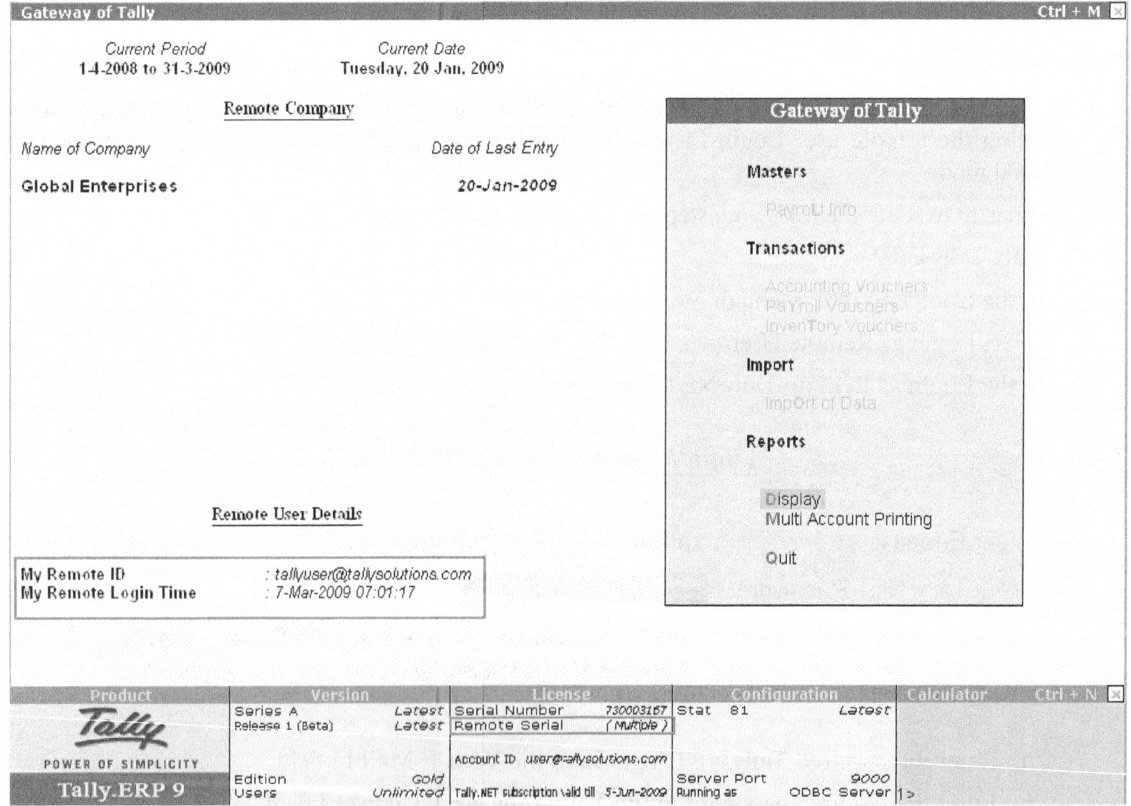

Fig. 10.16 Remote Company with connection

11 Fundamentals of Accounting and Inventory

Fundamentals of Accounting

This section tells you about the basic accounting features and how Tally handles them. Those of you who have accounting background must be very clear about these concepts and would probably find the following information quite childish but it is important for us to give these information specially for those of you who do not have the accounting background.

Let us start with some definitions.

Debit

It is what you receive.

Credit

It is what you give.

Debtor

It is that person who owes money to the business on account of credit sale of goods or advance given or services rendered to him.

Creditor

It is that person to whom the business owes money on account of credit purchase of goods or loan taken or services received from him.

Transactions

It means transfer of money or money's worth from one party to another.

Drawing

It means withdrawal. The amount of money or the value of goods taken by the proprietor from the business for his personal use.

Liability

It is that sum of money which the business owes to outsiders. Capital is that part of wealth which is contributed by the proprietor to start, run and further expand the business.

Assets

These are the things of value owned by the company. Cash, unsold stock, furniture, money due from the debtors fall under the category of assets.

Accounting Systems

There are two main accounting systems: Cash and Mercantile. In cash system enteries in the book are done only when the amount due has been received. It is not shown as due at any stage.

On the other hand in mercantile system, a record is made on the basis of amounts having become due for payment or receipt.

Transactions are also of two types: Double and Single entry. The double entry system is based on the fact that a transaction is a double-sided affair. If one receives something, somewhere something must have been reduced, or some service must have been rendered.

A single entry system on the other hand is concerned with only one side of the transaction, either you pay someone or you receive from someone.

The double entry system is more accurate, scientific and systematic.

Journal Accounts

Debiting and crediting each and every individual account for every transaction is very time consuming. This is overcome by recording the debit and its corresponding credit or the credit and its corresponding debit in a subsidiary book. Each journal transaction is recorded in the form of a voucher. A voucher is supposed to have the following information:

Date

It records the date of transaction with its month and year.

Particulars

This is what is usually known as narration. You can write here the details of the transactions in plain English.

Ledger Folio

Posting in the ledger accounts is done on the basis of journal entries. It is therefore, necessary that there should be certain reference to the page number of ledger, where the account in journal is being posted.

Debit

This contains the amount debited under a transaction.

Credit

This contains the amount credited under a transaction.

Cash Book

For a big company it is not possible to have only one journal to carry all the accounting information. So for this we have different books for different accounts. That is why we have Purchase Books, Purchase Return Books, Sales Books, Sales Return Books, Bill Receivable Books and Bills Payable Books. You will read about them later in the book.

Cash book records all the cash transactions. Cash does not mean hard cash only. It also means notes, coins, bank drafts, cheques and postal orders too. As in other transactions, here too you have Receipts and Payments. There are various types of cash books which the company's maintain depending upon the type of business that they have.

Simple Cash Book

It is the simplest form of the cash book, where all the cash transactions are recorded. It does not even records the banking and cash discount transactions. The following may represent a format of the same:

Dr.	*Receipts*				*Payments*		*Cr.*
Date	*Particulars*	*L.F.*	*Amount Rs. P.*	*Date*	*Particulars*	*L.F.*	*Amount Rs. P.*

Remember the cash book is maintained date wise and all the entries are totalled as per the date, *i.e.*, the balance is found out at the end of each date.

Petty Cash Book

It is a usual practice for a company to withdraw cash from the bank and then keep on using it for various purposes like Travelling, Postage, Carriage, Stationery, etc. So when the cash level reaches a minimum level more cash is added and thus this book keeps on working. This book is called the Petty Cash Book since it takes care of the cash transactions which are very petty in nature.

In this case the ledger has the various heads under which the usual amount is spent. The first column is receipt of the cash and then day to day cash activities are noted as per the details. At the end of week/ month the totals are done and balance taken.

A possible example of the petty cash book can be:

Receipts	Date	Particulars	V no.	Total	Conveyance	Stationary	Postage	Others
100.00	1.2.00	To cash A/c.						
	2.2.00	By conveyance		15.00	15.00			
	5.2.00	By Stationary		19.00		19.00		
	7.2.00	By Postage		22.00			22.00	
	10.2.00	By telephone		6.00				6.00
100.00		Total		62.00	15.00	19.00	22.00	6.00
		By balance C/d		38.00				
38.00		By balance B/d						

Next in line is the Ledger and Ledger accounts.

Ledger and Ledger Accounts

These reflect the main accounting picture of a company. All transactions dealing with a particular account are reflected here.

The ledger shown here is divided into two parts. The left hand side is debit side and right hand side is the credit side. Each side is further divided into 4 sections namely: Date, Particulars, Folio and Amount.

Dr.							Cr.
Date	Particulars	Folio	Amount	Date	Particulars	Folio	Amount

Date

These columns record the date of the transaction. The date of transaction is first recorded in the journal book, from the journal it is brought to the ledger account.

Particulars

As usual this column records the details of the transaction, *i.e.*, the name of the account in which the corresponding debit or credit is found.

Folio

This column works as reference. Here we write the Journal Page No. of the account which is being written in the Particulars column of ledger.

Amount

This is the amount which is debited or credited and is entered in this column.

Following is the example of an account where some transactions have taken place between the company and Sachin in the form of sale. Let us see how they are first recorded into journal, then into the accounts of Sachin and the cash account.

Date	*Particulars*	*Amount (in Rs.)*
2-1-01	Goods sold to Sachin	10,000
4-1-01	Received cash from Sachin	8,000
6-1-01	Brought goods on cash	20,000
8-1-01	Paid cartage	100
10-1-01	Goods returned by Sachin	2,000
12-1-01	Goods sold to Sachin	4,000
15-1-01	Received cash from Sachin	3,000

These entries in the journal will look like this.

Date	*Particulars*		*L.F.*	*Debit (Rs.)*	*Credit (Rs.)*
2-1-01	Cash Account	Dr.		10,000	
					10,000
	(being the sale of goods on cash)				
4-1-01	Cash Account	Dr.		8,000	
					8,000
	(being receipt of cash)				

6-1-01	Goods Account	Dr.	20,000	
	(purchase of goods)			20,000
8-1-01	Goods Account	Dr.	100	
	(cartage on goods)			100
10-1-01	Goods Account	Dr.	2,000	
	To Sachin Account			2,000
	(being the value of goods returned)			
12-1-01	Sachin Account	Dr.	4,000	
	To Goods Account			4,000
	(being the sale of goods on credit)			
15-1-01	Cash Account	Dr.	3,000	
	Sachin Account			3,000
	(being receipt of cash)			

Let us now see how the individual ledgers would look like.

Dr. Cash Account Cr.

Date	Particulars	J.F.	Amount (Rs.)	Date	Particulars	J.F.	Amount (Rs.)
2-1-01	To Goods A/c		10,000	6-1-01	By Goods A/c		20,000
4-1-01	To Sachin A/c		8,000	8-1-01	By Goods A/c		100
15-1-01	To Sachin A/c		3,000				
							20,100
					By Balance C/d	900	
			21,000				21,000
	To Balance b/d		900				

Dr. Goods Account Cr.

Date	Particulars	J.F.	Amount (Rs.)	Date	Particulars	J.F.	Amount (Rs.)
6-1-01	To Cash A/c		20,000	2-1-01	By Cash A/c		10,000
8-1-01	To Cash A/c		100	12-1-01	By Sachin A/c		4,000
10-1-01	To Sachin A/c		2,000				
					By Balance C/d		8,100
			22,100				22,100
	To Balance b/d		8,100				

Dr.			Sachin Account				Cr.
Date	Particulars	J.F.	Amount (Rs.)	Date	Particulars	J.F.	Amount (Rs.)
12-1-01	To Goods A/c		4,000	15-1-01	By Cash A/c		3,000
					By Balance C/d		1,000
			4,000				4,000
	To Balance b/d		1,000				

Trial Balance

At the end of an accounting period all the accounts are balanced and the balances listed. The total on both the sides of this, called the trial balance, should balance. Since we are working on the concept of every debit entry having a contra credit entry and vice versa. Thus the trial balance is an arithmetic check that all the double entries have been completed.

A company's trail balance could look like this:

Particulars	*Debit (Rs.)*	*Credit (Rs.)*
Cash Account	30,000	
Bank Account	4,000	
Goods Account	5,000	
Discount Account		200
Machinery Account	8,000	
Capital Account		50,000
Sachin Account	1,000	
Salary Account	3,000	
Rent Account		1,500
Interest Account	700	
	51,700	51,700

The total on the debit side equals the total of credit side, indicating that there are no mistakes in the calculations.

Trading and Profit and Loss Account

The result of all financial accounting amounts to two parts: income statements and position statements. The term income statement is better known as Trading and Profit & Loss Account and position statement is known as Balance Sheet.

Before you go any further you must understand the following terms:

Gross Profit = Net Sales – Cost price of goods sold

Net sales = Sales – Goods returned

Cost of goods sold = Sales – Gross profit

or in other words this can be written as:

Cost of goods sold = Opening stock + Net purchases + Direct Expenses – Closing stock

Gross loss = Cost of goods sold - Net sales

Net Purchases = Purchases – Purchases returned

Let us now take another example and try to calculate the profit from the following information about a company

	Amount (Rs.)
Opening Stock	20,000
Purchases	4,000
Sales	40,000
Salaries	5,000
Fuel	2,000
Closing Stock	4,000
Purchase returned	1,500
Sales returned	1,000
Transportation	1,500
Octroi	600

On the basis of above information, we can generate the following results:

Direct expenses = Fuel + Transportation + Octroi

= 2000 + 1500 + 600

= 4100

Net Purchases = Purchases – Purchases returned

= 4000 – 1500

= 2500

Net Sales = Sales – Sales Returned

= 40000 – 1000

= 39000

Cost of goods = Opening stock + Net Purchases + Direct expenses – Closing stock

= 20000 + 2500 + 4100 – 4000

= 22600

Gross Profit = Net Sales – Cost of goods

= 39000 – 22600

= 16400

Proforma of a Trading Account

The trading account of a company would look like the one shown below. Let me explain the various heads used in this.

Dr.	Trading Account		Cr.
Particulars	Amount (Rs.)	Particulars	Amount (Rs.)
To opening stock		By Sales Less: Sales return By closing stock	
To Purchases		By gross loss - transferred to Profit/Loss account (if debit side exceeds the credit side)	
To Carriage or Cartage			
To Octroi or Local Taxes			
To Wages			
To Fuel			
To Royalty			
To any other expenses related to purchases on production.			
To gross profit (transferred to Profit/Loss A/c if credit side exceeds the debit side)			

Firstly the ones on the left hand side of the account.

Opening Stock

It is the stock available with the company on the opening day of the accounting period. This stock is available from the debit side of trial balance, therefore it is shown on the debit side of the trading account. The opening stock does not exist for a newly started business but if the company has existed for more than one year it will definitely have an opening stock.

Purchases

This account includes all cash as well as credit purchases of goods made during the year. Two important points need to be mentioned here.

Firstly, we have to show net purchases in the trading account, hence we deduct here the purchases returned.

Secondly, it needs to be emphasized that the only purchases transferred to this account are the one in which business is being carried. The account does not include purchase of assets.

Carriage or Cartage

All expenses incurred during the purchase of goods are direct expenses and add to the cost of goods purchased.

Wages

Companies involved in manufacturing have to pay wages to the labour. These expenses are the part of the value of goods manufactured by the company. It is therefore necessary that these expenses are added to the cost of goods produced and debited to trading account.

Fuel

Just like cartage expenses, the amount of money spent on fuel which is used to fetch the raw material for producing goods adds up to the cost of goods and must be accounted for.

Royalty

It is the amount payable to the landlord of mines and tea gardens for the right to work at his place, or any other similar thing. In case of foreign collaboration it is the amount given to foreign principals as part of the agreement for the consultancy. It is paid by the company and is treated as direct expenses.

Now we come to the right hand side of the trading account.

Sales

It includes the total of both the cash and credit sales made during a financial year. As before two points have to be emphasized, first sale does not include the sales of assets and second the amount of net sales, goods sold-goods returned, is recorded here.

Closing Stock

It is the value of goods on the closing date of an accounting period. Stock is valued at cost price or market price, whichever is lower. Usually, the closing stock is not given in the trial balance but is given among other adjustments outside the trial balance. In order to bring the closing stock into account, it is necessary to pass an adjustment entry debiting stock account and crediting trading account. The following is the example of a trading account of a company.

	Amount (Rs.)
Opening Stock	60,000
Sales A/c	80,000
Purchases return	4,000
Royalty A/c	8,000
Fuel	2,000
Wages	5,000
Sales return	1,000
Purchase A/c	10,000
Closing Stock as on 31st Dec, 2001	4,000

This when put into the trading account would look like as shown below.

Dr.	Trading Account		Cr.
Particulars	**Amount (Rs.)**	**Particulars**	**Amount (Rs.)**
To opening stock	60,000	By Sales 80,000 Less: Sales return By closing stock	 1,000 79,000
To Purchases Purchase return	10,000 4,000 6,000	By gross loss - transferred to Profit/Loss account (if debit side exceds the credit side)	
		Closing Stock	6,000
To Wages	5,000		
To Fuel	2,000		
To Royalty	8,000		
To gross profit (transferred to Profit/Loss A/c if credit side exceeds the debit side)	4,000		
	85,000		85,000

Profit and Loss Account

It is prepared to calculate the net profit or net loss of the business for a given accounting period. As expected it is the summary of all income and expenses.

On the income side, you can have the entries like:

Dividend received

Interest earned

Discount and commission received

Whereas on the expenses side you can have expenses like:

Selling expenses

Such as rent for office premises, advertising expenses, travelling allowance, commission, etc.

Distributive expenses

Such as packing charges, vehicle maintenance, outward cartage, etc.

Administrative expenses

Such as staff salary, electricity bill and other office expenses.

Closing Entries

The entries that have to be made in the journal for preparing the trading account and profit & loss account are known as closing entries. Follow the steps mentioned below to make the necessary entries:

— In order to close the accounts of expenses or loses, debit the profit and loss account and credit the corresponding expense account. This entry will close all the expenses account in the ledger.

— In order to close the accounts of income or profit, debit the corresponding income account and credit the profit and loss account. This entry will close the income account in the ledger.

— In order to transfer the balance of profit and loss account, debit the profit and loss account and credit the capital account if there is net profit, otherwise credit the profit and loss account and debit the capital account.

On the basis of these available figures we would prepare the Trading Account and then Profit and Loss Account. So let's do it.

Trial Balance

Debit Balances	**Debit (Rs.)**	**Credit Balances**	**Credit (Rs.)**
		Capital Account	50,000
Stock Account	6,000		
Cash at Bank	10,000		
Cash in Hand	7,000		
Machinery Account	5,000		
Furniture Account	3,000		
Purchases Account	4,000		
Wages Account	6,000		
Fuel Account	6,000		
Electricity Bill Account	5,000		
Salaries Account	2,000		
Discount Allowed Account	8,000		
		Discount Receivd Account	1,000
Advertising Account	2,000	Sales Account	50,000
		Adjustments	
		(i) stock on 31st March	10,000
		(ii) Depreciation on Machinery & Furniture	10%
		(iii) Rent outstanding	1,000

Adjustment Entries

Stock (closing Account)	Dr.	10,000	
To Trading Account			10,000
(being the amount of closing stock brought into account)			
Profit & Loss A/c	Dr.	1,000	
To Outstanding Rent A/c			1,000

Dr. Trading Account Cr.

Particulars	Amount (Rs.)	Particulars	Credit (Rs.)
To Stock A/c	6,000	By Sales A/c	50,000
To Purchase A/c	4,000	By Closing Stock	10,000
To Wages A/c	6,000		
To Fuel A/c	6,000		
To Electricity Bill A/c	5,000		
To Gross Profit transferred to Profit & Loss A/c	33,000		
	60,000		60,000

Dr. Profit & Loss A/c Cr.

Particulars	Amount (Rs.)	Particulars	Credit (Rs.)
To Salaries A/c	2,000	By Gross profit transferred from the Trading A/c	33,000
To Discount Allowed A/c	8,000	By Discount Received A/c	1,000
To Advertising A/c	2,000		
To Net Profit transferred to Capital A/c	22,000		
	34,000		34,000

Balance Sheet

A balance sheet is a statement of the financial position of the company, in terms of capital, assets and liabilities. Let us see what goes into the balance sheet and what it reflects.

Assets – Liabilities = Capital

The two sides of the balance sheet show the following:

Left Hand Side	*Right Hand Side*
Capital and Liabilities	**Assets**
Sources	Uses
Where the finances came from	Where the finances went to
What the business owes	What the business owns

A balance sheet of the company may have the following information.

Balance Sheet

Liabilities	Amount (Rs.)	Assets	Amount (Rs.)
Sundry or Trade Creditors		Cash in Hand	
Bills Payable		Petty Cash	
Bank Overdraft		Cash at Bank	
Employees Provident Fund		Bills Receivable	
Loans (Cr.)		Sundry Debtors	
Mortage		Loans (Dr.)	
Reserve/Res. Fund Capital			
Capital		Closing Stock	
Add Interest on Capital		Investments	
Add Net Profit		Furniture and Fittings	
Less Drawings		Loose Tools	
Less Income Tax		Plant & Machinery	
Less Interest on Drawings		Horses & Carts	
Less Net Loss		Land and Buildings	
Outstanding Expenses		Freehold/Leasehold Land	

Fundamentals of Inventory

In the last section you read about Accounting. But, Tally is not about Accounting only, it takes care of the Inventory too. By inventory we mean the stocks and items. Before you go deep into understanding Tally for Inventory you must understand the basics of Inventory specially if you are a non-accounting person.

You can enter inventory details while entering Vouchers. For convenience of entry, Tally also permits to enter in invoice format where computation of Taxes, Duties or other charges can be automated. You can organize items into Groups and optionally Categorize them for better organization and reporting. You get numerous Reporting options on diverse parameters. To enter and maintain inventory details, in the Company Info screen, you should opt for Maintaining Accounts with Inventory option.

Let us understand the various inventory terms.

Stock Items

What you receive or issue, Sell or purchase, each item is a Stock Item. For example, for the Bookshop from you buy this book, this book is a Stock item. Similarly stock items can be clubbed together and can be called Stock groups. For example, in a department store of clothes, Gents clothes can be a group having Pants, Shirts, Coats, etc., for under that category. Similarly for Ladies and Children.

Usually Stock Items are measured in a Unit, *e.g.*, Pcs, Kg, Ltr, etc. Different items may be measured in different units. You can create Unit of Measurement as per your business need. You can specify the Unit in which the item is transacted—normally one Unit. However, some items may be transacted in 12 units also called dozens. Tally allows you to specify upto 2 Units for a single Stock Item, one as Unit and the other as Alternate Unit, you define relationship between the two Units.

A company has usually many places to store inventory items, they are called Godowns normally. Each godown has its inventory and that when combined with inventory of other godowns give the complete picture of the company's inventory. This helps in locating an item which may not be there at one location, then, it can be transfered from other godown where it is there. Tally allows you to create Stock items as per your requirement, its alternate Name (Aliases), Part Numbers, Description, Remarks, etc. You can optionally maintain Batchwise details, enter Purchase and Sale prices, specify Stock Valuation Method for an item.

Stock Group

As mentioned earlier, stocks items can be clubbed together to form stock groups. We had taken the example of Gents clothing. Normally thousands of Stock items are traded in an Organization. It may become unmanagable if the items are not properly grouped. You can arrange all Stock items into Stock Groups based on common features (*e.g.*, based on Brand, Quality, Specification, etc.) You can nest Groups to any depth, as such.

Gents Clothing

- Pants
- Shirts
- Coats, etc.

Women Clothing

- Sarees
- Dresses
- Other accessories, etc.

Children Clothing

- Toddler items
- Children clothing
- Toys, etc.

Grouping of stock items helps to get Group specific report. In above example, to get a Stock report of Sarees only, you can conveniently get it by selecting Saree Group. In fact Stock Group provides similar advantages as Account Groups provide for organization of Accounts.

Stock Categories

Stock Categories offer the benefit of classifying an item in another dimension - thus at any moment you can find similar items. In the above example, gents shirts may be of different types, for example, of brands like Live-in, Newman, Provouge, etc.

Such additional information for item help when a customer asks for one item which is not available in Stock or enquiries about similar items.

Godowns

It has been mentioned earlier while talking about Stock items, Godown (or Location) is a place to store materials. It may be a Warehouse, Rack, Shell, BIN or anything. You can extend this concept even to materials issued to Jobbers or Principal's goods held on Consignment basis. To monitor Locationwise movement of Stock, you may create Multiple Godowns and while entering transactions, specifications, specify the Godown.

On activating Godown option, Tally creates a default godown main Location under primary, you can alter its Name but cannot delete. Godowns can be nested to any level. So you can logically build Warehouses, Shed No., Godown Number, Rack Number, BIN Number, etc., to organize Godowns to get summarized totals for each level.

You can treat the Godwons as stockable/non-stockable. Non-stockable godowns does not appear in the List of Godowns in Voucher to prevent data entry errors.

Unit of Measure

As mentioned earlier, a stock item is measured in a Unit, e.g., Piece, Litre, Metre, etc. Select one of this option to create all such units. Many items are measured by a combination of 2 units (*e.g.*, Box of 100 pcs, strip of 4 capsules) which is termed as Compound Units.

Market Valuation Method

Inventory costing methods are various as per Tally. You can choose any one of them. A brief explation of the various options are:

FIFO

The full form is First In First Out. Tally considers oldest stock moved first.

LIFO Annual

LIFO is the abbreviation for Last In First Out. Tally considers movement of latest goods first, taking into account the current financial year.

LIFO Perpetual

It is similar to LIFO Annual but last purchase continues from previous Financial year.

Average Cost

The weighted average for the whole year is computed considering all Purchases.

Monthly Avg. Cost

It is similar to Average Cost but weighted average is computed for the month instead of whole year.

Last Purchase Cost

Values at latest Purchase Cost.

Standard Cost

At the rate that you entered in Stock item at Standard Purchase Cost applicable for the date of Report.

At Zero Cost

Cost of such item is considered at zero. For example, for defective items of no commercial value.

Reorder Levels

Reorder Level report is helpful for Manufacturing organisation or Assembling industry for timely procurement of materials (to ensure no production loss due to non-availability of raw materials or component). Traders will also be able to identify items for which order to be placed in time to ensure no customer is returned due to non-availability of Stock.

Besides specifying absolute quantity, you can also base re-order level on previous consumption during a specific period and ask Tally to compute whichever lower or higher with option for Rounding Off.

Many vendors fix a minimum ordering quantity which too you can specify for each item. In many trade, it becomes economical to buy a larger lot as compared to immediate requirement - you can specify such quantity to achieve economy of scale. All these helps placement of Purchase Order in time.

What is a Reorder Level?

Reorder level is the quantity for a Stock item, when stock-in-hand reaches that quantity, you should place order for supplies. Every organization desires to execute customer orders in time and have sufficient stock to serve them but at the same time over-stocking costs hight (in terms of blocked money, interest cost and space to store). Thus, re-order level figure is computed in such a manner that neither stock for an item becomes NIL at any point of time nor unwanted stock is carried.

Multiple Price List

During Stock item creation, you learned how to enter Standard Sales Price for each Stock item. Many organisation have different Price Lists for different class of Nuyers, for example, one Price List for Retail Customers and another for Wholesale Customer. Some Organization also offer different discount on different volume. With a single Standard Price List you cannot address all these issues. Besiders Cost and Sales Prices for Stock items. Tally provides you with the option of having multiple Price Lists.

Inventory Transactions

Like accounting, inventory too has vouchers with the help of which you can enter the information to Tally. All stock items information whether the item is going in or going out is given to Tally with the help of vouchers.

You can also give information with the help of invoice, order or challans.

Vouchers

Various voucher which are used in inventory are:

Stock Journal Vouchers

This voucher is used for transfer of materials. It allows you to move stock items from one godown to another without affecting the financial accounts.

Receipt note Vouchers

Whenever you buy goods, you pass a purchase voucher. However, if you have not received a bill then you can simply pas a Receipt Note. This updates the stock of that item but does not afffect the financial accounts. When you receive the bill, you can adjust it against the Receipt Note.

Rejections-in Vouchers

Sometimes the party to which you sell goods you can send them as rejections. If the buyer does not immediately send you a debit note, then you can pass Rejections in voucher to bring the goods back into your stock.

Delivery note vouchers

When you sell goods to a customer, you generally raise an invoice. However, sometimes you send goods out with a Delivery Note and later raise an invoice against this delivery note.

Rejections-out Vouchers

Sometimes, you reject some items from the goods you purchased but send its debit note to the seller later. In this case, you can pass a Rejection Out voucher and raise a Debit Note against this rejection note.

Physical Stock Vouchers

This voucher at any given date represents the confirmation of actual stock on that date. Whenever you check the actual stock, you pass a Physical Stock voucher to specify the correct stock value. The stock value at this point is considered the stock-in-hand and all the calculations are based on this value.

Invoice

Invoice entries are similar to Vouchers, the prime difference may be listed as under:

In Voucher you first enter Accounts allocation, then Inventory allocation. In Invoice, it is just the reverse, i.e., first inventory allocation, then accounting details. In Vouchers, you have to pre-compute the item transaction value, duties and taxes, etc., in order to compute the amount to debit/credit the party account. In Invoice, all the computation is done by the software Tally, you have to just enter the basic figures of quantity, rate, etc.

Order

Orders are optional documents of pre-invoice stage. You can prepare invoices even without incorporating ordering system. Orders do not affect inventory.

Tally provides you the following options for Purchase and Order Acceptance:

1. Entry and printing of Purchase and Sales Order Acceptance.
2. Staggering Deliver Time for the same item.
3. Item specific & common Rates for Discount, Tax and Other Billing Terms.
4. Bypassing of Orders, *i.e.*, Sales & Purchase transaction entry with & without orders.
5. Tracking of Outstanding Order status.
6. Other Terms and Conditions for Sales & Purchase.

Challans

Normally inventory transaction comprises of 2 principal elements, Movement of Materials and Financial Transactions. Thus, the Inventory and Accounting vouchers reflecting the transaction may be like:

1. Movement of Goods and Financial Trasaction simultaneously.
2. Movement of Goods and Financial Transaction are separate events.

Inventory Reports

Following reports can be generated from Tally with respect to inventory.

Movement Analysis — Stock Group Analysis

Movement Analysis of a selected stock group brings up the Total Inward and Outward movement of all the items in which slected Stock Group. The Quantaties shown are actual Quantaties of movement (which is some cases, may be different from the billed Qty in the transactions). The inward detail shows the Effective Rate or Final Landed Cost of the materials, after considering all overhead costs.

In case the Effective Rate is different from the basic invoice rate of the materials, it is shown in Bold — to highlight a possible candidate for further study. The Outward detail shown the Basic Invoice Rate and Value of Goods sold/transferred out.

Item Movement Analysis

Item Movement Analysis is the next level of information (press Enter on the stock item or Display Inventory - Books Stock Item Analysis). This brings up the Party-wise/Transfer wise detail of Movement In and Out. The inward details show the Basic Invoice Rate as well as the Effective Rate.

This is a greate comparative report to view the effect of Purchase costs from different suppliers. For example, Supplier A may have a lower Basic Invoice Rate as compared to Supplier B, but the Effective Rate may be higher — (perhaps due to differences in Taxes, Packaging Costs, Freight Costs, etc.)

Similarly, in context where a material is both manufactured in-house, as well as purchased — the difference in Purchase Costs and In-house Costs can be compared. Lastly, by selecting multiple columns for different periods, you would get to see the changes in Effective Rate for your purchases. The next level of information (press Enter on the Party Name or Stock Journal Name), gives the transaction level detail of information.

Here, the Date of goods received/sold, the Quantities, Basic Rates, Addl. Costs and Effective Rate for each transaction may be viewed pressing Enter expands into the Date, Type and Number of the Vouchers which have contributed to this transaction.

Ledger Analysis

Ledger Analysis is similar to Movement Analysis, except for bringing up the movements of the items for the selected Ledger (Party). Thus, you get an analysis of all purchases made from a supplier or all items sold to a customer. The next level of information brings up the transaction level detail.

Transfer Analysis

Transfer Analysis gives the movement details of each type of Stock Journal. This can be used powerfully by following a simple discipline of using different Stock Journal types for each nature of trnasaction. For example, item A Prod item B can be used for the production of items A and B respectively.

In this scenario, the report then represents the total of item A produced, as well as the Raw Materials used for its production, with overhead costs (as entered). This becomes a very useful costing and waste analysis too. In non-manufacturing segments, but with Multiple Godown, this report becomes a quick check to verify that all transfer have been entered correctly - since the Total Movement In and Out must watch.

Aged Stock Analysis (Ageing Analysis)

A very important function of Working Capital management is monitoring stocks. Money locked up in stocks can adversely affect the liquidity of company and every company strives or should strive to reduce stock levels to the optimum.

Every business (except perhaps the liquor and antiques dealers) would prefer to dispose of older stocks as they might deteriorate with time, go out of fashion or simply get forgotten. Tally's aged stock analysis or Stock agening enables you to know the age of stocks in hand according to when they were received and the purchase value.

Stock Transfers

This report displays the number of stock journal vouchers for the month.

Physical Stock Register

This report displays the monthly stock transfer vouchers in a register format.

Godown Summary (Location Summary)

The Godown/Location Summary statement shows the Stock Summary for different Godown/Locations. While the main Stock Summary shows the stock position for the entire company on a given date, the Godown/Location Summary is a statement of stock in hand at each location on a particular date.

As with all Tally statements, it is updated with every transaction so that it provides current stock position for any godown/location at any time.

Views of Godown/Location Summary Statement

Use options in the button bar to set up different information views. The Godown/Location Summary shows stocks at each location.

Godown/Location Stock Flow/Reconciliation

The reconciled flow of goods at each location is available.

Exception Reports

Excetion reports are reports that track transactions or balances. The different Exception reports are:

Negative Stock

This a list of all stock items that have a negative balance at the end of the period of display. If a negative balance occurs within the period but is adjusted by a purchase so that the balance is not negative at the end of the display period, the item will not be listed.

Change the period or select multi-column display, via auto-column and see the negative items.

Negative Ledgers

This is a list of ledger accounts that have observer balances, *i.e.*, balances that are opposite to the nature of the account. For example, a creditor amount having a debit balance and an asset account having a credit balance.

Overdue Receivables

This is list of all invoices that are overdue on the current date.

Overdue Payables

This is a list of all purchae bills that are overdue on the current date.

List of Memorandum Vouchers

This a list of Memorandum Vouchers entered during a period. Change the period as required.

List of Reversing Journals

This is a list of Reversing Journals entered during a period. Change the period as required.

List of Optional Vouchers

This is a list of vouchers marked as Optional during a period. This list includes all types of vouchers that are marked Optional.

Post-dated Vouchers

This is a list of vouchers that are marked Post-dated within a given period. This list includes all types of vouchers that are marked Post-dated.

12 Project in Tally.ERP 9

Manual Accounting Transaction

Journal Exercise

Ram Dayal & Co.

DATE	TRANSACTION	AMOUNT
JAN 1	Business started with cash	1,00,000
JAN 2	Cash Purchase goods	2000
JAN 2	Goods purchased from Malik Company on credit	1,000
JAN 7	Goods sold to Saligram Co.	800
JAN 10	Purchased goods from Vishnu Shankar	1,100
JAN 11	Goods sold to Kunj Bihari Co. for cash	2,000
JAN 11	Cash Sales Goods	2500
JAN 12	Cash received from Saligram Co.	500
JAN 16	Goods sold to Raj Nararain	3000
JAN 16	Payment given to Vishnu Shankar	400
JAN 22	Purchased goods from Gupta Co.	2500
JAN 28	Cash received from Rajnarain	2200
JAN 28	Salary paid to Worker	1500
JAN 30	Commission received	500
JAN 31	Trade expenses	1200

M/s Pradeep Kumar

FEB 1	Pradip Kumar started business with cash	20,000
FEB 1	Cash purchases	2,000
FEB 4	Brought furniture from Bareilly Furniture Depot.	3000
FEB 5	Goods purchased from Mushtak & Co.	5000
FEB 4	Cash sales	800
FEB 8	Goods sold to Hari Narayan	5000
FEB 9	Paid shop expenses	200

FEB 11	Purchased goods from Mushtak & Co.	3500
FEB 14	Drawing cash	400
FEB 18	Paid to Bareilly Furniture Depot in full settlement of his A/c	2900
FEB 26	Cash paid to Mushtak & Co.	2,000
FEB 27	Cash sales	1,325
FEB 28	Cash received from Hari Narayan	3000
FEB 28	Salary Paid by Cheque	2200

M/s Durga Prasad

MAR 1	Commenced business : Cash	20,000
	: Goods	8,000
MAR 2	Cash deposit in Bank	5,000
MAR 3	Goods purchased from Dinesh	6,000
MAR 6	Goods sold	1,475
MAR 10	Cash purchased	3,000
MAR 13	Goods sold to Dharamvir on Credit	6,000
MAR 16	Paid to Dinesh in full settlement of his A/c	5,910
MAR 18	Cash received from Dharamvir	5,940
	Discount allowed	60
MAR 22	Cash sales to Govind	1,000
MAR 26	Stationary purchased	500
MAR 28	Commission received	1,000
MAR 30	Rent paid	2,000
MAR 30	Salary paid	3,000
MAR 30	Charity given	501
MAR 30	Cash sales	4,000
MAR 31	Goods sold to Dina Nath on credit	3,000

M/s Kamta Nath & Co.

APR 1	Commenced business with cash	1,00,000
APR 3	Purchased furniture for office	50,000
APR 4	Goods purchased from Bharat Industries	25,000
APR 6	Goods sold for cash	10,000
APR 7	Deposit in Bank	50,000
APR 8	Paid Cash to Bharat Industries in full settlement of A/c	24,000

APR 10	Cash sales	15,000
APR 14	Telephone bill paid	1,200
APR 16	Deposit in Bank	10,000
APR 18	Goods withdrawn for personal use	1,500
APR 20	Goods sold to Manish Trading Corp.	20,000
APR 21	Received Cash from Manish Trading Corp.	19,000
APR 28	Rent paid	3,000
APR 30	Wages paid	5,000

M/s Asha Ram Baldeodas

M/s Asha Ram Baldeodas commenced business on 1st **January'2000** with a cash of Rs. 60,000 and goods of Rs 40,000.His transaction in the month of January were as follows :

JAN 1	Cash purchases	5,000
JAN 3	Furniture bought from Gupta Co.	3,000
JAN 5	Goods sold to Amar Nath	6,500
JAN 8	Cash sales	4,000
JAN 10	Stationary purchased	500
JAN 14	Payment given to Gupta Co.	2,950
	Received discount from him	50
JAN 15	Goods purchased from Naresh on credit	
	Costing Rs. 1,000 at trade discount of 5%	
JAN 20	Cash Received from Amar Nath	3,000
JAN 22	Full settlement of Naresh's A/c	925
JAN 25	Purchased cycle for business use	500
JAN 28	Salary paid to Worker	1500
JAN 30	Commission received	500
JAN 30	Trade expenses	1200
JAN 31	Paid salary Rs.2,000 wages Rs. 500	
	Rent Rs. 1,500 and office expenses Rs. 1,000	

M/s Chhedi Lal & Bros.

JUNE 1	Started business with Cash	1,00,000
JUNE 2	Cash purchases	48,00
JUNE 3	Sold goods to Vasudev	10,000
JUNE 6	Returned defective goods by Vasudev	1,000

JUNE 8	Received cash from Vasudev	8800
	And discount allowed	200
JUNE 9	Chanderkant sold goods to us	20,000
JUNE 10	Pritam purchased goods from us	12,000
JUNE 10	Paid insurance premium	500
JUNE 12	Paid for life insurance premium of Mr. Chhedi Lal	2,000
JUNE 15	Paid cash to Chanderkant	13,780
	And discount allowed by them	220
JUNE 18	Bought goods from Pawan ,list price 15,000 less 20% Trade discount	
JUNE 22	Paid to Pawan	8,000
JUNE 26	Received cash from Pritam	5,000
JUNE 31	Paid wages Rs.400, Advertisement Expenses Rs.250 and Salaries paid 1,500	
JUNE 31	Received interest	100
JUNE 31	Received Commission	600

Assignment In Tally

Prepare Inventory (Stock & Items)

M/s Ram Narain & Sons

JUNE 5 Bought of Mohan Lal & Co. Agra :— 20 quintal Sugar @ 1,200 per quintal. 40 bags Rice each containing one quintal @ Rs. 1,500 per quintal. Trade discount 15%

JUNE 10 Purchased from Bharat Bhushan & Sons, Mathura: — Desi Ghee 20 tins, each containing 16 kg, @ Rs 120 Per kg. coconut Oil 1,000 liter @ Rs 120 per litre Trade discount 10%

JUNE 14 Purchased from Anil Kumar Sunil Kumar, Delhi:—

Wheat 30 quintal @ Rs 500 per quintal,

Gram 20 quintal @ Rs 1,200 per quintal,

Rice 10 quintal @ Rs 1,400 per quintal,

Cartage and other expenses paid in Cash Rs 700

JUNE 25 Bought furniture for office use from New Furniture House, Faridabad on credit:

20 Godrej Chairs @ 300 per Chair.

2 Godrej Table @ 1,600 per Table.

JUNE 26 Purchased from Fashion House, Chennai: -

200 Shirts @ Rs 80 per Shirt

100 Tee –Shirts @ Rs 40 Per piece

	Add: Packing Charges Rs 10 & **Less**: Trade Discount 20 %	
JUNE 27	Purchased from Appolo Garments Mumbai: - 150 Bush Shirts @ Rs 60 Per piece 180 Tee Shirts @ Rs 50 Per piece Less: 15%	

M/s Kamal Cloth Store

2006		
DEC 1	Started business with cash	1,00,000
DEC 3	Deposited into Bank	15,000
DEC 4	Purchased from Jindal Trading Co.	
	200 metre Silk @ Rs 80 per metre	
	100 metre cotton @ Rs 40 per metre	
DEC 6	Sold to Radha Krishan & Co.	
	50 metre Silk @ Rs 125 per metre	
	40 metre Cotton @ Rs 60 per metre	
DEC 10	Returned to Jindal Trading co	
	20 metre Silk and 15 metre cotton	
DEC 12	Issued a cheque to Jindal Trading Co. in full settlement of their account.	
DEC 15	Received cash Rs 2000 and cheque for Rs 6,000 from Radha Krishan & Co The cheque was immediately sent to bank	
DEC 16	Sold to Brij Kishore	
	80 metre Silk @ Rs 130 per metre less 5% T.D.	
DEC 18	Returned by Brij Kishore 10 metre Silk	
DEC 20	Purchased from Mohan Silk Ltd	
	300 metre Silk @Rs 90 per metre	
	200 metre cotton @ Rs 50 per metre	
DEC 24	Received from Brij Kishore Rs 7500	
DEC 25	Goods purchased for cash	5,000
DEC 26	Withdrew from Bank	1,000
DEC 29	Paid salaries by cheque	3,500
DEC 30	Paid rent	500

Monika Department Store

1)	Business Started with cash	Rs. 5, 00,000
2)	Purchase Soaps - 300 Pcs **Lux 75gm** @ 12 each, 200 pcs Rexona @ 14 each,	
	100 Pcs Liril 75gm @18 each,	

150 pcs Closeup 100gm @ 25 each
60 Closeup 200gm @ 35 each,
200pcs Dove @ 30 each from **Deepa Agencies**.

3) Bought from Mohan Lal & Co. Agra :—
20 quintal Sugar @ 1,800 per quintal . with 5% Trade discount.
40 qtl Rice @ Rs.1,500 per quintal.Trade discount 10%
Desi Ghee 20 tins ,each containing 16 kg ,@ Rs 200 Per kg.

4) Purchased from Anil Kumar Sunil Kumar, Unnao :—
Wheat 30 quintal @ Rs 500 per quintal, Gram 20 quintal @ Rs 1,200 per quintal,
Rice 10 quintal @ Rs 1,400 per quintal, 30 qtl Sugar @ 1775 per qtl.
Cartage and other expenses paid in Cash Rs 700

5) Purchased for cash from Gopi Chand Haldi Ram , Delhi :—
50 bag of cotton @ Rs 1,500 per bag.

6) Bought furniture for office use from New Furniture House , Kanpur on credit :—
20 Godrej Chairs @ 300 per Chair. 2 Godrej Table @ 1,600 per Table.
30 Cupboards @ 500 each, 50 steel chairs @ 250 each with 5% trade discount.

7) Goods Sold to Janki Das CO.10 qtl Sugar @ 2000 per qtl. with 3% Trade discount.
15 qtl Rice @ Rs.1,800 per quintal.Trade discount 4%
Desi Ghee 5 tins ,each containing 16 kg ,@ Rs 250 Per kg.

8) Cash sales — 2 qtl Sugar @ 1950 per qtl. with 3% Trade discount.
5 qtl Rice @ Rs.1,750 per quintal.Trade discount 2%
Desi Ghee 2 tins ,each containing 16 kg ,@ Rs 240 Per kg.

9) Paid Freight Charges Rs. 1350

10) Purchased from Bharat Bhushan & Sons ,Mathura :—
200 Pcs Lux 75gm @ 12 each, 150 pcs Rexona @ 14 each,
50 Pcs Liril75gm @18 each, 120 pcs Closeup 100gm @ 25 each
30 Closeup 200gm @ 35 each, 140 pcs Dove @ 30 each
Packing Charges 3% & Freight 1500 extra.

11) Sold to Radhey Shyam Bros.
300 Pcs Lux 75gm @ 14 each, 200 pcs Rexona @ 15 each,
100 Pcs Liril75gm @20 each, 150 pcs Closeup 100gm @ 28 each
60 Closeup 200gm @ 38 each, 200 pcs Dove @ 32 each

Bank Transaction

S.NO.	TRANSACTION	ENTRY	
1.	When cash is deposited into the Bank	Bank A/c To Cash A/c	Dr.
2.	When cash is withdrawn from the Bank	Cash A/c To Bank A/c	Dr.
3.	When cheques, drafts, etc received from the customers are deposited into bank on the same day.	Bank A/c To Party Name	Dr.
4.	When cheques, drafts, etc received from the customers are not sent to bank on the same day	Cash A/c To Party Name	Dr.
5.	On the date when above cheques, drafts, etc are sent to Bank	Bank A/c To Cash A/c	Dr.
6.	When a customer directly deposits the amount in our bank account.	Bank A/c To Party Name	Dr.
7.	When a cheque previously deposited into the bank is dishonored.	Party Name Bank A/c	Dr.
8.A	Cheque is received from Customer and discount is allowed, cheque sent to Bank same day.	Bank A/c Discount A/c To Party Name	Dr. Dr.
B	In case the above cheque is dishonored & Discount will withdrawn from the customers a/c	Party Name To Bank A/c To Discount A/c	Dr.
9.	When payment is made by an issue of a cheque.	Party Name To Bank A/c	Dr.
10.	When expenses are paid by issue of a cheque.	Expenses A/c To Bank A/c	Dr.
11.	When cash withdrawn from the bank for the personal use of the proprietor	Drawing A/c To Bank A/c	Dr.
12.A	When interest is charged by bank.	Interest A/c To Bank A/c	Dr.
B	When interest is allowed by the bank.	Bank A/c To Interest A/c	Dr.

13.	When bank charges some amount for the services rendered by the bank.	Bank Charges A/c To Bank A/c	Dr.

Kamal Kishore & Vimal Kishore

APRIL		Rupees.
2.	Commencement of Business worth Cash 50,000/-, Bank 25000/-, Furniture 15000/- & Machinery 20,000/-	
3.	Goods Purchase from Hariya & co.	2000
6.	Wages paid Goods=500 & Cash =200	700
7.	Goods distribute for Advertisement	400
8.	Donation Cash =500 & Goods=250	750
9.	Commission received from Lala Ram	800
9.	Drawing Goods	300
10.	Goods sold to Gagan & Magan Co.	10000
10.	Cash drawn for own exp. from Bank	300
10.	Cash deposited in Bank	3000
11.	Goods return back from Gagan & Magan Co.	500
14.	Goods burn in Godown worth	1200
15.	Losses by theft (Goods)	450
18.	Gagan & Magan Co. declare insolvent & received 70% only	
19.	Issue a cheque for final payment to Hariya & Co.	1950
22.	Cash deposited in Bank	3500
25.	Cash Purchase & paid by cheque to Janki Das	8000
26.	Wages paid to Kallu	150
30.	Rent paid of shop by cheque	300
30.	Cash Sales with 10% Cash discount	1400
May 1.	Furniture sold to Naresh & co. with 12% Trade Discount	2500
3.	Cheque received from Naresh & co. and send to Bank	2200
5.	Wages paid to labour	500
5.	Postage Exps. Paid	100
8.	Legal charges paid	2000
10.	Purchase Raw Material = 4000 & Furniture = 3000	7000

12.	Paid electric charges	2200
15.	Machinery Purchase from J.K. Machineries	24700
20.	Salary paid to worker	2000
22.	Paid electric fitting charges	250
25.	Interest paid	1000
26.	Trade Exps. Paid	145
28.	Cash Sales	12500
30.	Final Payment to J.K. Machineries & received Cash Discount 5%	
31.	Rent paid of shop through Bank	300
June 1.	Goods Purchase by Cash with 12% Cash discount	5000
5.	Cash Sales to M/s Gopal Das & Sons	2300
7.	Machinery Purchase of Rs. 12000 and paid Rs. 50 as Carriage & Rs. 150 for Installation.	
10.	Cash withdraw from Bank	1000
15.	Cash Sales	2500
20.	Cash deposited in Bank	800
22.	Paid Advertisement exp. By cheque	500
25.	Wages paid	120
28.	Outstanding Salary	2500
30.	Rent paid of shop through Bank	300

Mona Chandani

1. Business started worth Rs.5,00,000
2. Goods Purchase of Rs. 25000 by Cash .
3. Goods sold to Kamal & Vimal Prasad. Rs. 15000
4. Amount received from Kamal & Vimal Prasad Rs. 14800 & allow 200 as discount
5. Purchase a Machinery of Rs. 20000 & paid 250 as Fitting Charges.
6. Cash Sales of Rs. 5000
7. Horse Purchase of Rs. 20000 & Cart of Rs. 5000
8. Rent received by Bank Rs. 5000
9. Purchase from s.k. Furniture 500 chairs @ 200 each , 250 tables @ 500 each & 250 cupboards @ 300 each.
10. Horse died and received 5000 by selling its body.
11. Wages Paid to Labour Rs. 800.

12. Machinery Purchase from Naresh & co. Rs. 50000
13. Sold to Keshu brothers. 200 chairs @ 300 each, 100 tables @ 750 each & 125 cupboards @ 450 each.
14. Cash received as commission Rs. 2500.
15. Losses by fire of Rs. 5000.
16. Losses by theft Rs.6000 (Cash).
17. Keshu brother declared insolvent received only 80 %.
18. Purchase a building Rs. 50000 from J.K. Industries.
19. Sold a building to R.K. Industries with 2% discount.
20. Paid exp. Subscription to Trading Society Rs. 500

    Lighting charges -1500. Wages -500. Telephone bill -1250

    Rent of shop – 350, Interest- 500.
21. Purchase from M/s Gagan & Sons, 50 tins of groundnut oil @ 500 each & tins of coconut oil @ 450 each.
22. Salary paid to workers Rs. 5000.
23. Depreciation @ 12% per annum on Machinery.
24. Furniture Purchase from Bareilly Furniture Rs. 4500
25. Purchase from Mustaq & Co. Rs. 3000.
26. Cash Sales 3000
27. Goods sold to Hari Narayan 2500.
28. Purchase from Mustaq & co. 1500.
29. Final payment to Bareilly Furniture 4500.
30. Cash paid to Mustaq & co. Rs. 4500.
31. Cash Sales to Kallu & ballu Rs. 2300.
32. Cash received from Hari Narayan Rs. 2200.

Sunder Lal

2 APRIL Commencement of business worth Rs.50000/-, Goods 20000 & Furniture of Rs. 15000.

2. Machinery Purchase by Cash 20000.
3. Furniture Purchase from Thakur Das Rs. 15200.
4. Stationary Purchase of Rs. 120.
5. Goods Purchase for Cash Rs. 5000.
8. Goods sold to Beni Singh Rawat Rs. 2600.
9. Goods Purchase from Jawahar & co & paid by cheque 4000.

10. Cash paid to Thakur Das & receive 6% Cash Discount.
11. Paid 102 as postage exp.
12. Cash Sales of Rs.3000.
13. Paid subscription 151 to Ram Leela Committee.
15 Cash & Goods drawn for own exp. 500 & 300.
20. Paid Salary by cheque 1500.
21. Wages paid to labour 150.
22. Paid printing charges 450
23. Wages Paid to Labour Rs. 800.
24. Received commission from broker 2500.
25. Purchase from Anupam Stores Rs. 6000 with 10% trade discount 12% Cash discount.
26. Deposited in Bank Rs. 2600.
27. Sold to Harish & co. Rs.15000.
28. Goods return back from Harish & co. 1000.
29. Cash received from Harish & co. 10000.
30. Paid subscription to trading society 200.
31. Rent paid 310 as shop Rent.

MAY4 Goods sold to Kallu Bros. Rs. 15000 & return back of Rs. 2000 for bad quality.
6. Commission paid Rs. 1500.
7. Cash withdraw of Rs. 800.
10. Cash received from Kallu Bros. 10000.
11. Wages Paid to Labour Rs. 800.
12. Interest paid Rs. 510.
14. Postage exp. paid 300.
18 Electric bill paid 1500.
19. Goods Purchase by Cash of Rs. 5000 with 12% Cash discount & 10% trade discount.
22. Purchase 20 chairs @ 350 each from H. S. Furniture.
25. Land Purchase of Rs. 20000
26. Cash paid to H. S. Furniture for full & final payment 6800.
27. Cash deposited in bank Rs.4000.
28. Wages paid 150.
29. Rent paid of shop 320.
30. Interest received 950.

30.	Telephone bill paid 1500.
30.	Cash Sales with 12% discount of Rs. 3500.
30.	Paid Rs. 1500 as tour & travel exp. to Jag Mohan Das.
30.	Cash Sales of Rs. 2500.

Gautam Brothers

1. JAN	Business started worth	100000
5.	Purchase from Kapoor Bros.	8500
5.	Furniture Purchase from Sohan & Co.	4000
10.	Cash Sales of Goods to Guru Prasad	9000
15.	Goods Purchase from Goyal & Pandit	5000
17.	Cash Sales	3000
23.	Cash paid to Goyal & Pandit	2950
28.	Amount paid to Sohan & Co.	1950
31.	Goods sold to Shyam	1500
31.	Salary paid to Changa Mal	4000
31.	Rent paid of shop	200
31.	Drawn for own exp.	500
31.	Cash Sales	5000
31.	Paid Subscription to Trading Society	501
31.	Wages Paid to Labour Rs.	800
1. Feb	Goods Purchase	2000
3.	Credit Sales to Murari Bros.	800
10.	Purchase from Keshav Das	5000
12.	Cash Sales	700
18.	Sales return from Murari Bros.	100
20.	Purchase return to Keshav Das	1500
24.	Cash Purchase from Prem.	1000
26.	Final payment to Keshav Das	3400
28.	Received from Murari Bros.	680
28.	Salary paid to workers	1000
28.	Rent paid of shop	300
28.	Commission received from the party	250

1. March	Cash Purchase	3500
1.	Furniture Purchase from Bareilly Furniture Depot	4500
4.	Purchase from Mustaq & co.	3000
6.	Cash Sales	3000
8.	Goods sold to Hari Narayan	2500
9.	Purchase from Mustaq & co.	1500
12.	Final payment to Bareilly Furniture Depot	4500
15.	Cash paid to Mustaq & co.	4500
20.	Cash Sales to Kallu & ballu	2300
30.	Cash received from Hari Narayan	2200
31.	Rent paid of shop	300
31.	Salary paid to workers	2000
2.April	Goods Purchase from Ashok & Sons by Cash	6000
3.	Goods sold to Pramod & Vinod co.	1800
5.	Furniture Purchase from Jawahar co. & paid by cheque	2600
5.	Machinery Purchase from Ram & Shyam	5000
7.	Fittings charges of Machinery	250
7.	Wages Paid to Labour	750
9.	Goods Purchase from Sanjay Bros.with 10% Trading discount	1000
10.	Cheque Received from Pramod & Vinod for final payment	1750
15.	Final payment to Sanjay Bros.	900
30.	Rent paid of shop	300

Final A/c

The Financial Statement → "OBJECTS..."

A) The Profit made by the firm during a particular year.

B) The Financial position of the firm at the end of the year.

Trading A/c :-

Gross Profit/ Gross Loss is determined by the preparation of Trading A/c

Gross Profit = Net Sales — Cost of Goods Sold

Net Sales = Total Sales made during the year

Cost of Goods Sold= Opening Stock + Purchases – Closing Stock

M/s __________________

Trading A/c

(For the year ending 31st March' 20__)

Particulars Amount		**Particulars Dr.**	**Particulars**		**Amount Cr.**
To Opening Stock			By Sales	-------	-------
To Purchases	-------		Less : Sales Return / Inward	-------	-------
Less : Purchase Return / Outward	-------	-------	By Closing Stock		-------
To Wages / Wages & Salary	-------		By Goods Send On Consignment		-------
Add : Outstanding Wages	-------		(At Cost)		
Less : Prepaid Wages	-------	-------	**By Gross Loss C/D**		-------
To Freight		-------			
To Carriage Inward		-------			
To Cartage		-------			
To Dock Charges		-------			
To Custom Duty (Import Duty)		-------			
To Royalty		-------			
To Excise Duty		-------			
To Gas, Electricity & Fuel		-------			
To Factory Expanses		-------			
To Packing Materials & Charges		-------			
To Consumable Stores		-------			
To Gross Profit C/D		-------			
		######			######

Profit & Loss A/c

The main aim of preparing the profit & loss a/c is to determine the Net Profit of Business. The profit & Loss A/c is also known as **Income – Statement**.

Net Profit = Gross Profit + Incomes & Gains – Expanses

Format of P/L

M/s ________________

Profit & Loss A/c

(For the year ending 31st March' 20__)

Particulars	**Amount Dr.**	**Particulars**	**Amount Cr.**
To Gross Loss B/d	———	By Gross Profit B/d	———
To Expanses Indirect	———	By Income Indirect	———
		By Net Loss	———
To Net Profit	———		
	######		######

M/s ________________

Profit & Loss A/c

(For the year ending 31st March' 20__)

Particulars		**Amount Dr.**	**Particulars**	**Amount Cr.**
To Gross Loss B/d	———	———	By Gross Profit B/d	———
To Salary / Salary	———	———	By Rent Received	
Add : Outstanding Salary		———	By Interest Received	
To Office Rent		———	(On Loan, Investment, Advances, Deposits)	
To Rate & Taxes		———	By Commission Received	———
To Office Lighting		———	By Discount Received	———
To Insurance	———	———	By Profit On Sale Of Assets	———
Add : Outstanding Interest	———	———	By Recovery Of Amounts	———
To Printing & Stationery		———	By Net Loss	
To Postage & Telegram		———	(less from capital a/c in Balance Sheet)	
To Legal Expanses		———		
To Trade Expanses		———		
To Audit Fee		———		
To Car Upkeep Expanses		———		
To Telephone Expanses		———		

To General Expanses	——
To Cash Discount Allowed	——
To Interest on Capital	——
To Interest Paid on Loan	——
To Interest Paid on Overdraft	——
To Interest Paid on Bills Overdue	——
To Rebate On Bill of Exchange	——
To Bad Debts	——
To Selling & Distribution Expanses	——
To Outward Freight	——
To Outward Cartage & Carriage	——
To Cost Of Samples	——
To Catalogue Expanses	——
To Salesman's Salary	——
To Commission Paid	——
To Advertisement Expanses	——
To Tour & Traveling Expanses	——
To Repairs – Motor / Building Etc.	——
To Depreciation on Fixed Assets	——
To Loss On Sale of Fixed Assets	——
To Bank Expanses	——
To Donation	——
To Subscription	——
To Subscription to Trading Society	——
To Export Duty	——
To Insurance of Goods	——
To Delivery Van Expanses	——
To Sales Tax	——

To Remuneration Of Representative	———		
To Salary of Agent	———		
To Agent's Commission	———		
To Net Profit			
(Add to capital a/c in Balance Sheet)			
	######		######

Balance Sheet

1) Balance Sheet show the financial position of a firm at a given point of time.
2) The Balance Sheet gives a picture of the financial position of the firm while the Profit & Loss a/c provides an explanation of the causes leading to the change in financial position.
3) A Balance Sheet May be defined as a statement summarizing the financial position of business as on a particular date. It is a statement of the Assets & Liabilities of the business as on a given date.

M/s ________________

Balance Sheet

(For the year ending 31st March' 20__)

Liabilities	**Amount Cr.**	**Assets**	**Amount Dr.**
SHARE CAPITAL		**FIXED ASSETS:**	
Authorized Share Capital		Goodwill	
Issued Share Capital		Land	
Subscribed Share Capital		Building	
Less : Calls Unpaid / Arrear		Less: Depreciation	
Add : Forfeited Share		Lease hold	
Less : Drawing		Plant & Machinery	
		Less: Depreciation	
RESERVE & SURPLUS		Furniture & fittings	
Capital Reserve		Development of property	
Capital Redemption Reserve		Patents, trademark & design	
Security Premium Amounts		Vehicles	
Other Reserve			

Surplus (Balance In P/L A/C)	**INVESTMENT**
	Govt. & trust securities
SECURED LOAN	Shares debentures & bonds
Debentures	Immovable properties
	Investment in the capital of partnership firm
Loan & Advances From Bank	
Loan & Advances From Subsidiaries	
Bank Overdraft	
Loan From Directors	**CURR_ASSETS / LOANS, ADV.**
Cash Credit (CC)	**CURRENT ASSETS**
	Interest accured on investment
UNSECURED LOAN	Shares & spare parts
Fixed Deposits	Stock – in – trade
Loan & Advances From Subsidiaries	Work – in - progress
Short Term Loans & Advances	Sundry debtors
(A) From Bank	Less : provisions
(B) From Others	Cash – in – hand
	Cash – at – bank
CURRENT LIABILITIES / PRO.	Live stock
A. CURRENT LIABILITIES	Bills receivables
Bills Payable	**LOANS & ADVANCES**
Sundry Creditors	Advances & loans subsidiaries
Outstanding Expenses	Advances& loan to partnership firm
Advance / Prepaid Incomes	In which the company / any its
Unclaimed Dividends	Subsidiaries is a members
Tax Payable Including Cr. Bal Of TDS	Bill of exchange
Advance From Customers	Prepaid expenses
Others Liabilities (If Any)	Balance with customs, port, trust

Interest Accrued But Not Due On Loan	
	MISCELLANEOUS EXPENDITURES
B. PROVISIONS	Preliminary expanses
	Expanses including commission or brokerage
Provision on Taxations	On underwriting or subscription of shares
Proposed Divided	
For Contingencies	Discount allowed on issue of Shares and debentures
For Provident Fund Scheme	
For Insurance, Pension	
Other Provisions	
######	######

Assets

Anything which is in the possession or is the property of a business enterprises including the amounts due to it from others, is called an assets. Assets Classified in Following categories:

1) Fixed Assets

   e.g. – Land & Building, Plant & Machinery, Motor, Vehicles, Furniture etc.

2) Current Assets

   e.g. – Cash in Hand, Cash at Bank, Bills Receivable, Short Terms Investment, Debtors, Stock, Live Stock, Prepaid Expanses etc.

3) Tangible Assets

   Tangible assets are those things which can be touched, felt, measured, purchased, sold etc.

   e.g. – Cash A/c, Stock A/c, Furniture a/c, Land a/c, Building A/c etc.

4) Intangible Assets

   These assets represent such things which cannot be touched, but their value can be measured in terms of money,

   e.g. – Goodwill, Patents, Trade Marks, Copyright A/c etc.

Stock - -

Stock is that a goods which is lying unsold at the end of accounting year. There are two types of stocks:- a) Opening Stock b) Closing Stock

Types of Stock:-

1) Stock of Raw Material: Raw Material purchase using them in the products manufactured but still lying unused, for eample, the value of cotton in the case of cloth mills is the stock of raw material
2) Stock Of Work In Progress: Incase of cloth mills the value of threads and the unfinished cloths will be the stock of work in progress.
3) Stock Of Finished Goods: In case of cloth mills the finished cloth will be the value of finished goods.

Calculation of Closing Stock:

Case -1

1- Goods, which have been sold but remain undelivered.

2- Goods Purchased and received but not been recorded in the purchase book.

Case - 2

Following the goods should be included in the list of stocks

1- Goods sent to customers on sales or return basis

2- Goods send to the agents for sales but remain lying with them as unsold.

Note: It should always be kept in mind the stock is valuate at cost price or market price which ever is less.

Adjustment Theory:

Objects or necessity of adjustments:

1. To ascertain the true net profit or loss of the business.
2. To ascertain the true financial position of the business.
3. To make a record of the transactions omitted from the books.
4. To rectify the errors committed in the books of accounts.
5. To make a records of such expenses which have accrued but have not been paid.
6. To make a record of such incomes which have accrued but have not been received.
7. To provide for depreciation and other provisions.

Important Adjustment

1. CLOSING STOCK
2. OUTSTANDING EXPANSES.
3. PREPAID EXPANSES.
4. DEPRECIATION
5. ACCRUED INCOME
6. UNEARNED INCOME
7. INTEREST ON CAPITAL

8. INTEREST ON DRAWING
9. INTEREST ON LOAN
10. BAD DEBTS
11. PROVISION FOR BAD & DOUBT. DEBTS
12. PROVISION FOR DISCOUNT ON DEBTORS
13. PROVISION FOR DISCOUNT ON CREDITOR
14. LOSS BY ACCIDENT
15. CHARITY IN FORM OF GOODS.
16. GOODS DISTRIBUTED AS FREE SAMPLE
17. DRAWING IN GOODS
18. USE OF GOODS IN BUSINESS
19. MANGER'S COMMISSION ON NET PROFIT.
20. CAPITAL EXPENDITURE TREATED AS REVENUE EXPENDITURE

Closing Stock

The amount of goods unsold at the end of year is called closing stock.

Closing Stock A/c **Dr.**

To Trading A/c

Outstanding Expanses

These are the expanses which have been incurred during the year but have been left unpaid on the date of preparation of final a/c.

Wages A/c Dr.

To Outstanding Wages

Salary A/c Dr.

To Outstanding Salary

Note :

Outstanding Wages add with wages in Trading A/c

Outstanding Wages shown in liabilities side of Balance Sheet

Prepaid Expanses

(Unexpired Exps. Or Expanses Paid in Advanced)

These are the expanses which have been paid in advanced for the next year during the current year itself.

Prepaid Insurance A/c Dr.

To Insurance A/c

Note:

Prepaid Insurance less in P/L by Insurance.

Prepaid Insurance shown in Assets side of Balance Sheet.

Accured Income

It is quite common that certain items of Income such as interest on Securities, Commission, Rent, etc., are earned during the current year but have **not be actually received** by the end of current year.

Also known as Accrued Income & Earned Income.

Adjustment: - Commission earned but not received.

Accrued Commission A/c Dr.

To Commission A/c

Note:

Accrued Income Add to Commission in P/L A/c.

Shown In Balance Sheet Assets side.

Unearned Income

It may also happen that a certain income is received in current year but the whole amount of it does not belong the current year. Such portion of this income which belongs to the next year is known as unearned income or income received but not earned.

Adjustment :- Rent received but not earned.

Rent A/c Dr.

TO Rent received in Advanced A/c

(for adjustment entry for unearned rent)

Note:

Unearned income less in P/L from Rent in Cr. Side.

Shown on Liabilities side in Balance side as "Unearned Rent"

Interest on Capital

Capital invested by the proprietor is treated as a loan to the business earning interest at a fixed rate. If this amount had not been invested in the business, it would even then have earned some interest outside. As such the proprietor wants interest for this capital and profit for the risk undertaken by him.

Adjustment :- 6% Interest on capital of Rs. 100000/-

Interest on capital A/c Dr.

To Capital A/c

(for interest allowed on capital)

Note:

Interest on capital should be shown on P/L debit site.

It is gain to the Proprietor so that added to his capital

Interest on Drawing

The proprietor draw cash or goods for his personal use. Such withdrawals treated as drawings. If the firm pays interest on capital, it is fully justified that is should also charge interest on the Drawing.

Adjustment: - Charge Interest on Drawing.

Drawing A/c Dr.

To Interest on Drawing

(Being Interest charged on drawings)

Note:

Interest on drawing, it is gain for business, so that show on Cr. Side of P/L.

Interest on drawing less in Liabilities from Drawing.

Interest on Loan

Loan is liabilities of the firm and the interest on such loan will be an expanse. If up-to-date interest has not been paid on the loan, the unpaid interest will have to be calculated and will be treated just outstanding expanses.

Adjustment:- Interest on loan is due for the whole year.

Interest on loan A/c Dr.

To Outstanding Interest

(for outstanding interest on loan)

Note:

INTEREST ON LOAN show in P/L as expanses.

INTEREST ON LOAN shown in balance sheet (Loan from Bank + Outstanding Interest)

Bad Debts

Bad Debts occur when Debtors fail to pay their dues to a firm.

Bad Debts. Dr.

To Debtors.

Note:

Bad Debts. Shown on P/L at debit site.

Bad Debts less in balance sheet from Debtors.

Bad Debts Recovered

Sometimes it is so happens that the bad debts previously written off are subsequently recovered.

Cash A/c Dr.

To Bad Debts. Recovered A/c

(For cash received form Xyz, Previously written off as bad – debts)

Note:

Bad debts Recovered shows in Cr. Side of P/L

Bad debts Recovered less in balance sheet from bad debts.

Closing Entries

Opening Stock- the Opening Stock is the stock of goods and material that the company has at the beginning of each accounting year.

Trading A/c Dr.

To Stock (opening)

Purchases – the purchases shows the total value of purchases of those goods in which the company is dealing.

Trading A/c Dr.

To Purchases

Direct Expanses – the direct expanses are those expanse incurred to manufacture, bring the purchased goods the godown and to run the factory, wages, fuel, carriage etc.

Expanses A/c Dr.

To Outstanding Expanses

....

Add: Prepaid Expanses A/c Dr.

To Expanses

....

Trading A/c Dr.

To Expanses

Sales – the sales of the during the year.

Sales A/c Dr.

To Trading A/c

Final A/c - "Exercise"
Trial Balance of Shri Rai Bahadur

DEBIT BALANCE	RS.	CREDIT BALANCE	RS.
STOCK	20,000	SUNDRY CREDITORS	15,000
PURCHASE	75,000	PURCHASE RETURN	3,000
SALES RETURN	8,000	SALES	2,50,000
FREIGHT & CARRIAGE	7,500	COMMISSION	3,300
WAGES	36,500	CAPITAL	1,70,000
SALARIES	12,000	INTEREST ON BANK DEPO.	2,000
REPAIRS	1,200	B/P	6,200
TRADE EXPANSES	4,000		
RENT & RATES	24,000		
CASH IN HAND'	5,700		
B/R	4,000		
DEBTORS	55,000		
PLANT & MACHINERY	1,60,000		
DRAWINGS	16,600		
BANK DEPOSITS	20,000		
	4,49,500		**4,49,500**

31 MARCH 2006 – CLOSING STOCK – **Rs. 25,000/-**

Trading & Profit and Loss A/c
(For the Year ending 31 March 2006)

PARTICULARS		AMOUNT	PARTICULARS		AMOUNT
To Opening Stock		20,000	By Sales	2,50,000	
To Purchase	75000		Less: Sales Return	8,000	2,42,000
Less: Purchase Return	3000	72,000	By Closing Stock		25,000
To Freight & Carriage		7,500			
To Wages		36,500			
To Gross Profit c/d		1,31,000			
		2,67,000			**2,67,000**
To Salaries		12,000	By Gross Profit b/d		1,31,000
To Repair		1,200	By Commission		3,300
To Trade Exp.		4,000	By Interest on Bank Deposit2,000		
To Rent & Taxes		24,000			
To Net Profit Transferred to Capital A/c		95,100			
		1,36,300			**1,36,300**

Balance Sheet
(As on 31st March 2006)

LIABILITIES		AMOUNT	ASSET	AMOUNT
B/P		6,200	Cash in Hand	5,700
Sundry Creditor		15,000	B/R	4,000
Capital	170000		Sundry Debtors	55,000
Add: Net Profit	95100		Closing Stock	25,000
	265100		Bank Deposit	20,000
Less: Drawing	16600	2,48,500	Plant & Machinery	1,60,000
		2,69,700		**2,69,700**

Trial Balance of M/s Gopi Chandra
(For the year ended 31st March' 2006)

DEBIT BALANCE	RS.	CREDIT BALANCE	RS.
OPENING STOCK	45,000	SUNDRY CREDITORS	22,100
PURCHASES	1,20,000	RETURN OUTWARDS	2,500
RETURN INWARDS	3,200	SALES	3,50,000
CARRIAGE INWARDS	2,400	CAPITAL	2,00,000
CARRIAGE OUTWARDS	1,500	LOAN FROM BANK	24,000
OFFICE FURNITURE	8,000	DISCOUNT RECEIVED	2,000
SUNDRY DEBTORS	68,000	COMMISSION	1,600
DOCK CHARGES	5,000		
ELECTRIC POWER	10,000		
FUEL, GAS & WATER	12,000		
BAD – DEBTS	1,100		
ADVERTISEMENT	25,000		
SALARY	36,000		
CASH IN HAND	8,100		
CASH AT BANK	30,000		
MOTOR VEHICLES	58,000		
MOTOR REPAIRS	3,000		
INTEREST ON BANK LOAN	2,400		
RENT & INSURANCE	24,500		
BUSINESS PREMISES	1,06,000		
HOUSEHOLD EXPANSES (Drawing)	33,000		
	6,02,200		**6,02,200**

STOCK AT THE END OF YEAR – **75,000/-**

Trading A/c
(For the year ending 31st March' 2006)

PARTICULARS		AMOUNT	PARTICULARS		AMOUNT
To Opening Stock		45,000	By Sales	3,50,0000	
To Purchase	120000		Less: Return inwards	3,200	3,46,800
Less: Return outwards	2500	1,17,500	By closing stock		75,000
To Carriage inwards		2,400			
To Dock charges		5,000			
To Electric Power		10,000			
To Fuel, Gas & Water		12,000			
To Gross Profit c/d		2,29,900			
		421800			**4,21,800**

Profit and Loss A/c
(For the year ending 31st March' 2006)

PARTICULARS	AMOUNT	PARTICULARS	AMOUNT
To Carriage outwards	1,500	By Gross Profit b/d	2,29,900
To Bad debts	1,100	By Discount	2,000
To Advertisement	25,000	By Commission	1,600
To salary	36,000		
To Motor Repairs	3,000		
To Interest on Bank Loan	2,400		
To Rent & Insurance	24,500		
To Net profit transfer to Capital	1,40,000		
	2,33,500		**2,33,500**

Balance Sheet
(As on 31st March' 2006)

LIABILITIES		AMOUNT	ASSET	AMOUNT
Loan From Bank		24,000	Cash in Hand	8,100
Sundry Creditor		22,100	Cash at Bank	30,000
Capital	2,00,000		Sundry Debtors	68,000
Add: Net Profit	1,40,000		Closing Stock	75,000
	3,40,000		Office Furniture	8,000
Less: Drawing	33,000	3,07,000	Motor Vehicle	58,000
			Business Premises	1,06,000
		3,53,100		**3,53,100**

M/s Ved Vyas
Trial Balance
(For the year ending 31st March' 2006)

LEDGER HEADS	Dr. Rs.	Cr. Rs.
PURCHASE AND SALES	2,75,000	5,20,000
RETURNS INWARDS	15,000	
RETURN OUTWARDS		9,000
CARRIAGE	12,400	
WAGES AND SALARIES	58,600	
TRADE EXPANSES	2,200	
RENT		13,000
INSURANCE	2,000	
AUDIT FEE	1,200	
DEBTORS & CREDITORS	1,10,000	62,100
B/R AND B/P	3,300	2,200

PRINTING AND ADVERTISEMENT	5,500	
COMMISSION		1,000
OPENING STOCK	36,000	
CASH IN HAND	12,800	
CASH AT BANK	26,800	
BANK LOAN		20,000
CAPITAL		2,50,000
INTEREST ON LOAN	1,500	
DRAWING	15,000	
FIXED ASSETS	3,00,000	
	8,77,300	8,77,300

Adjustment

1. Stock at end Rs. 60,000
2. Depreciate Fixed Assets by 10%
3. Commission earned but not received amt. Rs. 400.
4. Rent received in advance Rs. 1000
5. Interest on Bank Loan @15% P.A. is unpaid for the last six months.
6. Allow 8% interest on Capital and charge Rs. 900 as Interest on Drawing.

Raghu Nath Co.
Trial Balance
(For the year ending 31st March' 2006)

LEDGER HEADS	Dr. Rs.	Cr. Rs.
OPENING STOCK	12,000	
PURCHASES	40,000	
SALES		86,000
DISCOUNT		400

SALES RETURN	6,000	
BUILDING	50,000	
DEBTORS	16,000	
SALARIES	2,400	
OFFICE EXPANSES	1,200	
WAGES	10,000	
PURCHASE RETURN		4,000
INTEREST		800
TRAVELING EXPANSES	400	
FIRE INSURANCE PREMIUM	800	
MACHINERY	20,000	
CARRIAGE ON PURCHASE	700	
COMMISSION	400	
CASH IN HAND	2,300	
RENT & TAXES	1,800	
CAPITAL		62,000
CREDITORS		10,800
	1,64,000	1,64,000

Adjustement:

1. Closing Stock was valued at Rs. 16,000.
2. Wages Rs. 2,000 and Salaries Rs. 1,200 are outstanding.
3. Rent for two months @ of Rs 500 per month is outstanding.
4. Depreciate Building by 5% and machinery by 10%.
5. Prepaid Insurance Rs. 200

Ans: GP – Rs. 35,300, NP – Rs 23,000, B/S Total Rs. 1, 00,000/-

Gateway Of Tally → Account Info. → Ledger → Create

Ledger Heads	Debit/Credit	Under
Audit Fee	Dr.	Expenses (Indirect)
Bad Debts	Dr.	Expenses (Indirect)
Bank A/C	—	Bank A/C
Bank Exps.	Dr.	Expenses (Indirect)
Bills Payables	—	Current Liabilities
Bills Receivables	—	Current Assets
Building	—	Current Assets
Capital A/C	Cr.	Capital A/C
Cash A/C	—	Cash – In – Hand
D.D. Charges	Dr.	Expenses (Indirect)
Depreciation	Dr.	Expenses (Indirect)
Discount	Dr.	Expenses (Indirect)
Discount	Cr.	Income (Indirect)
Drawing A/C	Dr.	Capital A/C
Electric Goods	Dr.	Fixed Assets
Excise Duty	Cr.	Duties & Taxes
Export Duty	Dr.	Expenses (Indirect)
Fitting Charges	Dr.	Expenses (Indirect)
Freight Charges	Dr.	Expenses (Direct)
Furniture & Fixtures	—	Fixed Assets

Input Vat	Dr.	Duties & Taxes
Insurance Premium	Dr.	Expenses (Indirect)
Inter State Sales	Cr.	Sales
Interest	Cr.	Income (Indirect)
Interest	Dr.	Expenses (Indirect)
Interest On Capital	Dr.	Expenses (Indirect)
Losses By Fire	Dr.	Expenses (Indirect)
Losses By Live Stock	Dr.	Expenses (Indirect)
Losses By Theft	Dr.	Expenses (Indirect)
Machinery A/C	—	Fixed Assets
Name Or Party	Dr.	Sundry Debtors
Name Or Party	Cr.	Sundry Creditors
Office Expenses	Dr.	Expenses (Indirect)
Output Vat	Cr.	Duties & Taxes
Outstanding ………..	—	Current Liabilities
Plant & Machinery	—	Fixed Assets
Postage Expenses	Dr.	Expenses (Indirect)
Pre – Operative Exps.	Dr.	Expenses (Indirect)
Preliminary Expenses	Dr.	Expenses (Indirect)
Prepaid Expenses	—	Current Assets
Printing Expenses	Dr.	Expenses (Indirect)

Profit & Loss A/C	—	Expenses (Indirect)
Purchase A/C	Dr.	Purchase A/C
Purchase Return A/C	Cr.	Purchase A/C
Rent A/C	Dr.	Expenses (Indirect)
Rent A/C	Cr.	Income (Indirect)
Salary A/C	Dr.	Expenses (Indirect)
Sales A/C	Cr.	Sales A/C
Sales Return A/C	Dr.	Sales A/C
Share Application	Cr.	Current Liabilities
Share Capital A/C	Cr.	Capital A/C
Share Premium A/C	Cr.	Current Liabilities
Stationery A/C	Dr.	Expenses (Indirect)
Stock	—	Stock – In – Hand
Subscription A/C	Dr.	Expenses (Indirect)
Tour & Travel	Dr.	Expenses (Indirect)
Trading A/C	Dr.	Expenses (Direct)
Trading Expenses	Dr.	Expenses (Indirect)
U.P.T.T.	Cr.	Duties & Taxes
Wages	Dr.	Expenses (Direct)

13 Keyboard Shortcuts

Shortcut Keys in Tally

The shortcut keys appear in button names in the button bar (right side of the Tally screen). You can either click the button from the button bar or press the relevant function key or character underlined/ double-underlined.

The buttons have a function key before the button names (Eg. F1: Select Cmp) which means you need to press F1 key (Function Key) to select the 'Select Company' screen

The buttons have an underlined character (Eg:F3:Cmp Info) which means you need to press A lot + F3 to select the 'Company Info' Screen.

Some buttons have a double-underlined character (Eg: As Voucher) which means you need to press Ctrl + V to select the 'Voucher' in voucher mode.

The shortcut keys available in Tally are listed in the below table:

Function Key Combination

Windows	*Functionality*	*Availability*
F1	To select a company	At all masters menu screen
F1	To select the Accounts Button	At the Accounting Voucher creation and alteration screen
F1(Alt+F1)	To select the Inventory Button	At the Inventory Voucher creation and alteration screen
F2	To change the date	At almost all screens in Tally
F3	To select the company	At almost all screens in Tally
F4	To select the Contra voucher	At Accounting / Inventory Voucher creation and alteration screen
F5	To select the Payment voucher	At Accounting / Inventory Voucher creation and alteration screen
F6	To select the Receipt voucher	At Accounting / Inventory Voucher creation and alteration screen
F7	To select the Journal voucher	At Accounting / Inventory Voucher creation and alteration screen
F8	To select the Sales voucher	At Accounting / Inventory Voucher creation and alteration screen

F8 (Ctrl+F8)	To select the Credit Note voucher	At Accounting / Inventory Voucher creation and alteration screen
F9	To select the Purchase voucher	At Accounting / Inventory Voucher creation and alteration screen
F9 (Ctrl+F9)	To select the Debit Note voucher	At Accounting / Inventory Voucher creation and alteration screen
F10	To select the Reversing Journal voucher	At Accounting / Inventory Voucher creation and alteration screen
F10	To select the Memorandum voucher	At Accounting / Inventory Voucher creation and alteration screen
F11	To select the Functions and Features screen	At almost all screens in Tally
F12	To select the Configure screen	At almost all screens in Tally

Special Key Combinations

Windows	*Functionality*	*Availability*
Alt+2	To Duplicate a voucher	At List of Vouchers – creates a voucher similar to the one where you positioned the cursor and used this key combination
Alt+A	To Add a voucher	At List of Vouchers – adds a voucher after the one where you positioned the cursor and used this key combination.
Alt+C	To create a master at a voucher screen (if it has not been already assigned a different function, as in reports like Balance Sheet, where it adds a new column to the report)	At voucher entry and alteration screens, at a field where you have to select a master from a list. If the necessary account has not been created already, use this key combination to create the master without quitting from the voucher screen.
Alt+D	To delete a voucher	To delete a master (if it has not been already assigned a different function, as explained above) At Voucher and Master (Single) alteration screens. Masters can be deleted subject to conditions, as explained in the manual.
Alt+E	To export the report in ASCII, HTML OR XML format	At all reports screens in Tally
Alt+I	To insert a voucher	At List of Vouchers – inserts a voucher before the one where you positioned the cursor and used this key combination.

Alt+L	To select the Language Configuration	At almost all screens in Tally.
Alt+K	To select the Keyboard Configuration	At almost all screens in Tally.
Alt+O	To upload the report at your website	At all reports screens in Tally
Alt+M	To E-mail the report	At all reports screens in Tally
Alt+P	To print the report	At all reports screens in Tally
Alt+R	To remove a line in a report	At all reports screens in Tally
Alt+S	To bring back a line you removed using Alt + R	At all reports screens in Tally
Alt+ V	From Invoice screen to bring Stock Journal screen	At Invoice screen à Quantity Field à Press Alt + V to select the Stock Journal.
Alt+W	To view the Tally Web browser	At all reports screens in Tally
Alt+X	To cancel a voucher in Day Book/List of Vouchers	At all voucher screens in Tally
Alt+Y	To Register Tally	At almost all screens in Tally.
Ctrl+A	To accept a form – wherever you use this key combination, that screen or report accepted as it is.	At almost all screens in Tally, except where a specific detail has to be given before gets accepting.
Ctrl+B	To select the Budget	At Groups/Ledgers/Cost Centres/ Budgets/ Scenarios/Voucher Types/ Currencies (Accounts Info) creation and alteration screen
Ctrl+C	To select the Cost Centre	To select the Cost Category At Groups/Ledgers/Cost Centres/ Budgets/ Scenarios/Voucher Types/ Currencies (Accounts Info) creation and alteration screen At Stock Groups/ Stock Categories/ Stock Items/ Reorder Levels/ Godowns/ Voucher Types / Units of Measure (Inventory Info) creation/alteration screen
Ctrl+E	To select the Currencies	At Groups/Ledgers/Cost Centres/ Budgets/ Scenarios/Voucher Types/ Currencies (Accounts Info) creation and alteration screen
Ctrl+G	To select the Group	At Groups/Ledgers/Cost Centres/ Budgets/ Scenarios/Voucher Types/ Currencies (Accounts Info) creation and alteration screen

Ctrl+I	To select the Stock Items	At Stock Group/ Stock Categories/ Stock Items/ Reorder Levels/ Godowns/ Voucher Types / Units of Measure (Inventory Info) creation/alteration screen
Ctrl+L	To select the Ledger	At Groups/Ledgers/Cost Centres/ Budgets/ Scenarios/Voucher Types/ Currencies (Accounts Info) creation and alteration screen
Ctrl+O	To select the Godowns	At Stock Group/ Stock Categories/ Stock Items/ Reorder Levels/ Godowns/ Voucher Types / Units of Measure (Inventory Info) creation/alteration screen
Ctrl+Q	To abandon a form – wherever you use this key combination, it quits that screen without making any changes to it.	At almost all screens in Tally.
Ctrl+Alt+R	Rewrite data for a Company	From Gateway of Tally screen
Ctrl+S	Allows you to alter Stock Item master	At Stock Voucher Report and Godown Voucher Report
Ctrl+U	To select the Units	At Stock Groups/ Stock Categories/ Stock Items/ Reorder Levels/ Godowns/ Voucher Types / Units of Measure (Inventory Info) creation/alteration screen
Ctrl+V	To select the Voucher Types	At Groups/Ledgers/Cost Centres/ Budgets/ Scenarios/Voucher Types/ Currencies (Accounts Info) creation and alteration screen

Special Function Key Combinations

Windows	*Functionality*	*Availability*
Alt+F1	To close a company	At all menu screens
	To view detailed report	At almost all report screens
	To explode a line into its details	At almost all screens in Tally
Alt+F2	To change the period	At almost all screens in Tally
Alt+F3	To select the company info menu	At Gateway of Tally screen
	To create/alter/shut a Company	
Alt+F4	To select the Purchase Order Voucher Type	At Accounting / Inventory Voucher creation and alteration screens
Alt+F5	To select the Sales Order Voucher Type	At Accounting / Inventory Voucher creation and alteration screens
	To view monthly and quarterly report	At almost all report screens in Tally

Alt+F6	To select the Rejection Out Voucher Type	
	To change the Sales Order Voucher Type	At Accounting / Inventory Voucher creation and alteration screens
Alt+F7	To select the Stock Journal Voucher Type	To accept all the Audit lists
		At Accounting / Inventory Voucher creation and alteration screens
		At TallyAudit Listing screen
Alt+F8	To select the Delivery Note Voucher Type	At Accounting / Inventory Voucher creation and alteration screens
	To view the Columnar report	At Ledger Voucher screen
Alt+F9	To select the Receipt Note Voucher Type	At Accounting / Inventory Voucher creation and alteration screens
Alt+F10	To select the Physical Stock Voucher Type	At Accounting / Inventory Voucher creation and alteration screens
Alt+F12	To filter the information based on monetary value	At almost all report screens
Ctrl+Alt+F12	Advanced Config	At Gateway of Tally

Key Combination Used for Navigation

Windows	*Functionality*	*Availability*
PgUp	Display previous voucher during voucher entry/alter	At voucher entry and alteration screens
PgDn	Display next voucher during voucher entry/alter	At voucher entry and alteration screens
Enter	To accept anything you type into a field.	You have to use this key at most areas in Tally
	To accept a voucher or master	
	To get a report with further details of an item in a report.	At the receivables report – press Enter at a pending bill to get transactions relating to this bill (e.g., original sale bill, receipts and payments against this bill, etc)
Esc	To remove what you typed into a field	
	To come out of a screen	At almost all screens in Tally.
	To indicate you do not want to accept a voucher or master.	

Shift+Enter	Collapse next level details	At Voucher Register screen and Trial Balance report
Shift+Enter	To explode a line into its details	In almost all Reports: At a Group/Stock Group/Cost Category/Godown/Stock Category – displays Sub Groups and Ledgers/Stock Items/Cost Centres/Secondary Godowns/Secondary Stock Categories At a Voucher – displays its entries and narration At a Stock Item- displays its godowns and batch details At Voucher Register screen – displays the next level details At Trial Balance report - displays the next level details
Ctrl+Enter	To alter a master while making an entry	At voucher entry and alteration screens
	or viewing a report	At all reports